ASHGATE
RESEARCH
COMPANION

THE ASHGATE RESEARCH COMPANION TO POLITICAL VIOLENCE

A balanced, tight-knit collection of essays from experts who write on the subject of political violence with an authority founded both on meticulous scholarship and, in many cases, direct experience. Under the editorial hand of Breen-Smyth, political violence is never reduced to a mere academic concept but is instead scrutinised and explained as a real force with devastating ramifications.

Katy Hayward,
Queen's University Belfast, Northern Ireland

If you want to choose one book to introduce you to different perspectives on political violence then this is the one. The editor has gathered scholars, practitioners and activists together to clarify the meaning of political violence. They consider its diverse genealogies and short, medium and long term impacts. These are then woven into a series of discussions about how to end different kinds of political violence and transform the relationships that brought them into existence. It is a must read book for anyone interested in how to conduct politics by peaceful rather than violent means.

Kevin P. Clements,
National Centre for Peace and Conflict Studies,
University of Otago, New Zealand

ASHGATE
RESEARCH
COMPANION

The *Ashgate Research Companions* are designed to offer scholars and graduate students a comprehensive and authoritative state-of-the-art review of current research in a particular area. The companions' editors bring together a team of respected and experienced experts to write chapters on the key issues in their speciality, providing a comprehensive reference to the field.

Other Research Companions available in Politics and International Relations:

The Ashgate Research Companion to Religion and Conflict Resolution
Edited by Lee Marsden
ISBN 978-1-4094-1089-8

The Ashgate Research Companion to the Globalization of Health
Edited by Ted Schrecker
ISBN 978-1-4094-0924-3

The Ashgate Research Companion to Chinese Foreign Policy
Edited by Emilian Kavalski
ISBN 978-1-4094-2270-9

The Ashgate Research Companion to International Trade Policy
Edited by Kenneth Heydon and Stephen Woolcock
ISBN 978-1-4094-0835-2

*The Ashgate Research Companion to War
Origins and Prevention*
Edited by Hall Gardner and Oleg Kobtzeff
ISBN 978-0-7546-7826-7

The Ashgate Research Companion to Regionalisms
Edited by Timothy M. Shaw, J. Andrew Grant and Scarlett Cornelissen
ISBN 978-0-7546-7762-8

The Ashgate Research Companion to Secession
Edited by Aleksandar Pavkovic and Peter Radan
ISBN 978-0-7546-7702-4

The Ashgate Research Companion to Non-State Actors
Edited by Bob Reinalda
ISBN 978-0-7546-7906-6

The Ashgate Research Companion to Political Violence

Edited by
MARIE BREEN-SMYTH
University of Surrey, UK

ASHGATE

© Marie Breen-Smyth and the contributors 2012

All rights reserved. No part of this publication may be reproduced, stored in a retrieval system or transmitted in any form or by any means, electronic, mechanical, photocopying, recording or otherwise without the prior permission of the publisher.

Marie Breen-Smyth has asserted her right under the Copyright, Designs and Patents Act, 1988, to be identified as the editor of this work.

Published by
Ashgate Publishing Limited
Wey Court East
Union Road
Farnham
Surrey GU9 7PT
England

Ashgate Publishing Company
110 Cherry Street
Suite 3-1
Burlington, VT 05401-3818
USA

www.ashgate.com

British Library Cataloguing in Publication Data
The Ashgate research companion to political violence.
   1. Political violence.
   I. Research companion to political violence
   II. Breen-Smyth, Marie.

Library of Congress Cataloging-in-Publication Data
Breen-Smyth, Marie, 1953–
   The Ashgate research companion to political violence / Marie Breen-Smyth.
      p. cm.
   Includes bibliographical references and index.
   ISBN 978-0-7546-7752-9 (hardback) — ISBN 978-0-7546-9493-9 (ebook)
   1. Political violence. I. Title.
   JC328.6.S67 2012
   303.6 — dc23

2012018438

ISBN 9780754677529 (hbk)
ISBN 9780754694939 (ebk – PDF)
ISBN 9781409471820 (ebk – ePUB)

Printed and bound in Great Britain by MPG Books Group, UK

ASHGATE
RESEARCH
COMPANION

Contents

List of Figure and Tables   *ix*
Notes on Contributors   *xi*
Preface   *xvii*
Acknowledgements   *xix*
List of Abbreviations   *xxi*

Introduction   1

PART I   DEFINING POLITICAL VIOLENCE

1   Political Violence: An Overview   17
     John Darby

2   Orthodox Accounts of Terrorism   33
     Jason Franks

3   Critical Accounts of Terrorism   47
     Richard Jackson

4   State Violence as State Terrorism   63
     Ruth Blakeley

5   The 'War on Terror' as Political Violence   79
     Richard Seymour

6   The Concept of Security in Political Violence   99
     Jessica Wolfendale

PART II   MOTIVATIONS AND GOALS OF POLITICAL VIOLENCE

7   From Dissent to Revolution: Politics and Violence   119
     Harmonie Toros

The Ashgate Research Companion to Political Violence

8	Why Do Individuals Resort to Political Violence? Approaches to the Psychology of Terrorism *Jeff Victoroff and Janice Adelman*	137
9	The Motivation of the Irish Rebel and Resistance to the Label 'Terrorist' *Anthony McIntyre*	169
10	Martyrs without Borders: The Puzzle of Transnational Suicide Bombers *Mohammed M. Hafez*	185
11	The Origins and Inhibiting Influences in Genocide, Mass Killing and Other Collective Violence *Ervin Staub*	205
12	Religion as a Motivation for Political Violence *Jeroen Gunning*	225

PART III THEORISING, UNDERSTANDING AND RESEARCHING POLITICAL VIOLENCE

13	Social Movement Studies and Political Violence *Donatella della Porta*	243
14	Feminist Reflections on Political Violence *Laura Sjoberg*	261
15	National Identity, Conflict and Political Violence: Experiences in Latin America *Peter Lambert*	281
16	Staying Alive while Conducting Primary Research: Fieldwork on Political Violence *Jeffrey A. Sluka*	301

PART IV MANIFESTATIONS OF POLITICAL VIOLENCE

17	Genocide as Political Violence *Adam Jones*	329
18	War as Political Violence *R. Gerald Hughes*	347

PART V COUNTERING POLITICAL VIOLENCE

19 Intelligence and Political Violence: The Case of Counter-Terrorism 369
    Frank Gregory

20 Counter-Terrorism and its Effectiveness in the UK since 1969:
    Does it Pay to be Tough on Terrorism? 389
    Robert Lambert

21 Counter-Terrorism and Human Rights since 9/11 411
    Michael McClintock

22 Counter-Terrorism and Human Rights in the UK 443
    Clive Walker

PART VI ENDING POLITICAL VIOLENCE

23 The State's Role in the Management and Resolution of Violent
    Conflict: Learning from Northern Ireland? 467
    Bill Rolston

24 Political Violence and Peace Processes 493
    Roger Mac Ginty

25 Civil Society Actors and the End of Violence 507
    Avila Kilmurray

PART VII DEALING WITH THE AFTERMATH

26 Defining and Building the Rule of Law in the Aftermath of Political
    Violence: The Processes of Transitional Justice 529
    Richard J. Goldstone and Adam M. Smith

27 Political, Economic and Social Reconstruction after Political Violence:
    The Case of Afghanistan 549
    William Maley

Conclusions 569

Index 583

For Margaret Gregory, 1945–2011

Liz Breen, 1928–2009 and John Breen, 1921–2011

For Professor John Darby, 1940–2012

And for Cynthia Keppley Mahmood, a brave and most heroic anthropologist

Carrie Twomey, a rebel with a cause

J, I, B & M

and for Owen and all at Farrar Road, past and present

List of Figure and Tables

Figure

1.1 Graph to show the conflict cycle   20

Tables

8.1   Classification of approaches to the psychology of terrorism   139

10.1 Data on foreign fighters in Iraq   189

18.1 Revolutions in military affairs (RMA), AD 1301–2000   352

25.1 Summary of the menu of roles adopted by such actors over
      the course of the Northern Ireland troubles   522

Notes on Contributors

Janice Adelman is a Research Scientist at NSI, Inc. Her research focuses on factors of support for violent intergroup conflict, including multiple social identities and uncertainty. She has previously worked at the RAND Corporation and has taught classes on the psychology of terrorism. She is an active member of the Society for the Psychological Study of Social Issues and the International Society of Political Psychology. She holds a BA in neuroscience and psychology from Brandeis University and an MSc in neurobiology from the Hebrew University of Jerusalem. She earned her PhD in applied social psychology from Claremont Graduate University.

Ruth Blakeley is Senior Lecturer in International Relations at the University of Kent, Canterbury. She is author of *State Terrorism and Neoliberalism: The North in the South* (2009) and has published various articles on state terrorism and torture. She was awarded a UK Economic and Social Research Council grant in 2011 for her research on the globalisation of rendition and secret detention. She is an associate editor of the *Critical Studies on Terrorism* journal and is a friend of the International State Crime Initiative, run by Kings College London, Harvard and Hull Universities.

Marie Breen-Smyth is Associate Dean International in the Faculty of Arts and Human Sciences and Professor of International Politics at the University of Surrey and Co-Director of the Centre for International Intervention (cii). She was the founding director of the Centre for the Study of Radicalisation and Contemporary Political Violence (CSRV) at Aberystwyth University, the founder and CEO of the Institute for Conflict Research until 2004 and has held academic positions in Aberystwyth University, the University of Ulster and Smith College, MA. She was 2002–2003 Jennings Randolph Senior Fellow in the United States Institute of Peace and is a founding editor with Richard Jackson and Jeroen Gunning of the journal *Critical Terrorism Studies*. She has written extensively on political violence and its impacts.

John Darby was Professor of Comparative Ethnic Studies at the Kroc Institute, University of Notre Dame from 1999 until his death in 2012. In 1990 he was founding director of INCORE, a joint programme of the United Nations University and the University of Ulster. During his long and distinguished career, he held visiting positions at Harvard and Duke Universities, and fellowships at the Rockefeller

Foundation, the Woodrow Wilson Center, USIP and Fulbright. He wrote or edited 15 books and more than 150 other academic publications. He was founder and director of the Peace Accords Matrix (PAM) at Notre Dame, which provides comparable data on more than 30 comprehensive peace accords. Sadly, John died just before this volume was published. He is greatly missed by his fellow scholars, students, colleagues and many friends throughout the world.

Donatella della Porta is Professor of Sociology in the Department of Political and Social Sciences at the European University Institute. She has directed the Demos project, devoted to the analysis of conceptions and practices of democracy in social movements in six European countries, and a major ERC project 'Mobilizing for Democracy', on civil society participation in democratisation processes in Europe, the Middle East, Asia and Latin America. Her main fields of research are social movements, the policing of public order, participatory democracy and political corruption. Her most recent publication is (with M. Caiani and C. Wagemann) *Mobilizing on the Extreme Right* (2012).

Jason Franks is an independent researcher in terrorism, conflict and peace.

Richard J. Goldstone was a judge in South Africa for 23 years, the last nine as a Justice of the Constitutional Court. Since retiring from the bench, he has taught as a visiting professor in a number of US law schools. From August 1994 to September 1996, he was the chief prosecutor of the United Nations International Criminal Tribunals for the former Yugoslavia and Rwanda. He is an honorary Bencher of the Inner Temple, London and an honorary fellow of St John's College, Cambridge. He is an honorary life member of the International Bar Association and is Honorary President of its Human Rights Institute.

Frank Gregory is Emeritus Professor of European Security in the Division of Politics and International Relations in the School of Social Sciences at the University of Southampton. His continuing research interests are on the homeland security, terrorism, crime and policing aspects of the EU's internal security policy with special reference to the UK. He was a co-opted member of an ACPO-TAM subcommittee (Explosives Detection), a member of a UK government advisory panel on emergency responses (SAPER) and is a member of RUSI. In 2011, he was elected an Honorary Fellow of the Institute for Civil Protection and Emergency Management.

Jeroen Gunning is Reader in Middle East Politics and Conflict Studies at the School of Government and International Affairs, Durham University, and Director of the Durham Global Security Institute. His research focuses on the interplay between Islamist social movements, democratisation, religion and violence in the Middle East, with particular emphasis on Hamas and Hizballah. He is one of the founders of the field of critical terrorism studies. His publications include *Hamas in Politics:*

Democracy, Religion, Violence (2007/2008) and *Critical Terrorism Studies: A New Research Agenda* (2009; co-edited with Richard Jackson and Marie Breen-Smyth).

Mohammed M. Hafez is an associate professor of national security affairs at the Naval Postgraduate School in Monterey, California, and specialises in Islamic social movements, Middle Eastern and North African politics, and violent radicalisation. He is the author of *Suicide Bombers in Iraq: The Strategy and Ideology of Martyrdom* (2007); *Manufacturing Human Bombs: The Making of Palestinian Suicide Bombers* (2006); and *Why Muslims Rebel: Repression and Resistance in the Islamic World* (2003). He earned a PhD in international relations from the London School of Economics and is the recipient of major research grants from the United States Institute of Peace and the Harry Frank Guggenheim Foundation.

R. Gerald Hughes is Lecturer in Military History at Aberystwyth University, the Director of the Centre for Intelligence and International Security Studies and an assistant editor of the *Intelligence and National Security* journal. His recent publications include *Britain, Germany and the Cold War: The Search for a European Détente 1949–1967* (2007) and, as editor, *Intelligence, Crises and Security: Prospects and Retrospects* (2008); *Exploring Intelligence Archives: Enquiries into the Secret State* (2008); and *Intelligence and International Security: New Perspectives and Agendas* (2011).

Richard Jackson is Associate Professor, University of Otago, New Zealand and Deputy Director at National Peace and Conflict Studies Centre, University of Otago. He is the founding and senior editor of the *Critical Terrorism Studies* journal and is the author and editor of seven books on critical terrorism studies and international conflict resolution.

Adam Jones is a Professor of Political Science at the University of British Columbia Okanagan in Kelowna, Canada. He is author of *Genocide: A Comprehensive Introduction* (2nd edn, 2010) and is author or editor of a dozen other books. In 2010 he was selected as one of 'Fifty Key Thinkers on the Holocaust and Genocide' for the book project of that name.

Avila Kilmurray has been Director of the Community Foundation for Northern Ireland and a founder organisational member of the Foundations for Peace Network, a peer network of independent, indigenous foundations working in divided societies since 1994. Previously she was coordinator of the Northern Ireland Council for Voluntary Action's Rural Action Project, an EU Second Anti-Poverty Programme initiative. In 1990, she was appointed the first Women's Officer for the Ireland Transport and General Workers' Union. She has also served on the Northern Ireland Committee and on the Executive Council of the Irish Congress of Trade Unions. In addition, she was active in establishing the NI Women's Coalition.

Peter Lambert is Senior Lecturer in Latin American Studies at the University of Bath. Having worked in Paraguay as a political researcher for an NGO, he obtained his PhD from the University of the West of England (UWE), before moving to the University of Bath to set up the Spanish and Latin American Studies programme in 2000. He has researched and published extensively on contemporary Paraguayan politics and history, and has carried out consultancy work on Paraguay. He was President of the Society for Latin American Studies (SLAS) 2007–2009.

Robert Lambert is a lecturer at the Centre for the Study of Terrorism and Political Violence (CSTPV) at the University of St Andrews and is co-director of the European Muslim Research Centre (EMRC). In *Countering al-Qaeda in London: Police and Muslims in Partnership* (2011), he reflects on his experience as head of the Metropolitan Police Muslim Contact Unit (MCU) in the Metropolitan Police from January 2002 to December 2007 and on his subsequent PhD research examining the legitimacy and effectiveness of police and Muslim partnerships in London. He is currently examining the nature of anti-Muslim or Islamophobic violence against Muslims in the UK.

Roger Mac Ginty is Professor of Peace and Conflict Studies at the Humanitarian and Conflict Research Institute and the Department of Politics, University of Manchester. His latest book is *International Peacebuilding and Local Resistance: Hybrid Forms of Peace* (2011). He edits the *Peacebuilding* journal and the *Rethinking Political Violence* book series (Palgrave Macmillan).

Michael McClintock has worked in the human rights field for over 30 years – as a researcher and director of Amnesty International from 1974 to 1994; deputy programme director of Human Rights Watch (1994–2002); director of programme and research of Human Rights First (2002–2007); and currently as an independent consultant based in Mexico City. He has undertaken numerous fact-finding missions and has written extensively on human rights issues. As an independent authority, he is the author of *Instruments of Statecraft: U.S. Guerrilla Warfare, Counterinsurgency and Counterterrorism, 1940–1990* (1992) and histories of El Salvador and Guatemala.

Anthony McIntyre is a former IRA prisoner who has written extensively on modern Irish republicanism. He spent 18 years in Long Kesh and four years on the blanket and no-wash/no-work protests which led to the hunger strikes of the 1980s. In prison he obtained a First in politics from the Open University. Upon his release, he wrote a doctoral thesis on provisional republicanism in its formative years, for which he was awarded a PhD. He is author of the book *Good Friday: The Death of Irish Republicanism* (2008). He left the republican movement at the endorsement of the Good Friday Agreement and went on to become a journalist. He was a co-founder of *The Blanket*, an online magazine that critically analysed the Irish peace process.

William Maley is Professor and Director of the Asia-Pacific College of Diplomacy at the Australian National University. He is author of *Rescuing Afghanistan* (2006) and *The Afghanistan Wars* (2002, 2009); the editor of *Fundamentalism Reborn? Afghanistan*

Notes on Contributors

and the Taliban (1998); the co-author of *Regime Change in Afghanistan: Foreign Intervention and the Politics of Legitimacy* (1991) and *Political Order in Post-Communist Afghanistan* (2002); and co-editor of *The Soviet Withdrawal from Afghanistan* (1989), *From Civil Strife to Civil Society: Civil and Military Responsibilities in Disrupted States* (2003) and *Global Governance and Diplomacy: Worlds Apart?* (2008).

Bill Rolston is Professor of Sociology and Director of the Transitional Justice Research Institute at the University of Ulster. He has been involved over the last three decades in researching and writing about society, politics and culture in Northern Ireland, with a particular focus on the violent political conflict. In recent years, much of his research has concentrated on the issue of dealing with the past and with the role of various constituencies, particularly the politically motivated ex-prisoner groups, in conflict transformation.

Richard Seymour is a London-based writer. He is the author of *The Liberal Defence of Murder* (2008), *The Meaning of David Cameron* (2010) and *American Insurgents* (2012), and is currently researching a PhD at the London School of Economics.

Laura Sjoberg is Assistant Professor of Political Science at the University of Florida. She is author and editor of several books, including, most recently, *Feminism and International Relations* (2011, with J. Ann Tickner) and *Women, Gender, and Terrorism* (2011, with Caron Gentry). Her work has been published in more than two dozen scholarly journals and she is currently finishing *Gendering Global Conflict: Towards a Feminist Theory of War*.

Jeffrey A. Sluka earned his PhD from the University of California at Berkeley and is Associate Professor in the Social Anthropology Programme at Massey University, New Zealand. A political anthropologist with extensive fieldwork experience in Northern Ireland, he is an expert on political violence, the cultural dynamics of armed conflicts involving ethnonationalist movements and indigenous peoples, and managing danger in ethnographic fieldwork. He is the author of *Hearts and Minds, Water and Fish: Popular Support for the IRA and INLA in a Northern Irish Ghetto* (1989) and edited *Death Squad: The Anthropology of State Terror* (2000) and (with Antonius Robben) *Ethnographic Fieldwork: An Anthropological Reader* (2007).

Adam M. Smith is an international lawyer based in Washington DC and a commentator on human rights and international justice. He has written numerous articles and two books: *The Architecture of International Justice at Home and Abroad* (2008, with R. Goldstone) and *After Genocide: Bringing the Devil to Justice* (2009). He has held postings at the United Nations, the World Bank and the OECD, and been a visiting scholar at institutions in Africa, Europe and South Asia. He obtained a BA in political science and economics from Brown, an MPhil in politics from Oxford and a JD from Harvard, where he was a senior editor of the *Harvard International Law Journal*.

Ervin Staub is Professor Emeritus and Founding Director of the doctoral programme in the Psychology of Peace and Violence at the University of Massachusetts at Amherst. He is past president of the International Society for Political Psychology and of the Society for the Study of Peace, Conflict and Violence. His books include *The Roots of Evil: The Origins of Genocide and Other Group Violence* (1992) and a new book, *Overcoming Evil: Genocide, Violent Conflict and Terrorism* (2011). He has worked in many real-world settings, including Rwanda, Burundi and the Congo, to promote psychological recovery and reconciliation. He has received varied awards, including life-long contributions to peace psychology and distinguished contributions to political psychology. For more information and downloads of articles, see www.ervinstaub.com.

Harmonie Toros is Lecturer in International Conflict Analysis at the University of Kent, Canterbury. Her research focuses on developing a critical theory-based approach to terrorism and examining the potential for conflict transformation in conflicts marked by terrorist violence. In her latest publication (*Terrorism, Talking and Transformation: A Critical Approach*, 2012), she examines whether and how talking contributed to the transformation of conflicts in the southern Philippine region of Mindanao and in Northern Ireland.

Jeff Victoroff received his MA in social science from the University of Chicago and his MD from Case Western Reserve University. He completed residencies in both neurology and psychiatry at Harvard Medical School and a fellowship in neurobehaviour at UCLA. He currently serves as Associate Professor of Clinical Neurology and Psychiatry at the Keck School of Medicine of the University of Southern California. His main interests are aggression, terrorism and evolutionary neurobehaviour. In addition to studies of the biopsychosocial bases of violent behaviors, he has provided strategic advice regarding the struggle against violent extremism.

Clive Walker is Professor of Criminal Justice Studies at the School of Law, University of Leeds. He has written extensively on terrorism, with numerous published papers, and has also served as visiting professor in institutions such as Melbourne and Stanford Universities. He was a special adviser to the UK parliamentary select committee on civil contingencies, from which he published *The Civil Contingencies Act 2004: Risk, Resilience and the Law in the United Kingdom* (2006). His latest books on terrorism include *The Anti-Terrorism Legislation* (2nd edn, 2009) and *Terrorism and the Law* (2011).

Jessica Wolfendale is Assistant Professor of Philosophy at West Virginia University. She is the author of *Torture and the Military Profession* (2007) and has published extensively on military ethics, terrorism and torture.

Preface

This collection of essays aims to provide a broad overview of political violence, contemporary and historical ideas about such violence, together with a discussion of the nature, scale and effects of such violence and an overview of some of the key debates in the field. No one volume can possibly address the enormous range of concerns and issues raised about political violence and this volume can merely point the reader in the direction of some of the key issues within the field. In conclusion, other directions for further reading and inquiry are suggested and topics that could not be addressed in this volume are indicated.

The choice of title – 'political violence' – is deliberately broad and inclusive, rather than the other terms which are subsumed under that broad title: terrorism; counter-terrorism; war; ethnic conflict; insurgency; and the underlying conditions of security and insecurity. Similarly, the perspectives represented by the authors are on a spectrum, from a critical take on terrorism and state terrorism through feminist and human security approaches to rather more orthodox representations of intelligence, ethnic conflict and genocide. If we were to gather the contributing authors in one room, something that would be delicious, if expensive, to do, there would be many scholarly synchronicities, catalytic conversations but also many debates and disagreements. Indeed, the contributors themselves hail from a variety of backgrounds: lawyers concerned with transitional justice, an anthropologist seeking to immerse himself in the context in which non-state armed groups operate, psychologists seeking to discover whether such groups attract particular personality types, a political scientist arguing for dialogue as a method of ending violence and a former combatant, amongst others.

Although the book contains the work of scholars and professionals, it is designed to address a wide range of concerns and questions about political violence of interest not only to students but also to laypersons interested in politics and international relations and peace and conflict studies. I would invite the reader to imagine a series of seven encounters, whereby the reader can meet the authors in each of the seven main parts into which the book is organised and have the benefit of their respective expertise on some of the key questions about political violence, one of the most persistent, absorbing and urgent questions that face us locally and globally.

Marie Breen-Smyth
Vero Beach, Florida

Acknowledgements

The editorial assistance of Charlotte Heath-Kelly and Jennifer Pedersen in liaising with authors and keeping track of versions of chapters was invaluable. Louise Booth's work in preparing the final drafts for submission was also important. My colleagues at the University of Surrey, and previously at Smith College, Massachusetts and Aberystwyth University, provided a scholarly environment for the work. The commitment and flexibility of Margaret Younger and Kirstin Howgate at Ashgate have also been central to the success of the project. It is largely due to the work of the authors, however, who endured my often invasive and demanding editorial comments, not to mention the delays whilst I dealt with family illnesses, moved jobs and countries, with patience with good humour that the project was at all possible. They deserve the biggest thanks. Thanks to Leo and Bea Coyle for providing me with my 'office' at Vero Beach where I could escape and work on the project. Finally, but by no means least, my thanks is due to Ken Sparks, whose patience, love and support allowed me to neglect my other duties to my friends, family and garden, particularly during the final stages of production.

List of Abbreviations

ACPO	Association of Chief Police Officers
BCU	Borough Command Units
CBRN	Chemical, Biological, Radiological or Nuclear
CIA	Central Intelligence Agency
CoE	Council of Europe
CPNI	Centre for the Protection of National Infrastructure
CRS	Congressional Research Service
CTAC	Counterterrorism Analysis Centre
DCIS	Defence Criminal Investigation Service
DG MI5	Director General of MI5
DHS	Department of Homeland Security
DI&AS	Defence Intelligence & Analysis Service
DNI	Director of National Intelligence
DoD	Department of Defence
DVLA	Department of Vehicle Licensing
EAD-I	Executive Assistant Director for Intelligence
EU	European Union
FBI	Federal Bureau of Investigation
GAO	General Accountability Office
GCHQ	Government Communications Head Quarters
HMIC	Her Majesty's Inspectorate of Constabulary
HSA	Homeland Security Act
HUMINT	human sources intelligence
IED	Improvised Explosive Device
IMINT	imagery intelligence, e.g. from 'spy' satellites
IRTPA	Intelligence Reform and Terrorism Prevention Act 2004
JTAC	Joint Terrorism Analysis Centre
MASINT	measurements and signatures intelligence
NCA	National Crime Agency
NCS	National Clandestine Service
NCTC	National Counterterrorism Centre
NCTI	National Coordinator (of) Terrorist Investigations
NGA	National Geospatial-Intelligence Agency
NIS	National Intelligence Strategy of the US
NJTTF	National Joint Terrorism Task Force

NRO	National Reconnaissance Office
NSA	National Security Agency
OI	Office of Intelligence
OSINT	open source intelligence
PACE	Police and Criminal Evidence Act 1984
PES	Privacy Enhancing Strategies, e.g. avoidance of the Internet
PET	Privacy Enhancing Technologies, e.g. encryption
PTSD	post-traumatic stress disorder
RDA	Revolution in Diplomatic Affairs
RIA	Revolution in Intelligence Affairs
RMA	Revolution in Military Affairs
SAC	Supervisory Agents in Charge (in the FBI)
SARs	Nationwide Suspicious Activity Reports (US)
SIGINT/ELINT	various forms of communications intercept
TIDE	Terrorist Identities Datamart Environment
UAV	unmanned aerial vehicle
UN	United Nations
WMD	weapons of mass destruction

ASHGATE
RESEARCH
COMPANION

Introduction

Political violence is one of the great scourges of the world. For some of us, it was and is the leitmotif of our lives, punctuated by bombing, shooting, loss of life, devastation and militarisation of the environment in which we live, but also by fear, hatred, loss, grief, anger and despair, divided communities and families. Yet for others, political violence is sometimes a career, handed down from father to son, either in standing state armies or in militias, through which status and respect can be achieved as a defender of the community. Yet others see political violence and the armaments it involves as a business opportunity, or the reconstruction that follows as a chance to invest, make money in re-building the physical environment. For many political actors, combatants, policy-makers and elite decision-makers, it is one of a range of methods of intervention, and deployment is a decision that brings with it the burden of responsibility for the lives of others and the moral dilemmas of risking those lives alongside the imperative to act and be seen to act in robust defence of one's constituents.

As one who has taken to the pen following experience of the sword, I am ever conscious that this book is produced in the absence of any of these responsibilities or imperatives and in the haven of the luxury of quiet rooms and time to think. Amidst what Arundhati Roy[1] refers to as 'the terror of war and the horror of peace' that follows, there is rarely such luxury. Our very ideas are shaped by the context of urgency and the reductionism that intervention and decisive action in extreme circumstances seem to demand. The commentator in the quiet room must remember with humility that thinking is shaped by the context in which it is takes place. And hindsight and tranquillity are not readily available in the heat of battle.

The importance of scholarship is not diminished by this dilemma. Bringing to bear the lessons of the past on contemporary crises involving political violence requires the genius that can give audible and authoritative voice to reason in a maelstrom of emotions and vested interests. Whilst the audibility of that voice may be a matter of politics, its authority must be a matter of scholarship.

Thus, this book aims to provide an overview of some of the key issues that political violence raises. To begin with, what is political violence and how is it distinct, if at all, from terrorism? (The word 'terrorism' is used in some chapters and avoided or used in a circumscribed way in others. Whilst it is left to individual contributors to choose their own language, the editor generally prefers to use the term 'political

---

1   Roy, A. (1997) *The God of Small Things*. London: Harper Collins.

violence' in order to avoid the political judgment and de-legitimisation inherent in the use of the term, unless it is purposely deployed.) Other questions arise, such as why do people resort to such violence? What motivates them at an individual and a group level? How has human society collectively used political violence in war and genocide? What strategies are used to counter such violence and how can it be brought to an end? And when violence ends, what are the consequences and how are they addressed?

In order to address these questions, the volume is organised into seven parts: defining political violence; the motivations and goals driving violent actors; frameworks for theorising and researching political violence; forms of political violence and the ways in which political violence manifests itself; countering political violence; how political violence ends; and the aftermath of political violence.

Defining Political Violence

Part 1 deals with issues of defining political violence, the language used to describe it and contests over definitions and language. It considers whether or not 'political violence' is a distinct category from 'terrorism' and how political violence is related to the idea of security. The role of the state in political violence and how violence serves to render certain populations secure or insecure are examined, using the example of the War on Terror.

In Chapter 1, John Darby, an influential scholar of peace and conflict studies, raises a number of issues that are taken up at greater length in subsequent chapters. He engages with the tricky business of defining political violence, the disputed territory of differentiating political violence from conventional crime. He also offers clarification on protest and non-violence versus violence, criminality versus political violence and the role of political objectives and other factors in such differentiation. He provides a discussion of inter- and intra-state violence and raises the issue of violence by the state, taken up later in the volume by Blakeley and others. A survey of attitudes to political violence, the evolution of thinking about it and a summary of patterns of political violence over the last 30 years or so leads to a concluding discussion of successes and failures in transforming violent conflicts into peace.

Jason Franks, an independent researcher in the field of terrorism, peace and conflict, contributes Chapter 2, which provides an analysis of orthodox terrorism theory. Franks suggests that this is the principal paradigm and rational positivist approach used, primarily by state governments, to explain political violence. For him, such orthodox views of terrorism provide an understanding of terrorism that supports hegemonic, liberal agendas, while keeping a robust distinction firmly in place that prevents a creeping legitimation of terrorist agendas. Thus, orthodox accounts of terrorism are based on a dualistic legitimacy/illegitimacy split that constructs non-state violence as terrorist and state violence as legitimate. Using the example of the Israeli–Palestinian conflict, Franks points out that orthodox terrorism theory is a theoretically constructed discourse derived from key texts in terrorism studies. Its dominance is maintained by its monopoly of state government counter-terrorism and anti-terrorism policies. He offers an account of orthodox terrorism theory as a discourse, a description of how and why it is constructed, what it is used for and the associated problems. He concludes with a discussion of the implications this has, not only for the study of political violence, but also for finding ways of ending political violence.

In Chapter 3, Richard Jackson, one of the founding scholars of critical terrorism studies, provides an account of critical approaches to terrorism studies, investigating the nature of 'terrorist' violence from a number of critical perspectives. He explains how these accounts depart from the dominant orthodox rationalist and foundationalist accounts of terrorism, which Jason Franks discussed in the previous chapter and which, Jackson argues, have an explicit normative component. Critical scholars such as Jackson resist the application of the term 'terrorism', so he examines this 'terrorism' from the perspective of anthropology and critical terrorism studies, including a discussion of state terrorism. He explains that critical approaches to 'terrorism' are based on a broadly social constructivist as opposed to objectivist ontology, epistemology and methodologies.

This is followed in Chapter 4 by Ruth Blakeley's examination of state violence, which, she argues, is properly seen as state terrorism. Blakeley, who has written extensively on state terrorism and torture, explores state terrorism in relation to other forms of state violence, beginning by introducing the reader to the contested terrain of how terrorism generally, and state terrorism specifically, are defined. She argues that there is sufficient agreement among scholars on the key elements of terrorism to support a definition of state terrorism. A defining feature of state terrorism which distinguishes it from other forms of state violence, according to her, is that it involves the illegal targeting of individuals that the state has a duty to protect, in order to instill fear in a target audience beyond the direct victim. Thus, the monopoly on the legitimate use of violence that is granted to the state is contested insofar as there is neither a justification for excluding state terrorism from studies of terrorism, nor for affording states the right to use violence in any way they choose. The chapter charts the main difficulties in identifying state terrorism and distinguishing it from other forms of state violence, suggests how scholars can overcome these difficulties and examines the different forms that state terrorism can take.

In Chapter 5, Richard Seymour, who is a London-based writer, moves the discussion to how the 'War on Terror' has shaped recent debates and conceptualisations. Seymour shows how the term 'terrorism' both describes a form of (illegitimate) political violence and provides a primary justification for (legitimate) political violence. In the 'War on Terror', political violence that is branded 'terrorism' carries connotations of epic and indiscriminate violence. The humane values of states united in opposition to this terrorism purport to limit this epic violence, thus legitimising the violence of those states. Violence against troops in occupied Iraq and Afghanistan, though permissible under international law, is regarded as terrorism, whilst the violence of the USA and its allies is rationalised and legitimated. Anti-occupation violence is represented as anti-modern and illiberal, waged by a disarticulated network of criminalised non-state actors with whom there can be no negotiations. Seymour argues that this bifurcation of global violence mitigates against any consideration of the impact of race and caste on contemporary international politics. For him, political violence in the 'War on Terror' has been coded in the tropes of magnanimous, rational, humane empire versus illiberal, irrational, suspicious 'native fanaticism'. He argues that the reiteration of these tropes, which for him originate in an era in which white supremacy was the global norm, serves to remind us that the effects of such supremacy remain potent.

In Chapter 6, Jessica Wolfendale, who has published extensively on military ethics, terrorism and torture, engages with the field of security studies. She reviews definitions of security and provides a definition based on three dimensions of human identity. She discusses the relationship between these three dimensions (individual security, national security and the security of the state) and argues that national security can only claim a moral authority if the security of individual citizens is assured. She then sets out the conditions, according to her reading of just war theory and the responsibility to protect, under which external and internal threats to security can justify the use of force and political violence by states and non-state actors. She argues that in debates about political violence, the concept of security is used in misleading ways. She offers a consistent alternative account of security that has implications for how political violence is understood and concludes by advancing some theoretical frameworks for understanding political violence and pointing to issues for researchers in the field.

Motivations and Goals of Political Violence

Part 2 examines motivations for engaging in political violence, such as why people resort to such violence, whether they have a right to do so, how their motivations are understood and the methods they employ. It specifically addresses the methods of suicide attacks and genocide.

In Chapter 7, Harmonie Toros, who has conducted fieldwork in Mindanao and Northern Ireland, considers the 'right to resist' and attitudes to popular uprising, citizens' recourse to revolt and other extralegal measures in response to injustice. She considers contemporary arguments about the right to dissent, to resist or to revolt. She focuses on the relationship between dissent, resistance, revolution and political violence, and how the introduction of violence impacts on rights to dissent and to resist. Using Rawls, she examines the legal, moral and philosophical basis of the right to revolt and goes on to consider how non-violence is frequently considered to be an essential condition for the legitimation of the right to dissent. Is there a right to violently resist injustice in modern democratic states? She considers the argument that modern democratic states provide non-violent means to express dissent and thus there is no valid need to engage in violence. She examines how violence is understood and whether violence necessarily signals that an actor is attempting to overthrow the state or whether violence can be deployed in pursuit of the more limited goals of challenging oppressive laws or practices. She asks whether the right of self-determination legitimises the use of violence by minorities to overthrow the state in order to attain that right and indeed who has the right to self-determination – individuals, communities, nations and/or states. She concludes by asking if a theoretical discussion on the rights of dissent, resistance and revolution can be relevant or influential in the contemporary practice of political violence, its perceived legitimacy, the form that it takes and the responses to it.

There is a change of disciplinary approach in Chapter 8, which moves into a psychological exploration of the motivations and the psychological causes of violence at the individual level. Jeff Victoroff and Janice Adelman consider why individuals resort to political violence. Victoroff has studied the biopsychosocial basis of violent behaviour, and Adelman's research focuses on support for intergroup conflict. They begin by pointing out that political violence, and especially what is referred to as terrorism, is relatively rare. Only a small number of people resort to political violence to express their grievances or ambitions, even though comparatively large numbers of people feel politically aggrieved or ambitious. They provide a wide-ranging survey of theories that have been advanced to explain political violence. Their review covers the early psychopathological explanations and more recent accounts that point to the psychological normalcy of violent actors. They trace the history of debates about the psychology of terrorism, critically examining the fundamental claims of the key proponents of the various conceptual camps. Finally, they conclude by advocating the virtues of transdisciplinarity in understanding the motivations of violent actors.

Anthony McIntyre, a former IRA prisoner and commentator on Irish republicanism, contributes an account of the motivation of Irish republican rebels in Chapter 9. He provides an historical background to contemporary republican resistance to the terminology of 'terrorism'. In discussing the motivation of the Irish rebel, he traces the ideology of contemporary republicanism from its historical roots, through to its contemporary diverse manifestations. These are a constitutionalised and pacified rebellion on the one hand and a dissident pursuit of armed struggle on the other. He considers the implications of the recent republican embracing of electoral and constitutional politics for traditional positions on Irish freedom and the past use of violence as a method.

In Chapter 10, Mohammed Hafez, a specialist in Islamic social movements, considers why martyrdom operations have become a feature of conflict in the Muslim world. He argues that suicide bombings represent innovations in both tactics and ideology. In tactical terms, they contend with the gaping asymmetry of power such as that faced by Muslims challenging domestic regimes or foreign occupations. This provides the context in which martyrdom operations offer a tactical solution. Suicide missions offer the possibility of military, psychological and communication advantages over opponents' superior military might. Hafez explains that, ideologically, by interpreting suicide as martyrdom and drawing on obscure religious traditions that permit exceptional forms of violence in a defensive jihad, Islamists have circumvented religious prohibitions against suicide and the killing of civilians in order to legitimate suicide operations.

In Chapter 11, Ervin Staub, who has written extensively on genocide, engages with the issue of genocide and mass killing. He provides a survey of contemporary genocide, mass killing and violence directed at groups targeted because of their ethnicity, race, religion, culture or political affiliation. He explains and differentiates between the use of the terms 'collective', 'mass', 'group' and 'ethnopolitical' violence. He also provides an account of the motivations for such violence in terms of material interest, issues of identity, power and politics, or differentiation between 'us' and 'them', and describes the dynamics of devaluation of others that facilitate these practices. The chapter focuses on two related, intense forms of violence: mass killing and genocide in the context of the United Nations Genocide Convention of 1948, which defines genocide as 'acts committed with intent to destroy in whole or in part, a national, ethnical, racial or religious group'. He also discusses some of the limitations of the UN definition and the issues that these raise for effective definition, prevention and international justice processes.

Contemporary discussions, particularly after 2001, of political violence defined as terrorism have been greatly preoccupied with religion as a motivating factor for political violence and the practice of terrorism. In Chapter 12, Jeroen Gunning, based on his extensive studies of Hamas and knowledge of debates in the field of terrorism studies, discusses religion as a motivation for political violence. His chapter reviews the current state of the literature, from Rapoport's 1984 article introducing the notion of 'religious terrorism' to the 'new terrorism' and 'violent religions' debates. He concludes that, while religiously inspired frames have indeed shaped many a militant's motivation, it is misleading to create a separate category called 'religious terrorism' or 'religious violence'. He draws on (critical) terrorism studies, sociology of religion and conflict studies to argue that one cannot effectively distinguish between religious and secular politics either conceptually or empirically. Religion, he argues, is as likely to inspire violence as non-violence. The contemporary preoccupation with terrorism lies in the development of Western social science within the context of the Westphalian state system. The concept serves a political agenda of de-legitimising certain actors whilst legitimising exceptional responses to them. At the same time, he argues that such formulations obscure the manner in which the state has subsumed many of the functions of organised religion.

Theorising, Understanding and Researching Political Violence

Part 3 addresses some of the ways in which scholars explain political violence in terms of nationalism, social movement theory and feminist perspectives, and the challenges of developing scholarship about such violence.

In Chapter 13, Donatella della Porta, one of the key proponents of social movement theory as it applies to political violence, evaluates the social scientific engagement with extreme forms of political violence in the social sciences. She argues that such engagement has been episodic, with area study specialists focusing on ethnic and religiously motivated violence, 'breakdown' theories being applied to right-wing radicalism and social movement theories to left-wing violence. Her chapter provides an account of political violence from a social movement perspective and the challenges presented to this account by contemporary debates on terrorism and counter-terrorism. The chapter reviews research on violence as an escalation of action repertoires within cycles of protest. Della Porta points to the importance of understanding political opportunity and the role of the state in the escalation of violence. She describes the concept of resource mobilisation within organisations that use violence and discusses how such violence is narratively represented. She concludes by outlining and what such research tells us about how violent actors see the outside world.

Laura Sjoberg, a leading scholar of feminism in international relations, discusses key issues arising in contemporary feminist perspectives on political violence in Chapter 14. She explains how feminist approaches to the making and fighting of wars have required the broadening of the definition of 'war' in order to explore women's multiple roles in conflict. This exploration also uncovers the complex relationships between gender, gender-based stereotypes and political violence. She sets out the key components of feminist theories relating to the meaning of political violence, those who practise political violence and those who are impacted by political violence. She argues that political violence is constituted by gender 'all the way down'. Not only is political violence gendered, she argues, its actors are gendered and its impacts are gendered. Through exploring examples where women have been involved in commissioning acts of terrorist violence, she contends that contemporary orthodox explanations are inadequate and broader understandings are called for. A broader conceptualisation of what gender is and of what counts as 'political' violence, she argues, is necessary to a more comprehensive and thorough understanding of that violence. She concludes by proposing a feminist reading of political violence as a gendered concept.

The role of nationalism and national identity in political violence is the subject of Chapter 15. Taking examples from Latin America, Peter Lambert, a leading scholar of the region, considers how national identity (and how it is managed) can fuel, or be changed by, political violence. Contests over national identity have provided the context for violent political conflict and provide a consistent theme underlying political violence. National identity and nationalist sentiment can be easily manipulated, whilst being resilient and inherently flexible. Therefore, national identity is often politically deployed as a key device to obtain political advantage and power. Using Latin American history since independence, Lambert considers how conflict and the violent struggle for political power has been shaped and fuelled by such contests. He argues that, fundamentally, nationalism and national identity have been at the root of political violence, and the clash between conflicting interpretations of national identity is often used to legitimise certain struggles and to provide moral justification for political violence. He describes the relationship between violence and the construction of national identity in Latin America by reviewing conflict and the use of violence from the mid-twentieth century onwards. He analyses both dominant and dissident forms of nationalism and examines how historical myths, codes, symbols and discourse shape the construction and use of such violence. He also documents various aspects of the intimate relationship between national identity, nationalism and violence, with examples from across Latin America.

Finally in this part, the business of conducting research on political violence is addressed in Chapter 16 by Jeffrey Sluka. He considers the challenges of doing research in violent contexts, based on his own fieldwork experience in Northern Ireland. Researchers engaging in research on political violence must manage the danger that is often inherent in undertaking such research. This is a particular challenge for researchers conducting primary research on political violence or those working in locations where such violence is ongoing. Sluka points out that, while there is a burgeoning literature about how to conduct fieldwork, there is comparatively sparse material, beyond anecdotal accounts, about handling or managing danger as a methodological or indeed an ethical issue. He argues that although there has been growing interest in, and literature on, the study of political violence, hardly anything has been written about the practicalities of researcher survival in perilous field sites. He reviews what literature and current research there is in this area and discusses his own experience as an illustrative and reflexive case study of dangerous fieldwork in Belfast. He concludes by outlining practical strategies and ideas for dealing with threats to the safety and security, and for ensuring the well-being of researchers and informants who work amid the threat of violence.

Manifestations of Political Violence

In Part 4, two specific forms of wholescale political violence are examined, namely genocide and war.

In Chapter 17, Adam Jones who has written extensively on holocaust and genocide, considers the subject of genocide as a form of political violence. He provides an analysis of the significant points of overlap and confusion between the concepts of political affiliation and those of national/ethnic/religious identities, which lead to these identities being 'politicised' in the eyes of perpetrator forces. This process, he argues, renders it difficult to separate 'political groups' from those collectivities formally protected by the Genocide Convention. This leads to a consideration of the profound and ambiguous nature of the link between genocide as political violence. He points out that most acts of genocide occur during civil and/or international conflict, and entail atrocities committed by a politically hegemonic actor acting against a politically weaker one. He considers the role of political groups in the discourse of genocide and examines the implications of the exclusion of these groups from the United Nations Genocide Convention of 1948 (whose application is limited to 'national, ethnic, racial, or religious' groups). He argues that the targeting of populations on the grounds of political considerations is widely regarded as one of the most common, if not the most common, forms of contemporary mass violence. He points to some of the steps being taken to mitigate the limitations of the Convention and describes the efforts to re-interpret the legal provisions and re-define genocide to include genocidal acts by political groups in order to bring such groups under the umbrella of protection of the Genocide Convention. This is to be achieved using alternative means, namely by ascribing a political designation to the 'part' of a broader national or ethnic group that is specifically targeted for destruction. Thus, at the conceptual level and in a legal context, efforts have been made to re-define genocide to include political groups in international tribunal proceedings.

Gerry Hughes, a military historian and writer on intelligence issues, provides an historical survey of the phenomenon of war as a form of political violence in Chapter 18. Pointing to the constancy of war as an historical phenonmen, Hughes looks at the evolution war as a (mainly) state-centric political activity. Using Clausewitz, who describes war as a 'continuation of political intercourse, carried on with other means', he discusses why war, an essentially cultural entity, is not limited to any particular political formation, but rather is to be found in many and various types of political systems and societies. He provides a framework that borrows from many of the notable thinkers on war (Sun Tsu, Machiavelli, Clausewitz) within which he takes the reader from war in ancient times up to the contemporary phenomenon of war. The analysis assesses historical variations in the perceived utility of war to state and non-state actors. He discusses the role of technology in the evolution of war and its changing nature. In addition, he documents shifts in attitudes to and the prominence of questions of morality in war and considers how these questions have influenced societies in judging just when and where the use of force has been deemed acceptable. He provides an account of the 'just war' tradition alongside a consideration of how contemporary democracies see war and its utility to the modern state. He finishes by arguing the contemporary relevance of Plato's maxim 'Only the dead have seen the end of war', concluding that it has the same relevance today as when Plato wrote it.

Countering Political Violence

Part 5 offers perspectives on countering state and non-state political violence, emanating from both state and non-state actors, including the role of intelligence in countering or anticipating political violence and the effectiveness or otherwise of counter-terrorism and its impact on human rights.

In Chapter 19, Frank Gregory, who is an expert and government advisor on homeland security, terrorism, crime and policing, assesses the successes and failures of intelligence in prosecuting and countering political violence. He points out that the evaluation of the role of intelligence is necessarily contextualised at the macro-level of the particular political system and the operational and organisational contexts. He recognises that it is difficult and problematic to advance simplistic categorisations about democratic states' rule of law approaches to intelligence as compared to the practices in authoritarian states. To highlight this difficulty, he points to the record of the recent Presidency of George W. Bush in the USA. He examines the focus of intelligence activity relating to political violence with reference to three basic questions, namely: what information is sought from which the intelligence 'product'?; from whom or where is that information sought?; and for what purpose is it sought? He points out that there are important due process of law implications if intelligence is to be used for evidential purposes in criminal cases, whereas these may not apply if it is simply sought for disruption or target protection purposes. He provides an evaluation of the UK government's counter-terrorism 'CONTEST' strategy, based on the four Ps structure (Prevent, Pursue, Protect and Prepare), which provided the basis for the European Union's counter-terrorism strategy. He uses this comparative framework for cross-national comparisons. His chapter provides an account of intelligence-gathering organisations and their methods, including consideration of the 'tools' of intelligence, for example, open source, surveillance by intelligence officers or technical means, 'HUMINT' obtained via undercover agents and infiltration. He concludes by evaluating variations in structures, contexts and methods of various national intelligence organisations, in particular intelligence agency relationships with the government, the police and the military, and draws conclusions about the future implications for intelligence operations.

In Chapter 20, Robert Lambert, former head of the Muslim Contact Unit of the Metropolitan Police and now a critical terrorism studies researcher and writer, evaluates the effectiveness of counter-terrorism approaches and operations in the UK since 1969, and evaluates the effectiveness of 'tough' measures designed to counter terrorism. He focuses on political and operational counter-terrorism responses by the UK government to campaigns conducted by the Provisional IRA and allied Irish republican groups from 1969 onwards and by al-Qaeda and allied groups and individuals from 2001 onwards. He argues that both republican and violent jihadi movements have benefited from the retributive approaches taken by the UK government, which have been driven by a determination to appear to be tough on terrorism in the aftermath of violent attacks by these groups. He argues that the governments of Margaret Thatcher and Tony Blair produced responses to terrorist attacks that were insufficiently focused on the violent groups themselves and consequently stigmatised their constituent communities, thereby augmenting the sense of grievance represented by the violent groups in the first place. He argues that, in both instances, disproportionate government responses were capitalised upon by these groups' propagandists in order to reinforce their exhortations that communities adversely affected by draconian counter-terrorism measures should join their cause. He also examines the political impact of counter-terrorism policy on counter-terrorism policing and intelligence activity. He finds that there too, disproportionate operational activity has an adverse impact on communities sympathetic to the violent groups' cause and is therefore effectively counter-productive in that it increases the risk of increasing community support for violent methods. He concludes by advocating the merits of an operational counter-terrorism strategy that is focused on investigation and thus avoids alienating key sections of the community. This approach, he argues, pays dividends in terms of reducing proactive support for terrorism. He asserts that Tony Blair repeated the mistakes made by Margaret Thatcher's government and that this is indicative of the power of terrorist attacks to compel politicians to appease tabloid anger and outrage rather than to put in place effective counter-terrorist strategies and measures.

In Chapter 21, Michael McClintock, a former director of Amnesty International and an independent consultant, considers the impact of contemporary US counter-terrorism policies and practices on human rights. He describes how the attacks of 11 September 2001 led to a re-direction of American domestic and foreign policies. These policies, he argues, have undermined human rights protection both at home and abroad. He examines how counter-terrorism policies and practices have had serious consequences for human rights in the USA and the prospects for the restoration of the human rights protections that have been lost. He describes how, under the administration of George W. Bush, responses to the 9/11 attacks were established on multiple fronts, largely with widespread compliance, if not consent. Bush was granted a sweeping mandate for global action by Congress, which he used to enact an omnibus emergency law curtailing civil liberties. This was followed by a series of executive orders and secret legal memoranda, which in turn facilitated the introduction of torture, secret detention, clandestine international transfers, special courts and indefinite detention without charge or trial. These changes meant the undermining or setting aside of the fundamental rights of Americans and non-nationals to, amongst other things, due process of law, freedom of association, non-discrimination and privacy. Using government reports, court cases, the legislative record and newly declassified documents on counter-terrorism policies, he charts disagreements within the administration – and the military – over the direction taken. Nonetheless, the harm caused by the new normative framework is evident through the human rights record. He concludes by examining the promise of the Obama administration to deliver on a platform of change, whilst moving rapidly to reverse some of the abusive policies of the Bush administration. Yet much of the abusive framework of law and policy has remained in place. McClintock considers why this should be, and the indicators of public opinion and political direction in considering the prospects for change in such areas as domestic surveillance, preventive detention, fair trial and government secrecy.

Clive Walker, a former government advisor on civil contingencies and a prominent expert on anti-terrorism legislation, provides an analysis of the human rights implications of counter-terrorism measures in the UK in Chapter 22. In institutional terms, he argues that key decisions about the response to terrorism determine whether a predominantly military or policing strategy is to be used, who is to generate and own intelligence, and where financial support is to be directed. Choices about the legal regimes underpinning counter-terrorism approaches, from the rules of war and states of emergency to more nuanced uses of criminal justice approaches, will determine not only the nature of a society whilst it deals with terrorism but also how that society will emerge from terrorism and the residual scars it may bear. He argues that human rights discourse has emerged as a key determinant of counter-terrorist strategic choices and modes of delivery. He also sets out to assess the meaning and impact of this discourse, alongside the discourse of democratic accountability in counter-terrorism policy and practice in the UK. In spite of well-rehearsed human rights incursions, he argues that rights protection within counter-terrorism has strengthened since the entry into force (in October 2000) of the UK Human Rights Act 1998, which has helped to foster a more pervasive culture of rights beyond the Act's technical legal requirements. This culture is supported by three institutional support mechanisms: internal governmental 'Strasbourg proofing'; parliamentary scrutiny; and judicial review. These operate alongside the explicit reviews of the operations of counter-terrorism legislation itself.

Walker therefore argues that through the Act, observance of human rights standards is scrutinised within the domestic sphere and that these standards are applied to any sphere where effective British control exists – even if overseas. Although acknowledging the importance of the European Convention on Human Rights, the prime focus of Walker's chapter is on the impact of the Human Rights Act as the most important legal development in counter-terrorism over the past decade. He argues that counter-terrorism laws have become more permanently established and therefore human rights provisions can be seen as positive and growing in influence. However, he points out that, despite a broadly progressive picture, substantial paradoxes and weaknesses in the protection of human rights remain. He rejects the belief that a return to positivism in which the executive dominates the security agenda on the basis of subjective and secretive assessments will afford better protection against the excesses of counter-terrorism and consequently greater success against terrorism.

Ending Political Violence

Part 6 considers the way in which political violence ends or is brought to an end. The role of the state in 'managing' violence or resolving conflict, the significance of continuing political violence during political negotiations and the role of civil society in supplanting political violence with other processes are considered.

Bill Rolston, a prolific scholar on the Northern Ireland conflict and Director of the Transitional Justice Institute, considers whether Northern Ireland can provide a source of generalisable lessons about the role of the state in the management and resolution of conflict in Chapter 23. He argues that political events in Northern Ireland, such as Bloody Sunday, the firebombing of the La Mon House Hotel and the hunger strikes, have played a crucial role in radicalising both republican and loyalist activists in Northern Ireland. Focusing on republican activism, he asks why and how the state acts in effect as a recruiting sergeant for an insurgent group with which it is engaged in violent conflict. He considers the extent to which the state performs this role out of short-sightedness or lack of political imagination, and to what extent it is a result of the result of conflict management strategy wedded to military approaches and therefore regarding the mobilisation of enemies as 'collateral damage'. He concludes by examining whether the adherence to military approaches is due to opportunism, where politicians seek to enhance their political profile by responding to popular demands for action.

In Chapter 24, Roger Mac Ginty, a prominent analyst of peace processes, examines the prevalence and significance of violence during peace processes in the Israel–Palestine and Pakistan–India cases. He considers how and to what extent political violence can impact upon peace-making processes in civil wars and deeply divided societies. He argues that peace processes can be regarded as sustained attempts by major actors to reach an accommodation that lowers the cost of the conflict. Yet the peace process may be threatened by the continuation of violent conflict or by apparently 'new' forms and sources of violence. He examines how the pre-negotiation, negotiation, implementation and security sector reform stages of a process can be threatened or undermined by violence. Drawing on contemporary examples, he describes possible strategies in a peace process to counter such violence. Whilst treating terms such as 'spoiler' and 'crime' with caution, he emphasises the role of spoiler groups and spoiler violence.

The role of civil society actors in achieving an end to political violence is the focus of Chapter 25 by Avila Kilmurray. Taking the Northern Ireland case as her focus, Kilmurray uses her extensive experience as a civil society leader and expert on civil society in Northern Ireland to describe how organisations and activists in the community sector engaged with local issues and concerns during the period of violent conflict. Experiences of ongoing conflict were interwoven with perspectives on social and economic issues, although these were interpreted differently in republican and loyalist communities. She charts how social space was created to undertake community action in the midst of violence and how the meta-governmental narrative was communicated and understood within local communities. She argues that community initiatives acted as a catalyst for change, particularly in terms of both dealing with the implications of conflict and of emerging from violence. She illustrates how community-level action contributed to creating the conditions in which a transition from violence became possible. She holds that these experiences remain a largely hidden, if important history that played a critical part in achieving peace.

Dealing with the Aftermath

Part 7, the final part of the volume. considers issues of transitional justice after political violence has ended and the challenges of instituting social, political and economic formations that can support non-violent societal governance.

Richard Goldstone, a former chief prosecutor for the UN International Criminal Tribunals for the former Yugoslavia and Rwanda, and Adam Smith, an international lawyer based in Washington DC, set out the key issues in achieving the rule of law following the end of violent political conflict in Chapter 26. There has been a growing recognition that building 'rule of law' is an essential ingredient in sustaining the peaceful resolution of conflict. However, Goldstone and Smith argue that in spite of this growing consensus, there have been highly variable degrees of success in instituting and consolidating the rule of law in states emerging from political violence. Equivocation about the meaning of the rule of law does not assist its supporters. They point out that whilst some define the rule of law in hindsight (in that violence-prone countries have lacked a rule of law), others have adopted a functional approach (arguing that the rule of law is a system of enforceable, just regulations), while yet others advance a broader, systemic understanding that includes law, political and civil society. As a result, rule of law projects instituted in the wake of political violence have encountered a wide range of difficulties, three of the main obstacles being: difficulties in achieving a sense of local ownership; continuation of the distrust and division that previously fuelled violence; and the empowerment of spoilers of peace processes. The authors argue that the means by which the perpetrators of the violence are to be addressed, commonly referred to as transitional justice, is a key part of rebuilding rule of law. Transitional justice can help identify some of the obstacles facing broader rule of law projects. They conclude that transitional justice is important, yet fragile, and can either solidify or impede wider rule of law efforts.

Finally in Chapter 27, focusing on the case of Afghanistan, William Maley, an expert on Afghanistan and on international intervention, provides an account of political, economic and social reconstruction after political violence. The case of the Afghan transition process following the overthrow of the Taliban is an instructive case study. It clearly illustrates the challenges of achieving functioning institutions in a context of massive social dislocation and an absence of trust between key actors. Maley argues that the Afghan case, where the transition takes place in an environment of continuing violence, as opposed to a cessation of armed conflict, is typical of such transitions. This, he argues, has led to emerging scholarly attention to the challenges of 'conflictual peacebuilding'. The Afghan case provides a salutary warning that the commitment of international actors can easily drift and that after major political change, there may only be one opportunity to get things right. In the course of the chapter, he provides an account of the historical development of the Afghan state and its subsequent collapse which frames the challenges for the transition. He sets out and evaluates the approaches to political, economic and social development taken from 2001 onwards. He also examines the impact of the wider international environment that Afghanistan faced and assesses where Afghanistan finds itself after these reconstruction efforts, and draws lessons for other such endeavours in the future.

Together, these chapters provide an overview of many of the key issues relating to political violence. They raise issues of definition, motivation, how political violence is variously understood, the ethical, legal and political significance of political violence, why it happens, what drives it, how to intercept, manage and stop it, and how to deal with the aftermath. The reader is invited to explore these issues through the chapters in each part. In the conclusions, further questions that arise as a result of these chapters are set out, and a number of other issues and questions that are not explored here and can provide the subjects for further study are indicated.

PART I
Defining Political Violence

Political Violence: An Overview

John Darby[1]

This chapter sets out to consider some of the problems that cluster around the concept of political violence, starting with an examination of the boundaries between political violence and other forms of violence. It will review changes in the patterns of political violence over the last 30 years or so, from an earlier focus on international wars to more recent challenges, including those presented by the Global War on Terror in the early years of the twenty-first century. It will conclude by exploring exit routes from political violence and the consequences of its ending through military victory or through a negotiated settlement.

Contested Terms

Existing definitions of political violence tend to be all-inclusive rather than precise. One recent definition, aimed primarily at the business community, includes 'armed revolution, civil strife, terrorism, war, and other such causes that can result in injury or loss of property' (BusinessDictionary). Another definition, widely used by undergraduate students, goes on to include the motivation of the perpetrators: 'Politically motivated violence is commonly referred to by the terms terrorism, rebellion, war, conquest, revolution, oppression, tyranny, and many others. In general, it can be defined as committing violent actions against others with the intended purpose of effecting a change in their actions' (Wikipedia).

The presumption in most definitions is that political violence includes organized violence aimed at overturning the state. Can it also be used to describe violence by the state against its political rivals? What about the use of protest by either the state or its opponents in order to provoke a violent response from their opponents? Is it a useful term to apply to violence not involving the state, but directed against

---

[1] During the final stages of editing this volume, Professor John Darby, author of this chapter, died peacefully at his home in Portstewart, Northern Ireland after a short illness. He will be sadly missed by his friends and colleagues for his insightful wisdom, generosity and good humour.

political opponents or ethnic rivals, such as confrontations between republicans and loyalists in Northern Ireland, or wars with rival organizations inside their own ethnic community, such as the LTTE elimination of rival Tamil militant groups? Should the 'fundraising' activities conducted to finance the struggle – bank robberies, kidnapping and drug dealing – lose their *imprimatur* when the war ends and simply be classified as conventional crime?

Towards a Definition

So what conditions are necessary to qualify a conflict as political violence, in order to distinguish it from other forms of conflict? As already indicated, the two are far from discrete and the boundary between them is best regarded as a sliding scale located between the two extreme positions. Four propositions are suggested here. They are not definitive statements, but are intended to provoke a debate in search of a working definition of the term.

Proposition 1. Political violence's principal activities, and key aims, are primarily expressed within an existing political entity, but they may be inspired and strengthened by international movements.

Proposition 2. Political violence involves the use of violence rather than the use of protest. The use of protest in order to provoke violence lies in the no-man's land between protest and violence.

Proposition 3. The objective of political violence is to achieve changes in the political system rather than other forms of social change

Proposition 4. Political violence is an organized activity.

Three questions will be examined to test the border between political violence and other violent activities: is political violence always conducted within a specific state, or can the term ever be applied to international conflict? Does the motivation of the perpetrators, whether it is aimed at advancing a political position or personal gain, help to determine the definition? And how can a distinction be made between political pressure and political violence?

Inter-state or Intra-state?

One important distinction between armed conflicts within a state and wars between states is that inter-state wars are more likely to end decisively in victory. Internal political violence usually produces less decisive outcomes, for a range of reasons: the combatants permanently inhabit the same battlefield; even during periods of tranquillity, their lives are often intermeshed with those of their opponents; and it is not possible to terminate hostilities by withdrawal behind national frontiers. As a consequence, political violence is often characterized by internecine viciousness rather than by the more impassive slaughter of inter-state wars.

POLITICAL VIOLENCE: AN OVERVIEW

Political violence carried out within a state's boundaries, at its most extreme, can escalate into civil war. The distinction is one of scale and intensity. According to Toft and others, certain criteria must be satisfied for a local armed conflict to qualify as a civil war: it must be a dispute about governing the territory; at least two organized groups of combatants must be fighting; one of them must be the state; the stronger side must suffer at least five per cent of the casualties; and the war must be largely waged within the boundaries of a state (Toft 2006). More contentious is the common view that there must be at least 1,000 battle deaths a year, which appears to rule out the possibility of a civil war, however high the casualty rate proportionately, in places where the population is small, such as Fiji and Northern Ireland. Nevertheless, by all these measures, political violence is a term that is not applied to inter-state wars, but only to internal armed conflicts.

Unfortunately, the distinction between inter-state war and internal violence is undermined by a number of complications. First is the presumption by militants that their liberation struggles are actually legitimate wars. In virtually every peace process initiated since 1990, one of the preconditions required by militants for entering negotiations was the release of prisoners, in effect a claim that they are more than rebels or militants or criminals, but warriors engaged in a war. By implication, the violence preceding the peace process was a war rather than the plethora of other words – insurrection, rebellion, qualified terms such as guerrilla war or civil war – often used to describe it. For militant groups, this acknowledgement helps to provide the symmetry between governments and militants necessary for successful peace negotiations.

A second complication in distinguishing between inter-state and intra-national armed conflicts is the growing regionalization and internationalization of political violence. This partly arises from the social demography of ethnicity. Most ethnic minorities are not confined within a single nation-state and many disputes arise from a mismatch between the claims of particular ethnic groups and those of recognized states. Ted Gurr's (1992) international study of 'Minorities at Risk' found that 'of the 179 minorities identified in the survey, more than two thirds (122) have ethnic kindred in one or more adjacent countries'.[2] The cases of Serbs in Croatia and Bosnia, Russians within many of the successor states of the USSR, and the Kurds and the Chinese in many Asian countries illustrate that ethnic identity often ignores the borders of nation-states. A 1991 study by the Institute of Geographers in Moscow, for example, concluded that only three of the 23 borders between the former Republics of the USSR were not disputed (Anderson and Smith 2001). It is not uncommon for minority groups to look to neighbouring countries for protection, or for neighbouring countries to make irredentist claims, thus propelling local disputes onto the world stage. De Silva and May (1991, 10) have described this process as the 'second law of ethnic conflict, that once such a conflict breaks out,

---

2 As further illustration, Walker Connor (1994) estimated that, in the early 1970s, only about ten per cent of states could claim to be nation-states in the sense that the state's boundaries coincided with those of the nation and that the state's population shared a single ethnic culture.

sooner or later, indeed sooner rather than later in this era of instant communications, it will be internationalized'. It is no longer realistic to regard political violence, in contrast to international wars, as a second-level threat to world order.

Political Conflict or Political Violence?

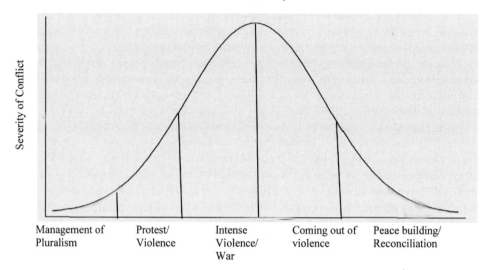

Figure 1.1　Graph to show the conflict cycle

At what point does political conflict become political violence? Consider all pluralist societies as positioned along a Bell curve, according to how effectively they deal with their component groups; the pattern might be presented as an ascending line.

At the bottom of the line are peacefully regulated multicultural societies currently experiencing little or no political violence, such as Canada and Australasia; both of these have experienced tensions, and sometimes political violence, in the past and may experience it again in the future.

Moving along the ascending line, a large number of communities suffer relatively low levels of political violence, including in the present or recent past the Basque Country, Guatemala and South Africa. In all these places violence has been conducted by organizations against the state or ethnic rivals, but has been controlled by the presence of an army or by indigenous social and economic mechanisms. If communal grievances are not addressed rapidly at this stage, violence tends to escalate and may ultimately spiral out of control into civil war.

At the top of the graph are societies in which political violence has spiralled out of control, such as those in Rwanda, Sri Lanka and Iraq. These are often characterized by open warfare conducted by organized armies. The down slope of the Bell curve is the post-violent phase of the violence cycle, following victory by one or other side, or a no-war no-peace stalemate. This is also the phase that includes the negotiation of a peace agreement and its implementation, or the resumption of violence. Permanent peace is not an attainable aspiration.

Individual societies may move along the line of the graph at different speeds. Some have completed the full course more than once, while others oscillate around one point over prolonged periods. The risk is that the violence may follow a succession of curves along the graph, as political violence rises, is suppressed or insufficiently addressed, and resumes at some future date.

It is sometimes possible, especially during the earlier phases of political violence, to address grievances and to initiate or strengthen progress towards a more peaceful accommodation by the introduction of appropriate policies. It is also possible for low-violence conflicts to be suppressed temporarily by force. But if serious grievances are not addressed rapidly, they tend to accelerate along the line of grievance and to become increasingly violent. In the absence of political reform, political violence is the default position.

Political violence enters the arena between the second and third phases of the graph. It is not always easy to draw a distinction between the more aggressive forms of peaceful protest and the beginning of violence. Are protesters against abortion clinics an illegitimate restraint on individual choice or a legitimate form of political expression? If the protest leads to violence – and at least eight people associated with clinics in the USA have been murdered since 1993, the most recent being Dr George Tiller in 2004 – does this constitute political violence? Similarly, it is not easy to draw a distinction between the state's obligation to maintain order and its use of force. Is the use of water cannons or taser guns to control a protesting crowd a legitimate means of control or the start of a progression towards the use of political violence by the state? Despite the difficulty in drawing a firm line between them, a distinction must be made between political protest and political violence. It is the use of violence that gives political violence one of its essential features.

Political Violence or 'Ordinary Decent Crime'?

Moser and Clark suggest that violent social and political conflicts can be classified in three different ways: economic, social and political. They conceptualize economic violence as 'street crime, carjacking, robbery/theft, drug trafficking, kidnapping, and assaults'. Social violence represents disturbances at a more interpersonal level such as domestic violence. Political violence includes 'guerrilla conflict, paramilitary conflict, political assassinations, armed conflict between political parties, rape and sexual abuse as political act and forced pregnancy/sterilization' (2001, 36). They acknowledge that the boundaries between social, economic and political violence often overlap and are difficult to distinguish. Political violence is defined as 'the commission of violent acts motivated by a desire, conscious or unconscious, to obtain or maintain political power' (2001, 36).

This seems straightforward, almost a tautology. In practice it can be much more complicated. Consider the following case. In the late 1970s IRA prisoners in Northern Ireland engaged in a 'blanket protest', during which they refused to wear prison uniforms; this soon escalated into a 'dirty protest', during which they smeared the walls of their cells with excrement; finally, in 1980 and 1981 the protests culminated in the deaths of ten prisoners during two hunger strikes and a resurgence of support for republicans in the nationalist community. The reason for the escalating protests was the government's decision in 1976 to withdraw 'Special Category Status', or political status, for prisoners convicted of paramilitary offences, and the prisoners' insistence that they were prisoners of war and should be treated differently from other prisoners. The other prisoners were equally eager to be distinguished from IRA prisoners. They had been incarcerated, after all, for what was described ironically in Northern Ireland as 'ordinary decent crime'. As such, the IRA prisoners denied that their actions were criminal and the 'ordinary decent criminals' would also have denied any political agenda.

The IRA hunger strikes and the response to them indicate how difficult it is to make a distinction between political violence and conventional criminality. Their manifestations are often indistinguishable. Militant organizations often feel justified in carrying out criminal acts to fund their armed struggle, including drug dealing (Colombia), blackmail (Sri Lanka), bank robberies (Northern Ireland), smuggling (Democratic Republic of the Congo) and kidnapping (Somalia). Indeed, there is a tendency to resort to indigenous forms of fundraising, and armed organizations sometimes follow the example of similar organizations in other countries. Consequently, the distinction between politically motivated violence and 'ordinary decent crime' is determined only by the intentions of the perpetrators.

Political Violence: Validity, Costs and Effectiveness

Popular attitudes to political violence are largely determined by subjective and situational variables. One perspective is that the price of political violence, as measured in human casualties, economic costs and inter-group tensions, will ultimately be higher than the grievances that led to the violence in the first place. What is the conclusion drawn by this position? Is it an argument that political violence is thus never justified because it is more costly? An alternative position holds that the continuing refusal by the state to redress fundamental minority rights, despite legitimate efforts to change the situation – through the elected assembly or the courts, through the media, through pressure from external authorities and through peaceful protest, for example – will inevitably reach a point when force is the only means available to the discontented. Again, what is the conclusion? Is this an argument that, by their refusal to reform, the state is therefore morally culpable for the violence that ensues?

Consider two examples: at the start of the twentieth century, anarchist movements in Europe and North America attempted to forcibly overthrow governments elected by popular vote; there was little dissention either internationally or nationally when various governments asserted their obligation to protect their citizens against anarchist terror by the introduction of what has been described as 'draconian anti-terrorist legislation and the official use of torture' (Carr 2008, 29–31). In this first case, the robust response by the state was justified in terms of ensuring the security of the population. During the 1980s and 1990s, the South African government cited a similar justification for its military campaign against the African National Congress (ANC). In this case, international reaction was more ambivalent. Many regarded the ANC campaign, especially following the introduction of apartheid, as partially or wholly justified by the intransigent and undemocratic nature of the South African government. Who was guilty of political violence here – the state that maintained its minority control over a majority by systematic discrimination under the apartheid system or the militants who resisted the state by a campaign of force? Despite the use of force by the ANC, the global community was sufficiently exercised by the innately discriminatory nature of the South African state to impose sanctions.

What factors determine these different responses? Political violence can arise from a number of sources, including the state, and at every stage of a conflict, from the inception of armed conflict itself to the implementation of a peace agreement. Attitudes towards the use of violence during the years of armed conflict become less ambivalent when the conflicting parties are moving towards a settlement. The Irish Taoiseach (Prime Minister), Bertie Ahern, suggested in *The Observer* in 1997 that: 'It is an observable phenomenon in Northern Ireland and elsewhere that tension and violence tend to rise when compromise is in the air.'[3] Almost three times as many people were killed in South Africa while the agreement was being negotiated between 1990 and 1994 than in the previous four years (Du Toit 2000, 32). The use of political violence also rose dramatically during the Middle East peace process, and more than two-thirds of victims were killed during the Rabin/Peres era (Hermann and Newman 2000). Nor does violence disappear when a ceasefire is declared and a peace process starts; indeed, the same actors, recently regarded as combatants or freedom fighters, are regarded as criminals the day after peace is declared. In addition, the forms of violence change in ways that may threaten the evolving peace process. The threats come from three principal sources: the state, the militants opposing it and the dynamics of violence at community level.

Political Violence by the State

Political violence, as demonstrated by the two definitions cited at the start of this chapter, is generally interpreted exclusively as the use of violence against a state, based on the premise that the state has a monopoly on the legitimate use of force. In many cases of armed conflict, however, the prime motor for violence against the

---

3   *The Observer*, 22 September 1997.

state is the failure of the state to satisfy the basic needs and demands of its citizens. Johan Galtung and others described this failure as structural violence (Galtung and Hoivik 1971). They argue that it inevitably produces social conflict and, if not modified, leads to violence against the state. Nor does political violence by the state end when the state attempts to end this violence by entering into negotiations with its opponent. Governments are often even more divided about peace processes than about the armed conflict that preceded them. During the war, the requirement to present a united front trumped any misgivings individual ministers might have had about waging it and ensured at least the appearance of unity. The decision to enter into negotiations with 'terrorists' is often accompanied by dissension. Governmental or quasi-governmental agencies may continue covert actions to undermine the process itself, as when the 'third force' in South Africa used violence to support the Inkatha Freedom Party (IFP). Even if such pressure is not applied, the security apparatus built up during periods of violence is a potential danger when they end. Militants are released instead of imprisoned. The security forces augmented during the violence are abruptly reduced in number, endangering their jobs and personal security. Demands are made to reform the police force that regarded itself as the bastion against terrorism. Unless handled carefully, disaffection within the security forces has the potential to undermine the peace process itself.

State violence may continue even after peace accords are signed. According to South Africa's Minister of Safety and Security, some members of both the state security services and the ANC were still active in crime syndicates as late as 1998 (Republic of South Africa 1998, 14). In Indonesia the inability or unwillingness of the government to control the actions of its security forces in East Timor in the build-up to the independence referendum in 1999 led to many deaths and the forced evacuation of 200,000 people. In the face of considerable international pressure, the Foreign Minister, Ali Alatas, eventually admitted that the military and the police had participated in the violence, but he attributed it to 'rogue elements' and 'criminal activities' (Lander 1999). Since then, a report commissioned by the United Nations concluded that, far from a few soldiers misbehaving, a systematic campaign of terror had been 'planned and carried out' by the Indonesian army, with militia participation, to undermine the vote for independence in the referendum. It concluded:

> Several of the senior officers named in this report not only sponsored the setting up of the militia, providing training, arms, money and in some cases drugs; they also encouraged its campaign of violence and organized the wave of destruction and deportation that occurred between 5 and 20 September [1999]. (*Sydney Morning Herald* 2001)

Ending Political Violence from Militants

Political violence from militant groups is a more obvious threat to peacemaking. Rather than the monoliths presented by their opponents, they are rather umbrellas that provide shelter for a range of diffuse and often contradictory interests – political fundamentalists, oppressed minorities, common criminals and psychopaths. Their internal differences are temporarily sidelined in the interests of the common cause. When the fighting stops, the interests sheltering under the umbrella go their separate ways, presenting at least four potential threats to peace processes.

A Return to Political Violence

Ceasefires are never unanimous, so the most obvious threat is that they will break down and that political violence will return. The more disaffected members of the militants may desert to form splinter groups. The less disaffected may go along with the majority view, but their continuing allegiance will depend on securing measurable benefits from negotiation, including prisoner releases and the dismantling of the security apparatus. These rewards are rarely immediate. Consequently, the pendulum may swing back towards militancy. It is worth remembering that negotiations broke down in both Northern Ireland and South Africa, leading to periods of renewed violence in 1996 and 1992 respectively, before the peace processes resumed.

'Tactical' Violence

A common fear among constitutional parties is that the pace of negotiation will be determined by the gunmen outside the negotiating rooms and that their political surrogates may use the threat of violence to get their own way; acts of violence during the process are taken as confirmation of this fear. The early stages of the Oslo Process were hampered by Israeli suspicion of the motives of the Palestine Liberation Organization (PLO), and later the government regarded atrocities carried out by Hamas as evidence that Yasser Arafat was either unable to control his own people or was colluding with it for strategic advantage. During the early stages of the Northern Ireland peace process, Unionists constantly warned that Sinn Féin would use IRA violence to remind other negotiators of its power. As the negotiations progressed, it became increasingly clear that violence threatened Sinn Féin's interests as much as those of the Unionists. The complaints diminished, as they had earlier in South Africa.

Spoilers: Zealots versus Dealers

The very involvement of paramilitary interests in negotiations implies that the purity of their cause has been compromised. It is difficult to find any instances when such a move was not accompanied by a split between the negotiators and zealots within their own communities. In Sri Lanka the result was a succession of assassinations of Tamil rivals by the Liberation Tigers of Tamil Eelam (LTTE); in 1998 they murdered the Tamil Mayor of Jaffna, having previously killed her husband, and went on to kill her successor as mayor. All major attempts to start negotiations in Israel-Palestine were accompanied by Palestinian attempts to bomb them away; the killing of 28 Muslims by the Israeli settler Baruch Goldstein in 1994 and the assassination of the Israeli Prime Minister Yitzhak Rabin in 1995 showed that zealots were eager to overturn the process. Both white and black dissidents threatened the South African process, although both were relatively well controlled during the period of negotiation.

Internal Paramilitary Violence

The determination of militants to exercise control over their own communities may not diminish when they enter a negotiation process. They are unlikely to hand over this negotiating card, even at the risk of destabilizing the peace process itself. Violence between factions within the Palestinian community continued long after the first transfer of land to Palestinian control in 1995 and intensified a decade later. Punishment beatings persisted in Northern Ireland after the Good Friday Agreement as both loyalists and republicans exercised what they regarded as their policing role.

Political Violence in the Community

Two other forms of quasi-political violence may also seriously undermine peace processes – the revival of direct confrontations between political rivals and a rise in the conventional crime rate.

When a ceasefire is declared, the discipline of the military campaign diminishes, but the underlying sectarian hatred remains, taking the form of riots and undisciplined confrontations with political rivals or the police. The paramilitary representatives who enter negotiations are not divorced from the instincts and antagonisms of their communities, and may feel the need to support them. During the early months of negotiation in South Africa, sectional violence was partly orchestrated between the ANC and the IFP, but spilled over into tit-for-tat killings and more general violence. In Northern Ireland the declaration of the 1994 ceasefires was marked by a return to more direct violence between Catholics and Protestants, especially during the marching seasons from 1996 to 1998.

In addition to growing confrontational violence, the level of conventional crime, especially violent crime, is also likely to rise after a peace agreement, fuelled by the arms stockpiled during the years of violence; in Angola an AK-47 could be bought for the price of a chicken (Naylor 1997). By 1998 violent crime had emerged as a serious problem in both Guatemala and San Salvador, raising concerns about a possible correlation between high crime rates and disrespect for new democratic institutions. During the 1990s, the crime rate rose to such a degree in South Africa as to seriously undermine post-settlement stability, something that was not helped by low conviction rates (Sidiropoulos et al. 1998); by 1998, the daily homicide rate was averaging 68, the world's highest (Du Toit 2000, 98). Although the crime rate included a potential political threat – 1,500 white farmers were attacked between 1994 and 1998, resulting in more than 200 murders – a review of post-war violence by Roger Mac Ginty (2006) concluded that conventional crime has not been identified as a major factor contributing to the outright failure of a peace accord, except insofar as it might erode confidence in the agreement among the general population.

Therefore, the effects of political violence on peacemaking are not universal or constant. They vary between different settings and between different stages in the peace process. Although a peace process usually follows open warfare between a highly militarized state and guerrilla-type opposition, the level of violence may intensify during the pre-negotiation phase as combatants try to optimize their negotiating positions. The negotiations themselves are often accompanied by the emergence of more extreme dissident groups. Negotiators also have to confront a new range of priority issues, including demands for the early release of prisoners, demobilization[4] and policing reform, as well as the re-integration of militants into society and consideration of their victims. Although these patterns generally apply, they are also heavily influenced by local distinctions. Each distinct form, however, demands different policy approaches, for governments, international and regional bodies, negotiators and non-governmental organizations (NGOs) attempting to move towards a fair and lasting settlement.

Changing Patterns of Political Violence

Is political violence increasing? The answer, as usual, depends on definitions. The second half of the twentieth century did not experience anything close to the number of deaths inflicted during the two World Wars. However, if violence is measured by the number of conflicts rather than by casualties, the pattern is quite different. Since the ending of the Cold War, there has been an increase in the number of localized conflicts. The University of Uppsala has been monitoring political violence internationally, classifying instances by the number of casualties as either minor armed conflicts (less than 25 deaths and involving at least one state), intermediate armed conflicts (more than 25 deaths in one year and more than 1,000 during the conflict) or major armed conflicts (more than 1,000 deaths in one year). In the three years between 1989 and 1992 alone, the amalgamated total came to 82; 35 of them were major armed conflicts. By 2008 there were 16 major armed conflicts active in 15 locations, two more than in the previous year. These were geographically widely spread – three in the Middle East, three in Africa, seven

---

4   There is a growing literature on demobilization, disarmament and reconstruction (DDR). 'Demobilization' usually refers to the reduction or removal of arms held by state agents, the army or the police, and the term 'disarmament' to describe the handing over of weapons held by militants. These common usages are somewhat complicated by the popular usage of 'decommissioning' in Northern Ireland to describe disarmament by paramilitary organizations.

in Asia and three in the Americas. Harbom and Wallensteen (2009, Appendix 2A) summarize the findings as follows:

> All of these conflicts are intrastate: for the fifth year running, no major interstate conflict was active in 2008. However, troops from another state aided one of the parties in four conflicts: USA, Afghanistan, Iraq and Somalia. Over the past decade, the total number of conflicts has declined overall from 21 in 1999. However, the decline has been uneven, with increases in 2005 and 2008.

Traditional Approaches to Political Violence

These figures only apply to major armed conflicts. If minor conflicts were included, the total would be significantly higher and would include racist tensions in Europe as well as religious and ethnic disputes trapped within the enormous territories of India, China and Russia. Galtung has claimed that only 20 states are nation-states (Galtung, Jacobsen and Brand-Jacobsen, 2000), but even this low figure may be exaggerated. In addition to suppressed ethnic minorities whose voices may not be heard, new minorities may emerge in previously relatively monolithic societies through the emergence of new grievances, the arrival of immigrants or international developments such as globalization. A permanently monolithic society is unrealizable.

So how have states traditionally dealt with political violence and complex minority tensions? Simpson and Yinger (1965) listed six policy approaches by which a politically dominant group may deal with its opponents: assimilation, either forced or permitted; pluralism; legal protection for minorities; population transfer (either negotiated or forced); continued subjugation; and extermination. Historically, the most common approach to handling inconvenient minorities has hovered between the most violent of these alternatives: subjugation and extermination. Primary responsibility for the resolution of internal disputes has traditionally resided with the nation-state. If the conflict was between groups within the state, any suggestion of external arbitration is often rigorously resisted, and the right of states to deal with their own internal affairs is a key component of the UN Charter. As a result, severe political violence – often effectively a war – may rage within countries while the international community stands by, as evidenced in Bosnia, Rwanda, and Burundi in the 1990s.

New Challenges: The Global War on Terror

Violence from within is the most usual contemporary manifestation of political violence, but regional and global contexts may also have a powerful effect on whether conflicts move toward violence or settlement. The context alters continually. During the Cold War, the two superpowers maintained their own form of order against threats of violence from within their own areas of control; the Soviet Union in Hungary, Yugoslavia and Russia, the USA in the Americas. The ending of the Cold War in the 1990s revealed the persistence of old national and ethnic allegiances. Mary Kaldor (1999) and others have argued that the challenges to state autonomy and authority internationally have led to a succession of 'new wars' in which the traditional state monopoly on the use of violence was increasingly undermined; the distinctions between traditional wars, international crime and human rights violations became increasingly blurred.

Developments following the events of 11 September 2001 again altered the global context for many armed conflicts. President Bush's declaration of a 'War against Terror' had a number of local and regional consequences. It became more difficult to distinguish between the war against al-Qaeda and long-standing political struggles in Indonesia, Palestine and Sudan. The effects of this conflation between terrorism and political violence have been critical, both for governments and for militants opposing them. Some governments, encouraged by the growing concern about terrorism, distanced themselves from the possibility of negotiations with militant minorities in their own countries. Others justified tougher security approaches as part of the Global War on Terror. Actions such as the torture of prisoners and assassinations of militant leaders, previously conducted covertly by governments in the interests of security, were more likely to be carried out more openly, encouraged by a new atmosphere of anti-terrorism.

The effects of these changes on militant opponents of government were twofold. The stronger actions angered many Muslim groups and nations. Violent resistance intensified, especially in parts of Asia and the Middle East. On the other hand, it is clear that the new global temperature reduced support from diaspora populations for the Tamil Tigers in Sri Lanka, for dissident republican groups in Ireland, etc. Military intervention by governments applied pressure on their campaigns. Paradoxically, the Global War on Terror provided a potential international safety net for some governments to engage in a peace process with political dissidents. If militants called off talks and re-started the war – and the sanctions against this increased – the international community seemed ready to provide substantial assistance to governments. One might argue about the relative benefits and costs. The Global War on Terror significantly altered the local climate within which political violence was conducted.

It also altered the model of peace processes developed during the 1990s, one that sought opportunities to negotiate rather than confront. The Global War on Terror encouraged an alternative model, one that saw the possibility of victory over dissent; its characteristics are strength and the presentation of stark choices. The two models co-exist, and the arrival of the Obama administration may swing the pendulum again, but the Global War on Terror demonstrates yet again the ability of global developments to affect traditional patterns of political violence.

Victory or Negotiation? Exit Routes from Political Violence

Once political violence intensifies into major armed conflict or civil war, its resolution is usually the result of either a decisive victory for one side or through a comprehensive peace agreement accepted by the main actors and addressing the central issues in contention. The balance between these two approaches has not been constant. The vast majority of the 41 civil wars between 1940 and 1989 ended through military victory, with only 20 per cent being resolved through negotiation (Walter 1997), but the pattern changed significantly when the Cold War ended. Ninety per cent of all civil wars during the 1980s ended through military victory and none through negotiated settlement. During the 1990s, 39 per cent of civil wars ended in victory, but 42 per cent ended through negotiated settlement. The Uppsala Conflict Data Program (UCDP), broadening the canvas to include all intra-state conflicts between 1946 and 2005, confirms the pattern. As many as 58.2 per cent of intra-state conflicts ended in victory between 1946 and 1989, but only 13.6 per cent between 1990 and 2005, while the percentage ended by peace agreement rose from 8.5 per cent to 18.4 per cent. While victory was the most common form of conflict termination during the Cold War, it has become the least common category since 1989 (Fortna 2004). The figures take on an additional significance if the duration of the fighting is considered. Almost 75 per cent of all intra-state conflicts that ended in victory were concluded in the first year of fighting (King 1997; Wallensteen and Sollenberg 2001; see also Marshall and Gurr 2003). If neither combatant is able to deliver a quick victory, it is more likely to be settled through mediation and negotiation, and most studies of peace processes have concentrated on how entry points may be found for external intervention in the conflict cycle. Zartman (1989) emphasized the importance of taking advantage of the 'ripe moment' when the parties in conflict have reached a 'hurting stalemate', when the costs and prospects of war outweigh the costs and prospects of settlement for the major combatants.

It has been suggested that military victory by one side or the other is more likely than negotiated settlements to lead to longer-term stability and is less likely to lead to a renewal of war. Luttwak has argued that if wars are allowed to reach their 'natural conclusion', the losers' ability to re-mobilize is diminished. The successful side was sufficiently powerful to win the war and is therefore more likely to ensure post-war order, especially if rebels rather than governments are the victors (Toft 2006). Negotiated settlements collapse, on the other hand, because, as Walter (1997, 335) put it, 'civil war opponents are asked to do what they consider unthinkable' – to demobilize at a time when disorder is endemic and guarantees are uncertain. A peace agreement would confirm the state's monopoly over the use of force, although the transfer of ex-militants into the police and security forces, as in the Palestinian territories and South Africa, may help to convert a potentially destabilizing armed threat into support for the new structures. Nevertheless, an agreement would require that non-state combatants dismantle their war machine, thus removing their safeguards against anarchy or the state's perfidy, and reducing their strength if war were to resume.

These arguments are somewhat persuasive, but underrate the advantages of negotiated peace agreements over military victories. At least three important qualifications challenge the claim that military victory is more likely than negotiations to lead to post-war stability. First, the stability achieved by a successful army often carries a high cost in terms of denied democratization and human rights; Burma, for example, was relatively stable from its military coup in 1962 until 2009, but its internal differences remain unresolved. Second, terminations of civil wars through conquest may appear to produce a temporary settlement while they actually lay the foundations for a revival of violence. In other words, the claim that 'wars ended by negotiated settlement are three times more likely to reignite than those ended by military victory' (Toft 2006, 13) adopts too short a timescale for measuring success. The victory may create only short-term stability while increasing the likelihood of recurrence, as it has in the countries of the former Yugoslavia and Chechnya.

Finally, not only do peace accords save lives, at least in the short term, but they are the product of compromise between the main actors in the war, following an attempt to confront basic political differences. Unlike military victories, they are less likely to concentrate power within one group in a contested society and are therefore less likely to lead to a resumption of the serious inter-group conflict that had led to violence in the first place. Certainly, the different aspirations of the new partners present them with a fundamental challenge. The challenge is worth facing if it starts a process towards normal politics and reconstruction.

References

Anderson, K. and Smith, S. (2001), 'Editorial: Emotional Geographies', *Transactions of the Institute of British Geographers* 26:1, 7–10.
BusinessDictionary, 1, 14.
Carr, M. (2008), 'Cloaks, Daggers and Dynamite', *History Today* 57:12, 29–31.
Connor, W. (1994), *Ethnonationalism: The Quest for Understanding* (Princeton: Princeton University Press).
De Silva, K.M. and May, R.J. (eds) (1991), *Internationalistion of Ethnic Conflict* (London: Pinter).
Du Toit, P. (2000), 'The Peace Process in South Africa', in J. Darby and R. Mac Ginty (eds), *The Management of Peace Processes* (London: Macmillan), 16–60.
Fortna, V. (2004), *Peace Time: Cease-Fire Agreements and the Durability of Peace* (Princeton: Princeton University Press).
Galtung J. and Hoivik, T. (1971), 'Structural and Direct Violence: A Note on Operationalization', *Journal of Peace Research* VIII:1, 73–6.
Galtung, J., Jacobsen, C. and Brand-Jacobsen, K.F. (2000), *Searching for Peace: The Road to TRANSCEND* (London: Transcend, Pluto).
Gurr T.R. (1992), 'Third World Minorities at Risk', in S.J. Brown and K.M. Schraub (eds), *Resolving Third World Conflict* (Washington DC: USIP).

Harbom, L. and Wallensteen, P. (2009), *SIPRI Yearbook* (Stockholm: Stockholm International Peace Research Institute).

Hermann, T. and Newman, D. (2000), 'Israel-Palestine: A Path Strewn with Thorns', in J. Darby and R. Mac Ginty (eds), *The Management of Peace Processes* (London: Macmillan), 107–53.

Kaldor, M. (1999), *New and Old Wars: Organised Violence in a Global Era* (Cambridge: Polity Press).

King, C. (1997), *Ending Civil Wars* (London: International Institute for Strategic Studies Adelphi Paper).

Kroon, R. (1999), 'Q & A/Ali Alatas, Foreign Minister: Jakarta Goal for East Timor: Autonomy', *New York Times*, 3 February, http://www.nytimes.com/1999/02/03/news/03iht-quanda.t.html [accessed 4 July 2012].

Lander, M. (1999), 'The Fate of East Timor: The Indonesian View; Jakarta Military is Taking Central Role in Crisis', *New York Times*, 10 September.

Mac Ginty, R. (2006), 'Post-Accord Crime', in J. Darby (ed.), *Violence and Reconstruction* (Notre Dame: University of Notre Dame Press).

Marshall, M.G. and Gurr, T.R. (2003), *Peace and Conflict 2003: A Global Survey of Armed Conflicts, Self-Determination Movements, and Democracy*, http://www.systemicpeace.org/PC2003.pdf [accessed 4 July 2012].

Moser, C. and Clark, F. (2001), *Victims, Perpetrators, or Actors? Gendered Armed Conflict and Political Violence* (New York: St Martin's Press).

Naylor, R.T. (1997), 'The Rise of the Modern Arms Black Market and the Fall of Supply-Side Control', in V. Gamba (ed.), *Society under Siege – Crime, Violence and Illegal Weapons* (Johannesburg: Institute for Security Studies), 43–72.

Republic of South Africa (1998), Interpellations, Questions and Replies of the National Assembly, Second Session, Second Parliament, Government Printer. Cape Town, 18 February.

Sidiropoulos, E. et al. (1998), *South Africa Survey 1997–98* (Johannesburg: South African Institute of Race Relations).

Simpson, G. and Yinger, J. (1965), *Racial and Cultural Minorities* (New York: Harper & Row).

Sydney Morning Herald (2001), 'East Timor Massacre Work of Indonesia's Army', *Sydney Morning Herald*, 20 April.

Toft, M.D. (2006), 'Peace through Security: How to Make Negotiated Settlements Stick', paper presented at the International Studies Association annual meeting, March, http://citation.allacademic.com/meta/p_mla_apa_research_citation/1/0/0/2/3/pages100235/p100235-1.php [accessed 4 July 2012].

Wallensteen, P. and Sollenberg, M. (2001), 'Armed Conflict, 1989–2000', *Journal of Peace Research* 38:5, 629–44.

Walter, B.F. (1997), 'The Critical Barrier to Civil War Settlement', *International Organization* 51:3, 335–64.

Wikipedia. http://en.wikipedia.org/wiki/Political_violence [accessed 4 July 2012].

Zartman, I.W. (1989), *Ripe for Resolution: Conflict and Intervention in Africa.* (New Haven: Yale University Press).

Orthodox Accounts of Terrorism[1]

Jason Franks

Introduction

Terrorism is essentially a contested concept. The aim of this chapter is to examine the concept of terrorism and explain the existence of the orthodox understanding of terrorism or orthodox terrorism theory. This theory, I suggest, is the principal paradigm and rational positivist approach used – primarily by state governments – to explain political violence. It is essentially a theoretical explanation and understanding of terrorism that is employed to suit hegemonic, liberal or other agendas, while keeping a distinction firmly in place that does not allow for a creeping legitimation of terrorist tactics agendas. It is, I suggest, a discourse based on the legitimacy/illegitimacy dualism that constructs non-state violence as terrorist while state violence is deemed to be legitimate. It is also a subjective understanding of political violence that professes to explain the act of violence from the perspectives of both the instigator and the recipient of the violence.

In this chapter, I suggest that far from the universal and single understanding of political violence that it portrays, orthodox terrorism theory is in fact a theoretically constructed discourse created from key texts in terrorism studies[2] (Laqueur 1987; Hoffman 1999; Wilkinson 2000) within the discipline of international relations, and its dominance in this field is maintained by its monopoly of state government counter-terrorism and anti-terrorism policies and practice.[3]

---

1   This chapter builds on a wider study of terrorism that has been published as a monograph by Palgrave Macmillan. I would like to thank Marie Breen-Smyth and the editorial team for their comments on an earlier draft. This chapter represents my own views and any errors are my responsibility.
2   This chapter uses a number of key texts in terrorism studies that laid the foundation for the accepted understanding of terrorism. The author would also like to point out that these texts relate particularly to the disciple of international relations.
3   The argument in this chapter is focused on the problems inherent in the state understanding of terrorism in international relations. It is important to point out that terrorism is also studied in different social science disciplines, such as psychology, sociology and anthropology, and in these fields the orthodox approach is not so dominant.

Although I argue in this chapter for the existence of orthodox terrorism theory as the dominant theoretical approach for explaining terrorism, it is not the only approach. Indeed, following an extensive review of the literature in terrorism studies, it is possible to identify a number of different perspectives on terrorism. Although these are based on different levels of analysis (Franks 2006), it is possible to identify from this survey a general differentiation between approaches, particularly in relation to explaining the causes of terrorism. These are as follows:

1. Orthodox terrorism theory: this is the predominant explanation and understanding of terrorism. It does not engage in a root causes debate as it favours the illegal/illegitimate binary approach to explaining terrorism that mirrors the realist, state-centric understanding. It is the basis for governmental anti-terror and counter-terrorism policies. The key texts that support this explanation of terrorism are provided by Hoffman (1999); Laqueur (1987, 2001); Schmid and Jongman (1988); and Wilkinson (1997, 2000). This academic fraternity has notably increased since 9/11.
2. Radical terrorism theory: this is occasionally apparent in the literature and explains terrorism largely from the perspective of the terrorist. It is a justification for violence and a defence of the root causes that exist predominantly in the structure. It is expressed by writers such as Camus (2000); Fanon (2001); Marx and Engels (1992); and Qutb (2006).
3. Moderate terrorism theory: this is a fast developing sub-field (particularly recently), but is still a limited approach in terrorism studies and attempts to engage with a root causes debate. It is a trend that tries to explain and understand the roots of terrorism in relation to socio-economic and structural as well as political causes, and also includes the developing field of critical terrorism studies. Examples of literature in this field include Berman (2003); Bjørgo (2005); Crenshaw (1995); Della Porta (1992); and Gurr (1970).

Orthodox Terrorism Theory

Orthodox terrorism theory, as I have argued above, is essentially an understanding of terrorism employed to suit hegemonic agendas that constructs non-state violence as terrorist while state violence is deemed to be legitimate. The subjective nature of this approach to terrorism professes to explain the act of violence from the perspectives of both the instigator and recipient of the violence, be it a terrorist group against a state or, indeed, vice versa. However, this theory tends to concentrate on acts of anti-state violence and views this as illegitimate violence against the established authority or state, not necessarily violence by the state. Whilst state terrorism is included in this theory, it is primarily seen as state-sponsored or proxy terrorism carried out by illiberal states (Hoffman 1999, 185–96; Wilkinson 2000, 62–9). Orthodox terrorism theory is essentially a Western model of understanding terrorism rooted in Western freedoms, the rule of law and the liberal democratic Westphalian state (O'Sullivan and Herman 1991, 44). By employing this legitimising discourse, the state is able to avoid engaging in a 'root causes' debate on terrorism, as this might legitimise non-state violence – at least in rhetorical terms. Terrorism is therefore employed as a pejorative term by hegemonic actors to make a moral justification of their claim to legitimacy and moral condemnation of their opponents, thus allowing the legitimate use of state violence and avoiding the necessity for negotiation and compromise. Although this suits the monopoly of state power, it is a problem not just for approaching and dealing with terrorism by the symptomatic management of the violence, but also for enacting long-term solutions that attempt to solve the root causes.

This orthodox understanding of terrorism is monopolised by state governments and forms the basis of anti-terrorism and counter-terrorism policies. As a result of this monopoly – which is also perhaps an indication of how co-opted academia can become – the orthodox understanding also dominates terrorism studies. According to the study of terrorism in the international relations literature, and in particular those scholars focusing on it from the perspective of the state, terrorism is thus defined (relative to the legitimacy of state governance) as an illegal and illegitimate act[4] (Hoffman 1999, 30), as a specific method of political violence against the state, such as hijacking or bombing[5] or as acts of violence against civilians protected by the state[6] (Wilkinson 2000, 17). As a result, the study of terrorism has become, in quarters associated mainly with states and governments and indeed academia, preoccupied with explaining *what* actually constitutes terrorism, *how* it functions and ultimately *how* to counter it. This has been to the clear detriment of examining *why* it actually occurs – particularly when it appears to challenge state power.

In the current security climate, orthodox terrorism theory has been imbued with further potency because of the growing political pressure to establish an accepted single definition of terrorism. This was a recommendation of the UN High-Level Panel Report, which suggested that a single definition be adopted, one that can be enshrined in law to institute a general scientific theory of terrorism.[7] The purpose of this, it seems, is to institute a common governmental and international basis on which to approach and deal with terrorism. Orthodox terrorism theory, it seems, looks to provide this service by offering a lens through which the state can explain terrorism, particularly in relation to state security.

In order to create a conceptual point of departure for examining the predominant state understanding of the phenomena of terrorism, the theory of orthodox terrorism discourse has been constructed from a thorough examination of the literature in terrorism studies (Franks 2006). This theory of terrorism comprises a number of

---

4   The US Department of Defence definition.
5   The United Nations defines terrorism in relation to international conventions, see www.un.org.
6   Terrorism is defined as violence against civilians.
7   Although the UN High-Level Panel did come up with a definition of terrorism, it was not adopted in the World Summit document. See UN High-Level Panel Report, www.un.org/secureworld [accessed 1 July 2012].

common themes that re-occur throughout the terrorism literature. Although it can be argued that this technique conflates the understanding of terrorism and creates a 'straw man',[8] nevertheless, in order to endeavour to understand a phenomenon in international relations, an attempt needs to be made to construct a conceptual framework through which the theory, and indeed the practice of the phenomenon, can then be unpacked and examined. Orthodox terrorism theory is just such a conceptual theory and can be constructed around three re-occurring themes – or suggested functions of terrorism – that are found in the literature of orthodox terrorism theory. These are; *functional, symbolic and tactical* (Bowyer Bell 1978, 50).

The *functional* pillar of orthodox terrorism theory relates to the belief that terrorism is intended to 'provoke a response [by the state] to further the [terrorist] cause by strategic manipulation' (Bowyer Bell 1978, 51). This is a central concept and suggests that the aim of the act of terrorism is to force a reaction – hopefully an overreaction – by the established power centre, governing authority or state against the instigators, their supporters and even the population in general. Rubenstein calls this 'heroic terrorism' and suggests that the aim is to 'provoke intense indiscriminate state repression in order to deprive the government of legitimacy and radicalise the masses' (Rubenstein 1987, 161).

Laqueur calls this 'the terrorist theory of provocation' and suggests that it is intended to produce state repression, draconian measures and thus ultimately undermine the 'liberal' façade (Laqueur 1987, 25–7). Furthermore, acts of terrorism are seen as attempts to demonstrate the unsuitability of the incumbent authority to govern and by exposing its 'true' nature, the terrorists endeavour to wrest legitimacy from the state and bestow it upon their own cause. The intention of the terrorists (according to orthodox terrorism theory) is to undermine the security of the population by demonstrating that the state is unable to provide adequate protection and therefore to force the population to turn to alternative sources, such as the instigators of the terrorist violence, to provide security and alternative governance. Examples of this understanding are suggested historically in the post-Second World War anti-colonial conflicts in Cyprus, Aden and Algeria, more recently in Northern Ireland, Spain and the Balkans, and currently in Chechnya, Kashmir, Nepal, Afghanistan and Iraq.

A second re-occurring theme contained in the literature of orthodox terrorism theory is the *symbolic nature of terrorism*. This function of terrorism is arguably the basis of orthodox terrorism theory, which, according to Hoffman, has its origins in the earliest forms of nineteenth-century terrorism and is encapsulated in Carlo Pisacane's 'theory of propaganda by deed'[9] (Hoffman 1999, 17). Orthodox terrorism theory uses this concept of symbolism to explain an act of terrorist violence as being

---

8   Many times when I have presented this work I have received this straw man critique. The first instance was from Professor Vivienne Jabri at Kings College, London, during my PhD Viva in December 2004.
9   Piscane suggested that ideas result from deeds and that violence was necessary not only to draw attention to or generate publicity for a cause, but also ultimately to inform, educate and rally the masses.

highly symbolic and an attempt to terrorise, intimidate and strike fear into those against whom the violence is directed – the targets (even if they are not the actual physical recipients of the violence, they are nevertheless affected, or terrorised, by it). Obviously, the actual targets of the act and the wider audience that witnesses it are directly affected by it. The orthodox explanation of the symbolic value of terrorism is regarded as 'coercive intimidation' or 'pure terrorism', which is 'the systematic use of murder and destruction or the threat of, to terrorise individuals, groups, communities and governments into conceding to terrorist demands' (Wilkinson 1977, 46). Classically, the conventional philosophy of terrorism is as a symbolic act, intended to affect more than just the target of the violence. As Sun Tzu suggested in *The Art of War*, the aim is to 'kill one and frighten ten thousand' (Sun Tzu 1963, 76).

Whilst much of the literature on orthodox terrorism theory supports these psychological implications, it also emphasises the communicative aspects of symbolic violence. The orthodox discourse suggests that acts of terrorism are committed in order to publicise and internationalise a political aim, thereby demonstrating the high propaganda and publicity value that can be gained from acts of terrorist violence. This understanding is particularly clear from analysis in terrorism studies of the 'hijacking period' in the 1960s and 1970s when Palestinian groups such as the Popular Front for the Liberation of Palestine (PFLP) attempted to internationalise the Palestinian-Israeli conflict. This concept is encapsulated by describing 'terrorism as theatre' (Hoffman 1999, 132).

This understanding of terrorism applies equally to the state, which is known to generate the symbolic terrorism of fear and intimidation against its own domestic population in order to ensure political loyalty and compliance to authority.[10] Wilkinson suggests that terrorism can be categorised depending on where it occurs; thus, domestic or *internal* terrorism is confined within a single state or region while *international* terrorism is an attack carried out across international frontiers (Hoffman 1999, 67; Wilkinson 2000, 15).

Nevertheless, regardless of the location of violence, both the psychology of fear and the role of publicity contained in the symbolic nature of orthodox terrorism theory demonstrate quite graphically the significance of media and communications in propagating the psychological implications of the terrorist message to an even wider audience (Alexander and Latter 1990; Hoffman 1999, 131; Wilkinson 2000, 174).

The third component of orthodox terrorism theory is *tactical*. This can be understood in two ways. The first is as a limited means to achieve short-term gains, such as the exchange of hijack hostages for prisoners or a bank robbery to fund the procurement of arms. The second is as a tactical part of a long-term strategic initiative. This has its roots in the theories of revolution and guerrilla warfare[11]

---

10 Much of the literature on orthodox terrorism theory suggests that the historical roots of terrorism existed in the French Revolution of 1789 when the ideology of the Revolution and the power of the new government was enforced and consolidated by the so-called 'Reign of Terror' which was enacted on the population.
11 Guerrilla warfare is defined as 'a series of operations by irregular forces, depending on mobility and surprise aimed at harassing a regular army' (Chaliand 1987, 12).

(Chaliand 1987, 12) by proponents such as Mao Tse-Tung[12] and Carlos Marighela[13] (Marighela 1971), who suggested that acts of terrorism should be part of the wider struggle for revolution or an initial stage preceding popular revolt. Schmid and Jongman define this phenomenon as 'the insurgency context of terrorism' (Schmid and Jongman 1988, 7).[14]

A Discourse of Terrorism

Orthodox terrorism theory is employed by the state to describe acts of terrorist violence and is based upon the assumptions discussed above. It is also interesting to note that by adopting this theory of terrorism, assumptions are made about the nature of the terrorist actor. Crenshaw investigates this and develops 'strategic choice theory', which she argues is a representation of the perpetrator of the act of violence as a rational actor, who has calculated the implications and has made a rational choice among alternatives as part of strategic reasoning (Crenshaw 1992b, 8). This suggests that acts of terrorist violence, whilst appearing to be indiscriminate and random, and the behaviour of mad and crazed individuals, are in fact – according to the understanding provided by orthodox terrorism theory – tactical parts of a carefully planned and calculated strategy to influence decision-making and effect political change.

In this rational understanding, orthodox terrorism theory is rooted in the social contract between the governed and the elites, according to the liberal values of democracy, the rule of law and human rights. Rational states, elites and citizens conform to and legitimise these norms, forming a social contract, and actors that deviate from this contract and act outside the boundaries are seen as terrorists. This constructs the classic positivist binary of in-group/out-group based upon state sovereignty and legality, and offers legitimacy to those who operate within these liberal values. Orthodox terrorism theory is thus a state-centric discourse created to enforce this social contract based on the legitimacy/illegitimacy dualism that constructs non-state violence as terrorist while state violence is deemed to be legitimate.

The above components of orthodox terrorism theory also help to construct the state definitions of terrorism and clearly illustrate the existence and dominance of this homogeneous and coherent theory of terrorism. Consider, for example, the

---

12 Mao developed a strategy of protracted war in three stages: the enemy's strategic offensive and the revolutionaries' strategic defensive; the enemies' strategic consolidation and the revolutionaries' preparation for a counter-offensive: and the revolutionaries' strategic retreat (Wilkinson 2000, 11).

13 Marighela's strategy was to convert a political crisis into an armed struggle by violent acts that force the government to transform the political situation into a military one.

14 Insurgency can be defined as 'a rebellion or rising against the government in power or civil authorities' (Wilkinson 2000, 2).

US Department of Defence definition of terrorism as the 'unlawful use of force or violence against individuals or property to coerce and intimidate governments to accept political, religious or ideological objectives'.[15] Schmid and Jongman suggest that terrorism is:

> a method of combat in which random or symbolic victims serve as instrumental targets of violence. These instrumental victims share group or class characteristics, which form the basis for the victimisation. Other members of that group or class are put in a chronic state of fear (terror) ... The purpose of which is to change attitudes or behaviour favouring the interests of the user of method of combat. (Schmid and Jongman 1988, 2)

This particular definition of terrorism was produced after an exhaustive survey of academics and practitioners in the field, has consequently had a profound influence on the general understanding of terrorism and certainly helps support orthodox terrorism theory.

Orthodox terrorism theory is a discourse in that it does not necessarily represent the 'truth' about terrorism but exists as a Foucauldian 'regime of truth' (Foucault 1985, 122) to provide *an* explanation of the violence. In the Coxian sense, it is just a theory, the purpose of which is to explain terrorism for the benefit of the state whereby it confirms the state's monopoly of legitimacy and therefore violence. It carefully helps to explain *how* terrorism works and *what* it is intended to achieve, but does little to explain *why* it occurs. This is perhaps the purpose for which terrorism discourse was designed – to provide an explanation of political violence that can allow the state the arbitrary use of force without any requirement for a 'root causes' debate whilst maintaining the integrity of the state. In this role, orthodox terrorism discourse serves the security needs of the Westphalian state particularly well.

Nevertheless, despite the parsimony that orthodox terrorism theory provides for the study of terrorism, it seems to be doing little to generate policies and practices that actually reduce the appearance of violence; indeed, it may well be exacerbating it, which in some instances may well be the devious objective. The orthodox understanding of terrorism makes the violence a global security problem and a growing concern, particularly in relation to the current conflicts in Iraq and Afghanistan. Terrorism in this context is also of wider concern in the development debate, as Duffield (2001) has pointed out. Therefore, is orthodox terrorism theory really the best approach for explaining and thus dealing with the roots of this type of violence or is it a discourse that is in some way manipulated to achieve an end result? In the next section I seek to illustrate how orthodox terrorism theory is employed in practice in the Palestinian-Israeli conflict.

---

15   United States Departments of the Army and the Air Force, *Military Operations in Low Intensity Conflict,* Field Manual 100-20/Air Force Pamphlet, 3–20 Washington DC: Headquarters, Department of the Army and Air Force, 1990, pp. 3–1 (Hoffman 1999, 38).

Israel and Palestine and Orthodox Terrorism Discourse

Orthodox terrorism theory is based on two principal assumptions. First is the primacy of state legitimacy. This suggests that the state is both unequivocally morally and legally right, compared to the terrorist actor, who is indisputably wrong. Second, the terrorist is considered a rational actor. According to orthodox terrorism discourse, the terrorist is acting outside the law and is punishable without recourse to reasons, circumstances or root causes. The terrorist is also acting to accomplish a particular aim or tactical goal that is part of a wider strategic plan into which the use of terrorism fits in order to achieve a desired political agenda. Ultimately, by employing this discourse, the state is actually incapable of engaging in a root causes debate and examining (publicly at least) why the violence might be occurring, as this would bestow some form of legitimacy on the terrorists and their cause, thus legitimating their violence and potentially that of any other group who might decide to oppose the state. Instances of terrorist violence are understood by the conventional terrorism discourse as part of a wider strategic plan to destabilise and undermine the political position of the state. This is apparent when acts of terrorism are seen in comparison to acts of violence, which take place within war or conflict, as it is a considered element of war to kill the enemy and not part of any particular coercion strategy.

Israel employs terrorism discourse to understand the conflict with the Palestinians because it allows it to locate the violence in an internal state security problem and external border dispute, instead of civil war, ethnic, separatist or independence conflict. It also views the conflict as 'internal', meaning between the Israeli state and individual Palestinian groups, and is made distinct from any 'external' conflict that may exist between Israel and the wider Arab world.[16] So, whilst the roots of terrorism are not explored, they are also often separated from any understanding of potential causes of the conflict with the Palestinians. Terrorism is also seen as the act of extremists and is divorced from the wider understanding of the conflict. It is seen as 'unacceptable and not part of the conflict'.[17] This is probably due to the way that Israel sees attacks by Palestinian 'terrorists' against Israeli 'innocents' as impossible to understand and therefore unequivocally condemns them as wrong without looking for the potential reasons why they are occurring.[18] This allows Israel to employ the full power of state machinery in the form of legal and military means to deal with the illegal security problem; this is the mainstay of Israeli counter-terrorist and anti-terrorist policies and actions, and was certainly used by Israel to justify the war against Gaza in 2009.

The orthodox understanding of terrorism benefits the power and authority of the state government and consequently the discourse of Zionism, which is focused on maintaining an ethnically homogeneous Jewish state. Whilst it is true to say that most state governments in general employ terrorism theory to maintain the security of the state, due to the precarious ethnographic nature of the Israeli situation, it is

---

16   Interview with Ilan Libovitch, MK Shinui, Knesset: Jerusalem, 1 April 2003.
17   Ibid.
18   Ibid.

even more useful for Israel as it can employ orthodox terrorism theory to discredit, delegitimise and consequently ignore any claims the Palestinians have against the Israeli state.

As I argued above, orthodox terrorism theory can be explained using a basic typology involving three conceptions of terrorism: functional terrorism, symbolic terrorism and tactical terrorism. Functional terrorism is the basis for the theory that terrorist groups employ acts of terrorism in order to provoke a response from the state, such as inciting ruthless reprisals. Laqueur calls this generalisation the 'mainspring of terrorism' and suggests that 'Seldom have terrorists assumed they could seize power but instead rely on a strategy of provocation ... which is intended to trigger intended events' (Laqueur 2001, 37). This theory is used by Israel to explain and justify its actions against Palestinian terrorism. For example, Israel was able to explain the rocket attacks by Hamas as murderous acts of terror and thus conduct a major military offensive against Gaza in the summer of 2007.[19] If the orthodox theory of terrorism is correct and the Palestinians' strategic intention is to elicit a harsh response from Israel, then their tactics have worked. Conversely, if Israel is manipulating terrorist theory to suggest that its actions are what the Palestinians intend but instead is forced to respond in order to 'fight terrorism', then either the Israelis are ignoring the lessons of orthodox terrorism theory, which advocate a measured response to terrorism, or they are free-riding on the orthodox terrorism discourse in order to destroy their political opponents. This contradiction was illustrated in an unprecedented statement by an Israeli Defence Force (IDF) Lieutenant-General, who stated: 'In our tactical decisions we are operating contrary to our strategic interest, as it [our hard-line tactics] increases hatred for Israel and strengthens the terror organisations.'[20]

The second pillar of terrorism theory, symbolic terrorism, suggests that terrorism is employed as a method or psychological weapon to coerce, intimidate, threaten, kill, and ultimately terrorise a particular target group. By this rationale, the attacks undertaken by Palestinian groups, especially inside Israel, are calculated to terrorise society. This is how terrorism is understood by Israel. For example, Hoffman suggests that 'the [Palestinian] suicide terrorists intend to make [Israeli] people paranoid and xenophobic and fearful of venturing outside their homes ... in order to compel the enemy's societies' acquiescence to their demands' (Hoffman 2003, 44).

This delegitimises the actions of the Palestinians and allows the Israeli society and government to openly condemn the Palestinians and suggest that they will not give in to the illegal and illegitimate demands of 'killers' and 'murderers'. As an Israeli politician suggested, the Palestinian use of terrorism 'broke the rules of the game'.[21] Israel is then able to exploit this understanding by publicly suggesting that the aim of the terrorist is to illegally attempt to threaten, coerce and terrorise. This enables the state to justify the adoption of tough counter-terrorism measures that pointedly refuse to acquiesce to terrorism in any way. This argument is found

---

19 *The Guardian*, 27 September 2007.
20 *The Guardian Weekly*, 6–12 November 2003, p. 3.
21 Interview with Yulie Tamir, MK Labour-Menad, Knesset: Jerusalem, 1 April 2003.

in orthodox terrorism theory and is expounded by Wilkinson as the 'hardline approach', and relates to a set of key elements that refuse negotiations, concessions, special status or deals (Wilkinson 2000, 94–5).

The orthodox discourse is not only a way for Israel to approach the problem of terrorism and deal with the violence generated by the Palestinians. It is also a useful method to publicly delegitimise and demonise them, whilst simultaneously explaining to the public – who ultimately bear the brunt of terrorism – that the state counter- and anti-terrorism policy is a legitimate course of action.

The last concept that helps explain terrorism theory – tactical terrorism – or terrorism employed to achieve short-term tactical gains or specific objectives is attributed by Israel to the proliferation of international terrorism in the form of hijacks, hostage taking and sabotage by Palestinian groups that is largely intended to generate international public opinion for the Palestinian political cause against Israel, as well as to raise funds and secure prisoner releases (Morris 2000, 204).

However, tactical terrorism can also imply the use of the methods of terrorism as a strategic weapons system, employed for example by groups with limited means and resources. Terrorist bombings have been described as the 'poor man's air force', and Hoffman, in reference to Palestinian suicide bombers, suggested they were the 'ultimate smart bomb' (Hoffman 2001, 40). Yet Israel does not see the attacks by the Palestinians as acts of retaliation for its own anti-terrorist actions, nor does it understand them in terms of asymmetric conflict. They are viewed through orthodox terrorism theory as unlawful acts designed specifically to achieve a particular tactical goal with the effect of illegally influencing the political situation. They are not seen as defence, revenge, the manifestation of vented frustrations or anger or the final desperate acts of a subjugated people. Instead, these acts of violence are tactical components of a wider, calculated and rational plan to illegally influence Israeli state policies. Terrorism for Israel is 'using immoral or unjust means of coercion, forcing decisions not according to power but according to emotional stress and fear'.[22]

As I have argued above, there are a number of reasons for the Israeli employment and practice of orthodox terrorism discourse. They are all linked, it seems, to state security, which is the main application for the orthodox approach. In fact, it can be seen as the raison d'être for terrorism studies, especially in the construction of state policy. The employment of the orthodox discourse by Israel is completely understandable, because, according to this doctrine, Israel, founded upon the discourse of Zionism, must remain an ethnically homogeneous and racially dominant Jewish state at all costs. The political, social and cultural dominance of Jewish identity is a vital core value for the existence of the Israeli state. As Marc Ellis argues, a civil war currently exists in which Jews fight to maintain their separation from the 'other', as only then can the essence of their Jewish identity be maintained (Ellis 1997, 58). It is vital, when considering the existence of the Israeli state and its relationship with the Palestinians, not to overlook the immense importance for the Israeli government in maintaining a pure Jewish state – that is, an Israeli state with an overwhelmingly ethnic Jewish majority in the population. Ethnic Jewish

---

22   Interview with Yulie Tamir, MK Labour-Menad, Knesset: Jerusalem, 1 April 2003.

security is integral to Zionism and the existence of a state because it is ostensibly an identity-based nationalist discourse and is deeply founded and enshrined in the Jewish national psyche. As the Prime Minister of Israel, Benjamin Netanyahu, has argued, 'a distinguishing feature of Jews raised in Israel is the absence of the sense of personal insecurity and whilst Israel itself may come under personal attack the sense of being a Jew does not' (Netanyahu 1993, 370).

The threat to the Jewish ethnic security of the Israeli state is particularly real as the Palestinians represent a political, social, cultural and ethnic challenge to the whole fabric of the society and the existence of its ethnic homogeneity. As Gershon Baskin suggested, the implications of annexation (of the West Bank and Gaza) would amount to 'Jewish national suicide', as the eventual assimilation of a population bigger than that of the Israeli Jews would mean the loss of Jewish national identity.[23] The Palestinian-Israeli conflict is viewed primarily by Israel as an identity conflict and principally by the Zionist discourse as a fight for the survival of the Jewish people, hence the absence of a root causes debate and the lack of understanding of the causes of the conflict in relation to the claims of the Palestinians. In Israeli terms, the conflict is understandably about the security needs of Israeli and particularly of the Jewish people. This is, above all, the protection and security of ethnic Jewish identity enshrined in the existence of the state of Israel: 'The conflict [with the Palestinians] is the interface between competing identities, which is not only an identity struggle but also a personal struggle.'[24] Orthodox terrorism theory is a vital theoretical tool employed by the Israeli state in this struggle. Nevertheless, serious problems exist for this approach.

Conclusion

This chapter is intended to introduce orthodox accounts of terrorism and is a theoretical study designed to examine orthodox terrorism theory as a theoretical framework grounded in the case study of the Palestinian-Israeli conflict. The aim has been to unpack the notion of orthodox terrorism theory, explain how it is constructed and examine how this approach or discourse is employed and what problems arise from using this understanding. As the arguments above have demonstrated, orthodox terrorism theory essentially becomes a critique of the state government's 'orthodox' approach to terrorism, which, I have argued, is the predominant discourse that is used to explain, understand and deal with terrorism. It is a theory supported by a substantial body of scholarly literature that is designed and employed to legitimise the violence used by the state to enforce its political will whilst simultaneously delegitimising the use of political violence by opposition movements or organisations. It is created and employed to deal with terrorism from the perspective of state security, without any recognisable form

---

23 The demographic problem: interview with Dr Gershon Baskin: IPCRI, 29 June 2007.
24 Interview with Yulie Tamir, MK Labour-Menad, Knesset: Jerusalem, 1 April 2003.

of 'root causes' debate in order to legitimise governmental anti-terrorism and counter-terrorism policies and actions.

Whilst this has obvious advantages for states when 'dealing' with terrorism, it is an increasingly problematic approach, not only because it fails to tackle the root causes but also because it actually serves to exacerbate the conflict and violence. Furthermore, as the international profile of terrorism has grown immeasurably since 9/11 and following ten years of the 'war on terror', the ignominious withdrawal from Iraq and the increasingly bloody conflict in Afghanistan, questions are being increasingly asked if this realist, state-centric and positivist approach to terrorism (and especially al-Qaeda) is the right one.

If the problem of terrorism is to be effectively understood and ultimately resolved, perhaps a new agenda for research is required, one that contains a much more holistic, multi-level and multi-dimensional approach to terrorism and one that allows the problem to be examined and explained from wider perspectives. This ontological shift would emancipate the study of terrorism from the chains of the political legitimacy debate and allow it access to other analytical tools, such as those provided by conflict studies, which provide a much more comprehensive understanding of the roots of terrorism and also provide a greater number of potential alternative pathways for resolving violence (Franks 2006).

However, the emphasis of this new agenda would need to come from state governments. If they intend to actually resolve the violence, they would need to move outside the orthodox terrorism discourse and bestow some form of legitimacy on the claims of the actors using terrorism. It would then be possible to engage in a 'root causes' debate to deal with the deep political and socio-economic reasons that are generating the cause of the violence. This is the development of a 'peace process' and is the established procedure – albeit an often very protracted one – for conflict transformation. This process of transition of understanding the violence, from terrorism to conflict to peace, would equate to a discourse shift from the 'management' of violence – through the orthodox understanding – to engaging with terrorists as legitimate actors in a more moderate approach in order to seek conflict resolution. Although this clearly contradicts the rationale and 'teaching' of orthodox terrorism theory, such as recognising and negotiating with terrorists, successful examples of these processes do exist, such as Northern Ireland, Nepal and Peru, and indeed most conflicts have an established peace process. It is also interesting to note that debate is currently in progress as to whether negotiations should be held directly with the Taliban in Afghanistan in order to end the violence there.

During this transition process, there is a change in the lexicon. Terrorist actors are no longer referred to as terrorists; instead, they are called militants or fighters in value-neutral conflict language and are engaged in negotiations as legitimate actors and in some instances pardoned for 'terrorist crimes' that they were once tried and imprisoned for (this is particularly damning for the orthodox approach, which stresses the criminality of terrorism – indeed, upon release, many 'terrorist' leaders have even become elected politicians). Furthermore, there is also progress in dealing with the political and socio-economic structural problems. So what changed? And why not adopt this agenda for dealing with terrorism from the beginning of the violence?

Questions that arise from this argument, such as when the transition occurs and why it happens, are probably the subjects of another study (Richmond and Franks 2009). Yet it illustrates clearly the unsuitability of the orthodox approach to terrorism because it questions how this shift occurs, given that orthodox terrorism theory gives no quarter to actors using violence. It also prompts a number of other uncomfortable questions, such as whether a peace process is a sign of victory for terrorists in an orthodox understanding. Does this show orthodox terrorism theory to be a flawed approach because – on closer examination – it is actually incapable of dealing with terrorism? Moreover, whilst the orthodox approach is being employed, can terrorism as illegal violence ever be eradicated?

The critical examination of orthodox terrorism theory contained in this study suggests that this might indeed be the case. The need now is to move beyond orthodox terrorism theory into a new agenda for terrorism research. This is vital for the survival of terrorism studies in the post-Westphalian and globalised world where the emphasis is shifting from state-centric to homocentric causes of conflict. A new research agenda is needed, one that accepts and engages the socio-economic and structural roots as well as the political causes of the violence. This means that terrorism can be studied contextually (instead of generically) according to individual and specific case studies and as part of a wider 'root causes' of conflict approach, where terrorism is seen as a further expression of violence alongside other forms of conflict. The new agenda needs to move away from the orthodox understanding completely, no longer considering acts of violence to be about political coercion or terrorising (functional, symbolic and tactical) but seen purely as acts of conflict in the context of conflict. These causes of conflict need to be centred on the individual and seen through human rights and human security issues. Ultimately, these developments, and a new agenda for research, may lead to a far deeper socio-economic and cultural understanding of the root causes of terrorism than the state and, indeed, orthodox terrorism theory can ever hope to provide and to which the state can ultimately respond.

References

Alexander, Y. and Latter, R. (1990), *Terrorism and the Media* (McLean, VA: Brassey's).
Berman, P. (2003), *Terror and Liberalism* (London: W.W. Norton & Co Ltd).
Bjorgo, T. (2005), *The Root Causes of Terrorism* (London: Routledge).
Bowyer Bell, J. (1978), *A Time of Terror* (New York: Basic Books).
Camus, A. (2000), *The Rebel*, 3rd edn (London: Penguin).
Chaliand, G. (1987), *Terrorism from Popular Struggle to Media Spectacle* (London: Saqi Books).

Crenshaw, M. (1992a), 'How Terrorists Think: What Psychology can Contribute to Understanding Terrorism', in L. Howard (ed.), *Terrorism; Roots, Impact and Responses* (New York: Praeger).
Crenshaw, M. (1992b), 'The Logic of Terrorism: Terrorist Behaviour as a Product of Strategic Choice', in W. Reich (ed.), *Origins of Terrorism* (Cambridge: Cambridge University Press).
Crenshaw, M. (1995), *Terrorism in Context* (Pennsylvania: Pennsylvania State University Press).
Della Porta, D. (1992), *International Social Movement Research* (Greenwich: Conneticut).
Duffield, M. (2001), *Global Governance and the New Wars* (London: Zed Books).
Ellis, M.H. (1997), 'The Future of Israeli/Palestine: Embracing the Broken Middle', *Journal of Palestinian Studies*, 26:3, Spring, p. 58.
Fanon, F. (2001), *The Wretched of the Earth*, 5th edn (London: Penguin).
Foucault, M. (1985), *Power and Knowledge* (London: Wheatsheaf).
Franks, J. (2006), *Rethinking the Roots of Terrorism* (Basingstoke: Palgrave Macmillan).
Gurr, T. (1970), *Why Men Rebel* (Princeton: Princeton University Press).
Hoffman, B. (1999), *Inside Terrorism* (London: Indigo).
Hoffman, B. (2003), 'The Logic of Suicide Bombers', *The Atlantic Monthly*, 291:5, June.
Laqueur, W. (1987), *The Age of Terrorism* (Boston: Little, Brown & Co).
Laqueur, W. (2001), *The New Terrorism*, 3rd edn (Oxford: Phoenix Press).
Marighela, C. (1971), *For the Liberation of Brazil* (Harmondsworth: Penguin).
Marx, K. and Engels, F. (1992), *Manifesto of the Communist Party* (Oxford: Oxford University Press).
Morris, B. (2000), *Righteous Victims, A History of The Zionist-Arab Conflict 1881–1999* (London: John Murray).
Netanyahu, B. (1993), *A Place Among the Nations: Israel and the World* (New York: Bantam Books).
O'Sullivan, G. and Herman, E. (1991), 'Terrorism as Ideology and Cultural Industry', in A. George (ed.), *Western State Terrorism* (Cambridge: Polity Press).
Qutb, S. (2006), *Milestones* (London: Islamic Book Service).
Reich, W. (1992), *Origins of Terrorism* (Cambridge: Cambridge University Press).
Richmond, O. and Franks, J. (2009), 'The Impact of Orthodox Terrorism Discourses on the Construction of the Liberal Peace: Internalisation, Resistance and Hybridisation', in *Critical Terrorism Studies: A New Research Agenda*, 2:2, August.
Rubenstein, R.E. (1987), *Alchemists of Revolution: Terrorism in the Modern World* (New York: Basic Books).
Schmid, A. and Jongman, A. (1988), *Political Terrorism: A Guide to Actors, Authors, Concepts, Data Bases, Theories and Literature* (Oxford: North Holland).
Sun Tzu, *The Art of War* (Oxford: Oxford University Press, 1963).
Wilkinson, P. (1977), *Terrorism and the Liberal State* (London: Macmillan).
Wilkinson, P. (2000), *Terrorism versus Democracy, The Liberal State Response* (London: Frank Cass).

Critical Accounts of Terrorism

Richard Jackson

Introduction

Before the early 1970s, 'terrorism' occupied a relatively minor place in political debate, the academic study of political violence and the public imagination. Since then, and particularly following the attacks of 11 September 2001, terrorism has become the focus of unprecedented political, academic and media attention. Notwithstanding ongoing debates over a universally accepted definition, there has over this period been a broad consensus that 'terrorism' refers to the actions of individuals and sub-state groups who use violence against civilians in pursuit of ideological goals. Along with this understanding of the essence of terrorism, a series of beliefs and knowledge claims has developed about the nature, causes and necessary responses to terrorism which has gained widespread acceptance politically, academically and culturally (see Jackson 2009; Stohl 1979; Zulaika and Douglass 1996). These ideas include, among others, the understanding that terrorism poses a major threat to modern societies, that it is caused by extremism, that it can be dealt with using force and that it can be studied objectively. In many respects, the dominant understanding of terrorism – the accepted orthodoxy – functions as a 'regime of truth' in society which constructs and maintains a common-sense view of the phenomenon. The terrorism truth regime is in part maintained by the activities of academics and officials in the 'terrorism industry' (Herman and O'Sullivan 1989), as well as by the institutions and activities of politicians, the media, the legal system, security officials, the police, religion and others.

This chapter aims to explore the nature and study of terrorism as a form of political violence from an openly 'critical' perspective. The term 'critical' is used here in two primary senses. First, in a broad sense, it simply means trying to stand apart from the existing order, questioning what passes for common-sense or accepted knowledge and asking deeper questions about how the existing order came to be and how it is sustained. Second, in a much narrower sense, 'critical' refers to approaches which draw upon the tools and insights of Critical Theory, a social theory oriented towards critiquing and changing society as a whole which is most commonly associated with the so-called Frankfurt School (Toros and Gunning 2009). All critical approaches – broad and narrow – share a number of key commitments, including: the continuous questioning and interrogation of that which is taken for granted, including widely accepted knowledge claims; the prioritisation of the gathering and analysis of primary data; sensitivity towards issues of knowledge and power, especially the understanding that knowledge always works for something and is never ideologically neutral; the acceptance that researchers always bring with them a set of attitudes and preconceptions that are rooted in their own context; and an ethical commitment to human rights, progressive politics and improving the lives of individuals and communities.

The first section of the chapter briefly outlines two of the earliest critical approaches to the study of terrorism. The next section examines in some detail the origins and characteristics of what has become known in recent years as Critical Terrorism Studies (CTS). It explains its primary ontological, epistemological, methodological, ethical and normative commitments. The final section briefly outlines a future critical research agenda, arguing for a widening and deepening of research on terrorism, as well as the inclusion of some long-ignored subjects. The conclusion to the chapter reflects on the successes of critical approaches to terrorism and highlights some potential pitfalls and problems.

Critical Approaches to Terrorism

A set of challenges to the dominant understanding and study of terrorism came from what can broadly be termed political-economy approaches. Scholars in this tradition produced a number of important critical works on the terrorism industry and state terrorism during the Cold War (Chomsky and Herman 1979; Herman 1982; Herman and O'Sullivan 1989; Klare and Kornbluh 1989; George 1991). Another wave of this kind of research followed the start of the war on terror in 2001 (see, for example, Gareau 2004; Burnett and Whyte 2005; Stokes 2005; Blakeley 2009; Raphael 2009; Miller and Mills 2009). This type of critical research sought to highlight the links between the orthodox terrorism studies field, counter-insurgency and the political establishment (see Burnett and Whyte 2005; Miller and Mills 2009); the political biases and propagandistic elements of much orthodox research on terrorism (see Chomsky and Herman 1979; Raphael 2009); the role of the terrorism discourse in legitimising Western imperialism and hegemony, particularly in the global South (see Herman and O'Sullivan 1989; Stokes 2005); and the ways in which the state terrorism of Western states and their allies has often been ignored and excused (see George 1991; Blakeley 2009).

Political-economy approaches have sought to demonstrate, and argue for, an alternative approach to terrorism in which terrorism is conceptualised primarily as a tactic or strategy of political struggle that any actor can employ, including states. They argue that this has two important consequences: first, it makes for a more objective rather than propagandistic study of terrorism; and, second, it re-prioritises research by individual scholars towards the much greater problem of state terrorism rather than the relatively rare occurrences of non-state terrorism.

Political-economy approaches also argue that terrorism research needs to examine the role that the language of terrorism and counter-terrorism plays in advancing Western state interests, the ways in which forms of Western state violence, such as counter-terrorism programmes, can sometimes constitute state terrorism, and the motives and interests underlying dominant Western states' use of terroristic forms of violence as a foreign policy tool (see Rolston, Chapter 23, this volume).

A second broad set of critical approaches comes from the disciplines of anthropology, history, sociology and area studies. Over the past few decades, scholars from these fields have produced a great many important works on aspects of terrorism which implicitly or explicitly adopt a critical approach to the dominant ideas of the orthodox field, even if they often do not use the term 'terrorism' at all in their work (see Feldman 1991; Mahmood 1996; Sluka 1989; Zulaika 1988; English 2003, 2009; Townshend 1983; Oliveiro 1998; Gunning 2007c). These studies suggest that much commonly accepted knowledge about terrorism and terrorist groups amounts to stereotypes and misconceptions, which is often a direct consequence of the failure to engage in primary research, especially in terms of 'talking to terrorists', or to fully appreciate the historical, cultural and social context in which terrorism takes place. Often, scholars from these perspectives start from the premise that the term 'terrorism' is an unhelpful and distorting frame through which to study political violence (see Zulaika 1988; Sluka 1989; Mahmood 1996).

By virtue of the methods and kinds of questions they adopt, these studies demonstrate an alternative, broadly 'critical' approach to terrorism research. First, they show how primary research among the groups under scrutiny is both possible and necessary for gaining an indepth, richly textured and nuanced understanding of the subject. Second, they prove that terrorism cannot be fully understood outside of the historical, political, social and cultural context in which it occurs. They argue that generalising about terrorism – comparing the IRA or ETA with al-Qaeda or Hamas, for example – is a largely fruitless exercise, as terrorism and the groups that employ it can only be fully understood within their local context. Finally, these approaches show how a range of different methodologies, from archival research to ethnographic observation, symbolic analysis and cultural studies, can produce different layers and types of understanding which produce a 'thick' account (Geertz 1973: 5–6) of this form of political violence.

Although these two broad sets of critical approaches have been present for several decades, they have not been brought together into a recognised body of research or a new field. Instead, they have tended to remain fairly isolated and idiosyncratic publications. They have also largely taken place outside of the orthodox field, having only rarely been published in the main terrorism studies journals or included in its conferences. In part, this is because scholars from these perspectives have generally shunned the orthodox field and have simply continued to research terrorism, but often without using the term. For these reasons and because of certain gate-keeping measures by the terrorism industry (see Reid 1993), these critical approaches have had little cross-fertilisation with or impact upon the orthodox field.

The Critical Turn and CTS

From 2006, a number of terrorism scholars began to organise a series of scholarly activities to discuss the need for, and the value of, an explicitly 'critical' approach to terrorism research. Consequently, a new network called the Critical Studies on Terrorism Working Group (CSTWG) was formed within the British International Studies Association (BISA), and an international, peer-reviewed journal called *Critical Studies on Terrorism* was established. Conferences and panels were organised to debate the emergence and future direction of what was being called 'critical terrorism studies', and a series of symposiums and articles on the subject were subsequently published (see Jackson 2007; Horgan and Boyle 2008; Hulsse and Spencer 2008; Weinberg and Eubank 2008; Burke 2009; Jarvis 2009; Joseph 2009; Stokes 2009). At the same time, an increasing number of PhD projects were started which examined issues and questions surrounding critical approaches to terrorism (see, for example, Toros 2008). This was accompanied by an increasing number of scholars who began to establish openly critically-oriented teaching programmes on terrorism-related subjects. Collectively, these developments suggested that a 'critical turn' was taking place within the wider terrorism studies field (Gunning 2007a).

CTS, as it has since become known, is rooted in the earlier critical approaches to terrorism research described above. However, unlike those earlier efforts, CTS has made a genuine effort to engage directly with the orthodox terrorism studies field and its scholars. Consequently, evidence is starting to emerge that CTS is beginning to have a measurable impact on the broader study of terrorism and it is now increasingly the case that any serious study or teaching of terrorism has to be willing to engage with its perspectives and ideas. It is important to note that, as with most academic approaches, CTS is a broad and evolving church made up of diverse perspectives and a series of ongoing disagreements over some important issues. In this sense, the version of CTS presented here is only one perspective on this dynamic new approach (for alternative perspectives, see Hulsse and Spencer 2008; Stokes 2009).

CTS can be understood first and foremost as a critical orientation, a sceptical attitude and a willingness to challenge received wisdom and knowledge about terrorism. In this sense, it can be conceived of as a broad scholarly movement that allows multiple perspectives, some of which have been considered outside of the mainstream, to be brought into the same forum. In other words, it seeks to engage with, and learn from, a range of perspectives and approaches, including excellent research within the orthodox field. Most importantly, CTS entails an ongoing process of intellectual engagement and debate with a wide range of perspectives and approaches, rather than a fixed position or endpoint.

However, beyond the adoption of a generally 'critical' attitude, CTS can be characterised by an identifiable set of important ontological, epistemological, methodological and ethical-normative commitments. These commitments distinguish CTS from the dominant orthodox approach to terrorism research (the following sections draw from Jackson 2007; Jackson, Gunning and Breen Smyth 2009; Jackson et al. 2011).

Ontological Commitments

CTS adopts the ontological position that terrorism is fundamentally a social fact rather than a brute fact, because deciding whether a particular act of violence constitutes an 'act of terrorism' relies on judgments about the context, circumstances and intent of the violence, rather than any objective characteristic inherent to it (Schmid and Jongman 1988: 101). As such, terrorism has no pure essence. For example, if a group of civilians is killed in a bomb blast or a policeman is shot, it is not immediately obvious whether either of these events is necessarily an act of terrorism, as there is nothing inherent or objective in the violence itself which makes it 'terrorism' per se. Instead, it requires a careful analysis of the circumstances and context of the events and the intentions of the perpetrators to determine whether it fits a particular definition of terrorism. In other words, while acts of violence are a brute physical fact for the victims and onlookers, the meaning or labelling of the acts – as a 'crime' or an act of 'war' or 'terrorism', for example – is a social process that depends upon different actors making judgments about its nature. In contemporary society, deciding which events come to be viewed as terrorism depends upon a series of social, cultural, legal and political processes of interpretation, categorisation and labelling (Zulaika and Douglass 1996). Crucially, the actors and actions understood as terrorist and terrorism can change over time and circumstance.

In addition, terrorism is not an ideology like socialism or liberalism; it is not a set of ideas or perspectives for making sense of the world or a set of goals for constructing a good society. Rather, it is a violent *strategy* or tactic of political struggle which actors can employ to try and achieve their goals; it is a *means* to some kind of political end. Groups specialising in terror and no other forms of political action do sometimes form, but they are extremely rare and typically they remain highly unstable and usually disappear within a short time. In reality, most terrorism occurs in the context of wider political struggles in which the use of terror is one strategy among other more routine forms of contentious action (Tilly 2004: 6). In other words, ontologically speaking, while there is the strategy of terror which actors can adopt or discard, there is no terror*ism* as such – although this is the common term used to describe the strategy.

Importantly, CTS adopts the same ontological position in relation to the terror*ist* label. It argues that calling a group or individual a 'terrorist' is not an ontological statement about the nature or status of a particular individual: 'terrorist' is not an identity like 'Amish' or 'Canadian', nor is it the case that 'once a terrorist, always a terrorist' (Schmid 2004: 205; Toros 2008). A number of former 'terrorists' have later become respected heads of state, and some like Menachim Begin, Nelson Mandela and Yasser Arafat have even won the Nobel Peace Prize. Most so-called 'terrorists' eventually stop using the terrorism strategy and go on to live relatively ordinary lives or continue pursuing their goals using non-violent political strategies. CTS argues that there is little intellectual value to be gained from reducing or essentialising a person or group to what is usually a subset of their overall behaviour, rather than a reflection of their ideological beliefs or political aims.

CTS scholars argue that there are some important implications and advantages to the ontological position they adopt towards terrorism. First, they suggest that recognising that terrorism is a social fact with no objective essence means that scholars should always be extremely careful in their use of the term and should remain vigilant about the politics of naming individuals or groups as 'terrorist'. A second implication is the rejection of the frequent tendency to universalise or generalise about terrorism from one context to another, to assume that terrorism has a single essential and recognisable nature, and to treat acts of terrorism as wholly exceptional kinds of events that have nothing in common with other forms of social and political activity. Finally, an advantage of this ontological position is that it permits the study of the legal, academic and cultural processes by which certain acts come to be accepted as 'terrorism', as well as the actual political violence in the 'real' world which may have 'terroristic' characteristics.

Epistemological Commitments

CTS adopts a number of important epistemological positions. First, it accepts that creating knowledge is ultimately a social process which depends on a range of contextual and process-related factors, such as the social position of the researcher, the institutional context within which they conduct research and the kinds of methods they employ. These sorts of factors impact on the kinds of knowledge produced, as well as the purposes to which it is put. In other words, CTS scholars argue that we must remain sensitive to, and be continuously aware of, the different ways in which context and process impact on knowledge about terrorism. In addition, the recognition that knowledge is a social process and that societies change means that what we 'know' about terrorism today differs from previous societies and will likely differ from future ones. Crucially, this means that there are few if any knowledge claims about terrorism today that cannot be challenged or questioned.

Second, CTS recognises that no individual, including academic researchers, can completely put aside their personal identity, values, perceptions and world view, and then engage in objective, dispassionate, value-free research. Rather, every researcher brings with them a particular culture and set of values and understandings which shapes their research in important ways. CTS scholars argue that recognising and acknowledging the personal subjectivity of the researcher is an important step (Breen Smyth 2009), not least because such continuous reflexivity acts as an antidote to the dangerous claim that some kinds of knowledge are objective and wholly unbiased – and therefore superior to others.

Third, CTS is deeply aware of the links between power and knowledge, particularly in terms of the different ways in which knowledge can be employed by actors as a political tool of influence and domination. CTS scholars are critical of the way in which certain kinds of knowledge claims about terrorism – the widely accepted knowledge that terrorism poses a serious ongoing threat to Western societies, for example – have been used by governments to increase their own power, suppress opposition, restrict civil liberties and attack other countries.

Consequently, CTS scholars begin by asking: who is terrorism research for? How does terrorism research support particular interests? And what are the ideological effects of terrorism research on society?

In effect, CTS begins with the acceptance that wholly objective or neutral knowledge – any kind of absolute or real 'truth' – about terrorism is impossible and that there is always an ideological, ethical-political dimension to the research process (Toros and Gunning 2009). Crucially, this does not mean that all knowledge of the social world is hopelessly insecure or that what can be called 'anchorages' – relatively secure knowledge claims – cannot be found and built upon (Booth 2008; Herring 2008; Toros and Gunning 2009). It also does not mean the rejection of rigorous scholarly standards and procedures in research on terrorism. Rather, it suggests that, in addition to a commitment to the highest standards of scholarship, those conducting research on terrorism should remain continuously aware of the ways in which the unique context in which acts of terrorism occur and the values of the individual researcher impact upon the nature and outcomes of the research, and how such research is always an inherently political or ideological process.

An important consequence of this epistemological position (and its related ontological position) is an opening up of the broader intellectual project of studying terrorism to new questions and topics which go beyond seeking to understand its causes and solutions, as well as new methods and approaches to its study. The acceptance of the socially constructed nature of terrorism and terrorism knowledge, for example, raises new kinds of questions about how the phenomenon we now know as 'terrorism' came to be viewed primarily as a kind of non-state (as opposed to state) violence and how the academic study of terrorism contributed to this process. Similarly, questioning the terrorism knowledge produced by the dominant social scientific approaches which stress objectivity and quantifiable data suggests that other kinds of knowledge produced by ethnography, discourse analysis, constructivism, sociology, history and many fields could also be extremely helpful in our understanding of terrorism and its processes.

Methodological Commitments

The ontological and epistemological commitments at the heart of CTS have a number of important consequences for method and approach in researching terrorism. First, CTS scholars are committed to transparency about their own values and standpoints, particularly as they relate to the interests and values of the societies in which they live and work. For Western-based scholars, this translates into an abiding commitment to being aware of, and trying to overcome, the Eurocentric, Orientalist and patriarchal forms of knowledge which currently dominate the terrorism studies and security studies fields, and social science more generally (see Gunning 2009; Sylvester and Parashar 2009; Toros and Gunning 2009), as well as honesty about any associations and relationships with state or private political actors, standpoints on important political issues and the nature of the sponsors of the research.

Second, CTS scholars are committed to taking subjectivity seriously, in terms of both the researcher and the research subject (see Breen Smyth 2009). This means being aware of, and transparent about, the values and impact of the researcher on the process and outcomes of the research, and being willing to seriously engage with the viewpoint and perceptions of the 'terrorist' other. This latter point implies an additional commitment to engaging in primary research when relevant, as opposed to the all too frequent habit of relying primarily on secondary sources (see Zulaika and Douglass 1996).

Third, CTS scholars are committed to methodological and disciplinary pluralism in terrorism research – a willingness to embrace the insights and perspectives of different academic disciplines, intellectual approaches and schools of thought. In particular, CTS sees value in post-positivist and non-international relations-based methods and approaches, including discourse analysis, post-structuralism, constructivism, Critical Theory, historical materialism, history, ethnography and others.

Finally, CTS refuses to privilege dominant social scientific methods and approaches to terrorism research which stress rationalism, empiricism and positivism. Instead, it argues that interpretive and reflectivist approaches can be equally valuable in expanding the study and understanding of terrorism. In one respect, this means refusing to be limited by the narrow logic of traditional social scientific explanation based on linear notions of cause and effect, in which terrorism is caused by 'Islamic extremism' or 'anti-Americanism', for example. Rather, CTS argues that adopting an interpretive 'logic of understanding' rooted in 'how possible' rather than 'what causes' questions can open space for subjects and perspectives that are often foreclosed by traditional social science (see Doty 1993). Asking 'how does terrorism become possible in a particular social and political context?', for example, can open up new possibilities of understanding which can be foreclosed by the question 'what causes terrorism?'.

Ethical-Normative Commitments

There are a number of ethical-normative commitments which flow directly from the ontological, epistemological and methodological commitments described above. First, CTS is committed to a permanent set of responsible research ethics which take account of, and try to avoid harming, the various end-users of terrorism research. These may include informants or interviewees (who may be considered 'terrorists' by the state), the 'suspect communities' from which terrorists often emerge and the populations or groups who bear the brunt of terrorist campaigns and counter-terrorism policies – as well as the wider public, other academics and policy-makers. In practical terms, these research ethics mean: the adoption of a 'do no harm' approach to research; operating transparently as a researcher in terms of aims and values; 'recognising the human behind the [terrorist] label' (Booth 2008: 73) and consequently the vulnerability of those being researched; honouring undertakings of confidentiality and protecting interviewees; utilising principles of informed consent; and taking responsibility for the anticipated impact of the research and the ways in which it may be utilised. For example, in the current legal and political environment, research on certain Islamist groups could lead to the arrest or persecution of individual Muslims and the demonisation of Muslims more broadly if the researcher does not take extreme care in how the research is conducted and how the results are later presented (see Fekete 2009).

Second, the broader CTS approach involves a shift from state-centrism and making state security the central concern to a focus on the security, freedom and well-being of human individuals and communities (Sluka 2009; Toros and Gunning 2009). Just as Critical Security Studies has argued that the primary actor to be secured should be the human individual and not the state, CTS scholars also tend to be more concerned with ending the avoidable suffering of human beings than with bolstering the state. In other words, CTS scholars tend to prioritise human security over national security, and they work towards minimising all forms of physical, structural and cultural violence (Toros and Gunning 2009). Related to this, they take seriously the scholarly and practical exploration of non-violence, conflict transformation and reconciliation as practical alternatives to terrorist and counter-terrorist violence.

Third, CTS scholars are committed to trying to influence public policy, because not being concerned with policy is not an option for scholars committed to improving human security and well-being (Gunning 2007b; Toros and Gunning 2009). Importantly, this does not mean that CTS scholars limit their research to being relevant to the needs of state elites. Instead, CTS argues that critical scholars need to engage equally with both policy-*makers* – the state elites who have to make policies to deal with non-state terrorism – and policy-*takers* – the groups and wider societies who have to bear the brunt of counter-terrorism policies. Engaging with policy-takers lessens the risk of co-option by the status quo, particularly if those thus engaged include members of communities labelled 'suspect' by the state, those designated 'terrorists' and so on. However, to be effective in realising the potential for positive change within the status quo, critical scholars must simultaneously strive to engage with those who are embedded in the state, members of the 'counter-terrorist' forces, the political elite and so on. While there are tremendous obstacles to such engagement, such as embedded institutional bias and gate-keeping practices by state intellectuals, there are rare occasions when critical scholars have the opportunity to inject their perspectives into the policy process.

Fourth, CTS involves a continuous process of 'immanent critique' of society's power structures and oppressive practices, and a simultaneous commitment to bringing about the positive transformation of existing structures (Herring 2008; Toros and Gunning 2009). More specifically, CTS scholars see an important task in questioning both morally and intellectually the dominant paradigm of political violence which promotes the idea that violence can be a rational instrument for bringing about positive change, whether by governments or non-state groups (Burke 2008). From this perspective, CTS can be understood as a kind of 'outsider theorising' which seeks to go 'beyond problem-solving within the status quo and instead … to help engage through critical theory with the problem of the status quo' (Booth 2007).

Collectively, these commitments – to human security over state security, to ending avoidable suffering, to minimising and questioning all forms of violence, to continuous immanent critique and to positively transforming existing structures – can be described as a broad commitment to the notion of emancipation. Despite objections to the term and its past implication in hegemonic projects, and rooted in a philosophical commitment to praxis, CTS scholars for the most part see emancipation as a process of trying to construct 'concrete utopias' by realising the unfulfilled potential of existing structures, freeing individuals from unnecessary structural constraints and the democratisation of the public sphere (Wyn Jones 2005: 229–32; McDonald 2009). In other words, as with all 'critical' research, CTS involves an underlying conception of a different social and political order (Alker 2004: 192; Wyn Jones 2005: 217–20). Importantly, as CTS understands it, emancipation is a continuous *process* of struggle and critique rather than any particular endpoint or universal grand narrative. Emancipation, then, can never be fully and finally achieved: it is something for us as scholars, students and practitioners of global politics to continuously aim towards.

Within the context of critical research on terrorism, emancipation expresses itself in a variety of ways, including, among others: efforts to end the use of terrorist violence, whether by state or non-state actors; the promotion of human rights and well-being in situations of terrorist and counter-terrorist violence; the refusal to sanction illegal and immoral practices such as targeted killings and torture; explorations in non-violent and conflict resolution-based responses to terrorism; and addressing the conditions and grievances that can be seen to impel actors to resort to terrorist tactics in the first place. In short, CTS imbues many of the values, concerns and orientations of peace research, conflict resolution and critical security studies.

A Critical Research Agenda

The value of any critical approach lies not just in the insights it can provide through a critique and deconstruction of an existing field, but also in the extent to which it can provide an alternative and credible future research agenda for the subject (Jackson, Gunning and Breen Smyth 2009). In relation to terrorism research, critical approaches such as CTS aim to encourage three broad developments. First, they argue for *broadening* the study of terrorism to include subjects that have often been neglected by the field, including subjects like the wider social context of political violence, the nature and causes of state violence, non-violent practices, gendered aspects of terrorism, and the nature and impact of terrorism and counter-terrorism in the developing world, among others. Second, they argue for *deepening* terrorism research by uncovering the field's underlying ideological, institutional and material interests, exploring the forms of knowledge and practice which socially construct terrorism, and making the values, perspectives and normative commitments of both researchers and the researched more open and explicit. Third, they argue for making a commitment to *emancipatory praxis* central to the terrorism research enterprise.

More specifically, CTS suggests that an initial critically-oriented research agenda should include the subjects listed below, among others. While there is a growing literature on some of these subjects already, much of this research occurs largely outside of the wider terrorism studies field. Indeed, one of the tasks of a critical approach is to gather in all these fragmented voices and serve as a tent under which research from other disciplines and approaches can coalesce and cross-pollinate (Gunning 2007a).

First, as suggested, there is a need to examine more thoroughly and systematically the linguistic, conceptual, ideological and institutional underpinnings of the terrorism studies field and its related practices of counter-terrorism. The language and widely accepted knowledge of terrorism, and the institutionalised practices of counter-terrorism, are actually a very recent invention; 50–100 years ago, the term 'terrorism' was rarely spoken in public discourse and there were few laws or counter-terrorism institutions in existence. Systematic research is needed to uncover how and why the term entered the public discourse and how it became such a powerful discourse able to generate vast amounts of research, political activity and public concern.

Directly related to this, there is a further need to explore in much more detail the political-economic contexts of both the terrorism studies field as a politically embedded domain of knowledge and the theory and practice of counter-terrorism. Although the popular perception is that counter-terrorism theory and practice is based on rational, evidence-led strategies and approaches, this is rarely the case. In other words, applying historical materialist approaches and taking material reality seriously, there is a need for further exploration of how counter-terrorism functions as a form of ideology; that is, how it works to promote certain kinds of material and class interests, maintain hegemony and sustain dominant economic relationships. There are a great many actors who benefit directly and materially from efforts to counter the terrorist threat as it is commonly understood, including, for example, all branches of the security services, the military, the police, private security companies, military contractors, pharmaceutical companies, the media, politicians, academics and many others. This means that critical analyses of the theory and practice of counter-terrorism need to be rooted within theories of class, capitalism, hegemony and imperialism (Herring 2008).

Third, there is a real need for more systematic research on the nature, causes and consequences of state terrorism and state repression more broadly. In particular, there is a need for wider research into those forms of state terrorism that have remained virtually invisible in terrorism research so far, such as the state terrorism of Western states (including Israel) and the state terrorism practised by many Western allies, such as Egypt, Saudi Arabia, Pakistan, Sri Lanka and Colombia, to name but a few (see Blakeley 2009). We also need more research into how state terrorism ends and how it might be more effectively dealt with.

Fourth, it is imperative to broaden the research agenda to include the wider social and historical context within which terrorism occurs, instead of artificially singling it out as a unique phenomenon. Terrorism is always part of a wider context in which other forms of violent and non-violent behaviour takes place, and militants are almost always part of a broader social movement struggling for a political goal. At present, too little is understood about the interaction between militants and non-militants within social movements and between militant and non-militant forms of behaviour. We also do not fully understand the role played by bystander publics, political elites, state forces and wider ideological debates in the evolution of violent militancy (Gunning 2009). Similarly, more research is needed into the effect of movement participation on individual motivation and behaviour, the effects of the Internet and wider international networks on militancy, the relationship between political and domestic violence, and the interactions between structural and political violence, among others.

Fifth, there is a need to take gender much more seriously in terrorism research. A number of important topics suggest themselves here, including: examining the gendered nature of the terrorism studies field itself, the kinds of masculinised forms of knowledge it produces and the silences it contains about women and gender; exploring the perspectives, motivations, ambitions, goals and political agency of female participants in terrorism, counter-terrorism and political violence more broadly; applying a gender-sensitive perspective towards militant groups and movements, and exploring how women join, mediate, subvert and resist such movements; comparative research on women in different societies who join terrorist and counter-terrorist groups; and the impact of counter-terrorist measures on women and children.

Sixth, there is a real need to address the Eurocentric and Western state-orientation of much terrorism research by expanding the study of terrorism to include the voices and perspectives of those in the global South who have in fact been the most frequent victims of both terrorism and counter-terrorism. It can be argued that the Global War on Terror has had its greatest impact on the global South, but this impact has yet to be the subject of systematic research. This concern is related to the emancipatory agenda of critical approaches, as it involves seeking to include and empower marginalised groups and individuals (McDonald 2009). Of particular importance is the need to move beyond explanations which suggest that violence in the developing regions is due to inherent cultural characteristics or pathological inclinations, or which assume that actors in the global South are passive victims lacking their own agency.

Finally, there is a need to further analyse the ethics, impacts and effectiveness of different approaches to counter-terrorism. In the first instance, there is a real need to find transparent and meaningful ways of evaluating the success of counter-terrorism policies and to critically examine accepted wisdom, such as the popular argument that 'we do not negotiate with terrorists'. Other questions which need to be explored in greater detail include: the impact of counter-terrorism policies on specific communities and individuals, the legal order, domestic society and the international system; the effects of counter-terrorism policy on human rights, social trust, community cohesion, democratic culture, academic research, the media and policing practices; the role of civil society and socio-economic change in ending campaigns of political violence; the effectiveness or otherwise of dialogue with groups practising terrorism; the precise role and dynamics of demilitarisation strategies, police reform, truth and reconciliation mechanisms and the like; and the successes and failures of the current Global War on Terror and other previous experiences of terrorism. In particular, the impact of the Global War on Terror is in need of much more systematic research, given its global reach and size, and the vast areas of social and political life it has thus far impacted upon.

Conclusion

It could be argued that critical approaches to terrorism amount to little more than criticism of the dominant orthodoxy and the call for better research. This chapter has tried to argue that they are much more than this because not only do they provide a critique of the existing field, they also suggest a comprehensive framework for understanding and studying terrorism which encompasses ontology, epistemology, methodology and praxis, as well as a concrete research agenda for the future. As such, critical approaches open up new kinds of questions, new areas of study and new ways of thinking about contemporary forms of political violence (both state and non-state).

Importantly, critical approaches to terrorism are beginning to have a major impact on the field as a whole. Their success is in part due to the unique historical juncture in which they have emerged. The failures and difficulties of counter-terrorism efforts in the Global War on Terror in Iraq, Afghanistan and elsewhere, combined with growing dissatisfaction with the overreaction and damaging consequences of domestic counter-terrorism efforts based on traditional ideas of terrorism, mean that policy-makers, scholars and the wider public are increasingly open to new, fresh approaches to the subject.

However, notwithstanding the impact that critical approaches have had thus far, there are a few dangers and obstacles which must be carefully negotiated by scholars of terrorism. For example, there is a danger that the growth of critical approaches will have the effect of splitting the broader field into critical and orthodox intellectual ghettos which then refuse to engage in a fruitful dialogue or, worse yet, engage in hostile attacks on each other (see, for example, Jones and Smith 2009). The understandable tendency to speak within rather than across theoretical and scholarly divides must be resisted in favour of a broad engagement. There is a related danger that the critical side of the field will remain isolated and marginalised and, as a consequence, will remain locked out of being able to influence policy-makers or compete for research funding. This has been the fate of other critical approaches to terrorism studies in the past; in spite of current efforts, the risk that CTS will go the way of the political-economy-based critiques of the 1980s cannot be discounted. There are also continuing debates and arguments between critical scholars and others over what it really means to be 'critical' and what 'emancipation' means in practice. Here, the risk is that critical scholars expend all their energy in deconstructing other approaches or debating theoretical nuances, and little new research on 'real world' political violence is undertaken. None of these challenges are insurmountable, but they will require careful attention and effort by critical scholars over the coming years.

References

Alker, H., 2004. 'Emancipation in the Critical Security Studies Project', in K. Booth (ed.), *Critical Security Studies and World Politics* (Boulder, CO: Lynne Rienner).
Blakeley, R., 2009. *State Terrorism and Neoliberalism: The North in the South* (Abingdon: Routledge).
Booth, K., 2007. *Theory of World Security* (Cambridge: Cambridge University Press).
Booth, K., 2008. 'The Human Faces of Terror: Reflections in a Cracked Looking Glass', *Critical Studies on Terrorism*, 1(1): 65–79.
Breen Smyth, M., 2009. 'Subjectivities, "Suspect Communities", Governments and the Ethics of Research on "Terrorism"', in Jackson, R., Gunning, J. and Breen Smyth, M. (eds), *Critical Terrorism Studies: A New Research Agenda* (Abingdon: Routledge), 194–215.
Burke, A., 2008. 'The End of Terrorism Studies', *Critical Studies on Terrorism*, 1(1): 37–49.
Burke, A., 2009. 'Metaterror', *International Relations*, 23(1): 61–7.
Burnett, J. and Whyte, D., 2005. 'Embedded Expertise and the New Terrorism', *Journal for Crime, Conflict and the Media*, 1(4): 1–18.
Chomsky, N. and Herman, E., 1979. *The Political Economy of Human Rights, Volume I: The Washington Connection and Third World Fascism* (Nottingham: Spokesman).
Doty, R., 1993. 'Foreign Policy as Social Construction: A Post-Positivist Analysis of U.S. Counterinsurgency Policy in the Philippines', *International Studies Quarterly*, 37: 297–320.
English, R., 2003. *Armed Struggle: The History of the IRA* (London: Pan Macmillan).
English, R., 2009. 'Review Article: The Future of Terrorism Studies', *Critical Studies on Terrorism*, 2(2): 377–82.
Fekete, L., 2009. *A Suitable Enemy: Racism, Migration and Islamophobia in Europe* (London: Pluto).
Feldman, A., 1991. *Formations of Violence: The Narrative of the Body and Political Terror in Northern Ireland* (Chicago: University of Chicago Press).
Gareau, F., 2004. *State Terrorism and the United States: From Counterinsurgency to the War on Terrorism* (London: Zed Books).
Geertz, C., 1973. *The Interpretation of Cultures: Selected Essays* (New York: Basic Books).
George, A., 1991. 'The Discipline of Terrorology', in George, A. (ed.), *Western State Terrorism* (Cambridge: Polity Press), 76–101.
Gunning, J., 2007a. 'A Case for Critical Terrorism Studies?', *Government and Opposition*, 42(3): 363–93.
Gunning, J., 2007b. 'Babies and Bathwaters: Reflecting on the Pitfalls of Critical Terrorism Studies', *European Political Science*, 6(3): 236–43.
Gunning, J., 2007c. *Hamas in Politics: Democracy, Religion, Violence* (London: Hurst).

Gunning, J., 2009. 'Social Movement Theory and the Study of Terrorism', in Jackson, R., Gunning, J. and Breen Smyth, M. (eds), *Critical Terrorism Studies: A New Research Agenda* (Abingdon: Routledge), 156–77.
Herman, E., 1982. *The Real Terror Network: Terrorism in Fact and Propaganda* (Boston, MA: South End Press).
Herman, E. and O'Sullivan, G., 1989. *The 'Terrorism' Industry: The Experts and Institutions that Shape our View of Terror* (New York: Pantheon Books).
Herring, E., 2008. 'Critical Terrorism Studies: An Activist Scholar Perspective', *Critical Studies on Terrorism*, 1(2): 197–212.
Horgan, J. and Boyle, M., 2008. 'A Case against "Critical Terrorism Studies"', *Critical Studies on Terrorism*, 1(1): 51–64.
Hulsse, R. and Spencer, A., 2008. 'The Metaphor of Terror: Terrorism Studies and the Constructivist Turn', *Security Dialogue*, 39(6): 571–92.
Jackson, R., 2007. 'The Core Commitments of Critical Terrorism Studies', *European Political Science*, 6(3): 244–51.
Jackson, R., 2009. 'Knowledge, Power and Politics in the Study of Political Terrorism', in Jackson, R., Gunning, J. and Breen Smyth, M. (eds), *Critical Terrorism Studies: Framing a New Research Agenda* (Abingdon: Routledge), 66–83.
Jackson, R., Gunning, J. and Breen Smyth, M. (eds), 2009. *Critical Terrorism Studies: A New Research Agenda* (Abingdon: Routledge).
Jackson, R., Jarvis, L., Gunning, J. and Breen Smyth, M., 2011. *Terrorism: A Critical Introduction* (Basingstoke: Palgrave Macmillan).
Jarvis, L., 2009a. 'The Spaces and Faces of Critical Terrorism Studies', *Security Dialogue*, 40(1): 5–27.
Jones, D.M. and Smith, M.L.R., 2009. 'We are all Terrorists Now: Critical – or Hypocritical – Studies on Terrorism?', *Studies in Conflict and Terrorism*, 32(4): 292–302.
Joseph, J., 2009. 'Critical of What? Terrorism and its Study', *International Relations*, 23(1): 93–8.
Klare, M. and Kornbluh, P. (eds), 1989. *Low-Intensity Warfare: How the USA Fights Wars Without Declaring Them* (London: Methuen).
McDonald, M., 2009. 'Emancipation and Critical Terrorism Studies', in Jackson, R., Gunning, J. and Breen Smyth, M. (eds), *Critical Terrorism Studies: A New Research Agenda* (Abingdon: Routledge), 109–23.
Mahmood, C., 1996. *Fighting for Faith and Nation: Dialogues with Sikh Militants* (Philadelphia, PA: University of Pennsylvania Press).
Miller, D. and Mills, T., 2009. 'The Terror Experts and the Mainstream Media: The Expert Nexus and its Dominance in the News Media', *Critical Studies on Terrorism*, 2(3): 415–38.
Oliverio, A., 1998. *The State of Terror* (New York: State University of New York Press).
Raphael, S., 2009. 'In the Service of Power: Terrorism Studies and US Intervention in the Global South', in Jackson, R., Breen Smyth, M. and Gunning, J. (eds), *Critical Terrorism Studies: A New Research Agenda* (Abingdon: Routledge).
Reid, E., 1993. 'Terrorism Research and the Diffusion of Ideas', *Knowledge and Policy*, 6(1): 17–37.

Schmid, A., 2004. 'Frameworks for Conceptualising Terrorism', *Terrorism and Political Violence*, 16(2): 197–221.
Schmid, A. and Jongman, A., 1988. *Political Terrorism: A New Guide to Actors, Authors, Concepts, Databases, Theories and Literature* (Amsterdam: North Holland).
Sluka, J., 1989. *Hearts and Minds, Water and Fish: Support for the IRA and INLA in a Northern Ireland Ghetto* (Greenwich: JAI Press).
Sluka, J., 2009. 'The Contribution of Anthropology to Critical Terrorism Studies', in Jackson, R., Gunning, J. and Breen Smyth, M. (eds), *Critical Terrorism Studies: A New Research Agenda* (Abingdon: Routledge), 138–55.
Stohl, M., 1979. 'Myths and Realities of Political Terrorism', in Stohl, M. (ed.), *The Politics of Terrorism* (New York: Marcel Dekker), 1–19.
Stokes, D., 2005. *America's Other War: Terrorising Colombia* (London: Zed Books).
Stokes, D., 2009. 'Ideas and Avocados: Ontologising Critical Terrorism Studies', *International Relations*, 23(1): 85–92.
Sylvester, C. and Parashar, S., 2009. 'The Contemporary "Mahabharata" and the Many "Draupadis": Bringing Gender to Critical Terrorism Studies', in Jackson, R., Gunning, J. and Breen Smyth, M. (eds), *Critical Terrorism Studies: A New Research Agenda* (Abingdon: Routledge), 178–93.
Tilly, C., 2004. 'Terror, Terrorism, Terrorists', *Sociological Theory*, 22(1): 5–13.
Toros, H., 2008. 'Terrorists, Scholars and Ordinary People: Confronting Terrorism Studies with Field Experiences', *Critical Studies on Terrorism*, 1(2): 279–92.
Toros, H. and Gunning, J., 2009. 'Exploring a Critical Theory Approach to Terrorism Studies', in Jackson, R., Gunning, J. and Breen Smyth, M. (eds), *Critical Terrorism Studies: A New Research Agenda* (Abingdon: Routledge), 89–108.
Townshend, C., 1983. *Political Violence in Ireland: Government and Resistance since 1848* (Oxford: Oxford University Press).
Weinberg, L. and Eubank, W., 2008. 'Problems with the Critical Studies Approach to the Study of Terrorism', *Critical Studies on Terrorism*, 1(2): 185–95.
Wyn Jones, R., 2004. 'On Emancipation: Necessity, Capacity, and Concrete Utopias', in Booth, K. (ed.), *Critical Security Studies and World Politics* (Boulder, CO: Lynne Rienner).
Zulaika, J., 1988. *Basque Violence: Metaphor and Sacrament* (Reno, NV: University of Nevada Press).
Zulaika, J. and Douglass, W., 1996. *Terror and Taboo: The Follies, Fables, and Faces of Terrorism* (London: Routledge).

4 State Violence as State Terrorism

Ruth Blakeley

Introduction

Much state violence is used to coerce populations into complying with the wishes of elites by using the violence to instil fear in an audience beyond the direct victim of the violence. State violence of this kind is usually intended to achieve certain political objectives, particularly curtailing political opposition. When used in this way, state violence constitutes state terrorism. With reference to specific empirical examples, this chapter explores state terrorism in relation to other forms of state violence. It will begin by introducing the reader to the debates on how terrorism generally, and state terrorism specifically, are defined, and will demonstrate that these are highly contested terms. Nevertheless, the chapter will show that there is sufficient agreement among scholars on the key constitutive elements of terrorism that we can adequately define state terrorism based on existing and accepted definitions of terrorism. A defining feature of state terrorism – and that which distinguishes it from other forms of state violence – is that it involves the illegal targeting of individuals that the state has a duty to protect with the aim of instilling fear in a target audience beyond the direct victim. In this regard, this chapter challenges the monopoly on legitimate violence that is frequently afforded to the state. It shows that any monopoly of violence that the state claims is neither a justification for excluding state terrorism from studies of terrorism, nor, more importantly, for affording states the right to use violence in any way they choose.[1] After discussing the ways in which state terrorism is defined, this chapter then outlines the main difficulties associated with identifying state terrorism

---

1   While not the focus of this chapter, it should be noted that in challenging the monopoly on violence that states claim, particularly where they use violence in illegitimate ways, it is logical to afford legitimacy to non-state actors involved in violent resistance to state tyranny. States deploy the self-defence principle to justify their recourse to violence, which they argue constitutes a legitimate use of force. Therefore, non-state actors resisting illegitimate violence by the state should also be afforded the same right, namely to deploy violence in self-defence when they are illegitimately attacked by agents of the state.

and distinguishing it from other forms of state violence. These difficulties relate primarily to questions of motive and agency. The discussion here explores the measures that scholars can take to overcome these difficulties, with reference to various forms that state terrorism can take.

Defining State Terrorism in Relation to State Violence

Totalitarian regimes throughout history, including those of Stalin, Hitler and Pol Pot, have used violence to terrorise populations into complying with the regime's demands. European colonial powers used violence in this way to establish and maintain their empires, and to try to thwart independence movements in their colonies. The allies during the Second World War bombed civilians in German cities to try and incite the public to turn against Hitler. The Latin American national security states during the Cold War, with significant support from the US, also deployed violence, including disappearances and torture, to try and curtail support for opposition movements. When non-state actors use violence to intimidate an audience beyond the direct victim of that violence, we refer to it as terrorism. Yet there has been considerable resistance within international relations scholarship to the notion that states can be perpetrators of terrorism, even though the vast majority of state violence, particularly against domestic populations, is intended to have a terrorising effect and results in far higher casualties than non-state terrorism does. It is frequently assumed that because the existence of the state is based on its monopoly of coercive power, there is a fundamental difference between terrorism perpetrated by non-state actors and violence perpetrated by the state. In other words, states are permitted to use violence, so we should not refer to their use of violence as terrorism. Non-state actors, on the other hand, are afforded no such right in pursuit of their political objectives, so we refer to their actions as terrorism. There are two significant problems with these assumptions. First, terrorism and state violence are being differentiated on the basis of who the perpetrator of the act is, rather than on the nature of the act itself. Second, this incorrectly assumes that because the state has a monopoly on violence, any use of violence by the state is permissible. I will show that definitions of terrorism should be based on the nature of the act, and not the actor, and that on these grounds, there is no reason why actions by the state cannot be labelled as terrorism if these acts fit the definition. I will then demonstrate that just because the state claims a monopoly on the use of violence in the interests of its survival, this does not mean that all forms of state violence are legitimate.

Debating Definitions

There is no consensus on how terrorism should be defined. Indeed, as Andrew Silke notes, most works on terrorism begin with a discussion of the various associated definitional problems of the term (Silke 2004: 2) and the failure of scholars to reach agreement (Badey 1998: 90–107; Barker 2003: 23; Cooper 2001: 881–93; Duggard 1974: 67–81; Jenkins 1980; Weinberg et al. 2004: 777–94). Nevertheless, there is a group of core characteristics that are common to competing definitions. Yet some scholars do not accept that terrorism by states should be equated with terrorism by non-state actors. Walter Laqueur, for example, argues: 'There are basic differences in motives, function and effect between oppression by the state (or society or religion) and political terrorism. To equate them, to obliterate them is to spread confusion' (Laqueur 1986: 89). He has also argued that including state terrorism in the study of terrorism 'would have made the study of terrorism impossible, for it would have included not only US foreign policy, but also Hitler and Stalin' (Laqueur 2003: 140). Laqueur's position shows that his analysis of terrorism is actor-based rather than action-based. Even if the motives, functions and effects of terrorism by states and non-state actors are different, the act of terrorism itself is not, since the core characteristics of terrorism are the same, whether the perpetrator is a state or a non-state actor. Laqueur's argument also serves to entrench the supposed moral legitimacy of state violence. He claims that those who argue that state terrorism should be included in studies of terrorism ignore the fact that 'the very existence of a state is based on its monopoly of power. If it were different, states would not have the right, nor be in a position, to maintain that minimum of order on which all civilized life rests' (Laqueur 2003: 237). Bruce Hoffman has made similar claims. He argues that failing to differentiate between state and non-state violence, and equating the innocents killed by states and non-state actors would 'ignore the fact that, even while national armed forces have been responsible for far more death and destruction than terrorists might ever aspire to bring about, there nonetheless is a fundamental qualitative difference between the two types of violence'. He argues that this difference is based upon the historical emergence of 'rules and accepted norms of behaviour that prohibit the use of certain types of weapons' and 'proscribe various tactics and outlaw attacks on specific categories of targets'. He adds that 'terrorists' have by contrast 'violated all these rules' (Hoffman 1998: 34).[2] This argument would only stand if it could be shown that states do not violate these rules, as set out in the Geneva Conventions. The reality is that they do. Any monopoly of violence that the state has is neither a justification for excluding state terrorism from studies of terrorism, nor, more importantly, for affording states the right to use violence in any way they choose (Stohl 2006: 4–5). Indeed, even in situations where, according to international law and norms, states have the legitimate right to use violence (*jus ad bellum*), it is not always the case that their conduct (*jus in bello*) is itself legitimate.

There are certain core characteristics common to the many definitions of terrorism. For Eugene Victor Walter, terrorism involves three key features: first,

---

2   A more detailed critique of the work of these scholars can be found in Sam Raphael, 'Putting the State Back In: The Orthodox Definition of Terrorism and the Critical Need to Address State Terrorism', *British International Studies Association Annual Conference* (Cambridge, UK, 2007).

threatened or perpetrated violence directed at some victim; second, the violent actor intends that violence to induce terror in some witness who is generally distinct from the victim (in other words, the victim is instrumental); and, third, the violent actor intends or expects that the terrorised witness to the violence will alter his or her behaviour (Walter 1969). Paul Wilkinson's widely quoted definition echoes that of Walter. Wilkinson argues that terrorism has five main characteristics:

> It is premeditated and aims to create a climate of extreme fear or terror; it is directed at a wider audience or target than the immediate victims of the violence; it inherently involves attacks on random and symbolic targets, including civilians; the acts of violence committed are seen by the society in which they occur as extra-normal, in the literal sense that they breach the social norms, thus causing a sense of outrage; and terrorism is used to try to influence political behaviour in some way. (Wilkinson 1992: 228–9)

Both Walter's and Wilkinson's definitions identify a specific logic in the use of terrorism, namely that it involves not simply harming the direct victim of the violence, but exploiting the opportunity afforded by the harm to terrorise others. Similarly, for both Walter and Wilkinson, terrorism is defined according to the actions carried out, rather than who the actors are, meaning that the state is not precluded as a potential perpetrator of terrorism. In an attempt to establish an agenda for research on state terrorism in the 1980s, Christopher Mitchell, Michael Stohl, David Carleton and George Lopez incorporated Walter's core characteristics into their definition of state terrorism. They argued:

> Terrorism by the state (or non-state actors) involves deliberate coercion and violence (or the threat thereof) directed at some victim, with the intention of inducing extreme fear in some target observers who identify with that victim in such a way that they perceive themselves as potential future victims. In this way they are forced to consider altering their behaviour in some manner desired by the actor. (Mitchell et al. 1986: 5)

While this is not far removed from Wilkinson's definition of terrorism, it retains one of the elements established by Walter, namely that the threat of violence is sufficient for a state to be perpetrating terror. This threat would only be sufficient in a pre-existing climate of fear induced by prior acts of state terrorism. As Ted Robert Gurr argues, a threat would not be adequate unless it was part of a pattern of activity 'in which instrumental violence occurs often enough that threats of similar violence, made then or later, have their intended effects' (Gurr 1986: 46).

Drawing on existing definitions, and specifically that of Walter, I propose that state terrorism involves the following four key elements: 1) there must be a deliberate act of violence against individuals that the state has a duty to protect, or a threat of such an act if a climate of fear has already been established through preceding acts of state violence; 2) the act must be perpetrated by actors on behalf of or in conjunction with the state, including paramilitaries and private security agents; 3) the act or threat of violence is intended to induce extreme fear in some target observers who identify with that victim; and 4) the target audience is forced to consider changing their behaviour in some way. With the exception of Walter's definition, the definitions discussed argue that the change in behaviour in the target audience has to be political. In line with Walter, I do not make the same claim, since states have frequently used violence to terrorise a wider audience so that they subordinate themselves to the wishes of the state. Those wishes may of course include lending political support to the state, but they may also involve citizens labouring in the interests of elites. This was frequently the case in colonial states, where imperialists used terror to coerce citizens into working, often as slaves, to extract resources (Blakeley 2009). The strength of Walter's criteria is therefore that changes in behaviour other than political behaviour are not precluded. As already implied, the key ingredient that distinguishes state terrorism from other forms of state repression is its instrumentality.

The Importance of the Target Audience

The key difference between state terrorism and other forms of state violence is that state terrorism involves the illegal targeting of individuals that the state has a duty to protect with the intention of creating extreme fear among an audience beyond the direct victim of the violence. That audience may be a domestic one and it may be limited, consisting of only the immediate acquaintances of the actual victim. This is significant because it helps us to make an important distinction between isolated incidents of criminal activity or state violence on the one hand and state terrorism on the other. The case of torture is helpful for exploring the significance of the target audience.

Many victims of state violence are subjected to torture. In some cases torture is carried out covertly and is aimed primarily at tormenting the victim. It of course violates international law, but for torture to constitute state terrorism, it must be aimed at, or have the effect of, terrorising an audience beyond the direct victim. Torture was used in history, very publicly, as a form of punishment, but also as a means of deterring criminal behaviour (Beccaria [1764] 1995; Foucault 1977; Peters 1985; Vidal-Naquet 1963). Torture continues to be used as a means of terrorising other incarcerated detainees in order to compel certain behaviour by ensuring that they hear the torture occurring or see the physical harm inflicted on their fellow captives. Torture is often intended to alter behaviour among a much wider audience well beyond the walls of the torture chamber. It was used in this way by the Guatemalan state during the counter-insurgency war of the 1970s and 1980s, during which, as Amnesty International reported, newspapers were permitted to publish photographs of dead torture victims:

> Guatemalan counterinsurgency operations in the early 1980s ... included the terrorisation of targeted rural populations in an effort to ensure that

> they did not provide support for guerrillas. Tortured, dying villagers were displayed to relatives and neighbours who were prevented from helping them. Newspapers in urban areas during this period were allowed to publish photographs of mutilated bodies, ostensibly as an aid to families seeking their missing relatives, but also as a warning to all citizens not to oppose the government. (AI 1976)

The publication of the photographs in the Guatemalan case clearly indicates that the target of the terrorism was a very general audience. Indeed, the intention was to terrorise the populations of entire cities. In some cases a much more specific organisation or set of individuals will be the intended audience. Had the victims in the Guatemalan case been members of a specific political group that the government opposed and had the victims' bodies been returned to the group's headquarters, the target of the terrorism would have been that political group, although others in the community may also have been terrorised if they came to know of the torture and murder of those individuals.

If torture occurs in complete secret and there is no audience to witness it, it is difficult to argue that this constitutes state terrorism. For example, if an isolated individual or group of prison guards or members of the armed forces secretly used torture and went to great lengths to ensure that no one else knew of it, and there was no evidence that higher authorities had sanctioned the torture, we might conclude that this was the criminal act of an individual or group rather than an act of state terrorism. On the other hand, if such an act was carried out with the sanction of higher authorities, but the perpetrators and the higher authorities went to great lengths to ensure that no one else knew of it, we might conclude that this was an act of state violence, since it was perpetrated very clearly on behalf of the state. We could not, however, conclude that it was state terrorism if there was no audience to witness it. In practice, most torture committed by state agents is part of a wider pattern of state repression and, in many cases, state terrorism. Nevertheless, it is important to make this distinction between criminal activities by individuals, state violence and state terrorism, thereby reserving the label of state terrorism for those acts which are both condoned at some level by the state and are intended to or have the effect of terrorising a wider audience. I will discuss in more detail below how we might determine when individual acts are part of a wider policy of state terrorism.

International Law, State Violence and State Terrorism

Before discussing the forms that state terrorism can take, we must first consider the status of state violence and state terrorism in relation to international law. While states claim a monopoly on the legitimate use of violence, in that they claim the right to resort to violence in self-defence, certain acts of state violence are nevertheless prohibited, even in the course of a defensive war. State terrorism, however, has no status as an illegal act in international law. Nevertheless, it may involve certain acts of state violence that are prohibited under international law. It is perpetrated with the aim of terrorising others through those illegal acts of state violence. In other words, state terrorism involves the deliberate use of violence against individuals that the state has a duty to protect in order to invoke terror in a wider audience. The deliberate targeting of civilians in this way, either in armed conflict or in peacetime, violates principles enshrined in the two bodies of international law that deal with the protection of human rights: international humanitarian law (IHL) and international human rights law (IHRL). Human rights are those rights which all citizens share under international law, both in peacetime and during armed conflict. The most fundamental of these are the right to life, the prohibition of torture or cruel, inhuman or degrading treatment or punishment, the prohibition of slavery and servitude and the prohibition of retroactive criminal laws (ICRC 2003). Targeting armed enemy combatants is legitimate in warfare, but certain acts are nevertheless prohibited. These include killing prisoners of war or subjecting them to torture or other inhuman or degrading treatment or punishment (ICRC 1949). These constitute illegitimate acts of state violence, Where the laws prohibiting such acts are violated, states may also be guilty of state terrorism if those illegal acts were intended to, or had the effect of, terrorising a wider audience, as I will show. IHL also deals with the thorny question of what acts are permissible in warfare where civilian casualties are likely to ensue. The targeting of civilians is prohibited, both by IHL and IHRL, in times of war and peace. However, it is acknowledged in IHL that civilian casualties are likely to be a secondary effect of certain actions deemed to be legitimate in armed conflict. IHL is therefore concerned with ensuring that maximum effort is made to protect civilians when such operations take place and with ensuring that any risks taken with civilian life are proportional to the acts being carried out. This is far from straightforward, as I will later show with reference to the use of strategic aerial bombardment.

Some IHRL treaties permit governments to derogate from certain obligations in situations of public emergency threatening the life of the nation, but there are some rights that are never to be violated:

> Derogations must, however, be proportional to the crisis at hand, must not be introduced on a discriminatory basis and must not contravene other rules of international law – including rules of IHL. Certain human rights are never derogable. Among them are the right to life, freedom from torture, or inhuman or degrading treatment or punishment, prohibition of slavery and servitude and prohibition of retroactive criminal laws. (ICRC 2003)

State terrorism involves the derogation from one or more of these against an individual or group in order to invoke fear in a wider audience. The illegally targeted individual may be a civilian or an enemy combatant who has been disarmed and is being detained. The law is clear that there should be no derogations at all from the provisions of IHL that uphold the right to life and the right to freedom from inhuman or degrading treatment or punishment. State terrorism, then, only exists through the illegal targeting of individuals that states have a duty to protect. In this regard, as with other forms of state violence, a key ingredient of state terrorism is that it involves acts that are illegal under international law. It is deemed illegal and inhuman when non-state actors commit those acts and it is no less inhumane if the perpetrator is a state.

The Difficulties of Identifying State Terrorism

Both state terrorism and the illicit use of other forms of violence by the state are prosecutable under international law. Nevertheless, it is important to try and determine when states are using illicit violence as a means of intimidating an audience beyond the direct victim of the violence, thereby committing state terrorism. This is because in so doing they are committing not just one but two serious crimes – illegal use of force and an act of terrorism. Determining the intentions of state actors is not easy. Often their purposes will, at best, be ambiguous. This is largely because in most cases, governments seek to conceal the extent to which they use terrorism, and when such activities are exposed, they tend to be justified as 'necessary measures' or more benignly as 'police action' (Mitchell et al. 1986: 2–3; Nicholson 1986: 31). Obtaining data on acts of terrorism committed by states is extremely difficult, since they tend not to advertise their terrorist activities or intent (Chambliss 1989: 203–4; Gibbs 1989: 330; Mitchell et al. 1986: 2; Nicholson 1986: 31). When such activities are exposed, considerable analytical effort is required to determine whether such an act does constitute state terrorism, since they are unlikely to be included in the major data sets of terrorist incidents. This also means that drawing concrete conclusions about whether certain acts constitute state terrorism may not always be possible, and instead we might need to make inferences from other, context-specific evidence. I will explore some of the difficulties involved in identifying state terrorism. They relate primarily to problems of motive and agency.

State Terrorism as a Secondary Effect

In some cases, groups within a society may be terrorised as a consequence of other acts of state violence. This raises the question of whether we can argue that state terrorism has occurred if it is not the primary or only outcome of state violence. According to Mitchell et al., if the terror was unintentional, we could not argue that this was 'true' terrorism. But this assumes that we can determine that the terror was not intentional, rather than one of a number of intentions of the act. If we apply this condition, an act of violence cannot be defined as state terrorism if it is primarily aimed at harming the victim, a secondary effect of which is to terrorise other groups within a population. Mitchell et al. illustrate their argument with the example of the policies of the Khmer Rouge that were aimed at the destruction of a particular sector of society and which therefore constituted genocide. While this will have instilled terror throughout society, this was not the primary intention. By contrast, they argue, policies such as the US Operation Phoenix in South Vietnam, which involved terrorising people associated with members of the National Liberation Front by publicly rounding them up, torturing and assassinating them, do constitute state terrorism, because terrorising the target audience was the primary objective (Mitchell et al. 1986: 6).

Such a sharp distinction should not be made between terrorism as a secondary effect and terrorism as the primary objective of an act, particularly in cases where the act itself is illegitimate. A parallel can be drawn with Michael Walzer's work on the legitimacy of acts in war which are likely to have evil consequences. He argues that, in line with the *jus in bello* principles, such an act is only permissible providing four conditions hold:

> that the act is good in itself or at least indifferent, which means ... that it is a legitimate act of war; that the direct effect is morally acceptable ... that the intention of the actor is good, that is, he aims only at the acceptable effect; the evil effect is not one of his ends, nor is it a means to an ends; that the good effect is sufficiently good to compensate for allowing the evil effect; it must be justifiable under the proportionality rule. (Walzer 2000: 153)

These conditions can be usefully applied to state terrorism where it appears to be a secondary effect of some other act of state violence. State terrorism in such cases is not the unintended secondary effect of some good or indifferent act. It is a consequence of a policy which itself is illegitimate, repressive and, on Walzer's terms, evil. Furthermore, if the state seeks to commit genocide, for example, against a specific group, are they not assisted because others outside of that group are sufficiently fearful of the consequences for themselves if they were to intervene in an attempt to prevent the genocide? And could the terror that arises among other groups not be an intended effect, whether primary or secondary? In the case of the genocide by Nazi Germany against Jews, gypsies and homosexuals, individuals outside of those groups may not have intervened because they had been sufficiently terrorised by the increasing intensity of efforts by the Nazis to single these groups out, round them up and transport them to unknown places, and subsequently by the rumours they had heard of concentration camps and of others outside these groups who had attempted to protect the vulnerable, themselves disappearing. Indeed, as Gurr notes, Adolf Hitler, while in power, was explicit about the fact that his genocidal policies also served as a tool of terror to deter opposition:

> I shall spread terror through the surprising application of all means. The sudden shock of a terrible fear of death is what matters. Why should I deal otherwise with all my political opponents? These so-called atrocities save me hundreds of thousands of individual actions against the protestors and discontents. Each one of them will think twice to oppose me when he learns

what is [awaiting] him in the [concentration] camp. (Adolf Hitler, cited in Gurr 1986: 46–7)

Even where the terrorism is not a secondary objective, it might prove expedient to the state and should be labelled state terrorism. Walzer argues that to conclude that a secondary effect was unintentional, there would have to be evidence that the actors involved sought to minimise the secondary effect. It is difficult to envisage that a state involved in a genocidal policy would be too concerned about minimising the ensuing terror among others outside of the targeted group, particularly where the terror may be instrumental to its overall objectives.

The same principle applies if terrorism ensues as a secondary effect of an act that may be considered legitimate. The case of the targeting of electrical power during the 1991 Gulf War is instructive here. In Operation Desert Storm, the US-led campaign against Iraq in 1990–1991, civilians were never intended as direct targets. According to the Gulf War Air Power Surveys (an analysis carried out by the US Air Force following the Gulf War), 'there was widespread agreement from the outset of the planning process that directly attacking the people of Iraq or their food supply was neither compatible with US objectives nor morally acceptable to the American people' (Keaney and Cohen 1993: 268). The target categories drawn up by the planners also indicate that civilians were not intended as direct targets. The authors of the Gulf War Air Power Surveys claim that the air campaign had not only been 'precise, efficient and legal, but had resulted in very few civilian casualties' (Keaney and Cohen 1993: 305). A Greenpeace International study in 1991 estimated that countrywide civilian casualties were 2,278 dead and 5,976 injured (Arkin et al. 1991: 46–7). The Greenpeace figure is cited by the Gulf War Air Power Surveys and is not disputed by the authors of the Surveys (Keaney and Cohen 1993: 482). There was, however, considerable controversy relating to the reporting of civilian casualties in the Gulf War, since the Pentagon made no attempt to keep records of civilian deaths. As the *Pittsburgh Post-Gazette* reported, Greenpeace later revised its estimates, but these differed from other estimates. In 1993 Greenpeace revised its estimate to 3,500 civilian deaths as a result of coalition bombing. The US Army War College estimated that 3,000 had been killed and the government of Iraq put the figure at 2,248 (Kelly 2003). Greenpeace did conclude that they found no evidence of deliberate targeting of civilians. They did, however, highlight the catastrophic human impact of the air campaign, resulting from the devastation of the Iraqi infrastructure and the intense environmental degradation caused by the bombings (Arkin et al. 1991: 5). This was a result of the intensity of the air campaign. As Greenpeace reported, 'In one day of the Gulf War, there were as many combat missions flown against Iraq as Saddam Hussein experienced in the entire Iran-Iraq war' (Arkin et al. 1991: 6).

There was, however, no indication in the Gulf War Air Power Surveys that measures were taken to minimise the secondary effect of terrorising the population, which would undoubtedly ensue from aerial bombardment of targets deemed to be legitimate, especially given the extensive nature of the bombing campaign. The opposite was true. There was a view among a number of those involved in the planning of the air campaign that harming the morale of the civilian population would be a welcome secondary effect of the targeting of Iraq's electricity generating capacity:

> As for civilian morale, some of the air planners, including General Glosson, felt that 'putting the lights out on Baghdad' would have psychological effects on the average Iraqi ... By demonstrating that Saddam Hussein could not even keep the electricity flowing in Baghdad, it was hoped the Ba'th Party's grip on the Iraqi population could be loosened, thereby helping to bring about a change in the regime. (Keaney and Cohen 1993: 292)

Aerial bombardment that was sufficient to cripple the entire electricity generation capacity of modern cities such as Baghdad and Basra is likely to have resulted in considerable levels of fear among the civilian population. This was not seen by the planners as an illegitimate secondary effect, but instead as a welcome means by which to undermine the regime. In warfare, attacking the morale of enemy soldiers is considered an appropriate means by which to attempt to avoid having to fight each and every battalion one by one. However, Walzer's argument requires that measures are taken to minimise the secondary effect, in this case, terrorising large sectors of the population. No such measures were taken by the air campaign planners. Indeed, they hoped that the population would be so 'psychologically affected', a euphemism for 'terrorised', that opposition to the regime would increase. Rather than try and prevent the terrorising of the population, those involved in planning the air campaign actively encouraged it, even though this is illegitimate according to IHRL.

The Problem of Agency: When are State Representatives Acting on Behalf of the State?

As discussed above, before concluding that an act of violence by a representative of the state was an act of state terrorism, we are confronted with a number of challenges relating to agency. We must first rule out the possibility that the act was simply an isolated, criminal act by an individual as opposed to an act of state violence. We then need to be able to demonstrate that the act was intended to or had the effect of terrorising a wider audience than the direct victim of the violence. Even then, however, the state still holds a degree of responsibility for the actions of its representatives. Whether we conclude that a state sanctioned the act, and therefore was complicit in state terrorism through its agents, might depend on how the state responds afterwards. If the state fails to prosecute the individual to the full extent of the law and fails to compensate the victims, and if it attempts to excuse the actions in some way, it is condoning the actions of that individual. Therefore, we can argue that the state was complicit. With reference to the use of torture at Abu Ghraib, I will demonstrate the importance of context-specific evidence in determining, first, whether acts of violence by state agents were acts of state terrorism and, second, whether those acts were part of an institutionalised policy of state terrorism.

To differentiate between the odd isolated criminal act of a prison officer or member of the armed forces and an act sanctioned by the state, it is important to examine the reaction of the relevant officials and the state. If measures are taken, swiftly, to try and punish the perpetrator(s) through proper legal and disciplinary channels, and there is no evidence of the state sanctioning such activities, we might conclude that this was a criminal act by an individual or group and not an act of state violence. This was indeed what the Pentagon and the Bush administration claimed once the photographs emerged in 2004 revealing that detainees at the Abu Ghraib prison in Iraq had been tortured by US personnel. Nevertheless, this claim cannot be sustained, since there have been very few prosecutions, sentences have been light and punitive measures have been limited to lower-ranking soldiers rather than the senior officers involved, or indeed the officials in the Bush administration who fought to ensure that methods tantamount to torture be permitted against terror suspects. In a speech on Iraq on 24 May 2004, shortly after the public had learned of the torture, President Bush declared:

> Under the dictator [Saddam Hussein], prisons like Abu Ghraib were symbols of death and torture. That same prison became a symbol of disgraceful conduct by a few American troops who dishonored our country and disregarded our values. (Bush, cited in Milbank 2004)

The same conclusions were drawn by Major General Antonio Tabuga in his initial inquiry. He concluded that the torture was the work of a few bad apples in need of improved training (Taguba 2004: 37).

Yet the record of events uncovered through various leaked documents, traced by Seymour Hersh (2004) and now compiled by Karen Greenberg and Joshua Dratel (2005), shows that despite the public statement condemning torture, the administration had been behind numerous attempts to allow the torture of detainees in the 'War on Terror'. Policies outlined in the various memos that passed between the upper echelons of the administration, including the White House, the Department of Justice and the senior Counsel to the president, were enacted. These included not affording protection under the Geneva Conventions to detainees and allowing torture, including the use of stress positions, extremes of temperature and light, hooding, interrogations for 20 hours, forced grooming and removal of clothing, water boarding and the use of scenarios designed to convince the detainee that death or severe pain was imminent, as advocated in a memo from Major General Dunlavey, dated 11 October 2002, requesting approval for such techniques (Dunlavey 2002). These techniques were subsequently sanctioned by Donald Rumsfeld on 2 December 2002 (Haynes 2002).

The response of the administration to the abuses at Abu Ghraib involved proceedings in military courts against nine reservists involved in the abuses, three of whom were convicted; the other six made plea deals (Gutierrez 2005). None of the senior officers implicated were brought to trial and there was no attempt to hold to account those in the Bush administration who had themselves been involved in efforts to legitimise torture. Without examining the wider context of the Abu Ghraib case, it would be possible to conclude that this was an isolated incident committed by a small number of miscreants, and this was certainly the message that the administration attempted to portray. The reality is that there have been many cases of abuse in the 'War on Terror' at numerous camps in Iraq and Afghanistan, as well as at Guantanamo Bay, at the hands of the US and allied forces. Furthermore, the policy of extraordinary rendition has resulted in torture and abuse, sanctioned by the US and various liberal democratic allies, and carried out by security agents from many countries with appalling human rights records (Blakeley 2009). Abu Ghraib was therefore not an isolated incident, but part of a much bigger pattern of state violence sanctioned by the US state. We can also conclude that it is indicative of a pattern of state terrorism, since these practices have had the effect of terrorising a wider audience than the direct victims of the disappearances and torture.

The case of Abu Ghraib underlines the importance of the wider context when considering whether acts of violence by state agents constitute state terrorism. Without evidence of intentions, we have to look to the broader context. A further indicator of intention concerns the reasonably anticipated likely consequence of an act. If, for example, a state chooses to bomb civilian areas of a city, knowing that this is almost certainly going to result in civilian casualties, it cannot claim that no harm was meant to civilians. Similarly, if state agents are in the business of kidnapping political activists, the state cannot claim that it did not intend to terrorise other political activists. If such acts are carried out repeatedly, despite the state having already seen that civilians are killed and terrorised by the bombing and that political activists are fearful, we can conclude that this was the intended outcome of those acts and that the state is therefore committing acts of terrorism against civilians.

As with various phenomena in the social sciences, determining whether state violence was used instrumentally to alter the behaviour of a wider audience than the direct victim, thereby constituting state terrorism, requires that we make judgments concerning the motives and agency behind specific acts. To legitimately label incidents of violence by representatives of the state as state terrorism, those incidents should not be analysed in isolation, but with reference to the wider context. This helps overcome some of the ambiguities we face when seeking to determine the degree of sanction from the state for those acts of violence, and the purpose that they were intended to serve. In some cases it simply may not be possible to make a decisive judgment and it may only be with the passage of time that sufficient evidence comes to light to confirm that an act of state terrorism was committed and to confirm that it was part of a wider institutionalised policy of terrorism.

Conclusion

States have frequently used violence against their own or external populations as a means of achieving their political objectives. State violence frequently also constitutes state terrorism, because it is used to instil fear in a wider audience than the direct victim of the violence. This is what distinguishes state terrorism from other forms of state violence. It also helps to explain why much of the violence deployed by states against their own or another population also constitutes state terrorism. States have found terrorism to be functional to the achievement of their political objectives, as the examples explored here demonstrate.

Despite the widespread use of state terrorism, there has been considerable opposition to the concept within international relations scholarship. I have shown that the justifications for excluding state terrorism as a category of state violence are based on flawed applications of the various definitions of terrorism. Existing definitions of terrorism adequately encompass acts by state agents. I have shown that state terrorism involves a deliberate threat or act of violence against a victim by representatives of the state, or a threat of such when a climate of fear already exists through prior acts of state terrorism, which is intended to induce fear in some target observers who identify with the victim, so that the target audience is forced to consider changing their behaviour in some way. They also reinforce the monopoly on legitimate violence afforded to the state, even though within international norms and law, it is clear that certain acts of state violence are never permitted. Where widespread state terrorism takes place, it may emerge from the use of other forms of state violence, where the main objective was not to terrorise, but where this was a secondary and often welcome consequence. With reference to the 'Just War' tradition, I have argued that where state terrorism appears to be a secondary effect (albeit an instrumental one) rather than the primary motive of some other act, legitimate or not, it still constitutes state terrorism.

Neither definitions of terrorism nor international law pertaining to human rights present significant obstacles to scholars of state terrorism. On the contrary, they provide helpful criteria by which to identify and oppose state terrorism. The challenge for scholars, however, is to determine whether acts of violence by state representatives can be labelled state terrorism and when acts of state terrorism are part of a wider, institutionalised policy. As with other atrocities, there is a scarcity of evidence that explicitly shows such acts to have been sanctioned by the state. We are therefore faced with considerable challenges in identifying motive and agency when atrocities are committed. We can overcome some of these challenges by situating specific acts of state violence within a much broader context. This involves analysing the circumstances surrounding the events in question, both at the local level and in relation to other events and broader policies and strategies.

References

AI (1976), 'Guatemala', London: Amnesty International Briefing Papers, No. 8.

Arkin, W., Durrant, D. and Cherni, M. (1991), 'On Impact: Modern Warfare and the Environment – A Case Study of the Gulf War', http://www.greenpeace.org/international/en/publications/reports/on-impact-modern-warfare-and [accessed 4 July 2012].

Badey, T. (1998), 'Defining International Terrorism: A Pragmatic Approach', *Terrorism and Political Violence*, 10(1): 90–107.

Barker, J. (2003), *The No-Nonsense Guide to Terrorism*. London: Verso.

Beccaria, C. ([1764] 1995), *On Crimes and Punishments and Other Writings*, ed. Richard Bellamy, trans. Richard Davies. Cambridge: Cambridge University Press.

Blakeley, R. (2009), *State Terrorism and Neoliberalism: The North in the South*, Routledge Critical Terrorism Studies. London: Routledge.

Chambliss, W. (1989), 'State-Organized Crime – The American Society of Criminology, 1988 Presidential Address', *Criminology*, 27(2): 183–208.

Cooper, H. (2001), 'Terrorism: The Problem of Definition Revisited', *American Behavioural Scientist*, 44: 881–93.

Duggard, J. (1974), 'International Terrorism: Problems of Definition', *International Affairs*, 50(1): 67–81.

Dunlavey, M. (2002), 'Counter-Resistance Strategies (Memorandum for Commander, US Southern Command)', 11 October, http://www.torturingdemocracy.org/documents/20021011.pdf [accessed 13 June 2012].

Foucault, M. (1977), *Discipline and Punish. The Birth of the Prison*, trans. Alan Sheridan. London: Penguin.

Gibbs, J. (1989), 'Conceptualization of Terrorism', *American Sociological Review*, 54(3): 329–40.

Greenberg, K. and Dratel, J. (eds) (2005), *The Torture Papers. The Road to Abu Ghraib*. Cambridge: Cambridge University Press.

Gurr, T.R. (1986), 'The Political Origins of State Violence and Terror: A Theoretical Analysis', in Michael Stohl and George Lopez (eds), *Government Violence and Repression: An Agenda for Research*. New York: Greenwood Press, 45–71.

Gutierrez, T. (2005), 'Lynndie England Convicted in Abu Ghraib Trial', *USA Today*, 26 September.

Haynes, W.J. (2002), 'Counter-Resistance Techniques (Action Memo from William J Haynes, General Counsel, to Secretary of State for Defence Donald Rumsfeld)', 27 November, http://www.torturingdemocracy.org/documents/20021127-1.pdf [accessed 13 June 2012].

Hersh, S. (2004), *Chain of Command. The Road from 9/11 to Abu Ghraib*. London: Penguin.

Hoffman, B. (1998), *Inside Terrorism*. New York: Columbia University Press.

ICRC (1949), 'Convention (III) Relative to the Treatment of Prisoners of War', http://www.icrc.org/ihl.nsf/7c4d08d9b287a42141256739003e636b/6fef854a3517b75ac125641e004a9e68 [accessed 13 June 2012].

ICRC (2003), 'International Humanitarian Law and International Human Rights Law: Similarities and Differences', http://www.icrc.org/eng/assets/files/other/ihl_and_ihrl.pdf [accessed 4 July 2012].

Jenkins, B. (1980), 'The Study of Terrorism: Definitional Problems', *The RAND Paper Series*. Santa Monica: The RAND Corporation, http://www.rand.org/pubs/papers/2006/P6563.pdf [accessed 13 June 2012].

Keaney, T. and Cohen, E. (1993), 'Gulf War Air Power Surveys (Volume II, Part II)', http://www.airforcehistory.hq.af.mil/Publications/Annotations/gwaps.htm [accessed 13 June 2012].

Kelly, J. (2003), 'Estimates of Deaths in First War Still in Dispute', *Pittsburgh Post-Gazette*, 16 February, http://www.post-gazette.com/nation/20030216casualty0216p5.asp [accessed 13 June 2012].

Laqueur, W. (1986), 'Reflections on Terrorism', *Foreign Affairs*, 65: 86–100.

Laqueur, W. (2003), *No End to War: Terrorism in the Twenty-First Century*. New York: Continuum.

Milbank, D. (2004), 'Bush Seeks to Reassure Nation on Iraq', *Washington Post*, 25 May 2004.

Mitchell, C. et al. (1986), 'State Terrorism: Issues of Concept and Measurement', in Michael Stohl and George Lopez (eds), *Government Violence and Repression: An Agenda for Research*. New York: Greenwood Press, 1–26.

Nicholson, M. (1986), 'Conceptual Problems of Studying State Terrorism', in Michael Stohl and George Lopez (eds), *Government Violence and Repression: An Agenda for Research*. New York: Greenwood Press, 27–44.

Peters, E. (1985), *Torture*. New York: Basil Blackwell.

Raphael, S. (2007), 'Putting the State Back In: The Orthodox Definition of Terrorism and the Critical Need to Address State Terrorism', paper given at British International Studies Association Annual Conference, Cambridge, UK, December 2007.

Silke, A. (2004), *Research on Terrorism: Trends, Achievements and Failures*. London: Frank Cass.

Stohl, M. (2006), 'The State as Terrorist: Insights and Implications', *Democracy and Security*, 2: 1–25.

Taguba, M.G.A. (2004), 'Article 15-6 Investigation of the 800th Military Police Brigade', Washington DC: US Department of Defense.

Vidal-Naquet, P. (1963), *Torture: Cancer of Democracy*. Harmondsworth: Penguin.

Walter, E.V. (1969), *Terror and Resistance*. Oxford: Oxford University Press.

Walzer, M. (2000), *Just and Unjust Wars*, 3rd edn. New York: Basic Books.

Weinberg, L., Pedahzur, A. and Hirsch-Hoefler, S. (2004), 'The Challenges of Conceptualizing Terrorism', *Terrorism and Political Violence*, 16(4): 777–94.

Wilkinson, P. (1992), 'International Terrorism: New Risks to World Order', in John Baylis and Nick Rengger (eds), *Dilemmas of World Politics: International Issues in a Changing World*. Oxford: Clarendon Press, 228–57.

The 'War on Terror' as Political Violence

Richard Seymour

While it is pardonable for the colonizer to have his little arsenals, the discovery of even a rusty weapon among the colonized is cause for immediate punishment.
Albert Memmi

Introduction

One of the oddities of the 'war on terror' is that there remains no clear, universally agreed-upon definition of its key referent, terrorism. Notwithstanding such indeterminacy, the term operates doubly in a descriptive and prescriptive capacity. Terrorism both describes a form of (illegitimate) political violence and a primary justification for (legitimate) political violence. In the context of the 'war on terror', connotations of epic and indiscriminate brutality accrue to that political violence branded terrorism, while its purported opposite is held to be limited by the humane values of states united in opposition to terrorism. Violence against troops in occupied Iraq and Afghanistan, though not targeting civilians, is routinely described as terrorism. The violence of the US and its allies is rationalised, while anti-occupation violence is pre-emptively pathologised, its motives ascribed to an anti-modern and illiberal reflux.

In the 'war on terror', a caste of Euro-American states is permitted the full range of kinetic force. They are opposed to a subterranean and disarticulated network of non-state actors with whom there can be no negotiations and whose means of violence are criminalised. Political violence in the 'war on terror' has been coded in the tropes of (magnanimous, rational, humane) empire versus (illiberal, irrational, suspicious) 'native fanaticism'. This binary stratification of global violence advises against what Robert Vitalis (2000) refers to as the 'norm against noticing' the impact of race and caste on contemporary international politics.

This chapter will consider the different forms of political violence that have been deployed in the major theatres of the 'war on terror', particularly in light of the language used about them. It will argue that the conduct of Euro-American states in these theatres contradicts their central claims as to what distinguishes their violence morally from that of their opponents – foremost among which is their concern to protect civilians. It will demonstrate that statespersons' depictions of oppositional violence in Iraq and Afghanistan are at variance with the realities described both in scholarly studies and US government reports. In order to delegitimise opposition violence, techniques of ascriptive diminution originally aimed at anti-colonial forces have been aggressively re-deployed for the purposes of the 'war on terror'. The codification of political violence according to the binary of 'just war' versus unjust terror, or of the magnanimous extension of the fruits of civilisation versus the vindictive attempt to destroy them, is a survival of colonial ideology. Finally, this chapter will conclude that such colonial ideas continue to be powerful because the international norms of statehood and property – and thus of 'just war' – that produced those ideas in the first instance continue to be relevant.

Civilians and the 'War on Terror'

A pivotal moral justification for Western political violence is that it operates within constraints that respect civilian life. It is a standard refrain of Western military sources that 'we do not target civilians'. The claim is an important part of the US State Department's overseas public relations strategy (Inskeep 2006). This is also what is held to separate 'terrorism' from those claiming to wage war against 'terrorism'. As George W. Bush explained (2004), 'Every life is precious. That's what distinguishes us from the enemy'. A look at the range of options that occupying forces have permitted themselves in Iraq and Afghanistan suggests that this claim is untenable.

Air Strikes

US military rules permit the killing of civilians during air strikes. As former Pentagon advisor Marc Garlasco explained, 'if you hit 30 as the anticipated number of civilians killed, the airstrike had to go to Rumsfeld or Bush personally to sign off', but otherwise no one need be told (Benjamin 2007). Such a standard is interesting for a number of reasons. First, it normalises a certain level of civilian killing, thus belying the claim that 'every life is precious' to war planners. Second, any 'anticipation' on the part of military tacticians clearly has a profound subjective element that enables greater latitude for civilian killing outside of executive authorisation than the figure of 30 suggests. When mass killings of civilians have been reported, the US military's response has often been to insist that most or all of those killed were in fact 'insurgents'. The definition of 'civilian' in the context of the 'war on terror' has proven highly malleable. Chief Warrant Officer Dave Diaz, heading Special Forces A-Team in Afghanistan, put the point bluntly:

Yes, it is a civilian village, mud hut, like everything else in this country. But don't say that. Say it's a military compound. It's a built-up area, barracks, command and control. Just like with the convoys: If it really was a convoy with civilian vehicles they were using for transport, we would just say hey, military convoy, troop transport. (Quoted in Mann 2003: 138)

Realistically, Western states engaged in warfare do operate within constraints applied by, for example, negative publicity. And if their aim is to control a territory, they have to consider how much their tactics alienate local populations. Nonetheless, such constraints on the targeting and killing of civilians would appear to be inadequate at best.

The detected consequences of aerial bombardment in the main frontiers of the 'war on terror' suggest that a terrible burden is being placed on civilian life by it. Two cluster studies of excess morality carried out in Iraq by researchers at Johns Hopkins University were published by *The Lancet* in 2004 and 2006.[1] The latter estimated/calculated a total of 601,027 violent deaths between March 2003 and June 2006. A total of 13 per cent of these were attributable to air strikes, accounting for over 78,000 deaths (Roberts et al. 2004, 2006). The Johns Hopkins University studies were unable to distinguish between civilians and combatants, though a separate survey of civilian deaths in Iraq, based on the Iraq Body Count database, found that 46 per cent of those killed by air attacks were women and 39 per cent were children (Hicks et al. 2009).

Similarly detailed studies have not been conducted in Afghanistan, though a study based on interviews with 600 groups in the nine months after September 2001 estimated some 10,000 civilian casualties, with 2,997 attributed to unexploded ordinance and mines, and 7,773 attributed to air strikes, rockets and gunfire (Benini and Moulton 2004). The rate of aerial attacks in Afghanistan has soared as the insurgency, initially relatively weak, has acquired momentum. In the summer of 2007, a study for the Center for Strategic and International Studies showed that air attacks had reached an unprecedented peak in Afghanistan, with 368 major strikes in July and 670 in August, higher even than in Iraq (Cordesman 2007). The following

---

1   These studies have been subject to searching scrutiny and criticism. Some of these criticisms were vexatious (see Edwards and Cromwell 2005), while others focusing on the report's implications were arguably circular: for example, the authors of the Iraq Body Count project suggest that the report's conclusions are improbable because, among other things, they imply that English-language media reports, which the Iraq Body Count bases its own estimates on, has failed to detect the majority of deaths in war zones (Dardagan et al. 2006). This missed the point that it was a central contention of the survey's producers that media reports systematically under-detected deaths in war zones (Burnham et al. 2006). One scholarly appraisal, building on the conclusions of the Iraq Body Count, maintained that the study suffered from 'main street bias' by surveying only the most accessible streets and thus missing areas likely to be exempt from combat (see Johnson et al. 2008). The authors of *The Lancet* studies have repeatedly refuted this argument, maintaining that it was untrue that they had restricted their research to more accessible surveys, and noting that their sample matched the population spread (Giles 2007; see also Karagiozakis 2009 for an account of the highly politicised nature of this controversy).

July, it was reported that air strikes had doubled on the previous year. On average, official figures said, allied air craft dropped ordinance ranging between 500lb and 2,000lb on Afghanistan 68 times every day (Wood 2008). Though there have not been *Lancet*-style surveys of excess mortality in Afghanistan, Human Rights Watch estimated that the rate of civilian deaths resulting from air attacks tripled in the year between 2006 and 2007 (Norton-Taylor 2008). A United Nations (UN) count of civilian deaths in 2008 estimated that 67 per cent of those killed by NATO-led forces were killed by air strikes (Filkins 2009).

Given the awesome force involved in such a strategy and the implications that it has for civilian life, military spokespersons often refer to the use of 'smart bombs' guided by satellite and radar technology. One rejoinder to this claim is that the munitions in question are only as 'smart' as the intelligence which provides the targets. A somewhat stronger rejoinder is that many of the other weapons used are 'dumb', in the sense of being designed to destroy without discrimination: examples would be cluster bombs, which disperse clusters of bomblets over wide areas, and 'daisy cutters', which have a lethal radius of up to 900 feet upon impact.

Paramilitaries and Local Proxies

America's initial conquest of Afghanistan was effected largely by proxy, with its aerial assault being mainly used to bolster Northern Alliance forces as they routed the Taliban. There were hardly any US troops on the ground until after the country was 'liberated' – a mere 316 special forces personnel and 110 CIA officers assisted the Northern Alliance. The main way in which such forces were aided was by the distribution of suitcases stuffed with dollars, up to a million per warlord depending on his status (Mann 2003: 127–8).

These proxy forces, which had in the early 1990s destroyed much of Afghanistan and killed tens of thousands of people through internecine wars, became the basis of the post-Taliban state. A number of warlords were invited to a UN conference in Bonn to negotiate the balance of power within the new regime, with the brutal General Rashid Dostum awarded control of the Ministry of Defence, while local commanders were depended on to impose order. General Dostum controlled the central northern provinces, General Mohammed Daud the northeast, and Ismail Khan controlled Herat with a 30,000-strong army. Southern provinces including Kandahar were given over to the control of Commander Gul Agha Sherzai. The Karzai administration itself was only able to control a small area of Afghanistan around Kabul. The 'order' imposed by these warlords and their private armies, initially characterised by 'revenge' attacks against suspected Talibs and mass executions, has remained particularly violent and arbitrary, with torture, rape and political murder a regular occurrence. By 2003, the International Crisis Group asserted that the country's already fragile legal system had essentially collapsed and the abusive rule of commanders, dependent on the opium economy, prevailed (Kolhatkar and Ingalls 2006: 95–116; Macdonald 2007: 110).

Similar patterns of coercive violence, often enacted through Iraqi clients, took place during and after the 2003 invasion of Iraq. This was partially conceived with the assistance of Iraqi exiles such as Ahmed Chalabi and, to a lesser extent, Kanan Makiya (Packer 2006: 66–8 and 77–97). Chalabi, it seems, had some role in persuading the US to forge an alliance with the Iran-backed Shi'ite movement, the Supreme Council for the Islamic Revolution in Iraq (SCIRI), later known as the Supreme Iraqis Islamic Council (SIIC) (Roston 2009: 222). This movement, founded in Tehran under the leadership of Muhammad Baqir al-Hakim, was initially sponsored by the Islamic Republic as part of a project to promote pan-Shi'ite unification. Unlike the movement of Muhammad Sadiq al-Sadr, SCIRI had little basis in Iraqi society.[2] Iranian officials managed the group's intelligence and military apparatus, integrating them into the Badr Army, a *de facto* Iranian auxiliary with a mandate to act as the provisional government of Basra in the event that Iranian forces captured the city. These units were integrated into the new post-Ba'ath security apparatus by the US, despite initial attempts to persuade them to disarm. They were able to take control of several southern Iraqi cities, notably Basra, replaced local police commanders with their own personnel by fiat and quickly became known for their brutality in countering opposition (Jabar 2003: 235–63; Herring and Rangwala 2006: 16, 53 and 126).

In 2005, policy planners began to raise the prospect of a 'Salvador Option' to defeat the growing Iraqi rebellion. Pentagon officials were reported to be debating whether or not to fund and train paramilitary outfits 'to target Sunni insurgents and their sympathizers'. The idea was modelled on death squads supported by the US in the Salvadoran Civil War of 1979–1992. A military source explained the rationale of offensive operations designed to intimidate the civilian population: 'The Sunni population is paying no price for the support it is giving to the terrorists … From their point of view, it is cost-free. We have to change that equation' (Hirsh and Barry 2005).[3]

Though the Secretary of Defense Donald Rumsfeld denied that such plans were being considered, the activity of paramilitary squads acting on behalf of the occupation has been widely reported. In particular, it emerged that Special Police Commandos (SPCs), an Iraqi paramilitary outfit created and maintained by the US

---

2 SCIRI's early cadres were drawn from exiles from Najaf and Karbala, but its estrangement from Iraq's main population centres can be gauged from its strategy. Throughout the 1980s, it engaged in a bombing campaign inside Iraq. Though this tactic was perhaps inspired by Hakim's espousal of a Maoist 'popular war', it was largely integrated into Iran's war effort during the latter's conflict with Iraq. Subsequently, its support for anti-Saddam insurgency in the aftermath of Operation Desert Storm was carried out in such a way as to alienate local populations by raising the divisive flag of Khomeinism (Jabar 2002: 252–4 and 270).

3 There is some support for the idea that layers of the Iraqi population sustained the insurgency, although this was by no means restricted to Sunnis. In fact, support for attacks on US troops among Iraqis of all ethnicities, including the broadly pro-US Kurds, rose to 61% by 2006, according to a study by the University of Maryland's Program on International Policy Attitudes (Schweid 2006).

military's General David Petraeus, were behind a large number of death-squad killings. Initially led by former Ba'athist General Adnan Thabit, the commandos were under the control of the Ministry of Interior and trained by the US military, as well as by 'USIS', a Virginia-based contractor which was alleged to have been directly involved in some killings by the commandos (Federal News Service 2007; Miller 2005). Though Paul Wolfowitz described the SPC as an 'Iraqi invention', Petraeus has explained his role in forming these 'paramilitary units' with some pride (Maass 2005; Petraeus 2006; Clark 2006).

The kinds of activities attributed to the SPC, subsequently dubbed the National Police, include torture, mutilation and murder (Buncombe and Cockburn 2006). A fearsome unit attached to the SPC, known as the Wolf Brigade, was composed of Badr Organisation members. It has launched notable counter-insurgency operations in cities such as Mosul, with the backing of US troops, and its leader Abul Walid became notorious for his interrogation of captured (and obviously beaten) 'terrorist' suspects on the television programme 'Terrorism in the Grip of Justice'. Broadcast on the Pentagon-funded Al-Iraqiya network, the programme augmented the terror that Walid's paramilitaries were promulgating in the streets (Macdonald 2005; Krane 2003). The Wolf Brigade was also held responsible for a detention centre discovered in the Iraqi Ministry of the Interior, in which bodies were found with signs of horrendous torture: burn marks, bruises from severe beating and drilling round the kneecaps (Beaumont 2005).

In one astounding incident, commandos contacted a Baghdad morgue demanding that the metal handcuffs found on the corpse of a tortured and murdered man be returned on the grounds that they were too expensive to replace (Sengupta 2006). It is unclear to what extent these murders comprised sectarian killings outside of the direct control of the occupiers and to what extent they resulted from a counter-insurgency strategy within the remit of the commandos. Indeed, there may be no hard distinction between the two, given that the populations targeted for sectarian attack were seen as a vital base of support for the insurgency.

Urban Assault

The twin assaults on the 'Sunni triangle' city of Fallujah in April and November 2004 quickly became emblematic of the occupation of Iraq. It had been one of the most peaceful cities in the early months of the occupation, but the first violent scenes broke out when US forces shot at a peaceful demonstration against the American decision to occupy a local school on 28 April 2003. Twenty people were killed; shots were also fired at those trying to recover the bodies, and even ambulance crews came under fire. An attempt was made to capture the city in April 2004, after the killing of four mercenary contractors by Iraqi crowds. The operation, known as Vigilant Resolve, saw 600 Iraqis, compared to only 27 US troops, killed. However, US troops were obliged to make a temporary retreat.

From then on, the US subjected the city to repeated raids and assaults and, in November 2004, launched its most fearsome assault yet, known as Operation

Phantom Fury. In the prelude to the attack, the US bombed the city to force those inhabitants who could to flee, and then sealed it off to prevent those remaining from escaping. War crimes such as the bombing of one hospital and the military takeover of another were openly reported, but less well reported were the beatings carried out on doctors and the attacks on ambulances. It later emerged that the US had used white phosphorus, a chemical that burns the flesh and melts right down to the bone. Non-governmental organisation (NGO) estimates maintained that between 4,000 and 6,000 were killed in the assault and that 36,000 houses, 9,000 shops, 65 mosques and 60 schools were demolished. And although the operation had been justified by the need to evict an 'al-Qaeda' cell said to be operating in the city, the leaders of the resistance there were found to be local. A total of 350,000 dispossessed refugees were eventually filtered back into the city, subjected to biometric scanning and prepared for forced labour (Holmes 2007: 1–25; Marqusee 2004). Eyewitness reporter Jo Wilding describes US attacks on civilians and ambulances (Holmes 2007: 30–64). Major General Richard Natonski later conceded that, although Abu Musab al-Zarqawi's presence had been suggested, US authorities did not expect to find him there (AP 2004).

In mid-2007, a detailed report by 30 NGOs for the Global Policy Forum (GPF)[4] analysed various aspects of the counter-insurgency, and particularly the modus operandi of the occupiers when it came to assailing major towns and cities. It outlined the main techniques of subduing major population centres in Iraq, citing seven of particular importance: 1) *encircle and close off the city*, as in Fallujah and Tal Afar, where the occupiers built an eight-foot-high wall around the entire city before launching an attack; 2) *forcefully evacuate those who remain*, as in Fallujah and Ramadi; 3) *cut off food, water and electricity*, as in Fallujah, Tal Afar and Samarra; 4) *confine reporters and block media coverage*, with the systematic exclusion of all non-embedded reporters during such assaults; 5) *conduct intense bombardment*, usually targeting the infrastructure; 6) *conduct a massive urban assault, using sniper fire, and put survivors through violent searches*; 7) *attack hospitals, ambulances and other medical facilities* (Global Policy Forum 2007).

This wide-ranging assault on life-supporting infrastructure and civilian targets could not but terrorise the population as a whole, as it was surely intended to do. Colonel Nathan Sassaman described the approach early on in the occupation: 'With a heavy dose of fear and violence, and a lot of money for projects, I think we can convince these people that we are here to help them' (quoted in Global Policy Forum 2007).

---

4 This report, though not covered in the press, has subsequently been cited in numerous scholarly articles (see, e.g., Bell 2009; Ferris and Hall 2007; Hamilakis 2009; İhsanoğlu 2007; Karagiozakis 2009).

Torture and Killings

In 2002, the US Justice Department issued a memorandum advising the White House that the torture of suspected terrorists 'may be justified' in order to prevent future terrorist attacks. Furthermore, the application of techniques designed to cause pain and stress alone should not be considered torture. The pain must be 'equivalent in intensity to the pain accompanying serious physical injury, such as organ failure, impairment of bodily function, or even death' (Smith and Priest 2004). This permitted considerable latitude for the application of painful physical punishment.

The subsequent torture of prisoners at Abu Ghraib included such techniques as forced stress positions, sexual humiliation, mock electrocution, sodomy and ultimately homicide. Much of this was overseen by military intelligence (Walsh et al. 2006; Hersh 2007). Further disclosures concerning the torture of prisoners in Bagram and Guantanamo have been accompanied by revelations about secret detention centres. Other less well-known cases also attest to the brutal practises of the occupation. For example, in a prison complex known as Camp Mercury on the outskirts of Fallujah, prisoners continued to be detained and subjected to brutal torture, known to the 82nd Airborne Division troops guarding the prisoners (who referred to themselves as 'Murderous Maniacs') as 'fucking' them. The American Civil Liberties Union (ACLU) gained sworn testimony that soldiers regularly 'beat the fuck out of' detainees (Human Rights Watch 2005; ACLU 2005). Importantly, torture has not been restricted to known combatants (see also McClintock, Chapter 21, this volume).

US soldiers have gone on record as saying that the deliberate and often random murder of Iraqis was a habitual occurrence, often legitimised by racist rhetoric about 'hajis'. Witnesses told BBC's *Newsnight* (2006b) that it was drummed into their heads that 'they're not humans, they're just "hajis"' and that if one wanted to kill an Iraqi, it was enough to drop a shovel near the corpse, so that it would appear that they were insurgents killed while planting an Improvised Explosive Device (IED). Fifty individual combat veterans interviewed for *The Nation* magazine described atrocities and casual killings (Hedges and Al-Arian 2007). Though disorganised, such actions clearly work to terrorise a population implicitly seen as an enemy. And this perception of the Iraqi population, according to the testimony, is one authorised and reinforced by military officials.

From Risk-Transfer War to Degenerative War

I maintain that in the above, an increasing propensity to target the civilian population for violence and intimidation is discernable. The sociologist Martin Shaw has developed two useful concepts which can help us to understand the way in which advanced capitalist states – 'the West' – deploy political violence overseas. The first tendency he identifies is that which he refers to as 'risk-transfer war', in which the war-making power opts for technologies of destruction, such as aerial bombardment, that knowingly transfer the risk of death from American or Allied combatants to civilians. Shaw maintains that while Western states operating in the post-Vietnam era have largely not treated civilians as enemy populations in the conduct of direct combat, the 'small massacres' resulting from 'risk-transfer' are both an inevitable component of the 'new Western way of war' and are 'intended' by the states waging war (Shaw 2003: 84–7).

The second tendency he identifies is towards what he calls 'degenerative war', in which the distinction between civilian and combatant is gradually lost in the course of battle. This tendency can arise where civilians are seen to provide an important support base for military rivals. The ultimate logic of such warfare can slide into genocide insofar as civilian population groups become the objects of at least partial destruction (Shaw 2005, 2007).

Without lingering on the details of Shaw's broader perspective, three observations arise out of the foregoing. First, the success of 'risk-transfer war' depends to some extent on the tacit acquiescence of the populations subject to its costs. That such passivity has not been forthcoming in the cases of Iraq and Afghanistan is often treated as a failure of tactics, the inability to 'win hearts and minds', but this implicitly adopts a purview in which those populations are objects for manipulation and conquest rather than potential shapers of their own destiny. They may see no advantage, or may see grave disadvantage, arising from an invasion whose costs they are expected to accept. Second, insofar as populations do attempt to hinder the objectives of war-making powers by military or other means, 'risk-transfer war' can shade directly into 'degenerative war', as local populations themselves become the enemy. Their recourse to political violence, though, is usually decoupled from the context that produced it and treated as a pathology to be neutralised. Third, as a corollary, the perception that grave acts of violence against civilians on the part of Euro-American states are aberrant and atypical can only be the result of the immense powers of ideological reproduction that those states possess.

Anti-occupation Violence in Iraq and Afghanistan

Characterisation of Insurgency as 'Terrorism'

In response to the US-led invasions of Iraq and Afghanistan, anti-occupation insurgencies have emerged in both countries. The character of these insurgencies was discussed by General Sir Richard Dannatt, then head of the British Army, addressing the International Institute for Strategic Studies in September 2007 as the Iraq War was at a violent nadir. Reflecting on the characterisation of the Iraqi insurgency as 'terrorists', he said: 'By motivation ... our opponents are Iraqi Nationalists, and are most concerned with their own needs – jobs, money, security – and the majority are not bad people.' He went on to make similar remarks about the insurgency in Afghanistan, regretting its lazy characterisation as 'Taliban' (Dannatt 2007).

This represented a significant break with the rhetoric of political leaders on both sides of the Atlantic, pointing to the complex and often disaggregated nature of military opposition that the US and its allies have encountered. In Iraq in particular, a variety of resistance movements embracing religious and nationalist opposition to the occupation have operated independently of one another and with diverse long-term aspirations for Iraq (for an overview of some of these groups, see Hashim 2006).

Although their activities have been classified as 'terrorist', the nature of insurgent violence calls this designation into question. Quarterly studies conducted by the US Department of Defense consistently show that the majority of insurgent attacks are directed at US troops. At the height of the insurgency in April 2007, it was estimated that of over 1,000 weekly attacks, almost 800 had been directed at US troops, while approximately 200 had been directed at Iraqi security forces, and less than 100 had targeted civilians (Kaplan 2006; BBC 2006a; Department of Defense 2007).

In response to this trend, the US military embarked on a campaign to demonise the insurgency as an invasion by 'foreigners'. Documents reproduced in the *Washington Post* (2006) discussed an American psychological operation aimed at demonising the armed resistance as foreign fighters and 'al-Qaeda'. The goal of the operation was to 'Eliminate Popular Support for a Potentially Sympathetic Insurgency' and deny the 'Ability of Insurgency to "Take Root" Among the People'. The main means of achieving this were to 'Villainize Zarqawi' and 'leverage' any 'xenophobic response' to foreign fighters.

However, the role of 'foreign fighters' has been limited, with their number accounting for approximately five per cent of the total insurgent force as it took off in 2005 (Pincus 2005). And the influence of Abu Musab al-Zarqawi, who declared loyalty to 'al-Qaeda' in 2005, has been greatly overstated – a fact surely indicated by the continued rise in insurgent attacks long after his death in June 2006 (Davies 2008: 205–57; Napoleoni 2005). Indeed, reports suggested that the mainstream of the insurgency were battling the minority Salafist elements that Zarqawi had represented, while seeking to defend Shi'ites from attacks (Knickmeyer and Finer 2005).

Afghanistan's insurgency has seen forces loyal to the Taliban, or 'neo-Taliban' as they have been called, establish a permanent presence in up to 80 per cent of the country's territory. Only in the northern province of Sari Pul, accounting for three per cent of the territory, was the Taliban's presence considered 'light' (International Council on Security and Development 2009). Again, the reduction of such a movement to 'terrorism' is problematic. Antonio Giustozzi has pointed out that though Taliban suicide attacks have largely killed civilians, civilians were not the target of such attacks; rather, the high civilian casualties were often the result of poor 'technical shortcomings' resulting in 'premature explosions'. The aim was 'not to terrorise the population' but to 'inflict casualties on the enemy' (Giustozzi 2007: 108–9).

None of this is to suggest that political violence by insurgent groups is insusceptible to critique on the humanitarian grounds cited by their opponents. Often, the tactics used, even if not directed against civilians, incur substantial civilian casualties as an anticipated byproduct. Yet, the way in which such violence has been proscribed and criminalised in advance as 'terrorism' has serious ideal and practical consequences. Terrorists are, after all, those with whom one does not negotiate (even if, after all else failed, US-led states were obliged to conduct negotiations with insurgents in both Iraq and Afghanistan). Three key reasons are given for refusing to negotiate with terrorists. The first is that they are irrational, deluded in their grievances and uncontrolled in their methods, so that negotiations are futile. The second is that they are not a legitimate party for negotiations or any communication other than the assurance that they will be destroyed. To negotiate with terrorists is to concede the impossible, which is that they merit cordiality and respect from the defenders of the 'Free World' and of civilisation. This has a great deal to do with the way in which the right to political violence has historically been distributed in a geopolitical space shaped by colonial and imperial relations. The third is that it incentivises the use of terrorism by insurgent groups as a means of obtaining a negotiating position.

Grand Narratives of Counter-insurgency

Discussions of terrorism are so hedged by uncertainty, doubt, qualifications and definitional disputes as to call into question whether the term has any use at all. For example, Alan Krueger's celebrated study of terrorism (2007) focused only on 'politically motivated violence carried out by sub-state actors' and then omitted examples that were of a counter-revolutionary character. He acknowledged that were he to write the book from the beginning, he would avoid all reference to terrorism (Krueger 2007: 145–6). What he was actually studying was a certain form of insurgency, his perspective informed by the paradigm of counter-insurgency. This approach, with its narrowness and exclusivity of focus, has been partially responsible for generating the school of 'critical terrorism studies' that is intended to challenge it (Jackson et al. 2007).

However, an equally pervasive and misleading approach to contemporary terrorism is that rooted in the grand narrative of civilisational combat. At stake, supposedly, are a set of Enlightenment values aggregated and attributed to a loose geopolitical entity known as 'the West' and its opponents. Yet, as Richard Jackson has pointed out, terrorism is 'not an ideology or form of politics in itself'. It is, he says, better understood as a form of political violence involving 'the deliberate targeting of civilians in order to intimidate or terrorise for distinctly political purposes' (Jackson 2007). Even so, in the context of the 'war on terror', terrorism has been discussed as though it were a political movement, and one with global authority. Jack Straw, as UK Foreign Secretary, described terrorism as the 'new totalitarianism' and the greatest threat to 'human freedoms' and 'human rights' (BBC 2004). Also worth considering are the remarks of then Prime Minister Tony Blair, who in 2005 had argued that:

> There is absolutely no doubt in my mind that what is happening in Iraq now is crucial for our own security. Never mind the security of Iraq or the greater Middle East. It is crucial for the security of the world. If they are defeated, this type of global terrorism and insurgency in Iraq, we will defeat them everywhere. (Blair 2005)

With his characteristic stridency, Blair had conflated a localised anti-occupation insurgency with 'global terrorism'. Early on in the war, President Bush repeatedly characterised the insurgency as 'terrorist' and, describing their 'strategic goal' as being to 'shake the will of the civilized world', he said:

> Two years ago, I told the Congress and the country that the war on terror would be a lengthy war, a different kind of war, fought on many fronts in many places. Iraq is now the central front. Enemies of freedom are making a desperate stand there – and there they must be defeated. (Bush 2003)

In this light, the insurgency was not a reaction to the invasion and occupation of Iraq, but was part of a global conspiracy against the 'civilized world'. Bush later characterised the 'war on terror' as one being waged against 'Islamic fascists' who 'will use any means to destroy those of us who love freedom' (Bush 2006). To speak of 'terrorism' in the context of the 'war on terror', then, is indeed to invoke not just a particular kind of political violence to be confronted and abated, but also an ideology that denigrates 'freedom' and 'civilization'.

The ideology in question, in this case, is Islam or a variant thereof. Thus, one authority on terrorism, Walter Laqueur (2004), has argued that there is an element of truth to Samuel Huntington's 'clash of civilizations' thesis insofar as it applies to Islam. He detects a 'greater incidence of violence and aggression in Muslim societies than in most others'. Muslims, he says, 'have a hard time living as minorities in non-Muslim societies', but also 'find it equally difficult to give a fair deal to minorities'. Huntington (2002) himself has described Islam as an expansionist civilisational form with 'bloody borders'. Throughout Laqueur's text, Orientalist tropes identifying 'modernity' with 'the West' in opposition to Islam and indoctrinated 'Muslim masses' continually appear, though Islam is important in his interpretation mainly as a subspecies of 'fanaticism' (Laqueur 2004: 19–25; on the misuses of the idea of 'fanaticism', see Toscano 2010).

To this extent, it can be seen as a mandarin version of the more demotic polemics by such writers as Melanie Phillips, Sam Harris, Christopher Hitchens and Martin Amis, each of whom regard political violence by Muslims as the result of a cultural pathology inherent in Islam, but also related to other 'totalitarian' fanaticisms. If, generally speaking, war leaders have been diplomatic enough to distinguish between what they refer to as 'moderate' and 'extremist' Islam, the more pedestrian ideologists of the 'war on terror' accept no such distinction. For Hitchens, no policy could incite or alleviate such violence, since 'the gates of Vienna would have had to fall to the Ottoman jihad before any balm could begin to be applied to these psychic wounds'. For Harris, '"Muslim extremism" is not extreme among Muslims', since the basic thrust of Islam is to 'convert, subjugate, or kill unbelievers; kill apostates; and conquer the world', and those 'who speak most sensibly about the threat that Islam poses to Europe are actually fascists.' For Phillips, 'Islamic terrorism' originates from 'the extremism within mainstream Islam itself'. Such a diagnosis pre-emptively delegitimises political violence by those groups currently bearing the costs of war, as well as mandating particularly savage responses by Western states. Thus, while Harris has defended torture as a mere form of 'collateral damage', Hitchens has defended the assault on Fallujah, asserting that too few died in its course since too many jihadists escaped (Seymour 2008: 13–20; Phillips 2008).

This way of stratifying political violence according to certain *a priori* assumptions about the civilisational and intellectual status of those deploying it has its origins in the colonial period.

Conclusion: How the Right to Political Violence is Distributed

The condemnations of insurgent violence in Iraq discussed above implicitly contain a theory of what constitutes a judicious use of political violence. The right to political violence has in the modern period been defined in various ways, from Grotian 'just war' theory to the foundation international law, in such a fashion as to exclude the majority of humanity from its use. This has its origins in a shift from pre-modern empires to modern colonial empires, changing conceptions of statehood and a corresponding transformation in conceptions of property rights.

For example, Vitoria, a medieval humanist, could have agreed with the early modern liberal Locke that a 'just war' could take place in defence of property rights. Yet, while Vitoria appealed to a universal natural law that credited Indians as rational beings with method in their customs and rights in the international order, Locke was already gesturing towards a new way of conceiving the global space. For him, the Americas which were subject to colonisation exemplified the 'state of nature' held to precede the emerging civilised European state form. It was the religious duty and right of Europeans to take possession of 'barren' territories where, supposedly, no sovereign authority operated. Those who interfered with this process broke the law of nature, and thus might be subject to punishments up to and including slavery. Barbara Arniel has written that 'the natural right to property' was from inception 'defined in such a way as to exclude non-Europeans from being able to exercise it' (Tuck 1999: 166–81; Bernasconi and Mann in Valls 2005: 91; Farr 1991: 666–89; Anaya 2004: 16–18; Arniel 1994: 591–609).

If the right to political violence was conceived of in a Eurocentric fashion in early modern Europe, this was bound up with the state-centrism of most jurisprudence, a bias that remains in effect, notwithstanding recent attempts to abridge the claims of sovereignty through such doctrines as 'Responsibility to Protect'. Antony Anghie argues (2007) that this organising principle has genetic roots in exclusionary nineteenth-century conceptions of the 'Family of Nations', in which the very idea of statehood was bound up with particularly European ways of internal social ordering. Though it has some precedent in the 'state sovereignty' jurisprudence of Emerich de Vattel in the eighteenth century (Anaya 2004: 22–3), the concentration of legitimate violence in sovereign states was particularly advanced during the zenith of European expansionism in the late nineteenth century. The emerging forms of international law legalised colonial relations on the basis of a binary stratification of civilisation versus its opposite. Thus, the rights of statehood could not be attributed to 'wandering tribes', while large areas of the planetary surface could be considered sufficiently 'lawless' and 'barbaric' as to lack rights to statehood (Anghie,2007: 52–65).

Since the colonial relationship was legally and normatively legitimate, attempts to subvert it were by definition illegitimate, particularly as these challenges happened to come from non-state bodies. Anti-colonial violence has typically been understood by its targets as a manifestation of what the English Orientalist Gertrude Bell once referred to as 'native fanaticism', or by reference to some similar cultural or racial trope (Bell 2005: 35). Thus, the Indian Rebellion of 1857 was interpreted by contemporaries in light of the supposed 'fanaticism of the Mohammedans of Lucknow and Delhi', and of the 'resentment for imaginary wrongs' and 'hatred and fanaticism' of the natives (Herbert 2007: 41 and 153). Later anti-colonial rebellions were given much the same treatment. The Mau Mau of Kenya were understood as a 'rabid and fanatical' cult which sought 'to lead the Africans of Kenya back to the bush and savagery'. Louis Leakey's account of how the Mau Mau acquired support among the Kikuyu was that the latter were forced to take an oath of loyalty which they in their pre-Enlightened state took to have some supernatural power over them (Presley 1988; Gluckman 2004: 139; Leakey 2004: 97–8). These examples may serve to indicate the general state of affairs when it comes to the assessment of 'native' insurgency against Western states.

The 'war on terror' is being acted out in an international political and legal environment decisively shaped by this colonial legacy. In their engagements with Afghanistan and Iraq, the US and its allies have created new states and new property regimes. In doing so, they have effectively appropriated both the rights of statehood and of property from the populations of the occupied countries. They have thereby accumulated a monopoly of legitimate violence consistent with legal norms.[5] They have asserted their corollary right to suppress violent opposition and to treat it as lawless and at variance with the mainstays of civilisation – which, naturally, include the rights of statehood and property. Therefore, the colonial tropes used to legitimise occupation violence and delegitimise anti-occupation violence are themselves a testament to the enduring effects of the colonial era on the international system.

References

ACLU (2005), 'Department of Defence Memoranda Released under the Freedom of Information Act', http://www.aclu.org/torturefoia/released/032505/index.html [accessed 14 June 2012].

Anaya, S. James (2004), *Indigenous Peoples in International Law*. Oxford: Oxford University Press.

---

5   Notwithstanding popular critiques of 'war on terror' jurisprudence, it is unwise to underestimate the virtuosity of pro-war legal arguments in the 'war on terror'. See Miéville 2009.

Anghie, Antony (2007), *Imperialism, Sovereignty and the Making of International Law*. Cambridge: Cambridge University Press.
AP (2004), 'Fallujah Invasion Called Success', *Associated Press*, 15 November.
Arniel, Barbara (1994), 'Trade, Plantations, and Property: John Locke and the Economic Defense of Colonialism', *Journal of the History of Ideas*, 55(4): 591–609.
BBC (2004), 'Terror "is New Totalitarianism"', 13 March, http://news.bbc.co.uk/1/hi/uk_politics/3507730.stm [accessed 14 June 2012].
BBC (2006a), 'Iraq Violence: Facts and Figures', *BBC News*, 17 August, http://www.bbc.co.uk/news/world-middle-east-11107739 [accessed 4 July 2012].
BBC (2006b) 'Newsnight', 30 March.
Beaumont, Peter, 'Revealed: Grim World of New Iraqi Torture Camps', *The Guardian*, 3 July.
Bell, Colleen (2009), 'War by Other Means: The Problem of Population and the Civilianisation of Coalition Interventions', Department of Politics, University of Bristol, Working Paper 02-09.
Bell, Gertrude (2005), *Persian Pictures*. London: Anthem Press.
Benini, Aldo A. and Moulton, Lawrence H. (2004), 'Civilian Victims in an Asymmetrical Conflict: Operation Enduring Freedom, Afghanistan', *Journal of Peace Research*, 41(4): 403–22.
Benjamin, Mark (2007), 'When is an Accidental Civilian Death Not an Accident?', *Salon.com*, 30 July.
Blair, Tony (2005), interview with Andrew Marr, 'BBC Sunday AM', 25 September.
Buncombe, Andrew and Cockburn, Patrick (2006), 'Iraq's Death Squads: On the Brink of Civil War', *The Independent*, 26 February.
Bush, George W. (2003), 'President George W. Bush's Address to the Nation Regarding Iraq', 7 September, http://2001-2009.state.gov/p/nea/rls/rm/23897.htm [accessed 4 July 2012].
Bush, George W. (2004), Presidential Debate, Bush-Kerry, University of Miami, *MSNBC*, 1 October.
Bush, George W. (2006), 'Transcript of Bush Remarks in Green Bay, Wisc., 8/10/06', http://2001-2009.state.gov/s/ct/rls/prsrl/70204.htm [accessed 4 July 2012].
Clark, Todd (2006), 'Forging the Sword: Conventional U.S. Army Forces Advising Host Nation; HN Forces', *Armor*, 1 September.
Cordesman, Anthony H. (2007), 'US Airpower in Iraq and Afghanistan: 2004–2007', Centre for Strategic and International Studies, 13 December, http://csis.org/files/media/csis/pubs/071213_oif-oef_airpower.pdf [accessed 14 June 2012].
Dannatt, General Sir Richard (2007), 'Address to the International Institute for Strategic Studies', 21 September, http://www.mod.uk [accessed 5 December 2007].
Dardagan, Hamit, Slobodan, John and Dougherty, Josh (2006), 'Reality Checks: Some Responses to the Latest Lancet Estimates', *Iraq Body Count*, 16 October.
Davies, Nick (2008), *Flat Earth News*. London: Chatto & Windus.
Department of Defense (2007), 'Measuring Stability and Security in Iraq', June, Report to Congress, in accordance with the Department of Defence Appropriations Act 2007 (Section 9010, Public Law 109–289), www.defenselink.mil/pubs/pdfs/9010-Final-20070608.pdf [accessed 14 June 2012].

Edwards, David and Cromwell, David (2005), 'Burying The Lancet – Part 1', *MediaLens*, 5 September and 'Burying The Lancet – Part 2', *MediaLens*, 6 September.
Farr, James (1991), '"So Vile and Miserable an Estate": The Problem of Slavery in Locke's Political Thought', in Richard Ashcraft (ed.), *John Locke: Critical Assessments*, vol. 2. London: Routledge.
Federal News Service (2007), 'Department Of Defence Bloggers Roundtable with Brigadier General David Phillips, Deputy Commanding General, Civilian Police Assistance Training Team', 21 September.
Ferris, Elizabeth and Hall, Matthew (2007), 'Update on Humanitarian Issues and Politics in Iraq', Bern, Switzerland: Brookings-Bern Project on Internal Displacement, University of Bern, 6 July.
Filkins, Dexter (2009), 'Afghan Civilian Deaths Rose 40 Percent in 2008', *New York Times*, 17 February.
Giles, Jim (2007), 'Death Toll in Iraq: Survey Team Takes on its Critics', *Nature*, 446, 1 March.
Giustozzi, Antonio (2007), *Koran, Kalashnikov, and Laptop: The Neo-Taliban Insurgency in Afghanistan*. New York: Columbia University Press.
Global Policy Forum (2007), War and Occupation in Iraq', June, http://www.globalpolicy.org/iraq/war-and-occupation-in-iraq.html [accessed 14 June 2012].
Gluckman, Max (2004), *Order and Rebellion in Tribal Africa*. London: Routledge.
Hamilakis, Yannis (2009), 'The "War on Terror" and the Military–Archaeology Complex: Iraq, Ethics, and Neo-Colonialism', *Archaeologies: Journal of the World Archaeological Congress*, 5(1): 39–65.
Hashim, Ahmed S. (2006), *Insurgency and Counter-Insurgency in Iraq*. London: Hurst & Company.
Hedges, Chris and Al-Arian, Leila (2007), 'The Other War: Iraq Vets Bear Witness', *The Nation*, 9 July.
Herbert, Christopher (2007), *The Indian Mutiny and Victorian Trauma*. Princeton, NJ: Princeton University Press.
Herring, Eric and Rangwala, Glen (2006), *Iraq in Fragments: The Occupation and its Legacy*. London: Hurst & Company.
Hersh, Seymour M. (2007), 'The General's Report', *The New Yorker*, 25 June.
Hicks, Madelyn Hsiao-Rei, Dardagan, Hamit, Guerrero Serdán, Gabriela, Bagnall, Peter M., Sloboda, John A. and Spagat, Michael (2009), 'The Weapons That Kill Civilians – Deaths of Children and Noncombatants in Iraq, 2003–2008', *New England Journal of Medicine*, 360(16): 1585–8.
Hirsh, Michael and Barry, John (2005), 'Special Forces May Train Assassins, Kidnappers in Iraq', *Newsweek*, 14 January.
Holmes, Jonathan (2007), *Fallujah: Eyewitness Testimony from Iraq's Besieged City*, Constable.
Human Rights Watch (2005), 'Leadership Failure: Firsthand Accounts of Torture of Iraqi Detainees by the U.S. Army's 82nd Airborne Division', *Human Rights Watch*, 17(3), September, http://www.hrw.org/reports/2005/us0905/index.htm [accessed 14 June 2012].

Huntington, Samuel P. (2003), 'The Clash of Civilizations?', *Foreign Affairs*, Summer, reproduced in *America and the World: Debating the New Shape of International Politics*, W.W. Norton & Co., 2003.
İhsanoğlu, Ekmeleddin (2007), 'Assessing the Human Tragedy in Iraq', *International Review of the Red Cross*, 89(868): 915–27.
Inskeep, Steve (2006), 'State Department Defends America's Image Abroad', National Public Radio, 27 March.
International Council on Security and Development (ICOS) (2009), 'Eight Years after 9/11 Taliban Now Has a Permanent Presence in 80% of Afghanistan', press release, 10 September, http://www.icosgroup.net/modules/press_releases/eight_years_after_911 [accessed 14 June 2012].
Jabar, Faleh A. (2003), *The Shi'ite Movement in Iraq*. London: Saqi Books.
Jackson, Richard (2007), 'The Core Commitments of Critical Terrorism Studies', *European Political Science*, 6(3): 244–51.
Jackson, Richard, Gunning, Jeroen and Smyth, Marie Breen (2007), 'The Case for a Critical Terrorism Studies', prepared for delivery at the 2007 Annual Meeting of the American Political Science Association, 30 August–2 September.
Johnson, Neil, Spagat, Michael, Gourley, Sean, Onnella, Jukka-Pekka and Reinert, Gesine (2008), 'Bias in Epidemiological Studies of Conflict Mortality', *Journal of Peace Research*, 45(5): 653–63.
Kaplan, Fred (2006), 'Western Targets: The Iraqi Insurgency is still Primarily an Anti-occupation Effort', *Slate.com*, 9 February.
Karagiozakis, Maria (2009), 'Counting Excess Civilian Casualties of the Iraq War: Science or Politics?', *Journal of Humanitarian Assistance*, 22 June, http://sites.tufts.edu/jha/archives/559 [accessed 4 July 2012].
Knickmeyer, E. and Finer, J. (2005), 'Iraqi Sunnis Battle To Defend Shiites', *Washington Post*, 14 August.
Kolhatkar, Sonali and Ingalls, James (2006), *Bleeding Afghanistan: Washington, Warlords, and the Propaganda of Silence: How America's Policies Destroyed a Nation*. New York: Seven Stories Press.
Krane, Jim (2003), 'Pentagon Funds Pro-U.S. Network in Iraq', *Associated Press*, 28 November.
Krueger, Alan B. (2007), *What Makes a Terrorist: Economics and the Roots of Terrorism*. Princeton, NJ: Princeton University Press.
Laqueur, Walter (2004), *No End to War: Terrorism in the Twenty-first Century*. London: Continuum.
Leakey, L.S.B. (2004), *Mau Mau and the Kikuyu*. London: Routledge.
Maass, Peter (2005), 'The Way of the Commandos', *New York Times*, 1 May.
Macdonald, David (2007), *Drugs in Afghanistan: Opium, Outlaws and Scorpion Tales*. London: Pluto Press.
Macdonald, Neil (2005), 'Iraqi Reality-TV Hit Takes Fear Factor to Another Level', *Christian Science Monitor*, 7 June.
Mann, Michael (2003), *Incoherent Empire*. London: Verso.
Marqusee, Mike (2004), 'A Name that Lives in Infamy', *The Guardian*, 10 November.

Miéville, China (2009), 'Multilateralism as Terror: International Law, Haiti and Imperialism', *Finnish Yearbook of International Law*, 18: 63–92.
Miller, T. Christian (2005), 'Soldier's Journey Ends in Anguish', *Los Angeles Times*, 4 December.
Napoleoni, Loretta (2005), *Insurgent Iraq: Al-Zarqawi and the New Generation*. London: Constable & Robinson.
Norton-Taylor, Richard (2008), 'US Air Power Triples Deaths of Afghan Civilians, Says Report', *The Guardian*, 28 September.
Packer, George (2006), *The Assassin's Gate*. New York: Farrar, Strauss & Giroux.
Petraeus, Gen. David (2006), 'Gangs of Iraq: Interview General David Petraeus', PBS, 11 October.
Phillips, Melanie (2008), 'Sleepwalking into Islamisation', *Daily Mail*, 8 July.
Pincus, Walter (2005), 'CIA Studies Provide Glimpse of Insurgents in Iraq', *Washington Post*, 6 February.
Presley, Cora Ann (1988), 'The Mau Mau Rebellion, Kikuyu Women, and Social Change', *Canadian Journal of African Studies/Revue Canadienne des Études Africaines*, 22(3): 502–27.
Roberts, Les, Burnham, Gilbert, Lafta, Riyadh and Doocy, Shannon (2006), 'Mortality after the 2003 Invasion of Iraq: A Cross-sectional Cluster Sample Survey', *The Lancet*, 11 October.
Roberts, Les, Lafta, Riyadh, Garfield, Richard, Khudhairi, Jamal and Burnham, Gilbert (2004), 'Mortality before and after the 2003 Invasion of Iraq: Cluster Sample Survey', *The Lancet*, 29 October.
Roston, Aram (2009), *The Man Who Pushed America to War: The Extraordinary Life, Adventures, and Obessions of Ahmad Chalabi*. New York: Nation Books.
Schweid, Barry (2006), 'Poll: Iraqis Back Attacks on US Troops', *Washington Post*, 27 September.
Sengupta, Kim (2006), 'Operation Enduring Chaos: The Retreat of the Coalition & Rise of the Militias', *The Independent on Sunday*, 29 October.
Seymour, Richard (2008), *The Liberal Defence of Murder*. London: Verso.
Shaw, Martin (2003), *War and Genocide: Organised Killing in Modern Society*. Cambridge: Polity Press.
Shaw, Martin (2005), *The New Western Way of War*. Cambridge: Polity Press.
Shaw, Martin (2007), *What is Genocide?* Cambridge: Polity Press.
Smith, R. Jeffery and Priest, Dana (2004), 'Memo Offered Justification for Use of Torture', *Washington Post*, 8 June.
Toscano, Alberto (2010), *Fanaticism: On the Uses of an Idea*. London: Verso.
Tuck, Richard (1999), *The Rights of War and Peace: Political Thought and International Order from Grotius to Kant*. Oxford: Oxford University Press.
Valls, Andrew (ed.) (2005), *Race and Racism in Modern Philosophy*. New York: Cornell University Press.
Vitalis, Robert (2000), 'The Graceful and Generous Liberal Gesture: Making Racism Invisible in American International Relations', *Millennium – Journal of International Studies*, 29: 331–56.

Walsh, Joan, Scherer, Michael, Benjamin, Mark, Rockwell, Page, Carstensen, Jeanne, Follman, Mark and Clark-Flory, Tracy (2006), 'Other Government Agencies', in 'The Abu Ghraib Files', *Salon.com*, 14 March.

Washington Post (2006), 'Leverage Xenophobia', *Washington Post*, 10 April, http://www.washingtonpost.com/wp-dyn/content/graphic/2006/04/10/GR2006041000097.html [accessed 4 July 2012].

Wood, David (2008), 'Afghan Air War Grows in Intensity', *Baltimore Sun*, 28 July.

The Concept of Security in Political Violence

Jessica Wolfendale

During the last 100 years, the concept of security has been used to justify war, revolution, torture, assassinations and invasions. The post-9/11 US invasions of Afghanistan and Iraq were justified partly by reference to the need to protect national security, and the threat of terrorism to domestic and international security was invoked to justify radical counterterrorism measures such as extended police and intelligence powers, as well as torture, extraordinary rendition and detention without charge (see Michaelsen 2005; Waldron 2006).

Yet despite the frequency with which the concept of security is invoked in debates about political violence, there is little agreement about the meaning of security. Should the term 'security' refer to a state's military power, as traditional security studies have claimed (Buzan 1983)? Or should security be understood as human security – the security of individual persons (Duffield and Waddell 2006)? If so, how does national security relate to human security and how are we to assess threats to these different forms of security? Without answers to these questions, the idea of security could easily become a meaningless concept that could be used to justify almost any policy that a state wishes to pursue.[1]

A definition of security must fulfil several requirements if appeals to security are to justify political violence. The definition must clarify what constitutes security as a political goal for states and individuals, what constitutes threats to security, how security is to be weighed against other political ideals, and which measures will increase security for states and individuals. Only then can we be in a position

---

[1] Steve Smith has argued that the concept of security is 'essentially contested'; that any definition of security 'depends upon and in turn supports a specific view of politics', and so a neutral definition of security is impossible (2005: 27–8). As will become apparent, I disagree with this view. The fact that it may be impossible for states and international actors to agree on a definition does not mean that no neutral definition is possible. It is possible, I believe, to develop a definition of security that is independent from a particular political theory and that captures the moral importance of security.

to assess how security is to be weighed against other political goals and what measures might increase security.

In this chapter I aim to provide such a definition.[2] In the first section, I propose a definition of individual security as the security of the conditions of identity – a multi-faceted definition of security that captures the physical, psychological and moral aspects of security that form the basis of our common-sense intuitions about when we are and are not secure. In the second section, I consider what constitutes threats to security, as I have defined it, and what a state's duties are in relation to the security of its citizens. In the third section, I analyse the connection between security, national security and state legitimacy. I argue that any plausible definition of national security must be grounded in the protection of the security of citizens, where security is understood as the security of the conditions of identity. In this view, protecting national security may justify the resort to violence *only* in order to protect the fundamental security of citizens. In addition, it is now widely believed that a state's legitimacy and its right to non-interference are connected to the duty of the state to protect the fundamental human rights of citizens, including the right to security. Thus, if a state fails to protect or itself threatens citizens' security, external intervention to protect citizens may be justified.

In the final section of this chapter, I consider the possibility that the appeal to security may justify the resort to violence by non-state actors if those actors genuinely promote or protect citizens' security. We cannot ignore the possibility that non-state actors might be justified in resorting to violence to protect the security of groups of citizens, particularly if the state is failing to provide protection or is itself threatening the security of those groups.

What is Security?

Security as a political goal could have several different aims. Following the human security approach adopted by many contemporary critical security studies theorists and international organizations (see Commission on Human Security 2003; Duffield and Waddell 2006), any plausible definition of security must refer to the security of individual citizens. Understood in this sense, security policies are those policies that aim to protect or promote the security of a state's citizens, however security is understood. Security policies could also refer to the security of sub-state communal groups, such as religious, ethnic or political communities. At the state level, national security could refer to the security of a state's political apparatus or institutions of government. But the referent of the term 'security' is only one part of the question. As David Baldwin (1997: 17) argues, any definition of security must

---

[2] My aim in this chapter is to offer a definition of security that explores the implications of that definition for questions about the moral justification of political violence at the state and non-state levels. Empirical questions about the current security policies of different nations are beyond the scope of this chapter.

clarify 'the actor whose values are to be secured, the values concerned, the degree of security, the kinds of threats, the means for coping with such threats, the costs of doing so, and the relevant time period'. It is also worth noting that total security of any kind is not a realistic political goal. Security is a relative state: individuals and states may be more or less secure in different areas of public and private life (secure from crime, not secure from terrorism), but absolute security is impossible.

Individual Security

What is individual security and what conception of individual security should be the appropriate aim of state security policies? As Jeremy Waldron (2006: 463) argues, any serious candidate for a definition of security as a political goal must at least refer to basic physical safety – security from threats to physical well-being. A state that systematically and deliberately failed to protect citizens from the threat of physical attack from other citizens and from external enemies would arguably fail to meet the basic requirements for state legitimacy.[3]

However, this conception of security (which Waldron (2006: 461) terms the 'pure safety' account) is deficient as an account of security for human beings. Being safe from physical attack is a necessary but not sufficient condition of security. As Ken Booth (2006: 22) notes, 'security is not synonymous with survival. One can survive without being secure'. The conception of security as physical survival does not account for other important aspects of our common-sense notion of security. Merely being currently free from the threat of violent attack while one's future well-being is far from assured is certainly not sufficient to enable one to feel secure.

A plausible conception of security for human persons must therefore take into account the characteristics of persons. Unlike other animal species, typical human persons are characterized by the ability to develop and form a coherent self-conception over time, as well as the ability to rationally assess goals and life plans (Griffin 2001: 310–311). As David Velleman (2000: 363) argues, the motivation to see ourselves as unified agents – as 'explicable and predictable'– is necessary in

---

3   It is true that a state may sometimes deliberately place citizens in threatening situations, for example, when a state sends troops to war, without undermining state legitimacy. The difference between these cases and cases where a state fails to protect citizens from unjust attacks from other citizens or external enemies lies in the reason for exposing citizens to risk. A state fighting a just war is protecting the survival of the community, and so arguably the state is justified in risking the safety of individual soldiers in order to protect the survival of nation as a whole (although there are limits on the level of risk that soldiers may legitimately be exposed to – most military forces go to some lengths to protect soldiers from harm). In addition, most military forces today are volunteer forces, and so soldiers in those armies have consented to accept the risks associated with war. This would not apply to conscript military forces, however, and in that case I would argue that a state that uses a conscript army would only be justified in threatening the safety of troops if doing so was necessary to protect to overall security or survival of the state. I thank an anonymous reviewer for encouraging me to clarify this point.

order to make sense of our ordinary concept of an agent. Agents, as we ordinarily conceive of them, are more than creatures who use reason; they are 'causes rather than the mere vehicles of behaviour; they would be guided by the normative force of reasons for acting; and they would find such force in principles requiring them to be moral' (Velleman 2000: 363). In other words, moral agents are those who are able to understand and act on moral reasons, and who are capable of seeing themselves as unified selves existing over time.

So a plausible definition of security for human beings must take into account what it means for beings *such as ourselves* to be secure. For creatures such as ourselves, whose lives revolve around future-oriented preferences and goals, security has a temporal as well as a physical component.[4] We are unlikely to feel secure unless we believe that we can plan for the future with some assurance that the basic structure of our lives will remain intact over time – that our homes, our freedom and our families – what Waldron (2006: 466) calls 'our mode of life' – will not suddenly be taken from us. But what is important for our mode of life? As noted above, being secure must involve being free from the threat of physical harm. But economic and material security is also important to our sense of security (Waldron 2006: 462). Being secure from the threats of poverty, starvation and homelessness is essential if we are to feel confident in planning for our future.[5]

However, our security is not just a matter of objectively assessing the relative safety of the basic goods that we need in order to pursue our life plans. Security also has a subjective component (Booth 2006: 22). Security involves both an objective assessment of the probability of a specific threat occurring and also an individual's emotional or mental state relative to that threat, a state that may or may not accurately reflect the objective assessment. We may *feel* more insecure in relation to one kind of threat, such as the threat of a terrorist attack, even if that threat is much less likely to occur than many other threats to our physical safety, such as the threat posed by, for example, driving a car. So how we *perceive* our security may bear little relation to how physically secure we are, objectively speaking. Why is there this discrepancy between objective and subjective security?

One way of explaining the discrepancy between objective and subjective security is in terms of the nature of the threats that we face. As Waldron (2006: 462) correctly notes, we tend to fear violent death or injury (particularly when due to intentional human action) to a greater extent than we fear death by water or fire or other natural events. One plausible explanation for this difference in

---

4 In his definition of security as 'an instrumental value that enables people(s) some opportunity to choose how to live' (Booth 2006: 23), Ken Booth recognizes the importance of the capacity to choose and to plan for human flourishing. However, Booth does not explain what degree or kind of choice is necessary for security to be achieved. Unless we have some understanding of what *kinds* of life choices are necessary for human security, this definition remains too vague. Nor does his definition capture the moral aspect of human security.

5 Thus, the Commission on Human Security (2003) identifies economic security, health, and education as central goods that are necessary to promote human security.

our fear responses is that we fear malevolent harm more than we fear accidental harm. Karen Jones (2004: 10) describes this feature of human psychology. In her discussion of the impact of terrorism, she notes that our emotional reactions to harm caused by someone's deliberate actions are very different from our responses to harm caused by accidents, natural disasters or unintentional human actions. As she says: 'We are more likely to be psychologically devastated by harms caused by the active ill will on the part of other agents than by other kinds of harms ... There is also suggestive empirical evidence that post-traumatic stress is more likely to follow from sudden man-made violence than natural disaster' (2004: 11).

This explains why the random nature of terrorist attacks (from the victims' perspective) contributes to the fear such attacks cause, as well as the sense of powerless and lack of control that victims experience. There is nothing a potential victim can do to avoid a terrorist attack, as he or she cannot know where and when an attack might occur.

Jones argues that random acts of violence can undermine what she calls 'basal security' – the unarticulated affective sense of safety and trust through which we (sometimes unconsciously) judge and assess risks. An individual's level of basal security 'shapes the agent's perception of those reasons that she has that concern risk and vulnerability where such risk and vulnerability arise from the actions of others' (Jones 2004: 15). Jones' account describes this phenomenon clearly, but it is less clear *why* malevolent harm undermines our basal security so severely. I suggest that malevolent attacks undermine our basal security because such attacks undermine what I shall call our *moral security* – our belief that we matter, morally speaking; our belief that we have intrinsic moral value that limits what others may legitimately do to us. I am not suggesting that we consciously hold this belief as we go about our everyday activities. Instead, our reactions to malevolent harm suggest that we implicitly hold such a belief in relation to our interactions with and expectations of other people.

We typically go about our everyday lives assuming that we have some degree of control over what happens to us, that other people are not intending to harm us, that other people will respect us in the sense of recognizing that it would be seriously wrong to hurt us, and that our interests and our desires matter. So if we are victims of a violent attack from another person, this radically shakes our belief in our own moral worth – the belief that others may not use us as a mere means to their ends. The wrongdoer has demonstrated to us in the most vivid way that they do not see us as morally important; that our pain and our suffering are less important than their desires.

This loss of faith in our basic moral worth can have profound consequences. Once attacked, we may believe that we can no longer trust other people – the basic security of our everyday lives can seem like an illusion. Victims of serious physical attacks often report such a loss of faith in others and an ongoing inability to trust other people (see Brison 2002). Where once we felt secure in our self-worth, now we can no longer be sure that other people will treat us with the respect that we once took for granted. The basic fabric of our moral security has been destroyed.

This analysis of moral security suggests that security for human persons is a multi-faceted state involving objective facts about our relative physical, economic and material safety, our subjective interpretations of those threats and the strength of our belief that we matter, morally speaking. I am secure, in this sense, if I am able to go about my life without fearing the loss of my life, property, economic and material goods, and without fearing that I will be treated in ways that ignore or undermine my basic moral standing. Only when I am secure in this sense will I be able to develop and express my identity as a person. For this reason, I refer to this conception of security as the *security of the conditions of identity*. The term 'identity' captures the relevance of these different aspects of security to our capacity to develop our self-conception as persons. Security of the conditions of identity therefore refers to those basic goods – both objective and subjective – that individuals require in order to develop and sustain a coherent self-conception over time.[6]

This conception of security does not imply that individuals are only secure if they are able to express every possible aspect of their identity or actively pursue any life-plan they wish. Nor does it imply that security policies must actively support or encourage specific expressions of identity. Instead, security of the conditions of identity refers to the security of a set of basic conditions that, combined, allow individuals the physical safety and basic moral standing they require in order to develop as persons, regardless of the content of their individual self-conceptions.[7]

The importance of the conditions of identity to human persons is recognized by many theorists. Most liberal political philosophers, for example, recognize the importance of allowing individuals to exercise their autonomy and cultivate new ways of living (see Mill (1912) 2002). However, by incorporating the conditions of identity in the meaning of security, my account offers a new perspective on security that has several significant advantages over more simplistic accounts of security.

First, my account enables us to explain why a state that subjected its citizens to a campaign of psychological fear, yet fed and clothed them and provided them with police and military protection, would be undermining its citizens' security even though their basic physical security was assured. In the next section, I clarify the connection between my account of security and a state's duties to its citizens, but for now it is sufficient to note that my account permits a broader understanding of how state (and non-state) actions may violate and threaten human security. This, as I will explain in the final section of this chapter, has important implications for conceptions of state legitimacy and justifications for the resort to political violence.

Second, my account provides a starting point from which to begin analysing the connection between security and liberty – two values that have often been portrayed in conflict with each other in debates about the fight against terrorism (see Waldron 2006). Liberty is neither identical nor reducible to security, as I have defined it.

---

6   Thus, my account is consistent with but more conservative than that of Booth (2006) in that I define security by reference to the protection of the basic goods necessary for security of identity, rather than (as Booth does) defining security in an open-ended fashion as 'the possibility to explore human becoming' (2006: 22).
7   As such, my account does not presuppose a racially or culturally homogeneous state.

However, some forms of liberty, such as freedom of association and freedom of speech, are connected to the development and expression of personal identity. Arguably, the value of freedom of association and freedom of speech derives from the connection of these freedoms to the security of persons, and so may not be straightforwardly traded off against the security of persons. Thus, freedom and security do not stand in clear opposition to each other and may not be balanced against or traded off against each other in a simplistic fashion. Under my definition of security, some restrictions of liberties (for example, restrictions on freedom of religion or freedom of association) might count as undermining security if those restrictions seriously undermined the ability of individuals to form and develop a sustained self-conception or undermined their basic moral standing. So a further advantage of my account is that it provides a theoretical basis for understanding which liberties are central to security and when restrictions of liberties would undermine security. This can then provide a framework for examining the validity of counter-terrorism legislation and policies that are claimed to be justified by the need to balance liberty against security.

Third, my account illuminates the connection between individual security and the security of sub-state groups such as religious and ethnic communities. Security of the conditions of identity is connected to communal security in two ways. First, our assessment of our moral standing depends to some extent on how integrated or secure we believe our community to be – where 'community' could refer to anything from a geographically bounded community such as a small village or a large metropolis to what Benedict Anderson (2006) calls an 'imagined community' such as a nation.[8] We often identify ourselves by reference to our membership of communities that are defined by shared values (such as religious or political values), as well as by reference to physically located communities. We are more likely to feel morally secure when we believe that our relationships with others in our community are governed by shared moral and social norms. If we come to believe that the communities with whom we have identified do not share our moral and social norms, we may feel deeply insecure – our trust in our moral standing will have been undermined. As noted earlier, one of the reasons why violent attack is so disruptive on the victim's sense of trust and security is that it throws into stark relief how easily our belief in our moral standing can be shattered and how fragile is our faith in the commitment of others to shared moral norms.

Second, our self-conception is intimately connected to our relationships with our close friends and family, and the communities (religious, political, social) with which we identify. Even if we do not endorse the communitarian belief that

---

8   According to Anderson (2006: 6), our identification with the nation is 'imagined' because 'members of even the smallest nation will never know most of their fellow-members, meet them, or even hear of them, yet in the minds of each lives the image of their communion'. The same could also apply to religious communities and political communities (for example, one might identify as a member of the Catholic community or as part of the Communist community without ever meeting the vast majority of Catholics or Communists).

the self is formed primarily through identification with communities (see Sandel 1981; Taylor 1985), it is certainly true that our identities are closely linked with those communities that we are part of. We experience ourselves not as atomistic individuals but as embedded in a web of relationships that contribute to (without being reducible to) our self-conception and, to an extent, colour how we express our identities through our everyday activities. So, in order for us to form a coherent self-conception, we must be able to be part of communities. Community security, while clearly distinct from the security of the individuals within a community, therefore has moral value that is derived from the moral value of individual security. As such, ensuring the security of communities is an important moral good and a legitimate focus of a state's security policies.[9] Such security protects the ability of communities to form and sustain shared moral, religious or other values believed to be important by community members, subject to the constraint that a community's activities do not seriously harm community members and/or other citizens.

However, the connection between individual security and community security does not entail that all sub-state communities have an equal claim to protection from threats to their cohesion and integrity. First, as noted above, a community's moral value is connected to how well it treats members of the community. Arguably, a community that mistreated its members would not be justified in claiming state protection from threats to its existence and might be a legitimate subject of state interference and restrictions (Chambers 2002). Second, communities that pose a serious threat to non-members (for example, White supremacist groups in the US who attack African-American citizens) could legitimately be subject to restrictions even if they treat their own members well. But there is an important distinction between individuals *within* a community who pose a danger to others and dangerous communities. Muslim terrorists are dangerous *individuals*, but the existence of such individuals does not provide a sufficient reason to conclude that the Muslim *community* is therefore a dangerous community. White supremacist communities, on the other hand, encourage violence towards others through cultivating shared norms and beliefs that support such violence (Berlet and Vysotsky 2006). Thus, they are dangerous communities even if they do not threaten the security of their own members and even if not all individual members of the community are dangerous.

In summary, the connection between individual security and community provides a strong *prima facie* reason for states to protect the integrity of communities within their boundaries when those communities form an important part of the self-conception of their members and when those communities do not pose a threat to the security of members and/or non-members. The security of communities should therefore be an important goal of the security policies of states.

---

9   Conversely, the security of communities can be harmed by state policies that attack citizens on the basis of community membership. For example, the security of Muslim communities in the UK was arguably undermined by counter-terrorism measures that treated the community as a 'suspect community' (Hillyard 1993; Pantazis and Pemberton 2009). Banning religious practices, banning specific cultural practices and banning the use of specific languages would also be attacks on community security.

Threats to Security and Duties of the State

What Counts as a Threat to Security?

We are now in a position to consider threats to security. Given the importance of basic physical safety, it is uncontroversial that individual security will be threatened by external attacks such as invasions or terrorist attacks, as well as by internal criminal violence. However, security of the conditions of identity also incorporates subjective security (how secure we feel ourselves to be) and moral security (the security of our belief in our moral standing). What would threaten these aspects of security?

We feel secure when we believe ourselves to be safe from harm, particularly malevolent harm, and we feel morally secure when we believe ourselves to have moral worth in the eyes of those around us. As I explained earlier, malevolent violent attacks threaten moral security as well as physical security, but moral security can also be threatened in more subtle ways. Discriminatory policies can undermine the moral security of those individuals who are the targets of such policies, particularly when such policies are long-standing and deeply ingrained in a community, thereby significantly altering the attitudes and behaviour of community members. Racist, sexist, homophobic or ageist policies communicate to the subjects of those policies the message that they are intrinsically inferior – morally, socially and physically – simply because they are members of a particular group. In extreme cases, discriminatory policies can lead to denial of the subjects' humanity, with devastating consequences for their self-worth and identity. Primo Levi eloquently describes the devastation of self-identity that results from being treated in an extremely dehumanizing manner: 'Imagine now a man who is deprived of everyone he loves, and at the same time of his house, his habits, his clothes, in short, of everything he possesses: he will be a hollow man, reduced to suffering and needs, forgetful of dignity and restraint, for he who loses all often easily loses himself' (1987: 33).

So moral security can be threatened by state actions and policies aimed at particular groups or individuals believed to be intrinsically inferior. Such policies, under my account, should be understood as attacks on the security of the conditions of identity.

Our sense of security is also strongly shaped by how we *perceive* threats to our well-being, even if the likelihood of those threats eventuating is statistically very small. This means that our security can be threatened if we are led to believe that we might be attacked, even if the probability of an attack occurring is actually quite small. So citizens' subjective security can be undermined if government statements, media reports and other public reports misrepresent or seriously exaggerate the likelihood of a specific threat occurring. For example, a 1987 US survey found that 68–80 per cent of those surveyed believed that terrorism was a 'serious' or 'extreme' threat, even though the probability of a terrorist attack occurring at that time was miniscule and there had been no terrorist attacks by foreigners on American soil (Jackson 2005: 95, 98–103). Since the terrorist attacks of 11 September 2001, a similar discrepancy between the perception of the threat of terrorism and the actual likelihood of an attack has developed (Mueller 2006). After 9/11, several US public officials made statements portraying terrorism as an ongoing and omnipresent threat that might strike at any moment with terrifying force. For example, the then Chairman of the Joint Chiefs of Staff, Colin Powell, stated that: 'Even as I speak, terrorists are planning appalling crimes and trying to get their hands on weapons of mass destruction' (Jackson 2005: 104), former US Attorney General John Ashcroft claimed that: 'Terrorism is a clear and present danger to Americans today', and former Department of State Coordinator for Counter-terrorism Cofer Black announced: 'The threat of international terrorism knows no boundaries' (Jackson 2005: 100). Combined with extensive media coverage of terrorism, statements such as these, which are not supported by clear evidence, can seriously undermine citizens' subjective security (Mueller 2006; Wolfendale 2007).

Security and the Duties of the State

I have argued that security of the conditions of identity can be threatened by physical attacks, discrimination and the belief that malevolent violent attacks are imminent. What does this analysis of threats to security imply about a state's duties in relation to the security of its citizens?

A growing number of scholars, politicians and international organizations argue that states have a 'Responsibility to Protect' their own citizens (Bellamy 2010; ICISS 2001). According to this doctrine, states that fail to protect or actively threaten the basic physical security of their citizens (for example, through the use of torture,[10] extra-judicial executions and other serious human rights abuse) have lost the right to non-interference that for many years was central to a state-based view of international relations (see Altman and Wellman 2008; Coady 2002; Waldron 2006).

The responsibility to protect doctrine was unanimously adopted by the heads of state and government at the 2005 UN World Summit and re-affirmed twice by the UN Security Council (Bellamy 2010: 143). Together with the rise in humanitarian and peacekeeping operations over the last 20 years, this points to an increasing international consensus that a state's right to sovereignty is not absolute, but rests to an important degree on whether the state is protecting the basic rights of its citizens.[11]

So the claim that states have a duty to protect the physical safety of their citizens and the integrity of the communities within their borders is now relatively uncontroversial. It is more controversial but certainly not outrageous to argue that states also have a duty to provide their citizens with basic material and economic

---

10 The prohibition against torture is a peremptory norm that is binding on all states regardless of whether they have signed specific treaties relating to torture (see Foot 2006).
11 Not all states accept this belief, however. According to the International Coalition for Responsibility to Protect (ICRtoP), at the UN General Assembly's 63rd Session in 2009: 'A handful of member states rejected the use of coercive action in any circumstance … Yet far more states were of the view that, should other measures have failed, coercive action and even the use of force is warranted by the UN Charter to save lives' (ICRtoP 2009). Exactly what forms of external interference are justified is a separate question.

security by, for example, offering some forms of welfare or other protections against life's vicissitudes (Commission on Human Security 2003). However, the question of whether states have a duty to protect or promote the subjective and moral security of their citizens is largely unexplored. I argue that such a duty exists and forms part of the state's fundamental duty to protect the basic rights of its citizens.

States, to a large extent, exercise significant control over how their populations perceive threats to their safety. How a state chooses to portray the seriousness of certain threats, such as the threat of terrorism, will strongly affect how safe the state's citizens believe themselves to be. As I have argued elsewhere (Wolfendale 2007), states that depict the threat of terrorism, for example, as all-pervasive, constant and a threat to the very foundation of society can do more to spread the fear of terrorism than terrorist acts themselves. Therefore, I argue that states have a duty not to inflate or exaggerate threats to the safety of citizens, particularly if such exaggeration is then used to justify changes to civil liberties.[12] States have a duty to realistically assess threat levels and to present information to citizens in a way that is sensitive to the impact of threat assessments on the subjective security of citizens.[13]

It is less obvious that states have a duty to protect or promote citizens' moral security in the sense that I have outlined earlier. States do not have a duty to ensure that all their citizens firmly believe that they are morally valuable – such a duty would be both unrealistic and far too demanding. However, states do have a duty not to endorse or implement discriminatory policies that will seriously undermine the self-worth and identity of the subjects of those policies, and a duty to take positive steps to prevent and punish extreme discrimination. Protecting the security of the conditions of identity therefore involves three aspects: protecting citizens' physical safety; protecting citizens' subjective security; and protecting citizens' ability to see themselves as having basic moral standing in the eyes of their community.

Having established a definition of security that encompasses the different aspects of human identity, I shall now turn to the relationship between individual security and national security, before considering the question of security as a justification for political violence.

---

12   This does not imply that states should intentionally lie to citizens and encourage them to believe that they are safe when in fact they are under serious threat, or that states should pander to those citizens whose fears are irrational (Waldron 2006: 468). Paternalistic withholding of the truth would be a violation of autonomy and would thus be unjustified.

13   How this duty would be enforced is an important question and one that requires more attention that I can give it in this chapter. I would suggest that, like the duty of states to protect their citizens' basic physical safety, this duty would require external monitoring to encourage compliance (forcing compliance is a different matter, as is clear from the general failure to enforce the international prohibitions against torture). Organizations such as Human Rights Watch could report on the media and government publications of different states, and international pressure could be brought to bear on states that systematically deceived their populations.

National Security, State Legitimacy and Political Violence

National security is a term that is used with abandon in political discourse. Yet it is often unclear what the term 'national security' is intended to refer to or how specific security policies either enhance or threaten national security. As Arnold Wolfers (1952: 481) noted, this lack of clarity means that a statesman can easily invoke national security 'to label whatever policy he favours with an attractive and possibly deceptive name'.

In the context of debates about political violence, national security must refer to a good, the protection of which would justify the resort to force. This means that any plausible definition of national security must carry significant moral weight. We must not accept the current freewheeling use of the term in debates in international relations and politics.

What is National Security?

A good place to start when thinking about national security is the definition of a nation. As the term is typically employed in debates about political violence, 'nation' refers not to a specific ethnic or political community, but rather to one particular *form* of political community: the state, understood as the system of government over a designated geopolitical region (Luban 1980: 168). Given this conception of the nation, a possible definition of national security would refer to the safety and integrity of a state's political apparatus – the institutions that together make up the functioning of the state (Waldron 2006: 460). However, such a definition would fail to justify the use of political violence in defence of national security, since there is no necessary correlation between the security of a state's institutional apparatus and how well that apparatus protects the security of the citizens of that state. A totalitarian dictatorship may have secure institutional apparatus, and yet at the same time torture and murder its citizens. Thus, protecting national security so defined could not justify the resort to political violence since a state's institutional apparatus does not have intrinsic moral value that is independent from how effectively that apparatus functions to protect citizens' basic rights.

National security should therefore not simply refer to the relative safety of a particular political entity. The term 'national security' must retain its normative force. As William Bain argues:

> Individual security is assumed to follow from national security by virtue of our membership in a particular political community. Thus national security presupposes the assumption that states express something worth preserving: they are moral communities in their own right and, as such, they are entitled and competent to determine the nature of their security interests and how best to address them. (2001: 278)

Bain is correct to link national security to individual security, but he has the connection backwards. The value of individual security does not derive from the value of national security; the moral value of national security derives from the moral importance of individual security. Promoting national security only counts as a moral good if protecting national security genuinely protects the security of citizens. Thus, a state's right to self-defence, as enshrined in the UN Charter (Bain 2001: 278) can only be understood as a moral right if it is defence of the citizens of the state. If the goal of promoting national security is to justify the use of extreme violence, then it must refer to the protection of a substantive moral good. The moral good protected by states is most plausibly understood as the lives of the citizens of those states. The security of the state is therefore best thought of as the most effective way of protecting the security of the individual citizens.[14] This latter interpretation of national security reduces the likelihood that there could be a genuine moral conflict between the security of the state and the security of citizens. In addition, this interpretation is consistent with the widely accepted belief that the resort to war is only justified in order to defend a nation from external attack (subject to the constraints of the principles of proportionality and last resort)[15] where this is typically interpreted as defence of the nation's integrity as a geopolitical entity, and hence defence of the lives and basic rights of the nation's citizens.[16] In traditional just war theory, the use of military aggression to defend national interests (as opposed to national survival), such as trade interests or spheres of political influence, is not considered a just cause for war (see Walzer 2000).

So a state's right to self-defence is based on its role in protecting the security of its citizens (the state's 'Responsibility to Protect') – and thus protecting the security of citizens is one of the fundamental requirements for state legitimacy and, as I argued earlier, a state's right to non-interference.[17] Resorting to political violence in defence of national security can therefore only be justified in response to a threat to the nation's integrity that seriously threatens the security of the nation's citizens.

Thus far, I have only considered when war could be justified to protect a state from *external* threats to national security. But what if the threat to national security comes

---

14 This is the basic idea behind social contract theories of state authority. For contemporary discussions of social contract theories, see Waldron 2006: 493–4.

15 In traditional just war theory, war is justified in national defence only if war is the last resort (all other available means of resolving the conflict have been attempted) and the resort to war will not cause more suffering that it is aiming to prevent. Other commonly accepted criteria of a just war include legitimate authority (war must be authorized by a legitimate authority and publicly declared), right intention and probability of success. For a discussion of these principles and the concept of just war, see Luban 1980; McMahan 2006; and Rodin 2005.

16 As I noted earlier, many authors now believe that the resort to war to defend others from unjust attack is also justified (Walzer 2000: 86–109).

17 It is not the only requirement for state legitimacy, however. David Luban (1980), for instance, argues that a state is legitimate only if it governs with the consent of its citizens. As such, a benevolent dictatorship would not be legitimate even if it did not harm the security of its citizens.

from *within* a state? Ordinary criminal violence is unlikely to seriously threaten a state's integrity, but revolution, insurgencies and domestic terrorism could all pose a serious threat to national security. Yet using military force to respond to such threats would directly harm the security of the citizens who are responsible for the threats and thus, contrary to my earlier claim, it appears that a genuine conflict between the security of the state and the security of (some of) the state's citizens is possible.

A detailed analysis of how states should respond to internal threats is beyond the scope of this chapter. However, a number of factors should be taken into account when considering whether a state would be justified in using military force against its own citizens if those citizens posed a serious threat to national security. First, I argued earlier that the right of sub-state communities to state protection depends on how well those communities treat their members and whether they threaten the security of non-members. Communities that threaten the security of members and/or non-members may not be entitled to state protection. Similarly, if individual citizens or groups of citizens pose a threat of unjust harm to others, they may also be legitimately subject to restrictions and punishment – and even the use of force – by the state. Just as a state's right to non-interference depends on the state's treatment of its citizens, so an individual's right to non-interference depends on whether that individual poses a threat of serious harm to others.

Thus, I argue that if a state is upholding its responsibility to protect its citizens, then that state may defend itself against unjust internal threats to national security. But the use of force in such cases must meet the criteria discussed earlier in relation to the resort to war. The use of force must be necessary to prevent the threat (all other means of preventing the threat must have been attempted), the use of force must have some chance of success in stopping the threat and the harm caused by the use of force must be proportional to the harm being prevented.

But what if a state is failing (or actively violating) its responsibility to protect the basic rights of its citizens? What may citizens do in response? Could non-state groups legitimately use violence against the state?

Non-state Violence and Security

If a state is justified in resorting to violence in order to protect the security of its citizens, understood as the security of the conditions of identity, then could non-state actors also be justified in resorting to violence to the protect the security of citizens? It is clear from the above discussion that states do not have a moral monopoly on the justification of self-defence. If a state is failing to protect the security of its citizens or is actively undermining that security, then it is plausible that a sub-state group could legitimately act on behalf of citizens in order to protect their security (for more on this, see Victoroff and Adelman, Chapter 8, this volume). How we would know whether a sub-state group is genuinely acting on the behalf of (or with the consent of) citizens is an important question. Democratic states typically have institutional procedures that allow citizens to express consent, and so it can be relatively easy to ascertain whether or not a state genuinely acts on behalf of and with the consent of its citizens, but this is much more difficult to ascertain in the case of sub-state groups. Yet, as Virginia Held argues (2005: 184–6), this difficulty in establishing whether a sub-state acts on behalf of and with the consent of citizens does not imply that no such group could genuinely so act.

Sub-state groups could act to protect the physical safety of all or a sub-set of citizens, as in the case of a resistance movement or an insurgency that aims to protect citizens from government violence, but they could also act to protect citizens from threats to their moral security. As I argued above, certain kinds of policies undermine moral security by communicating to their targets the message that they are intrinsically inferior, and so may be treated in ways that would otherwise be wrong. If a state supported or endorsed severe forms of discrimination – even while protecting the physical safety of citizens – those discriminated against could justly complain that their security is being undermined by the state. Given the importance of moral security to the conditions of identity, I argue that those so discriminated against would be justified in taking action to protect their moral security from further attack. But whether *violent* action would be justified would depend on whether non-violent forms of protest (for example, mass demonstrations, lobbying, strikes and civil disobedience) had been attempted and proved unsuccessful, and whether violent protest would have a chance of success and be proportional to the harm being averted. Given the potential harm to innocent people caused by violent protest, genuine attempts to remedy the situation through non-violent means must have occurred before violence could be justified.[18] That said, the importance of moral security to the basic conditions of identity would justify the use of violence to protect moral security if the threat to moral security was profound and such violence was necessary, proportionate and a last resort.

Such violence need not take the form of terrorism. While some definitions of terrorism, notably those of the US Department of State and the US National Counterterrorism Center (NCTC 2008), rule out the possibility of state terrorism, any consistent and non–arbitrary definition of terrorism cannot make a distinction between state and non-state actors. Terrorism is, I suggest, best understood as a *tactic* that can and has been used by both state and non-state actors, a tactic that many define as the use or threat of violence against civilians or innocents with the intention of spreading fear in order to influence a wider group (see Primoratz 2002). However, as Held (2005: 178) notes, terrorists attack military and police targets as well – the attacks on the Pentagon in 2001 and the *USS Cole* in Yemen in 2000, for example, were widely described as terrorist attacks even though the targets were military. To incorporate this usage of the term, Held defines terrorism as 'political violence that usually involves sudden attacks to spread fear to a wider group than those attacked, often doing so by targeting civilians'. Thus defined, terrorism may be used by both state and non-state actors, although it should be remembered that state terrorism has been by far the most deadly form of terrorism during the last 200 years (Held 2005: 178).

---

18   This parallels the requirements of last resort, necessity, and proportionality in just war theory, discussed earlier.

Terrorism bears a particularly high burden of justification not only because it often deliberately targets civilians, but also because it attacks the victims' moral and subjective security by seeming (from the victims' point of view) arbitrary and random, and because the direct victims of the attack are treated as means to the terrorists' end – the victims' deaths and injuries are used to influence a different group (for instance, the government) to take a particular course of action (Primoratz 2002). Terrorism is thus a paradigmatic case of treating individuals as mere means and it thus radically undermines the victims' moral security (for more on the use of individuals as mere means, see Blakely, Chapter 4, this volume). Hence, without taking a firm stand on the issue here, it is a consequence of my view that terrorism would rarely, if ever, be justified.

That said, my account leaves open the possibility that non-state groups may legitimately resort to other forms of political violence to protect the security of citizens. By emphasizing the importance of moral security to the conditions of identity, my account allows for the possibility that political violence may be justified not only to protect citizens' physical security but also their moral security in cases where a state's policies are so discriminatory that they seriously undermine the victims' moral well-being. In order to justify a resort to violence, such threats to moral security would have to be extremely severe, but need not be threats to physical safety. Therefore, a state that routinely subjected a sub-set of its citizens to ongoing and extreme discrimination, leaving those citizens unable to develop their capacity for self-conception and their belief in their basic moral worth, without actually physically harming them, would still be failing in its positive duty to its citizens and could, other things being equal, be a legitimate target for political violence aimed at protecting the security of those citizens.

Conclusion

In this chapter I offered an account of security based on an assessment of the nature of persons – typical human beings – in order to clarify what security for human persons means. I argued that security for human persons involves not only physical safety, but also subjective security and, importantly, moral security. These three aspects combine to form the security of the conditions of identity – a definition of security that captures the basic physical, psychological and moral components necessary for human identity and self-conception. Applying this conception of security to the relationship between security and national security illuminated how a state's duty to protect its citizens goes beyond ensuring their physical safety and how state actions may undermine security in a number of different ways. Thus, I argued that national security as a moral value is intimately connected to individual security, and so protecting national security may in some cases justify the resort to political violence. However, the importance of the security of the conditions of identity also left room for the possibility that the use of violence by sub-state groups to protect the security of citizens may also be justified.

The implications of my account of security for debates in political violence go beyond what I was able to discuss in this chapter. However, the conception of security of the conditions of identity that I have argued for in this chapter provides an important starting point for further investigation.

References

Altman, A. and Wellman, C.H. (2008), 'From Humanitarian Intervention to Assassination: Human Rights and Political Violence', *Ethics* 118, 228–57.
Anderson, B. (2006), *Imagined Communities*, 2nd edn (London: Verso).
Bain, W. (2001), 'The Tyranny of Benevolence: National Security, Human Security, and the Practice of Statecraft', *Global Society* 15:3, 277–74.
Baldwin, David. (1997), 'The Concept of Security', *Review of International Studies* 26, 5–16.
Bellamy, A. (2010), 'The Responsibility to Protect – Five Years On', *Ethics and International Affairs* 24:2, 143–69.
Berlet, C. and Vysotsky, S. (2006), 'Overview of U.S. White Supremacist Groups', *Journal of Political and Military Sociology* 34:1, 11–48.
Booth, K. (2006), 'Introduction to Part 1', in Booth, K. (ed.), *Critical Security Studies and World Politics* (Boulder: Lynne Rienner).
Brison, S. (2002), *Aftermath: Violence and the Remaking of a Self* (Princeton: Princeton University Press).
Buzan, B. (1983), *People, States, and Fear* (Boulder: Lynne Rienner).
Chambers, C. (2002), 'All Must Have Prizes: The Liberal Case for Intervention in Cultural Practices', in Kelly, P. (ed.), *Multiculturalism Reconsidered: 'Culture and Equality' and its Critics* (Cambridge: Polity Press).
Coady, C.A.J. (2002), *The Ethics of Armed Humanitarian Intervention* (Washington DC: US Institute of Peace).
Commission on Human Security. (2003), 'Final Report', http://ochaonline.un.org/humansecurity/CHS/finalreport/index.html [accessed 4 July 2012].
Duffield, M. and Waddell, N. (2006), 'Securing Humans in a Dangerous World', *International Politics* 43:1, 1–23.
Foot, R. (2006), 'Torture: The Struggle over a Peremptory Norm in a Counter-Terrorist Era', *International Relations* 20:2, 131–51.
Griffin, J. (2001), 'First Steps in an Account of Human Rights', *European Journal of Philosophy* 9:3, 306–27.
Held, V. (2005), 'Legitimate Authority in Non-state Groups Using Violence', *Journal of Social Philosophy* 36:2, 175–93.
Hillyard, P. (1993), *Suspect Community: People's Experience of the Prevention of Terrorism Acts in Britain* (London: Pluto Press).
ICRtoP (International Coalition for the Responsibility to Protect) (2009), 'Implementing the Responsibility to Protect the 2009 General Assembly Debate: An Assessment: Report by the Global Center for the Responsibility to Protect',

http://www.responsibilitytoprotect.org/index.php/component/content/article/35-r2pcs-topics/2522-report-by-the-global-centre-for-r2p-the-2009-general-assembly-debate-an-assessment- [accessed 14 June 2012].

ICISS (International Commission on Intervention and State Sovereignty). (2001), *The Responsibility to Protect: Report of the International Commission on Intervention and State Sovereignty* (Ottawa: International Development Research Centre).

Jackson, R. (2005), *Writing the War on Terror: Language, Politics and Counter-terrorism* (Manchester: Manchester University Press).

Jones, K. (2004), 'Trust and Terror', in DesAutels, P. and Walker, M.U. (eds), *Moral Psychology: Feminist Ethics and Social Theory* (Lanham: Rowman & Littlefield).

Levi, P. (1987), *If This is a Man* (London: Abacus Books).

Luban, D. (1980), 'Just War and Human Rights', *Philosophy & Public Affairs* 9:2, 160–81.

McMahan, J. (2006), 'Just Cause for War', *Ethics and International Affairs* 19:3, 1–21.

Michaelsen, C. (2005), 'Antiterrorism Legislation in Australia: A Proportionate Response to the Terrorist Threat?', *Studies in Conflict and Terrorism* 28:4, 321–39.

Mill, J.S. (1912 (2002)), *On Liberty*, Casey, K. (ed.) (Toronto: Dover Publications).

Mueller, J. (2006), *Overblown: How Politicians and the Terrorism Industry Inflate National Security Threats, and Why We Believe Them* (New York: Free Press).

NCTC (National Counterterrorism Center) (2008), *2008 NCTC Report on Terrorism* (Washington DC: National Counterterrorism Center).

Pantazis, C. and Pemberton, S. (2009), 'From the "Old" to the "New" Suspect Community: Examining the Impacts of Recent UK Counter-Terrorist Legislation', *British Journal of Criminology* 49:5, 646–66.

Primoratz, I. (2002), 'State Terrorism', in Coady, C.A.J. and O'Keefe, M. (eds), *Terrorism and Justice* (Melbourne: Melbourne University Press).

Rodin, D. (2005), *War and Self-Defence* (Oxford: Oxford University Press).

Sandel, M. (1981), *Liberalism and the Limits of Justice* (Cambridge: Cambridge University Press).

Smith. S. (2005), 'The Contested Concept of Security', in Booth, K. (ed.), *Critical Security Studies and World Politics* (Boulder: Lynne Rienner).

Taylor, C. (1985). *Philosophy and the Human Sciences: Philosophical Papers 2* (Cambridge: Cambridge University Press).

United States Government Department of State. (2004), 'Patterns of Global Terrorism', http://www.state.gov/documents/organization/31912.pdf [accessed 4 July 2012].

Velleman, D. (2000), 'Self Psychology to Moral Psychology', *Philosophical Perspectives* 14, 349–77.

Waldron, J. (2003), 'Security and Liberty: The Image of Balance', *Journal of Political Philosophy* 11:2, 191–210.

Waldron, J. (2006), 'Safety and Security', *Nebraska Law Review* 85, 454–507.

Walzer, M. (2000), *Just and Unjust Wars: A Moral Argument with Historical Illustrations*, 3rd edn (New York: Basic Books).

Wolfendale, J. (2007), 'Terrorism, Security, and the Threat of Counterterrorism', *Studies in Conflict and Terrorism* 30:1, 75–93.

Wolfers, A. (1952), '"National Security" as an Ambiguous Symbol', *Political Science Quarterly* 67:4, 481–502.

PART II
Motivations and Goals of Political Violence

From Dissent to Revolution: Politics and Violence

Harmonie Toros

I like a little rebellion now and then.

Thomas Jefferson

Introduction

Dissenters, resisters and révoltés have been shunned and hounded but also glorified and protected over the centuries as political regimes and philosophers have debated whether, why and how dissent, disobedience and revolution should have a place in their system of governance. Prior to social contract theory, dissenters were generally perceived as the worst kind of traitors – traitors that no one was willing to protect (Baumgold 1993; Post 2006). But with the espousal of theories such as those of Jean Jacques Rousseau and John Locke, dissenters came to be seen as respectable 'competitors', and by the early days of the French Revolution, dissent was encouraged by some as a healthy bulwark against tyranny (Kittrie 1981; Mably 1972). French legal scholar Georges Vidal (quoted in Kittrie 1981: 292–3) wrote in 1916 that the 'political criminal' once treated as a 'public enemy' had become 'a friend of the public good, as a man of progress, desirous of bettering the political institutions of his country, having laudable intentions, hastening the onward march of humanity'.

By the middle of the twentieth century, however, Nicholas Kittrie (1981: 294) noted that 'middle-of-the-road governments, dependent upon fragile coalitions of divergent parties for survival, were no longer willing to pay the price for dissenting political views'. Today, even the Frantz Fanon-reading US President Barack Obama (Mendell 2007: 57) is unlikely to repeat the words of Jefferson quoted at the start of this chapter. Indeed, replacing the theory of 'the divine and absolute sovereignty' is the 'theory of constitutional perfection, holding that self-correcting procedures under the constitution obviate the need, and therefore abolish the citizens' right, to resort to extra-legal measures of reform' (Kittrie 1981: 295). But has this right indeed been abolished? Do we no longer have the right to dissent, to resist or to revolt?

While providing an overview of the main issues surrounding dissent, resistance and revolution, this chapter will focus in particular on their relationship with political violence and how the latter impacts on the question of an individual's right to dissent, resist and revolt. Unorthodoxly, I will begin by examining the *right to revolt*. Indeed, although revolution is the most violent and radical form of engagement against a regime, the right to revolt is arguably the least controversial. As Deborah Baumgold (1993: 6) argues, it 'is one of the great resolved issues in political philosophy'. In the first section of the chapter, I will therefore examine how the right to revolt is enshrined in both law and political philosophy, and will discuss how political violence is seen as a right of 'the people'.

The second section of the chapter will engage with the more complex *right to dissent* and investigate how non-violence is often presented as a prerequisite for dissent to be a legitimate practice. Engaging with the work of John Rawls on civil disobedience, I will examine whether non-violence is indeed a necessary requirement for civil disobedience to be justified and whether the distinction to be drawn should be between persuasion and coercion rather than between the absence and presence of physical violence.

This will lead to the far more controversial question of whether there exists a *right to resist* violently to injustice in modern democratic states. This question is particularly relevant as modern democratic states claim to allow for non-violent means to dissent, thus arguably invalidating the need to engage in violent ones.[1] This question will be addressed in three parts. I will first examine how violence is understood in the context of resistance. I will then question whether the use of violence necessarily means that an actor is revolting against the state as a whole or whether violence can be used to achieve the more limited goals of challenging oppressive laws or policies. Lastly, I will engage with the question of whether minorities may also engage in violence to overthrow the state or regime by examining the right of self-determination and the use of political violence to attain that right. Questions such as who has the right to self-determination – individuals, communities, nations and/or states – and what they may do to achieve it will be examined.

Finally, I will conclude by asking whether and how such a theoretical discussion on the rights of dissent, resistance and revolution is relevant to the practices of political violence today. What difference does it make if a group engaging in political violence has, according to philosophical or international legal approaches, the right or not to engage in such violence? Does it have any impact on their violence or on the response to such violence?

---

1   It is arguably easier to justify violent means of dissent in authoritarian states as non-violent forms of dissent are often banned or de facto repressed. This does not necessarily mean that violence is the only means of expressing dissent in repressive states, as can be seen by non-violent campaigns for example in Chile against the regime of Augusto Pinochet or in Denmark against Nazi rule (see Ackerman and DuVall 2000). A discussion of the right to violent dissent in repressive regimes and how it differs from the case of modern democratic states is very interesting but is beyond the scope of this chapter.

The Right to Revolt

The right of revolution has been described variously as 'the great and fundamental right of every people to change their institutions at will'; a 'legal right' of the people; 'the reserved right' of a people, 'an original right' of the people, a 'natural right'; a 'most sacred right'; 'an indubitable, inalienable, and indefeasible right' of the community; and a 'revolutionary right' (Paust 1983: 567–8).

The *right to revolt* or the right of revolution is the right to change government or government structure (Paust 1983; Williams 1997). Since according to democratic theory, 'sovereignty over a politically demarcated territory is vested in the resident population' and 'governmental authority is derived from the consent of that population' (Kapitan 2008: 13; see also Baumgold 1993), the resident population or 'the people' have the right to withdraw their consent. Furthermore, Jordan J. Paust (1983: 569) adds that the principles of necessity and proportionality may apply to *how* the revolution is carried out (whether through violent or non-violent means) but 'are not needed for the justification of a revolution'. The people have the right to revolt for whatever reason.

As noted by Baumgold in the introduction, the right of revolution has become enshrined in both law and political philosophy. The 1776 American Declaration of Independence stated that since just power was derived 'from the consent of the governed', 'whenever any Form of Government becomes destructive of these ends, it is the Right of the People to alter or to abolish it'.[2] A few years later, the 1789 French Declaration of the Rights of Man and of the Citizen established the right of resistance to oppression – a right that by 1793 became the duty of insurrection in the case of oppression (Bertrand 1900). When the 1948 Universal Declaration of Human Rights declared that 'it is essential, if a man is not to be compelled to have recourse, as a last resort, to rebellion against tyranny and oppression, that human rights should be protected by the rule of law', international legal experts concluded 'that the right of a people to revolt against tyranny is now a recognized principle of international law' (Paust 1983: 560).

The right to revolt is generally viewed exclusively as the right of 'the people' – usually understood as the majority of the resident population (Paust 1983). Although I will discuss at length later in the chapter the difficulties in identifying who 'the people' are, what is important to note here is that in modern democracies the people have the right of revolution since authority is understood as ultimately lying with the people.

As noted above, the principles of proportionality applicable more broadly to the *jus in bello* branch of Just War Theory may be applicable to the use of violence in revolution, and the right to revolt should not be understood as a licence for indiscriminate violence. It is nonetheless a right of all peoples at all times.

---

2 The Americans later established, through the Second Amendment, the right to bear arms against tyranny, a right that is still referred to today by groups defending gun freedom in the USA.

The Right to Dissent and to Disobey

The *right to dissent* is also a broadly accepted right. Dissent – the right to disagree with the policies of a monarch or a democratic majority – in itself is rarely questioned. What is questioned is how one expresses that dissent. Indeed, as long as individuals choose legal means to express their opposition or disapproval of laws and policies, dissent is largely uncontroversial in modern democratic states. Debate arises when such legal means prove to be a dead end, and when individuals and groups consider disobedience as a means to express their dissent.

A few key political thinkers, such as Thomas Hobbes and Immanuel Kant, believe that disobedience can never be legitimate (see Mavelli 2012 for a discussion of Hobbes' approach to dissent). Hobbes argues that 'one is obligated to obey any state whatsoever, irrespective of its origins or policies', since 'even the worse state would be better than the best war' (Frazier 1972: 320–21). From this perspective, disobedience means the collapse of order and a return to the state of nature. Similarly, Kant believes that not only is there no right to resist but also that resistance is never right (Nicholson 1976). 'Kant is explicit that his prohibition on resistance is absolute and applies even to unjust sovereigns' as any resistance makes all systems of law and order insecure (Nicholson 1976: 222).

Although they remain key political thinkers, Hobbes' and Kant's approach to disobedience represent minority positions in contemporary political theory. Indeed, most would agree with Clyde Frazier (1972: 333) when he argues that 'as long as we cannot devise a procedure which guarantees that only good laws will be passed (and we cannot), the possibility of justifiable disobedience will exist'. Anyone who does not buy into the 'theory of constitutional perfection' needs to accept that legal means may not suffice to change an unjust law or practice.

Citizens are indeed considered to have the right, if not the duty, to follow the higher moral imperative of justice over legality and, in the words of political philosopher and civil disobedient Henry David Thoreau (1991: 32) there are times when 'a people, as well as an individual, must do justice, cost what it may'. John Rawls (1991: 103) stresses that such disobedience – limited by a set of strict conditions – is not a destabilizing force but rather 'one of the stabilizing devices of a constitutional system, although by definition an illegal one'.

Indeed, there can be no *legal* right to disobedience, since if disobedience were legalized, it would no longer constitute disobedience (Frazier 1972: 330). It is its very illegality that confronts individuals with a conflict of duties. 'At what point does the duty to comply with laws enacted by a legislative majority (or with executive acts supported by such a majority) cease to be binding in view of the right to defend one's liberties and the duty to oppose injustice?' asks Rawls (1991: 103).

How does one make this calculation and what kind of disobedience in authorized? The most broadly accepted form of disobedience is *civil* disobedience. Rawls (1991: 104) sets up several conditions regarding the justification of civil disobedience in its very definition as 'a public, non-violent, conscientious yet political act contrary to law usually done with the aim of bringing about a change in the law or policies of the government'. It must address the general sense of justice of the majority and cannot be 'grounded solely on group or self-interest' (Rawls 1991: 106), and must be engaged in as a last resort. This does not mean that legal means have been exhausted, but rather that they have not led to any change and that one may reasonably believe that they will continue to be ineffective (Rawls 1991: 110).[3]

Many authors engaging with civil disobedience put forward similar conditions and insist that it be non-violent (see Bedau 1961; Martin 1970). For Rawls, the reason for this is twofold: a) violence 'obscures the civilly disobedient quality of one's acts'; and b) civil disobedience is meant to express 'disobedience to the law within the limits of fidelity to law', a fidelity which violence would contravene (Rawls 1991: 106). Others argue that civil disobedience cannot use violent means because its means 'are bounded by a recognition of the fundamental rights of other citizens within a community' which distinguishes it from 'wide-scale subversion, rebellion or treason' (Gosling 1990: 86). I shall engage with these arguments put forward about the need for disobedience to be non-violent in the next section.

What should to be noted here is that even authors who insist that civil disobedience should be non-violent accept that sometimes it may not be sufficient to enact change and thus there may be occasions in which violence can be used to disobey or protest. Rawls (1991: 108) for example, argues that 'militant action and other kinds of resistance are surely justified' when 'the basic structure is thought to be so unjust or else to depart so widely from its own professed ideals that one must try to prepare the way for radical or even revolutionary change'. However, violence of this kind is no longer disobedience but revolution, as it is 'not within the bounds of fidelity of the law' (Rawls 1991: 108). Although Rawls does not specify this, such an understanding of violence as revolutionary brings us back to the right to revolt that requires that *the people* as a whole choose to revolt. What it does not address is whether there is an individual and group right to resist violently, that is, a resistance of a minority against the majority.

The Right to Resist

Rawls places great faith in the public 'sense of justice', a faith that arguably is 'not justified by experience' (Gosling 1990: 85). Indeed, the public sense of justice is 'made up of fragmented, contradictory, intuitive, unsystematic beliefs within wide variations of class-based, religious, cultural and ethnic practices' (Gosling 1990: 87) and, as such, is capable of great injustice. What if, for example, 'a majority supports the notion that the state exists for the sake of a single national group' (Kapitan 2008: 33)? What if the majority is responsible for the systematic and continued violation of a minority group? What if the majority does not respond to appeals – legal and

---

3   Not all scholars of civil disobedience believe that it may only be used as a last resort after legal means have failed. Thoreau (1991: 36) states that legal means of dissent 'take too much time, and a man's life will be gone'.

illegal but non-violent ones – to their sense of justice? Can a minority engage in violent resistance?

This question needs to be broken down into three parts: the first looks at how the concept of last resort that is used to justify civil disobedience could allow for the possibility of engaging in violent resistance; the second addresses how violence should be understood and how it changes the act of dissent/disobedience; while the third examines whether there needs to be, as Rawls and others argue, a correspondence between means and ends. Does violence necessarily imply that actors reject the system of government as a whole and are seeking to overthrow it? Each of these will be examined in turn.

As noted earlier, the concept of last resort appears to be broadly accepted in the civil disobedience literature. *If* legal means are not fruitful, *then* actors may disobey the law through non-violent action. Rawls (1991: 106) also accepts that in some cases, 'if the final appeal fails in its purpose, forceful resistance may later be entertained'. Thus, the logic of last resort does not end with disobedience but passes on to resistance and, indeed, the notion of last resort is often used by armed groups to justify their use of violence. Nelson Mandela, for example, stated in 1989 that the African National Congress turned to violence (through its armed wing, the MK) as 'a legitimate form of self-defence against a morally repugnant system of government which will not allow even peaceful forms of protest' (quoted in Maharaj 2008: 12). Similarly, republican leader Gerry Adams (2004: 32) in Northern Ireland argued that 'in the absence of any alternative, armed actions represent a necessary form of struggle against the British administration and in pursuance of national independence'.[4]

Nonetheless, Andrew Valls (2000: 73) points out that although the argument of last resort will always be open for debate (were all legal and non-violent means really attempted?), if it can be used to justify the resort to war by states (as required by Just War Theory), it may also be used in the case of non-state actors. Thus, it is arguably a state-centric bias that accepts the possibility of fulfilling the last resort condition for states, but rejects it when examining an individual's or group's right to resist the state. If the former is possible, so is the latter, and the very logic used to justify non-violent civil disobedience can be passed on to justify violent resistance.

But what does the use of violence entail? Paul Gilbert (1994: 77, emphasis in original) argues that this question is misleading and makes 'it appear as if the choice of political acts involving violence is always the choice of a certain kind of *tactic* for securing one's ends, so that one could then use a general formula to assess whether such a tactic can be defended given the probability of its achieving its ends and the certainty of the suffering it causes'. On the contrary, Gilbert (1994: 78) points out that violence is not necessarily a calculated act and 'can be a spontaneous expression of

---

[4] Some, such as Michael Walzer (2002), remain entirely unconvinced by non-state armed groups' use of this argument, stating that 'terror is commonly the first resort of militants' who 'are neither interested in nor capable of organizing their own people for any other kind of politics'.

indignation or apprehension'.[5] Violence can be and often is unplanned, occurring, for example, during a demonstration originally planned as non-violent, often as a result of state violence. Violence can thus be a calculated thought-through choice of opposition groups, but may also be a spontaneous response to state violence or other triggers.

Authors also assume that they know what violence is and equate it with physical force. This may be misleading. Indeed, John Morreall (1991: 132) argues that 'the essence of violence does not lie in the use of great physical force' as there are instances of great physical force that are not violent and instances of violence that do not involve any physical force or contact. Thus, when a car is brought to the dump and crushed with the approval of its owner, it is not violent, although it involves great physical force. Meanwhile, parents who berate and belittle their children without using physical force against them are in fact using violence on then (Morreall 1991; Wilkins 1992). Other forms of violence that do not necessarily involve physical force can be economic violence or cultural violence as well as what Johan Galtung (1969: 171) terms 'structural violence', i.e. violence that is 'built into the structure and shows up as unequal power and consequently as unequal life chances'.

Violence should instead be understood through the concept of violation and must 'have a direct or indirect reference to *persons*' (Morreall 1991: 132, emphasis in original). Violence is the violation of *prima facie* rights of individuals, such as the right to one's body, but also the right to 'make free decisions and to carry them out' and the right to the product of one's labour (Morreall 1991: 123–33). Morreall challenges the common understanding of violence put forward by scholars of civil disobedience by stating that:

> The line is usually drawn between physically violent means of changing laws and physically nonviolent means of doing so (a distinction which is supposed to give us a way of separating the justifiable from unjustifiable acts); when in reality the important distinction is between tactics which achieve change by forcing those in power to change the law or policy, and tactics which work by *changing people's minds*. The significant line to be drawn here is between *coercion* – physical and psychological – and *persuasion*. (1991: 135–6, emphasis in original)

Thus, violent tactics are aimed at coercing others, while non-violent tactics are aimed at persuading others.

If this understanding of violence is used, then civil disobedience, according to Morreall, Frazier and Gosling, nearly always involves some form of violence. Sit-ins impede access to one's own property or public property, stopping trains from carrying troops to an unjust war impedes the railway workers' right to work unimpeded and so on (Frazier 1972: 325–9; Gosling 1990: 84; Morreall 1991: 135–6).

---

5   Gilbert (1994: 78) adds that 'it need not be done on the spur of the moment to be spontaneous, in the sense of arising naturally from such passion; anger or fear can smoulder long before they are expressed'.

'If we are going to respect all the *prima facie* rights of persons to their bodies, to their autonomy and to their property, and merely try to *convince* others of the rightness of our cause, then it would seem the rare situation in which we could ever break a law in carrying out this persuasion' (Morreall 1991: 136).

Thus, if civil disobedience nearly always involves the violation of others' *prima facie* rights, what distinguishes it from forms of resistance, such as guerrilla warfare or terrorism?[6] Why is the first justifiable and the latter often not? Indeed, according to Carl Wellman (1979: 251), 'the internal objective and defining end of every act of terrorism is coercion'. But if coercion is acceptable in civil disobedience and one accepts that some *prima facie* rights will be violated, the question becomes one of degrees of violation of *prima facie* rights: how much coercion is acceptable in resistance? There is no longer an ontological difference between disobedience and violent resistance.

Wellman (1979: 257), however, puts forward another reason why political violence such as terrorism may not be justified: 'Terrorism necessarily violates the most fundamental of all human rights, the right to be treated *as* a human being', rather than as a means through which to coerce others. When actors kill someone with the aim of impacting on state policy, they are using their victim as a means, not as a person. But does civil disobedience not do the same thing, although violating the human being to a much lesser degree? Again, with a sit-in, are activists not, for example, *using* those whose movement they are impeding to influence state policy?

It is important to stress that although civil disobedience and forms of political violence such as terrorism may follow the same process that violates rights and uses coercion, this does not mean that the two should be equated. The degree of the violation of rights and the degree of coercion constitute important, substantial differences, which characterize both the initial act of protest and reactions to it. Nevertheless, it seems that the distinction between civil disobedience (a broadly accepted form of protest) and political violence such as terrorism (a form of action generally viewed as unjustifiable) is not as clear-cut as generally argued. Indeed, both violate the *prima facie* rights of others – although often to radically different degrees.

But *prima facie* rights are precisely that: *prima facie* – subject to circumstances as opposed to absolute (Wilkins 1992; Bunnin and Yu 2004) – and thus by definition can be violated if a higher moral imperative warrants such action. Of course, the greater the degree of violation of *prima facie* rights, the greater the moral imperative needed to justify such a violation. As examined earlier, for Rawls (1991: 121), violent

---

6   Although there are numerous forms of political violence that minority groups may engage in, from guerrilla warfare to sabotage, I will focus particularly on the question of terrorism, which is often presented as the form of violence to which individuals and groups have the least right to turn to. There is of course a long and tortuous debate on whether terrorism can be defined and what such a definition would look like. I argue that terrorism can be broadly understood as 'the threat or use of politically motivated violence aimed at affecting a larger audience than its immediate target that is broadly deemed illegitimate' (Toros 2009).

resistance may be justified when 'the coercive apparatus of the state [is employed] in order to maintain manifestly unjust institutions'. Wellman (1979: 255) argues that terrorism can be 'morally justified because it prevented the even greater harm of a continuation of the *status quo* or because it was also a means of bringing about some much greater good'.

There is likely to be considerable debate over what could constitute a high enough moral imperative to justify violence and, indeed, some argue that 'unless we would be justified in overthrowing the whole political-legal system, we could not be justified in using any kind of violence' (see a discussion of this point in Morreall 1991: 140). This brings us back to Rawl's argument earlier that violence amounts to revolting rather than resisting. As such, it is based on the moral imperative of needing to overthrow an unjust government or state system and implies a rejection of the entire social order.

Several authors, however, contest this automatic coupling of violence with the decision to overthrow the regime. Gosling (1990: 84) argues that 'action is not necessarily transformed from civil disobedience to subversion by virtue of there being violence against person or property'. Indeed, Morreall (1991: 141, emphasis in original) stresses that 'not all acts of violence threaten the existence of the government; many of them do not even threaten our lives or bodily security' and thus 'the justifiability of a revolution is not a prerequisite for justifying the *limited* use of violent means to achieve selective ends'.[7] Justifiable disobedience can thus turn into justifiable resistance and does not necessarily involve revolution.

This right to resist, unlike the right to revolt, is an individual right of each person (and each collective) and does not require a majority, as does the right to revolt. Of course, it requires facing certain hard questions such as: was it necessary to cause this much harm? Was violence the most effective way to achieve the set goals?[8] Are the goals worth the cost of achieving them (Wellman 1979: 255)? However, if one can answer these questions positively – and one cannot *a priori* exclude this possibility – then one may consider that there exists the right to resist.

Crucially, the right to resist is inextricably linked to the notion of injustice. It is as a last resort to injustice that an individual or minority group has the right to use violence to redress the situation. Indeed, the right to resist requires such injustice and cannot – according to the arguments put forward so far – be used by an individual or minority group to challenge or overthrow the government simply because they wish to. This conclusion, however, leaves us with the final

---

7   Authors stress that they do not include a blanket right to use any means in what I have called the right to resist. Morreall (1991: 141), for example, states that 'starting mass fires and throwing grenades into restaurants' would indeed require justifying revolution.
8   It is important not to over-rationalize violence. As noted earlier, both state and non-state parties may plan violence but may also engage in it spontaneously or as a reaction to the other. Indeed, political violence carried out by non-state actors needs to be understood as a relational form of violence that exists, reacts to and feeds into state violence as well as structural violence (see also Toros and Gunning 2009).

question surrounding the right of self-determination. Do individuals and most importantly stateless nations or communities have the right to decide how to govern themselves? And do they have the right to use political violence if they are denied self-determination?

The Right of Self-Determination: Who Can Revolt?

Just as a civil disobedient is not so clearly distinct from an actor using political violence, the difference between minorities protesting specific discriminatory policies and those attempting to overthrow the system of government may not be as clear-cut as is generally assumed. Indeed, Frazier (1972: 326) argues that 'rather than attempting to speak of resistance and revolution as two distinct modes of action it seems preferable to consider them as part of a continuum of actions that vary in their degree of opposition to the given order'. When does a movement protesting over the denial of its right to use its own language or protesting against an oppressive legal system turn into a group demanding the right to decide on taxation levels or on court systems? When does it become a movement demanding a different system of governance or independent self-government?

Indeed, contemporary non-state groups using political violence often have both the aims of protesting the violation of the rights of their community *and* challenging the existing government or system of government. The Moro Islamic Liberation Front (MILF) in Mindanao is fighting the Philippine state to protest decades of anti-Muslim discrimination and to attain self-rule in Mindanao. The Irish Republican Army (IRA) engaged in political violence to protest discrimination and violence against the Catholic community of Northern Ireland *and* to dismantle the Northern Irish state and unite the island of Ireland. Indeed, resistance and revolution are often combined in the rhetoric of non-state armed groups (Dudouet 2009: 45).

Accepting this fluid boundary, there are nonetheless groups that espouse revolutionary goals, which can entail simply a change of government or a challenge to the system of government based on ideological (socialist, fascist, anarchic) or nationalist (independence or autonomy within a loose state structure) ideals, or both. The primary right involved in each case is the right of self-determination. I examined above how the right of self-determination allowed 'the people' to revolt. But who are 'the people'?

Simply defining the people as the majority of the resident population does not necessarily solve the problem. As Tomis Kapitan (2008) and David Gosling (1990) argue, the majority may not be acting in the interests of all 'the people' and may only serve a single sub-national group. In such cases, do minorities have the right to revolt on behalf of the people? Paust (1983) also raises the problem of whether individuals or a minority group can engage in a battle for self-determination when the will of the majority is not known. This is likely to be the case very often, particularly in the early days of revolt in a totalitarian regime. How can an individual or even a group of individuals, however large, know that they have 'the people' behind them? Paust thus concludes that:

> For this reason, no easy, mechanistic test of permissibility concerning strategies or tactics of private violence will suffice. As several writers recognize, an adequate analysis of strategies or tactics of revolution or 'civil disobedience' demands consideration of all relevant features of context, including, of course, an examination of the larger social process in which such strategies or tactics operate. (1983: 577)

Although a close analysis of the context is important, it may not be sufficient to allow the outsider to understand whether the majority supports a violent uprising. More importantly, in a context of censorship and repression, it is also particularly difficult for the insider to understand the majority's will.

Even if one can determine what the will of 'the people' is, one still has not solved the issue of *who* the people are. Indeed, Phillips (1990: 70) argues that the principle of self-determination is 'fatally flawed by vagueness' as it does not 'specify which sample of a given population is to "count"' in who is to decide how a territory is governed. Although the right of self-determination is generally understood to require 'that governing institutions are to derive from the consensus of the entire community, not by the preferences of internal minorities or agencies' (Kapitan 2008: 20–21), there are strong arguments to be made for opposing a state-centric conception of the right of self-determination. Kapitan (2008: 13) points out that:

> States come and go, and sometimes a territory is stateless. Also, large-scale demographic shifts during upheavals and peacetime immigrations change the assessments of who belongs where. Does everyone residing in a place at a particular time have a right to share in its governance then? What about illegal immigrants?

Furthermore, following the overall completion of the decolonization process, it is usually what are called 'exceptional beneficiaries' that appeal to the right of self-determination rather than the majority of the population in a given state (Kapitan 2008: 21), once again opening the question of what kind of group has such a right.

For Kapitan (2008: 21), 'exceptional beneficiaries' includes 'non-autonomous groups desirous of self-governance, whether recently liberated from previous rulers as a result of war, de-colonization, or the break up of a state, or, currently engaged in secessionist struggles'. But how does one 'demarcate the class of exceptional beneficiaries?' (Kapitan 2008: 21). If any group appealing to the right of self-determination were to be considered exceptional beneficiaries – not only every ethnic and national group, but also groups who coalesce around ideological goals (such as socialism, fascism, etc.), around religious precepts (from Christian groups to Muslim communities), or a combination of the above – then one could witness endless 'fragmentation and tribalism' (Etzioni 1992: 21).[9] One must therefore find a way to differentiate between those groups that can claim the right of self-determination and those that cannot.

Kapitan (2008: 21) begins by specifying that such groups must be politically coherent – they must represent 'an intergenerational community capable of political independence whose members share adequate means of communication and enough normative moral ideals capable of sustaining their adherence to the same political and legal institutions'. It must also have a connection to a territory that is both 'geographically unified' and politically integrable – i.e. an area 'in which the exercise of normal state functions (e.g. maintaining a police force) would not violate the sovereign rights of existing states in distinct regions outside its boundaries'.

Yet, even these conditions are insufficient as:

> If every politically coherent collective residing in a politically integral region claimed a right of self-determination in that region, the world would be faced with a bewildering justification not only for conflicting claims between populations and sub-populations, but also for the fragmentation of virtually all existing states. (Kapitan 2008: 22)

Kapitan therefore adds two conditions for groups to have the right of self-determination: they either need to inhabit regions that are 'unsettled'[10] and thus within which any coherent group may make a claim, or they must be classified as 'endangered' because of the serious and persistent violation of their rights. I shall focus on the second case as in the first – a situation in which a territory is 'up for grabs' – there is arguably no recognized overarching authority against which the group is revolting.

In the latter case, however, self-determination becomes a right of self-defence (Valls 2000). Indeed, the right of self-determination 'derives from the right of individuals to appeal to collectives to which they belong, and whose other members might face similar abuse, to take collective action in the defense of individual rights' (Kapitan 2008: 27). This not only strengthens the requirement that a group, if not inhabiting an unsettled territory, be the subject of serious rights violation,

---

9   It is interesting to note that Rosecrance (2006: 279) argues that 'the process of state formation has largely run its course and come to an end' and that national groups are less likely to be seeking independence or secession as they realize that globalization would make them particularly vulnerable and in all likelihood unviable economically due to their size.

10 'Such regions include those that (i) were formerly dominated by another community but are currently free from that domination, due to wars or decolonization; (ii) are currently under some form of internationally sanctioned trusteeship; (iii) have been accorded the right of secession by a larger state of which it is presently a part or (iv) are presently under the control of an illegitimate state' (Kapitan 2008: 26).

but also requires that their demand of self-determination excludes the aim of a state or system of government that violates the rights of other groups. As Daniel Philpott (1995: 371) argues: 'Advocates of autonomy must object to the curtailment of basic liberal freedoms, as they must to the denial of the right to participate and be represented, which would undermine the essential democratic justification of self-determination.' Thus, one may argue that minority groups have the right of self-determination if they inhabit unsettled territories or if their rights have been persistently and seriously violated. However, they may not use that right to violate the rights of others.

Of course, having the right of self-determination does not automatically mean that a group has the right to use political violence to achieve it. However, the right of self-determination may be considered a higher moral imperative than the right to life or liberty. They are all *prima facie* rights (Philpott 1995; Wilkins 1992), and thus the right of self-determination could arguably override the right to life and liberty. Indeed, Antonio Cassese (1995: 198, emphasis in original) argues that although international law does not bestow on groups a legal right to use violence to achieve self-determination, such movements had 'the *license* to use force' in response to the 'forcible denial of self-determination'. Political violence may thus be potentially legitimate for minority groups intent on changing the system of government *if* they inhabit an unsettled region or *if* their rights have been persistently violated and all other means of protest and redress have proved ineffective.

Therefore, individuals or minority groups do not, unlike the established majority in recognized states, have the right to revolt – that is, use violence to overthrow the government or system of government – unless their rights have been persistently and seriously violated. Their use of violence to overthrow the government or system of government is in fact based on a collective right to resist rather than a right to revolt. Individuals or minority groups whose rights have not been violated must instead resort to persuasion and do not have the right to coerce the majority. Such coercion would arguably amount to 'demanding more political power than is rightly (theirs)', turning such action into 'the essence of unjust force' (Phillips 1990: 77). The right to revolt remains, it appears, that of the majority.

Rights and the Practices of Political Violence

One crucial question remains to be addressed: What difference do such rights – discussed in abstract principally by political philosophers and international lawyers – make to the practices of political violence today? Does a discussion of rights impact on an individual's or group's decision to engage in political violence? Does it impact on the state's or international community's response to the violence?

One could argue that men and women determined to achieve their goals and intent on using political violence will do so whether or not they have been subjected to persistent and serious violations or form a politically and geographically coherent group. For example, the militia movement in which Timothy McVeigh found a home for his 'antigovernment sentiments' argued that violent resistance was necessary to stop the government from violating 'individuals' rights with impunity' (DeSa and McCarthy 2009: 45), but it would be difficult for them to argue that they formed a politically and geographically coherent group subjected to serious violations. Likewise, states will reject non-state violence as an aberration that is entirely unconnected from any social realities such as discrimination against minority groups, regardless of whether any such discrimination occurred. The Turkish state, for example, rejected for decades any link between the violence of the Kurdistan Workers' Party (PKK, now KADEK) and political, economic and structural violence of the state against the country's Kurdish population (see Aydinli and Ozcan 2011).

Nonetheless, such a rights-based analysis of political violence may not be entirely extraneous to the practices of political violence today. Indeed, the very fact that non-state armed groups use rights-based arguments to justify their violence is potentially an indication of two things: either such arguments are part of their own understanding of the means and ends of their struggle; or the group feels that they need to use rights-based arguments to be able to convince the various constituencies involved of the justifiability of their struggle; or both. Even if only the latter were true, one could still argue that rights – the right to dissent, disobey, resist and revolt as well as the rights to life, liberty and the pursuit of happiness – are inextricably part of the politics of political violence.

Indeed, the strength of the rights claims of non-state groups is likely to actually have an impact on the various constituencies involved in the struggle. The violence of a group whose rights are known to be seriously and persistently violated is likely to be received differently – at least by third parties if not by the targeted population – than that of a group which is not deemed to have been persecuted. Such a public perception may in turn lead to pressure on states to respond in different manners to the violence. For example, the bombing in Oklahoma City by Timothy McVeigh in 1995, allegedly in protest at an overbearing US federal government, only brought messages of condolence and assistance to that government from across the world, while bomb attacks in Baghdad have led to a widespread international questioning of US policy in Iraq and in the Middle East more broadly. McVeigh's racism and anti-government paranoia (Crothers 2003) did not inspire compassion or concern, while the fate of Iraqis, occupied and at times abused, does. In another example, the known persistent and serious violations of the Catholic community in Northern Ireland gave Irish republicans important international support that helped pressure the British government into seeking a political dialogue with the IRA (see, for example, Mitchell 1999).

Thus, a rights-based analysis of contemporary political violence can be useful. Whether a group engaging in political violence has suffered persistent and serious rights violations, whether they engaged in violence as a last resort and whether they fulfil the various requirements to have the right of self-determination can make a difference in how states, international organizations, non-governmental organizations and the various constituencies affected by the violence respond to it. Such evidence may be useful, for example, in pressing or persuading states and third parties to address such violations or to talk to the armed group to reach a political solution to the violence on all sides. Scepticism about the prospects for success for discussions may be justified, but one cannot rule out the possibility that it may contribute to transforming political violence. As such, when applied to specific cases of political violence, a rights-based discussion can be both analytically and prescriptively relevant.

Conclusion

From the above discussion, one can reach a series of conclusions: a) 'the people' have the right to revolt; b) we, as individuals, have the right to dissent; c) our sense of justice and our perceptions of state obstinacy also give us the right to disobey; d) if our rights are being persistently and seriously violated and if the state will not change its practices through disobedience, we have the right to resist. None of these rights imply carte blanche to use any form of violence, and each act of violence and coercion must only be engaged in after a calculation of the cost in terms of violations of others' rights and the chance of success through the use of violence.

This highlights how the boundaries between disobedience, resistance and revolution, and between violence and non-violence are often fluid and difficult to determine. The right to disobey merges into the right to resist, while violence and non-violence do not always constitute starkly separate categories. Furthermore, it is never entirely clear who 'the people' are. These conclusions brings the discussion closer to the practices of political violence in which boundaries are rarely easily delineated and concepts are always fluid.

A second point to emerge is that rights-based arguments are already part both of state and non-state discourses on political violence. These discourses can be examined and potentially challenged by engaging in an analysis of the rights to dissent, disobey, resist and revolt. This allows us to move past the state-centric view that rejects all rights-based claims of non-state violence as well as the past the glorification of all rebellion. It provides one lens through which to examine political violence that may serve policy-makers in shaping their responses. Finally, it demands that the academic and policy world analyse whether a specific non-state group has the right to dissent, disobey, resist or revolt based on the specifics of its situation and then consider how such a right should be addressed.

References

Ackerman, P. and DuVall, J. (2000), *A Force More Powerful: A Century of Nonviolent Conflict* (Basingstoke: Palgrave).

Adams, G. (2004), *Hope and History: Making Peace in Ireland* (Dingle, Co. Kerry: Brandon).
Aydinli, E. and Ozcan, N.A. (2011), 'The Conflict Resolution and Counterterrorism Dilemma: Turkey Faces its Kurdish Question', *Terrorism and Political Violence* 23:3, 438–57.
Baumgold, D. (1993), 'Pacifying Politics: Resistance, Violence, and Accountability in Seventeenth-Century Contract Theory', *Political Theory* 21:1, 6–27.
Bedau, H. (1961), 'On Civil Disobedience', *Journal of Philosophy* 58:21, 653–65.
Bedau, H. (ed.) (1991), *Civil Disobedience in Focus* (London: Routledge).
Bertrand, A. (1900), *La Déclaration des Droits de L'Homme et du Citoyen de 1789* (Paris: Librairie Delagrave).
Bunnin, N. and Yu, J. (2004), *The Blackwell Dictionary of Western Philosophy* (New York: Blackwell).
Cassese, A. (1995), *Self-Determination of Peoples: A Legal Reappraisal* (Cambridge: Cambridge University Press).
Crothers, L. (2003), *Rage on the Right: The American Militia Movement from Ruby Ridge to Homeland Security* (Landam, MD: Rowman & Littlefield).
DeSa, T.M. and McCarthy, K.E. (2009), 'The Solo Crusader: Theodore Kaczynski and Timothy McVeigh', in Haberfeld, M.R. and von Hassell, A. (eds), *A New Understanding of Terrorism: Case Studies, Trajectories and Lessons Learned* (Dordrecht: Springer).
Dudouet, V. (2009), 'From War to Politics: Resistance/Liberation Movements in Transition', *Berghof Report No. 17*; available at http://www.berghof-center.org/std_page.php?LANG=e&id=183&parent=10 [accessed 15 June 2012].
Etzioni, A. (1992), 'Anarchy Rules: The Evils of Self-Determination', *Foreign Policy* 89:4, 21–35.
Frazier, C. (1972), 'Between Obedience and Revolution', *Philosophy and Public Affairs* 1:3, 315–34.
Galtung, J. (1969), 'Violence, Peace and Peace Research', *Journal of Peace Research* 6:3, 167–91.
Gilbert, P. (1994), *Terrorism, Security, and Nationality: An Introductory Study in Applied Political Philosophy*. (London and New York: Routledge).
Gosling, D. (1990), 'Rawls in the Nonideal world: An Evaluation of the Rawlsian Account of Civil Disobedience', in Warner, M. and Crisp, R. (eds), *Terrorism, Protest and Power* (Aldershot: Edward Elgar).
Haberfeld, M.R. and von Hassell, A. (eds) (2009), *A New Understanding of Terrorism: Case Studies, Trajectories and Lessons Learned* (Dordrecht: Springer).
Halwani, R. and Kapitan, T. (eds) (2008), *The Israeli-Palestinian Conflict: Philosophical Essays on Self-Determination, Terrorism, and the One-State Solution* (Basingstoke: Palgrave Macmillan).
Jackson, R., Breen Smyth, M. and Gunning. J. (eds) (2009), *Critical Terrorism Studies: A New Research Agenda* (London: Routledge).
Kapitan, T. (2008), 'Self-Determination', in Halwani, R. and Kapitan, T. (eds), *The Israeli-Palestinian Conflict: Philosophical Essays on Self-Determination, Terrorism, and the One-State Solution* (Basingstoke: Palgrave Macmillan).

Kittrie, N. (1981), 'Patriots and Terrorists: Reconciling Human Rights with World Order', *Case Western Reserve Journal of International Law* 13, 291–313.
Mably, G. (1972), *Des Droits et des Devoirs du Citoyen* (Paris: Librairie Marcel Didier).
Maharaj, M. (2008), 'The ANC and South Africa's Negotiated Transition to Democracy and Peace', Berghof Series: Resistance/Liberation Movements and Transition to Politics, http://www.berghof-center.org/std_page.php?LANG=e&id=337 [accessed 4 July 2009].
Martin, R. (1970), 'Civil Disobedience', *Ethics* 80:2, 123–39.
Mavelli, L. (2012), 'Security and Secularization in International Relations', *European Journal of International Relations* 18:1, 177–99.
Mendell, D. (2007), *From Promise to Power* (New York: Amistad Press).
Mitchell, G., (1999), *Making Peace: The Inside Story of the Making of the Good Friday Agreement*. (London: William Heinemann).
Morreall, J. (1991), 'The Justifiability of Violent Civil Disobedience', in Bedau, H. (ed.), *Civil Disobedience in Focus* (London: Routledge).
Nicholson, P. (1976), 'Kant on the Duty Never to Resist the Sovereign', *Ethics* 86:3, 214–30.
Paust, J. (1983), 'The Human Right to Participate in Armed Revolution and Related Forms of Social Violence: Testing the Limits of Permissibility', *Emory Law Journal* 32, 545–81.
Phillips, R. (1990), 'Terrorism: Historical Roots and Moral Justifications', in Warner, M. and Crisp, R. (eds), *Terrorism, Protest and Power* (Aldershot: Edward Elgar).
Philpott, D. (1995), 'In Defense of Self-Determination', *Ethics* 105:2, 352–85.
Post, G. (2006), *Studies in Medieval Legal Thought: Public Law and the State, 1100–1322* (Clark, NJ: The Lawbook Exchange).
Rawls, J. (1991), 'Definition and Justification of Civil Disobedience', in Bedau, H. (ed.), *Civil Disobedience in Focus* (London: Routledge).
Rosecrance, R.N. (2006), 'Who will be Independent?' in Rosecrance, R.N. and Stein, A.A. (eds), *No More States? Globalization, National Self-Determination and Terrorism* (Lanham, MD: Rowman & Littlefield).
Rosecrance, R.N. and Stein, A.A. (eds) (2006), *No More States? Globalization, National Self-Determination and Terrorism* (Lanham, MD: Rowman & Littlefield).
Thoreau, H.D. (1991), 'Civil Disobedience', in Bedau, H. (ed.), *Civil Disobedience in Focus* (London: Routledge).
Toros, H. (2009), *Terrorism, Talking and Transformation: Northern Ireland and Mindanao*, unpublished thesis submitted at Aberystwyth University.
Toros, H. and Gunning, J. (2009), 'Exploring a Critical Theory Approach to Terrorism Studies', in Jackson, R., Breen Smyth, M. and Gunning. J. (eds), *Critical Terrorism Studies: A New Research Agenda* (London: Routledge).
Valls, A. (2000), 'Can Terrorism be Justified?', in Valls, A. (ed.), *Ethics in International Affairs: Theories and Cases* (Lanham, MD: Rowman & Littlefield).
Valls, A. (ed.) (2000), *Ethics in International Affairs: Theories and Cases* (Landam, MD: Rowman & Littlefield).

Walzer, M. (2002), 'Five Questions about Terrorism', *Dissent* (Winter), http://www.dissentmagazine.org/article/?article=622%3Cbr%20/%3E [accessed 15 June 2012].

Warner, M. and Crisp, R. (eds) (1990), *Terrorism, Protest and Power* (Aldershot: Edward Elgar).

Wellman, C. (1979), 'On Terrorism Itself', *Journal of Value Inquiry* 13:4, 250–58.

Wilkins, B.T. (1992), *Terrorism and Collective Responsibility*. (London, Routledge).

Williams, D. (1997), 'The Constitutional Right to "Conservative" Revolution', *Harvard Civil Rights-Civil Liberties Law Review* 32, 413–48.

Why Do Individuals Resort to Political Violence? Approaches to the Psychology of Terrorism

Jeff Victoroff and Janice Adelman

Introduction

> The ignorant mass looks upon the man who makes a violent protest against our social and economic iniquities as upon a wild beast, a cruel, heartless monster, whose joy it is to destroy life and bathe in blood; or at best upon an irresponsible lunatic. Yet nothing is further from the truth. As a matter of fact, those who have studied the character a personality of these men, or who have come in close contact with them, are agreed that it is their super sensitiveness to the wrong and injustice surrounding them which compels them to pay the toll of our social crimes. (Emma Goldman (1930: 2))

Anarchist Emma Goldman refers to 'those who have studied the character and personality' of politically violent men as if such a group of scholars existed. It is not clear to whom Ms Goldman is referring. If, in 1930, there existed a cadre of psychologists who studied the 'character and personality' of politically violent men, they apparently failed to publish their results. However, at the time of writing, a decade into the twenty-first century, there is indeed a cadre of scholars of the psychology of terrorism, and a body of literature that earnestly wrestles with the troubling question: 'Why do individuals resort to political violence?' Terrorism is arguably a major threat to global security. Some fear that the dreaded nexus of terrorist intention and nuclear capability may be the next occasion for nuclear holocaust. It would seem to be very much in the interests of peoples and nations to prevent terrorism. It is possible that knowledge of terrorist psychology might contribute to that project, so it would seem very much in the interests of peoples and nations to understand why terrorists do what they do.

At the outset, it is important to clarify the boundaries of this endeavour. First, a robust twentieth- and early twenty-first-century literature evolved discussing the psychology of human aggression and violence (e.g. Archer and Brown, 1989;

Averill, 1982; Barash, 2000; Baron and Richardson, 2004; Dollard et al., 1939; Englander, 2003; Geen, 2001; Lorentz, 1963; Montagu, 1976; Moyer, 1976; Niehoff, 1999; Scherer, Abeles and Fischer, 1975, Selg, 1975; Stoff, 1996; Storr, 1968). Political violence is merely a modest subset of the human spectrum of intraspecific violence. Second, within the domain of the psychology of political violence, one might elect to examine matters as diverse as the psychology of leaders deciding on war (e.g. Cashman, 1993; Geller and Singer, 1998; Hymans, 2006; Schelling, 1960; Stoessinger, 2005), the psychology of the soldier facing combat (e.g. Adler, Castro and Britt, 2006; Bourke, 2001; Brit, Castro and Adler, 2006; Grossman and Christensen, 2008; Nadelson, 2005; Shalit, 1988; Siddle, 1995), the specific psychology of killing in warfare (e.g. Bourke, 2000; Grossman, 1995), the psychological aftermath of soldiering (e.g. Gabriel, 1988; Nadelson, 2005) or the psychology of terrorism (e.g. Horgan, 2005; Victoroff, 2005). Third, even within the psychology of terrorism, it is vital to acknowledge that multiple actors commit such acts, from lone wolves to small or large groups of non-state actors with popular political goals, to states themselves. The present chapter will focus, for the sake of concision, on terrorist political violence committed by substate actors. And, while multiple definitions of substate terrorism exist (Schmid and Jongman, 1988), for the purposes of this chapter, terrorism means deliberate attacks by non-state actors on non-combatants to advance a political agenda.

A review of the efforts to date in this regard raises concerns. Relatively few of the published commentaries report empirical research. Relatively little funding has been invested – and the distribution of this funding may not have been well targeted to produce actionable knowledge. This review will highlight both the major theoretical approaches to understanding terrorist behaviour and the controversies regarding the optimum conceptual framework and methods of study. A pragmatic agenda will be proposed for advancing the field.

A Classification of Approaches to the Psychology of Terrorism

First, within the literature of the psychology of terrorism, there persists a debate: should terrorists be regarded as probably normal or abnormal? As we shall discuss, this debate embraces the false dichotomy that is common to efforts to apply a medical model to the tremendous complexity and variability of human behaviours. Maxwell Taylor offered a sophisticated discussion of this ambiguity, cautioning: 'There are no clear-cut technical definitions of abnormality which command general authoritative acceptance' (1991: 59). We propose that an alternative model may resolve the debate and be more helpful to the cause of understanding terrorism.

Second, psychological approaches to atypical behaviour are divided into dispositional versus contextual approaches, the first focusing on traits that predispose individuals to exhibit behavioural a typicality and the second focusing on environmental circumstances that might motivate atypical behaviour. This classification is hardly a dichotomy. Modern psychology long ago set aside the barren nature-versus-nurture debate with the recognition that individuals become who they are due to the influences of both factors. Nonetheless, threads of commentary in the literature of the psychology of terrorism appear in which the authors emphasize supposedly innate versus acquired behaviours.

Third, political deviance contains an additional complexity: the need to factor in group dynamics. While lone-wolf terrorism occurs, most strategically important terrorism is committed by modest-sized groups, embedded to various degrees within even larger human collectives, such as political parties or states that purportedly sponsor terrorism. So the literature on the causes of individual terrorist behaviour must transcend the traditional boundaries of individual psychology and include social psychological, sociological theories and perhaps even anthropology.

With this as an introduction, Table 8.1 offers a simple framework for classifying the literature on the psychosocial bases of political violence.

Table 8.1   Classification of approaches to the psychology of terrorism

Individual factors
- *Abnormal psychology*
  - Psychosis
  - Paranoia
  - Narcissism
  - Psychopathy/sociopathy
  - Atypical personality traits
- *Normal psychology*
  - Rational response to political grievance
  - Perceived injustice
  - Victimization, trauma and revenge
  - Prejudice
  - Moral disengagement
  - Humiliation
  - Developmental influences
  - Cognitive style
  - Social identity theory

Group dynamics
- Collective versus individual identity
- Small group pressures to conform
- Culture of martyrdom
- Social network theory

Socio-political factors
- Poverty/relative deprivation
- Governance model
- Societal attitudes

Abnormal Psychology

Some early accounts of the mind of the terrorist contained striking generalizations and claims that terrorists were psychologically abnormal. McKnight (1974: 89), for instance, wrote '[Nikos Sampson] suffers today from the same disorders common to most terrorists: the stress symptoms brought on by his murderous form of activity'. No evidence was offered that 'most' terrorists suffered from stress symptoms. 'Terrorists can be roughly divided into three groups: the crazy, the criminal, and the crusading', wrote Hacker (1976). Hacker's terminology implies that terrorists neatly fall into crazy and non-crazy categories, again without presenting evidence. In contrast, many modern accounts of the psychology of terrorism begin with an equally unsupported rejection of the possibility that terrorists are psychologically different from non-terrorists. Silke (1998), for instance, dismissed the effort to investigate the possibility that terrorists might be different from non-terrorists, opining that 'terrorists are normal people'. This opinion apparently derives: (1) from the paucity of systematically collected evidence regarding terrorist psychology; and (2), one senses, as a reaction to the claims of some earlier contributors that terrorists might be insane.

Indeed, several studies report little evidence of insanity among terrorists. The renowned West German Ministry of the Interior study of 250 1970s-era terrorists and extremists (Jäger, Schmidtchen and Siillwold, 1981) did not find elevated rates of clinical psychiatric disorders. Based on psychological autopsies he performed, Merari (2005) reported that none of 34 Palestinian suicide bombers were determined to have exhibited clear pre-morbid symptoms of psychopathology. And Sageman (2008) claimed that in a sample he describes as 'about 500', thought disorder was perhaps seen in four (although no valid or reliable method of assessing thought disorder is reported). Thus, with the exception of the German study, insufficient descriptions of methods and results are provided in the few reports to justify the published conclusions. Still, giving these authors the benefit of the doubt, the limited available data does not indicate that insanity is common among terrorists. Personality is an entirely different issue and will be addressed further below.

Setting aside more general declarations of terrorist normality versus abnormality, five specific psychological domains have been suggested as possibly distinguishing terrorists from non-terrorists: psychosis, paranoia, narcissism, psychopathy or sociopathy, and atypical personality traits.

Psychosis

It seems likely that some terrorists are actively psychotic, that is, genuinely out of touch with reality. Laqueur claimed with regard to nineteenth-century terrorists that 'some were half mad' (1987: 91) and that the terror committed by Irish rebels, American workers and Spanish peasants 'was perpetrated by unstable individuals' (1987: 91). Similarly, Ferracuti and Bruno claimed: 'In the right-wing terrorism, the individual terrorists are frequently psychopathological' (1981: 197). The basis for these psychiatric claims is not clear. Terrorists Theodore Kaczynski and Shoko Asahara, both probably schizophrenics, are modern exemplars of the exceptional thought-disordered terrorist. However, psychosis is probably rare among modern members of organized terror groups.

Paranoia

Robins and Post claimed: 'The terrorist group is particularly attractive to individuals with paranoid personalities.' (1997: 103). This 1997 statement was, unfortunately, not supported by any data. Taylor offered a more conservative opinion: 'The fanatic and the paranoid may well share many elements, and in practice, it may prove difficult to distinguish between them' (1991: 67). He did not suggest that terrorists necessarily exhibited paranoia, but rather that: 'The selectivity of perception of the fanatic certainly comes close to that of the paranoid.' This claim of similarity may come closer to expressing a plausible relationship between a suspicious, put-upon mindset and the typical world view of extremists, whether or not they engage in violence. Since the forensic psychiatric literature demonstrates an association between paranoid thought disorder and violence, it is worth investigating whether paranoid traits are more common among terrorists than among non-terrorists sharing the same political grievances. Moreover, it is plausible that the stress of underground life itself might cause anxiety that, in vulnerable individuals, could precipitate paranoia. In one empirical study (Gottschalk and Gottschalk, 2004), incarcerated Muslim extremists scored higher on the paranoia scale of the Minnesota Multiphasic Personality Inventory-2 (MMPI-2) than did community comparison subjects. However, these results with a select sample cannot be generalized to the universe of extremists, so the possibility of a relatively higher prevalence of paranoid traits among terrorists remains unresolved.

Narcissism

Crayton wrote of 'The narcissistic aspects of terrorist behaviour' (1983: 40). Agreeing with this essential thesis, Pearlstein reported his psychoanalytic analysis of nine cases of terrorists: 'the external psychological determinants or sources of political terrorism appear to lie in what are termed narcissistic injury and narcissistic disappointment' (1991: 171).

Such psychoanalytic formulations have, for the most part, been discredited as failing to satisfy minimal criteria for falsifiable scientific theories. Yet, setting aside the terminology 'narcissistic injury', abundant literature exists that links early developmental trauma to later psychological atypicality – including criminality and aggression (e.g. Caspi et al., 2002; Cassel and Bernstein, 2007; Downes and Rock, 2007; Etain et al., 2008; Goodman, New and Siever, 2004; Heide and Solomon, 2006; Heim et al., 2008; Petit, 1997; van Winkel, Stefanis and Myin-Germeys, 2008;

Wilson, Stover and Berkowitz, 2009). The issue of trauma will be addressed further below.

Psychopathy and Sociopathy

Cooper claimed that: 'Given the closeness, the near identity of this fundamental characteristic [indifference to the rights of others] in both the psychopath and the terrorist, it is small wonder that, on occasion at least, the distinction between them seems scarcely worth making' (1977: 256). Taylor stated: 'Thus, terms like "sociopath" and "psychopath" recur in the literature on terrorism' (1988: 80). The terms 'psychopath' and 'sociopath' both overlap to some degree with the more modern psychiatric diagnosis, Antisocial Personality Disorder (ASPD), insofar as all three terms connote a lack of normal conscience and insensitivity to the rights of others. Since terrorists often attack innocent non-combatants, sometimes in gruesome ways, it is reasonable to speculate that perhaps they lack conscience. A chicken-versus-egg conundrum is worth considering: exposure to combat – and even to depictions of violence – is potentially brutalizing, desensitizing individuals to committing aggression. It is not clear to what degree, and among what subgroups of extremists, callousness is innate, socially learned, a result of virtual exposures (e.g. videos of beheadings) or a result of direct exposure to violence.

Sageman claims to have done empirical research on this issue: 'Underlying the entire criminality issue is the commonly held belief that terrorists are simply psychopaths or sociopaths. This also turns out not to be so' (2008: 63). Again, giving this author the benefit of the doubt with regard to his poorly documented methodology, Sageman's report does not support a high prevalence of ASPD in one subset of global Salafist jihadis. On the other hand, the far more rigorous West German Ministry of the Interior study reported, with regard to left-wing terrorists, that 33 per cent reported severe conflict with parents and 33 per cent had a history of juvenile court convictions. Both facts are consistent with conduct disorder – the precursor of ASPD.

Limited conclusions are possible. The well-known drift into common criminality by such groups as the Ulster Defence Association, the Irish National Liberation Army, Columbia's FARC and the Abu Sayef group – and the well-established statistical association between violent criminality and ASPD (see e.g. Fountoulakis, Leucht and Kaprinis, 2008; Hare, 2006; Kirsch and Becker, 2007; Vien and Beech, 2006) – suggest that this condition may in fact be more common in the world's diverse community of terrorists than among matched non-terrorists. Sufficient modern data are lacking to resolve this question.

Atypical Personality Traits

Multiple authorities have opined that there is no terrorist personality. Borum, for example, declares: 'There is no "terrorist personality", nor is there any accurate profile – psychologically or otherwise – of the terrorist' (2004: 3). Crenshaw states that 'most analysts of terrorism do not think that personality factors account for terrorist behaviour' (2000: 409). Sageman claims that 'I saw little evidence for any personality disorder' (2008: 64). Again, no validated method of assessment or quantification of results is reported.

The statement 'there is no terrorist personality' is both (a) probably true and (b) a gratuitous swipe at a straw man. No serious scholar has claimed that all terrorists are alike and that they all exhibit a uniform and deterministic 'terrorist personality'. The scientifically interesting and unresolved question is whether any personality traits are measurably more common among a group of terrorists than among a reasonably matched comparison group of non-terrorists.

Personality traits are associated with aggression and/or criminality, and individuals in certain careers are more likely to exhibit certain traits. For instance, although one would not state that there is a 'policeman personality', police have been reported to exhibit more than usual extraversion, venturesomeness and impulsivity (Gudjonsson and Adlam, 1983), defensiveness and guardedness (Detrick, Chibnall and Rosso, 2001) and authoritarianism (Rubinstein, 2006). Robbers also seem to be different, exhibiting more aggression and extraversion, on average, than non-robbers (Inciardi, 2003; Johnston, 1978; Rosenfeld and Fornango, 2007; Schwaner, 2000). More generally, a very large literature reports that early developmental factors, cognitive styles and personality traits correlate with career choice (e.g. Ackerman and Beier, 2003; Alvi et al., 1988; Brown, Lum and Voyle, 1997; Burton and Topham, 1997). Based upon this robust literature regarding differences in average traits among those who pursue different life paths, it would be extremely illogical to declare, prior to study, that those who choose to participate in terrorist acts are psychologically identical to those who do not.

The West German Ministry of the Interior study, in this regard, possibly offers some insights. The investigators reported that two personality patterns were common among their groups of terrorists and extremists, the first an extroverted, stimulus seeking, dependent pattern, and the second a hostile, suspicious, defensive pattern. However, it is difficult to interpret this major report, since this study did not utilize the types of normed and validated instruments that have subsequently become required for peer-reviewed publication.

This raises an important methodological issue: the threat of terrorism has inspired a sense of urgency among stakeholders (e.g. Western governments) who wish to understand terrorist psychology. Yet the rush to understand has sometimes led to the publication of conclusions drawn from scientifically weak empirical studies or from theoretically based 'expert' opinions. The only way to determine whether any personality or behavioural trait is disproportionately common among terrorists would be to conduct a study that includes a matched comparison group and employs a validated measure. In other words, one needs to:

a. identify a behavioural trait that may be important in the motivation or restraint of violent extremism, for example, aggressiveness, depression, paranoia, etc.;
b. identify a measure of that trait that has been shown to distinguish between those who have more or less of that trait;
c. determine the normal population distribution of that trait (e.g. 'average aggressiveness among 20-year-old second-generation Muslim immigrants in the UK is X';
d. compare measures of that trait in groups of extremists versus age, sex, religion and socio-economically matched non-extremists; and
e. quantitatively determine whether any statistically significant difference emerges.

In the case of violent extremism, multiple practical barriers make such studies challenging to conduct. One is obliged to obtain data, for instance, from public records that provide biographical hints, interviews with 'retired' extremists or interviews with the subset of incarcerated extremists who are willing to cooperate. Such interviews should be carefully structured or should utilize valid psychological measures, but often do not. Hence, many of those regarded as authorities on the psychology of terrorism have generated articles and books that fail to distinguish between levels of evidence, from the lowest – personal opinion – to the highest – replicable studies employing scientific methods. Qualitative ethnography, theoretical speculation and even psychodynamic interpretations have been important in opening the door to serious study of the mind of the terrorist. Ultimately, scholarship in this field will benefit from open-minded dialogue across disciplines, each of which may inspire the others to re-formulate their inquiries and, by successive approximations that take advantage of both instinct and data, refine our understanding of this multi-faceted phenomenon. However, one hopes that the applied social science of counter-terrorism will increasingly be informed by empirical studies using validated methods.

While admittedly challenging, it is possible to conduct such studies. Gottschalk and Gottschalk (2004) reported that 90 Palestinian and Israeli Jewish terrorists had significantly higher psychopathic deviate, paranoid, depressive, and hypomanic scale scores on the MMPI-2 as compared with 60 very roughly matched non-terrorists living freely in the community. This paper may be the sole controlled, direct, open-source psychological investigation of Middle-Eastern terrorists using a well-validated measure (better-controlled similar studies using an official and normed Arabic translation of the MMPI-2 are underway (Merari, personal communication, 2008)). Although no firm conclusion can be based on any single study, one must acknowledge the implications of the best available scientific evidence: some groups of terrorists perhaps exhibit atypical personality traits more often than expected.

Normal Psychology

Again, we caution against the assumption that any bright line can be drawn between normal and abnormal human psychology. Still, recognizing the popularity of this conceptual framework, one may identify specific themes in the literature of the psychology of terrorism that begins with the assumption that the subjects are essentially normal, healthy humans. We will examine these in turn.

Rational Response to Political Grievance

Decision-making and rational choice science has advanced rapidly in recent decades. The essence of this science is the assumption of free will and conscious deliberation: humans are assumed to possess a capacity to seek goals via strategic cost-benefit analysis that, in the popular economic terminology, will maximize utility under conditions of uncertainty (e.g. Camerer, 2003; Nash, 1950; Neumann and Morgenstern, 1944). In an excellent essay, Martha Crenshaw addressed how this approach can play a role in understanding terrorist behaviours: 'Terrorism can be considered a reasonable way of pursuing extreme interests in the political arena. It is one of many alternatives that a radical organization can choose' (1990: 24). Some economists have applied quantitative rational choice theory to specific aspects of terrorism. As Enders and Sandler (2000) comment, for example, the employment of X-ray screening devices in airports and the fortification of high-profile targets led to a predictable, rational shift to other modes of terrorism. Since then, a small group of authorities have examined the terrorist as a rational actor and shown how government behaviour does and does not influence terrorist behaviour, primarily employing time-series analyses, cross-sectional and discrete choice models (e.g. Rosendorff and Sandler, 2005; Weiman and Brosius, 1988; also see Li and Schaub, 2004).

The rational choice approach to terrorist collectives may indeed offer insights into group dynamics and predictions of responses to contingencies. The rational choice argument for why an individual becomes a terrorist is more problematic. Unless a rational choice argument can accurately predict that every person, given certain circumstances, will commit terrorism, decision-making science fails to account for this individual behaviour. Terrorism is extraordinarily rare. Hafez (2007), for instance, identified just 53 Saudi Arabians who committed jihad-related suicide bombing in Iraq. Thus, approximately 0.00024 per cent of Saudis – less than one-thousandth of one percent of persons who might plausibly resent the presence of US troops in the Middle East – seem to have committed terrorist acts. Some explanation other than rational pursuit of desired ends might better explain who does and who does not choose this career.

Perceived Injustice

Anger at unfairness is a universal human trait (Batson et al., 2007). Perceived injustice may be an important explanatory variable in the occurrence of juvenile delinquency (Moon, Blurton and McCluskey, 2008) and workplace violence (e.g. Barling, Dupré and Kelloway, 2009). The question is whether, and to what degree, this natural phenomenon plays a contributory role in political violence.

Hacker (1976) claimed that 'remediable injustice is the basic motivation for terrorism'. Based on a review of some terrorist biographies, Borum stated that: 'Perceived injustice, need for identity and need for belonging are common vulnerabilities among potential terrorists' (2004: 3). Pyszczynski, Rothschild and Abdollahi (2008) tie the concept of perceived injustice to the cognitive strain of mortality salience – or a heightened conscious awareness of the inevitability of eventual death. These authors opine that terrorism can be provoked when prejudice, discrimination and unjust treatment are felt as threats not only to one's group of identity but also to one's very survival. It makes sense that perceived injustice is a common and critical factor in the genesis of political anger. Perceived injustice, perceived prejudice, perceived victimization and the experience of personal humiliation may comprise a hard-to-disentangle tetrad of psychological provocations. Some individuals will be exposed to more social injustice, discrimination and potentially humiliating treatment than others. Some individuals may be more sensitive to such provocations than others. And a subset of provoked persons may be predisposed to violent responses. The determination of the relative frequency of these feelings among terrorists versus non-terrorists seems a promising avenue for further study.

Victimization, Trauma, and Revenge

> I am one, my liege,
> Whom the vile blows and buffets of the world
> Hath so incensed, that I am reckless what
> I do to spite the world.
> (Second murderer, *Macbeth*, Act III, Scene I)

The notion that trauma might contribute to participation in terrorism needs to be clarified. Three different mechanisms are pertinent. First, a person might be driven to participate in an extremist act because of a traumatic loss (e.g. loss of a loved one or romantic disappointment) entirely apart from a political conflict. Thus, for example, Bloom (2007: 159–60) cites the case of Dhanu, a woman who was reportedly a victim of rape, who could not therefore get married and who then joined the Tamil Tigers, strapped on a bomb and died while killing Indian Prime Minister Rajiv Gandhi. As noted above, a great deal of evidence supports the association between early traumatic experiences and later violence. Second, a person might have experienced a personal conflict-related loss to which they respond via extremist action. In Speckhard and Akhmedova's interviews with the families of Chechen suicide terrorists (2006), for example, a specific traumatic event – typically the imprisonment or death of a relative at the hands of the Russians – was often cited as a motivation that changed the life course of the bomber. In our own studies of teenaged boys in Gaza (Victoroff et al., 2006), there was a significant association between support for attacks on Israeli civilians and a family member having been wounded or killed by the Israeli Defence Forces. And Moghadam (2003) cites the example of Nafez al-Nether, a Palestinian who blew up himself and several Israeli soldiers on 9 July 2001, having declared a desire to avenge the death of his brother, Fayez, who had been killed during the first intifada. On the other hand, Merari reports that, based on his study of Palestinian suicide terrorists from 1993 to 1998, 'a personal grudge has not been a necessary factor ... although it presumably was a contributing factor in some of the cases' (2005: 76).

Suffice it to say that psychological research indeed supports both the notion that life trauma might be associated with violence and that some terrorists seem to have acted in response to trauma. Yet trauma cannot be assumed to be either a necessary or a sufficient cause of terrorism. More evidence is required to determine (a) the proportion of terrorists who seem primarily motivated by traumatic stress and (b) (an issue with policy implications) the degree to which potentially remediable stressors account for radical violence in different conflicts.

Prejudice

The bias and discriminatory behaviour of terrorists towards members of another group are so self-evident that they hardly inspire comment. But even between two societies in conflict, some persons are more prejudiced than others. As Taylor writes, 'it does seem ... that we can identify some constitutional psychological processes that relate to the psychological basis of fanaticism, and these processes may well have links with the origins of prejudice' (1991: 71). This raises the reasonable question of whether more prejudiced individuals are more likely than less prejudiced individuals to become terrorists.

As with regard to other proposed atypicalities of terrorists, formal comparative measures of prejudice against members of the out-group are lacking. But prejudice may deserve the attention of policy-makers as a modifiable risk factor for terrorism. This is particularly so in view of the history of interventions to ameliorate prejudice and their possible role in reducing extremist violence.

The other side of the coin is perceived prejudice. Psychological theory strongly supports the notion that unfair or biased treatment can provoke aggression (e.g. Smart Richman and Leary, 2009). And recent experiments with prisoners demonstrate that raising the salience of perceptions of disrespect increases the risk of violence (Butler and Maruna, 2009). To the best of our knowledge, no findings have been published regarding whether those who support or participate in terrorism feel victimized by the prejudice of their perceived oppressors. Sageman opines that: 'Low-level local discrimination usually does not by itself become a direct cause of terrorism' (2008; 83). Again, no data are offered. This opinion may underestimate a critical point: victims of prejudice may become enraged. Rage at exclusion itself may lower the threshold for participation in political violence. The role of perceived prejudice in motivating political violence deserves empirical study.

Moral Disengagement

Psychologist Albert Bandura (1986) proposed a theory that moral regulation can be deliberately activated or deactivated. He proposes that when a person elects to disengage his or her controls, four mechanisms will liberate the person to commit detrimental conduct: reconstruing conduct (for instance, euphemistic labelling of one's abhorrent act), obscuring casual agency (for instance, blaming the circumstances for making the act necessary), distorting consequences (for instance, minimizing the severity of the injuries one perpetrates) and blaming and devaluing targets. Such 'moral disengagement' supposedly occurs in many forms of combat (Grossman, 1995). Bandura has explicitly claimed that terrorists are taught to employ these selective mechanisms. He writes: 'Terrorist behaviour evolves through extensive training in moral disengagement' (1990: 185).

This theory seems weak for two reasons. First, self-selection occurs prior to training. The tiny minority of individuals who feel a political grievance and who then join a terrorist group are already presumably different from the vast majority who do not. Thus, Bandura's theory does not explain who becomes a terrorist. Second, modern psychological theory recognizes that a great deal of motivation is unconscious. It does not seem to be a promising line of inquiry to propose that harming others occurs due to pre-emptive and 'selective' switching off of cognitive controls.

A more defensible theory, consistent with modern research, would be that a person's restraint against committing violent action is the product of both innate and acquired factors. Some of these are emotional or affective, while others are cognitive, but little if any of these restraints are conscious and 'selective'. Taylor and Quayle point out one of those cognitive mechanisms, positing that the Fundamental Attribution Error (mistakenly attributing ill-intent to threatening others) and the 'Actor-Observer' effect 'can help us to understand how the terrorist can in a sense evade the responsibility for his or her actions by locating the causes of his or her behaviour in the actions of others' (1994: 31). More generally, under conditions in which an out-group is systematically demonized by leaders or within society, or in which military training teaches aggression without deliberation, significant but largely unconscious changes occur in the brain that lead a person to essentialize and infra-humanize members of the other group (e.g. Demoulin, Saroglou and van Pachterbeke, 2008; Epley, Waytz and Cacioppo, 2007; Harris and Fiske, 2007; Pratto and Glasford, 2008; Sherman et al., 2009).

Humiliation

Terrorism expert Jessica Stern opined that humiliation is an important factor in motivating terrorists. As she put it: 'It is not just the violence; it is the pernicious effect of repeated, small humiliations that add up to a feeling of nearly unbearable despair and frustration, and a willingness on the part of some to do anything – even commit atrocities – in the belief that attacking the oppressor will restore their sense of dignity' (2003: 62). Humiliation might be personal or felt on behalf of the group. Juergensmeyer, for instance, states that, in Kahane's estimation, Baruch Goldstein committed his infamous 1994 massacre of 29 Muslims in Hebron because 'Anything that humiliated the Jews was not only an embarrassment but a retrograde motion in the world's progress toward salvation' (2003: 54). Linder (2006) also warns that humiliation may provoke conflict and terrorism. It seems reasonable that either individual insults or group insults are factors that sometimes lower the threshold for a person to participate in political violence (see also McCauley, 2007). Again, Sageman claims to have researched this issue: 'In looking at the background of the terrorists in the sample, I was not struck by any common theme of personal humiliation' (2008: 73). A study using replicable and valid methodology would help test this theory.

In partial summary, Borum's formulation regarding the psychologically related issues of trauma, perceived injustice and humiliation seems worthy of consideration:

> Histories of childhood abuse and trauma appear to be widespread. In addition, themes of perceived injustice and humiliation often are prominent in terrorist biographies and personal histories. None of these contribute much to a causal explanation of terrorism, but may be seen as markers of vulnerability, as possible sources of motivation, or as mechanisms for acquiring or hardening one's militant ideology. (2004: 40)

Acknowledging the need for quantitative confirmation of Borum's claims regarding the frequency of these 'themes' and the need for psychometrically valid methods to measure vulnerability to these perceptions, we nonetheless suspect that experiential and personality risk factors may indeed lower the threshold for aggrieved persons to turn to terror.

Developmental Influences

A massive body of research supports the notion that developmental influences may alter the trajectory of psychological life. Therefore, it is possible that the difference between a person's responding to a political grievance with non-violent protest or with terrorism might have something to do with early development. Braungart and Braungart (1992), for instance, speculated that psychological needs based in early developmental experiences were especially common among those who became weathermen. Again, the danger is in over-interpreting fragmentary biographical information using a scientifically insupportable theoretical framework. Post, for example, opined that: 'Like many of his generation, the developmental experiences of Amar Rezaq shaped his attraction to the path of terrorism ... The psychological soil had already been prepared by his mother's recounting of their family's expulsion from Jaffa ...The father's harsh discipline ... did leave Rezaq ripe to idolize an alternative model, which he found in his Palestinian teacher' (2000: 175). One must set aside such post-hoc psychodynamic formulations but not reject the valuable underlying observation: certain early developmental events such as maternal deprivation are well-established risk factors for later criminal and/or aggressive behaviour (e.g. Petit, 1997). While such early developmental factors do not seem likely to be necessary or sufficient to make a terrorist, it is worth considering that such factors may increase the risk that a person will respond more aggressively to a political grievance.

Cognitive Style

One theme in modern psychology is that different people think about the same things differently. Variation in cognitive style, or traits describing the relative weight that persons give to different cognitions, may account for a number of political phenomenon (Tetlock, 1983; also see Jost et al., 2003). Dogmatisim/close-mindedness (Rokeach, 1960; Smithers and Lobley, 1978), right-wing authoritarianism (RWA) (Altemeyer, 1998), social dominance orientation (SDO) (Sidanius and Pratto, 1999), intolerance of ambiguity (Frenkel-Brunswik, 1949; Sidanius, 1978), need for cognitive closure (Webster and Kruglanski, 1994) and low integrative complexity (Sidanius, 1985; Tetlock, 1984) all represent common variants in cognitive style. It has been proposed, for example, that politically conservative persons tend to exhibit resistance to change, RWA, SDO, intolerance of ambiguity and, as a result, also exhibit fear and aggression (Adorno et al., 1950; Altemeyer, 1998; Fibert and Ressler, 1998; Jost et al., 2003; Oreg et al., 2008; Pratto et al., 1994; Thorisdottir et al., 2007). Terrorists cross the political spectrum. It would be simplistic to propose (and has yet to be meaningfully studied) that one narrowly defined cognitive style is more common among terrorists than among non-terrorists. Yet specific groups that support or act in extreme ways might indeed exhibit a higher prevalence of given cognitive styles. Canetti and Pedahzur (2002), for example, reported that the traits of authoritarianism and supernatural beliefs were associated with right-wing extremism among Israeli students. Locicero and Sinclair (2008) hypothesized that some terrorist leaders might exhibit a dangerous combination of 'entrenched cognitive simplicity' with regard to ideology and cognitive complexity in regard to tactics. Victoroff (2005) theorized that differences in cognitive style perhaps underlie differences in the tendency to respond to political grievances with violence.

Little systematic research has explored possible links between cognitive style and political violence. However, Liht, Suedfeld and Krawczyk (2005) studied the

1995 San Andrés Peace Talks between Mexico's Chiapas guerrillas, government representatives and mediators. Consistent with predictions regarding extremism, and potentially problematic for the prospect of peaceful mediations, the guerrillas exhibited the lowest integrative complexity (the capacity to perceive different elements of an issue and their relationship) of the three parties.

Social Identity Theory

Tajfel introduced social identity theory (SIT) in the 1970s to help account for out-group prejudice (Tajfel, 1972, 1981; Tajfel and Turner, 1979). SIT posits that individuals tend to think and feel that they belong to a specific subset of humans. Corollaries of belonging include loyalty to the in-group and often negative emotions and cognitions towards the out-group, including fear, social distance, rejection and discriminatory behaviour (see e.g. Abrams and Hogg, 1990; Crocker and Luhtanen, 1990; Ethier and Deaux, 1994; Gagnon and Bourhis, 1997; Hogg, Terry and White, 1995; Turner, 1985). Grant and Brown (1995) suggested that social identity helps drive not only ethnocentrism but also collective political action. Staub (2004) discusses how both group and territorial identity contribute to the intractability of the Israeli/Palestinian conflict. These notions together provide a theoretical springboard for the possibility that collective aggression, including terrorism and war, are driven, in part, by social identity.

Some theorists have gone much further. Moghaddam, for example, opines that SIT is the key social psychological explanation for Islamist terrorism: when in-group loyalty is combined with the perception of little alternative, he theorizes, the ends justifies terrorist means: 'a "superordinate factor" … explains terrorism far better', he writes, 'and this is to do with identity and the deep and pervasive crisis of identity being experienced by Islamic communities' (2006: 26). Identity crises could also be used to describe the stresses of membership in any politically subordinate community, such as black South Africans in the apartheid era or Tamils under Sinhalese rule. This position may overvalue one aspect of a complex phenomenon. Yet we agree that SIT provides a useful framework for understanding 'Us versus Them' emotions and cognitions. The more strongly a politically aggrieved person identifies himself or herself as a group member, the more fearful he or she may be about threats to his or her group, and the more incentives he or she may perceive for displays of loyalty to his or her group, including rewards for action against the out-group.

Since SIT describes an individual's mental relationship to his or her group, this discussion of SIT provides a natural segue from the consideration of individual to group psychology in the genesis of political violence.

Group Dynamics

Collective versus Individual Identity

For more than a century, social psychologists have written about the contrast between societies that are 'collectivist' versus 'individualist' (e.g. Kelly, 1901; Triandis, 1988, 1995). The 'collectivist' versus 'individualist' distinction supposedly captures one aspect of human identity: the extent to which people think of themselves as independent agents whose meaning and purpose comes from their own aspirations versus group members whose meaning and purpose is inextricable from that of their group. The relationship between individualism, collectivism and violence has been studied. As Forbes et al. reported (2009), people in more individualistic societies (e.g. the USA) are more likely to commit violence than those in collectivist societies (e.g. China). Nonetheless, from another point of view, a person's willingness to commit violence on behalf of his or her group might reasonably relate to his or her degree of identification with group goals.

Based on semi-structured interviews with 35 incarcerated Middle Eastern terrorists, Post, Sprinzak and Denny wrote: 'Once recruited, there is a clear fusing of individual identity and group identity ... An overarching sense of the collective consumes the individual' (2003: 175–6). The data and methods upon which this conclusion is reached are not available. Methodological critiques aside, the interviewers may have accurately detected signs of a theme common to the development of group cohesion: identity shifts towards a sense of the collective. While this phenomenon is by no means special to terrorist groups, it may indeed represent one common facet of group dynamics pertinent to such groups.

Small Group Pressures to Conform

Conformity – a concept perhaps closely related to group identity and to collectivist orientation – might play several roles in the phenomenon of terrorism. First, when one's society rewards expressions of prejudice, it is difficult to stand up for a more balanced view of members of another group. Second, when valued peers are participating in an activity (e.g. a Hamas-run summer camp or a left-wing student radical organization), it may be both attractive to join and unappealing to be left out. Third, once an extremist group is established, conformity to a flawed collective decision-making process might lead to the selection of violent means. As Taylor notes: 'Cohesive groups tend to engage in a number of faulty decision-making processes. These involve rigidity in the appraisal of situations, simplified and stereotyped views about the outcomes of decisions, and belief in the morality of their decision and its invulnerability to failure' (1991: 78). He is describing so-called Group-think. And, fourth, as shown by Milgram's famous experiments (1963, 1974), otherwise normal individuals may be willing to conform to authority (or even peer) encouragement to commit serious aggression against innocent victims.

These psychological mechanisms of conformity plausibly contribute to the phenomenon of terrorism. Taylor, for example, states: 'Thus, in the developmental process of fanaticism ... the notion of obedience may well be important' (1991: 260). However, it is not clear that conformity is any more important to terrorism than to gang, corporate or military behaviour.

Culture of Martyrdom

Multiple writers have commented that suicide terrorism is due, at least in part, to a 'culture of martyrdom' (e.g. Ali and Post, 2008; Brooks, 2002; Hafez, 2007; Post, 2009; Post et al., 2009; Slavicek, 2008). The notion of a 'culture' of martyrdom rests on the assumption that humans living in some cultures are especially encouraged to display altruistic fervor that includes self-destruction on behalf of the group. Whether or not given cultures are dispositionally more supportive of martyrdom, this supreme sacrifice is hardly new and hardly confined to a single tradition. As Juergensmeyer writes: 'Though suicide bombing and self-sacrifice appear to be newly discovered devices of religious activities around the world, the idea of martyrdom has a long history within many religious traditions. Christ himself was a martyr, as was the founder of the Shiite Muslim tradition, Husain' (2003: 417).

While martyrdom behaviours have become especially frequent in the recent annals of terrorism, soldiers in many battles, not to mention parents, throughout history have sacrificed themselves for those they value. Further research might uncover some social psychological factor uniquely associated with this phenomenon, but it seems premature to judge that a given religion, cultural tradition or pattern of social organization lends itself to martyrdom.

Social Network Theory

Forensic psychiatrist Marc Sageman is known for contributing what he calls the 'bunches of guys' theory of terrorism. He states that 'social bonds play a more important role in the emergence of the global Salafi jihad than ideology' (2008: 178). His theory is that, whatever an individual's political ideology, being friends with another person who is already invested in jihad will 'transform him from an alienated Muslim into a dedicated global Salafi mujahed'. Atran (2008) echoes Sageman, stating: 'It is the *social networks* [emphasis in original] and group dynamics of these networks that are critical to understanding how terrorist networks form and operate, not the demographic profiles of individuals and whole populations' (see also della Porta in Chapter 13 of this volume).

This theory deserves consideration due to its counter-terrorism policy implications. If true, then a major focus of counter-terrorism efforts would involve identifying, disrupting and eliminating hubs. Indeed, good evidence exists that closely bonded individuals influence one another's behaviours (see e.g. Christakis and Fowler, 2008). But the social network enthusiasts in this field do not consider the potential of individual psychological traits to influence the likelihood that given person will (a) come into contact with an extremist or (b) become radicalized as a result of that contact. Moreover, a substantial body of research on youth gang membership strongly contradicts the main contention of the network theorists. Every urban male in certain neighbourhoods has regular contact with gang members. A minority of these males join gangs. Joining is reportedly associated with individual factors such as a learning disability, a previous history of social adjustment problems, negative life events, single-parent households, depressive symptoms or ready access to marijuana (see e.g. Decker and Curry, 2000; Eitle, Gunkel and van Gundy, 2004; Hill et al., 1999; Rizzo, 2003). These findings help expose the weakness of the social network theory of terrorism: while contacts are surely important, they are often sought. It is psychologically unrealistic to entirely attribute a profound behavioural change to a friend's behaviour.

Socio-political Factors

Poverty/Relative Deprivation

In a classic paper, Krueger and Maleckova explored multiple lines of evidence and found that, on the whole, terrorists were not poor: 'The evidence we have presented, tentative though it is, suggests little direct connection between poverty or education and participation in terrorism' (2003: 141). Moreover, the evidence also shows that impoverished nations are not disproportionate places of origin of terrorists: 'The cross-country evidence that we have assembled suggests that, once civil liberties are taken into account, a country's income level is unrelated to the number of terrorists who originate from that country' (2003; 142). Citing the important work of Fearon and Laitin (2003), Kruger and Maleckova offer a caveat: 'Poverty at the national level may indirectly affect terrorism through the apparent connection between economic conditions and the proclivity for countries to undergo civil wars' (2003: 141).

Krueger and Maleckova's excellent research, however, does not address whether the very existence of economic disparities, either on a country or a global level, and the sympathy they inspire represent a risk factor for terrorism. Richardson, for example, states: 'Rather than causing terrorism, poverty or inequality are risk factors that increase the likelihood of terrorism' (2006: 57). She cites what we propose might be an important mediating or moderating variable for the influence of poverty on terrorism risk: the existence of large numbers of unemployed young men. Li (2005) suggested another approach to this issue, testing the hypothesis that either income inequality or real GDP per capita might predict the frequency of terrorist attacks. Based on his analysis of the International Terrorism: Attributes of Terrorists Events (ITERATE) database, there was a positive but not statistically significant association between terrorism and income inequality, and level of economic development, based on GDP, was negatively associated with terrorism – suggesting that socio-economic factors indeed play a role in political violence.

A closely related hypothesis states that relative deprivation (RD) can cause political violence. Building on previous conceptual and empirical work by Stouffer et al. (1949), Davis (1959) and Runciman (1966), Gurr wrote: 'Discontent arising from the perception of relative deprivation is the basic, instigating condition for participants in collective violence' (1970: 13). During the subsequent four decades, Gurr's theory has become a popular explanation for intergroup aggression. Recently, several authors have opined that RD plays some role in terrorism (e.g. Gurr, 2006, Rice, 2009; Smelser and Mitchell, 2002). Richardson suggests that: 'What appears to drive some people to violence is not their absolute levels of poverty but rather their position relative to others' (2006: 56). Gurr's (2006) essay clarifies that terrorism cannot be attributed to deprivation by itself but that two intervening variables must also contribute: 'the political circumstances that dispose militants to use violence and the ideologies used to justify terror'. But Hogg and Abrams (1998) object that Gurr ignores a distinction originally made by Runciman (1966) between an individual's personal deprivation ('egoistic deprivation') and an individual's sense that they belong to a deprived group ('fraternal deprivation'). We agree that this distinction might help to explain the heterogeneity of findings with regard to socio-economic risk factors for terrorism.

One must still explain the fact that many terrorists come from individually privileged backgrounds. Socio-economic advantage perhaps provides individuals with more resources to act politically and perhaps inspires a sense of responsibility towards the less fortunate. But it is not clear whether the economically secure terrorist typically identifies with the underprivileged, or instead takes up the banner of those with whom he or she sympathizes, while firmly maintaining his or her identity as a member of the privileged class.

Governance Model

In a series of classic papers, Weinberg and Eubank (1994; see also Eubank and Weinberg, 2001; Weinberg and Eubank, 1998) investigated whether democracy encourages or discourages terrorism. They concluded, based on analysis of both the RAND-St Andrews Chronology and ITERATE databases, that civil liberties and democracy promote terrorism. Terrorist attacks occur most often in stable democracies and both the perpetrators and victims are most likely to come from such democracies.

Li (2005) re-examined this question. Again employing the ITERATE database, and contrary to the findings of Eubank and Weinberg, he found that voter turnout (interpreted as a measure of democratic participation) was significantly negatively associated with terrorist attacks. But Li explored another and deceptively complex question: do civil liberties increase or decrease the risk of terrorism? We agree with his ultimate conclusion: while civil liberties sometimes tie the hands of governments and slow the response to grievances, democracies have potent tools to protect themselves: 'By improving citizen satisfaction, electoral participation, and political efficacy, democratic governments can reduce the number of terrorist incidents within their borders' (2005; 294).

Societal Attitudes

A natural question is whether the existence of widespread negative attitudes among a large group towards another group, nation or leader increases the likelihood that some members of the first group will undertake terrorist actions. Few empirical studies have examined potential links between societal attitudes and terrorism, and, unfortunately, much of that data is confined to the narrow question of relations between Muslims and non-Muslims. Surveys such as the Pew Global Attitudes Survey (2006), the surveys of the Palestinian Centre for Policy and Survey Research (2009) and the Gallup World Poll (2009) have reported that significant proportions of some Muslim populations harbour negative feelings toward the West. Victoroff and Adelman (2008) reported preliminary evidence that such attitudes are associated with support for suicide bombing in Iraq. Krueger and Maleckova (2009) addressed a closely related question by studying the relationship between job disapproval of Western leaders by residents of Middle Eastern and North African countries (as reported in the Gallup World Poll) and terrorist acts. They reported as follows: 'We found a sizable and robust positive relationship between the number of terrorist incidents occurring from country i against country j and the rate at which people in country i disapprove of the job performance of country j's leaders' (2009: 1535). This finding contributes a new wrinkle to the understanding of, and perhaps the response to, terrorist motivations. If widely held social attitudes or affects cause more members of a social group to become terrorists, then surveys that detect such attitudes may serve as early warnings – and might even be used to guide terrorism-preventive policies.

Discussion

The psychology of terrorism is perhaps better conceived, as Jerrold Post has advised (personal communication, 2008) as the 'psychologies' of terrorism. Multiple well-reasoned arguments suggest that individual psychological factors, group psychological factors and socio-political circumstances all contribute to a given person's election of political violence as his or her response to a grievance. There exists no formula that predicts who will become a terrorist. But as terrorology matures, thinkers are gaining footholds, as they did in the early days of criminology, on the mountain of information, the impartial analysis of which might reveal modifiable risk factors. What is obviously missing is a body of research testing the many promising hypotheses.

Moreover, unfortunately, resistance remains to acknowledging some justifiable tentative conclusions from the available data. For example, Gottschalk and Gottschalk (2004) provide empirical evidence of an elevated frequency of certain personality traits in one cohort of terrorists. In spite of these published findings, one continues to encounter adamantine resistance to the notion that terrorists might exhibit atypical personalities, or indeed to the very idea that individual psychological factors may play a role in politically violent behaviour. A related conundrum is the likely differences in motives between those participating in different forms of political aggression, as well as the likely heterogeneity of motives among those participating in similar extremist actions. This heterogeneity belies any universal psychology of terrorism. Nonetheless, the field increasingly exhibits signs of maturity, with earnest scholars hard at work untangling fragile threads of evidence to better understand the complex warp and weave of extremist psychology.

We arrive at five conclusions from our review of this disparate literature. These five conclusions, insofar as they may be helpful to future efforts, might be characterized as a third way – a mediator's position that acknowledges the strengths of multiple arguments but asks for participants to attend to that which deserves agreement.

First, there is more consensus among authorities than some writings might imply. The majority of contributors now agree that both individual and group factors, both dispositional and circumstantial factors, play a role in the genesis of terrorist behaviour.

Second, much of the challenge of finding a consensus framework seems to arise from a straightforward error in conceptualization. Terrorism is not a psychological condition, like depression or schizophrenia. Terrorism is simply a rare form of aggression. As Alex Schmid has put it (2005, personal communication), 'why all this fuss about the psychology of terrorism? Isn't it a tactic, like Blitzkrieg? We don't try to analyze the psychology of Blitzkrieg'. It is obviously futile to seek a single, simple, uniform psychological trait explaining the cognitions, attitudes and behaviors of those who employ a given conflict tactic. Yet, observing the extreme rarity of the behaviour, we recognize the potential fruitfulness of systematic inquiries to determine whether individuals with different traits might be more prone to commit such extraordinary acts. A substantial body of research confirms that people with different experiences, personalities and cognitive styles tend to end up on different life paths, including risky ones (e.g. Ackerman and Heggestad, 1997; Alvi et al., 1988; Brown, Lum and Voyle, 1997; Burton and Topham, 1997; Chusmir, 1990; Goma-i-Freixanet and Wismeijer, 2002; Gudjonsson and Adlam, 1983; Harrison, 1998; Lorr and Strack, 1994; Lounsbury, Hutchens and Loveland, 2005; Low et al., 2005; Oakland et al., 2001; Rubenstein, 2006; Schwartz and Bilsky, 1987; Spokane, 1985; Wertheim, Widom and Wortzel, 1978; Woolnough and Guo, 1997). This massive body of research speaks volumes against the notion that the tiny minority who choose a very atypical life course, such as becoming terrorists, have nothing in common. Scholars of terrorism can work to discover factors that, among a group sharing a political grievance, help predict those who will be silent sufferers, peaceful protestors or plotting bombers.

Third, many accounts of the psychology of terrorism treat terrorism as a unitary phenomenon and terrorists as a particular species of actors. Osama bin Laden was a multi-millionaire terrorist and his behaviour was attributable to one individual psychology. His driver, Salim Hamdan, was a $200 per month lackey convicted of providing material support, and his participation in al-Qaeda is probably attributable to a different psychology. Thus, not only is terrorism not a psychological disorder, trait or condition, but the motives for and expected outcomes from participation in this conflict tactic surely vary contextually/historically/geographically. One should eschew the literature that treats terrorists as if they were a homogeneous class.

Fourth, there is nothing whatsoever incompatible about stating that: (a) certain innate predispositions and/or early experiences represent plausible risk factors for participation in terrorism; and (b) ideological, sociological, political, cultural, historical, economic and social contexts are important. The either/or debate is as embarrassing to the discipline of psychology as the nature-versus-nurture debates of the 1950s and 1960s. Surely one can transcend this debate and employ theoretically open-minded impartial data analysis in the interest of progress and security. What seems to be required is a transdisciplinary approach. For practical academic reasons, most contributors will focus on one piece of this multi-dimensional puzzle. But awareness of the virtues of other conceptual approaches and enthusiasm for figuring out how that one piece fits into the whole – for instance, by novel collaborations across often Balkanized academic domains, by methodologically rigorous controls for potential confounding factors and by humility in the face of complexity – may accelerate progress.

Fifth, even if the discipline overcame its preoccupation with theoretical polarities, and even if one overcame the obvious practical barriers to obtaining the type of data common to other social science research, one must have modest expectations regarding the application of psychological insights to solving the problem of terrorism. As Merari has stated (personal communication, 2003), there is no psychological solution to terrorism, only a political solution. Advances in psychological knowledge are well worth seeking. With sufficient funding of creative data gathering and analytic strategies, new scientific discoveries may inform multiple aspects of the struggle against violent extremism. Knowing that certain psycho-social-economic-political risk factors favour a greater number of individuals joining the ranks of terrorists groups, policy-makers might be better able to choose terror-damping alternatives. But that requires a step that does not always occur: the translation of social science knowledge into policy.

References

Abrams, D. and Hogg, M.A. (1990). *Social Identity Theory: Constructive and Critical Advances*. London: Harvester Wheatsheaf.

Ackerman, P.L. and Beier, M.E. (2003). 'Intelligence, personality, and interests in the career choice process'. *Journal of Career Assessment*, 11, 205–18.

Ackerman, P.L. and Heggestad, E.D. (1997). 'Intelligence, personality, and interests: evidence for overlapping traits'. *Psychological Bulletin*, 121, 219–45.

Adler, A. B., Castro, C.A., and Britt, T.W. (2006). *Military Life: The Psychology of Serving in Peace and Combat: Operational Stress*, vol. 2. Westport, CT: Praeger Security International.

Adorno, T.W., Frenkel-Brunswik, E., Levinson, D.J. and Sanford, R.N. (1950). *The Authoritarian Personality*. New York: Harper.

Ali, F. and Post, J. (2008). 'The history and evolution of martyrdom in the service of defensive jihad: an analysis of suicide bombers in current conflicts'. *Social Research*, 75, 615–54.

Altemeyer, B. (1998). 'The other "Authoritarian personality"', in M.P. Zanna (ed.), *Advances in Experimental Social Psychology*, vol. 30. New York: Academic Press, 47–91.

Alvi, S.A., Khan, S.B., Hussain, M.A. and Baig, T. (1988). 'The relationship between Holland's typology and cognitive styles'. *International Journal of Psychology*, 23, 449–59.

Archer, J. and Browne, K. (1989). *Human Aggression: Naturalistic Approaches*. New York: Routledge.

Atran, S. (2008). 'Who becomes a terrorist today?' *Perspectives on Terrorism*, 2, http://www.terrorismanalysts.com/pt/index.php?option=com_rokzineandview=articleandid=37andItemid=54 [accessed 25 June 2012].

Averill, J.R. (1982). *Anger and Aggression: An Essay on Emotion*. New York: Springer Verlag.

Bandura, A. (1986). *Social Foundations of Thought and Action: A Social Cognitive Theory*. Englewood Cliffs, NJ: Prentice Hall.

Bandura, A. (1990). 'Mechanisms of moral disengagement', in W. Reich (ed.), *Origins of Terrorism: Psychologies, Ideologies, Theologies, States of Mind*. New York: Cambridge University Press; Woodrow Wilson International Center for Scholars, 161–91.

Barash, D.P. (2000). *Understanding Violence*. New York: Allyn & Bacon.

Barling, J., Dupré, K.E. and Kelloway, E.K. (2009). 'Predicting workplace aggression and violence'. *Annual Review of Psychology*, 60, 671–92.

Baron, R.A. and Richardson, D.R. (2004). *Human Aggression*, 2nd edn. New York: Springer.

Batson, C.D., Kennedy, C.L., Nord, L-A., Stocks, E.L., Fleming, D.A., Marzette, C.M., Lishner, D.A., Hayes, R.E., Kolchinsky, L.M. and Zerger, T. (2007). 'Anger at unfairness: is it moral outrage?' *European Journal of Social Psychology*, 37, 1272–85.

Bloom, M. (2007). *Dying to Kill: The Allure of Suicide Terror*. New York: Columbia University Press.

Borum, R. (2004). *Psychology of Terrorism*. Tampa, FL: University of South Florida Press.

Bourke, J. (2000). *An Intimate History of Killing: Face-to-Face Killing in Twentieth-Century Warfare*. New York: Basic Books.

Bourke, J. (2001). 'The emotions in war: fear and the British and American military, 1914–45'. *Historical Research*, 74, 314–30.
Braungart, R.G. and Braungart, M.M. (1992). 'From protest to terrorism: the case of SDS and the weathermen', in D. della Porta (ed.), *Social Movements and Violence: Participation in Underground Organizations*. Greenwich, CT: JAI Press, 45–78.
Britt, T.W., Castro, C.A. and Adler, A.B. (2006). *Military Life: The Psychology of Serving in Peace and Combat: Military Performance*, vol. 1. Westport, CT: Praeger Security International.
Brooks, D. (2002). 'The culture of martyrdom'. *Atlantic Monthly*, 289, 18–20.
Brown, M.T., Lum, J.L. and Voyle, K. (1997). 'Roe revisited: a call for the reappraisal of the theory of personality development and career choice'. *Journal of Vocational Behaviour*, 51, 283–94.
Burton, M. and Topham, D. (1997). 'Early loss experiences in psychotherapists, Church of England clergy, patients assessed for psychotherapy, and scientists and engineers'. *Psychotherapy Research*, 7, 275–300.
Butler, M. and Maruna, S. (2009). 'The impact of disrespect on prisoners' aggression: outcomes of experimentally inducing violence-supportive cognitions'. *Psychology, Crime and Law*, 15, 235–50.
Camerer, C.F. (2003). *Behavioural Game Theory: Experiments in Strategic Interaction*. New York: Russell Sage Foundation.
Canetti, D. and Pedahzur, A. (2002). 'The effects of contextual and psychological variables in extreme right-wing sentiments'. *Social Behaviour and Personality*, 30, 317–34.
Cashman, G. (1993). *What Causes War?: An Introduction to Theories of International Conflict*. Lanham, MD: Lexington Books.
Caspi, A., McClay, J., Moffitt, T.E., Mill, J., Martin, J., Craig, I.W. et al. (2002). 'Role genotype in the cycle of violence in maltreated children'. *Science*, 297, 851–4.
Cassel, E. and Bernstein, D.A. (2007). *Criminal Behaviour*, 2nd edn. Mahwah, NJ: Lawrence Erlbaum.
Christakis, N.A. and Fowler, J.H. (2008). 'The collective dynamics of smoking in a large social network'. *New England Journal of Medicine*, 358, 2249–58.
Chusmir, L.H. (1990). 'Men who make nontraditional career choices'. *Journal of Counseling and Development*, 69, 11–16.
Cooper, H.H.A. (1977). 'What is a terrorist? A psychological perspective'. *Legal Medical Quarterly*, 1, 16–32.
Crayton, J.W. (1983). 'Terrorism and the psychology of the self', in L.Z. Freedman and Y. Alexander (eds), *Perspectives on Terrorism*. Wilmington, Delaware: Scholarly Resources Inc., 33–41.
Crenshaw, M. (1990). 'The logic of terrorism: terrorist behaviour as a product of strategic choice', in W. Reich (ed.), *Origins of Terrorism: Psychologies, Ideologies, Theologies, States of Mind*. Washington DC: The Woodrow Wilson Center Press, 7–24.
Crenshaw, M. (2000). 'The psychology of terrorism: an agenda for the 21st century'. *Political Psychology*, 21, 405–20.

Crocker, J. and Luhtanen, R. (1990). 'Collective self-esteem and ingroup bias'. *Journal of Personality and Social Psychology*, 58, 60–67.
Davis, J.A. (1959). 'A formal interpretation of the theory of relative deprivation'. *Sociometry*, 22, 280–96.
Decker, S.H. and Curry, G.D. 'Addressing key features of gang membership: measuring the involvement of young members'. *Journal of Criminal Justice*, 28, 473–82.
Demoulin, S., Saroglou, V. and Van Pachterbeke, M. (2008). 'Infra-humanizing others, supra-humanizing gods: the emotional hierarchy'. *Social Cognition*, 26, 235–47.
Detrick, P., Chibnall, J.T. and Rosso, M. (2001). 'Minnesota Multiphasic Personality Inventory-2 in police officer selection: normative data and relation to the Inwald Personality Inventory'. *Professional Psychology: Research and Practice*, 32, 484–90.
Dollard, J., Doob, L.W., Miller, N.E., Mowrer, O.H. and Sears, R.R. (1939). *Frustration and Aggression*. New Haven, CT: Yale University Press.
Downes, D.M. and Rock, P.E. (2007). *Understanding Deviance: A Guide to the Sociology of Crime and Rule-Breaking*, 5th edn. New York: Oxford University Press.
Eitle, D., Gunkel, S. and Van Gundy, K. 'Cumulative exposure to stressful life events and male gang membership'. *Journal of Criminal Justice*, 32, 95–111.
Enders, W. and Sandler, T. (2000). 'Is transnational terrorism becoming more threatening? A time-series investigation'. *Journal of Conflict Resolution*, 307–32.
Englander, E.K. (2003). *Understanding Violence*, 2nd edn. Mahwah, NJ: Lawrence Erlbaum.
Epley, N., Waytz, A. and Cacioppo, J.T. (2007). 'On seeing human: a three-factor theory of anthropomorphism'. *Psychological Review*, 114, 864–86.
Etain, B., Henry, C., Bellivier, F., Mathieu, F. and Leboyer, M. (2008). 'Beyond genetics: childhood affective trauma in bipolar disorder'. *Bipolar Disorders*, 10, 867–76.
Ethier, K.A. and Deaux, K. (1994). 'Negotiating social identity when contexts change: maintaining identification and responding to threat'. *Journal of Personality and Social Psychology*, 67, 243–51.
Eubank, W.L. and Weinberg, L. (2001). 'Terrorism and democracy: perpetrators and victims'. *Terrorism and Political Violence*, 13, 155–64.
Fearon, J.D. and Laitin, D.D. (2003). 'Ethnicity, insurgency, and civil war'. *American Political Science Review*, 97, 75–90.
Ferracuti, F. and Bruno, F. (1981). 'Psychiatric aspects of terrorism in Italy', in J.L. Barak and C.R. Huff (eds), *The Mad, the Bad and the Different: Essays in Honor of Simon Dinitz* Lexington, MA: Lexington Books, 179–213.
Fibert, Z. and Ressler, W.H. (1998). 'Intolerance of ambiguity and political orientation among Israeli university students'. *Journal of Social Psychology*, 138, 33–40.
Forbes, G., Zhang, X., Doroszewicz, K. and Haas, K. (2009). 'Relationships between individualism-collectivism, gender, and direct or indirect aggression: a study in China, Poland, and the US'. *Aggressive Behaviour*, 35, 24–30.

Fountoulakis, K.N., Leucht, S. and Kaprinis, G.S. (2008). 'Personality disorders and violence'. *Current Opinion in Psychiatry*, 21, 84–92.
Frenkel-Brunswik, E. (1949). 'Intolerance of ambiguity as an emotional and perceptual personality variable'. *Journal of Personality*, 18, 108–43.
Gabriel, R.A. (1988). *The Painful Field: The Psychiatric Dimension of Modern War*. New York: Greenwood Press.
Gagnon, A. and Bourhis, R.Y. (1996). 'Discrimination in the minimal group paradigm: social identity or self-interest?' *Personality and Social Psychology Bulletin*, 22, 1289–301.
Gallup World Poll. (2009). http://www.gallup.com/consulting/worldpoll/24046/About.aspx?CSTS=ADhp&to=SERVIC-Gallup-World-Poll [accessed 25 June 2012].
Geen, R.G. (2001). *Human Aggression*, 2nd edn. Buckingham and Philadelphia: Open University Press.
Geller, D.S. and Singer, J.D. (1998). *Nations at War: A Scientific Study of International Conflict*. Cambridge: Cambridge University Press.
Goldman, E. (1930). *The Psychology of Political Violence*. Indore City, India: Modern Publishers.
Goma-i-Freixanet, M. and Wismeijer, A.A.J. (2002). 'Applying personality theory to a group of police bodyguards: a physically risky prosocial prototype?' *Psicothema*, 14, 387–92.
Goodman, M., New, A. and Siever, L. (2004). 'Trauma, genes, and the neurobiology of personality disorders'. *Annals of the New York Academy of Sciences*, 1032, 104–16.
Gottschalk, M. and Gottschalk, S. (2004). 'Authoritarianism and pathological hatred: a social psychological profile of the Middle Eastern terrorist'. *The American Sociologist*, 35, 38–59.
Grant, P.R. and Brown, R. (1995). 'From ethnocentrism to collective protest: responses to relative deprivation and threats to social identity'. *Social Psychology Quarterly*, 58, 195–212.
Grossman, D. (1995). *On Killing: The Psychological Cost of Learning to Kill in War and Society*. Boston, MA: Back Bay Books.
Grossman, D. and Christensen, L.W. (2008). *On Combat: The Psychology and Physiology of Deadly Conflict in War and in Peace*, 3rd edn. Illinois: Warrior Science Publications.
Gudjonsson, G.H. and Adlam, K.R.C. (1983). 'Personality patterns of British police officers'. *Personality and Individual Differences*, 4, 507–12.
Gurr, T.R. (1970). *Why Men Rebel*. Princeton, NJ: Princeton University Press.
Gurr, T.R. (2006). 'Economic factors', in L. Richardson (ed.), *The Roots of Terrorism*. New York: Routledge, 85–102.
Hacker, F.J. (1976). *Crusaders, Criminals, Crazies: Terror and Terrorism in our Time*. New York: Norton.
Hafez, M.M. (2007). 'Martyrdom mythology in Iraq: how jihadists frame suicide terrorism in videos and biographies'. *Terrorism & Political Violence*, 19, 95–115.
Hare, R.D. (2006). 'Psychopathy: a clinical and forensic overview'. *Psychiatric Clinics of North America*, 29.

Harris, L.T. and Fiske, S.T. (2007). 'Social groups that elicit disgust are differentially processed in mPFC'. *Social Cognitive and Affective Neuroscience*, 2, 45–51.

Harrison, W.A. (1998). 'The occupations of drunk drivers: using occupational information to identify targetable characteristics of offenders'. *Accident Analysis and Prevention*, 30, 119–32.

Heide, K.M. and Solomon, E.P. (2006). 'Biology, childhood trauma, and murder: rethinking justice'. *International Journal of Law and Psychiatry*, 29, 220–33.

Heim, C., Newport, D.J., Mletzko, T., Miller, A.H. and Nemeroff, C.B. (2008). 'The link between childhood trauma and depression: insights from HPA axis studies in humans'. *Psychoneuroendocrinology*, 33, 693–710.

Hill, K.G., Howell, J.C., Hawkins, J.D. and Battin-Pearson, S.R. (1999). 'Childhood risk factors for adolescent gang membership: results from the Seattle social development project'. *Journal of Research in Crime and Delinquency*, 36, 300–322.

Hogg, M.A. and Abrams, D. (1998). *Social Identifications: A Social Psychology of Intergroup Relations and Group Processes*. London and New York: Routledge.

Hogg, M.A., Terry, D.J. and White, K.M. (1995). 'A tale of two theories: a critical comparison of identity theory with social identity theory'. *Social Psychology Quarterly*, 58, 255–69.

Horgan, J. (2005). *The Psychology of Terrorism*. London and New York: Routledge.

Hymans, J.E.C. (2006). *The Psychology of Nuclear Proliferation: Identity, Emotions, and Foreign Policy*. New York: Cambridge University Press.

Inciardi, J.A. (2003). 'The American bandit', in M. Silberman (ed.), *Violence and Society: A Reader*. Upper Saddle River, NJ: Prentice Hall/Pearson Education, 312–25.

Jäger, H., Schmidtchen, G. and Siillwold, L. (1981). *Analysen zum terrorismus* [*Analysis of Terrorism*]. Oplanden: Verlag.

Johnston, D.A. (1978). 'Psychological observations of bank robbery'. *American Journal of Psychiatry*, 135, 1377–9.

Jost, J.T., Glaser, J., Kruglanski, A.W. and Sulloway, F.J. (2003). 'Political conservatism as motivated social cognition'. *Psychological Bulletin*, 129, 339–75.

Juergensmeyer, M. (2003). *Terror in the Mind of God: The Global Rise of Religious Violence*. Berkeley, CA: University of California Press.

Juergensmeyer, M. (2008). 'Martyrdom and sacrifice in a time of terror'. *Social Research: An International Quarterly*, 75, 417–34.

Kelly, E. (1901). *Government or Human Evolution*, vol. II, *Individualism and Collectivism*. Oxford: Longman.

Kirsch, L.G. and Becker, J.V. (2007). 'Emotional deficits in psychopathy and sexual sadism: Implications for violent and sadistic behaviour'. *Clinical Psychology Review*, 27, 904–22.

Krueger, A.B. and Maleckova, J. (2003). 'Education, poverty and terrorism: is there a causal connection?' *Journal of Economic Perspectives*, 17, 119–44.

Krueger, A.B. and Maleckova, J. (2009). 'Attitudes and action: public opinion and the occurrence of international terrorism'. *Science*, 325, 1534–6.

Laqueur, W. (1987). *The Age of Terrorism*. Boston, MA: Little Brown and Company.

Li, Q. (2005). 'Does democracy promote or reduce transnational terrorist incidents?' *Journal of Conflict Resolution*, 49, 278–97.

Li, Q. and Schaub, D. (2004). 'Economic globalization and transnational terrorism: a pooled time-series analysis'. *Journal of Conflict Resolution*, 48, 230–58.

Liht, J., Suedfeld, P. and Krawczyk, A. (2005). 'Integrative complexity in face-to-face negotiations between the Chiapas guerrillas and the Mexican government'. *Political Psychology*, 26, 543–52.

Lindner, E. (2006). *Making Enemies: Humiliation and International Conflict.* Westport, CT: Praeger Security International.

Locicero, A. and Sinclair, S.J. (2008). 'Terrorism and terrorist leaders: insights from developmental and ecological psychology'. *Studies in Conflict and Terrorism*, 31, 227–50.

Lorentz, K. (1963). *On Aggression*. New York: MFJ Books.

Lorr, M. and Strack, S. (1994). 'Personality profiles of police candidates'. *Journal of Clinical Psychology*, 50, 200–207.

Lounsbury, J.W., Hutchens, T. and Loveland, J.M. (2005). 'An investigation of big five personality traits and career decidedness among early and middle adolescents'. *Journal of Career Assessment*, 13, 25–39.

Low, K.S.D., Yoon, M., Roberts, B.W. and Rounds, J. (2005). 'The stability of vocational interests from early adolescence to middle adulthood: a quantitative review of longitudinal studies'. *Psychological Bulletin*, 131, 713–37.

McCauley, C. (2007). 'Psychological issues in understanding terrorism and the response to terrorism', in B.M. Bongar, L.M. Brown, L.E. Beutler, J.N. Breckenridge and P.G. Zimbardo (eds), *The Psychology of Terrorism*. Oxford: Oxford University Press, 13–31.

McKnight, G. (1974). *The Mind of the Terrorist*. London: Michael Joseph.

Merari, A. (2005). 'Social, organizational and psychological factors in suicide terrorism', in T. Bjorgo (ed.), *Root Causes of Terrorism: Myths, Reality and Ways Forward*. London and New York: Routledge, 70–86.

Milgram, S. (1963). 'Behavioural study of obedience'. *Journal of Abnormal and Social Psychology*, 67, 371–8.

Milgram, S. (1974). *Obedience to Authority: An Experimental View*. New York: HarperCollins.

Moghadam, A. (2003). 'Palestinian suicide terrorism in the second intifada: motivations and organizational aspects'. *Studies in Conflict & Terrorism*, 26, 65–92.

Moghaddam, F.M. (2006). *From the Terrorists' Point of View: What They Experience and Why They Come to Destroy*. Westport, CT: Praeger Security International.

Montagu, A. (1976). *The Nature of Human Aggression*. New York: Oxford University Press.

Moon, B., Blurton, D. and McCluskey, J.D. (2008). 'General strain theory and delinquency: focusing on the influences of key strain characteristics on delinquency'. *Crime and Delinquency*, 54, 582–613.

Moyer, K.E. (1976). *The Psychobiology of Aggression*. New York: Harper & Row.

Nadelson, T. (2005). *Trained to Kill: Soldiers at War*. Baltimore, MD: Johns Hopkins University Press.

Nash, J.F. (1950). 'The bargaining problem'. *Econometrica*, 18, 155–62.
Neumann, J.V. and Morgenstern, O. (1944). *The Theory of Games and Economic Behaviour*. Princeton, NJ: Princeton University Press.
Niehoff, D. (1999). *The Biology of Violence*. New York: Free Press.
Oakland, T., Stafford, M.E., Horton, C.B. and Glutting, J.J. (2001). 'Temperament and vocational preferences: age, gender, and racial-ethnic comparisons using the student styles questionnaire'. *Journal of Career Assessment*, 9, 297–314.
Oreg, S., Bayazit, M., Vakola, M., Arciniega, L., Armenakis, A., Barkauskiene, R. et al. (2008). 'Dispositional resistance to change: measurement equivalence and the link to personal values across 17 nations'. *Journal of Applied Psychology*, 93, 935–44.
Palestinian Center for Policy and Survey Research. (2009). Palestinian public opinion poll no. 33; 13–15 August 2009, http://www.pcpsr.org/survey/polls/2009/p33e1.html [accessed 25 June 2012].
Pearlstein, R.M. (1991). *The Mind of the Political Terrorist*. Wilmington, DE: Scholarly Resources Inc.
Petit, G.S. (1997). 'The developmental course of violence and aggression: mechanisms of family and peer influence'. *Psychiatric Clinics of North America*, 20(2), 283–99.
Pew Global Attitudes Research Project. (2006). 'Muslims in Europe: economic worries top concerns about religious and cultural identity few signs of backlash from Western Europeans', http://pewglobal.org/reports/display.php?ReportID=254 [accessed 25 June 2012].
Post, J., Sprinzak, E. and Denny, L. (2003). 'The terrorists in their own words: interviews with 35 incarcerated Middle Eastern terrorists'. *Terrorism and Political Violence*, 15, 171–84.
Post, J.M. (2000). 'Terrorist on trial: the context of political crime'. *Journal of the American Academy of Psychiatry and the Law Online*, 28, 171–8.
Post, J.M. (2009). 'Reframing of martyrdom and jihad and the socialization of suicide terrorists'. *Political Psychology*, 30, 381–5.
Post, J.M., Ali, F., Henderson, S.W., Shanfield, S., Victoroff, J. and Weine, S. (2009). 'The psychology of suicide terrorism'. *Psychiatry: Interpersonal and Biological Processes*, 72, 13–31.
Pratto, F. and Glasford, D.E. (2008). 'Ethnocentrism and the value of a human life'. *Journal of Personality and Social Psychology*, 95, 1411–28.
Pratto, F., Sidanius, J., Stallworth, L.M. and Malle, B.F. (1994). 'Social dominance orientation: a personality variable predicting social and political attitudes'. *Journal of Personality and Social Psychology*, 67, 741–63.
Pyszczynski, T., Rothschild, Z. and Abdollahi, A. (2008). 'Terrorism, violence, and hope for peace: a terror management perspective'. *Current Directions in Psychological Science*, 17, 318–22.
Rice, S.K. (2009) 'Emotions and terrorism research: a case for a social-psychological agenda'. *Journal of Criminal Justice*, 37, 248–55.
Richardson, L. (2006). *What Terrorists Want: Understanding the Enemy, Containing the Threat*. New York: Random House.
Rizzo, M. (2003). 'Why do children join gangs?' *Journal of Gang Research*, 11, 65–75.

Robins, R.S. and Post, J.M. (1997). *Political Paranoia: The Psychopolitics of Hatred*. New Haven, CT: Yale University Press.
Rokeach, M. (1960). *The Open and Closed Mind*. New York: Basic Books.
Rosendorff, B.P. and Sandler, T. (2005). 'The political economy of transnational terrorism'. *Journal of Conflict Resolution*, 49, 171–82.
Rosenfeld, R. and Fornango, R. (2007). 'The impact of economic conditions on robbery and property crime: the role of consumer sentiment'. *Criminology*, 45, 735–69.
Rubinstein, G. (2006). 'Authoritarianism among border police officers, career soldiers, and airport security guards at the Israeli border'. *Journal of Social Psychology*, 146, 751–61.
Runciman, W.G. (1966). *Relative Deprivation and Social Justice: A Study of Attitudes to Social Inequality in Twentieth-Century England*. Berkeley, CA: University of California Press.
Sageman, M. (2008). *Leaderless Jihad: Terror Networks in the Twenty-First Century*. Philadelphia: University of Pennsylvania Press.
Schelling, T.C. (1960). *The Strategy of Conflict*. Cambridge, MA: Harvard University Press.
Scherer, K.R., Abeles, R.P. and Fischer, C.S. (1975). *Human Aggression and Conflict: Interdisciplinary Perspectives*. Oxford: Prentice.Hall.
Schmid, A.P. and Jongman, A.J. (1988). *Political Terrorism: A New Guide to Actors, Authors, Concepts, Data Bases, Theories, and Literature*. Amsterdam: North Holland.
Schwaner, S.L. (2000). 'Stick 'em up, buddy': robbery, lifestyle, and specialization within a cohort of parolees'. *Journal of Criminal Justice*, 28, 371–84.
Schwartz, S.H. and Bilsky, W. (1987). 'Toward a universal psychological structure of human values'. *Journal of Personality and Social Psychology*, 53, 550–62.
Selg, H. (1975). *The Making of Human Aggression: A Psychological Approach*. New York: St Martin's Press.
Shalit, B. (1988). *The Psychology of Conflict and Combat*. New York: Praeger.
Sherman, J.W., Kruschke, J.K., Sherman, S.J., Percy, E.J., Petrocelli, J.V. and Conrey, F.R. (2009). 'Attentional processes in stereotype formation: a common model for category accentuation and illusory correlation'. *Journal of Personality and Social Psychology*, 96, 305–23.
Sidanius, J. (1978). 'Intolerance of ambiguity and socio-politico ideology: a multidimensional analysis'. *European Journal of Social Psychology*, 8, 215–35.
Sidanius, J. (1985). 'Cognitive functioning and sociopolitical ideology revisited'. *Political Psychology*, 6, 637–61.
Sidanius, J. and Pratto, F. (1999). *Social Dominance: An Intergroup Theory of Social Hierarchy and Oppression*. New York: Cambridge University Press.
Siddle, B.K. (1995). *Sharpening the Warrior's Edge: The Psychology and Science of Training*. Millstadt, IL: PPCT Research Publications.
Silke, A. (1998). 'Cheshire-cat logic: the recurring theme of terrorist abnormality in psychological research'. *Psychology, Crime & Law*, 4, 51–69.
Slavicek, D.J. (2008). 'Deconstructing the Shariatic justification of suicide bombings'. *Studies in Conflict and Terrorism*, 31, 553–71.

Smart Richman, L. and Leary, M.R. (2009). 'Reactions to discrimination, stigmatization, ostracism, and other forms of interpersonal rejection: a multimotive model'. *Psychological Review*, 116, 365–83.

Smelser, N.J. and Mitchell, F. (2002). *Terrorism: Perspectives from the Behavioural and Social Sciences*. Washington DC: National Academy Press.

Smithers, A.G. and Lobley, D.M. (1978). 'Dogmatism, social attitudes and personality'. *British Journal of Social and Clinical Psychology*, 17, 135–42.

Speckhard, A. and Ahkmedova, K. (2006). 'The making of a martyr: Chechen suicide terrorism'. *Studies in Conflict & Terrorism*, 29, 429–92.

Spokane, A.R. (1985). 'A review of research on personality congruence in Holland's theory of careers'. *Journal of Vocational Behaviour*, 26, 305–43.

Staub, E. (2004). 'Understanding and responding to group violence: genocide, mass killing, and terrorism', in F.M. Moghaddam and A.J. Marsella (eds), *Understanding Terrorism: Psychosocial Roots, Consequences, and Interventions*. Washington DC: American Psychological Association, 151–68.

Stern, J. (2003). *Terror in the Name of God: Why Religious Militants Kill*. New York: Ecco.

Stoessinger, J.G. (2005). *Why Nations Go to War*. Belmont, CA: Thomson Wadsworth.

Stoff, D.M. and Cairns, R.B. (1996). *Aggression and Violence*. Hillsdale, NJ: Lawrence Erlbaum.

Storr, A. (1968). *Human Aggression*. New York: Atheneum.

Stouffer, S.A., Suchman, E.A., DeVinney, L.C., Star, S.A. and Williams Jr., R.B. (1949). *The American Soldier: Adjustment during Army Life*, vol. 1. Princeton, NJ: Princeton University Press.

Tajfel, H. (1972). 'La categorization sociale' ['Social categorization'], in S. Moscovici (ed.), *Introduction a la psychologie sociale*, vol. 1. Paris: Larousse.

Tajfel, H. (1981). *Human Groups and Social Categories: Studies in Social Psychology*. Cambridge: Cambridge University Press.

Tajfel, H. and Turner, J. (1979). 'An integrative theory of intergroup conflict', in W.G. Austin and S. Worchel (eds), *The Social Psychology of Intergroup Relations*. Monterey, CA: Brooks-Cole, 94–109.

Taylor, M. (1988). *The Terrorist*. London: Brassey's Inc.

Taylor, M. (1991). *The Fanatics: A Behavioural Approach to Political Violence*. London: Brassey's Inc.

Taylor, M. and Quayle, E. (1994). *Terrorist Lives*. London: Brassey's Inc.

Tetlock, P.E. (1983). 'Cognitive style and political ideology'. *Journal of Personality and Social Psychology*, 45, 118–26.

Tetlock, P.E. (1984). 'Cognitive style and political belief systems in the British House of Commons'. *Journal of Personality and Social Psychology*, 46, 365–75.

Thorisdottir, H., Jost, J.T., Liviatan, I. and Shrout, P.E. (2007). 'Psychological needs and values underlying left-right political orientation: cross-national evidence from Eastern and Western Europe'. *Public Opinion Quarterly*, 71, 175–203.

Triandis, H.C. (1988). 'Collectivism vs. individualism: a reconceptualization of a basic concept in cross-cultural psychology'. *Cross-cultural Studies of Personality, Attitudes, and Cognition*, 60–95.

Triandis, H.C. (1995). *Individualism and Collectivism: New Directions in Social Psychology*. Boulder, CO: Westview Press.

Turner, J.C. (1985). 'Social categorization and the self-concept: a social cognitive theory of group behaviour'. *Advances in Group Processes*, 2, 77–121.

Van Winkel, R., Stefanis, N.C. and Myin-Germeys, I. (2008). 'Psychosocial stress and psychosis. A review of the neurobiological mechanisms and the evidence for gene-stress interaction'. *Schizophrenia Bulletin*, 34, 1095–105.

Victoroff, J. (2005). 'The mind of the terrorist: a review and critique of psychological approaches'. *Journal of Conflict Resolution*, 49, 3–42.

Victoroff, J. and Adelman, J.R. (2008). 'Ingroup relations, prejudice reduction, and the threat of jihadi violence. In the changing face of terrorism: suicide terrorism and radicalization in emigre populations'. Paper presented at the American Psychiatric Association Annual Meeting, Washington DC.

Victoroff, J., Quota, S., Celinska, B., Abu-Safieh, R.Y., Adelman, J.R. and Stern, N. (2006). 'Sympathy for terrorism: possible interaction between social, emotional, and neuroendocrine risk factors', in J. Victoroff (ed.), *Tangled Roots: Social and Psychological Factors in the Genesis of Terrorism*. Amsterdam: IOS Press, 227–34.

Vien, A. and Beech, A.R. (2006). 'Psychopathy: theory, measurement, and treatment'. *Trauma Violence & Abuse*, 7, 155–74.

Webster, D.M. and Kruglanski, A.W. (1994). 'Individual differences in need for cognitive closure'. *Journal of Personality and Social Psychology*, 67, 1049–62.

Weimann, G. and Brosius, H.B. (1988). 'The predictability of international terrorism: a time-series analysis'. *Studies in Conflict & Terrorism*, 11, 491–502.

Weinberg, L.B. and Eubank, W.L. (1994). 'Does democracy encourage terrorism?' *Terrorism and Political Violence*, 6, 417–43.

Weinberg, L.B. and Eubank, W.L. (1998). 'Terrorism and democracy: what recent events disclose'. *Terrorism and Political Violence*, 10, 108–18.

Wertheim, E.G., Widom, C.S. and Wortzel, L.H. (1978). 'Multivariate analysis of male and female professional career choice correlates'. *Journal of Applied Psychology*, 63, 234–42.

Wilson, H.W., Stover, C.S. and Berkowitz, S.J. (2009). 'Research review: the relationship between childhood violence exposure and juvenile antisocial behaviour: a meta-analytic review'. *Journal of Child Psychology and Psychiatry and Allied Disciplines*, 50, 769–79.

Woolnough, B.E. and Guo, Y. (1997). 'Factors affecting student choice of career in science and engineering: parallel studies in Australia, Canada, China, England, Japan and Portugal'. *Research in Science & Technological Education*, 15, 105–21.

Wright, R. and Decker, S.H. (1997). *Armed Robbers in Action: Stickups and Street Culture*. Boston, MA: Northeastern University Press.

The Motivation of the Irish Rebel and Resistance to the Label 'Terrorist'

Anthony McIntyre

The men of the IRA are rebels.

Sean Cronin, cited in Flynn 2009: 10

Introduction

Sean Cronin, the IRA chief of staff for part of the organisation's failed border campaign in the middle of the twentieth century, was hardly inaccurate in his depiction of IRA members as being the quintessential rebels (Flynn 2009: 10). When chants of 'up the rebels' were reported (Hart 1998: 62), it was with the IRA in mind that they were shouted and heard. While no longer in frequent use, having being displaced by the equally subversive description 'Fenian' (O'Tuama 1998), the term 'rebel' was for a long time synonymous with IRA members, and rebellion was indivisible from the body to which they belonged. The rebellious sentiment was expressed by one Provisional IRA Maze escapee, who put it thus: 'I do not recognise the Brit legitimacy in my country. I do not give a sweet fuck what the Brits in a sense impose. If it is against my will then I will rebel' (Toolis 1995: 189).

Despite the association with the IRA, the Irish rebel long predated the emergence of any of the IRAs that Ireland has come to know since the name 'Irish Republican Army' first entered the public domain (Neeson 1998: 179). Some republican narratives trace that particular rebellious specimen back more than 800 years. As the newspaper columnist Patrick Murphy (2009) points out, struggles between the rebels and the authority they have rebelled against over definition of their seditious activity have had a similar lifespan. Pejorative labelling of opponents by all sides has featured prominently throughout the centuries. It is beyond the scope of this chapter to look at the labelling strategies employed by the rebel, of which there were many; rather, its purpose is to note that rebels were the target of labelling, in particular the label 'terrorist', and to permit them to use their own voices to illustrate the dogged resistance with which they responded to such labelling. This also dovetails with an exploration of the motives of the rebel. These are invariably framed in terms which seek to dissolve the adhesive substance of the labels which their opponents try to stick onto them.

Irish rebel history can be so elongated and its acts of rebellion so frequent that a narrative focusing on the rebel has to arbitrarily select its timeframe, otherwise it risks becoming crammed with detail. This chapter will look at the motivation of the Irish rebel and the resistance to being labelled as terrorist in its more recent manifestation of the Provisional IRA. Such was the intensity – some might prefer the term ferocity – of Provisional rebellion that on a number of occasions the Provisional IRA found itself either praised or lambasted as being 'one of the world's leading revolutionary movements' (English 2003: xxv). The longevity of the Provisional IRA meant that it operated in a context where acts of political violence against established governments were so pervasive that commentators could say 'terrorism remains a condition that affects us all … It is immediate and real … terrorism has become a universal tool that is easy to use and difficult to counter' (Taylor 1993: ix). Labelling the Provisional IRA 'terrorist' was easy against such a backdrop.

A Brief Historical Overview

Rebels in Ireland have long waged violent sedition against the British presence in the country. Those most identified with rebellion in the public mind, republicans and their sympathisers, trace the history of republicanism back to its 'father' Wolfe Tone, who died in British custody in 1798 after the failed United Irishmen Rebellion (Metress 1983: 32). Since 1798, a series of events in the republican calendar has been woven into a narrative which, as it has grown and been elaborated upon, has been handed down through generations within the republican tradition. The most significant of these events have been the 1803 rebellion led by Robert Emmet, for which Emmet was executed, the activities of the Young Ireland Movement of the 1840s, the Fenian movement of the 1860s, the Easter Rising of 1916 and the War of Independence of 1919–1921 (Kee 1972). And in terms of modern Provisional republicanism, 'the IRA campaigns in Northern Ireland and Britain in the 1930s, 1940s, 1950s and 1960s provide an important line of descent' (English 2003: xxiii). Coupled with the growing list of British atrocities in the republican cultural memory, such as the famine of the 1840s and the execution of the leaders of the 1916 Rising, there has been no shortage of grievances upon which rebellious sentiment could be nourished.

At many points during their rebellious forays, the rebels went to great lengths – including the forfeiture of their own lives – to reject all attempts by the British to label them pejoratively. One famed rebel in republican folklore was the Fenian agitator Jeremiah O'Donovan Rossa, who recorded his own harsh prison experiences (O'Donovan Rossa 2007) His graveside was the site for Padraic Pearse's most influential and motivational funeral oration:

> The defenders of this realm have worked well in secret and in the open. They think that they have pacified Ireland. They think that they have purchased half of us, and intimidated the other half. They think that they have foreseen everything. They think that they have provided against everything; but the fools, the fools, the fools! They have left us our Fenian dead, and while Ireland holds these graves, Ireland unfree shall never be at peace. (Macardle 1999: 137)

Pearse's references to the Fenian dead and their graves tapped into a deep and turbulent reservoir of Irish nationalist sentiment that could often be excoriating of the rebel up until the point of death, something O'Donovan Rossa had articulated so vividly:

> The heart of the country always goes out to the man who lives and dies an unrepentant rebel. The rebel can rely upon nothing in life; he is sure to be calumniated, he is likely to be robbed, and may even be murdered but let him once go out of life, and he is sure of a fine funeral. (Cronin 1980: 90)

O'Donovan Rossa's uncompromising example and Pearse's oration have become a core part of the rebel tradition. The Provisional IRA was a recent but not the last manifestation of this tradition. As has been stated by one historian:

> They, as volunteers, in a brutal and mean crusade, are burdened by history, enhanced by past example, dedicated and determined in spite of all, because of all. All the tradition and experience and all the practice and all the old ideals. They carry with them into the IRA a past often misread, misused, misunderstood but never forgotten ... First, the never failing source of all Irish political evils has always been the English connection. This ... must be destroyed to free the nation. And, second, the only and appropriate means to do this is through physical force. (Bowyer Bell 1990: 10)

However, the events that brought the Provisional IRA into being and sustained that organisation and the rebels within its ranks are arguably much less ideological in character. This does nothing to lessen the sense of legitimate grievance that fuelled the campaign of the Provisional IRA, nor does it add ballast to British state accusations of terrorism. However, it does raise questions and invite deeper reflection about the complexity and multiplicity of motivations.

This is all the more important when it is considered that today, in the context of a peace settlement, the Provisional movement through Sinn Fein has become part of a British state administration in Ireland which it long sought to overthrow. This movement now stands virtually no chance of securing the united Ireland its volunteers killed and died in pursuit of. As one observer of the Northern Ireland conflict put it, 'Sinn Fein's vision for a United Ireland by 2016 – the 100th anniversary of the Easter Rising – is entirely illusory' (McDonald 2009). The motivations of yesteryear seem to have been abandoned as the rebels of the Provisional IRA function as poachers turned gamekeepers with their participation in the devolved administration. In order to make the flip, the rebel had to be subject to influences other than the purely traditional. Extra-republican motivations either in place of or running in tandem with those traditionally framed had to factor themselves into the interpretative framework of the rebel. As the former IRA prisoner Alex McCrory asked in stunned disbelief, how otherwise is the ability of the seemingly most militant of nationalist movements to comprehensively accomplish a volte face without massive organisational rupturing to be explained (McIntyre 1999: 441)?

There remain inward-looking groups like the Real and Continuity IRAs that are impervious to the logic of those outside their loop and who, in spite of the lessons of past failure, continue to persist in rebellious acts (Mooney and O'Toole 2003; White 2006). While they use the same motivational logic as the Provisional IRA did, there is no evidence that there has been a mass haemorrhaging from the Provisional ranks into these rival IRAs. One would expect such wholesale defection if affinity to traditional republican ideology were to trump all other factors. Seemingly, the erstwhile rebels of the Provisional IRA, rather than follow in the seditious tradition of post-Provisional republican groups, are now content to label as 'criminal' the very rebels who have filled their shoes.

One former republican prisoner, Willie Gallagher, who served in both the IRA and the Irish National Liberation Army (INLA), vented his dismay at seeing republicans who dissented from the Sinn Fein line being labelled by the party of devolved government in a manner that the British had used against the Provisional IRA. Here Gallagher faithfully echoes the critique made of the 'mimic men' in post-colonial Africa (Gourevitch 1999):

> As time went on it was more difficult to accept similar labels that other fellow republicans, who were following directives from their leadership, were attaching to those who were affiliated to smaller republican organisations. It was difficult to understand how those who suffered great injustices could in turn mete out the same injustice to others. Nowadays, as an individual, I could not care in the slightest what these people say or think in their demonisation and use of terminology to that end despite frequently challenging those involved and being vociferous in doing so. (McIntyre 2009e)

Rebel Motivation

For a long time, the historiography of the Provisional IRA was bedevilled by a simple problem. Mainstream analysis such as that of Toolis (1995) and Kelley (1988) tended to import conceptualisations from first works on the Provisional IRA in their earlier studies of pre-Provisional Irish republicanism. As historians of the pre- Provisional IRA, writers like J. Bowyer Bell (1989) and Tim Pat Coogan (1984) simply extended that earlier history to cover the Provisional period when in fact an epistemological break with what had gone before was required. Such linear continuation was inadequate. The Provisional IRA, far from being the unalloyed and uninterrupted outgrowth of the pre-1960 IRA tradition, represented a periodised insurrection located within a specific conjuncture. It was characterised more by discontinuity than continuity.

A standard explanation for the motivation of the Provisional IRA rebel in the literature was established early on and shaped subsequent perceptions. Even two-and-a-half decades later, authors writing about the IRA were still offering the same type of explanation:

> Irish republicanism is deeply embedded in the whole Irish national psyche. It is the founding philosophy of the Irish republic. It is the case to which the state's first leaders gave their lives in the 1916 Easter Rising and are now revered for their sacrifice. Its ideals, of a united Ireland, would be affirmed by every living Irish man woman and child. (Toolis 1995: 331)

This idealised version of motivation is to be found in a typical obituary one republican newspaper carried for a dead IRA volunteer:

> Volunteer Frankie Ryan was a young man who came into the republican struggle because of his deeply held political convictions that led him ... to see for himself the struggle for Irish freedom and to play his part fully in that struggle. (Toolis 1995: 271)

Thus, rebels, through the creation of powerful counter-narratives and discourses constructed around issues like prison protests (Campbell, McKeown and O'Hagan 1998) successfully avoided becoming ensnared in the 'regime of truth' (Foucault 1980: 131) that is the terrorist narrative promoted by the state. However, the question of rebel motivation is more complex than either Bowyer Bell or Toolis suggest. Explanations unmediated by extrinsic factors not within the sphere of normative republican tradition are perhaps based on what Patterson has described as a tendency to acquiesce in the republican movement's monochrome remembrance of itself (Patterson 1989: 6). In republican memory, its activists are presented as being idealists fuelled by a selfless sense of unifying their country. Missing from this account is the range of contextual motivating factors identified by Alonso (2007), namely emotional factors such as status within the community, community defence, the youthful pursuit of excitement exuberance, hatred and defiance.

Even analysts who regard the IRA as terrorists find it hard to definitively establish a motivation for that terrorism. Gupta has shown the difficulties of using profiles of terrorists to establish what motivates their behaviour. After such an exercise, he concludes that it is not possible to do so (Gupta 2008: 60).

There is no compelling tradition reason to ascribe 'old school' traditionalist motivations to the rebel at the expense of 'new school' conjunctural ones. When Taylor argues that to 'understand the "Provos" you have to look at where they came from and why' (Taylor 1997: 8), he arbitrarily selects the 1916 Easter Rising. However, given the ease with which the Provos eventually came to reject the traditional values of 1916, with their emphasis on an inviolable right to wage armed insurrection and a total rejection of British administration, it makes more sense to trace much of their origins elsewhere. As the Provisional movement morphed from a revolutionary body determined to smash the Northern Ireland state into a entity that became central to the administration of that state, the ease with which the rebel abandoned virtually all beliefs that previously motivated him and embraced beliefs he opposed to the point of resistance through arms illustrates the differentiated mosaic that is motivation.

The challenge to republicanism's one-dimensional remembrance of itself is most pronounced in those who previously populated its ranks, such as Martin McGuinness, who displays a striking lack of republican historical awareness. The standard explanation for motivation which stresses the rebels' political awareness of the need to break the connection with England, 'the never failing source of all our political evils', to cite Wolfe Tone (Boylan 1997: 17), sits uneasily alongside the motivation outlined by McGuinness, the Provisional IRA's chief of staff from 1978 to 1982 (Clarke and Johnston 2001: 103, 134):

> Suddenly people were not prepared to turn the other cheek anymore. The RUC became the enemy. The Stormont government was the enemy. I cannot say at that stage that I had worked out that the people who were responsible for all this were in Downing Street. That came later. (Toolis 1995: 301)

For McGuinness, the motivation was anchored in events on the ground rather than being shaped by some long-standing sense of historical grievance. The same was true of the Provisional IRA's most celebrated volunteer, Bobby Sands. He viewed British soldiers as heroes in his childhood days. However, this changed because of the actions of British soldiers on the streets of Belfast:

> no longer did I think of them as my childhood 'good guys', for their presence alone caused food for thought. Before I could work out the solution it was answered for me in the form of early morning raids. (Feehan 1983: 66–7)

Again, Brendan Hughes, a much-feted IRA leader, would claim:

> The Provisionals were seen as Catholic, nationalist, reactionary – and to a large extent they were. I certainly reacted to the situation. I was a Catholic and I seen the Catholic community under attack. My whole reason for joining the Provisionals at that time was not to bring about a thirty two county democratic socialist republic, and I had no ideology at that time. (Stevenson 1996: 36)

In its formative years, the Provisional IRA was associated with explosions of insurrectionary (McIntyre 1999). When volunteers enlisted in substantial numbers, their motives are often read as event-induced. The crucial events that fed the formation and growth of the Provisional IRA occurred in the first three years of the Northern Irish conflict, and each of three defining moments provides a window through which republican motivation can be viewed.

In August 1969 the British state allowed the Stormont government to manage security, which led to the police joining in armed arson attacks on nationalist communities. Many nationalists felt their lives, homes and communities were in danger and responded defensively. The difference in perception between those new rebels and the old 'keepers of the flame' was encapsulated in an encounter in 1969 between two people representative of each school. An 18 year old, Bernard Fox, seeking a gun for the purposes of protecting his family and friends, approached an IRA leader and was asked 'could you shoot a British soldier?'. Fox was shocked. 'At that time I hadn't the idea that it was the British Government's fault' (Trainor 1998).

In July 1970 the British government introduced a curfew a week after the Provisional IRA had successfully defended a small nationalist enclave in East Belfast against attack from armed loyalists while the British Army stood by and refused to intervene. The curfew republican weaponry, considered by many vulnerable nationalists as the last line of defence against conflagration, was confiscated by British troops who at the same time paraded triumphalist unionist ministers around the Lower Falls, another nationalist area. One rebel described how his rebelliousness increased as a result of this one event:

> From 1970 I had sold *Republican News* from underneath my coat outside mass but it was only after the British Army curfew of the Falls Road in July 1970 that I decided to go one step further and hold guns for the IRA. (English 2006: 370)

In August 1971 the British state introduced internment without trial. The measure alienated broad sections of the nationalist community. Rather than depleting the ranks of the IRA as the British intended, it had the opposite effect. According to Brendan Holland, who had earlier drifted into the Official IRA but left to work in England, 'leaving all the ideology aside and theory and so on, as much as we knew about it ... when internment broke out then, we left London and joined the Provisionals' (Alonso 2007: 36). Tommy McKearney describes a similar motivational urge:

> I joined the IRA in late 1971 in the months after the beginning of internment in August 1971, and I imagine that was the incident above all else that would have propelled me into the IRA, in common with hundreds if not several thousand others at the time. (Alonso 2007: 45)

In January 1972 British paratroopers launched an armed attack on unsuspecting civilians attending a demonstration in Derry, massacring 14 people in the process and injuring many others. One rebel who had by then left the IRA found himself back in its ranks in response to the British state violence of Bloody Sunday:

> I knew that I would report back to the IRA to compete for operations within days. I now definitely viewed the British forces as terrorists in my country, murdering my people, and saw violence directed against them as a moral imperative. (O'Doherty 1993: 115)

But motivation is complex, is not static and evolves over time. In his comprehensive study of rebel motivation, Alonso points out that the reasons that a person has for joining an organisation may not be the same as the reasons for remaining in it over a period of time. (Alonso 2007). Robert White (1993) found that there were four types of republicans. He divided republicans into those originating in the Republic of Ireland and those from Northern Ireland and then divided these into two types: pre-1969 and post-1969. This matrix helps address the complexity of motivation, showing how pre-1969 republicans were motivated by a sense of historical grievance anchored in a British state denial of a united Ireland. Post-1969 republicans, on the other hand, were motivated by anger at the treatment of Catholics in the northern state, coupled with British state repression on the streets, thus promoting a desire amongst these rebels to protect their community:

> From the perspective of the outsider, Provisional Irish Republicans appear to be of one mind and one objective – to continue their struggle until the British leave Ireland. Although all republicans may agree with this objective, two social conditions, the timing and geography of recruitment into Republican politics, combine to produce four blocs of Irish Republicans: pre-1969 Northern and Southern Republicans and post-1969 Northern and Southern Republicans. Within these blocs, persons share experiences, ideas and conceptions of 'Irish Republicanism', all of which builds within-bloc camaraderie. In contrast, across these blocs, experiences, ideas, and conceptions of Republicanism vary. (White 1993: 131)

While traditional rebel ideology certainly does not seem to be the primary consideration in rebel recruitment from 1969 onwards, substantial political motivations cannot be discounted. In acknowledging such motivations and seeking to understand what creates them, the ease with which rebel activity is labelled and dismissed as terrorism becomes problematic.

Terrorism

The Irish rebel struggled against the British labelling of their struggle. The label most likely to raise rebel ire was 'criminal', a term applied by the British authorities to the Irish rebel from 1916 onwards. During the rebellion that led to the establishment of the modern Irish state, 'the British government of the day did not regard the conflict as a "war" but a criminal conspiracy to be countered by the police' (Taylor 1997: 10) A republican, writing in 1971, wryly elucidated the labelling strategy: 'funny how it is that all those countries engaged in resisting rule from Britain are full of criminal types' (*Republican News* 1971).

The 'criminal' label has been the most common term applied to republican rebels in the discursive contestation. Rebel refutation of it was more difficult in the years before the IRA officially ceased to function in 2005. By then the IRA was deeply involved in activities suggesting it more closely resembled a national crime syndicate than a national liberation army: extortion, robberies, mutilations, intimidation and the occasional murder of members of its own community (*Los Angeles Times* 2005). Its indisputable thuggery after its ceasefires made it easier to make the criminal label stick, something that was all but impossible in the previous IRA era of Bobby Sands (Jordan 2009). In spite of this derogation from republican standards, the determination of rebels to refuse the 'criminal' label placed on Irish rebellion by the British state endured, in spite of the deprivations they endured while prisoners. The defiance of republican prisoners in refusing to be labelled criminal by wearing prison uniform or doing prison work culminated in the fatal hungers strikes of 1981. The struggle of the Irish rebel was a challenge not only to a physical British presence in Ireland but also to discursive labelling strategies which sought to narrate the rebel into a pejorative and derogatory interpretive framework.

Originating in the Reign of Terror of the French Revolution, terrorism as a public discourse has flourished exponentially since the 2001 al-Qaeda attack on the USA. Gupta points out that ten times the number of books with terrorism in their title were published in the six and a half years following 2000 than were published in the previous six decades (Gupta 2008: 2). Initially, those accused of being terrorists wore the label like a badge of honour rather than being repelled by it. However, when the authorities who were being rebelled against appropriated the term and loaded it with moral opprobrium, those once happy to be labelled terrorists began using other terms like 'freedom fighter' to describe themselves. 'Lehi ... the Jewish extremist group operating in the British mandate of Palestine, was perhaps the last self-identified terrorist group in history' (Gupta 2008: 5).

The British authorities, as the primary target for the aggression of the Irish rebel, have consistently attempted to depict rebellious Irish activity as something less than the result of political idealism. A very specific strategic logic has governed labelling by the British state. Resistance to British rule and republican strategies and behaviour tend to be framed in terms that legitimise British authorities and delegitimise those who rebel. Shortly after the onset of the Provisional IRA campaign, the British state assiduously managed a propaganda campaign aimed at labelling and delegitimising its armed opponents in Ireland and any element in civil society or politics that may have been prepared to 'understand' the rebels (Curtis 1998). Successive secretaries of state referred to the conflict in terms of terrorism (Rees 1985: 211; Whitelaw 1989: 95).

Throughout the Northern Irish conflict, the British use of the label 'terrorism' played a role in a wider propaganda effort to show that the IRA campaign became 'the alpha and omega of the problem' (Curtis 1998: 276) the British state faced governing Northern Ireland. The British could have used the term 'political violence', but this would not have carried the same 'pejorative overtones' (Hogan and Walker 1989: 3). Its purpose was to re-capture the imagery so graphically traced by Conrad in his novel *The Secret Agent*:

> a bloodstained inanity of so fatuous a kind that it was impossible to fathom its origins by any reasonable or even unreasonable process of thought. For

perverse unreason has its own logical processes ... one remained faced by the fact of a man blowing to bits for nothing even most remotely resembling an idea. (Conrad 1975: 9)

According to the British narrative, the rebel in the form of the IRA had 'refined terrorism into an art form' (Geraghty 1998: xiv). The Northern Ireland Office periodically 'ran extensive TV and press advertising campaigns aimed at persuading the public in the six counties to renounce "terrorism"' (Curtis 1998: 257). Even when the armed conflict had concluded, senior British officials could not resist falling back on old habits and labelling the IRA actions as 'terrorist' (Powell 2008: 29). Jonathan Powell, the British Prime Minister's chief of staff, for example, when able to write about intricate rounds of negotiations with Britain's one-time enemies and no longer apparently harbouring the same degree of hostility towards rebel leaders, persisted in using the term.

The words of Gerry Adams in 2001 demonstrate an awareness of the dangers of failing to refute the allegation of terrorism. Adams has frequently faced accusations of being a terrorist himself (Sharrock and Devenport 1997: 449) which were fuelled by his role as a former Provisional IRA chief of staff (Moloney 2002: 172). However, in his more public political role as President of Sinn Fein, he has lambasted, after the attacks of 9/11, 'ethically indefensible terrorism' (Simms 2008). With the sense of evasiveness that Adams is renowned for, he made his criticism at a time when the USA had been attacked by al-Qaeda without reference to the fact that the organisation on whose governing body he had served for decades had also engaged in wilful attacks on civilians.

That the IRA was involved in terrorism was a view advanced by one of its former volunteers who had been convicted of killing a British soldier. While he did not regard the death of the soldier as an act of terrorism, the volunteer said of some IRA attacks in England: 'I disagreed with the likes of the Birmingham bombings and Guildford bombings ... I said they were acts of terrorism' (Alonso 2007: 180).

If we accept Stepanova's definition of terrorism as 'the form of violence that most closely integrates one sided violence against civilians with asymmetrical violent confrontation against a stronger opponent, be it a state or a group of states' (Stepanova 2008: 2), it seems that only part of the IRA's campaign could be regarded as terrorist. For example, the IRA operation that wiped out numerous members of the notorious British Parachute Regiment in August 1979 would not be included in the terrorist bracket, whereas the cold-blooded execution of ten unarmed Protestant workmen in January 1976 would fit.

The application of the term 'terrorist/terrorism' is part and parcel of the war of ideas and the production of propaganda. Throughout its existence, the Provisional IRA rebels ran an effective propaganda campaign. Through their two main organs *Republican News* and *An Phoblacht* (later amalgamated as *An Phoblacht/Republican News* in 1979), they constructed a counter-narrative to that of the state. Whereas the British state categorised the Provisional IRA as terrorists, republican propaganda outlets placed great emphasis on the historical legitimacy of armed resistance against the British state. Protesting prisoners resisting the label of criminal were depicted as political rebels within a long republican tradition. The political poetry and writings of Bobby Sands featured prominently in the paper, placing both him and his struggle at the heart of the prisoners' politically rebellious resistance (Beresford: 1987: 64).

Patrick Magee, one of the IRA's most prominent volunteers, was convicted of carrying out the Brighton bombing in 1984, which came close to wiping out the British Cabinet. Magee wrote a book challenging the dominant narrative in which 'Britain's highly partial and partisan view had achieved hegemonic status' (Magee 2001: 23). So too, in a ballad written in honour of the IRA H-Block hunger Joe McDonnell, the dead man becomes the narrator and the words he utters to the British are 'and you dare to call me a terrorist' (Celtic Lyrics Collection). McDonnell's death on hunger strike along with nine of his comrades was the quintessential rejection of the label 'terrorist' and that of 'criminal', for, as O'Hearn has observed, 'at its core the protest was about legitimating armed struggle *outside* of jail' (O'Hearn 2006: 227, emphasis in original).

The voices of other former IRA combatants offer a clear narrative through which to understand their perspective on the label 'terrorism'. As one study pointed out, IRA members found the term alien. Gupta reports one IRA volunteer as saying 'to me "terrorist" is a dirty word. And I certainly don't … nor have I ever considered myself to be one' (Gupta 2008: 6).

Tommy McKearney, a former Tyrone IRA volunteer who spent 53 days on hunger strike in 1980 resisting being labelled a 'terrorist' by the British, claimed:

> It is difficult to find an agreed definition of what today constitutes 'terrorism'. The great powers too often use the term as one of convenience to undermine the status of any non-state opposition bearing against them. Nor is the glib definition that the purpose of terror is to terrorise much help either. It would, for example, be difficult to differentiate between the objectives of those, supported by the great powers, who recently bombarded civilians in Gaza and those, excoriated by the same powers, who launched missiles into Israeli settlements. A century back, Marxists tended to use the term 'terrorism' a lot more scientifically. They argued that the violent actions of small and unrepresentative groups demanding political change without the support of a significant mass of the people were terrorism. They viewed these actions dispassionately, opposing them saying that those practising it were doomed to failure and were therefore wrong. By the older definition, the Provisional IRA cannot be deemed simply to have been a terrorist organisation. They enjoyed significant popular support and while their tactics were often bloody they strove at most times (apart from some parts of their English campaign) to prevent the Northern state functioning with the objective of gaining a desired political objective. This rather than merely trying to intimidate their enemy into abandoning the field was a military strategy adopted by an insurrectionary organisation. Whether their strategy was right or wrong or whether they were morally justified in their use of force is a separate argument. (McIntyre 2009a)

Richard O'Rawe, another IRA member who endured the deprivation of the prison blanket protest alongside McKearney, compared his own armed actions to those of the French Resistance fighters during the Second World War (O'Rawe 2005):

> Having been reared within an ethos of Irish republicanism, I was conditioned to believe that it was the patriotic duty of every right-thinking Irishman to join the IRA and to fight to remove the British presence from Ireland. That may sound simplistic, but for me, there was never any ambiguity: I was a resistance fighter, similar to the resistance fighters who fought to liberate their countries from the Nazis during World War II. What I never was, nor could be, was a terrorist; that was a British propaganda term whose sole purpose was to denigrate and stigmatise their enemy (McIntyre 2009b).

Thomas Elliot, another IRA veteran of the prison blanket protest, felt it was more legitimate to attach the label 'terrorist' to the British state than to him or his comrades:

> The day following Bloody Sunday I stood on Rossville Street as a 15 year old schoolboy and stared at the blood stains that marked the various places where 13 and later 14 of Derry's sons, brothers and fathers had fallen, cut down by a wanton act of terrorism. This wasn't the actions of the IRA which the British government labelled as terrorists but the actions of the Paratroops sent by that same government to instill fear in a risen people. People who had grown up in these very streets, hemmed in by over 50 years of Unionist misrule until they could take no more. When I later joined the IRA, I didn't do so to travel to other countries and kill people for the very ground they existed on, I did so to free the people of my country from the tyranny of a foreign government. Therefore I have never been a terrorist nor a criminal or whatever they chose to label me as, but I am an Irish man who took up arms for my people. (McIntyre 2009c)

Other IRA volunteers, while acknowledging why the label 'terrorist' ought to be rejected, were not as hostile to being described in such terms. Brendan Shannon, another prison blanket protester, commented:

> Well of course we rejected the label 'terrorism'. That is because we were concerned with public opinion. We were afraid of the Brits winning the propaganda battle. We were not terrorists. That was my problem, not the labelling. I had a problem with us going to great lengths to avoid being called terrorist. I thought one of our shortcomings was that we were not terrorising the British enough. We should have been using terrorism against them. Was it Winston Churchill who once said that if you are going to be called a name you may as well benefit from being what you are called? (McIntyre 2009d)

Other IRA members expressed a sense of indifference to how they were labelled. Willie Gallagher, a former member of both the IRA and the INLA, said:

> I have always viewed labels such as 'terrorist', 'criminal', 'gangster', etc. as words which were used as weapons by political opponents in a dehumanisation campaign in order to justify whatever draconian measures they choose to adopt. During my involvement in the early 1970s it was very much straightforward regarding this type of terminology which was coming from the Brits. I simply didn't care what labels they attached to me as an individual. (McIntyre 2009e)

Yet these are ultimately not matters of indifference, as Bhatia's observation about the important strategic advantages of labelling illustrates:

> Once assigned, the power of a name is such that the process by which the name was selected generally disappears and a series of normative associations, motives and characteristics are attached to the named subject. Indeed, the long historical relationship between the naming of opponents, empire and colonialism, as well as the manner in which the global media frame armed conflict, only provide further reason to doubt the truthfulness of the names assigned, and their ability to address the micro-realities involved in these conflicts and movements. Discourse is thus a tool for armed movements and a battleground and contested space in contemporary conflicts … The actual ability to name, and to have that name accepted by an audience, holds great power. (Bhatia 2005)

Conclusion

Irish republican rebel motivation is more nuanced than is allowed for in many of the standard accounts. In substantial numbers of the orthodox accounts, an irrational motive rooted in a history with little contemporary relevance is advanced to explain their motivation and the rebel is consequently depicted as devoid of reason; armed only with irrational ideology, rebellion is portrayed as a form of violent activity which is essentially nihilistic. Framing the rebel in such a manner has obvious propaganda advantages for the governments against which rebellion is being waged.

However, it is clear from what the rebels discussed here say that such a presentation is alien to their own understanding of motivation in taking up a cause that can often lead to enormous deprivation and death for themselves and considerable anguish and grief for their families. While many of their stated motivations are not fuelled by a developed sense of political awareness or framed within a coherent ideological framework, to use that as a basis for lending credence to government labelling strategies absolves the government of its responsibility for producing the circumstances in which the transformation from peaceful citizen to rebel occurs. Basically, because motivation may have been raw and emotionally reactive rather than intellectually pondered, this does not mean that validation should be extended to British or indeed other governments' labelling strategies. As much as the rebel narrative can be contested, so too can the British state's own narrative. As much as the observer should avoid acquiescing in the rebels' one-dimensional remembrance of themselves, it should equally avoid the British government's own one-dimensional remembrance of itself.

Typically, governments aspire to mask the deeply unethical nature of their own activities, whether they involve the use of torture, massacre or collusion – as was the case with the British government – with armed loyalist opponents of the rebels who ironically were also termed 'terrorist' by the British state. Clearly, 'the term "terrorism" suffers from a terminal dose of ambiguity' (Gupta 2008: xvii). For this reason, Bhatia contends that 'many governments, both in the West and those subject to internal armed contest, cannot be relied upon responsibly and ethically to name their opponents' (Bhatia 2005).

Essentially, the rebel examined here is not in the first instance an ideological creature, but one whose rebellion was a response to events initiated by the British state. The acquisition of ideological motivation was a longer process and the extent to which it ever took hold is questioned by the general acquiescence in an outcome that was anything but republican. There is a clear dialectic between state political violence and rebellion. The state, unwilling to accept this, prefers to describe its rebellious adversaries as terrorists. It is a zero-sum game where in terms of legitimacy the state takes all and the rebel loses everything.

Sean MacStiofáin, the Provisional IRA's first chief of staff, was a man deeply steeped in the republican rebel tradition. Yet even he noted that it was not his ideological convictions and those of his comrades that fuelled the growth of the Provisional IRA, but the aggressive actions of the British state which conjured into existence a guerrilla army against itself (MacStiofáin 1975: 167). The rebels of the Provisional IRA, regardless of the movement's ideological stance, were motivated less by the presence of the British state in the North of Ireland than they were by the manner in which the British state behaved in the North. In order to address these complaints, the British state has not had to withdraw from Ireland as demanded by the traditional rebel ideology, but merely to change its behaviour. With British behaviour changed, the rebel has finally been brought to heel. However, it does not follow that his lack of a strong sense of attachment to their movement's ideology makes his rebellion any less justified or any more terroristic.

There is no particular reason for thinking that those who employ the label 'terrorist' are themselves motivated by something other than egregious values. In his work on the 1944 Normandy landings, Beevor illustrated how the armies of Nazi Germany were deeply concerned by the 'terrorists' resisting their occupation of France (Beevor 2009). Few today outside neo-Nazi circles would agree that the French armed resistance movement was comprised of terrorists.

While a definite space exists for the rebel to resist the label 'terrorist', this partly results from the absence of any agreed international definition of terrorism which suggests that those wishing to employ the term against adversaries may well be doing so in a manner which is self-serving. Each state, confronted with its own particular adversary, labels oppositional activity 'terrorist' whereby another state may highlight a different aspect of adversarial behaviour for the same label.

References

Alonso, Rogelio, 2007. *The IRA and Armed Struggle*. London: Routledge.
Beevor, Antony, 2009. *D-Day*. London: Penguin Viking.
Beresford, David, 1987. *Ten Men Dead*. London: HarperCollins.
Bhatia, Michael V, 2005. 'Fighting Words: Naming Terrorists, Bandits, Rebels and other Violent Actors' *Third World Quarterly*, 26:1, 5–22.
Bowyer Bell, J, 1989. *The Secret Army*. Dublin: Poolbeg.
Bowyer Bell, J. 1990. *IRA Tactics & Targets*. Dublin: Poolbeg.
Boylan, Henry, 1997. *Wolfe Tone*. Dublin: Gill & Macmillan.
Campbell, Brian, McKeown, Laurence and O'Hagan, Feilim, 1998. *Nor Meekly Serve My Time*. Belfast: Beyond the Pale.
Clarke, Liam and Johnston, Kathryn, 2001. *Martin McGuinness*. Edinburgh: Mainstream.
Conrad, Joseph, 1975. *The Secret Agent*. Middlesex: Penguin
Coogan, Tim Pat. 1984. *The IRA*. London: Fontana.
Cronin, Sean, 1980. *Irish Nationalism*. Dublin: Academy Press.
Curtis, Liz, 1998. *Ireland: The Propaganda War*. Belfast: Sasta.
Diary of a Walking Butterfly, 'And You Dare to Call Me a Terrorist', http://www.walkingbutterfly.com/2011/07/24/and-you-dare-to-call-me-a-terrorist/ [accessed 15 June 2012].
English, Richard, 1998. *Ernie O'Malley: IRA Intellectual*. Oxford: Clarendon.
English, Richard, 2003. *Armed Struggle*: London: Macmillan.
English, Richard, 2006. *Irish Freedom*. London: Macmillan.
Feehan, John M, 1983. *Bobby Sands and the Tragedy of Northern Ireland*. Dublin: Mercier.
Flynn, Barry, 2009. *Soldiers of Folly*. Cork: Collins.
Foucault, Michel, 1980. *Power/Knowledge*. New York: Pantheon.
Geraghty, Tony, 1998. *The Irish War*. London: HarperCollins.
Gourevitch, Philip, 1999. *We Wish to Inform You That Tomorrow We Will Be Killed with our Families*. London: Picador.
Gupta, Dipak K., 2008. *Understanding Terrorism and Political Violence*. London: Routledge.
Hart, Peter, 1998. *The IRA and its Enemies*. Cork: Clarendon.
Hogan, Gerard and Walker, Clive, 1989. *Political Violence and the Law in Ireland*. Manchester: Manchester University Press.
Jordan, Hugh, 2009. 'Adams Hit by Fallout from Family Feud', *Sunday World*, 18 October.
Kee, Robert, 1972. *The Green Flag*. London: Chaucer.
Kelley, Kevin, 1988. *The Longest War*. London: Zed Books.
Los Angeles Times. 2005. 'The IRA is Morphing into the "Raffia"', 10 March.
Macardle, Dorothy, 1999. *The Irish Republic*. Dublin: Wolfhound.
McDonald, Henry, 2009. 'This is a Dramatic Blow to Sinn Féin's Dream of a United Ireland', *The Observer*, 4 October.
McIntyre, Anthony, 1999. *A Structural Analysis of Modern Irish Republicanism: 1969–1973*. Unpublished doctoral thesis. Belfast: Queen's University Belfast.

McIntyre, Anthony, 2009a. Interview with Tommy McKearney.
McIntyre, Anthony, 2009b. Interview with Richard O'Rawe.
McIntyre, Anthony, 2009c. Interview with Thomas Elliot.
McIntyre, Anthony, 2009d. Interview with Brendan Shannon.
McIntyre, Anthony, 2009e. Interview with Willie Gallagher.
MacStiofáin, Sean, 1975. *Memoirs of a Revolutionary*. Edinburgh: Gordon Cremonesi.
Magee, Patrick, 2001. *Gangsters or Guerrillas?* Belfast: Beyond the Pale.
Metress, Seamus, 1983. *The Hunger Strike and the Final Struggle*. Toledo: Centre for Irish Studies.
Moloney, Ed, 2002. *A Secret History of the IRA*. London: Penguin.
Mooney, John and O'Toole, Michael, 2003. *Black Operations*. Meath: Maverick House.
Murphy, Patrick, 2009. 'Defining Political Causes not an Irish Strong Point', *The Irish News*, 3 October.
Neeson, Eoin, 1998. *Birth of a Republic*. Dublin: Prestige.
O'Doherty, Shane, 2003. *The Volunteer*. London: Fount.
O'Donovan Rossa, 2007. *Irish Rebels in English Prisons*. Montana: Kessinger.
O'Hearn, Denis, 2006. *Bobby Sands*. London: Pluto.
O'Rawe, Richard, 2005. *Blanketmen*. Dublin: New Island.
O'Tuama, Sean, 1998. 'Banned History', *An Phoblacht*, 6 August.
Patterson, Henry, 1989. *The Politics of Illusion*. London: Hutchinson Radius.
Powell, Jonathan, 2008. *Great Hatred, Little Room*. London: Bodley Head.
Rees, Merlyn, 1985. *Northern Ireland*. London: Methuen.
Republican News, 1971. 'Dry Clean', August.
Sharrock, David and Devenport, Mark, 1997. *Man of War – Man of Peace?* London: Macmillan.
Simms, Brendan, 2008. 'The Long Good Friday', http://www.socialaffairsunit.org.uk/blog/archives/001745.php [accessed 15 June 2012].
Stepanova, Ekaterina, 2008. *Terrorism in Asymmetrical Conflict*. Oxford: Oxford University Press.
Stevenson, Jonathan, 1996. *We Wrecked the Place*. New York: Free Press.
Taylor, Peter, 1993. *States of Terror*. London: BBC.
Taylor, Peter, 1997. *Provos*. London: Bloomsbury.
Toolis, Kevin, 1995. *Rebel Hearts*. New York: St Martin's Press.
Trainor, Liz, 1998. 'Peace Welcome but no IRA "Surrender"', *Irish News*, 24 November.
White, Robert, 1993. *Provisional Irish Republicans*. Westport: Greenwood.
White, Robert, 2006. *Ruairi O'Bradaigh*. Indiana: Indiana University Press.
Whitelaw, William, 1989. *The Whitelaw Memoirs*. London: Aurum.

10

ASHGATE
RESEARCH
COMPANION

Martyrs without Borders: The Puzzle of Transnational Suicide Bombers

Mohammed M. Hafez

Introduction

Suicide bombings evoke shock and incredulity, yet they have become a prevalent method of violence around the globe, especially in the Muslim world. Since the 1980s, we have seen suicide attacks in the Middle East, Africa, South, Southeast and Central Asia, Europe and North America. More ominous perhaps is the growth of transnational suicide bombers who migrate from their relatively tranquil societies to conflict zones in the hope of fighting and dying as martyrs: Tunisians from Belgium carrying out suicide attacks in Afghanistan; Saudis killing and dying in Iraq; and a young Nigerian seeking to detonate explosives on an American plane on behalf of an extremist group in Yemen.

What explains the growth of this phenomenon in the Muslim world? Why are so many Muslims eager to embrace a tactic that leads to their demise? How can we explain the rise of transnational suicide bombers and how are they recruited? Answers to these questions are urgently needed to address one of the most daunting security challenges of our times. The widespread use of 'martyrdom operations' in recent years means that terrorism has become more lethal in its intent and now constitutes a major threat to national and international stability.

Experts are not in agreement on the causes of suicide terrorism and have produced competing narratives to explain this puzzle. Some, like Pape (2005), argue that suicide attacks are driven by strategic calculations. Others attribute it to organizational competition between insurgent factions (Bloom 2005). Yet others argue that suicide terrorism is rooted in a variety of ideological, organizational and strategic as well as tactical considerations (Pedahzur 2005; Moghadam 2008). A definitive explanation of transnational martyrdom is not readily available, but it is possible to sketch in broad terms the underlying *structural*, *organizational* and *ideological* variables that make this phenomenon possible. Structurally, suicide terrorism in the Muslim world emerged in a context of a radical transnational Islamist movement with network ties across many continents. The first generation of global jihadists, often referred to as 'Arab Afghans', which came out of the crucible of the anti-Soviet struggle in Afghanistan between 1979 and 1989, extolled the ethos of volunteerism and self-sacrifice in defence of suffering Muslims. These Arab Afghans did not engage in suicide attacks per se, but they venerated martyrdom and carried forward their newfound zeal to places like Tajikistan, Bosnia, Chechnya and other conflict zones in which Muslims seemed to bear the brunt of foreign domination and violence during the 1990s (Hafez 2009). Most importantly, they organized and operated al-Qaeda's training camps in Afghanistan during the second half of the 1990s, where they trained a second generation of global jihadists on the ways and means of jihad and self-sacrifice (Tawil 2007). This second generation along with the first planned and executed major suicide bombings in Kenya and Tanzania in 1998, Yemen in 2000, and the USA on 11 September 2001. These second-generation warriors served as the network infrastructure necessary for the emergence of a third generation that carried forward the banner of jihad and martyrdom after 2001 and 2003, when the USA invaded Afghanistan and Iraq, respectively. Thus, the spread of suicide attacks in the last decade has its roots in a subculture of volunteerism and martyrdom that was born in Afghanistan in the 1980s; honed in Bosnia, Chechnya and other civil wars and insurgencies in the 1990s; and reached its apex with the US invasion and occupation of Iraq in 2003.

Organizationally, suicide bombings spread because they provide small organizations confronting powerful adversaries with many advantages over conventional terrorism. Three advantages in particular – tactical effectiveness, strategic communication and socio-political destabilization – motivate the deployment of suicide bombers. Tactically, suicide bombers kill more people than conventional terrorists. They also capture media attention much more efficiently than ordinary insurgent attacks because of the extraordinary nature of their violence. Strategically, suicide attacks signal commitment to a cause and a determination to succeed by the mere fact that people are willing to give up their lives to achieve their objectives. They also help organizations deter neutral parties from collaborating with their enemies by threatening them with terrifying violence. Finally, the destructive potential of suicide bombers make them especially effective weapons for groups seeking to spoil efforts at political stabilization, societal reconciliation and economic reconstruction. Suicide bombers, on average, kill and injure more people than conventional terrorism because they can choose and adjust the place and timing of detonation to enhance their kill rate. Furthermore, the taboo nature of suicide bombings intensifies terrorism's psychological trauma, making it difficult for the authorities to justify compromise or reconciliation with 'wanton killers'.

Ideologically, the growth of transnational martyrdom benefits from earlier discursive support given by Islamic authorities to Lebanese and Palestinian suicide bombers against Israel beginning in the 1980s. This ideological environment in which the Muslim world hailed the suicide bomber as the ultimate response to oppression and injustice (i.e. Israel) opened the proverbial Pandora's Box, unleashing violent extremists outside of the Arab-Israel conflict. These extremists draw upon earlier religious arguments venerating self-immolation and replicate the ritualistic repertoires deployed by the widely celebrated Lebanese and Palestinian suicide bombers.

A detailed case study of volunteerism for jihad and martyrdom in Iraq sheds theoretical light on the process of transnational radicalization and illustrates the structural, organizational and ideological underpinnings of globalized martyrdom. Iraq is where most suicide attacks have taken place since the resurgence of this phenomenon in the early 1980s. At least 19 nationalities were present among the ranks of suicide bombers in Iraq, but the majority have come from Saudi Arabia and North Africa (Hafez 2007a; Felter and Fishman 2008).

The Iraqi insurgency offers a treasure trove of documents, videos and audio recordings by insurgent groups and their foreign recruits. Nearly all of this material is in Arabic and has been distributed via the Internet. Organizations like the SITE Monitoring Service (https://news.siteintelgroup.com) and the IntelCenter (http://www.intelcenter.com) regularly translate insurgent documents into English and keep an extensive archive, usually for a fee. These documents, videos and audio recordings are by no means perfect sources of information about the underlying motivations of transnational martyrs. The evidence they offer is fragmentary and replete with propagandistic narratives, and no researcher can randomly select examples from the universe of cases. Findings from this data cannot be considered conclusive by any measure. However, a thorough reading of the available data and carefully drawn inferences can help us piece together the strategies of recruitment by which foreign militants are drawn to a conflict zone. They also offer clues as to why some individuals volunteered to fight and die in Iraq. I begin by providing the basic background context to transnational martyrdom in Iraq. I then explore the demographics of the volunteers and discuss three pathways that led to their recruitment before discussing the structural, organizational and ideological underpinnings of their radicalization.

Background Context of Transnational Martyrdom in Iraq

Foreign fighters made their way to Iraq in at least two waves. The first came prior to the toppling of the Baathist regime in 2003. They included both experienced jihadists fleeing Afghanistan and new volunteers inspired by the goal of defending a neighbouring Arab state (Sulieman 2003). Many of the initial fighters were inspired by a nationalist impulse to defend an Arab land from foreign aggression. According to Samih Khrais, a lawyer who takes on security cases in Jordan, the initial volunteers were mainly motivated by the desire to protect fellow Arabs from an invader and antipathy toward the USA for its 'hostile' politics.[1] The quick collapse of the Baathist state forced many of these volunteers to go back home, denying them the opportunity to fight or even die as martyrs.

The story of Nadim Khadr is illustrative of the first wave. A Lebanese national in his mid-twenties, he travelled with his friends to Iraq before the fall of the regime.

---

1   Interview with Samih Khrais in Amman, Jordan, 3 March 2007.

Khadr was not an Islamist, nor was he religious. As a matter of fact, he owned a barbershop and was known for his Western style of dress and taste in music. After seeing images of bombardment during the 'shock and awe' phase of the US invasion of Iraq, he, along with a group of 14 young men from Tripoli, Lebanon, decided to make the journey to fight. Shortly after arriving in Kirkuk, a land mine blew away Khadr's legs and unsympathetic Iraqis subsequently captured him. He returned to Lebanon bitter from the entire experience (al-Sheikh 2007).

Those who could not return or did not wish to do so found no outlet other than jihadist groups that began to form in the Western regions of Iraq, especially the city of Fallujah. According to Abu Rumman (2005), a Jordanian expert on Abu Musab al-Zarqawi and his al-Qaeda in Iraq (AQI) network, 'most of the youths originally had nothing to do with al-Qaeda and al-Zarqawi group, which before the occupation of Baghdad had very few Arab followers. [However] after the occupation of Baghdad hordes of Arab volunteers, surprised by the sudden collapse of the Iraqi Army and the astounding fall of Baghdad, could not find an embrace other than al-Zarqawi's group, which managed to attract large numbers of Arabs and Iraqis'.

The experienced jihadists like al-Zarqawi came to Iraq with plans to stay indefinitely. The war in Afghanistan following the 9/11 attacks forced many jihadists to seek a new haven like the one they had under the Taliban regime. In 2002 many of them scattered throughout Iran and along the Pakistan-Afghanistan border. They knew that returning to their home countries was not an option because they were hunted men (they had gone to Afghanistan in the 1990s precisely for this reason). This is the quintessential story of al-Zarqawi and his Jordanian cohorts. Iraq's northern region on the border with Iran became an ideal place to gather immediately before and after the invasion (Krekar 2006).

The second wave of volunteers came after resistance appeared to be growing, especially after the battle of Fallujah in November 2004. The apparent success of the insurgents and their ability to strike and confuse the occupation forces injected experienced jihadists with a new spirit of resistance. The jihadi networks around the world saw an opportunity to strike which was missing in other conflict zones, whether in their home countries or in Afghanistan since the fall of the Taliban. These networks began to mobilize in the direction of Iraq.

Given the paucity of reliable data, it is difficult to provide conclusive evidence regarding who these volunteers were and where they came from. However, a number of analysts have collected fragments from various sources to put together a general profile (see Table 10.1).

Israeli researcher Reuven Paz (2005) analysed 154 names of dead Arab volunteers in Iraq (not all of whom were suicide bombers). As of March 2005, 94 (61 per cent) were from Saudi Arabia, 16 were from Syria (10.4 per cent), 13 were from Iraq (8.4 per cent) and 11 were from Kuwait (7.1 per cent). The remaining fighters came from Jordan, Algeria, Morocco, Yemen, Palestine, the United Arab Emirates and the Sudan. Paz noted that the ages of the volunteers ranged from 25 to 30 years. Some of them were married, some had degrees in higher education and most of them went to Iraq with the help of a friend or relative.

Table 10.1 Data on foreign fighters in Iraq

Study	N=	Mean age	Gulf	Levant	North Africa	Other
Paz (2005)	154	NA	~70%	~15%	~6%	~9%
Obaid and Cordesman (2005)	350	NA	29%	18%	48%	5%
al-Shishani (2005)	429	27	57%	~19%	~4%	20%
Felter and Fishman (2008)	595	24–25	49%	10%	37%	4%

Another study by Obaid and Cordesman (2005) drew on estimates from countries self-reporting the number of volunteers coming from their territory. As of September 2005, they estimated that 20 per cent came from Algeria, 18 per cent came from Syria, 17 per cent came from Yemen, 15 per cent came from the Sudan, 13 per cent came from Egypt and 12 per cent came from Saudi Arabia. Another study (al-Shishani 2005) that came out in December 2005 looked at the names of 429 volunteers in Iraq posted on the al-Saha web forum. It found that 200 fighters (53 per cent) came from Saudi Arabia. The rest came from Syria (13 per cent), Iraq (8 per cent), Jordan (5.8 per cent), Kuwait (4 per cent) and Libya (3.8 per cent). The remaining percentages were unknown.

Out of the 429 fighters listed by al Shishani (2005), only the ages of 85 were known. Based on these statistics, the average age of foreign fighters in Iraq was 27. Moreover, only 22 (5.1 per cent) have had fighting experience in other regions, 'demonstrating that the foreign fighters in Iraq do indeed constitute the third generation of Salafi-jihadists' (al-Shishani 2005).

A report by Felter and Fishman (2008) citing official US military figures declares that of 595 known foreign volunteers, 45 per cent came from Saudi Arabia, 10 per cent came from Syria and Lebanon, and about 37 per cent came from North Africa, especially Libya. While Saudis produced the majority of volunteers in an absolute sense, Libyans produced the most volunteers on a per capita basis. Given the high number of Saudis in all the aforementioned studies, it is important to scrutinize this category of volunteers. The Norwegian researcher Thomas Hegghammer (2007) has carried out an extensive study of Saudis in Iraq, looking at 205 biographies of their volunteers. His findings reveal the following:

- the average age of volunteers was 23;
- only nine of the 205 were known to have had previous combat experience from Afghanistan, Bosnia or elsewhere;
- the socio-economic backgrounds reveal diverse recruitment sources – some were very poor, while others came from rich and privileged families;

- although information about educational levels is sparse, it indicates that many were highly educated: '14 of the 16 for whom we know the education level attended higher education, one even had a doctorate';
- the professional occupations of the volunteers were also diverse. Of the 26 individuals for whom data is available, 14 were students, three were private sector workers, two were government clerks, two were healthcare workers, two were police/military officers, one was a teacher, one was a car mechanic and one was a meteorologist;
- as for regional patterns within Saudi Arabia, the most overrepresented regions were Riyadh and Qasim, as well as the northwestern regions of Tabuk, Jawf and Hail. The most under-represented regions were in the south – Jizan, Najran, Asir and Baha.

Hegghammer concludes: 'This socio-economic, geographic and tribal diversity tells us two important things. First, it shows that militancy is not confined to a particular section of Saudi society (the 'poor', the 'southerners', the 'Bedouins', etc). Second, it indicates that sympathy for the Iraqi cause cuts across Saudi society' (2007: 13).

In summary, based on the aforementioned studies of the demographics of volunteers in Iraq, we can conclude that Arab volunteers came from many parts of the Arabic-speaking Muslim world. The volunteers were mainly men in their early to late twenties, which suggests that they were either newcomers to jihadism or 'second generation' jihadists perhaps weaned on militancy in the Afghan training camps of the 1990s. Hardly any came from the first generation of 'Arab Afghans'. There were, however, no other salient patterns in terms of socio-economic status, educational levels or regional affiliations.

Three Patterns of Transnational Recruitment

Stories of dead and captured recruits for jihad in Iraq invariably reveal one of three patterns of mobilization: experienced jihadists seeking to extend their militant careers in Iraq; inexperienced volunteers motivated to fight and die in Iraq; and recruits selected in a top-down process. This analysis of mobilization and recruitment is based on reviewing over 400 published 'biographies' of jihadists in Iraq, not just suicide bombers. Insurgent groups seeking to commemorate their cadres publish these biographies on jihadi forums. These biographies range from one or two lines to several pages. The following analysis also draws upon informed news stories by investigative reporters who have interviewed the families of dead or wanted militants. The first involves individuals who are jihadists or wanted militants with a history of activism either in Afghanistan or in their home countries. Many reports reveal individuals who fled Afghanistan after the fall of the Taliban regime and could not go back to their home countries. These individuals saw the war in Iraq as an opportunity to extend their militant careers, set up a new haven for global jihad or die as martyrs fighting the USA. The following are some of the stories that reflect the first pattern of recruitment.

Abu Ahmad al-Kuwaiti, Abu al-Bara al-Kuwaiti and Abu Bakr al-Kuwaiti were all commanders within AQI responsible for dispatching several Kuwaiti suicide bombers. According to their biographies, they were killed in an unspecified battle. Abu Ahmad was in Afghanistan and became a commander of one of the groups in Fallujah. Abu al-Bara fought in Chechnya and spent time in Afghanistan. After the fall of the Taliban regime, he returned to Kuwait and was immediately arrested. In November 2003 he made his way to Fallujah and was subsequently killed in a non-suicide operation near Baghdad. Abu Bakr wanted to go to Afghanistan after the 9/11 attacks but was stranded at the Iranian border until he eventually returned to Kuwait. The Kuwaiti authorities repeatedly arrested him. After the fall of Baghdad, he went to Iraq with two others, Abu Salih al-Kuwaiti (Nayif Salih al-Subayi) and Abu Wadha al-Kuwaiti (Mansoor al-Hajari), both of whom carried out suicide attacks there.

Mohammed Afalah carried out a suicide attack in Iraq in May 2005. He drove a car packed with explosives into an Iraqi army checkpoint in Baghdad's Dora neighbourhood, killing one soldier and injuring eight. Previously he had been indicted for his involvement in the Madrid bombings. Within hours of the Madrid bombings, Afalah retreated to a safe house in the Leganes district along with eight others involved in the plot. On 3 April 2004, as Spanish security officers closed in, Afalah escaped, leaving the rest of the conspirators to blow themselves up rather than be captured. Before departing for Iraq, Afalah spent some time in Brussels at the home of Mourad Chabarou, one of 13 Moroccan militants tried for connections to the Madrid bombings.

Fadhal Saadi was a Tunisian suicide bomber living in Italy. Born in Haidra, Tunisia, on 28 July 1979, Saadi lived in Milan with his brother Nassim. In September 2001, they both left Italy with a number of volunteers to fight in Afghanistan against the USA. At the end of the war in Afghanistan in late 2001, the Saadi brothers fled to Iran, where they were briefly arrested. Eventually they were allowed to return to Europe. In the autumn of 2002, Saadi left France for Iraqi Kurdistan to join Ansar al-Islam, apparently seeking to flee from European authorities. US air strikes forced Saadi and others to cross the border into Iran, where he was arrested once again. It is not clear how he managed to leave Iran a second time, but in July 2003 he carried out a suicide attack in Iraq.

The second pattern of recruitment involves ordinary Muslims (not just Islamists) who were enraged by images of Muslim suffering in Iraq, Afghanistan and Palestine, and sought out experienced jihadists who could help transport them to Iraq, usually via Syria or Turkey. Some of the volunteers are said to have travelled from mosque to mosque along the Syrian-Iraqi border looking for facilitators to take them to fighting groups in Iraq. These individuals usually came with money to pay experienced smugglers along the borders. Their biographies reflect the common theme of fighting in defence of one's land, coreligionists and honour. Even when captured, they rarely expressed remorse and instead affirmed their desire to try again if the opportunity arose. Most often they travelled in small groups. Rarely did they go to Iraq on their own. The following stories illustrate the second pattern of recruitment.

In the autumn of 2006, Abu Ibrahim, a young man in his early twenties, along with five of his friends from Zarqa, Jordan, left for Iraq. They were not recruited directly by militants; rather, they gradually radicalized each other. They watched videos of tortured and dead Muslims and began to engage in discussions over them. Abu Ibrahim considered Abu Musab al-Zarqawi a hero, but his decision to go, he told Mekhennet and Moss (2007), was influenced by his friends: 'I decided to go when my friends went.' They managed to get the phone number of a smuggler and the address of a safe house in Iraq. In his earlier days, Abu Ibrahim was not religious: 'I was just looking to have fun', as he recounted how four of his friends died in Iraq. 'I was happy for them because they were going to paradise, but I was upset at myself.' He left home in October 2006 with only a sports bag full of clothes. His seat in a group taxi to the Syrian border cost $11. Neither the Jordanian nor the Syrian border guards asked many questions, he said. He slept in a Damascus hotel and then took a six-hour bus ride east to the Iraq border area, where he had the name of a smuggler who took travellers across the border for about $150 apiece. 'It is hard to leave our families', he said. 'But it is our duty, and if we don't defend our religion who should do it? The old people or the children?'

Bordj Bou Arreridj is an Algerian who was released by the Algerian authorities in March 2006 after being detained for attempting to fight in Iraq. He explained his failed attempt by saying: 'I spent several months on the Jordanian border before being forcefully turned back to Algeria, but many Algerians were luckier than I was and right now are fighting with their Arab brothers who have enlisted in the Iraqi resistance' (Oukaci 2006).

In interviews with Nawaf Tell and Muhammad al-Masri, both Jordanian experts at the Centre for Strategic Studies in Amman, Jordan, I was told that volunteerism often involves a group of friends or relatives talking politics, expressing outrage at events in Iraq and framing that rage in the conspiratorial language of an American war on Muslims for the sake of oil and to keep Israel safe from regional powers that can challenge its hegemony. Thus, the prevailing feeling among ordinary people was that the entire region is targeted in order to remake the Middle East into subservient 'puppet' regimes that answer to the USA and end all resistance to Israel.[2] To be sure, these views are common in the region and therefore cannot explain why these individuals decided to make the journey to Iraq. However, these widely held beliefs create fertile soil for radicalism, recruitment and volunteerism.

The third pattern of recruitment involves top-down selection and socialization by experienced jihadists seeking recruits in regions where one finds pre-existing networks of radical Islamists. For example, at least nine volunteers, and perhaps as many as 30, have connections to a single mosque, El Midway, in Titian, Morocco (Elliot 2007; Whitlock 2007). In Lebanon, many of the volunteers came from the Ain al-Hilweh refugee camp, where secular and Islamist Palestinian factions deploy their own security forces instead of the official Lebanese security apparatus. These recruiters emphasize the humiliation of Muslims at the hands of foreigners, the

---

2   Interview with Nawaf Tell and Muhammad al-Masri at the Centre for Strategic Studies at the University of Jordan, 6 March 2007.

religious duty to fight when Muslims are attacked and the rewards of martyrdom for Islam (Hafez 2007b). Recruiters often download insurgent videos and online propaganda material from the Internet and create DVDs that show images of Muslim suffering and jihadist resistance in Iraq to be used for one-on-one or group discussions. They also show the successful operations of jihadists to motivate recruits and fill them with a sense of empowerment. The following story illustrates some aspects of top-down recruitment.

J. Abdel-Haq (aka Noufal) was 29 years old when the Algerian authorities arrested him in late 2006 for recruiting other Algerians to fight in Iraq. He admitted to frequenting the Badr mosque in the al-Bisbas district in al-Tarif. He recruited three individuals to Iraq prior to the fall of the regime. However, the three only made it as far as to Syria and came back because the regime fell before they could enter the country. The three decided to go one more time in 2004. One of the three was Abu Jihad. He was to meet with a Syrian handler named Abu Adnan. The latter was responsible for transporting the militants to an Iraqi named Abu Ubaydah, the leader of an AQI training camp in Rawah, Iraq. Abdel-Haq travelled regularly to Syria under the pretext of being a clothes salesman (Muqaddam 2007).

According to the journalist Muhammad Sulieman (2004), who has written extensively on jihadism in Jordan, kinship and tribal relations play a big role in spreading the radical ideology from the top down, especially in Salt, Ma'an and al-Mafraq. Recruitment usually arises through social ties in which individuals are identified as potential members. These individuals are then invited to religious studies sessions. Initial lessons do not broach the topic of jihad or current politics. Those who appear interested are drawn in gradually through more politicized discussions where the possibility of action is presented.

Hegghammer (2008) describes the top-down recruitment of Saudis for jihadist activities including but not limited to Iraq. Returnees from the Afghanistan training camps in the late 1990s and after 9/11 constituted the network that generated further recruits within the kingdom. These returnees drew upon friendship, kinship and activist ties to expand their ranks. Direct recruitment took place in informal religious study groups and lectures organized by returnees from Afghanistan and by sympathetic clerics. Hegghammer describes the recruitment process: 'Typically, the recruiter and the recruit would meet at informal gatherings in private homes. Then the recruiter would invite the recruit to smaller gatherings or one-to-one conversations in order to assess his motivation and qualifications. If the recruit was promising, he would be introduced to the recruiter's superior, who would decide on how to integrate the recruit in the organization' (2006: 52).

In all three patterns of mobilization – whether by experienced jihadists seeking to extend their militant careers in Iraq or by newcomers who either volunteered or were selected for recruitment in a top-down process – the journey to Iraq was usually conducted in small groups. Rarely did individuals go to jihad alone, which suggests that group dynamics may have reinforced initial commitments to join the fray in Iraq. Insurgent videos often reveal jihadists training in small groups in farms or desert areas. The send-off the suicide bombers receive involves a group ceremony in which the 'living martyr' reads his last will and testament, gives general advice to Muslims and is embraced by his friends in a final farewell.

Iraqi and American interrogators often say that recruiters coerce the suicide bombers, using drugs, sexual enticements or brainwashing children and the mentally ill. The insurgents, on the other hand, often portray their recruits as eager martyrs who beseech their handlers to hasten their suicide attacks. The truth, perhaps, is somewhere in between these two narratives. It is safe to say that once volunteers make it to Iraq and are in the hands of insurgent groups, they are physically and psychologically entrapped – the radical group becomes their sole source of information, validation and protection. The act of travelling to Iraq is a form of bridge-burning in two ways. First, once a person is privy to the modus operandi of smugglers and identity of recruiters, it is difficult for that person to request to be returned back to where he came from. One Iraqi I interviewed speaks of subtle coercive tactics in which volunteers are deprived of their passport, which prevents them from leaving the country and keeps them dependent on the host group.[3] Second, recruits have limited communication with loved ones who may urge them to return home. They rarely tell their families of their plans until they have reached Iraq. Even then, contact is limited to a call or two (at least for the suicide bombers). This suggests that the volunteer or the insurgent group seeks to minimize counter-appeals that invariably attend conversations with family members. The following stories are revealing.

Abdelmonem Amakchar El Amrani was a 22-year-old Moroccan from the Tetouan. He carried out a suicide attack in Iraq on 6 March 2006, driving a Volkswagen Passat into a funeral tent in a village near Baqubah. He was a day labourer, was married and was the father of an infant girl. He travelled to Iraq with at least two friends – Moncef ben Masaoud, a 21-year-old suicide bomber, and Yones Achebback, a 23-year-old whose fate is not known. It appears that all of those who went to Iraq attended El Mizwaq Mosque in Terouan. According to El Amrani's family, he began spending more time at the mosque, grew a beard and one day disappeared. They learned of his fate only after he had carried out the suicide attack. Masaoud's father reports that his son, who also died in a suicide attack, left home as usual for school, but did not hear from him until his son called him for the last time to tell him that he was in Syria (Whitlock 2007).

Khalaf Allah al-Qatinah (Walid) was a 24-year-old Algerian from an impoverished neighbourhood in al-Wadi. He died in Iraq in a military operation (it is not clear if it was a suicide bombing). He was the oldest son in a family of six. He played handball in a local team. One day his family received a call from a man with an Iraqi accent informing them that their son was in Iraq and that he would call them shortly. However, they never heard from their son. Instead, in late 2006, they received a call from another Iraqi informing them that their son had died in a military operation against US forces.

---

3   Interview with Usama Abdul Jabbar, former Baathist who worked as a military industry technician in Baghdad before leaving to Amman, Jordan, in 2005. Interview conducted in Amman on 26 February 2007.

The recruit, it seems, is completely reliant on his handlers for information, security and daily support. The recruit is immersed in martyrdom veneration while residing in safe houses and training farms with other, presumably willing martyrs. According to Said Mahmud Abdel Aziz Haraz (Abu Umar al-Kurdi), a Kurdish Iraqi recruiter captured by Coalition forces, the recruits live in a house run by one of the groups. In one of the rooms, dubbed the 'martyr's room', a list is posted and volunteers for suicide missions enter their names and dates of arrival. This system is ostensibly used to establish a queue for suicide attacks (Grignetti 2006). Thus, to the extent that coercive recruitment for suicide attacks takes place at all, in all likelihood it takes the subtle form of coercion associated with dynamics of peer pressure, entrapment through bridge-burning and psychological priming for suicide missions.

Structural Underpinnings of Transnational Martyrdom

One of the strongest findings in the literature on political mobilization is that informal network ties are necessary for collective action, insurgency and terrorism (Gerlach and Hine 1970; Freeman 1973; McAdam 1986; McAdam and Paulsen 1993; Opp and Gern 1993; Sageman 2004). The concept of networks refers to private and public ties, whether direct or indirect, between individuals, clusters of individuals (such as social clubs or tribes) and organizations. These links could include friendship and family ties, ties with co-workers and neighbours, acquaintances and colleagues in social or religious organizations, activist ties across a number of political organizations or even borders and so on (Diani 2003). Formal mobilization structures are rarely the starting point for social movement activism, especially in the context of repressive political systems in which vigilant authorities heavily monitor or suppress formal organization.

In the case of Iraq, pre-existing transnational networks played, in a short timeframe, an important role in mobilizing volunteers, including suicide bombers, to go to Iraq. Both experienced activists and new jihadists were linked by activist networks in a number of countries. Those activists, in turn, constituted a transnational network of second-generation jihadists with ties to the Afghan-Pakistan training camps during the 1990s or to jihads in Bosnia, Chechnya or their home countries. Recruitment to Iraq shows that many of the individuals were either connected to someone who knew about the ways and means of jihad or else travelled in small groups to countries bordering Iraq in the hope of making connections with experienced smugglers. Smugglers in Syria clear the potential volunteers, making sure they come from reliable sources that can vouch for them.

Stories of dead militants as well as those captured by Iraqi and Coalitions forces indicate that at least some volunteers came with a name of a person who could vouch for them. Some of these volunteers could spend days in safe houses on the border before getting the signal to cross.[4] The volunteers then paid cash for their passage

---

4 Al-Jazeera documentary, 'The Road to Baghdad', viewed on 18 May 2006.

into Iraq, usually in a car to a Fallujah neighbourhood or border towns such as Al-Qaim, Tal Afar or al-Karabilah. All these security precautions suggest an elaborate network with experienced smugglers at the helm (Felter and Fishman 2008).

Earlier patterns of volunteering to participate in international conflicts served as templates for mobilizing recruits to Iraq. When the Soviet Union invaded Afghanistan in 1979, it took Arab volunteers several years to travel to the conflict zone. Moreover, estimates of no more than 3,000–4,000 volunteers made it there at any one time and many of those did not participate in the fighting because they had no prior experiences in jihad (Hafez 2009). When the war in Iraq began in 2003, however, jihadists had plenty of experience fighting in Afghanistan, Bosnia, Chechnya and their home countries. Activist ties that developed during earlier jihads and in training camps generated the necessary relationships and bonds of trust for future jihads.

The modality of volunteerism was accompanied by new media that brought the suffering of Muslims to the homes of their coreligionists. The spread of satellite television and the Internet made it possible to publicize the suffering of Muslims in distant places and engender among some youth a sense of an 'imagined community' based on the bond of faith and shared grievances, in the same way that the print media made European nationalism possible two centuries earlier (Anderson 1991). The war on terrorism, which was limited to fighting Islamist movements, further solidified 'Islam' and 'Muslims' as singular categories that were increasingly under threat by hegemonic powers. Moreover, the discourse surrounding the war on terror increasingly stereotyped and securitized the Islamic identity, producing feelings of humiliation among Western Muslims.

Vivid imagery of Muslim suffering in Iraq was disseminated via the Internet, fostering righteous indignation among potential recruits and shaming them into avenging their coreligionists. Internet material did not supplant face-to-face recruitment, nor did it obviate the need for on-the-ground facilitation for those seeking to make their way to conflict zones. The Internet and online forums, however, enabled transnational networks to circumvent the physical and legal limits on the dissemination of their ideological messages, which included the veneration of martyrdom in defence of Muslims. They also offered a counter-narrative to official rationale for the wars on terror, Iraq and Afghanistan.

Organizational Underpinnings of Martyrdom Operations

Why would groups deploy their recruits for suicide attacks when they could possibly use them repeatedly for conventional insurgent violence? Suicide terrorism enables weak groups to punch above their weight when striking at stronger opponents. Observers of suicide terrorism point out many advantages that accrue to groups deploying this tactic (Pape 2003; Hoffman and McCormick 2004; Bloom 2005; Hafez 2007a).

Suicide terrorism on average kills and injures more people with a single attack than any other form of terrorism. According to one estimate, conventional terrorist attacks since the early 1980s have killed on average less than one person per incident, whereas suicide attacks during the same period have killed on average 12 people per incident (Pape 2003). Through suicide terrorism, those seeking to coerce opponents can impose unacceptable human and material losses for the targeted countries.

In addition, suicide terrorists are 'smart bombs' that can pinpoint their targets, walk into highly secure areas, make last-minute adjustments in their plans and choose the time of detonation to inflict the greatest damage. In Israel, in at least two incidents, bombers changed their targets minutes before their operation because they noticed an extra security presence near their original targets. In one recent incident in Iraq, the suicide bomber waited for crowds to gather before setting off his explosives, killing scores of civilians. This tactical flexibility is rare in conventional terrorist attacks or even with the most expensive and technologically advanced conventional weaponry.

Furthermore, suicide bombing is an attractive option for terrorist groups seeking a cost-effective way to inflict the greatest possible damage on their opponents with the lowest number of cadres. In highly repressive environments where recruitment is difficult, terrorist groups become conscious of the need to cause the greatest damage without sacrificing many valued assets. Suicide terrorism allows them to inflict mass casualties with one or a few bombers. If we assume that a suicide attack kills on average 12 times as many people as a conventional terrorist attack, it would require 12 separate attacks to achieve what one suicide bomber could achieve in a single mission. Also, suicide operations do not require complicated escape plans that put other organizational personnel at risk of capture. Captured terrorists can be forced to reveal their recruiters' modus operandi, thus diminishing the operational security of violent groups.

Suicide terrorism has been used to kill a lot of people, but it is also an effective form of strategic communication (Hoffman and McCormick 2004). Suicide bombings, like other tactics of terrorism, are a form of psychological warfare. Observers of this phenomenon point out at least two strategic messages that suicide terrorists seek to communicate: determination and deterrence (Pape 2003; Hoffman and McCormick 2004).

Suicide bombings are intended to demonstrate commitment to a cause by highlighting the level of sacrifice that an insurgent group is willing to endure to achieve its objectives. Suicide attackers send the message to the targeted country that they are so determined to achieve their goals that they are willing to die for their cause. The willingness of suicide terrorists to sacrifice their lives voluntarily is sometimes interpreted as the ultimate testimony to the righteousness of the cause. This extraordinary commitment cannot be deterred easily by the threat of counter-terrorism.

The extraordinarily destructive nature of suicide terrorism sends a message to uncommitted allies to stay on the sidelines lest they become targets of mass-casualty attacks at the hands of people who will go to any lengths to achieve their goals. For example, the suicide attacks in the UK on 7 July 2005 – clearly intended to coerce the UK to abandon its support of the USA in Iraq and Afghanistan – also included a message to other governments, including Italy and Australia, to reconsider their current alliance with the USA. In Pakistan, violent extremists target the security forces to deter the state from further cooperation with the USA in the war on terror.

Mass-casualty suicide attacks can also be used to destabilize regimes and incite opponents into an overreaction, much like the 9/11 attacks laid the groundwork for US interventionism around the globe. Organizations seeking to destabilize vulnerable states, foster societal polarization or entangle opponents in a long war can do so by the destructive impact of suicide terrorism and the psychological shock that these attacks engender.

AQI's deployment of suicide attacks is intended to fulfil these strategic objectives in addition to others. Consequently, it uses suicide bombers to attack political, civic and humanitarian organizations in Iraq, such as the United Nations and Red Cross facilities, foreign embassies, party offices and state bureaucracies. Rampant chaos and insecurity adds to the public's frustration with its own government and the Coalition forces – both are ultimately blamed for failing to provide adequate security and services. Second, AQI wants to deprive the Iraqi state of having the monopoly over the use of force by intimidating and annihilating the emerging security forces. If the Iraqi state is allowed to raise a new army and security service with the support of the USA, AQI in all likelihood will be beaten back by the Shi'ite-led government. Therefore, AQI directs suicide bombers to attack Iraqi security forces, recruitment centres and local militias. Third, AQI in general is politically marginal in Iraq. To foster a base of support within the Sunni population, it has been enflaming sectarianism through direct attacks on Shi'ite civilians and their religious institutions and symbols. Sectarian polarization allows marginal extremists to present themselves as the indispensable defenders of the Sunnis.

Ideological Underpinnings of Transnational Martyrdom

A pre-existing ideological environment supportive of martyrdom in the Muslim world bolstered the spread of transnational suicide terrorism. Earlier clerical and popular support for Lebanese and Palestinian suicide bombers set the conditions for other groups unconnected to the Arab-Israeli conflict to exploit the template of 'martyrdom operations' (Hafez 2006). Religious scholars from various traditions and political orientations hailed the suicide bombers in the Palestinian territories as martyrs destined for paradise and eternal salvation in the company of prophets, saints and adored martyrs. Support for martyrdom came not only from radical bastions of Islamism such as Iran or Hezbollah in southern Lebanon, but also from traditionally conservative institutions such as Egypt's al-Azhar. Notable religious figures such as Sheikh Ahmed al-Tayyeb, mufti of Egypt, and Sheikh Muhammed Tantawi, imam of al-Azhar, affirmed the right of Palestinians to carry out 'martyrdom operations' against Israelis. Yusuf al-Qaradawi, a widely respected Muslim leader who has a weekly programme, *al-Sharia wal-Hayat* (*Islamic Law and Life*), on Al Jazeera satellite television, repeatedly issued religious rulings upholding the legitimacy of suicide attacks. Although al-Qaradawi and other religious authorities did not openly endorse suicide attacks in Iraq, their support for these attacks in the Palestinian-Israeli context was sufficient to lead jihadists in Iraq to ask what is different about occupation in Palestine and occupation in Iraq?

Dispatchers of suicide bombers in Iraq built on this culture of martyrdom. They cited the Quranic verses that state sanctioned clerics used in support of Palestinian suicide bombers:

> 9:111 – Allah hath purchased of the believers their persons and their goods; for theirs (in return) is the garden (of Paradise): they fight in His cause, and slay and are slain: a promise binding on Him in truth.

> 2:154 – And call not those who are slain in the way of Allah 'dead'. Nay, they are living, only ye perceive not.

For jihadists, what distinguishes despicable suicide from praiseworthy martyrdom is the intention of the bomber. The former is the act of a depressed person who has given up on life and cannot bear his hopelessness. His suicide is about escapism, the deviation of a weak mind. Martyrs, on the other hand, are about noble sacrifice by strong-willed individuals. The argument is best exemplified by Abu Qatada al-Falistini (Hafez 2007a). He argues that during the time of the Prophet Muhammad, two paradigms presented themselves. The first paradigm involved a Muslim killing himself by leaning on his sword after suffering an unbearable wound in battle. Rather than endure the pain, he intentionally killed himself to bring relief only to himself. When people asked about his destiny, the Prophet Muhammad declared that he is eternally in hellfire, which is the judgment of any person who commits suicide. The second paradigm involved what is termed 'plunging into the ranks' (*al-inghimas fi al-saf*). In this paradigm, Muslims, after hearing the Prophet Muhammad cite the rewards of martyrdom, intentionally took extraordinary risks in battle against unbelievers, including single fighters rushing headlong into a group of combatants, in order to achieve martyrdom. In both paradigms the end result is the same, which is the death of the Muslim fighter, but the intention of each differed significantly. In the case of the fighter 'plunging into the ranks' of the infidels, he was sacrificing himself for the benefit of others. In the case of the wounded fighter, he killed himself to benefit no one other than himself.

Jihadists also benefited from earlier state-sanctioned veneration of foreign volunteers to conflict zones. For example, jihad in Afghanistan, Bosnia, Chechnya and elsewhere during the 1980s and 1990s was widely portrayed by the Saudi government and the Wahhabi religious establishment as the legitimate defence of Muslim territories against non-believers (Hegghammer 2008). When the USA invaded Iraq in 2003, many Saudis saw the war in Iraq as a defensive jihad that required all Muslims to come to the aid of their coreligionists. It was hardly credible for the Saudi authorities to claim that it was not the individual obligation of Saudis to support their fellow Muslims in Iraq. As one Saudi intelligence officer put it: 'We encouraged our young men to fight for Islam in Afghanistan. We encouraged our young men to fight for Islam in Bosnia and Chechnya. We encouraged our young men to fight for Islam in Palestine. Now we are telling them you are forbidden to fight for Islam in Iraq, and they are confused' (Windrem 2005).

Conclusion

The case of Iraq suggests that at least four elements make the phenomenon of martyrs without borders possible: widespread grievances against a target group or country; pre-existing transnational networks of militants with a history of venerating volunteerism and self-sacrifice; tactical and strategic advantages of suicide attacks; and ideological rationalization rooted in authoritative sources. Transnational mobilization for jihad in Iraq highlights the complex interplay among these four variables. It is not possible to understand the rise, pace and scope of transnational suicide attacks without looking at how individual motivations, organizational networks and strategies, and ideological contexts interact.

The apex of transnational martyrdom had taken place in a context of wars in Iraq and Afghanistan in which Muslim publics, generally speaking, were suspicious of US intentions and rejected their reasons for occupying these countries. In addition, the war on terrorism unleashed by the USA and its allies in the aftermath of the 9/11 attacks has been widely perceived as singling out Muslims and Islamists. The securitization of the Islamic identity and images of Muslim suffering have enraged many of their coreligionists. Volunteering for jihad in Iraq became one way for some aggrieved youth to express their rejection toward aggressive interventionism on the part of the USA and its allies.

Suicide attacks have become a form of resistance that is perceived as both effective and culturally venerated in the Muslim world. The appeal of martyrdom lies not just in its efficacy, but also in its perceived normative value. The use of suicide attacks in Lebanon and Palestine gave martyrdom special legitimacy in the Muslim world. Religious scholars have insisted that these actions are genuine forms of jihad and devotion to the faith. The Muslim public supported them because they served as an 'equalizing weapon' in the face of 'arrogant' powers and demonstrated Muslim loyalty and sacrifice when governments were viewed as impotent collaborators. Transnational jihadists took advantage of this normative environment and drew on the texts, arguments and symbolism of earlier suicide attackers to justify their extreme tactics in Iraq.

The diffusion of this tactic is linked not only to the normative context, but also to relational ties between radical networks and ordinary Muslims enraged by wars in their regions. Pre-existing radical networks that have their origins in the first and second generations of global jihadists became the conveyor belts on which a third generation of foreign fighters made their way to Iraq. These networks were not only experienced in the ways and means of transnational volunteerism, which were honed in places like Afghanistan, Pakistan, Bosnia and Chechnya , they were diffused in several regions around the globe, including Europe, North Africa, the Middle East and South Asia. Those who were part of the al-Qaeda network had deployed suicide attacks before, at least as early as 1998 in Kenya and Tanzania. Their crowning achievement, however, was the 9/11 attacks in the USA.

The specific tactical and strategic rationale for adopting this mode of violence may vary from one conflict to another, but it seems that suicide attacks offer transnational jihadists certain advantages that conventional terrorism is incapable of delivering. These include a high kill rate, the ability for small groups to capture the media spotlight through extraordinary violence and the capacity to derail stabilization, reconciliation and reconstruction. The tactical and strategic logic of suicide terrorism is what drives groups to adopt this method, not just the normative legitimacy it has received from religious authorities.

In summary, by the time the insurgency developed in Iraq, suicide attacks had become modular, diffused and normatively accepted in the Muslim world. It did not require great imagination to apply this tactic in the Iraqi context. Nor is it a surprise that the wide use of this tactic in Iraq has carried over to other conflict zones such as Algeria, Afghanistan and Pakistan, given the relational ties between insurgents in these countries and al-Qaeda operatives that date back to the 1980s and 1990s. Transnational jihadists have shown a keen ability to advance their tactical and strategic plans by aligning their rhetoric and ideological appeals with the cultural norms and political grievances of their target recruits. What we witnessed in Iraq and elsewhere, however, was not merely the capacity of global jihadists to win over new cadres to their struggle against foreign 'invaders' and local 'apostates'; it was also the collective radicalization of Muslim communities and societies from which transnational martyrs stepped forward willingly and eagerly.

References

Abu Rumman, M. 2005. The Road to Baghdad (Arabic). *Al-Ghadd* (Amman, Jordan), 13 March.
Al-Sheikh, B. 2007. Those Who Went to Iraq Will Not Do It Again Because the Levant has Become 'A House of War' (Arabic), *Al Hayat* (London), 13 April.
Al-Shishani, M. 2005. The Salafi-Jihadist Movement in Iraq: Recruitment Methods and Arab Volunteers. *Terrorism Monitor*, 3(23), 6–8.
Anderson, B. 1991. *Imagined Communities: Reflections on the Origin and Spread of Nationalism*. London: Verso.
Bloom, M. 2005. *Dying to Kill: The Global Phenomenon of Suicide Terror*. New York: Columbia University Press.
Diani, M. 2003. Social Movements, Contentious Actions, and Social Networks: 'From Metaphor to Substance?', in M. Diani and D. McAdam (eds), *Social Movements and Networks: Relational Approaches to Collective Action*. New York: Oxford University Press.
Elliott, A. 2007. Where Boys Grow Up to Be Jihadis. *New York Times*, 25 November.
Felter, J. and Fishman, B. 2008. Al-Qa'ida's Foreign Fighters in Iraq: A First Look at the Sinjar Records. *Combating Terrorism Center at West Point*.

Freeman, J. 1973. The Origins of the Women's Liberation Movement. *American Journal of Sociology*, 78, 792–811.

Gerlach, L., Hine, V. 1970. *People, Power, Change: Movements of Social Transformation*. Indianapolis: Bobbs-Merrill.

Grignetti, F. 2006. One of Al-Nasiriyah Suicide Bombers Identified (Italian). *La Stampa*, 11 January.

Hafez, M.M. 2006. *Manufacturing Human Bombs: The Making of Palestinian Suicide Bombers*. Washington DC: United States Institute of Peace.

Hafez, M.M. 2007a. *Suicide Bombers in Iraq: The Strategy and Ideology of Martyrdom*. Washington DC: United States Institute of Peace.

Hafez, M.M. 2007b. Martyrdom Mythology in Iraq: How Jihadists Frame Suicide Terrorism in Videos and Biographies. *Terrorism and Political Violence*, 19, 95–115.

Hafez, M.M. 2009. Jihad after Iraq: Lessons from the Arab Afghans. *Studies in Conflict and Terrorism*, 32(2), 73–94.

Hegghammer, T. 2006. Terrorist Recruitment and Radicalization in Saudi Arabia. *Middle East Policy*, XIII(4), 39–60.

Hegghammer, T. 2007. Saudi Militants in Iraq: Backgrounds and Recruitment Patterns. *Norwegian Defence Research Establishment*, 5 February.

Hegghammer, T. 2008. Islamist Violence and Regime Stability in Saudi Arabia. *International Affairs*, 84, 701–15.

Hoffman, B. and McCormick, G. 2004. Terrorism, Signaling, and Suicide Attack. *Studies in Conflict and Terrorism*, 27(4), 243–81.

Husayn, F. 2005. Al-Zarqawi: The Second Generation of Al-Qaeda (Arabic). *Al-Quds al-Arabi* (London), 13–30 May.

Krekar, F. 2006. The Zarqawian Vision and its Heavy Burden (Arabic). *Al Jazeera*. Available at www.aljazeera.net [accessed 1 July 2006].

McAdam, D. 1986. Recruitment to High Risk Activism: The Case of Freedom Summer. *American Journal of Sociology*, 92, 64–90.

McAdam, D. and Paulsen, R. 1993. Specifying the Relationship between Social Ties and Activism. *American Journal of Sociology*, 99, 640–67.

Mekhennet, S. and Moss, M. 2007. In Jihadist Haven, a Goal: To Kill and Die in Iraq. *New York Times*, 4 May.

Moghadam, A. 2008. *The Globalization of Martyrdom: Al Qaeda, Salafi Jihad, and the Diffusion of Suicide Attacks*. Baltimore, MD: Johns Hopkins University Press.

Muqaddam, M. 2007. Investigation Continues to Determine Returnees' Connection with the Al-Qaeda Organization in the Islamic Maghreb (Arabic). *Al-Hayat*, 14 April.

Obaid, N. and Cordesman, A. 2005. *Saudi Militants in Iraq: Assessment and Kingdom's Response*. Washington DC: Center for Strategic and International Studies.

Opp, K. and Gern, C. 1993. Dissident Groups, Personal Networks, and the East German Revolution of 1989. *American Sociological Review*, 58, 659–80.

Oukaci, F. 2006. Algerian Jihadists in Iraq: The 'Syrian Networks' (French). *L'Expression*, 10 July.

Pape, R. 2003. The Strategic Logic of Suicide Terrorism. *American Political Science Review*, 97, 343–61.

Pape, R. 2005. *Dying to Win: The Strategic Logic of Suicide Terrorism*. New York: Random House.
Paz, R. 2005. Arab Volunteers Killed in Iraq: An Analysis. *Global Research in International Affairs Centre*, 3(1), 1–7.
Pedahzur, A. 2005. *Suicide Terrorism.* Cambridge: Polity.
Sageman, M. 2004. *Understanding Terror Networks*. Philadelphia: University of Pennsylvania Press.
Sulieman, M. 2003. An Invitation to Reflect on and Discuss 'The Phenomenon of Arab Volunteers' (Arabic). *Al-Asr* (Amman, Jordan), 4–5 October.
Sulieman, M. 2004. The Jihadist Current in Jordan: Harvesting the Fruits of a Decade of Confrontation (Arabic). *Al-Asr*, 10–16 October.
Tawil, C. 2007. *Al-Qaeda and Its Affiliates: The Story of the Arab Afghans* (Arabic). London: Dar Al-Saqi.
Whitlock, C. 2007. Terrorist Networks Lure Young Moroccans to War in Far-Off Iraq. *Washington Post*, 20 February.
Windrem, R. 2005. Saudi Arabia's Ambitious al-Qaida Fighter. *NBC News*, 11 July.

11

The Origins and Inhibiting Influences in Genocide, Mass Killing and Other Collective Violence

Ervin Staub

Introduction

In our contemporary times, genocide, mass killing and other violence by groups of people directed at other groups defined by their ethnicity, race, religion, culture or political affiliation have been widespread. Conflict between groups, and violence, can be based on material interest, issues of identity, power and politics, or differentiation between 'us' and 'them' and devaluation of others that is magnified or even created by difficult life conditions. Such violence between groups, most often part of the same country, can be called collective violence, mass violence or group violence. Sometimes the term ethnopolitical violence has been used.

The level of violence between groups can vary. I will focus on two related, intense forms of violence: mass killing and genocide. The United Nations Genocide Convention of 1948 defines genocide as 'acts committed with intent to destroy in whole or in part, a national, ethnical, racial or religious group' (see http://www.un.org/millennium/law/iv-1.htm). However, the Genocide Convention does not appropriately clarify when killing of part of a group is genocide, nor does it include the killing of political groups as genocide.

There are many definitions of genocide. Helen Fein (1993b: 24) defines it as 'sustained, purposeful action by a perpetrator to physically destroy a collectivity directly or indirectly, through interdiction of the biological and social reproduction of group members, sustained regardless of the surrender or lack of threat offered by the victim'. My definition is similar: 'a government or some group acts to eliminate a whole group of people, whether by directly killing them or creating conditions that lead to their deaths or inability to reproduce' (Staub, 2011). In contrast to genocide, mass killing is 'killing (or in other ways destroying) members of a group without the intention to eliminate the whole group, or killing large numbers of people' without a focus on group membership (Staub, 1989: 8). Studies of origins suggest that similar influences lead to mass killing and genocide, and the former can be a way-station to the latter (Staub, 1989: 2011).

There was hope after the Second World War that the horrors of the Holocaust, Nazi Germany's crusade against Jews and the killing of millions of other people would bring such violence to an end forever. Instead, collective or group violence has become commonplace in the second part of the twentieth century and has continued into the twenty-first century. Cambodia, China, Indonesia, Tibet, East Timor, Sri Lanka, Argentina, El Salvador, Chile, Guatemala, Colombia, Bosnia, Rwanda, the Democratic Republic of the Congo (DRC) and Darfur are only some of the better-known places where such violence has been perpetrated. Its forms have also been numerous, including genocide, mass killing, mutually violent conflict, abductions or disappearances of large numbers of individuals, widespread torture (Suedfeld, 1990; Staub, 2011) and in recent times wide-ranging terrorism.

There has been research and writing in various disciplines about the origins of such violence, especially genocide (e.g. Fein, 1979, 1993b, 2007; Harff, 2003; Kuper, 1981; Smith, 1998; Staub, 1989, 2011, 2012; Waller, 2007). Whereas collective violence in general has received limited attention in psychology, this has been changing (see Cairns and Darby, 1998; Comas-Diaz, Lynes and Alarcon, 1998; Kressel, 1996; Rouhana and Bar-Tal, 1998; for earlier work, see also Kelman, 1973; Kelman and Hamilton, 1989). In varied fields there has been increasing attention given to prevention (Carnegie Commission on the Prevention of Deadly Conflict, 1997; Chamy, 1991; Fein, 1994, 2007; Hamburg, 2007; Staub, 1996b, 2011) and to reconciliation between groups (Hewstone et al., 2008; Nadler et al., 2008; Staub, 2006, 2011; Staub et al., 2005; Wheeler, 2000).

Without effective prevention, the frequency of such violence is likely to rise further in the twenty-first century. Poverty, the experience of injustice, and social and psychological disorganisation that prevents the meeting of basic human needs in a rapidly changing world tend to lead people to turn to ethnic, religious, national or other 'identity' groups to strengthen individual identity and to gain support and security. This, combined with ideologies that groups adopt in difficult times, whether Nazism, communism, nationalism, racial supremacy or something else, frequently leads to antagonism and violence against other groups.

To understand collective violence requires an interdisciplinary perspective. Individual psychology, group psychology, culture, social institutions, the social conditions in a country, the political system and the system of international relations all have roles to play in both causation and prevention. This chapter provides a review of a conception of the origins of such violence (Staub, 1989, 1996a, 2011) before considering factors that limit and prevent such violence (see Staub, 2011). Understanding the influences that lead to collective violence is necessary for prediction; both understanding and prediction are essential for prevention. For effective prevention, it is highly important to further our understanding of commonalities in both causes and methods of prevention as well as to respect the particulars of each potentially violence-producing situation.

The conception of origins that follows has been applied to analyses of the Holocaust, the genocide of the Armenians, the 'autogenocide' in Cambodia (the killings by the Khmer Rouge of Khmer), and the disappearances in Argentina (Staub, 1989). It has also been applied in a limited analysis to the group violence in Bosnia (Staub, 1996a). As I further elaborated on the principles of origins, I applied the conception to the genocide in Rwanda, to the tremendous violence in the DRC that between 1996 and 2011 led to the death of about six million people due to violence, disease and starvation, and to the Palestinian-Israeli conflict and others (Staub, 2011).

As the applications of the concept in other publications have shown, genocide and lesser violence by groups – such as mass killing and even intractable, violent conflict – have shared determinants. This chapter discusses origins and then examines inhibitors of violence that in some cases of group conflict, when violence-generating conditions existed, helped to limit the level of violence (Staub, 2011).

Instigators of Violence

Like individual violence, group violence has instigators. Difficult conditions of life in a society, singly or in combination, are frequent instigators: severe economic problems, great political turmoil, great and rapid societal change. At times when there are other potential instigators, difficult life conditions may magnify their instigating power. In most of the instances mentioned above – the Holocaust, the genocide of the Armenians, the 'autogenocide' in Cambodia, the disappearances in Argentina, Bosnia and Rwanda – one significant starting point for genocide or mass killing was intense, persistent difficulties of life, usually of varied kinds. In all of these cases except the Holocaust, there was also conflict between the groups, related to material issues, identity or both.

Difficult life conditions frustrate basic human needs (Staub, 1989, 1996a, 1998, 1999, 2003a, 2011; Burton, 1990; Kelman, 1990), such as the needs for security, a feeling of effectiveness and control, a positive identity and positive connections to other people. Difficult life conditions also involve chaos and turmoil that frustrate the need to understand the world and one's own place in it. The frustration of basic needs does not directly lead to group violence. Instead, it leads to psychological processes in individuals and social processes in groups that can result in turning against and harming members of another group.

Another instigating condition is conflict involving vital interests, such as territory needed for living space, as in the case of the conflict between Israelis and Palestinians. Although living space and other vital interests are 'objective' needs, they have powerful psychological elements, such as the intense need for security that groups feel the territory will provide or intense identification by some groups with a particular territory.

A further instigating condition is conflict between a dominant group in a society and a subordinate group that has limited rights and receives few of the society's resources. Since the Second World War, demands by subordinate groups for greater rights and more resources have been frequent instigators of genocide (Fein, 1993a, 1993b) or other forms of inter-group violence. Other contributing conditions are abrupt transitions in government, difficulty on the part of a new government in effectively governing, and ethnic or revolutionary wars (Institute for Genocide Studies, 1999).

Poverty by itself does not appear to be a primary instigator of collective violence (Harff, 2003). Deteriorating economic conditions, relative deprivation and the experience of injustice are likely to be more important. The experience of injustice in economically difficult times, where members of a less privileged group are severely affected by life problems in comparison to others, seems to enhance the instigating power of difficult life conditions (Staub, 1989, 2011). As in Argentina at the time of the disappearances, demands for better conditions and, when unsuccessful, limited violence by the subordinate group can lead to mass killing or genocide by the dominant group. Occasionally, as in the case of Cambodia, fighting that ended in victory for the subordinate group was followed by genocide or mass killing by the previously subordinate group (Staub, 1989).

Violence against groups is at times also motivated by self-interest. For example, an indigenous group may live in a territory that others want to own or develop economically, as in the case of Native Americans in the USA (Sheehan, 1973) or the Ache Indians in Paraguay (see also Totten, Parsons and Charny, 1997).

Identity, Scapegoating and Ideologies

Certain psychological and social processes that arise under instigating conditions begin an evolution that can lead to extreme violence. Difficult life conditions can lead individuals to turn to their already-existing ethnic or religious group, or to new ideological movements for identity and connection. The members of the group may join in scapegoating, claiming that some other group is responsible for life problems. They can also adopt or create ideologies, visions of a better life for the group, of ideal social arrangements. Scapegoating and ideologies do not by themselves improve life conditions, but they satisfy needs for identity, connection and comprehension of reality.

All groups have ideologies, and positive visions in difficult times can be very valuable. But in response to difficult life conditions, especially when certain cultural conditions are in place, the ideologies that are adopted or created tend to identify enemies, which make them destructive. These ideologies usually identify a devalued, vulnerable group, often the scapegoated group and sometimes a historical antagonist, as an enemy that stands in the way of the group realising the fulfilment of its ideology. The presence of such an ideology, leaders propagating it and it acquiring wide appeal are all important sources and indicators of potential violence.

Some form of destructive ideology is almost always present before group violence. 'Better world' ideologies, like communism, claim to improve the welfare of all human beings. Nationalistic ideologies come in two forms: the desire to create one's own nation, which at times is a reasonable and constructive goal (Kelman, 1997), but which often creates conflict and is pursued by violent means; and the desire to enhance the power, wealth and purity of one's group. Dominant groups usually develop 'hierarchy legitimizing myths' (Sidanius and Pratto, 1999) or legitimising ideologies that justify subordinating other groups. They often see themselves as superior and deserving of their status due to their race, religion, intelligence, hard work, world view or other characteristics. Groups can also embrace 'ideologies of development', visions of economic progress, identifying the victim group as standing in the way.

A history of conflict and antagonism between groups can create an ideology of antagonism (Staub, 1989, 2011), a view of the other as a mortal enemy and a view of one's group as the enemy of the other. This ideology is then activated by life problems, conflicts or even by improvement in the condition of the other group. Implicit in ideologies of antagonism is the vision of a world without the historical enemy. Ideologies of antagonism often arise from – and in turn give rise to – continuing cycles of violence, often over generations (Fisher, 1997).

People can become intensely committed to the mode of thinking, goals and social movements created by an ideology. The ideals that the ideology propagates can become a higher morality that overrides conventional morality. Although human beings need positive visions, especially in difficult times, when such visions identify others as enemies, they tend to become destructive and should be important danger signals to those interested in prevention (Staub, 2011).

The Evolution of Violence and the Continuum of Destruction

Violence usually evolves. Harmful acts by individuals make further and more intensely harmful acts probable (Buss, 1966; Goldstein, Davis and Herman, 1975). As an examination of instances of group violence clearly shows (Staub, 1989, 1996a, 2011), limited discrimination changes to progressively greater discrimination, persecution and violence against the victimised group. With 'steps along a continuum of destruction' (Staub, 1989), this can lead to mass killing or genocide. Lesser acts of discrimination and violence change and ultimately transform the perpetrators of those acts. Progressively, the whole group to which they belong also changes. Perpetrators justify their actions by devaluing their victims more. They come to see them as less human and exclude them from the moral universe (Fein, 1993b; Opotow, 1990; Staub, 1989, 1990, 2011). The 'bystanders', the rest of the population, also change. As they remain passive, to reduce their own empathic suffering, they distance themselves from the victims and accept the justifications of violence against them. Those hostile to the victim group move into prominent positions in the perpetrating group (Merkl, 1980). Public norms of behaviour and the institutions of the perpetrating group change, or new ones are created that serve the goals of persecution and violence. Increases in the level of harm inflicted on a historically victimised group are an indicator of current danger, of progression in the evolution of violence.

The Role of Leaders and Elites

The way a population turns to destructive leadership in the presence of the instigating conditions described above (and the cultural characteristics described below) highlights the important role of followers in generating violence. In previous analyses I have focused on how such conditions lead people to be open to or seek and select leaders, and even generate leadership that turns the group against others (Staub, 1989). While followers are crucial, so are leaders. Except under the most extreme conditions, leaders have some latitude in how they deal with difficult life conditions or group conflict. They can offer positive visions that unify rather than divide people. They can attempt to engage in the difficult task of fostering community and cohesion, so that people join in efforts to improve life conditions (Staub, 2011).

Instead, leaders and a country's elite frequently intensify pre-existing hostility. They often work to maintain differences in power and status between groups. They may use propaganda to enhance fear and devaluation of the other. They can propagate a destructive ideology and represent action against the other as serving 'high ideals'. They often create organisations that are potential agents of violence (Staub, 2011; Zartman, 1989). Paramilitary organisations, broadly defined, have been created and used as tools of collective violence in many places, including Bosnia (Kressel, 1996), Rwanda (des Forges, 1999; Prunier, 1995), Argentina (Nunca Mas, 1986) and other South American countries.

Bystander Actions

Bystanders are witnesses who are in a position to know about events and to take action (Staub, 1989, 2011). Bystanders have crucial roles in situations where mass violence occurs. Often, when they are in a position to know what is happening, they close their eyes and ears to events and information that would make them feel responsible to act. Passivity by internal bystanders (members of the population where the violence is occurring) and by external bystanders (outside groups and nations) encourages perpetrators. It allows the evolution of increasing violence. Such passivity is common.

Internal bystanders are affected by difficult life conditions and feel loyal to their group in a conflict. They, too, have learned to devalue victims (see below) and like perpetrators are affected by the other cultural preconditions. Their passivity further changes them. Rationalising (justifying) their passivity distances them from victims and leads them to further devalue them. It diminishes their capacity to empathise with those in distress and neutralises their sense of guilt about their inaction. In the end, they go along with and frequently even support persecution and violence, as they did in 1915–1916 at the time of the genocide of the Armenians in Turkey (Dadrian, 1995) and during the increasing persecution of the Jews in the 1930s in Germany.

External bystanders in the form of nation-states or international actors frequently continue commercial, cultural and other relations with a country that engages in violence against a group of its citizens (Simpson, 1993), thereby expressing tacit acceptance. Often countries actively support perpetrators. Many countries supported Iraq before its invasion of Kuwait, even though it had started a war against Iran and used chemical weapons against its Kurdish citizens. The USA increased its aid to El Salvador in 1984, even though about 40,000 people were killed there between 1979 and 1983, a large percentage of them in extrajudicial executions by security forces. The USA has trained South American military personnel in 'counter-insurgency' techniques and has continued to do so when it was already evident that the techniques were employed during the disappearances in Argentina (Nunca Mas, 1986) and in violence against the populations in other South American countries (Staub, 2011).

Research on individual behaviour in emergencies (Latane and Darley, 1970; Myers, 1996; Staub, 1974) and on the behaviour of bystanders in real-life situations – such as the rescuers of Jews in Nazi Europe (Hallie, 1979; Oliner and Oliner, 1988; Staub, 1989, 1993, 2011) – has demonstrated the great power and potential of bystanders to influence the behaviour of other bystanders and even of perpetrators. Outside nations, international actors, also had great influence on the rare occasions when they acted as committed bystanders, with boycotts in South Africa, through early preventive actions and peacekeeping in Macedonia (Staub, 2011), and militarily in Bosnia.

Predisposing Cultural Characteristics

Certain cultural or societal characteristics, including political arrangements, make mass (ethnopolitical) violence more likely (see Staub, 1989, 2011). In every case of such violence, there had been a history of a differentiation between 'us' and 'them' and usually devaluation of a subgroup of society, which made it easier and more likely that the group would be scapegoated and chosen as the ideological enemy (Staub, 2011). In some contexts there are rifts in a society, indicated by mutual devaluation which may take a number of different forms and may vary over time in intensity. In Cambodia, there was a historical rift between peasants in the countryside and people in the cities who owned the land and administered the country (Kiernan and Boua, 1982). Devaluation ranges from seeing the other as inferior to seeing the other as morally bad, even evil, and finally to seeing the other as an enemy bent on one's destruction. The more intense the devaluation, the more easy and likely the violence against the other. Ideologies of antagonism described earlier are intense, mutual devaluations, where each group devalues the other and this devaluation is a stable characteristics of each group, its identity and world view.

Another important predisposing characteristic is a monolithic (in contrast to pluralistic) society. A plurality of values and ways of life with all groups having access to the public domain reduces the chances of the population engaging in intense devaluation or remaining passive in the face of escalating harm inflicted on a subgroup of society. An aspect of true pluralism is the reasonable distribution of rights and privileges. This is especially important in multi-ethnic, multicultural states.

Rummel (1994) argues that democracies neither engage in genocide nor start wars against other democracies. However, this is primarily true of 'mature' democracies, in which pluralism and democratic process are deeply rooted in culture and social institutions, and the rights of varied groups are respected. In Germany, a new democracy during the Weimar Republic, many Germans mourned the collapse of the monarchy and opposed the Republic. Consequently, under difficult life conditions, Germany soon became a totalitarian system under the Nazis. In Argentina prior to the disappearances, military dictatorships regularly unseated elected governments. In Colombia there have been great disparities in rights and privileges between the population and the military and other segments of society (drug lords, guerrillas, large landowners, paramilitary groups) who had the power to subvert democratic processes (US Department of State, 1996).

A strong' authority orientation' (Staub, 1989, 2011) is another predisposing cultural characteristic (Kelman and Hamilton, 1989; Milgram, 1974). While all societies are based on some degree of respect for and obedience to authority, there is great variation in that degree. For example, long before Hitler came to power, Germans were regarded as especially respectful of and obedient to authority (Girard, 1980). Similarly, there is evidence from Serbia of authoritarian child-rearing practices and strong respect for authority (Kressel, 1996). In strongly authority-oriented societies, people will be more impacted by difficult life conditions when the capacity of their leaders and the authorities to provide security and effective leadership breaks down. In such circumstances, the population is likely to have more difficulty dealing with conditions of uncertainty (Soeters, 1996) and is likely to turn to leaders who offer hopeful visions of the future, even if destructive, and blame other groups for their life problems. They will be less likely to speak out against leaders who may lead them to discrimination and violence against other groups and they will be more obedient when ordered to perpetrate violence.

Another important societal characteristic is unhealed group trauma. When a group has experienced great suffering, especially (but not only) due to persecution and violence at the hands of others, it is more likely to respond to renewed threat with violence. Trauma affects people's assumptions about and orientation to the world (Herman, 1992; Janoff-Bulman, 1992; Pearlman and Saakvitne, 1995). It creates insecurity, a feeling that the world is a dangerous place. It leads to experiencing threat intensely. In the case of conflict, it may make it difficult to consider the needs of others. Without healing from psychological wounds and without constructive social processes, in response to threat, psychologically wounded groups are therefore more likely to engage in what they see as the defensive use of force (Staub, 1998, 2011; Staub at al., 2008). In Rwanda, for example, Hutus, the perpetrators of the genocide, were severely oppressed by Tutsis before 1959, under Belgian colonial rule. The resulting psychological wounds were one likely contributor to the genocide (Mamdani, 2001; Staub, 2011)

These and some other (Staub, 1989, 2011) predisposing characteristics are present to some degree in many societies. When they are strongly present and in combination, they make group violence more likely. When they are absent or present to a lesser extent, processes that might lead to violence are less likely.

The Example of Rwanda

Instigators

Intensely difficult economic and political conditions preceded the genocide in 1994 in Rwanda. Hutus, who constituted about 85 per cent of a population of eight million people (with Tutsis making up about 14 per cent), killed somewhere between 600,000 and 800,000 Tutsis. About 50,000 Hutus were also killed, either because they were politically moderate or because they came from the southern part of the country and were mistrusted by the contemporary Hutu leadership from the northwest (for historical information, see des Forges, 1999; Gourevich, 1998; Kressel, 1996; Mamdani, 2001; Malvern, 2004; Prunier, 1995; Smith, 1998; Staub, 2011). In an already densely populated country, there had been substantial population growth in the years leading up to the genocide. In the late 1980s the price of coffee, the primary export of Rwanda, sharply declined, as did the price of tin, the major mineral produced in Rwanda. In a highly authoritarian political system, where the elite grew rich while the population suffered, demands for greater rights by various groups emerged. The economic problems and political pressures created divisions among the Hutu elite, who were vying for positions of advantage.

The invasion by the Tutsi Rwandan Patriotic Front (RPF) in 1990, consisting of refugees or children of refugees who had fled after previous massacres, intensified the political turmoil. Although the invasion was stopped, the RPF went on the offensive in 1992 and again a year later after massacres of Tutsi peasants. Thus, in addition to difficult life conditions created by economic problems, Rwanda experienced intense conflict between Hutus and Tutsis which led to a civil war. A peace agreement was signed in 1993 that was to create a multi-party system, with power-sharing by several groups. The RPF, which propagated national unity, would have controlled five out of 21 ministries.

Evolution

Under Belgian colonial rule, the long-dominant Tutsi minority was given the power to administer the country; while they were elevated, Hutus were oppressed. In 1959 there was a Hutu uprising, with Tutsis killed during the course of it. After the country gained independence in 1962, there were mass killings of Tutsis in the early 1960s and 1970s. From that time until the 1990s, there was only limited violence, with the Hutus firmly in control. Substantial discrimination excluded or marginalised Tutsis in the administration of the country. In the early 1990s, there were small-scale massacres of Tutsis. A simple but powerful ideology of 'Hutu power' developed and was propagated by the elite, which included advocacy of the destruction of Tutsis (des Forges, 1999; Gourevich, 1998; Mamdani, 2001; Prunier, 1995; Staub, 2011). The history of intense devaluation and discrimination, an ideology of antagonism and repeated mass killings were all part of the evolution that led to the genocide. They joined with difficult life conditions and the civil war in leading to a reversal of morality (Staub, 1989, 2011), the killing of Tutsis becoming the right thing to do.

The Role of Elites

An extensive media campaign, especially involving radio, was used against Tutsis, traditionally called cockroaches by Hutus, which incited fear and hatred. People were told that the Tutsis were going to reclaim all their property seized by the Hutus after the Tutsis escaped from earlier violence to neighbouring countries, and even that they were going to kill all Hutus. Paramilitary groups were created. The plane of the Hutu president, who had agreed to a multi-party system and power-sharing with Tutsis, was shot down (it is unclear by whom). The genocide began immediately after this.

The genocide was organised and systematic, its aim being the elimination of the Tutsi population. Many authors, including des Forges (1999) and Straus (2006) present evidence that an extremist Hutu leadership strategically exploited the image of the Tutsi as an absolute menace, alongside threats to and violence against dissidents. What these accounts do not sufficiently stress is that even when such images are strategically exploited, they are based on psychological realities, such as intense devaluation of the out-group, antagonism and fear.

Although the genocide was primarily perpetrated by the army and paramilitary groups, the tactics used by the leadership, combined with the historical division between Tutsis and Hutus and the tendency to obey authorities, succeeded in involving a significant, although still relatively small portion of the population as perpetrators (Straus, 2006). However, some Hutus tried to protect Tutsis. Most of the few who did so publicly were killed. Others succeeded in rescuing individuals (Africa Rights, 2002). At the beginning of the genocide, Hutus were killed for political reasons, while later some were killed for their property (des Forges, 1999). As violence evolves, such expansion of targeting is quite common (Staub, 1989, 2011).

The Role of Bystanders

In response to the first invasion by the RPF, the French sent troops to support the government. The French did not intervene in the 'small-scale' massacres of Tutsis that followed, such as the killings of about 2,000 Tutsi peasants in 1993. As passionately described by Gourevich (1998), the international community remained passive in the face of reports from varied sources, including Human Rights Watch, of the impending violence against the Tutsis. The United Nations (UN) failed to act on information about plans for a genocide, received by General Dallaire, the head of the UN peacekeeping troops, from a highly placed Rwandan.

As the genocide began, some Belgian peacekeepers were killed. Partly under Belgian influence, the UN removed its peacekeepers. In order not to invoke the Genocide Convention, which would have created strong pressure to take action, the world, including and in part led by the US government, avoided the use of the term 'genocide' (see des Forges, 1999). With the genocide in progress, the French sent troops that helped some Tutsis to escape being killed, but also helped huge number of perpetrators escape to Zaire (soon renamed the DRC) (Malvern, 2004).

Cultural Predispositions

Tutsis were cattle-herding warriors, believed to have been conquerors of ethnically diverse farming peoples in the fifteenth century, and Hutus were farmers. The division between them over time became primarily a division of economic status and political power. The Tutsis ruled, in a complex relationship with the Hutus, until the early twentieth century. The Belgian colonisers created structural changes in the relation between the Hutus and the Tutsis that greatly enhanced Tutsi dominance and exploitation of Hutus, intensifying Hutu hostility towards Tutsis. Soon after the Hutu revolution in 1959, when some Tutsis were killed, Rwanda gained independence, leaving the Hutu majority to rule the country.

The Hutu government had total control over the population. Everyone was registered as either Hutu or Tutsi. People had to carry ethnic identity cards and movements were restricted according to group membership. Tutsis had no access to the public domain. Observers have reported that child-rearing was authoritarian (Smith, 1998), the culture was characterised by strong respect for and obedience to authority and society was organised in a highly hierarchical fashion. There also had to be collective trauma and psychological woundedness among the Hutu, due to their past experiences as a subordinate, badly treated group (Staub, 2011). Even though the Tutsis suffered discrimination, their past history, culture and better education enabled them to have good jobs in the small but important private sector. This situation of a devalued, disliked group doing relatively well intensifies hostility, as many instances show, including the Jews in Germany and the Armenians in Turkey (Staub, 1989).

Genocide and After the Genocide

It was in this cultural and societal context that intensely difficult life conditions developed, consisting of economic problems, social injustice, political unrest and escalating demands by the population, divisions within the Hutu leadership and the invasion by a Tutsi army. Intense anti-Tutsi feelings were propagated by the leadership and effective machinery for the destruction of the Tutsi was developed that centred around the use of paramilitary groups and sections of the army. The motivations discussed in previous sections, the anti-Tutsi ideology and propaganda, fear of the Tutsi, violence against Hutus who did not cooperate and obedience to leaders, resulted in segments of the population participating in the killings. The killings were finally brought to an end by the victory of the RPF.

The renewed passivity of external bystanders following the genocide has contributed to new waves of violence. Huge numbers of Hutus left the country after the victory of the RPF and were settled in refugee camps outside the border. Among them were the perpetrators of the genocide. They were not separated from the rest of the refugees, ruled the camps and used aid provided to the camps to buy arms. They renewed their violence against the Tutsis, conducting incursions into the country from their base in the camps. The international community, which supplied the camps, did nothing. The Rwandan army invaded in 1996 into the DRC, killing both perpetrators and other Hutus (Prunier, 1995, 2009; Staub, 2011). Many refugees, including some of the perpetrators, returned to Rwanda. But some remained in the DRC, continuing their violence, leading to a second invasion by the Rwandan army in 1998. Years of violence between militaries from a number of countries, and then among various militias that were created or emerged, disease and starvation, led to about six million deaths in the DRC from 1996 onwards.

In recent instances of mass violence, such as Bosnia, Rwanda, the DRC and Darfur, rape has been widespread (for more on this, see Sjoberg, Chapter 14, this volume on feminist reflections on political violence). It is used as an additional means of destruction of the other group. As women are impregnated and/or infected with HIV, the women who are raped are seen as disgraced by their group, and the men, unable to protect them, are humiliated. A policy of rape also leads to rape becoming indiscriminate, as men come to use it for personal satisfaction.

Restraining Forces and Positive Evolution

In a number of other situations that might well have led to mass killing or genocide, the escalation of violence was limited. Understanding the influences leading to violence can help us at least in part to explain the forces that contained violence. In many instances the role of bystanders was crucial. In Bosnia, after years of hesitation and confusion, NATO took military action that stopped the violence and led to negotiations. There were continued efforts by third-party nations, by NGOs and by individuals (Agger, 2001; Staub, 2011) to bring about healing and reconciliation and to prevent future violence. While violence did not re-start, as of 2012 deep divisions remain.

Before its resolution, an upsurge of the seemingly intractable conflict between mainly Catholic Nationalists and mainly Protestant Unionists in Northern Ireland resulted in close to 4,000 deaths from the 1960s to the late 1990s. Although in a small country this is a substantial number, the level of violence was probably limited by the presence of the British army and a substantial police force. The agreement between the parties may have been reached in part because of the positive roles played by Britain, as well as the USA, in bringing the parties together. Along the way there was reform of previous discriminatory practices, improvement in the material existence of the Catholic minority and more contact between groups (Cairns and Darby, 1998). Even as violence continued, there were persistent and repeated – albeit unsuccessful – attempts at political solutions, all contributing to a positive evolution and the later agreement (Breen-Smyth, 2008; Pruitt, 1998). In Israel and the West Bank, limitations in the scale of violence may have been due to the continuous involvement of outside parties (Staub, 2011). Even though the USA has been an imperfect bystander – for example, apart from a suspension in 2010 that was limited in both scope and length of time, it failed to exert enough influence to halt the building of the settlements – its involvement, together with the involvement of others, contributed to the world focusing on the conflict. This is likely to have played a significant role in limiting violence. In addition, disapproval of violence against Palestinians by significant segments of the Israeli population at various times has impacted on Israel's democratic politics. Many groups have been working on creating positive contact between Jews and Palestinians, originating outside as well as within the region (Kelman, 1990; Rouhana and Bar-Tal, 1998; Rouhana and Kelman, 1994; Staub, 2011).

Two factors – bystanders and a prior positive evolution – limited violence in response to the civil rights movement in the USA. As the marches and sit-ins proceeded in the South, a significant segment of the population in the North came to support civil rights for African Americans, as did the government. With the readiness of the National Guard and the military to intervene, the effect of their physical presence and their symbolic role as representatives of the government and the people, the outcome was in stark contrast to the indifference and impunity surrounding the lynchings in the South in earlier times (Ginzburg, 1988). The Supreme Court's decision on the desegregation of schools, the desegregation of the military, and the contact between Southern Blacks and Whites in the military and around military bases (Reed, 2001) were all part of a prior positive evolution.

As violent societal dynamics evolve step by step, so too can resistance to escalation. More constructive relations between groups can also develop step by step. Certain kinds of interventions can help. Working in Rwanda, my associates and I have conducted workshops for groups at the community level for the media, as well as for national leaders, and have developed educational media such as a radio drama (which were also introduced in Burundi and the DRC) to promote healing and reconciliation. We have found that information about the origins of violence as briefly described in this chapter, about the impact of violence on people and about the role of active bystanders has positive effects. It has led to more positive orientation by members of hostile groups, Hutus and Tutsis, towards each other, lower trauma symptoms and a greater willingness to forgive under certain conditions (Staub et al., 2005). After only one year, exposure to an educational radio drama (which is in its eighth year in 2011) increased empathy (for survivors, leaders and even perpetrators), led to a greater willingness by people to say what they believe and to greater independence from authority (Paluck, 2009; Staub and

Pearlman, 2009). (For a review of all this work in Rwanda and similar work in the DRC, and for extensive discussion of principles and practices of prevention and reconciliation, see Staub, 2011.)

A positive evolution can lead both to the selection of new leaders and new directions chosen by leaders. It is likely that changes in the public mood within South Africa, at least partly due to the actions of the international community, led to the election of De Klerk. On becoming president, he legalised Black liberation organisations, which had been outlawed for 30 years. The changing public mood may have had a role in affecting other bystanders as well. A White South African lawyer, the husband of a friend of Winnie Mandela, took it upon himself to influence his friend, the justice minister Jacobus Coetsee, to initiate contact with Nelson Mandela (Sparks, 1994). The character of Nelson Mandela, as it later showed itself to the world and as it appeared to Coetsee on their first meeting, was also important. Coetsee, in turn, seems to have influenced De Klerk to initiate contact. Both the macro and the micro processes involved in such positive evolutions are worthy of further study.

Conclusion

The more the basic physical and psychological needs of groups of people are satisfied by constructive means, the less likely it is that psychological and social processes that lead to group violence arise. But without significant efforts at prevention, group violence is likely to become more widespread. There are a number of reasons for this. In our interconnected world, where communication is instant and pervasive, people see the riches that others possess, feelings of deprivation and injustice are likely to arise, and people turn to their group as a means of improving their lives. In a rapidly changing world where small, local communities are often undermined or destroyed, people turn to ethnic, religious or ideological groups for security, identity, connection and support.

In a world where sub-national conflict gives rise to new nation-states, the disengagement from, and continuing conflict with, former ethnic, religious or national rivals are potential sources of violence. Competition for resources and economic crises – with their impact on poor people and their tendency to increase inequality between groups – also have significant impacts (Staub, 2011). Psychologists, other social scientists, government officials, diplomats and leaders, journalists and many others must develop and use their professional knowledge and skills to work for the prevention of group violence. Late prevention, involving sanctions and especially military force, usually comes after great suffering, many deaths and also involves huge financial costs. We must engage in early prevention that addresses the conditions that give rise to violence and leads people to respond to them in constructive rather than destructive ways (Staub, 2011).

Striving for a world in which basic psychological needs can be satisfied by constructive means is an important means of prevention. Both multi-disciplinary scholarship and its applications in the real world to emerging and escalating conflicts are essential. Scholars, researchers and practitioners in the various disciplines involved in the field must act as morally committed persons, creating public education on a wide scale, both for citizens and leaders, and acting as morally courageous bystanders. And it requires citizens as active bystanders to help generate the motivation for action by relevant parties and to influence governments to create systems that respond to warning signs and engage in the early prevention of group violence (Staub, 2011).

References

Africa Rights. (2002). *Tribute to Courage*. Kigali, Rwanda.
Agger, I. (2001). Psychosocial 'during ethnopolitical warfare in the former Yugoslavia'. In Chirot, D. and Seligman, M.E.P. (eds), *Ethnopolitical Warfare: Causes, Consequences and Possible Solutions*. Washington DC: American Psychological Association, 305–19.
Breen-Smyth, M. (2008) Frameworks for peace in Northern Ireland; an analysis of the 1998 Belfast Agreement. *Strategic Analysis*, 32(6), 1–23.
Burton, J.W. (1990). *Conflict: Human Needs Theory*. New York: St Martin's Press.
Buss, A.H. (1966). The effect of harm on subsequent aggression. *Journal of Experimental Research in Personality*, 1, 249–55.
Cairns, E. and Darby, J. (1998). The conflict in Northern Ireland. *American Psychologist*, 53, 754–60.
Carnegie Commission on the Prevention of Deadly Conflict. (1997). *Preventing Deadly Conflict: Final Report*. New York: Carnegie Corporation of New York.
Chamy. I. (1991). Genocide intervention and prevention. *Social Education*, 124–7.
Comas-Diaz, L., Lynes, M.B. and Alarcon, R.D. (1998). Ethnic conflict and the psychology of liberation in Guatemala, Peru, and Puerto Rico. *American Psychologist*, 53, 778–92.
Dadrian, V. N. (1995). *The History of the Armenian Genocide*. Providence: Berghahn Books.
Des Forges, A. (1999). *Leave None to Tell the Story: Genocide in Rwanda*. New York: Human Rights Watch.
Fein, H. (1979). *Accounting for Genocide: Victims and Survivors of the Holocaust*. New York: Free Press.
Fein, H. (1993a). Accounting for genocide after 1945: theories and some findings. *International Journal on Group Rights*, 1, 79–106.
Fein, H. (1993b). *Genocide: A Sociological Perspective*. London: Sage.
Fein, H. (1994). *The Prevention of Genocide. A Working Paper of the Institute for the Study of Genocide*. City University of New York.
Fein, H. (2007). *Human Rights and Wrongs: Slavery, Terror, Genocide*. Boulder, CO: Paradigm Publishers.
Fisher, R.J. (1997). *Interactive Conflict Resolution*. Syracuse, NY: Syracuse University Press.

Ginzburg, R. (1988). *100 Years of Lynching*. Baltimore, MD: Black Classic Press.
Girard, P. (1980). Historical foundations of anti-Semitism. In Dimsdale, J. (ed.), *Survivors, Victims and Perpetrators: Essays on the Nazi Holocaust*. Washington DC: Hemisphere, 55–79.
Goldstein, J.H., Davis, R.W. and Herman, D. (1975). Escalation of aggression: experimental studies. *Journal of Personality and Social Psychology*, 31, 162–70.
Gourevich, P. (1998). *We Wish to Inform You that Tomorrow We Will Be Killed with our Families*. New York: Farrar, Straus & Giroux.
Hallie, P.P. (1979). *Lest Innocent Blood Be Shed. The Story of the Village of Le Chambon, and How Goodness Happened There*. New York: Harper & Row.
Hamburg, D. (2007). *Preventing Genocide: Practical Steps Toward Early Detection and Effective Action*. Boulder, CO: Paradigm Publishers.
Harff, B. (2003). No lessons learned from the Holocaust? Assessing risks of genocide and political mass murder since 1955. *American Political Science Review*, 97(1), 57–73.
Herman, J. (1992). *Trauma and Recovery*. New York: Basic Books.
Hewstone, M., Kenworthy, J.B., Cairns, E., Tausch, N., Hughes, J., Tam, T., Voci, A., von Hacker, U. and Pinder, C. (2008). Stepping stones to reconciliation in Northern Ireland: intergoup contact, forgiveness and trust. In Nadler, A., Malloy, T. and Fisher, J.D. (eds), *Social Psychology of Intergroup Reconciliation*. New York: Oxford University Press, 199–227.
Institute for Genocide Studies. (1999). *Ever Again? Evaluating the United Nations Genocide Convention on its 50th Anniversary*. New York: University of New York.
Janoff-Bulman, R. (1992). *Shattered Assumptions*. New York: Free Press.
Kelman, H.C. (1973). Violence without moral restraint: reflections on the dehumanization of victims and victimizers. *Journal of Social Issues*, 29(4), 25–61.
Kelman, H.C. (1990). Applying a human needs perspective to the practice of conflict resolution: the Israeli-Palestinian case. In Burton, J. (ed.), *Conflict: Human Needs Theory*. New York: St Martin's Press.
Kelman, H.C. (1997). Nationalism, patriotism and national identity: social-psychological dimensions. In Bar-Tal, D. and Staub, E. (eds), *Patriotism in the Lives of Individuals and Nations*. Chicago: Nelson-Hall, 165–90.
Kelman, H.C. and Hamilton, V.C. (1989). *Crimes of Obedience*. New Haven: Yale University Press.
Kiernan, B. and Boua, C. (eds) (1982). *Peasants and Politics in Kampuchea. 1942–1981*. Armonk, NY: Shatpe.
Kressel, N.J. (1996). *Mass Hate: The Global Rise of Genocide and Terror*. New York: Plenum.
Kuper, L. (1981). *Genocide. Its Political Use in the Twentieth Century*. New Haven, CT: Yale University Press.
Latane, B. and Darley, J. (1970). *The Unresponsive Bystander: Why Doesn't He Help?* New York: Appleton-Crofts.
Malvern, L. (2004). *Conspiracy to Murder: The Rwanda Genocide*. London: Verso.
Mamdani, M. (2001). *When Victims Become Killers: Colonialism, Nativism, and the Genocide in Rwanda*. Princeton, NJ: Princeton University Press.

Merkl, P.H. (1980). *The Making of a Stormtrooper*. Princeton, NJ: Princeton University Press.
Milgram, S. (1974). *Obedience to Authority: An Experimental View*. New York: Harper & Row.
Myers, D. (1996). *Social Psychology*. New York: McGraw-Hill.
Nadler, A., Malloy, T. and Fisher, J.D. (eds) (2008). *Social Psychology of Intergroup Reconciliation*. New York: Oxford University Press.
New York Times Conference on the Internet. (1996). *Bosnia: Uncertain Path to Peace*. Forum on Healing and Reconciliation.
Nunca Mas. (1986). *The Report of the Argentine National Commission on the Disappeared*. New York: Farrar, Straus & Giroux.
Oliner, S. B. and Oliner, P. (1988). *The Altruistic Personality: Rescuers of Jews in Nazi Europe*. New York: Free Press.
Opotow, S. (ed.) (1990). Moral exclusion and injustice. *Journal of Social Issues*, 46(1), 1–20.
Paluck, E.L. (2009). Reducing intergroup prejudice and conflict using the media: a field experiment in Rwanda. *Journal of Personality and Social Psychology*, 96, 574–87.
Pearlman, L.A. and Saakvitne, K. (1995). *Trauma and the Therapist*. New York: Norton.
Pruitt, D. (1998). *Resolving Seemingly Intractable Conflict*. Paper presented at the conference on *Ethnopolitical Warfare: Causes and Solutions*. Londonderry. Northern Ireland.
Prunier. G. (1995). *The Rwanda Crisis: History of a Genocide*. New York: Columbia University Press.
Prunier, G. (2009). *Africa's World War: Congo, the Rwandan Genocide, and the Making of a Continental Catastrophe*. New York: Oxford University Press.
Reed, J.S. (2001). Why there has been on race war in the American South? In Chirot, D. and Seligman, M.E.P. (eds), *Ethnopolitical Warfare: Causes, Consequences and Possible Solutions*. Washington DC: American Psychological Association, 275–87.
Rouhana, N.N. and Bar-Tal, D. (1998). Psychological dynamics of intractable ethnonational conflicts: the Israeli-Palestinian case. *American Psychologist*, 53, 761–70.
Rouhana, N.N. and Kelman, H.C. (1994). Promoting joint thinking in international conflicts: an Israeli- Palestinian continuing workshop. *Journal of Social Issues*, 20, 157–78.
Rummel, R. (1994). Democide in totalitarian states: Mortacracies and megamurders. In Chamy, I. (ed.), *Genocide: A Critical Bibliographic Review*. New Brunswick, NJ: Transaction.
Sheehan. B. (1973). *Seeds of Extinction*. Chapel Hill, NC: University of North Carolina Press.
Sidanius, J. and Pratto, F. (1999). *Social Dominance: An Intergroup Theory of Social Hierarchy and Oppression*. New York: Cambridge University Press.
Simpson, C. (1993). *The Splendid Blond Beast*. New York: Grove.

Smith, N.S. (1998). The psychological roots of genocide. *American Psychologist*, 53, 743–53.
Soeters, J. (1996). Culture and conflict: an application of Hofstede's theory to the conflict in the former Yugoslavia. *Peace and Conflict: Journal of Peace Psychology*, 2, 233–44.
Sparks, A. (1994). Letter from South Africa: the secret revolution. *The New Yorker*, April, 56–89.
Staub, E. (1974). Helping a distressed person: social, personality and stimulus determinants. In Berkowitz, L. (ed.), *Advances in Experimental Social Psychology*. New York: Academic, Vol. 7, 203–342.
Staub, E. (1989). *The Roots of Evil: The Origins of Genocide and other Group Violence*. New York: Cambridge University Press.
Staub, E. (1993). The psychology of bystanders, perpetrators and heroic helpers. *International Journal of Intercultural Relations*, 17, 315–41.
Staub, E. (1996a). Cultural-societal roots of violence: the examples of genocidal violence and of contemporary youth violence in the United States. *American Psychologist*, 51, 117–32.
Staub, E. (1996b). Preventing genocide: activating bystanders, helping victims and the creation of caring. *Peace and Conflict: Journal of Peace Psychology*, 2, 189–201.
Staub, E. (1998). Breaking the cycle of genocidal violence: healing and reconciliation. In Harvey, J. (ed.), *Perspectives on Loss: A Source Book*. Washington DC: Taylor & Francis.
Staub, E. (1999). The roots of evil: personality, social conditions, culture and basic human needs. *Personality and Social Psychology Review*, 3, 179–92.
Staub, E. (2003a). Basic human needs and their role in altruism and aggression. In Staub, E., *The Psychology of Good and Evil: Why Children, Adults and Groups Help and Harm Others*. New York, Cambridge University Press.
Staub, E. (2003b). *The Psychology of Good and Evil: Why Children, Adults and Groups Help and Harm Others*. New York: Cambridge University Press.
Staub, E. (2006). Reconciliation after genocide, mass killing or intractable conflict: understanding the roots of violence, psychological recovery and steps toward a general theory. *Political Psychology*, 27(6), 865–95.
Staub, E. (2011). *Overcoming Evil: Genocide, Violent Conflict and Terrorism*. New York: Cambridge University Press.
Staub, E. (2012). *The Panorama of Mass Violence: Origins, Prevention, Reconciliation and the Development of Caring and Active Bystandership*. New York: Oxford University Press.
Staub, E. and Pearlman, L.A. (2009). Reducing intergroup prejudice and conflict: a commentary. *Journal of Personality and Social Psychology*, 96, 588–94.
Staub, E., Pearlman, L.A., Gubin, A. and Hagengimana, A. (2005). Healing, reconciliation, forgiving and the prevention of violence after genocide or mass killing: an intervention and its experimental evaluation in Rwanda. *Journal of Social and Clinical Psychology*, 24(3), 297–334.

Staub, E. and Vollhardt, J. (2008). Altruism born of suffering: the roots of caring and helping after experiences of personal and political victimization. *American Journal of Orthopsychiatry*, 78, 267–80.

Straus, S. (2006). *The Order of Genocide: Race, Power, and War in Rwanda*. Ithaca, NY: Cornell University Press

Suedfeld, P. (ed.) (1990). *Psychology and Torture*. Washington DC: Hemisphere.

Totten, S., Parsons, W.S. and Charny, I.W. (eds) (1997). *Century of Genocide: Eyewitness Accounts and Critical Views*. New York: Garland Publishing.

US Department of State (1996). *Country Report on Colombia*. Washington DC: US Department of State.

Waller, J. (2007). *Becoming Evil: How Ordinary People Commit Genocide and Mass Killing*, 2nd edn. New York: Oxford University Press.

Wessells, M. (2007). *Child Soldiers: From Violence to Protection*. Cambridge, MA: Harvard University Press.

Wheeler, N. (2000). *Saving Strangers: Humanitarian Intervention in International Society*. Oxford: Oxford University Press.

Zartman, I.W. (1989). *Ripe for Resolution, Conflict and Intervention in Africa*. New York: Oxford University Press.

Religion as a Motivation for Political Violence

Jeroen Gunning

On the eve of his 'self-martyrdom' operation, a young Palestinian recorded the following video testament:

> Tomorrow is the day of encounter … the day of meeting the lord of the Worlds … [We] will make our blood cheap for the sake of God, out of love for this homeland and for the sake of the freedom and honour of this people, in order that Palestine remain[s] Islamic, and in order that Hamas remains a torch lighting the roads of all the perplexed and all the tormented and oppressed [and] that Palestine might be liberated. (Hamas videotape, quoted in Juergensmeyer 2000: 70)

Suicide bombing, or self-martyrdom as Hamas calls it, is often portrayed as the perfect example of 'religious terrorism'. It is (supposedly) carried out in the name of God by people claiming religion as their motivation. It involves behaviour that a secular rationality assumedly abhors and thus fits faultlessly into a paradigm which characterises religion as an 'irrational' phenomenon. And yet, as the above quote shows, all is not as it seems. For sure, the suicide bomber declares his religious motivation – his longing to '[meet] the lord of the Worlds' and ensure that 'Palestine remain[s] Islamic'. But in the same breath, he places his impending death in the service of not only liberating Palestine – 'out of love for this homeland and for the sake of the freedom and honour of this people' – but so that Hamas 'remains a torch lighting the roads of all the perplexed and all the tormented and oppressed'. If his testament is anything to go by, this young man's motivation is as much nationalist – even, to an extent, internationalist and anti-colonialist – as it is religious. It is also partisan, in terms of seeking to ensure Hamas' continued survival in the intense competition between rival Palestinian groups.

Religion clearly plays a role in this man's motivation. But it is not the only factor and, without further investigation, we cannot be sure that it is the most important one or that it can explain his behaviour better than other factors. Religion, after all, has inspired groups like Hamas and the Palestinian Islamic Jihad since the

1980s. Yet, they did not turn to suicide bombing until 1993, and since 2005, Hamas has ceased carrying out suicide attacks altogether, even while continuing to claim religious inspiration for its politics. The causes of this man's actions can thus not be found solely in religion.

If religion were a primary cause of groups adopting suicide bombing as a tactic, one would expect suicide bombing to be limited to groups claiming religious inspiration. However, when Robert Pape carried out his famous study, the group responsible for the highest number of suicide attacks globally was the secular and 'explicitly antireligious' Tamil Tigers in Sri Lanka (Pape 2005: 16). The organisation which is often cited as pioneering the tactic, the Lebanese Shi'i Islamist party Hizballah, meanwhile, has long ceased using it, and almost as many attacks have been carried out by Lebanon's myriad secular groups (Pape 2005: 17). Moreover, suicide tactics had already been experimented with by the deeply anti-religious Viet Cong in the 1960s (Weinberg 2006) and one could even say that militants among the nineteenth-century anarchist movements had laid the groundwork for suicide bombing by welcoming their death or subsequent execution in pursuit of what Leonard Weinberg calls, borrowing from Robert Jay Lifton, 'revolutionary immortality' (2006: 110).

Furthermore, suicide tactics tend to be adopted in very specific circumstances. To stay with Pape's analysis (2005: 21–3), the situation most likely to witness a turn to suicide tactics is when a militarily stronger democracy occupies a land inhabited by people who belong to a different religious group from those doing the occupying. Religion, in this scenario, plays a role as a marker of differentiation – although one can query whether it is religion per se or also ethnic differences and leaders playing on these differences that do the work. But other factors, such as the level of (nationalistic) attachment to a territory, the political system of the occupying state (whether it is a democracy and thus more susceptible to public pressure) and the level of asymmetry between the military capacities of the antagonists play arguably more central roles. This is because if religious difference were the primary cause, we would expect to see suicide tactics emerging in every conflict involving religiously differentiated groups. That this is not the case suggests that neither religion nor religious difference is a primary cause, or at least not on its own.

Religion and Violence in the Social Sciences

There is a long and problematic tradition linking religion and violence in the social sciences. Religion has, for many years, sat uneasily within the panoply of political science. For years, it was either ignored, quarantined from the study of politics because of its supposedly private, cultural nature or catapulted to centre stage as a fundamentalist, and fundamentally irrational, force spurring otherwise rational people to commit heinous acts of violence. Within the study of social movements, for instance, religious social movements were until relatively recently discarded as displacement phenomena, lulling the downtrodden into an obsession with the afterlife, away from the political activism that social movements were supposed to mobilise around (Hannigan 1991). Within the field of international relations, religion has similarly until recently been largely ignored as a serious object of study (cf. Philpott 2009) – unless, that is, religion was intertwined with conflict.

However, even where religion has been cited as a cause, the role of religion has not typically been studied in sufficient detail. Rather than engaging with the meaning of religious beliefs and the networks sustaining them, authors have tended to either treat religion as an inherent cause of division and fanatical hatred (thus lessening the need to investigate it further) or to see it as a mere byproduct of socio-economic changes, such as globalisation or urbanisation.

For the former, variously called culturalists, essentialists or (neo)-Orientalists (cf. Wolff 1998), religion is a marker of civilisation essence, differentiating an allegedly 'enlightened', rational West from an irrational, religiously driven 'Rest'. For these scholars, religion is a key factor in explaining violence, and particularly in explaining why conflicts become disproportionately violent. Other factors, such as Western imperialism, occupation, 'youth bulges' and legacies of territorial conquests, feature in their analyses (cf. Lewis 1990; Huntington 1996; Juergensmeyer 2000; Hoffman 2006). But religion is the clincher. Samuel Huntington argued in his controversial *The Clash of Civilizations and the Remaking of World Order* that: 'The frequency, intensity, and violence of fault line wars are greatly enhanced by beliefs in different gods' (1996: 254). Bernard Lewis (1990: 60, 48–9) famously explained the rise of militant political Islam by arguing that 'this is no less than a clash of civilizations – the perhaps irrational but surely historic reaction of an ancient rival against our Judeo-Christian heritage, our secular present, and the worldwide expansion of both'. The 'hatred' motivating these militants, he argued, 'goes beyond hostility to specific interests or actions ... and becomes a rejection of Western civilization as such ... as innately evil, and those who promote or accept [its values] as the "enemies of God"' – a view Lewis explicitly traced back to classical Islam's division of humanity into the 'House of Islam' and the 'House of War'. Religion, on this reading, is the driver. It is fuelled by political and socio-economic frictions. But without religion, conflict would be both less likely and less violent. Curiously, though, religion is treated in this literature by and large as a 'black box' – a phenomenon analysed in terms of its inputs and outputs, without serious analysis of its inner dynamics and how these interact with external dynamics.

For the second group of scholars, variously called structuralists or (neo)-Third Worldists (cf. Wolff 1998), the turn towards religiously inspired politics – including violent politics – is a byproduct of wider structural changes (cf. Ayubi 1991; Anderson 1997; Halliday 2002; Pape 2005). Islamist militancy, for instance, is explained as a response to the alienation and frustration produced by rapid modernisation, political exclusion or state repression (cf. Ayubi 1991; Anderson 1997). Religion plays a role as a source of identity and authenticity, as a marker of difference vis-à-vis the secular state elite, or as a beacon of hope and guidance in an increasingly baffling, hostile and alien globalised world. But it is seen as an instrument, (ab)used by elites and counter-elites alike (cf. Hasenclever and Rittberger 2000; De Juan 2008), a useful network of resources rather than a cause. Instead, the cause is seen to be located in structural changes.

Neither approach is particularly satisfactory. Adherents of the culturalist school tend to reify religion and treat it as an unchanging essence, almost autonomous from its surrounding context. Adherents of the structuralist school tend to relegate religion to being a secondary factor, a product of its environment more than an independent cause. Neither approach is capable of adequately capturing the complex roles beliefs play, as both products and producers of their environment, as both causes and effects, constantly shifting as interpretations and implementations are contested, altered and reproduced.

Linking Religion and Violence

The notion that religion has a propensity to inspire its adherents towards violence has a long pedigree within religious studies. In his critique of this literature (which overlaps with the fields of international relations and anthropology), William Cavanaugh singles out three types of argument that have traditionally been made to explain the supposed link between religion and violence. First is the argument that it is religion's claims to absolutism and its concomitant sense of superiority vis-à-vis non-believers that inspires its followers towards violence. Because believers 'absolutize what is merely relative' and come to believe in their (God-given) superiority over others, violence, it is argued, is a constant temptation, whether to protect oneself from threats from inferior others or to force those inferior others into submission to one's superior God (Cavanaugh 2004: 4–5).[1] Religion, on this reading, was one factor in the violence that accompanied colonialism.

Closely linked to this is a second type of argument, namely that religion's supposedly inherent divisiveness propels people to violence. Because religion is believed 'to divide people into friends and enemies, good and evil, us and them', it is said to encourage the use of violence 'by "satanizing" the other and ruling out compromise or peaceful co-existence' (Cavanaugh 2004: 9–10). Religious images of struggle, self-sacrifice and a cosmic war against sin or evil facilitate this demonisation of the enemy (see, for example, Juergensmeyer 2000). Andreas Hasenclever and Volker Rittberger (2000) make this same point when they argue that religion is particularly suitable to demonise the enemy and depict the conflict as a zero-sum struggle for existential survival.

The third argument is that it is religion's inherent irrationality and concomitant fanaticism that causes violence. On this count, religion is 'especially prone to violence because it produces a particular intensity of non-rational or irrational passion that is not subject to the firm control of reason' (Cavanaugh 2004: 19). Here, religion is contrasted with the supposedly rational conduct of secular states and science, a theme we will return to later.

---

1   The argument put forward in Cavanaugh (2004) has been expanded upon in Cavanaugh (2009).

A poignant illustration of how these arguments drive analysis can be found within the terrorism studies literature, where a separate category of 'religious terrorism' has been created.[2] Those who subscribe to this notion argue that 'religious terrorists' are more violent, more fanatical, more radical and less willing to compromise than their secular counterparts, and that it is religion which causes them to be thus. Bruce Hoffman (2006: 88–9), for instance, suggests that 'religious terrorists' are less inhibited about killing innocent civilians because they divide the world into believers and unbelievers, and see their violence as driven by divine imperative rather than rational this-worldly calculations. He also argues that they are less likely to compromise because of the absolutism of their claims and because they see themselves as divinely ordained outsiders. To support their claims, these scholars point to the fact that, statistically, groups labelled 'religious' have been more lethal over the past 40 years than groups that have ostensibly been inspired by secular ideologies (Hoffman 2006: 86–8; for statistics, cf. Robison, Crenshaw and Jenkins 2006; Masters 2008). However, as we will see, leaving aside difficulties in labelling groups 'religious' or 'secular', this in itself is not sufficient proof that it is religion that is causing these groups to be more violent rather than religion in the context of other factors.

There is a growing body of scholarship within the various literatures on religion and violence which emphasises that religion does not necessarily lead to violence (cf. Johnston and Sampson 1995; Appleby 2000; Abu-Nimer 2003; Gopin 2005). R. Scott Appleby, for instance, named his seminal book *The Ambivalence of the Sacred* (2000) precisely to signal that religion has given rise to both militants and peacemakers and thus that its impact on behaviour is ambiguous. Hasenclever and Rittberger (2000) similarly argue that religion can be interpreted in different ways and show how tendencies towards absolutism, divisiveness and irrational fanaticism can be countered by emphasising the more tolerant, unifying, grievance-transcending aspects of religious traditions. In *Religion: The Missing Dimension of Statecraft* (1995), Johnston and Sampson illustrate precisely this peaceful potential by analysing a number of cases where religious communities played a role in bringing conflicts to an end. Even Lewis (1990: 48), the originator of the 'clash of civilisations' thesis, starts his discussion by underlining that 'Islam is one of the world's great religions … It has taught people of different races to live in brotherhood and people of different creeds to live side by side in reasonable tolerance'. But, by and large, the emphasis of the various literatures dealing with religion and violence is on religion's propensity to propel people towards violence.

Rethinking the Link between Religion and Violence

All this raises the following question: is religion indeed inherently inclined towards violence? Is it particularly divisive, absolutist and irrational compared to other belief systems? Is it necessarily so or does it become so under specific circumstances

---

2   For a more detailed analysis, see Gunning and Jackson (2011).

– in which case, should we not investigate these circumstances rather than religion as such?

Much of what has been said about religion in conflict holds true for other belief systems. Nationalists have at times been every bit as absolutist, divisive, irrational and violent as some religiously inspired groups. The same can be said of Marxists, fascists, secularists and liberals, to name but a few. One could argue that it is profoundly irrational to believe that those who do not belong to one's national group are subhuman or that one's leader has superhuman qualities. Nationalism and ethno-centric beliefs have inspired people to massacre their erstwhile neighbours, as for example in the numerous wars between Germany and France, or, more recently, in Rwanda. Various forms of Marxism have been used to justify killing those labelled enemies of the proletariat (cf. della Porta 1995a, 1995b; Chernick 2007). The German Red Army Fraction (RAF) and the Italian Red Brigades (RB) both pursued a utopian world order with absolutist conviction, regarded themselves as being part of a form of 'cosmic war' and described their enemies in much the same eschatological language as that used by al-Qaeda (della Porta 1995a, 1995b).

Conversely, many of those labelled 'religious' rationally weigh up cost-benefit calculations and adapt accordingly, have clearly identifiable this-worldly goals (as opposed to acting on some other-worldly divine imperative) and this-worldly constituencies (as opposed to acting solely on behalf of God), and have shown themselves to be capable of restraint. Compared to the secular FARC (Colombia), the Tamil Tigers (Sri Lanka) and the Kurdish PKK (Turkey), so-called 'religious' groups such as Hamas (Palestinian territories) and Hizballah (Lebanon) have been far less lethal and more restrained, and have adjusted their methods in the light of changing circumstances, like any 'rational' secular organisation (cf. Gunning 2007; Gunning and Jackson 2011; Wiktorowicz and Kaltner 2003). The tactics of many supposedly 'religious' insurgents show a clear strategic rationality which follows the logic of asymmetric warfare rather than the logic of some imagined wild-eyed religious fanatic. Even the behaviour of al-Qaeda, the presumed epitome of religious violence, can more readily be explained with reference to the theories of terrorism developed by nineteenth-century Italian anarchists than in religious terms (Sedgwick 2004).

At the same time, religion has inspired many to forgo violence, even in the face of violent attack, and instead work towards peace. Within most religious traditions, there are both antecedents and justifications for violence and for forsaking violence. Which aspect of these traditions becomes operative is dependent on the context. In this, religion is far from unusual. Marxism has similarly inspired people to both violent and non-violent activism. In 1970s Italy, for instance, the Communist Party turned its back on the emphasis on violent revolution found in earlier Marxist thinking and embraced democratic party politics in what came to be known as 'the historic compromise'. Yet, simultaneously, the Red Brigades drew inspiration from the very same ideological tradition to justify their escalating use of violence against factory foremen, trade unionists, estate agents and politicians. The fact that both were inspired by Marxist ideology cannot explain these very different trajectories.

To do that, we have to look at the internal dynamics within the Italian Left, the shifting fortunes of the Communist Party vis-à-vis the Italian political system, the dynamics of the student and workers' revolution of the late 1960s, and how the police and their right-wing auxiliaries treated left-wing protesters (della Porta 1995a, 1995b).

A further problem is that mere statistical correlation does not necessarily mean that there is a causal link. The argument that 'religious terrorists' are more violent than 'secular terrorists' rests to a significant degree on the claim that the former have, taken together, perpetrated more violence than the latter over the past 40 years. But even if we can be certain that groups labelled 'religious' are indeed primarily motivated by religion – which is far from clear, as we will see shortly – we cannot be certain that it is religion that causes these groups to be more violent. To be able to claim this, we need further analysis of the precise role religion plays and of the context within which the violence takes place.

From Religion to Goal Type, Organisational Structure and the Wider Context

A closer look at the data underpinning the argument that 'religious terrorists' are more lethal than their secular counterparts suggests that it is not religion per se that is correlated to greater lethality but what types of goals groups pursue and whether the group is embedded in wider society or isolated from it. Following James Piazza (2009), the statistics on which the 'religion = greater lethality' argument is based are skewed by a few exceptionally deadly attacks by a particular subset of 'religious' militants, namely those broadly sympathetic to al-Qaeda. Once these groups have been removed from the sample, Piazza (2009: 71–2) notes: 'Islamist groups [which form the largest set of contemporary 'religious' militants] are no more likely than non-Islamist groups to commit higher casualty attacks.' If the militants are re-classified according to whether they are pursuing 'strategic' goals (such as liberation of a territory) or 'universal/abstract' goals (such as the establishment of a global government), all groups in the 'utopian' category are more prone to commit high-casualty attacks – regardless of whether they are motivated by utopian religion, utopian Marxism or other utopian belief systems (see also Tucker 2001: 5–7).

On this reading, rather than religion causing violence, the correlation seems to be between what types of goals are pursued, organisational structure and the level of violence that a group is willing to engage in. Group goals are in turn influenced by how socially integrated a group is, and thus how bound it is by such 'mundane' concerns as the effect of violence on the wider community. Utopian groups are often isolationist, separating themselves from what they see as a corrupted society, and thus less concerned with how they are perceived by society, or indeed with killing civilians (since no one is considered innocent). Therefore, whether a group claims religious inspiration or not cannot in and of itself explain what level of violence a group engages in. Instead, we have to look at how religion is interpreted by a particular group, what goals are pursued and how the group relates to wider society, all of which affects what methods are deemed legitimate.

Indeed, whether or not religion is interpreted as justifying violence is profoundly influenced by the context within which it is interpreted, contested and lived. Whether the prevailing political system is inclusive or repressive, whether it promotes divisiveness or consensus, whether there is a tradition of violence (whether state, colonial or societal) – all this affects how religion is interpreted, just as this process is affected by whether there are prevailing perceptions of inequality between different religio-ethnic groups or by the level and the nature of competition between rival groups.

Staying with the example of political Islam – one can find similar examples among any cluster of groups inspired by a particular set of ideas, religious or secular – a good illustration of the effect of context can be found in the diversity of how different Islamist movements have translated their interpretation of Islam into practice. Many Sunni Islamist movements in the Middle East adhere to a broadly similar interpretation of Islam, namely that pioneered by the Egyptian Muslim Brotherhood. Islam plays a central role in all. But many have not turned to violence and those who have have often started non-violently or have since turned away from violence.

The AKP (Turkey), the Justice and Development Party (Morocco), Hizb al-Wasat (Egypt) and the Islamic Action Front (Jordan), to name but a few, have each by and large eschewed violent tactics in their respective evolutions.[3] Others, such as Hamas (Palestine), the Islamic Salvation Front (Algeria) and the Egyptian Muslim Brotherhood (in its early years), have opted for violence, despite drawing on the same ideological heritage as their non-violent counterparts. Yet all three have foresworn violence at various stages in their evolution. Others still, such as the Jama'a al-Islamiyya (Egypt), the Armed Islamic Group (Algeria) and al-Qaeda, have engaged in much more indiscriminate violence than their more mainstream counterparts, despite emerging from the same ideological tradition (although it has to be stressed that they have diverged both ideologically and organisationally from the mainstream path, and their decision to engage in higher levels of lethality can be linked in part to that divergence; moreover, the Jama'a has since foresworn violence; see, for instance, Ashour 2009). If religion, or rather this particular interpretation of religion, was the cause of violence, one would expect all Islamists, or at least a significant majority, to be violent and to be consistently violent. Yet, as we can see, there is great variety, both over time and among Islamist groups, even among those adhering to broadly the same ideological interpretation of Islam.

To explain why some have turned to violence while others have not or why some turned to violence at a particular stage but foreswore it at another, we have to look at the wider context. Hafez (2003), for instance, has argued that the decision of the Jama'a Islamiyya in Egypt and the Armed Islamic Group in Algeria to begin

---

3   The AKP and the JDP are not part of the Muslim Brotherhood network, yet their ideologies are broadly comparable.

targeting civilians can be explained in part by looking at the interaction between political exclusion, indiscriminate state repression and the organisational dynamics of groups trying to evade repression. These particular turns towards violence were justified by a particular interpretation of Islam that emphasised the permissibility of violence against hypocrites and unbelievers, and the corruption of wider society, while downplaying other, more conciliatory interpretations of Islam. However, that this particular interpretation became dominant at a specific point in time was itself largely a result of the political context of exclusion and state violence (and thus a lack of perceived opportunities for other forms of political action, although ideology played a role in how these opportunities were perceived), and the corresponding development of exclusionary group structures. Beliefs played a role by shaping how the problem and its supposed solution were interpreted. But these beliefs were shaped by the structural and organisational context within which the activists operated.

In a similar vein, one can explain both Hamas' turn towards suicide bombing and its turning away from the tactic towards enforcing ceasefires by looking at changes in the political and organisational context of the movement (Gunning 2007: 39–54, 195–240). In both instances, the Palestinian-Israeli political landscape had changed dramatically. In 1993–1994, for instance, Hamas was confronted with an end to the uprising which had inspired its birth, a resurgent Fatah (its chief rival) and a peace process that was both popular and threatened to lead to its political marginalisation. Its leadership, meanwhile, had been able to forge closer links with the pioneer of suicide tactics in the Levant, Hizballah, during its forced exile to Lebanon from December 1992 onwards, while its cadres were restless following the end of the Intifada. Islam provided a justificatory framework. But Islam cannot be said to have caused this change in behaviour, since Hamas' reliance on Islam long predated its turn towards suicide tactics and until 1993 it frowned on the practice. Rather, it was the confluence of external political and internal organisational factors which led to a re-interpretation of Islam and a re-evaluation of the legitimacy and the costs and the benefits of the tactic. A similar contextual analysis can shed light on why Hamas abandoned the tactic in 2005, as political participation in a system that seemed more inclusive to Hamas came to be seen as more advantageous than a continuation of resistance.

More broadly, both the increase in religiously motivated militancy over the past few decades – which proponents of the 'religion-causes-violence' thesis put forward as a defence of their position – and the increase in lethality of militants (usually labelled 'terrorists') can be said to be, at least in part, a product of global structural and ideational changes. The increase in religiously motivated violence is part of the wider 'religious turn' in politics which, in turn, has been variously explained as a response to the breakdown of the polarity imposed by the Cold War, an increase in the speed of globalisation or a response to the alienation engendered by modernisation, to name but a few (cf. Eisenstadt 2000; Keane 2002; Robison, Crenshaw and Jenkins 2006; Neumann 2009: 83–116). Religion played a causal role in this by providing not just an alternative framework of identity, meaning, explanation and solution but also a ready set of social and institutional networks.

However, the specific way in which religion became a political rallying cry cannot be explained by looking at religion alone. To be sure, many of these contextual explanations suffer from both a structuralist and a secularist bias, and do not adequately engage with the meaning of the 'religious turn' or indeed acknowledge the constant presence of religiously motivated activism throughout the modern era. But they nevertheless underline that religiously motivated activism, whether of the violent or the non-violent variety, is in part a product of profound structural changes and is thus not simply 'caused' by religion.

Similarly, the observed increase in lethality can be explained with reference to both technological changes and to changes in the political and ideational context. Factors such as the gradual desensitisation of people to the portrayal of violence in the media, the effects of globalisation and a proliferation of bloody civil wars as well as technological innovation have been cited as reasons for the increase in lethality (cf. Neumann 2009). If this is so, then religion as such is not the cause of this increase in lethality. It may have facilitated this turn by providing moral justifications, existential explanations or deeply felt motivations, but religion per se cannot explain this increase in lethality. After all, all militants appear to have become more lethal, regardless of their ideological persuasion (Masters 2008: 412).

None of this is to downplay the role of beliefs and interpretation. Hafez, for example, has been criticised for being too deterministic by placing too much emphasis on structural factors. Katerina Dalacoura (2006), for instance, has rightly noted that political exclusion and state repression have not led to violence everywhere, while political inclusion, coupled with a relaxing of state repression, has often led to an *increase*, not a *decrease*, in oppositional violence. Much depends on the type and timing of repression, the way in which the political system is opened up or closed down, the strength of the opposition groups, the level of popular support they enjoy and how oppositional groups interpret state violence or its absence. But none of this undermines the claim that religion per se is an insufficient cause for violence and that other factors need to be in place for violence to occur.

Rethinking the Religious–Secular Divide

More fundamentally, the distinction between religious and non-religious groups is not as clear-cut as is typically assumed, raising serious questions about the validity of the claims made. Within the field of religious studies, debate continues to rage over how to distinguish religion from other belief systems. Because not all religions believe in a deity, or indeed in a transcendental world, we cannot define religion with reference to belief in a deity or the transcendental without excluding recognised religions such as non-theistic Hinduism or Buddhism. Conversely, defining religion more broadly as concern with the ultimate meaning of life would cast the net too widely and include political ideologies such as Marxism, or indeed the belief system of football supporters (cf. Cavanaugh 2004: 4–9, 14–18, 28–30; Hervieu-Léger 2000: 53–7). Even some of those who uphold the religious/secular dichotomy acknowledge that the distinction is deeply problematic. Ethnic identity, for instance, has a transcendent dimension, invokes the sacred and is maintained through ritual – all traits usually associated with religion. It is thus of little surprise that a leading scholar such as R. Scott Appleby concedes that 'it is virtually impossible to disaggregate the precise roles of religion and ethnicity' (quoted in Cavanaugh 2004: 24).[4]

Even if we can reach agreement on what we mean by religion, this does not necessarily resolve how we are to label groups which display both religious and non-religious qualities (Gunning and Jackson 2011). To return to the example at the start of this chapter, can we label Hamas 'religious', given that religion is only one of the motivations mentioned? In contrast to Hamas' main rival, Fatah, it may be useful to label Hamas 'religious', since Fatah is, at least officially, a 'secular' organisation. But such labels downplay both the 'religious' elements in Fatah – its 'religious' wing, the 'religious' motivations of many of its supporters, and its placing of Islam and Islamic holy sites at the centre of its nationalism – and the 'non-religious' elements in Hamas – its secular supporters, its nationalism, the largely secular logic informing much of its behaviour, and its modern roots. Hamas's conflict with Israel, for instance, and the dynamics of its violence has as much, if not more, to do with such 'non-religious' factors as territorial occupation, the logic of asymmetric conflict and political exclusion as with Hamas' religious beliefs or with religious differences between Hamas and the Israeli army, government and society. Most of its targets, for instance, are not religious in nature, while the changing nature of its violence, from popular resistance, to suicide tactics, to rockets and ceasefires, can be better explained with reference to changes in its political fortunes and the dynamics of revenge and competition than with reference to religion (cf. Hafez 2006; Gunning 2007: 195–240; Araj 2008). Its leaders, meanwhile, are predominantly secular professionals and their authority is based as much on secular as on religious values (Gunning 2007: 116–26, 160–175), while both its ideology and its members can be said to be, in part, products of modernity (Robinson 1997, Gunning 2007: 55–94; more broadly, about Islamism's indebtedness to modernity, cf. Euben 1999). This is not to say that religion does not play a role, but if religion alone cannot explain Hamas' behaviour, how useful is it to label Hamas 'religious' – with the implication that religion is the cause of its behaviour?

Another group to consider is the Tamil Tigers. The Tigers are usually classified as an anti-religious, Marxist-inspired, ethno-nationalist group. However, the supposedly secular Tigers use burial rituals that were traditionally reserved for Hindu saints to elicit divine energy from their martyrs, while they style their infamous resort to cyanide pills – to be swallowed upon capture – on religious practices of sacrifice, believed to give militants extra powers (Roberts 2005; Natali 2008). Labelling the Tigers 'secular' obscures such practices, rendering any conclusions based on too sharp a division between 'religious' and 'secular' dubious. This is because if the data we use to explain the role of religion include 'religious' groups which are heavily influenced by ethno-nationalism, while

---

4   Juergensmeyer, Wentz and Marty concede the same point (Cavanaugh 2004: 13, 28–9).

excluding ostensibly 'secular' groups that are influenced by religion, how can we deduce anything conclusive about the role of religion in causing the violence?

Why is the Assumption that Religion Causes Violence so Prevalent?

If the link between religion and violence is so ambiguous, why is the notion that religion gives rise to violence so prevalent? Why is it acceptable to assume that religion renders conflicts more violent, without (much) further analysis, or to paint religiously inspired activists as an inherent threat to democracy?

One reason, put forward by various scholars, concerns the way religion has come to be conceptualised in Western social sciences and philosophy. The notion of religion, as we know it today, emerged in the context of the rise of the modern European state in the early modern era and in response to both ideational shifts and the 'religious wars' of the sixteenth and seventeenth centuries. Ideationally, over the course of the Renaissance and its aftermath, the focus of intellectuals shifted from God and the Hereafter to humanity and the world it inhabited. Science and a concern with civic values began to undermine religion's intellectual dominance, and religion came to be defined in opposition to science and its supposedly rational, empirical pursuit of truth. Politically, the modern state began to take shape in opposition to traditional authority structures such as the Church and the notion of the divine right of kings. The so-called 'religious wars' of the sixteenth and seventeenth centuries ushered in a new era, embodied by the Peace of Westphalia which, at least according to the dominant historical narrative, established the modern state as a bastion against future religious strife, relegating religion and its institutions to the margins of private life (cf. Asad 1993; Salvatore 1997: 29–32; Cavanaugh 2004: 35–8; Thomas 2005) – although in practice religion and religious institutions continued to play a role in public life in most secular states (Keane 2002; Burgat 2003: 122–39).

Whether the modern state was in fact born with the Peace of Westphalia and whether it was indeed a bastion against religious strife has been the subject of much debate (cf. Inayatullah and Blaney 2004). What concerns us here is not the veracity of this narrative, but its impact on the way in which religion came to be conceptualised. Within this framework, any attempt to merge the political and religious realms (if one can indeed make such a distinction) and bring religion out of the private and cultural spheres becomes suspect. Indicative of this approach is Carsten Laustsen and Ole Waever's assertion that religion ceases to be religion and becomes ideology as soon as it is hitched to an earthly political project (Laustsen and Waever 2000: 726). This attitude, reinforced by the dominance of materialist and realist traditions in the social sciences (Thomas 2005), has meant that scholars have for a long time either written religion out of politics and left it unstudied (for example, ignoring the role religion plays in secular Western states – cf. Keane 2002;

Philpott 2009) or, as with 'religious terrorism' scholars, depicted it as abnormal, irrational and dangerous (see also Esposito 1999: 198–9). But terrorism scholars are far from alone in this. Within Middle Eastern studies, for instance, it has led to scholars treating 'an Islam that is comprehensive in scope, with religion integral to politics and society, [as] "abnormal" ... and nonsensical', with the result that Islamists were readily depicted as incontrovertibly intolerant, dogmatic and violent in contrast to the allegedly tolerant and pragmatic secularists, despite a wealth of contradictory evidence. In democratisation studies, religion has similarly long been treated as a fundamental threat to democracy, supposedly inevitably inspiring the kinds of fanatical loyalties, hatreds and irrational behaviour that are anathema to the democratic ideal. Only recently have scholars begun to look at religion's contribution to the development and indeed continuing sustaining of democracy (cf. Stout 2004).

Overlaying this secular bias in the social sciences are the remnants of a colonialist, Orientalist bias (cf. Said 1978), especially where the study of Islamic movements is concerned (cf. Wolff 1998; Sayyid 2003; Jackson 2007). The same conceptual division between religion and politics that came to dominate the social sciences within the West was used in the colonial enterprise to neutralise indigenous religions and impose a Western-type secular rationality (Cavanaugh 2004: 36–7). Within this scheme, indigenous peoples elsewhere came to be categorised as religious, in contrast to the West's 'superior' (and supposedly universal) secularism – and with it, irrational, fanatical and violent, thereby reinforcing the negative stereotypes of ethnic prejudices. It is no coincidence, argues Russell McCutcheon, that 'the centre of the study of religion moved along with the centre of imperialism from Europe to America in the 20th century' (paraphrased in Cavanaugh 2004: 37; see also Hannigan 1991). Religious studies, on this reading, continue to play a central role in dividing the world into 'those cultures still bound by non-rational tradition and group identity, and the "modern" rationalistic and individualistic culture [of the West] toward which the former are fated to evolve' (Cavanaugh 2004: 37) – and thus to provide a conceptual blueprint for 'managing' and gradually colonising these so-called indigenous 'Others'. The religious–secular dichotomy has thus been instrumentally useful in managing the world, in particular in conflicts where opponents can be categorised as 'religious' and hence delegitimised and marginalised (although not necessarily successfully). But it also forms the rallying cry for an identity that is deeply embedded in Western society, as can be witnessed in the various struggles over headscarves and minarets in the European context.

Because scholars of Islamic movements – which have come to feature prominently the literature on religion and violence, especially after 9/11 – are influenced by the legacies of both the general secular bias in the social sciences and this more specific Orientalist bias, it is of little surprise that it is here that the temptation to regard religion as a fundamental cause of violence is especially strong, although this temptation is by no means limited to those studying Islamic movements (cf. Cavanaugh 2004; Murphy 2011). Questions about religion's supposed propensity towards violence are thus as much about the observed as about the observer. Yet too often, analyses of religious militancy proceed as if the analyst is a neutral observer, unencumbered by such historical legacies.

References

Abu-Nimer, M. 2003. *Nonviolence and Peace Building in Islam: Theory and Practice*. Gainesville, FL: University Press of Florida.
Anderson, L. 1997. Fulfilling prophecies: state policy and Islamist radicalism, in J. Esposito (ed.), *Political Islam: Revolution, Radicalism, or Reform?*. Boulder, CO: Lynne Rienner, 17–31.
Appleby, R.S. 2000. *The Ambivalence of the Sacred: Religion, Violence, and Reconciliation*. Lanham, MD: Rowman & Littlefield.
Araj, B. 2008. Harsh state repression as a cause of suicide bombing: the case of the Palestinian-Israeli conflict. *Studies in Conflict & Terrorism*, 31(4), 284–303.
Asad, T. 1993. The construction of religion as an anthropological category, in *Genealogies of Religion: Discipline and Reasons of Power in Christianity and Islam*. Baltimore, MD: Johns Hopkins University Press.
Ashour, O. 2009. *The Deradicalization of Jihadists: Transforming Armed Islamist Movements*. London: Routledge.
Ayubi, N. 1991. *Political Islam: Religion and Politics in the Arab World*. London: Routledge.
Burgat, F. 2003. *Face to Face with Political Islam*, London: I.B. Tauris.
Cavanaugh, W. 2004. *The Violence of 'Religion': Examining a Prevalent Myth*. Online: Kellogg Institute for International Studies Working Papers no. 310. Available at: http://www.nd.edu/~kellogg/publications/workingpapers/WPS/310.pdf [accessed 25 June 2012].
Cavanaugh, W. 2009. *The Myth of Religious Violence*. New York: Oxford University Press.
Chernick, M. 2007. FARC-EP: from liberal guerrillas to Marxist rebels to post-Cold War insurgents, in M. Heiberg, B. O'Leary and J. Tirman (eds), *Terror, Insurgency and the State: Ending Protracted Conflicts*. Philadelphia, PA: University of Pennsylvania Press, 51–81.
Dalacoura, K. 2006. Islamist terrorism and the Middle East democratic deficit: political exclusion, repression and the causes of extremism. *Democratization*, 13(3), 508–25.
De Juan, A. 2008. A pact with the devil? Elite alliances as bases of violent religious conflicts. *Studies in Conflict and Terrorism*, 31(12), 1120–35.
Della Porta, D. 1995a. Left-wing terrorism in Italy, in M. Crenshaw (ed.), *Terrorism in Context*. University Park, PA: Pennsylvania State University Press.
Della Porta, D. 1995b. *Social Movements, Political Violence, and the State: A Comparative Analysis of Italy and Germany*. Cambridge: Cambridge University Press.

Eisenstadt, S.N. 2000. The resurgence of religious movements in processes of globalisation: beyond end of history or clash of civilisations. *International Journal on Multicultural Societies*, 2(1), 4–15.

Esposito, J. 1999. *The Islamic Threat: Myth or Reality?*, 3rd edn. New York: Oxford University Press.

Euben, R. 1999. *Enemy in the Mirror: Islamic Fundamentalism and the Limits of Modern Rationalism*. Princeton, NJ: Princeton University Press.

Gopin, M. 2005. *Holy War, Holy Peace: How Religion Can Bring Peace to the Middle East*. New York: Oxford University Press.

Gunning, J. 2007. *Hamas in Politics: Democracy, Religion, Violence*. London: Hurst.

Gunning, J. 2011. Rethinking religion and violence in the Middle East, in Andrew Murphy (ed.), *The Blackwell Companion to Religion and Violence*. Oxford: Blackwell, 511–23.

Gunning, J. and Jackson, R. 2011. What's so 'religious' about 'religious terrorism'? *Critical Studies on Terrorism*, 4(3), 369–88.

Hafez, M. 2003. *Why Muslims Rebel: Repression and Resistance in the Islamic World*. Boulder, CO: Lynne Rienner.

Hafez, M. 2006. Rationality, culture, and structure in the making of suicide bombers, *Studies in Conflict & Terrorism*, 29(2), 165–85.

Halliday, F. 2002. *Two Hours that Shook the World – September 11, 2001: Causes and Consequences*. London: Saqi Books.

Hannigan, J. 1991. Social movement theory and the sociology of religion: toward a new synthesis. *Sociological Analysis*, 52(4), 311–31.

Hasenclever, A. and Rittberger, V. 2000. Does religion make a difference? Theoretical approaches to the impact of faith on political conflict. *Millennium*, 29(3), 641–74.

Hervieu-Léger, D. 2000. *Religion as a Chain of Memory*. London: Polity.

Hoffman, B. 2006. *Inside Terrorism*. Revised and expanded edn. New York: Columbia University Press.

Huntington, S.P. 1996. *The Clash of Civilizations and the Remaking of World Order*. New York: Simon & Schuster.

Inayatullah, N. and Blaney, D. 2004. *International Relations and the Problem of Difference*. London: Routledge.

Jackson, R. 2007. Constructing enemies: 'Islamic Terrorism' in political and academic discourse. *Government & Opposition*, 42(3), 394–426.

Johnston, D. and Sampson, C. (eds) 1995. *Religion: The Missing Dimension of Statecraft*. New York: Oxford University Press.

Johnston, H., Laraña, E. and Gusfield, J. 1994. Identities, grievances, and new social movements, in E. Laraña, H. Johnston and J. Gusfield (eds), *New Social Movements: From Ideology to Identity*. Philadelphia, PA: Temple University Press.

Juergensmeyer, M. 2000. *Terror in the Mind of God: The Global Rise of Religious Violence*. Berkeley, CA: University of California Press.

Keane, J. 2002. The limits of secularism, in A. Tamimi and J. Esposito (eds), *Islam and Secularism in the Middle East*. London: Hurst, 29–37.

Laustsen, C. and Wæver, O. 2000. In defence of religion: sacred referent objects for securitization. *Millennium*, 29(3), 705–39.

Lewis, B. 1990. The roots of Muslim rage. *Atlantic Monthly*, 266, 47–60. Available at www.theatlantic.com/doc/199009/muslim-rage [accessed 25 June 2012].

Masters, D. 2008. The origin of terrorist threats: religious, separatist, or something else? *Terrorism and Political Violence*, 20(3), 396–414.

Murphy, A. (ed.) 2011. *The Blackwell Companion to Religion and Violence*. Oxford: Blackwell.

Natali, C. 2008. Building cemeteries, constructing identities: funerary practices and nationalist discourse among the Tamil Tigers of Sri Lanka. *Contemporary South Asia*, 16(3), 287–301.

Neumann, P. 2009. *Old & New Terrorism*. Cambridge: Polity.

Pape, R. 2005. *Dying to Win: The Strategic Logic of Suicide Terrorism*. New York: Random House.

Philpott, D. 2009. Has the study of global politics found religion? *Annual Review of Political Science*, 12, 183–202.

Piazza, J. 2009. Is Islamist terrorism more lethal? An empirical study of group ideology, organization and goal structure. *Terrorism and Political Violence*, 21(1), 62–88.

Roberts, M. 2005. Tamil Tiger 'martyrs': regenerating divine potency? *Studies in Conflict & Terrorism*, 28(6), 493–514.

Robinson, G. 1997. *Building a Palestinian State: The Incomplete Revolution*. Bloomington, IN: Indiana University Press.

Robison, K. Crenshaw, E. and Jenkins, J. 2006. Ideologies of violence: the social origins of Islamist and leftist transnational terrorism. *Social Forces*, 84(4), 2009–26.

Said, E. 1978. *Orientalism*. London: Routledge.

Salvatore, A. 1997. *Islam and the Political Discourse of Modernity*. Reading: Ithaca Press.

Sayyid, S. 2003. *A Fundamental Fear: Eurocentrism and the Emergence of Islamism*. London: Zed Books.

Sedgwick, M. 2004. Al-Qaeda and the nature of religious terrorism. *Terrorism and Political Violence*, 16(4), 795–814.

Stout, J. 2004. *Democracy and Tradition*. Princeton, NJ: Princeton University Press.

Thomas, S. 2005. *The Global Resurgence of Religion and the Transformation of International Relations*. New York: Palgrave Macmillan.

Tucker, D. 2001. What is new about the new terrorism and how dangerous is it? *Terrorism and Political Violence*, 13(3), 1–14.

Waterbury, J. 1994. Democracy without democrats? The potential for political liberalization in the Middle East, in G. Salamé (ed.), *Democracy without Democrats? The Renewal of Politics in the Muslim World*. London: I.B. Tauris.

Weinberg, L. 2006. Secular forms of suicide terrorism, in Ami Pedahzur (ed.), *Root Causes of Suicide Terrorism: The Globalization of Martyrdom*. London: Routledge, 108–21.

Wiktorowicz, Q. and Kaltner, J. 2003. Killing in the name of Islam: Al-Qaeda's justification for September 11. *Middle East Policy*, X(2), 76–92.

Wolff, K. 1998. New new Orientalism: political Islam and social movement theory, in A. Moussalli (ed.), *Islamic Fundamentalism: Myths & Realities*. Reading: Ithaca Press, 41–73.

PART III
Theorising, Understanding and Researching Political Violence

Social Movement Studies and Political Violence

Donatella della Porta

Political Violence and Social Movements: An Introduction

In contemporary social sciences, political violence has been studied mainly inside two broad traditions that very rarely interacted with each other: *terrorism studies* (which emerged within security studies as a branch of international relations) and social movement studies. According to data presented by Jeroen Gunning (2009), a key word search for 'social movements' found that of the 1,569 articles in two of the core terrorism studies journals, only 17 articles related to social movements; a search for terrorism-terrorist under the heading 'social movements' of the International Bibliography of the Social Sciences database yielded 81 articles, but most of them were published after 2000.

Concentrating on the most radical forms of political violence, the first approach has stressed either its macro- or micro-pathological causes. Within a functionalist perspective, the causes for high levels of intra-state violence are singled out in various strains at the macro-level – such as the strength of ethnic or class cleavages, the repressiveness of a regime, and cultural traditions. Conjunctural conditions such as the intermediate stages of economic development, the crises of modernization, periods of ineffective state coercion and rapid cultural change have also been mentioned. At a micro-analytic level, explanations for terrorism mentioned the psychological characteristics of violent militants, as well as significant levels of relative deprivation and frustration.

These explanations have been challenged on theoretical and empirical grounds. Specifically, isolating violence from social and political conflicts seems to reduce our capacity to understand it. Additionally, these interpretations have missed 'meso-level' factors that include organizational dynamics as well as specific interactions in any movement's organizational field. Most fundamentally, there has been a tendency to reify terrorism (and terrorists) on the basis of their use of some forms of collective action, with the risk of lumping together different phenomena under the same definition (Tilly 2004: 8). In particular, research has been more oriented towards developing anti-terrorist policies than developing a social science understanding of the phenomenon. In fact, 'many who have written about terrorism have been directly or indirectly involved in the business of counterterrorism, and their vision has been narrowed and distorted by the search for effective responses to terrorism, often very loosely defined' (Goodwin 2004: 260).

In the social movement studies of the 1970s and 1980s, much attention was paid to the interaction between political opportunities and organizational resources (della Porta and Diani 2006). However, 'social movement scholars, with very few exceptions, have said little about terrorism' (Goodwin 2004: 260). Research on extreme forms of political violence has been episodic, with some peaks during periods of high visibility of terrorist attacks, but little cumulative knowledge. Moreover, studies of different forms of political violence have followed different approaches, and for the most part 'breakdown' theories – explaining protest as a sign of breakdown of social ties – are used to analyse right-wing radicalism. In addition, mobilization theories – stressing instead the need for social ties in order to stage collective activities – are deployed in research on left-wing radicalism, whilst area study specialists focus on ethnic and religious forms of political violence. Finally, explanations tend to focus on either macro-systemic causes, meso-organizational characteristics or micro-individual motivations, with little synthesis between these different levels of analysis (della Porta 1995).

Recently, however, attention to the contribution of social movement theories to explaining political violence has increased. First, in the social movement field, political violence entered the agenda with the 'contentious politics' turn, a label under which research on social movements, revolutions, civil wars and so on were bridged and contrasted instead with routine-type of politics (McAdam, Tarrow and Tilly 2001). Moreover, radicalization has been addressed, especially in the (rare) research on non-Western democracies (discussed below). On the other hand, a school of 'critical terrorism studies' (developed along the path opened by critical security studies) brought about in international relations and area studies an interest in the application of social movement theories to political violence (Jackson, Breen Smyth and Gunning 2009). As Jeroen Gunning (2009) has recently suggested, social movement studies can indeed contribute in a number of ways to de-exceptionalizing violence by locating it within broader contexts and complex processes.

In both social movement studies and critical terrorism studies, some of the research on extreme forms of political violence has been able to trace processes of conflict escalation through the detailed examination of historical cases. Some cross-national research has focused on either small-N comparison of similar cases or large-N comparison of heterogeneous sets of cases.

Social movement studies have developed from within different traditions: in Europe and in the USA, but also in sociology and in political science as well as within different branches of both disciplines. Although these different paths met in growing dialogue in the 1980s (della Porta and Tarrow 2005; della Porta and Diani 2006), it is still possible to single out the specific contributions of each to research on political violence. In what follows, I will summarize some of the knowledge acquired in this research as well as the challenges coming from the new wave of debate on terrorist and counter-terrorist action and discourses. In this contribution, using some of the main categories developed within social movement theory, I will summarize some research findings, looking at the actors that worked as entrepreneurs of violence, activating some political and discursive opportunities formed during the escalation of protest. Additionally, I shall observe which relational, cognitive and affective mechanisms link the macro- and meso- with the micro-level, sustaining the development of militant identities.

Polarized Environments: Violence in Context

Research on social movements has contributed to the understanding of determinants of forms of action by locating political violence within a focus on the *repertoires of action*, that is, the historically developed set of collective action forms which are available to people when they want to protest (Tilly 1978). If we see social movement organizations and activists as value-oriented and as rational, instrumental actors attempting to mobilize both material and symbolic resources in their environment, radicalism or moderation would depend, in particular, on the response the movements meet with in their environment, the reactions of the authorities, and the strength and postures of their potential allies and opponents.

In his influential model of collective action, Charles Tilly (1978: 52–5 and 172–88) related the use of violence to the emergence of new social groups. In his terminology, political violence increases when new challengers fight their way into the polity and old polity members refuse to leave. In his pivotal research on protest strategies, William Gamson (1990) observes that the use of violence increases the probability of success of the challengers. In a similar vein, in their well-known study on what they called poor-people movements, Frances Fox Piven and Richard A. Cloward (1977) suggest that radical action facilitates mobilization as well as success.

However, using violence has many limitations and constraints. A key dilemma for protest leaders is that forms of action, such as the violent ones that are more likely to attract media attention, are also those that could be more stigmatized by potential allies, thus deterring those allies. While direct action has on occasion been associated with substantive success, it has also been noted that violent action often leads to an escalation in conflict. Violence polarizes conflict, transforming 'relations between challengers and authorities from a confused, many-sided game into a bipolar one in which people are forced to choose sides, allies defect, bystanders retreat and the state's repressive apparatus swings into action' (Tarrow 1994: 104). Violent action may cause an increase in repression and may alienate sympathizers. According to a rational choice approach, the use of more extreme tactics is constrained 'by the erosion of support occasioned by repression and moral backlash. The crucial question, therefore, is whether the government's additional responsiveness to violent protest will provide sufficient compensation for the movement's smaller size' (DeNardo 1985: 219). In a democratic regime, the state holds a monopoly on the legitimate use of force and most challenges to that monopoly are doomed to fail, transforming political conflict into a military confrontation in which the state has by far the greater firepower (della Porta 1995).

The choice of the forms of action is characterized by several dilemmas, and social scientists within the social movement tradition have stressed the relational characteristics of the process of radicalization that develop from the interactions between challengers and elites (Tilly 1978). Repertoires of protest techniques/ methods have, in fact, traditionally been seen as influenced by a *political opportunity structure*, defined as the existing institutional and cultural opportunities and constraints for those who mobilize. In general, exclusive political systems and unstable democracies have been shown to produce the most radical opposition and violent escalation (see della Porta and Diani 2004 for a synthesis). Research within the new social movements perspective has reflected, in particular, on how some political and social conditions facilitate a sort of implosion of social actors into violence (Wieviorka 1988).

Closing political opportunities were in fact present in many cases of development of political violence. In Italy, the use of violence has been interpreted as signalling a closure of political opportunities, with the end of the centre-left governments and a turn to the political right, as well as the development of the so-called 'strategy of tension' (*strategia della tensione*, oriented towards fomenting disorder in order to legitimize an authoritarian coup d'état) with alleged participation of the parts of the secret services in the so-called 'state massacre' in Piazza Fontana on 12 December 1969. Similarly, protests in Northern Ireland escalated as the inclusive and reformist mobilizing message of the 1960s civil rights movement lost ground in the face of a lack of political responsiveness by the state, which led to the development of an exclusivist nationalist frame in the 1970s among protestors. Right-wing political violence in Europe also appears to be motivated more by a lack of political opportunities than by grievances related to the presence of migrants or economic strains (Koopmans 2005).

A lack of/narrowing of opportunities alone is a necessary but not sufficient precondition for sustained waves of political violence. Mechanisms that cause radicalization are activated by interactions between movement activists and their opponents during cycles of protest, that is, moments of intensified protest mobilized by many different actors. In particular, during cycles of protest, the development of the forms of protest actions follows a dynamic of reciprocal tactical innovation between the activists and their opponents. Social movements change their tactics as their adversaries adapt their tactics to those of the movement (McAdam 1983). Seeing violence as an escalation of the protest repertoire points to the fluid borders between different strategies, and the reciprocal adaptation and learning as a result of interaction between social movements and external actors, namely the police and other adversaries. In this dynamic, escalating protest, policing as well as the presence of counter-movements have a relevant impact.

Research into cases as different as the Italian and German left-libertarian movement families in the late 1960s and early 1970s, and the ethno-nationalist conflicts in Northern Ireland and the Basque countries, illustrates how violence escalated in much the same way and followed much the same timing during cycles of protest, even though they involved different political and social actors (Waldman 1993; White 1993; Wieviorka 1988). In all these cases, the forms of action were initially disruptive but peaceful and the aims were moderate, comprised mainly of demands for the reform of existing institutions, although remaining mainly non-violent, protest repertoires radicalized at the margins, especially during street battles with adversaries and the police. In all of these cases, escalating police strategies contributed to radicalization. In particular, in Italy a tradition of militarized and partisan interventions re-emerged, with dramatic effects in terms of activists killed during police charges (della Porta and Reiter 2004).

Comparing these cases with other cases where little or no radicalization occurred (such as the police repression of the global justice movement in Genoa and the protests against the building of a high-speed railway in Val di Susa), we might observe, however, that radicalization develops not only when opportunities for peaceful conflicts are closing down and repression hits hard, but also when discursive opportunities for violence are made available, that is, when discourses that legitimize violence are widespread in the population. In particular, influential actors can contribute to the discursive opportunities by certifying violence as an acceptable form of action. In Italy, even though they were critical of terrorist forms of violence, a large part of the left-libertarian social movement in the 1970s accepted that forms of defensive violence were unavoidable when faced with violent opponents. In Italy, as in many other cases where protest escalated, the absence of a consolidated democratic culture influenced the frames that elites have used to emphasize the 'dangers' of protest. This absence also induced activists to resort to their particular national tradition (or lack of tradition) of resistance to the autochthon, authoritarian regime or to the occupying, foreign power (della Porta 1990). The development of narratives of violence was also relevant in social movement organizations themselves. Feeling excluded from the political system, social movements have escalated their demands, with both the elaboration of radical frames of meaning and a revolutionary rhetoric. This does not mean that political violence derived directly from the presence of ideologies that justified violence. In fact, the choice of violent forms of action was often debated within radical milieus, in both instrumental and in normative terms, and is often linked to contingent elements. However, a common mechanism is the (appropriation of a) narrative construction of a violent past by the entrepreneurs of violence where leaders within the movement locate themselves and their followers in a continuous historical line with violent antecedents.

A narrative of violence constitutes a discursive opportunity. When the student movements emerged in the 1960s, the governing elites of the young Italian and German democracies felt particularly endangered. In Germany, recollections of the end of the Weimar Republic were often quoted in the press, and the students' 'breaking the rules' was compared to the political violence that preceded the rise of Nazism. In Italy, the state justified its repression of the student movement by appealing to 'anti-fascist' sentiments. A similar dynamic was at play in the Japanese case (Zwerman, Steinhof and della Porta 2000).

In the aforementioned historical cases, those social movements who felt excluded from the political system escalated their demands, using elaborated radical frames of meaning and a revolutionary rhetoric which addressed the very nature of democracy. The Italian activists claimed they had to carry on their ancestors' partisan movement against a 'fascist state' – a movement that, according to them, the Old Left had abandoned. The German activists asserted that they had to resist by all possible means the new 'Nazi' state to avoid repeating the previous generation's mistakes and redeem their shame. In Ireland and the Basque country, the ethno-nationalists resorted to the long-lasting narrative of oppression of the Catholic minority in Ireland or the ethnic, Basque minority in Spain. In the Basque country, the 'pacted transition' was not sufficient to legitimize a Spanish state that stood accused of following the fascist tradition established during the lengthy Francoist regime where torture had been used against Basque patriots. Similar memories of colonial rule fed the conflict in Northern Ireland. In Cyprus, but also in Ireland, nationalist narratives were also used to justify other forms of nationalist violence, and the use of violence was supported by powerful actors (Demetriou 2007). Violent organizations of the extreme right motivate individuals to action through justify the use of violence by referring to a number of discourses that often refer to previous narratives. These narratives, including the superiority of one race (religion, gender, sexual orientation, etc.) over others (O'Boyle 2002, 28), religious fundamentalism, 'blood' and 'honour', are some of the common discourses used to justify violence (Bjørgo 2004; della Porta and Wagemann 2005).

This does not mean that political violence derives directly from the presence of ideologies that justify violence. In fact, the choice of violent forms of action is often debated within the radical milieu, in instrumental but also ethical terms, and the choice of violence is often linked to contingent moments. In Italy and Germany, radical ideologies engendered radical violent repertoires only when political opportunities triggered escalation (della Porta 1995). In Ireland, as already mentioned, changing political opportunities affected the shift from a civil-rights to an ethno-nationalist discourse (Bosi 2006). Some of the results of this body of research can indeed be useful in singling out contextual opportunities for the recent waves of radicalization discussed below.

As for *diminishing political opportunities*, while mainstream approaches to Islamic activism have tended to stress psychological distress, the political opportunity approach proves useful in understanding the adaptation of groups such as the Muslim Brotherhood or Hamas to changing (both the opening and closing of) windows of opportunity. The development of Hamas (up to their justification of suicide bombings) was influenced by the repression of protest by the Israeli and Palestinian authorities. This repression also increased Hamas' capacity to develop support for suicide bombings among the Palestinian population (Gunning 2007). In all these cases, state violence interacted with social movement violence. Political processes, rather than clashes of civilization, are the basis for explaining the very different forms taken by Islamic activism in Algeria, Egypt, Palestine or Bahrain (Wicktorowiz 2004) as well as in Central Asia (Karagiannis 2010).

As for the policing of dissent, similar dynamics can be identified in recent radicalization processes in Egypt and Palestine. The adoption of violent forms of action must be located within broader repertoires of contention in order to facilitate the understanding of Islamic political activism (usually addressed within 'breakdown' approaches – see above) and stimulate reflection on forms of protest in non-democratic polities. In particular, Muslim rebellion has been linked to political and institutional exclusion, as well as to reactive and indiscriminate repression. Moreover, the 'war on terrorism', read as war on Islam, contributed to the spread of injustice frames (that is, the perception of being mistreated) among Muslims and the politicization of religious identities (Hafez 2007). Pictures of tortured Muslim prisoners in Abu Ghraib or testimonies from Guantanamo and coverage of battles in Iraq, Afghanistan and Chechnya contributed to the spread of moral shock at what was perceived as deep injustice towards Muslims all over the world (for a summary, see Olesen 2009). In Egypt, political repression played an important role in the radicalization of Islamic fundamentalist militancy, as the suppression by the Nasser regime radicalized elements of the Brotherhood and led individuals to transform the ideology of modernist Islamists into a 'rejectionist call to arms' (Esposito 2002). In Europe as in the USA, anti-terrorist legislation, focusing especially on Muslim groups, has spread a feeling of discrimination (Schiffauer 2008). In several of these cases, interactions with counter-movements facilitated radicalization.

Finally, religious and non-religious authorities provided a sort of certification for the use of violence by legitimating it. In the case of radical Islam in the UK, Quentin Wiktorowicz (2005) argues that possessing the reputation of having the crucial ability to interpret sacred text is an important resource for the leadership of radical groups.

Closing opportunities, reciprocal tactical innovation and certification of violence are observable in both previous and more recent cases of radicalization. Recent forms of political violence, originating in geographical areas outside of those traditionally covered by social movement studies, point to the need to understand the specificities of polarization processes in non-democratic states. In fact, state responses are particularly brutal in authoritarian states (see e.g. Boudreau 2004).

Additionally, recent cases point to the need to consider the global dimension of current forms of political conflict as well as political violence within particular countries, both in the global North and in the South. In studies of political violence as well as in social movement studies, research has taken the nation-state as the main unit of analysis. This is increasingly less tenable, as both terrorism and counter-terrorism go global and factors such as geopolitical issues, wars, diaspora politics and the like acquire more and more explanatory power. For instance, Muslim rebellion has been linked to political and institutional exclusion and to reactive and indiscriminate repression that developed, at the same time, in various countries, both in the global North and in the South. As observed by Hafez:

> Muslims rebel because they encounter an ill-fated combination of political and institutional exclusion on the one hand and reactive and indiscriminate repression on the other. When states do not provide their Islamist opposition movements opportunities for institutional participation, and employ

repression indiscriminately against these movements after a period of prior mobilisation, Islamists will most probably rebel. (2003: 200)

Muslim experiences in both Muslim homelands and countries that Muslims have migrated to are said to create a sense of humiliation (Khosrokhavar 2006). So, repression experienced at the national level is increasingly implicated in a global form of radicalization.

Violent Entrepreneurs: The Mobilization of Resources

The development of political violence up to the point where it goes underground cannot be understood simply in terms of environmental (macro) preconditions. Addressing the meso level, social movement research seems particularly valuable in directing our attention towards the organizational fields in which violent organizations move, at their relations of competition but also of cooperation with other organizations.

First of all, radicalization develops in dense organizational fields from competition between various organizations that conflict with each other over the use of violence, among other issues. Underground organizations have evolved within and then broken away from larger, non-violent social movement organizations. Exploiting environmental conditions conducive to militancy, these splinter groups undergo further radicalization and eventually create new resources and opportunities for violence. In the late 1960s in Italy, both the decline of the student mobilization and the consequent reduction in available resources increased competition among the various formal and informal networks that constituted the left-libertarian social movement family. The large New Left organizations Potere Operaio and Lotta Continua split on the issue of violence, after they created semi-clandestine bodies devoted to military activities (such as 'defending' the marches from the police or fighting right-wing radicals). In Germany, a similar dynamic developed in the Sozialistische Patientenkollektive, which was initially mobilized on similar issues to those supported by other anti-psychiatry groups that remained pacific or in the youth counter-culture of the *Gammlerbewegung* (hippies) (della Porta 1995). In the USA, the Weather Underground developed as a faction of the Students for a Democratic Society (SDS) when they split over, among other things, the issue of the use of violence. Similar dynamics were found amongst radical groups in Japan (Zwerman, Steinhoff and della Porta 2000; Steinhoff 1991). Militant nationalist movements develop through a process of interaction, competition and coalition-building among different streams of Irish or Basque nationalists (Irvin 1999). Given environmental conditions conductive to militancy, these splinter groups underwent further radicalization and eventually created new resources and opportunities for violence.

Organizational dynamics develop in the underground through processes of 'implosion' or encapsulation (della Porta 1995). In many cases (ranging from the

Italian Red Brigades to Argentinean Montoneros or the Japanese Red Army – see della Porta 1995; Moyano 1995; Zwerman, Steinhoff and della Porta 2000), groups that went underground in order to perform low-level violence tended to escalate in terms of the forms of violence they used, moving towards lethal and sometimes indiscriminate violence under the pressure from the state as well as from internal competition for leadership positions. Isolated from potential supporters and forced to engage in self-financing through robbery and kidnapping, clandestine organizations sometimes enter into relationships with criminal groups. When underground, the organizations become more and more compartmentalized and closed to the outside world.

Perceiving radical political organizations as capable of instrumental action does not imply a denial of the relevance of cultural processes to the understanding of these groups. Cultural processes are, in fact, particularly important to take into account in research on radical organizations, since political violence is mainly symbolic. Political violence develops in contexts in which cultural resources are available; radical forms of protest lead to heated debates on the use of violence itself; and, over and above the material damage it causes, violence is aimed at producing emotional effects. Research on social movements elucidates symbolic processes through an analysis of the specific narratives that accompany the development of political violence. In the Italian case, radical and eventually underground organizations have produced justifying frames for violence. Once underground, their language tends to become more and more obscure and difficult for outsiders to understand; it becomes a code for internal consumption within the group. The formulation of the exclusive identity of the group and the consolidation of a robust identification with the group by each of its members facilitates the management of spoiled identities and the maintenance of self-esteem.

Research on recent waves of political violence emanating from Jihadis can build upon this knowledge. The emphasis of social movement studies on organizational resources could be particularly fruitful for the analysis of Islamist activism, composed, as it is, mainly of extreme forms of armed groups. Attention to broader organizational fields (including armed groups, but also NGOs, unions and even political parties) can be particularly relevant for understanding these recent forms of political violence.

As for organizational competition, the attacks on 9/11 re-invigorated a declining movement because they shifted attention from the traditional focus of religious nationalism against the autocrats in the Muslim world and dismissal of violent methods *tout court* (Karagiannis and McCauley 2006) and brought attention to the global war (Gergez 2005; see also Kepel 2002). Similarly, Hamas emerged from lengthy debates (about, among other issues, the use of violence) among the various factions in the Palestinian Muslim Brotherhood (Gunning 2007). During the second Intifada, some Palestinian groups adopted violent methods while others relied on non-violence.

Processes of encapsulation within clandestine organizations have been observed in the 1990s in Algeria (Hafez 2003) and in Egypt. Groups engaged in underground violence in the past, however, seem to differ from contemporary groups in terms of organizational structure. In the past, underground organizations developed mainly into hierarchical, although compartmentalized, structures, whereas groups engaged in contemporary extreme forms of political violence seemed to follow a different model, with a strongly networked structure which is made possible by new technology and is legitimized by a widespread organizational culture. In particular, Jihadi groups are reported to have moved from a hierarchical organizational model towards a more horizontal one. In the same vein, research on recent forms of political violence, especially violence occurring within authoritarian regimes, suggests that more attention should be paid to informal networks, such as those occurring within religious movements.

As for the construction of a narrative of violence, both in recent years (as well as in the past) various religious narratives have been used to justify violence (Juergensmeyer 2000). In the past, the discourses were more easily classified as political (left-right or ethno-nationalist) and were easier to address within the traditional categories of research on social movements, whereas nowadays the use of the 'clash of civilizations' metaphor (in different forms by the different actors involved) requires some new reflections. Although differences in religions are hardly a genuine source of political conflict per se, some scholars suggest that such differences can shape conflict behaviour in the direction of either escalation or de-escalation of violence (Hasenclever and Rittberger 2000). With reference to religious fundamentalism and the radicalization that can result from it, it has been remarked that culture provides a 'tool kit' of concepts, myths and symbols from which militant organizations can selectively draw to construct strategies of action (Hafez 2004). As Snow and Byrd (2007) have recently observed with reference to Islamic terrorism, ideology is too monolithic a concept to be able to explain the ideological variations among Islamic groups and to account for the flexibility required in order to use general ideas to justify specific violent actions and events. It is not a religious belief or a specific stream within that religion that is more or less conducive to violence, but rather the concrete institutional balances impose tolerance on both the state and the religious institutions (as, for example, Stepan's critique of Huntington's 'clash of civilization theory' clearly indicated). Even though they share some beliefs with Jihadist groups, Hizb al-Tahir has eschewed violence and the Jihad is referred to in justifying the armed struggle in some countries and by some groups, but not in and by others (Kepel 2005). Analysing these specificities without falling into 'Orientalist' prejudice is a challenge that research has to address (Wictorowitz 2004).

Freedom-Fighter Identities: Militant Constructions of External Reality

Organized violence – and groups specializing in violent repertoires – develops gradually, affecting the activists' construction of their external realities. Insights from symbolic interactionism, later revisited in the cultural turn in social movement studies, can help to identify some micro-dynamics of escalation and especially the ways in which social movement activists perceive and construct their social (macro- and meso-level) reality.

Polarized environments alongside violent entrepreneurs affect social movement activists through relational, cognitive and affective mechanisms that produce a freedom-fighter identity. First, militant networks play a significant role at all stages of the political careers of those who have, at times, ended up underground. In Italy (but also in Germany), activists' narratives indicate that relational circumstances such as going to a certain school, living in a certain neighbourhood, attending a certain demonstration or chance encounters with movement milieus or organizations often instigated the beginning of violent political careers (della Porta 1995). One particular condition seemed to increase the likelihood that a particular individual would participate in a radical movement organization, namely his or her involvement in those milieus that serve as relays – or connections/points of contact – for the radical movement. Additionally, one's chance of being recruited into a movement increased with participation in specific personal networks that were actually connected to more militant groups. The peer groups to which individuals belonged played a very important role in determining their subsequent political choices (for instance, joining a more structured movement), and in particular subsequent transitions from low-risk to high-risk activism. Throughout the networks of comrade-friends, friendship reinforced the importance of political commitment, while political commitment strengthened some ties of friendship, and these groups of political friends became closed units. Within the environment of the movement, personal networks are connected to each other and new networks emerge from old ones. Similar patterns have been identified in the Basque and Irish cases, where participation in the radical nationalist milieus was facilitated by family and friendship ties, and this was then escalated by everyday experiences of violent confrontations with the police and militias.

Throughout the networks of comrade-friends, friendship reinforces the relevance of political commitment, while political commitment strengthens some friendship ties, and the groups of political friends become closed units. An affective focusing on the militant networks has been vital in supporting recruitment and sustaining commitment to radical organizations; this emotional bond tended to increase after the more risky political activities, which increased the closeness of the group. The more radical the group, the more isolated from the wider movement culture it became, and the more the members' shared risks intensified the 'us versus them' mentality. In Italy and Germany in the 1970s, the activists' commitment to violence grew along with their emotional investment in politics, and their emotional investment grew with their experience of violence. Increased levels of solidarity within radical groups coincided with intensified hatred for their opponents, members of right-wing groups and the police, who, in their eyes, became progressively dehumanized. Engaging in daily fights thus created a rationale for violence and 'militarized' the activists' attitudes, infusing their politics with a kind of 'battle spirit'. At the same time, the militants' commitment to politics deepened.

Affective ties were ultimately vital in recruitment to clandestine organizations. Both the Italian and German militants testified that 'loyalty' to friends compelled them to descend into the underground and that underground organizations were founded by cliques of friends-comrades. Affective ties also provided important constraints against leaving the underground: the group relationship was, in fact, so intense and individual identities so embedded in the group that the members believed it was impossible to live outside it. Also, exiting the underground was often a collective choice (della Porta 2008b).

This communal solidarity also affected the militants' cognitive closure insofar as all the information the militant activists received was filtered through the group and this information defined their external reality, thus providing shared frames of meaning. Although radical beliefs are not themselves the cause of violence, the ideological frames through which the militants interpreted their daily encounters with political violence tended to dramatize the significance of these events. Again in Italy, the state became the fascist state of the bourgeoisie and the neo-fascist groups were the most evil enemies. Police charges were viewed as evidence of an imminent fascist evolution of the state; street fights with young political opponents became episodes of a civil war; violent encounters with the police were perceived as a stage in the social revolution. Those militants who eventually chose, or were drawn into, the underground then developed a freedom-fighter identity, seeing themselves as members of an embattled community of idealistic and altruistic people fighting a heroic war against 'evil'. Because of their isolation, the underground organizations eventually became the sole point of reference for their members, which led to them progressively losing a sense of external reality. The longer the life of the organization or the longer the individual's experience in it, the more demanding participation became, so that those militants living clandestinely came to depend on the underground formations as their only means of survival, and indeed for their identity. Consequently, commitment became ever more 'total'. As the underground group became the militants' only source of information, or at least the only source they were supposed to believe, their grasp of external reality became more and more tenuous with the passage of time. The emphasis on cognitive coherence is all the more important since the process of individual socialization in radical organizations involves a dramatic change in the militants' images of the external world. Internalizing the use of violence as ethically 'right' increases an individual's propensity to take part in violent confrontations.

However, a group's image of external reality was not just the product of small group dynamics: in the social construction of reality, the frames of meaning provided by the cliques of comrade-friends interacted with their interpretation of the reality of everyday experience. The militants' immersion in violence distorts their perceptions of the external reality: direct experiences of violence produced, in fact, frames of meaning that justified violence.

Commitment to radicalism is, however, often short term. It is necessary to analyse the process of individuals exiting from radical organizations in order to understand the functioning of the (reverse) causal mechanisms that produces the shifting towards non-militant networks, affective diffusion and cognitive opening (see, for example, Bjørgo and Horgan 2009).

Insights on relational, affective and cognitive mechanisms in social movement studies are certainly helpful in terms of understanding contemporary forms of fundamentalist violence. In particular, the presence of these mechanisms at the individual level challenges the idea (widespread in a branch of terrorism studies) that the 'new' forms of terrorism are fundamentally different from past historical cases. This view holds that militants who act on the basis of religious beliefs are by definition more fanatical, sadist and unrestrained than previous historical groups that were motivated by left- and right-wing or nationalist ideologies. Although this is clearly erroneous, these new waves of political violence nevertheless present some challenges to the ways in which processes of individual radicalization have been understood in the past.

First of all, the relevance of kinship ties (Sageman 2004) as well as of informal, religious *networks* has been emphasized in other cases, from the (Christian) anti-abortion terrorism in the USA to Islamic fundamentalism (Juergensmeyer 2000). In particular, sociological research on the Jihad has stressed the role of informal networks, using intense *affective focusing*, in the recruitment of suicide bombers. Whilst it is clear that activism in radical groups is not a result of economic frustration, the Muslim Brotherhood and European fundamentalist groups have often recruited among student groups (Gunning 2007; Wiktorowicz 2005). The former militants of the US-supported Mujahadiin in Afghanistan are particularly important in the spreading of a military vision of jihad in the numerous armed conflicts in the Middle East, Chechnya and former Yugoslavia, which helped the spreading of a military vision. After 9/11, the war in Afghanistan has pushed Salafi jihadists to look for protection in other countries, such as Pakistan and Iran, spreading military skills and ideological motivations (Hafez 2007: 166ff). Similarly, resistance to the American invasion of Iraq involved a heterogeneous coalition, comprised of Salafi jihadists but also of Ba'athists, where an important role was also played by former soldiers and secret service officers (Hafez 2007: 37).

These militaristic cultures gave a particular flavour to 'cognitive closure'. Moreover, specific cognitive dynamics are set in motion as a result of some of the religious discourses involved in the development of oppositional identities. In research on the Islamic al-Muhagirun in the UK, Quentin Wiktorowicz (2005) describes a process of cognitive change in future members which is linked to their identity crisis (and experiences of discrimination), but also to the encounter with the organization. Given the heterogeneity of the Muslim population by language, nationality and ethnic groups, in the countries to which Muslims have emigrated, a common/unitary Muslim identification entails a 'reinvention' of Islam (Roy 2004). Among second-generation migrants in particular, religious conversion takes place in the context of tensions between traditional values and pressures to assimilate into Western society. Similarly, in the Middle East, the impact of political repression on activists' lives helps to explain the radicalization of Islamic fundamentalist militancy, as the suppression by the Nasser regime radicalized elements of the

Brotherhood and led individuals to re-interpret the ideology of modernist Islamism into a 'rejectionist call to arms'.

Radicalization and Social Movements: Some Conclusions

Social movement research has not paid much attention to violence, preferring the study of more widespread (and accepted) forms of protest. However, some explanations of violence could be borrowed from social movement research, especially the research on repertoires of protest.

Forms of protest involve different degrees of radicalism and only a few forms of protest involve political violence. Leaders of social movements face a series of strategic dilemmas in choosing one or other form of action, since each form sends a different message to a range of audiences, each with different demands: the movement activists who seek to reinforce internal solidarity; the media, in search of 'news'; potential allies, who prefer more moderate forms of action; and, finally, decision-makers, who seek partners whom they can trust.

However, repertoires of actions are not just instruments of protest. They also reflect the activists' values. Historical traditions handed down through institutions and political socialization limit the range of options that can be considered, yet forms of protest spread from one movement to the other and from one country to the other, with frequent innovation and adaptation to local conditions. Additionally, repertoires of tactics are produced as a result of relational mechanisms, during long-standing interactions between various actors both inside and outside the movement. In these interactions, all actors develop socially constructed images of the external reality, and these guide their motivation and decisions.

Past research on social movements and violent radicalization can offer new (and helpful) lenses through which to read contemporary challenges. One of the lessons of this research is the importance of macro-contextual, meso-organizational and micro-individual levels of analysis. More thought and research are needed in order to successfully adapt existing tools to the new characteristics of recent processes of radicalizations. Such adaptation and application of these insights to contemporary preoccupations might well fill some gaps in the social science literature.

References

Bjørgo, T. (2004), 'Justifying Violence: Extreme Nationalist and Racist Discourses in Scandinavia', in A. Fenner and E.D. Weitz (eds), *Fascism and Neofascisms* (Houndsmills: Macmillan), 207–18.

Bjørgo, T. and Horgan, J. (2009), *Leaving Terrorism Behind: Individual and Collective Disengagement* (Abingdon: Taylor & Francis).

Bosi, L. (2006), 'The Dynamics of Social Movement Development: Northern Ireland's Civil Rights Movement in the 1960s', *Mobilization* 11, 81–100.
Boudreau, V. (2004), *Resisting Dictatorship. Repression and Protest in Southeast Asia* (Cambridge: Cambridge University Press).
Crenshaw, M. (2005), 'Political Explanations', in *Addressing the Causes of Terrorism*, Report of the Working Group at the International Summit on Democracy, Terrorism and Security, 8–11 March, Madrid, Club de Madrid Series on Democracy and Terrorism, Vol. 1, 13–18.
Davenport, C. (2005), 'Repression and Mobilization: Insights from Political Science and Sociology', in C. Davenport, H. Johnston and C. Mueller (eds), *Repression and Mobilization: Social Movements, Protest, and Contention* (Minneapolis: University of Minnesota Press).
Davenport, C. and Armstrong, D.A. (2004), 'Democracy and the Violation of Human Rights: A Statistical Analysis from 1976 to 1996', *American Journal of Political Science*, 538ff.
Della Porta, D. (1990), *Il terrorismo di sinistra* (Bologna: Il Mulino).
Della Porta, D. (1995), *Social Movements, Political Violence and the State* (Cambridge/New York: Cambridge University Press).
Della Porta, D. (1996), 'Protest, Protesters and Protest Policing', in M. Giugni, D. McAdam and C. Tilly (eds), *How Social Movements Matter* (Minneapolis: University of Minnesota Press), 66–96.
Della Porta, D. (2008a), 'Research on Social Movements and Political Violence', *Qualitative Sociology* 31(3), 221–30.
Della Porta, D. (2008b), 'Leaving Left-Wing Terrorism in Italy: a Sociological Analysis', in T. Bjorgo and J. Horgan (eds), *Leaving Terrorism Behind* (London: Routledge).
Della Porta, D. and Diani, M. (2006), *Social Movements: An Introduction*, 2nd edn (Oxford: Blackwell).
Della Porta, D., Peterson, A. and Reiter, H. (eds) (2006), *The Policing of Transnational Protest* (Aldershot: Ashgate).
Della Porta, D. and Reiter, H. (eds) (1998), *Policing Protest: The Control of Mass Demonstrations in Western Democracies* (Minneapolis: University of Minnesota Press).
Della Porta, D. and Reiter, H. (2004), *Polizia e Protesta* (Bologna: Il Mulino).
Della Porta, D. and Tarrow, S. (1987), 'Unwanted Children. Political Violence and the Cycle of Protest in Italy, 1966–1973', *European Journal of Political Research* 14, 607–32.
Della Porta, D. and Wagemann, C. (2005), *Patterns of Radicalization in Political Activism: Research Design*, Veto project Report (Florence: EUI).
Demetriou, C. (2007), 'Political Violence and Legitimation: The Episode of Colonial Cyprus', *Qualitative Sociology* 30, 171–93.
DeNardo, J. (1985), *Power in Numbers: The Political Strategy of Protest and Rebellion* (Princeton, NJ: Princeton University Press).
Ellison, G. and Smyth, J. (2000), *The Crowned Harp: Policing Northern Ireland* (London: Pluto Press).

Esposito, J.L. (2002), *Unholy War: Terror in the Name of Islam* (New York: Oxford University Press).
Francisco, R. (2000), 'Why Are Collective Conflicts Stable?', in C. Davenport (ed.), *Paths to State Repression: Human Rights Violations and Contentious Politics* (Lanham, MD: Rowman & Littlefield).
Gamson, W. (1990, original edition 1975), *The Strategy of Social Protest*, 2nd edn (Belmont, CA: Wadsworth).
Gamson, W.A, Fireman, B. and Rytina, S. (1982), *Encounters with Unjust Authorities* (Homewood, IL: Dorsey Press).
Gergez, F.A. (2005), *The Far Enemy. Why Jihad Went Global* (Cambridge: Cambridge University Press).
Goodwin, J. (2004), 'Review Essays: What Must We Explain to Explain Terrorism?', *Social Movement Studies* 3, 259–65.
Graham, H.D. and Gurr, T. (1969), 'Preface', in H.D. Graham and T. Gurr (eds), *Violence in America: Historical and Comparative Perspectives* (New York: Praeger).
Gunning, J. (2007), *Hamas in Politics: Democracy, Religion and Violence* (London: Hurst).
Gunning, J. (2009), *Social Movement Theory and the Study of Terrorism*, in R. Jackson, M. Breen Smyth and J. Gunning (eds), *Critical Terrorism Studies: A New Research Agenda* (London, Routledge), 156–77.
Gurr, T.R. (1970), *Why Men Rebel* (Princeton, NJ: Princeton University Press).
Hafez, M. (2003), *Why Muslims Rebel* (Boulder, CO: Lynne Rienner).
Hafez, M. (2004), 'From Marginalization to Massacres: A Political Process Explanation', in Quentin Wiktorowicz (ed.), *Islamic Activism. A Social Movement Theory Approach* (Bloomington, IN: Indiana University Press), 37–60.
Hafez, M. (2007), *Suicide Bombers in Iraq: The Strategy and Ideology of Martyrdom* (Washington DC: United States Institute of Peace).
Hasenclever, A. and Rittberger, V. (2000), 'Does Religion Make a Difference? Theoretical Approaches to the Impact of Faith on Political Conflict', *Millennium: Journal of International Studies* 29, 641–74.
Irvin, C.L. (1999), Militant Nationalism: Between Movement and Party in Ireland and the Basque Country (Minneapolis: University of Minnesota Press).
Jackson, R., Breen Smyth, M. and Gunning, J. (eds) (2009), *Critical Terrorism Studies: A New Research Agenda* (London, Routledge).
Jaspers, J., Goodwin, J. and Polletta, F. (2001), *Passionate Politics: Emotions and Social Movements* (Chicago: University of Chicago Press).
Johnston, H. and Klandermans, B. (eds) (1995), *Social Movements and Culture* (Minneapolis/London: University of Minnesota/UCL Press).
Juergensmeyer, M. (2000), *Terror in the Name of God: The Global Rise of Religious Violence* (Berkeley, CA: University of California Press).
Karagiannis, E. (2010), *Political Islam in Central Asia. The Challenge of Hizb Ut-Tahrir* (London: Routledge).
Karagiannis, E. and McCauley, C. (2006), 'Hizb ut-Tahrir al-Islami: Evaluating the Threat Posed by a Radical Islamic Group That Remains Nonviolent', *Terrorism and Political Violence* 18:2, 315–34.

Kepel, G. (2002), *Jihad: The Trail of Political Islam* (London: I.B. Tauris).
Kepel, G. (2005), *The Roots of Radical Islam* (London: Saqi).
Khosrokhavar, F. (2006), *Quand al-Quaïda Parle* (Paris: Points).
Koopmans, R. (2005), 'The Extreme Right: Ethnic Competition or Political Space?', in R. Koopmans et al. (eds), *Contested Citizenship: Immigration and Cultural Diversity in Europe* (Minneapolis: University of Minnesota Press), 180–204.
Kriesi, H. (1989), 'The Political Opportunity Structure of the Dutch Peace Movement', *West European Politics* 12, 295–312.
McAdam, D. (1983), 'Tactical Innovation and the Pace of Insurgency', *American Sociological Review* 48, 735–54.
McAdam, D., Tarrow, S. and Tilly, C. (2001), *The Politics of Contention* (Cambridge: Cambridge University Press).
Maney, G., (2007), 'From Civil War to Civil Rights and Back Again: The Interrelation of Rebellion and Protest in Northern Ireland 1955–1972', *Research in Social Movements, Conflicts, and Change* 27, 3–35.
Mayntz, R. (2004), *Organizational Forms of Terrorism: Hierarchy, Network, or a Type Sui Generis?* MPIfG Discussion Paper 04/4 (Cologne: Max Planck Institute for the Study of Societies).
Mees, L. (2003), *Nationalism, Violence and Democracy: The Clash of Identities* (Basingstoke and New York: Palgrave Macmillian).
Melucci, A. (1982), *L'Invenzione del Presente: Movimenti, Identità, Bisogni Individuali* (Bologna: Il Mulino).
Moyano, M.J. (1995), *Argentina's Lost Patrol: Armed Struggle, 1969–1979* (New Haven, CT: Yale University Press).
Norris, P. (2002), *Democratic Phoenix: Reinventing Political Activism* (New York: Cambridge University Press).
O'Boyle, G. (2002), 'Theories of Justification and Political Violence: Examples from Four Groups', *Terrorism and Political Violence* 14, 23–46.
Olesen, T. (2009), 'Islamism as Social Movement', Working Paper of the Center for Studies in Islamism and Radicalization, University of Aarhus.
Piven, F.F. and Cloward, R. (1977), *Poor People's Movements* (New York: Pantheon).
Pruitt, D.G. and Kim, S.H. (2004), *Social Conflict: Escalation, Stalemate, and Settlement*, 3rd edn (New York: McGraw-Hill).
Reiter, H. (1998), 'Police and Public Order in Italy, 1944–1948: The Case of Florence', in D. della Porta and H. Reiter (eds), *Policing Protest. The Control of Mass Demonstrations in Western Democracies* (Minneapolis: University of Minnesota Press), 143–65.
Rochon, T.R. (1988), *Between Society and State: Mobilizing for Peace in Western Europe* (Princeton, NJ: Princeton University Press).
Roy, O. (2004), *Globalized Islam. The Search for a New Ummah* (London: Hurst).
Sageman, M. (2004), *Understanding Terror Networks* (Philadelphia: University of Pennsylvania Press).
Schiffauer, W. (2008), 'Suspect Subjects: Muslim Migrants and the Security Agencies in Germany', in J. Eckert (ed.), *The Social Life of Anti-terrorism Laws* (Bielefeld: Transcript), 55–77.

Snow, D.A. and Byrd, S.C. (2007), 'Ideology, Framing Processes and Islamic Terrorist Movements', *Mobilization* 12, 119–36.
Steinhoff, P. (1991), *Red Army Faction: A Sociological Tale* (in Japanese) (Tokyo: Kabade Shobo Shinsha).
Stepan, A. (2000), 'Religion, Democracy, and the "Twin Tolerations"', *Journal of Democracy* 11(4), 37–57.
Tarrow, S. (1989), *Democracy and Disorder: Protest and Politics in Italy, 1965–1975* (Oxford/New York: Oxford University Press).
Tarrow, S. (1994), *Power in Movement: Social Movements, Collective Action and Politics* (New York/Cambridge: Cambridge University Press).
Tilly, C. (1978), *From Mobilization to Revolution*. (Reading, MA: Addison-Wesley).
Tilly, C. (2003), *The Politics of Collective Violence* (Cambridge: Cambridge University Press).
Tilly, C. (2004), 'Terror, Terrorism, Terrorists', *Sociological Theory* 22, 5–13.
Waldmann, P. (ed.) (1993), *Beruf: Terrorist* (Munich: Becks).
White, R. (1993), *Provisional Irish Republicans: An Oral and Interpretative History* (Westport, CT: Greenwood Press).
Wieviorka, M. (1988), *Société et terrorisme* (Paris: Fayard).
Wiktorowicz, Q. (2004), *Islamic Activism in social Movement Theory*, in Q. Wiktorowicz (ed.), *Islamic Activism: A Social Movement Theory Approach* (Bloomington, IN: Indiana University Press), 1–33.
Wiktorowicz, Q. (2005), *Radical Islam Rising: Muslim Extremism in the West* (Lanham, MD: Rowman & Littlefield).
Zwerman, G., Steinhoff, P.G. and Della Porta, D. (2000), 'Disappearing Social Movements: Clandestinity in the Cycle of New Left Protest in the US, Japan, Germany and Italy', *Mobilization* 5, 83–100.

Feminist Reflections on Political Violence

Laura Sjoberg

In 1985, Betty Reardon's *Sexism and the War System* made the argument that there are 'interrelationships between sexist oppression and militarization' such that 'the two problems not only are symbiotically related, but twin manifestations of the same underlying cause' (Reardon 1985: 2). The link between these, according to Reardon, is patriarchy – a system of dualism where there are 'aggressors and victims who play through the deadly combative ritual to achieve status' (Reardon 1985: 37). Because she sees political violence and gender subordination as products of the same root problem, Reardon suggests that it is a good idea to take on 'as one goal the two major transformative tasks of our generation: achieving equality for women and complete disarmament' (Reardon 1985: 97).

While over the 25 years since the publication of Reardon's book, a vibrant research programme on gender and political violence has expanded on, critiqued and re-formulated her argument, the fundamental point that political violence cannot be understood without reference to its intrinsic links to gender subordination has remained a mainstay in feminist reflections on political violence. Feminist research on the making and fighting of wars has urged students of security to broaden the definition of 'war' and to explore women's multiple roles in conflict with an eye for the complex relationships between gender, gender-based stereotypes and political violence. In this research, feminists argue from a variety of perspectives that gender is conceptually, empirically and normatively essential to studying international security and that, as such, accurate, rigorous and ethical scholarship on political violence cannot be produced without taking account of the gendered nature of political violence and the violent reproduction of gender in global politics.

This chapter provides an overview of the theoretical arguments that lead feminists to this understanding, alongside a number of examples illustrating those points. It begins by chronicling some important components of feminist work on the meaning of political violence, the people who commit political violence and the people who are impacted by political violence. It then argues that political violence is constituted by gender 'all the way down', that is, that political violence is gendered, its actors are gendered and its impacts are gendered. Looking theoretically at women who commit terrorist violence, this chapter contends that a broader understanding of both what gender is and what counts as 'political' violence is essential to a comprehensive understanding of the subject matter of political violence. The chapter concludes with a proposed feminist reading of political violence as a gendered concept.

Feminism and the Meaning of Political Violence

Feminist scholarship in international relations (IR) is, in Marysia Zalewski's (1996) terms, theory as practice – theorizing that is both research in the traditional sense and a part of a daily life as a political movement to end gender subordination. In feminist terms, gender subordination is the devalued status assigned in social and political life to characteristics and people associated with femininity. In this reading, 'gender' is divisible into *masculinities* and *femininities*, which are 'stereotypes, behavioural norms, and rules' assigned to those people perceived to be men and those people perceived to be women (Sjoberg 2006: 33). In this way, gender categorizations are socially constructed, but are reliant on the male/female dichotomy, which is associated with a number of other dichotomies in social and political life, including rational/emotional, public/private, strong/weak, public/private and aggressive/passive.

Feminists in IR study how gender influences and is influenced by global politics. In this research, they frequently understand gender as 'a system of symbolic meaning that creates social hierarchies' which organizes social and political life, where 'both men and women tend to place a higher value on ... masculinity' (Sjoberg 2009: 181). Feminists recognize that there is not just one 'masculinity' and one 'femininity', but hierarchies of masculinities and femininities positioned within the hierarchy between masculinity and femininity. These gender-based hierarchies construct, change and enforce meaning in global social and political life, and political violence. As a result, feminists tend to conceptualize the category of 'political violence' more broadly than traditional notions, questioning the personal/political and public/private divides. They argue that gender matters in political violence in three main ways: it is necessary, conceptually, for understanding what political violence is; it is important in analysing causes and predicting outcomes; and it is essential to thinking about solutions and promoting positive change.

Feminist scholarship, then, looks at the world through 'gender lenses', which 'focus on gender as a particular kind of power relation [and] trace out the ways in which gender is central to understanding international processes' (Steans 1998: 5). Still, there is not one 'women's experience', 'experience of femininity' or 'experience of gendered power' in the world. Instead, gender is lived by different people in different cultures and across time. As a result, there are a number of different ways in which feminists look through gendered lenses – in IR terms, as realists, liberals, constructivists, critical theorists, post-structuralists, postcolonialists and ecofeminists, to name but a few.[1] These 'perspectives yield different, sometimes

---

1   This typology comes from Tickner and Sjoberg (2010), but others exist (like the one

contradictory, insights about and predictions for global politics' (Sjoberg 2009: 183). Still, this work shares a normative and empirical interest in the gender-hierarchical nature of the international system.

In research on political violence, feminists have demonstrated the gender bias in the core concepts of international relations, such as the state, violence, war, peace and even security itself, urging re-definition in light of that bias (Peterson 1992; Pettman 1996; Tickner 2001). Feminist scholars have also gained empirical and theoretical insights from analysing the various roles of women and gender in conflict and conflict resolution. Feminists have found gender-based language and assumptions at the foundation of debates about nuclear strategy (Cohn 1987), the non-combatant immunity principle (Kinsella 2005; Sjoberg 2006), peacekeeping (Whitworth 2004) and various aspects of militarization and soldiering (for example, Enloe 2000). In addition to critiquing concepts traditionally employed in the study of security, gender-based perspectives have also uncovered new empirical knowledge about sexual violence in war and gendered participation in armed conflict (Card 1996). For example, feminist scholars have pointed out that rape is more prevalent in times of war than in times of peace (Enloe 1993). In addition to pointing out the serious threat to women's security posed by wartime rape (Hansen 2001), feminists have demonstrated that rape is institutionalized in war as recreational and as a weapon (Peterson and Runyan 2009: 127) (see also Staub on ethnopolitical violence in this volume, Chapter 11).

Still, as some scholars point out, feminist approaches to defining and dealing with political violence differ, and sometimes conflict, offering different research foci through gendered lenses. For example, feminist work from a realist perspective focuses on the role of gender in strategy and power politics between states (see Whitworth 1989). Liberal feminist work (for example, Caprioli 2004; Hudson et al. 2009) focuses on the subordinate position of women in global politics and argues that gender oppression can be remedied by including women in the existing structures of global politics and protecting them from political violence, as traditionally defined. Critical feminism explores the ideational and material manifestations of gendered identity and gendered power in world politics, contributing particularly to understandings of discursive violence as political violence (for example, Chin 1998; Steans 2006). Feminist constructivism focuses on the ways that ideas about gender shape and are shaped by political violence specifically and global politics generally (Locher and Prugl 2001). Feminist post-structuralism focuses on how gendered linguistic manifestations of meaning, particularly strong/weak, rational/emotional and public/private dichotomies, serve to empower the masculine, marginalize the feminine and (violently) constitute global politics (for example, Hooper 2001; Shepherd 2008). Postcolonial feminists, while sharing many of the epistemological assumptions of post-structural feminists, focus on the ways that colonial relations of domination and subordination established under imperialism are reflected in gender relations, and even relations between feminists, in global politics and academic work (Mohanty 2003).

Kimberly Hutchings' work uses, discussed later in this chapter).

In addition to diverse foci in the study of political violence, feminists have diverse approaches to the ethical questions surrounding political violence. Kimberly Hutchings outlines the parameters of these approaches, characterizing 'enlightenment feminisms' as a school of thought which 'makes the justification of uses of political violence', particularly in 'situations of gross threats to human rights, including rights of women, where no alternative means to address the threat are available' (Hutchings 2007: 95). This approach suggests women contest men's monopolies over the means of political violence and support women's rights to be a part of the persecution of just wars (Carter 1998; Hutchings 2007).

The second categorization that Hutchings uses is that of 'care' feminism. Care feminism argues 'for an ethics that is self-consciously based on the recognition of human inter-dependence and the generalization of the values inherent in women's caring work' (Hutchings 2007: 95). In global politics, then, care feminism guides students and practitioners of global politics to overturn masculine assumptions about the nature of political actors (as rational, unitary and independent) and the nature of politics (as competitive and zero-sum) (Hutchings 2007: 95; Robinson 1999). This feminist lens 'renders the legitimation of the use of violence highly problematic' because any such legitimation would be seen to reflect 'the masculine distortion of enlightenment feminism's model of the human' (Harris and King 1989; Hutchings 2007; Ruddick 1989). 'Care' feminism sees non-violence as a core value.

The third category of feminist approaches to political violence that Hutchings discusses is that of postcolonial feminism. Postcolonial feminism argues that the enlightenment approach is exclusive, lacking context and privileging Western values (Mohanty 2003). As Hutchings explains, 'for postcolonial feminism, the ethical significance of context is twofold: firstly, because it affects the meaning of a particular right, value or principle; secondly, because it affects the way in which the effects of measures promoting particular values and principles are experienced' (Hutchings 2007: 95). Still, in contrast to care feminism, postcolonial feminism does not posit a generic, feminist/feminine framework for ethical decision-making or a generic understanding of the meaning or definition of political violence. As such, postcolonial approaches evaluate political violence situationally.

While each of these approaches looks at and understands political violence through gendered lenses, they come to different conclusions. To illustrate this point, Hutchings uses Jean Elshtain's just warriors/beautiful souls dichotomy (see Elshtain 1987a). In Elshtain's understanding, the 'just warrior' trope links masculinity to protection of women/femininity, while the 'beautiful soul' trope links femininity to non-violence and the need for protection. In Hutchings' understanding, then, enlightenment feminism sees the just warrior as the ideal political actor (and the problem with the tropes is that they are gendered), while care feminism sees the beautiful soul as the ideal political actor (where the problem is the existence of the just warrior trope) and postcolonial feminism problematizes the gendered/hierarchical nature of the protected/protector dichotomy. As such, different feminist approaches (however categorized, and Hutchings' categorization is one of many) to political violence differ on questions as fundamental as whether or not it is ever a justifiable tool to use as a means to political ends.

Hutchings concludes that 'debates between different accounts of feminist ethics in world politics cannot be definitely resolved' considering that they, in effect, critique each other (2007: 98). Still, John Hoffman provides a framework through which we can see feminism's approaches to political violence and the ethics thereof as diversity within commonality. Hoffman introduces the idea of a 'momentum concept', which can accommodate difference, interpretational gaps, internal conflict and change, while still holding conceptual validity in a way that makes analysis possible (Hoffman 2001: 8). Momentum concepts are concepts which have an egalitarian and anti-hierarchical 'logic' (Hoffman 2001: 23). In other words, an idea is defined by the dialogue about it rather than strictly as one thing or another. Therefore, the boundaries are constantly changing both size and shape to accommodate new interpretations, internal disagreement and change over time. This flexibility, Hoffman contends, means that 'momentum concepts are therefore inherently subversive. They demonstrate an inner movement which transcends the formulations of their creators' (2001: 25). This means that feminisms, though they are diverse, can be seen as a singular research project and theoretical agenda. Hoffman asserts that this flexibility is also commensurate with a feminist concern for reflexivity (Hoffman 2001: 25). He argues that 'if feminism is to be coherently defined, then, in my view, it needs to be conceived as one river with numerous currents rather than as a series of rivers flowing in different and even contradictory directions' (Hoffman 2001: 48).

This chapter views feminist approaches to defining political violence and considering the ethical questions surrounding political violence as a momentum concept, in Hoffman's terms. While the research programme addressing gender and political violence is diverse, it has several common tenets. The first common tenet is a broad understanding of what counts as violence and who or what merits protection from that violence. Feminist approaches to security define security broadly in multi-dimensional and multi-level terms. In this view, violence includes not only war but also domestic violence, rape, poverty, gender subordination and ecological destruction (Tickner 1992). The second common theme in feminist studies of political violence is an understanding of the gendered nature of the values prized in the realm of international security. If 'masculinism is the ideology that justifies and naturalizes gender hierarchy by not questioning the elevation of ways of being and knowing associated with men and masculinity over those associated with women and femininity', then the values socially associated with femininity and masculinity are awarded unequal weight in a competitive social order, violently perpetuating inequality in perceived gender difference (Hooper 1998). A third common theme for the feminist study of political violence is the broad and diverse role that feminist scholars see gender playing in the theory and practice of global politics. These observations lead to a final common theme for the feminist study of political violence: that the omission of gender from work on political violence does not make that work gender-neutral or unproblematic. Instead, feminist work on issues of political violence has served to 'question the supposed nonexistence of and irrelevance of women in international security politics', interrogate 'the extent to which women are secured by state "protection" in times of war and peace', contest 'discourses where women are linked unreflectively with peace' and critique 'the assumption that gendered security practices address only women' (Blanchard 2003: 1290).

While most theorists of security think about political violence only on the levels that it is a direct product of or producer of international security, feminists understand physical, structural, ecological and sexual violence as political violence (Tickner 2001). This approach emphasizes individual human safety, especially at the political margins, re-focusing the object of violence from the state towards peoples' lives. Definitions of war as state action omit many of the political concerns about women and femininity that feminism emphasizes (Sylvester 2002: 116). Feminist theory calls attention to the suffering that traditional understandings of security normally ignore, including the impacts of war on individual women's lives and the different manifestations of political violence. It is appropriate to theorize political violence in militaries, on battlefields, with planes and with attention to terrorism. But it is also appropriate to theorize political violence as it relates to 'civilian casualties, power outages, structural violence, food shortages, militarism, and human rights' (Sjoberg 2006: 51, citing Steans 1998). In this interpretation, 'war is best understood as a continuum, or a process, rather than as a discrete event' (Cuomo 1996: 31). Crisis-based understandings of political violence can omit the suffering that leads up to and follows wars and takes attention away from everyday violence. As Chris Cuomo explains, references to 'war as a separate, bounded sphere indicate assumptions that war is a realm of human activity vastly removed from normal life' (1996: 30). Instead, 'war is a process that affects and is affected by daily political life' (Sjoberg 2006: 52).

Feminists' concern for the political margins inspires the insight that states are not monolithic entities, but diverse amalgamations of people and experiences. States claim to be unitary, however, and have become a symbolic substitute for the individual (Steans 1998). Feminisms, by contrast, prioritize women's individual subjectivity as a tool against the power of gender subordination. If individual subjectivity is important, then states are not the only actors in international politics. Instead, gendered lenses reveal that people, with their multiple relationships and multiple experiences, are political actors (Goldstein 2001: 53).

Feminism and Agents of Political Violence

Many traditional theories of political violence, particularly in political science (with the possible exception of terrorism studies), focus on states as the agents of political violence. Feminist approaches, as mentioned above, pay attention to a broader spectrum of political actors and define political action more broadly. The root of this theoretical difference, and of feminist theorizing about agency in political violence, is feminist criticisms of the public/private dichotomy, which were mentioned in the introduction to this chapter.

The gendered basis of the public/private dichotomy is the expectation that men's realm is outside the home (in business and in politics) and women's realm is inside the home (as homemakers). The public sphere, and thus men's lives, are of concern to other members of the public sphere, while the private sphere, and thus women's lives, are not of concern to the public sphere. As such, the private sphere is devalued socially, politically and economically. As Hilary Charlesworth, Christine Chinkin and Shelley Wright argue, the 'public realm ... where power and authority are exercised, is regarded as the natural province of men; while the private world ... is seen as the appropriate domain of women ... greater significance is attached to the public, male world' (1991). In other words, 'the things that happen in these private spaces (such as domestic violence or marital rape) have been treated as private matters beyond the control or authority of the state' (Eckert 2008).

While 'the terms of the public/private divide differ from domestic to international society', it has a similar function, calling attention to the public sphere and shielding the private sphere from visibility (Eckert 2008). Though the private sphere in international politics is multi-layered and includes a range of actors from non-state armed groups to civilians, it shares marginalization in war theorizing. In most theorizing about political violence, then, the 'public' sphere of the state has been visible (perhaps even over-visible) while the 'private' sphere in its various iterations (civilians who suffer in war or 'non-state' actors who make war) have been marginal or invisible. Feminist theorizing to denaturalize the public/private dichotomy ranks states as the agents in political violence and ignores the agency of non-state actors (Sjoberg 2006).

Replicating this public/private dichotomy, most theories of individual political violence either explicitly or implicitly exclude women. Those theories that are not explicitly *about men only* or gendered in their appraisal still rely on a male actor (as a man) as a stereotype and masculinized understandings of knowledge, values and actions. Many of the theories of individual violence have been shaped by attention to men and, even when applied to women, are adding women to an analysis, the terms of which have already been set by masculine discourses. Adding women to theories of individual (men's) violence shows *not only* that these theories omitted women, but the ways that they are gendered has made them inadequate to explain *both* men's violence and women's violence. One major point of contention that feminist critics have had with theories of agency in political science is the idea of (state) actors' autonomy.

Most theories of political violence begin with the assumption that actors, through explicit consent or social contract, have accepted some limitations on their decision-making capacity in exchange for the right to live in a society which provides them with protection and easy access to a number of human necessities (Hirschmann 1989: 1228). This understanding of an individual's role in political decision-making, however, comes up short in two important areas: first, consent is not always explicit or voluntary; and, second, the process of consent, even when voluntary, is complicated by a number of mitigating factors.

The contention that consent in the social contract is not always voluntary has been a tenet of feminist theory throughout its history (see MacKinnon 2001). There are many obligations that 'people do not choose, actively or passively' (Sjoberg 2006: 124). Gendered lenses see the incompleteness of choice because they recognize gender bias in the structure of political obligation and social agency (Hirschmann 1989: 1228–9). Women often are assigned obligations that they have not agreed to, either implicitly or explicitly. Seeing this as true of women allows for the interrogation of the general assumption that obligation is assumed freely by men or women.

Further, non-voluntary obligation is assigned to human beings on gendered terms. Traditional understandings of political agency and responsibility emphasize freedom (Hirschmann 1989: 1233) while traditional understandings of femininity emphasize control, headed by a laundry list of obligations that women must perform in households (Tickner 2001). In other words, obligatory relationships are always governed by gendered power. These limitations differ based on social group membership, where oppressed social groups have less access to powers and freedoms (and thus to agency) (Hirschmann 2004: 204). Often, in social relationships, women are the obliged and men the obligor, meaning women must recognize men and men need not return the recognition (Hirschmann 1989: 1239). As a result, 'unfair bargaining positions belie the freedom implicit in free choice' (Hirschmann 1989: 1239).

This brings us to the second shortcoming of the idea of consent: the many complexities surrounding it serve as mitigating factors. The first complexity, discussed above, is that people come to the 'consent table' with differential power and thus have different capacities to choose and ignore obligations. The second complexity, as Hirschmann describes, is that consent is mitigated by the fact that in almost all situations in which choice is required, there are limited choices, which narrow the possible gains from this (or any other) choice, giving people less incentive to want to choose some other option. Actor choice, then, is constrained by its (occasional) unavailability, individuals' (gendered) power differentials, limited choice and the social construction of internal will and desire. Yet, within this complex maze of limits on human agency and the freedom of choice, individual identity remains (Sylvester 1992). A feminist approach to the question of agency critiques the idea that all choices are made and responsibilities are assumed fully freely (Hirschmann 1989). Instead, a relational autonomy approach sees responsibility as intersubjective. Responsibility is *responsive* and interactive, based on the social and political interaction. If not all choices are made fully freely and not all obligations are assumed voluntarily, then obligation is relational.

In a world of relational autonomy, decisions can be made within constraints or with fellow constrainees, but are never entirely unavailable and never without any constraint. Accordingly, 'decisions are not made without others, but instead either with or around them' (Sjoberg 2006). Given this interdependence, actors can choose to use their limited autonomy to act against, around or with others. In this interpretation, the existence and identity of the self and other are mutually dependent, mutually vulnerable and mutually socially constructed. This mutual construction is not accomplished by harmony and cooperation, but by the ambivalence and conflict inherent in the environment.

Any move towards a gender-conscious theory of individual violence in global politics would need to at the same time account for political and social motivations, gendered context and individuality. Including previously hidden gender inequalities in the analysis of individual violence in global politics 'allows us to see how many of the insecurities affecting us all, women and men alike, are gendered in this historical origins, their conventional definitions, and their contemporary manifestations' (Tickner 1992: 129).

In short, feminist accounts of agency in political violence suggest that theories of political violence should complicate both who they look at as actors in the commission of political violence and how they consider the agency of those actors. I will conclude this section with an application of those ideas to an area of central concern to feminist thinking: women's multiple roles in war.

Women have agency in a number of different aspects of political violence and are victims of a number of different forms of political violence. Feminist theorizing notes this, and looks for women in the planning, making, fighting, supplying, ending and reconstructing of war. One of the trends that feminists note is the gendered nature of the treatment of women both in the policy world and in the study of political violence.

Across women's multiple roles in war, expectations that women are feminine and behave according to traditionally accepted standards of femininity are constant. Women are a crucial *casus belli* (justification) for fighting wars. For example, the US invasion of Afghanistan was justified in part by a claim that it would protect Afghan women from the Taliban government. It was also justified by an interest in protecting the 'way of life' of Americans, which was described in terms of soccer moms and beauty queens or idealized images of femininity.

Women are often abused and raped in war because belligerents see the opponent's women as productive and reproductive of the opponent's nation (see Staub, Chapter 11, this volume). Genocidal rape is seen as a way to corrupt and eliminate an ethnic group, at least in part because women are seen as the bearers of the culture. For example, in advocating ethnic cleansing, it is alleged that former biologist and then-President of the Serb Republic Biljana Plavsic argued that women's purity was the mark of cultural purity; eliminating one could eliminate another.

Women are also often incorporated into peace-building processes because it is perceived that women, because they are expected to be more emotional, sensitive, cooperative and peaceful than men, will be better at ending conflicts than men, who are expected to be more competitive and aggressive. Security Council Resolution 1325 argues that women and gender should be taken into account in peace-building processes *because* women are crucial to international peace and security. The inclusion of gender quotas in post-conflict constitutions and the election of women to public office in states recovering from conflicts have also been attributed to the perception that women are *better at peace* than men are.

Feminist work on the question of agency in political violence, then, broadens the actors considered agents, suggests more complex interpretations of those agents' actions and questions the gendered nature of the analysis of that agency in studies of political violence. Feminists point out that not only are states agents of political violence, but so are individuals, both in mainstream positions of power and at the margins of global politics. These agents are not entirely autonomous of their socio-political environments, but are relationally tied to others. Further, women's agency is not and should not be limited to perceived gender-appropriate roles: women commit, participate in, plan and prevent political violence, both in ways traditionally associated with femininity and in ways which defy gender-essentializing stereotypes.

Feminism and the Victims of Political Violence

Feminist theorizing is particularly interested in questions of gender and victimization in political violence. Catherine MacKinnon calls international reactions to gendered political violence 'the double-edged denial of their [women's] humanity – the denial that sex-specific violations are commonly committed and that they are inhuman' (2006: 1). Political violence affects women in different ways – from barely to completely – but most of the ways in which women are affected by political violence are gender-specific. In wartime, women often experience accession to household head with limited resources, which they must manage in addition to other duties in times of financial hardship. Women are often subject to increased medical and social vulnerability in times of conflict, resulting from infrastructural attacks on their homes and communities. Women are confronted with an increased threat of sexual violence in wartime, as rape rates are higher during conflicts than in any other political situation. Sexual violence is exacerbated in conflicts where rape is used as a weapon of ethnic cleansing or genocide. Women are the majority of civilian casualties in most conflicts. Women also comprise the majority of persons displaced by wars and conflicts. Women are oppressed and discriminated against in refugee camps, since camp managers often feed men first to prepare them for fighting and turn a blind eye to sexual abuse. Many women are subjected to war-structured sex work, serving as prostitutes, voluntarily or involuntarily (Giles 2011). Target misestimation and indiscriminate warfare often cause substantial female casualties. While states and international organizations often stop counting civilian casualties when the shooting stops, many women feel the effects of war for years or even decades later. These impacts come in the form of preventable disease, infrastructure damage, job losses, resource shortages and lapses in the rule of law.

For example, in the struggles for power in Afghanistan prior to the US invasion, women bore the brunt of conservative governance. They were forbidden to work, not allowed to leave the house without a male escort and forced to cover themselves from head to toe. During the US invasion, thousands of women died in the crossfire between the US military and the Taliban. While the conservative policies of the Taliban are gone, women today deal with the challenges of an unstable government that is often unable to protect them from men's violence. Even in the new, more liberal, post-conflict regime, only 30 per cent of Afghan girls have access to education, 70–80 per cent of women face forced marriages and one in three Afghan women have experienced sexual or domestic violence related to the conflict (Kandiyoti 2007; Shepherd 2006).

Two messages arise from these brief understandings of the sex differential in victimization in political violence: first, that gender subordination and victimization overlap; and, second, that asking the question 'where are the women?' in the impacts of political violence inspires researchers to look in a broader range of places for the commission and impacts of political violence.

In particular, feminist peace researchers have focused on the concepts of 'structural violence' and 'positive peace' (Brock-Utne 1989: 44). 'Structural violence' is a term that originated in the work of Johann Galtung, who describes it as physical, economic, domestic and other forms of violence which stop individuals from living to their potential (Galtung 1975: 110–11). Structural violence manifests itself in gender-unequal ways in the form of the gendering of poverty, the gender-disproportionate long-term impacts of war and conflict, and the gender-unequal structure of social welfare and social justice systems. Many feminist scholars have defined political violence as including structural violence. In this vein, feminist peace researchers have used the term 'positive peace' to describe a desire to eliminate not only war, terrorism and other things traditionally characterized as 'political violence', but also structural violence. Brigit Brock-Utne lays out a number of necessary conditions for the existence of positive peace, specifying the concept. These include: absence of unorganized, personal, physical and direct violence (intimate partner violence); absence of organized, personal, physical and direct violence (war); absence of unorganized, indirect violence which decreases lifespan (unequal working conditions on the basis of gender); absence of organized, indirect violence which decreases lifespan (nuclear dumping); absence of unorganized indirect violence which decreases quality of life (inequality of leisure time and freedom of speech); and absence of organized, indirect violence reducing quality of life (mass-media oligopoly) (Brock-Utne 1989: 44–50).

Political Violence is Constituted by Gender

Feminist research has shown that the meanings of political violence, understandings of agency in political violence and understandings of victimization in political violence are laced with gendered politics and gendered understandings. In this research, the association between masculinity and war has been central to feminist investigations. While the manliness of war is rarely denied, militaries must work hard to turn men into soldiers through misogynist training thought necessary to teach men to fight (see Goldstein 2001). Importantly, such training depends on the denigration of anything that could be considered feminine; to act like a soldier is not to be 'womanly'. 'Military manhood', or a type of heroic masculinity, which goes back to the Greeks, attracts recruits and maintains self-esteem in institutions where subservience and obedience are the norm (Eichler 2006; Enloe 2008). Another image of a soldier is a just warrior, self-sacrificially protecting women, children and other vulnerable people (Elshtain 1987a; Tickner 2001). The notion that young males fight wars to protect vulnerable groups, such as women and children, who cannot be expected to protect themselves has been an important motivator for the recruitment of military forces at both the state and non-state levels.

As Nancy Huston explains, images of femaleness as a justification for political violence simultaneously enable war and subordinate women. It is men's masculine duty to protect women; this duty fuels men's desire and ability to fight in wars. Huston explains that men will fight for women, even if they have no other reason:

> But there always remains at least *one* good reason to make the supreme sacrifice, at least *one* transcendental value that justified rushing headlong into as insane an undertaking as war; very often it is Woman; the virtue she represents for the warrior, the love she bears him, the tears she will shed when he is slain. (Huston 1983: 279, emphasis in original)

This stereotype initially appears to benefit women; after all, they are to be protected while they are not expected to make or fight wars. However, this appearance is only skin-deep and the image of women as 'the protected' actually subordinates them. As the objects to be fought for, women are without either choice or agency in war-making or war-fighting. Elshtain explains that 'certain social divisions got sealed as historical preliminaries to bourgeois beautiful souldom: between home life and public life; peace and war; family and state; the immediacy of desire and the self-conscious power of universal life' (1987a: 142). Being without choice might be acceptable if women really were protected by the making and fighting of war. The illusion of protection, however, is just that, as women's lives are detrimentally affected by war on almost every level. Not only are women not protected by the gendered immunity norm, but the gender stereotypes affect the meaning of gender outside of wartime (Elshtain 1987b: 4). According to just war narratives, women are a liability to be protected, which decreases the respect they merit during wartime and afterwards.

Yet, it is not only in the question of who is fighting a war that feminists find the gendering of war. Instead, feminists see a number of components of war, conceptually and in practice, as gendered. Definitions of war as state action omit many political concerns that women and other feminized members of the state might prioritize (Sylvester 2002: 116). Feminist security studies calls attention to suffering that security analysts normally ignore, including the gendered nature of war at the state level and the impacts of war on the lives of individual women. While conventional interpretations of security see it as a zero-sum game, feminist work argues that there are other paths to security than the competitive use of force. As a result, there is a relationship between the sort of violence traditionally understood as 'war' and unsafe working conditions, unemployment, foreign debt, structural violence, ethnic violence, poverty, and family violence (Tickner 2001) – they are a continuum (Cuomo 1996).

In a recent book, Laura Shepherd (2008) combines six critiques of the 'national security' literature and six critiques of the international security literature to articulate a feminist critique not only of the making of war but of the very intellectual possibility of separating 'war' and other 'everyday' forms of violence. Shepherd argues that 'national security' discourses are gendered because they hold certain interlocking assumptions: that all human existence is bound by the state;

that behaviour derives from human nature or the anarchic system; that violence is eternal and external to the state; that security can never be achieved; and that militarization needs to be increased (Shepherd 2006: 68). She contends that the scholarly literature on international security also contains erroneous assumptions, including: the existence of a benign global civil society; that security can be achieved in absolute terms; that security should be conceptualized in terms of emancipation; and that a liberal world is desirable (Shepherd 2008: 71). She proposes that 'the violent reproduction of the international and the violent reproduction of gender ... share common elements across conceptualizations of international security and gender violence' (2008: 171). Hers and other feminist work argues that violence in global politics is necessarily both gendered and interlinked. Feminists argue that gender can link together scholarship on the meaning, causes and consequences of war that emphasizes different causal factors, different levels of analysis and different eras in history by showing the continuity of gender as a variable, a constitutive force and an analytic category.

The consistency of gendered discourses of political violence – even as women's roles in war-making and war-fighting resonate with it less – has two possible explanations: first, it could be residue from decades and even centuries of the perception that women were the pure, innocent victims of war in need of protection from it; and, second, it could be that there is something that fundamentally links gender subordination and the justification of modern warfare. While it is likely that the first explanation has some influence, I suggest that it is fruitful to consider the possibility of the second in order to understand both the meaning of war and the meaning of gender in global politics.

Earlier in this chapter, I cited Nancy Huston's (1983) argument that a gendered victorious narrative about a war is key to a belligerent's ability to justify the war and rally the resources and troops needed to fight it. Jean Elshtain (1987b) then contended that each belligerent's victorious narrative about war included a story about brave, just (masculine) citizen-warriors rescuing or protecting pure, innocent (feminine) beautiful souls. If, as Huston argues, a victorious narrative has been key to the practice of all war and, as Elshtain argues, in practice, these victorious narratives have relied on differentiated gender roles to sustain them, then the practice of war itself could be seen to rely on differentiated gender-ideal types. In this understanding, the presence of a feminized other is crucial both to political violence and its justificatory narratives. The feminized other requires protection; the protection of the feminine can then be read as a crucial cause of war. The images of femaleness in the gender-stereotypical beautiful soul narrative, then, simultaneously enable war and provide space for its gender-subordinating justifications and effects.

If this reading of political violence as constituted by gender is correct, the gendered nature of political violence will not disappear as the nature of war changes and women's roles in conflict evolve. Instead, violence and protection are not opposites, but complementary concepts which necessitate each other: protection requires violence; violence requires protection. Without the feminized other to protect, the masculinized politically violent actor has nothing to excuse (his) fighting, and the justificatory narratives behind the making and fighting of wars are stalled without their victorious conclusion. There is, then, theoretical and empirical leverage to be gained from considering the mutual constitution of gender stereotypes and war. If the feminization of the other is central to political violence, and political violence is central to the building and maintenance of gender hierarchy, gender is a lynchpin of war-making and the war system is a lynchpin of gender subordination. In the next section of this chapter, I use the example of feminist studies of women's political violence to demonstrate that not only are gender subordination and politically violence intrinsically interlinked, but that they constitute each other.

Feminism and Women who Commit Political Violence

Several scholars of gender and international relations have identified a paradox of women's integration into global politics: women are doing more of the things that were traditionally understood as the exclusive domain of men, but stereotypes about what women should and should not be doing are not disappearing at the same pace (Enloe 2000). Instead, women's integration into global political life has sacrificed as little white male privilege as possible and has paid little attention to the discursive and performative elements of gender subordination (like stereotypical narratives) (for example, Butler 1993).

Women participate in political violence on almost every level (Sjoberg and Gentry 2007) – as soldiers, as insurgents, as terrorists, as protesters, as perpetrators in genocide and genocidal rape, and as war criminals in almost every conflict around the world. The increasing presence of women in arenas of political violence has been heralded by some as proof of the victory of gender equality (Ehrenreich 2004). At first, this appears to be a logical deduction: certainly, political and criminal violence are some of the last domains of male hegemony. This initial perception is rebutted, however, by the continuing differences in the scale of male as compared with female participation in violence, as well as how these women's acts of violence are portrayed. The fact that there are women committing the same crimes as men does not mean they have a gender-equal or gender-neutral role in global politics (Cockburn 1991). First, the relatively small percentage of women who commit war crimes and terrorism received a disproportionate amount of media attention (Enloe 1993). Cynthia Enloe argues that, in the beginning of the First Gulf War (when the percentage of deployed soldiers who were women went up from less than half of one per cent in the Vietnam War to seven per cent in that war), there was an concentration of media attention for female soldiers which was far disproportionate to women's actual representation as members of the fighting force. She attributes this to a rise in the salience of femininity: people were interested in women soldiers not as soldiers but as *women soldiers*, a distinction which, rather than highlighting the gender equalities in an integrated military, demonstrates that even an integrated military can maintain gender stereotypes. Women who commit violence are often told not as terrorists or war criminals, but as *women* terrorists and *women* war criminals.

The gendered nature of these portrayals stems from the understanding that women's crimes are different from and more deviant than those of men. Studying women's crimes in the USA, Carol Smart recognized that girls with a criminal record are three times more likely to be recommended for institutionalization than boys, because girls' crimes were viewed as sexually deviant (Smart 1995). Smart found that many in the criminal justice system viewed female deviancy as due to a 'much deeper pathology than deviancy by a male' (Smart 1995: 133). It is this perceived gender difference that produces the disproportionate attention that violent women attract. Indeed, Helena Kennedy finds that female terrorists, such as women in the Weather Underground and the Baader-Meinhof Gang, 'have all provoked more interest and speculation than their male comrades' (Kennedy 1992: 261). This interest, however, has little to do with the politics of female terrorists. Instead, it betrays a fascination with women terrorists' 'sexual liberation', which sparks the interest of 'their male voyeur' (Kennedy 1992: 262).

These characterizations of violent women link sexual deviance and engagement in violence. In these stories, women are not terrorists and violent criminals but sexually disturbed or, worse, sexual victims. Instead, an unhealthily strong sexual drive *or* sexual deviance and dependence are seen as the root causes of female violence. Given the link between sex and women's violence, a woman is not responsible for her violent actions because she is compelled to commit them by a combination of sexual instinct and victimization (Morgan 1989). This is where the 'double transgression' of women's political violence becomes clear: a woman who can decide to commit a violent crime defies the stereotype of both female helplessness and female peacefulness (Keitner 2002). Instead of acknowledging the falseness of the underlying stereotype, public and publicized stories emphasize the singularity of violent women through sexual depictions (Keitner 2002; Shapiro 2000).

The reality is that women who commit violence interrupt gender stereotypes. Instead of requiring protection, they are the people from whom others should be protected (Young 2003). These depictions, however, are buried under the language of sex, because stories of women's agency in violence would interrupt dominant discourses about women's roles generally and about women's relationship to violence specifically. A violent woman has committed two crimes: her violence, and her defiance of gender stereotypes that deem her incapable of that violence in the first place (Keitner 2002: 40). As such, acknowledging that women might choose to engage in violence would change both the way we see women and the way we see global politics. Therefore, though women's violence receives a disproportionate amount of media attention, violent women's stories are marginalized by their obfuscation within stylized narratives, couched in terms that deny women's agency. Gender tropes are preserved even in narratives that discuss women who are breaking them – stories of women's violence at once separate violent women from ideal-typical femininity and maintain the feminized other as the victim of and justification for political violence.

Conclusion

Different feminist perspectives on political violence have different insights about the gendered nature of political violence and the violent reproduction of gender in global politics. Different schools of feminist thought focus on different aspects of the relationship between gender and political violence, and offer contrasting understandings of the ethics of political violence. Still, as John Hoffman suggests, there are two ways to think about gendering political violence: as in conflict or as parts of a whole. This chapter takes the latter approach, considering feminist theorizing to be a 'momentum' concept, where diverse feminist theorizing on political violence contributes to knowledge accumulation through their commonalities and through their differences. Feminist approaches define security in multi-level terms, understand political violence as gendered, see gender playing a broad and diverse role in the theory and practice of political violence, and understand gender as a necessary component of understanding political violence.

Feminist scholars therefore work not only to re-define political violence, but also to revise understandings of agency and victimization in political violence through gendered lenses. Feminists note that it is not only states that are agents of political violence, but individuals and non-governmental organizations too. In addition to expanding the range of people who are considered actors in political violence, feminists questioned what constitutes agency in political violence, critiquing the assumption prevalent in most literature on political violence that actors are rational, unitary and autonomous. Feminist theorists also critique traditional understandings of victimization in political violence, pointing out that not only does political violence disproportionately affect women, but examining political violence's effects on women is instructive in broadening the definition of political violence to include structural violence and gender subordination.

Feminist insights about the nature of political violence also hold that political violence is constituted by gender, and that gender subordination and political violence are intrinsically interrelated concepts. Using the example of women's political violence in global politics, this chapter argues that the depth of the link between gender subordination and political violence is just beginning to be explored. Feminist scholarship thus far has noted that political violence is gendered and gendering is reproduced violently in global politics, and several feminist research programmes are now exploring the dynamics of that relationship.

References

Blanchard, E. (2003), 'Gender, International Relations, and the Development of Feminist Security Theory', *Signs: Journal of Women in Culture and Society* 28:4, 1289–313.
Brock-Utne, B. (1989), *Feminist Perspectives on Peace and Peace Education* (New York: Pergamon Press).

Butler, J. (1993), *Bodies That Matter: On the Discursive Limits of 'Sex'* (New York: Routledge).
Caprioli, M. (2004), 'Feminist IR Theory and Quantitative Methodology: A Critical Analysis', *International Studies Review* 6:2, 253–69.
Card, C. (1996), 'Rape as a Weapon of War', *Hypatia* 11:4, 5–17.
Carter, A. (1998), 'Should Women Be Soldiers or Pacifists?', in J. Lorentzen and L. Turpin (eds), *The Women and War Reader* (New York and London: New York University Press).
Charlesworth, H., Chinkin, C. and Wright, S. (1991), 'Feminist Approaches to International Law', *American Journal of International Law* 85:4, 613–45.
Chin, C. (1998), *In Service and Servitude: Foreign Female Domestic Workers and the Malaysian 'Modernity' Project* (New York: Columbia University Press).
Cockburn, C. (1991), *In the Way of Women: Men's Resistance to Sex Equality in Organizations* (London: Zed Books).
Cohn, C. (1987), 'Sex and Death in the World of Rational Defence Intellectuals', *Signs: Journal of Women in Culture and Society* 12:4, 687–718.
Cuomo, C.J. (1996), 'War is Not Just an Event: Reflections on the Significance of Everyday Violence', *Hypanthia* 11:4, 30–45.
Eckert, A. (2008), 'Just War Theory and the (Re)Privatization of Force', Paper presented at the annual meeting of the MPSA Annual National Conference, Palmer House Hotel, Hilton, Chicago, IL, 3 April.
Ehrenreich, B. (2004), 'Prison Abuse: Feminism's Assumptions Upended: A Uterus is Not a Substitute for a Conscience', *Los Angeles Times*, 16 May.
Eichler, M. (2006), 'A Gendered Analysis of the Chechen Wars', *International Feminist Journal of Politics* 8:4, 486–511.
Elshtain, J.B. (1987a), 'Against Androgeny', in Phillips, A. (ed.), *Feminism and Equality* (New York: New York University Press).
Elshtain, J.B. (1987b), *Women and War* (New York: New York University Press).
Enloe, C. (1993), *The Morning After: Sexual Politics at the End of the Cold War* (Berkeley, CA: University of California Press).
Enloe, C. (2000), *Maneuvers: The International Politics of Militarizing Women's Lives* (Berkeley, CA: University of California Press).
Enloe, C. (2008), *Globalization and Militarism: Feminists Make the Link* (New York: Rowman & Littlefield).
Galtung, J. (1975), *The Specific Contribution of Peace Research to the Study of the Causes of Violence* (Oslo: University of Oslo Press).
Giles, W. (2011), 'Women Forced to Flee', in Cohn, C. (ed.), *Women and Wars* (London: Polity).
Goldstein, J. (2001), *War and Gender: How Gender Shapes the War System and Vice Versa* (Cambridge: Cambridge University Press).
Hansen, L. (2001), 'Gender, Nation, Rape: Bosnia and the Construction of Security', *International Feminist Journal of Politics* 3:1, 55–75.
Harris, A. and King, Y. (1989), *Rocking the Ship of the State: Towards a Feminist Peace Politics* (Boulder, CO: Westview Press).

Hirschmann, N. (1989), 'Freedom, Recognition, and Obligation: A Feminist Approach to Political Theory', *American Political Science Review* 83:4, 1217–44.

Hirschmann, N. (2004), *The Subject of Liberty: Towards a Feminist Theory of Freedom* (Princeton, NJ: Princeton University Press).

Hoffman, J. (2001), *Gender and Sovereignty: Feminism, the State, and International Relations* (New York: Palgrave).

Hooper, C. (1998), 'Masculinist Practices and Gender Politics: The Operation of Multiple Masculinities in International Relations', in M. Zalewski and J. Parpart (eds), *The 'Man' Question in International Relations* (Boulder, CO: Westview Press).

Hooper, C. (2001), *Manly States: Masculinities, International Relations, and Gender Politics* (New York: Columbia University Press).

Hudson, V., Caprioli, M., Ballif-Spanvill, B., McDermott, R. and Emmett, C.F. (2009), 'The Heart of the Matter: The Security of Women and the Security of States', *International Security* 33:3, 7–45.

Huston, N. (1983), 'Tales of War and Tears of Women', in J. Steihm (ed.), *Women and Men's Wars* (Oxford: Pergamon Press).

Hutchings, K. (2007), 'Feminist Ethics and Political Violence', *International Politics* 44, 90–106.

Kandiyoti, D. (2007), 'Old Dilemmas or New Challenges? The Politics of Gender and Reconstruction in Afghanistan', *Development and Change* 38:2, 169–99.

Keitner, C. (2002), 'Victim or Vamp? Images of Violent Women in the Criminal Justice System', *Columbia Journal of Law and Gender* 11, 38–80.

Kennedy, H. (1992), *Eve was Framed: Women and British Justice* (London: Vintage).

Kinsella, H. (2005), 'Securing the Civilian: Sex and Gender in the Laws of War', in Barnett, M. and Duvall, R. (eds), *Power and Global Governance* (Cambridge: Cambridge University Press).

Locher, B. and Prugl, E. (2001), 'Feminism and Constructivism: Worlds Apart or Sharing the Middle Ground?', *International Studies Quarterly* 45:1, 111–29.

MacKinnon, C. (2001), *Sex Equality* (New York: Foundation Press).

MacKinnon, C. (2006), *Are Women Human?* (Cambridge, MA: Harvard University Press).

Mohanty, C. (2003), *Feminism without Borders: Decolonizing Theory, Practicing Solidarity* (Durham, NC: Duke University Press).

Morgan, R. (1989), *The Demon Lover: The Roots of Terrorism* (New York: Washington Square Press).

Peterson, V.S. (1992), 'Transgressing Boundaries: Theories of Knowledge, Gender, and International Relations', *Millennium: Journal of International Studies* 21:2, 183–206.

Peterson, V.S. and Runyan, A.S. (2009), *Global Gender Issues*, 3rd edn (Boulder, CO: Westview Press).

Pettman, J.J. (1996), *Worlding Women: A Feminist International Politics* (London and New York: Routledge).

Reardon, B. (1985), *Sexism and the War System* (New York: Teachers' College Press).

Robinson, F. (1999), *Globalizing Care: Ethics, Feminist Theory, and International Relations* (Boulder, CO: Westview Press).

Ruddick, S. (1989), *Maternal Thinking: Towards a Politics of Peace* (New York: Houghton-Mifflin).
Shapiro, A. (2000), 'Unequal Before the Law: Men, Women, and the Death Penalty', *American Journal of Gender, Social Policy, and Law* 8, 427–70.
Shepherd, L. (2006), 'Veiled References: Constructions of Gender in the Bush Administration Attacks on Afghanistan Post-9/11', *International Feminist Journal of Politics* 8:1, 19–41.
Shepherd, L. (2008), *Gender, Violence, and Security: Discourse as Practice* (London: Zed Books).
Sjoberg, L. (2006), *Gender, Justice, and the Wars in Iraq* (New York: Lexington Books).
Sjoberg, L. (2009), 'Introduction to *Security Studies*: Feminist Contributions', *Security Studies* 18:2, 183–213.
Sjoberg, L. and Gentry, C. (2007), *Mothers, Monsters, Whores: Women's Violence in Global Politics* (London: Zed Books).
Smart, C. (1995), *Law, Crime, and Sexuality* (London: Sage).
Steans, J. (1998). *Gender and International Relations: An Introduction* (New Brunswick, NJ: Rutgers University Press).
Steans, J. (2006). *Gender and International Relations: Issues, Debates, and Future Directions* (London: Polity).
Sylvester, C. (1992), 'Feminists and Realists View Autonomy and Obligation in International Relations', in Peterson, V.S. (ed.), *Gendered States: Feminist (Re) Visions of International Relations* (Boulder, CO: Lynne Rienner).
Sylvester, C. (2002), *Feminist International Relations: An Unfinished Journey* (Cambridge: Cambridge University Press).
Tickner, J.A. (1992), *Gender in International Relations* (New York: Columbia University Press).
Tickner, J.A. (2001), *Gendering World Politics* (New York: Columbia University Press).
Tickner, J.A. and Sjoberg, L. (2010), 'Feminism', in Smith, S., Dunne, T. and Kurki, M. (eds), *International Relations Theories: Discipline and Diversity*, 2nd edn (Oxford: Oxford University Press).
Whitworth, S. (1989), 'Gender in the Inter-paradigm Debate', *Millennium: Journal of International Studies* 18:2, 265–72.
Whitworth, S. (2004), *Men, Militarism, and UN Peacekeeping: A Gendered Analysis* (Boulder, CO: Lynne Rienner).
Young, I.M. (2003), 'The Logic of Masculinist Protection: Reflections on the Current Security State', *Signs: Journal of Women in Culture and Society* 29:1, 1–25.
Zaleswki, M. (1996), '"All These Theories Yet the Bodies Keep Piling Up": Theorists, Theories, and Theorizing', in Smith, S., Booth, K. and Zalewski, M. (eds), *International Relations: Positivism and Beyond* (Cambridge: Cambridge University Press).

15

ASHGATE RESEARCH COMPANION

National Identity, Conflict and Political Violence: Experiences in Latin America

Peter Lambert

Introduction: Political Violence and Constructed Identities

Latin American history since independence has been marked by the violent struggle for political power. While there were exceptions, the vast majority of countries failed to escape the violence generated in the process of independence and the creation of nation-states in the early to mid-nineteenth century. Likewise, few Latin American countries escaped the political instability and, in many cases, political violence associated with the emergence of mass-based politics in the early part of the twentieth century or the subsequent emergence of military dictatorships in the 1960s and 1970s, which were characterized by an unprecedented level of state violence.

This has led to a portrayal of Latin America as inherently violent, subject to recurrent authoritarian tendencies due to some innate trait that can be traced back to a cultural or historical heritage rooted in pre-Columbian culture and Spanish colonialism. The Mexican writer Octavio Paz saw his own nation as 'the child of double violence, imperial and unifying: that of the Aztecs and that of the Spaniards' (Paz 1985: 100), a perspective that seeks to explain its past but also condemns its future development. Similarly, a cultural determinist argument, put forward by scholars such as Howard Wiarda, interprets violence in Latin America as rooted in the colonial legacies of extreme hierarchical relations, Catholicism, patrimonialism and the autonomy of the armed forces (Wiarda 1992). Latin America, it might seem, is condemned by its past to continuous cycles of authoritarianism and violence, as suggested in Gabriel García Márquez's landmark novel, *One Hundred Years of Solitude*.

Foreign intervention has of course also played a central role in political violence. As Eduardo Galeano has argued, Latin America is 'the region of open veins' (Galeano 1973: 12), victim of the violence inflicted by foreign colonial and neo-colonial forces in their search for raw materials and cheap labour. Historical dependency, he argued, has produced prolonged political crisis and violence, especially in those regions, such as Central America, that have been most prone to foreign intervention and invasion. If we add to this the structural violence of endemic poverty, inequality, discrimination and exclusion, Latin America may well seem in some way condemned to ongoing political instability, crisis and violence.

However, violence is no more cultural in Latin America than anywhere else. Indeed, despite some exceptional cases, most notoriously the infamous destruction of Paraguay in the War of the Triple Alliance (1864–1870), Latin America has been surprisingly free from the scale and quantity of conflicts between states that have beset, for example, Europe over the past two centuries.[1] Moreover, despite persisting images of dictatorship, revolution and political violence, Latin America (with the exception of Colombia) has avoided much of the political violence that has plagued other areas of the world over the past 20 years. It has not suffered wars based on ethnic conflict, regional separatism, religious conflict, state collapse or even, more recently, terrorism, and has enjoyed a comparatively non-violent, if disappointing and difficult, process of transition to democracy since the late 1970s. Stereotypes can be misleading.

There are perhaps two striking elements about political violence in Latin America. First, violence has tended to take place not outside the state, or due to state collapse, but rather within established political systems with formal constitutional frameworks. In the worst cases, especially in the recent periods of authoritarian rule, it has been planned, deliberate, perpetrated by state agents against citizens, and justified by elites as a legitimate form of protection of the national interest (Rosenberg 1992: 8). Second, nationalism and the struggle for national identity has been used (and abused) in order to justify and legitimize much of the political violence. Indeed, the struggle over national identity has accompanied political violence from independence onwards, with nationalism representing a constant (if constantly evolving) discourse among a vast array of political actors and projects, from nineteenth-century *caudillos* to generals and populist leaders, and from revolutionary guerrillas to counter-insurgency operations, often used to justify the unjustifiable and legitimize the illegitimate.

At its heart, nationalism is intimately connected to relations of political power (Breuilly 1993). Independence in Latin America gave rise to new, previously non-existent nations, as well as new ruling elites that sought order and legitimacy through a constructed interpretation of the nation in order to instill in the population what Anderson terms the concept of shared 'imagined community' (Anderson 1983: 15). Such interpretations were constructed around the interests, needs and world views of the dominant elites to unite different classes and socio-political groups, and coordinate diverse interests, values and aims behind a certain political project (Larrain 2000: 35). National identity thus becomes an ideological construct (Kedourie 1960), a political tool used to capture and maintain power or,

---

[1] Since independence there have been relatively few major conflicts, the most significant being the Argentine Brazilian war (1825–1828), two wars between Chile and a Peruvian-Bolivian Alliance (1836–1839 and again in 1879–1883), the Mexico–US war (1846–1848), the War of the Triple Alliance (1864–1870) and the Chaco War (1932–1935).

as Eric Hobsbawm has argued, a conscious and deliberate exercise in ideological manipulation and social engineering for political gain (Hobsbawm 1983).

However, the construction of national identity is not simply an exercise in political manipulation and control. True, it may involve a significant amount of construction by elites, states and intellectuals, as they attempt to select and fashion their own readings of the past to serve their political interests. However, shared histories, myths, images, traditions and symbols cannot be arbitrary invention, but must have some root in national consciousness and a shared historical memory (Smith 1999). They do not exist in a political void, but rather their success depends on the relationship with the 'private sphere' of the daily practices, beliefs and traditions of the people (Larrain 2000: 38). As Roland Barthes argues, national identity may be a construct, a fabricated fiction designed in a particular context, but if it does not ring true with a significant part of the population, it will never gain credibility (Barthes 2000: 126). In short, the discourse 'must resonate with large numbers of the designated co-nationals, otherwise the project will fail' (Smith 1998: 198).

National identity is therefore, as Anthony Smith has argued, dynamic, flexible and malleable – inherently open to the possibility of re-interpretation, re-writing and regeneration (Smith 1999). The selection, interpretation and codification of values, symbols, myths and traditions are ongoing processes, developed by different political interests and thus 'subject to the continuous play of history, culture and power' (Hall 1990: 223). Despite the tendency of hegemonic versions of national identity to present themselves as the (only) authentic expression of national identity, all versions are inherently 'terrains of conflict' (Larrain 2000: 35) which may be contested and challenged by dissident versions. National identity is therefore open to constant contestation, rejection, re-invention and political struggle.

As a result, more often than not, facades of uniformity and consensus over national identity, even if achieved, conceal the existence of diversity, opposition, resistance and the seeds of violent conflict. Given the heterogeneity of Latin America in terms of ethnicity, language, culture and wealth, the construction of narrow interpretations of national identity designed to justify and legitimize power has generally failed precisely because the interpretations have been exclusive, narrow and inflexible and thus have marginalized large swathes of the population, which do not see themselves in the construct (Fowler 2006). It is the failure of leaders to embrace more pluralistic, inclusive and consensual interpretations of the nation that has been at the heart of much of the political violence that has plagued Latin American politics since independence.

Although the relationship between political violence and national identity in Latin America remains remarkably understudied, this chapter argues that the struggle over competing interpretations of national identity is a major explanatory tool in terms of understanding and analysing political violence.[2] Indeed, the prominence of

---

2   Political violence is defined for the purposes of this chapter as violence perpetrated in order to challenge, alter or defend the incumbent regime, the political system and the structures of economic and political power.

nationalism in hegemonic and dissident political discourse to justify and legitimize the use of violence is a striking feature of modern Latin American history.

Concretely, the chapter briefly analyses the relationship between political violence and emerging interpretations of the nation in the nineteenth century, before focusing on the rise of nationalism and its relationship with political violence in two specific periods; the beginnings of mass-based politics in the early to mid-twentieth century; and the resulting rise of authoritarianism in the 1960s and 1970s, using brief case studies to better illustrate trends and tendencies. It then briefly examines the post-authoritarian period (1980s to the present) before the final section draws tentative theoretical conclusions regarding the complexity of the relationship between political violence and national identity.

Violence and Nation-Building

Independence from Spain was not peacefully negotiated, but was won on the battlefields between 1810 and 1825 in conflicts that involved considerable violence, setting the scene for the political conflict that would become endemic throughout the process of nation-building in the nineteenth century. The high hopes among the new republics of an age of peace, liberty, stability and freedom soon degenerated into disillusionment and violent struggles for political power, associated with and generated by the process of nation-building (Keen and Haynes 2000). Indeed, the formative years of the post-independence period witnessed the almost continuous struggle for power over the state, economy and monopoly of force between competing elites (offering little social change or vision of the nation) and was characterized by civil wars, political instability, *caudillo* rule[3] and military-backed coups for the next half-century, exacerbated by the tendency of the armed forces to see themselves as political arbiters of national politics (Vanden and Prevost 2002). Despite the promises and ideals of the struggles for independence, the exclusionary social order of the new republics remained virtually untouched.

While the political violence may generally have been associated with the struggle between competing elites for 'the private appropriation of public power' (Koonings and Kruijt 1999: 7), elites were also fully aware of the delicate nature of the hierarchical structure. As Centeno has argued, the vision of the new nation was almost entirely exclusive and was based more on the fear of the 'enemy from below', the potential power of the poor and/or indigenous majority, than on any liberating ideal (Centeno 2002: 67). In this sense, early ideas of nationhood were often a mechanism of social control to justify and facilitate the preservation of systems based on extreme hierarchies of race, class and wealth.

---

3   Caudillo refers to regional political leaders (landowners and or military leaders) with an independent economic and political base. The term has gradually become synonymous with the idea of strong, charismatic, authoritarian national (and nationalist) leaders.

The violent struggles and civil wars between conservative and liberal elites[4] which dominated much of the continent in the mid-nineteenth century eventually led to the emergence of authoritarian developmentalism and conservative liberalism, the combination of economically liberal, but politically authoritarian states, to a position of hegemony between 1870 and 1930 (Fowler 2002). Modernization and development came not in the form of citizenship, political rights or any attempt to break the dominance of entrenched landowning elites or export-based economic development, but rather in the form of infrastructural development, such as in the fields of communications, education, technology and trade – fuelled by foreign investment – and the creation of a new dependency on Britain and later the USA.

Imported ideas of export-led modernization, modernism and positivism[5] reflected visions of the nation that sought inspiration in European ideas of the Enlightenment. Thus, constructs of the nation were generally exclusive of subordinate majorities and bore little resemblance to the reality of the majority. Instead, they saw progress in the form of emulation of European models of development, culture and politics, as reflected in Domingo Faustino Sarmiento's highly influential and controversial work, *Facundo: or Civilization and Barbarism* (1845).[6] In the most extreme cases they simply represented the continuation of the civilizing project of colonialism, suggesting a duty to bring European, Christian ideas of civilization and progress to indigenous or other subordinate groups. Paradoxically, the most extreme cases of such exclusive visions of national identity (Colombia, Argentina, Peru and much of Central America) tended to lead not to unity but to more prolonged social conflict and political violence.[7]

---

4   Conservatives broadly stood for the interests of traditional powers and the maintenance of traditional structures of power (Church, land, armed forces) whilst liberals, strongly influenced by European enlightenment and trade policies, advocated individual rights and freedoms within a modernizing, secular state, with few barriers to free trade and international commerce.

5   Modernism was shaped by the belief that order and progress would emerge through emulation of Northern models of development, culture and politics. Positivism, as a form of modernism, stressed the concepts of order and progress, and the role of science, education and technology in a developmental path inspired by European ideas of scientific progress and modernization.

6   In this work, Domingo Faustino Sarmiento, the Argentinian writer and later president, sets out the past, present and future of Argentina in terms of the struggle between civilization (embodied by Buenos Aires, liberalism and Europe) and barbarism, represented by uneducated, violent, uncivilized and 'barbarian' inhabitants of the interior of the country. The work became (and remains) a fundamental reference point for Latin American political thought and literary expression.

7   The process across Latin America was of course not uniform. In Paraguay, for example, a sense of national difference had emerged under colonialism and an inclusive national identity was constructed, based on national sovereignty, independence and racial integration. This was reflected in the extraordinary (although doomed) defence of the country against the combined forces of Brazil, Argentina and Uruguay in the War of the Triple Alliance.

The Mexican Revolution (1910–1917) revealed the limitations of liberal authoritarianism and signalled a fundamental political shift towards the emergence of mass-based politics, which would replace the traditional oligarchic order. The case of Mexico was exceptional in terms of the scale of the resulting violence (one million or approximately 10 per cent of the population were killed), its protracted nature, the level of mass involvement and its long-term consequences, but it was also emblematic of the underlying problems of the age (Knight 1986). At the root of the heterogeneous alliances, goals and aims of the revolutionary forces was a dual struggle; on the one hand, for political power amongst elites previously excluded from power under the dictatorship of Porfirio Diaz (1876–1880, 1884–1910) and, on the other hand, the revolutionary struggle of the excluded masses to gain greater political and civil rights (Hamnett 1999).

The betrayal of the peasantry and of the revolutionary ideals of land, freedom and equality is a dominant feature of political and literary writing that emerged on the period.[8] What is striking about the wars between 1910 and 1917 is that even though the final victory of Venustiano Carranza was as much about defeating General Huerta and the forces of reaction as about defeating Emiliano Zapata and the forces of revolution, the new reformist government rapidly presented itself as a revolutionary force by adopting, moulding and assuming the ideals, images and myths of the Revolution. The identity of the Party (and the state) rapidly became synonymous with the Revolution and thus the nation. By inverting traditional discrimination against the *mestizo* and indigenous majority, figures such as the politician, philosopher and Secretary of Public Education (1921–1924) José Vasconcelos sought to create a national revolutionary identity based on the inclusion and, indeed, symbolic celebration of the previously excluded majority. Although there were certainly areas of continuity and failure, the Revolution gradually led to mass participation in politics, greater access to land, education and civil rights, and broke the power of the traditional elites. It also consciously created an inclusive vision of a national identity, past, present and future, which justified and made sense of the horrific violence of the Revolution. So effective was the construction of revolutionary national identity that Mexico, the country that had experienced the most violent political upheaval in the twentieth century, avoided the political instability and violence that plagued much of Latin America over the next 100 years.

Mass Politics and Populism

The Mexican Revolution heralded the collapse of liberal oligarchic rule. Although the most immediate cause was related to the collapse of the traditional export-based model following the First World War and, more dramatically, the Wall Street Crash of 1929, the oligarchic order had been steadily eroded by social changes

---

8   See e.g. Juan Rulfo's Works, *Pedro Páramo* (1955) and *El Llano en llamas* (1953), as well as Mariano Azuela's *Los de abajo* (1915).

throughout the period 1870–1930. The inability of the old order to deal with the 'social question' (associated with rising urban and rural poverty and inequality), mass immigration from Europe, the growth of an urban working class and a middle class, eager for a share of political power, led to a slow transition towards wider political participation and limited formal democracy (Tella 1972). By the 1920s, the political domination of the landowning oligarchy was rapidly collapsing.

The awareness and rejection of economic dependency resulting from the series of economic crises between 1914 and 1930 led to the emergence of nationalist economic development programmes in terms of industrialization (Import-substituting Industrialization: ISI)[9] and agricultural development (Import-substituting Agriculture: ISA). The clear intention of such programmes was to address the inherent vulnerability of Latin American in the international free market and to promote greater economic independence and development. By the 1950s, the region was fully committed to the model which UNECLA[10] would later term and promote as 'inward oriented development' and which would last until the economic and political crisis of the 1970s.

Economic nationalism was accompanied by important cultural changes in terms of a growing rejection of the modernist and positivist orientation towards Europe and the USA as a model for development, civilization and identity. Influenced by political and economic changes, including the rise of working-class and peasant militancy, this evolved into an anti-imperialist and anti-elitist narrative, a rejection of US and European cultural values and a parallel re-evaluation and celebration of Latin American cultural and ethnic roots. A new generation of writers and thinkers emerged, including José Martí (Cuba), Rubén Darío (Nicaragua), José Vasconcelos (Mexico) and José Enrique Rodó (Uruguay), who rejected the cultural and political obsession with the USA and Europe (or *nordomanía* as Rodó entitles it), as well as positivism and concepts of superiority implicit in Sarmiento's opposition between civilization and barbarism. Instead, they sought to celebrate a national identity based on cultural and ethnic legacies, including the previously invisible black and indigenous populations, alongside a strong critique of the prevailing social and political order (Zea 1993).

Economic and cultural nationalism was paralleled by the dramatic rise of political nationalism. Indeed, by the 1930s, nationalist rhetoric had rapidly became almost hegemonic throughout Latin America, spanning the political spectrum, employed as much by brutal military dictators such as Rafael Trujillo in the Dominican Republic (1930–1961) or the Somoza dynasty in Nicaragua (1936–1979) as by democratic reformers such as Lázaro Cardenas in Mexico (1934–1940) and Juan José Arévalo (1945–1951) in Guatemala. However, it was in the wide variety of what Alain Touraine (1989) has termed 'national popular' – or nationalist populist – regimes that nationalism found its most important expression, as

---

9   ISI and ISA were based on concepts of proactive state intervention in the economy, including support, investment and planning, protectionism, infrastructure development and the construction of an internal market.
10   United Nations Economic Commission for Latin America.

leaders sought to establish broad alliances (including with organized labour, the middle class, industrialists, women and the armed forces) in favour of mass political mobilization, economic planning and a strong, interventionist state (Dix 1985). This was complemented by the adoption of more assertive expressions of national identity, which replaced exclusive and elitist concepts of the nation with more inclusive narratives, which, rhetorically at least, celebrated the poor and marginalized, offering them a protagonistic role in the development of the nation.

Nationalism was moulded by populist regimes to develop a distinct Latin American identity, which embraced a new, supposedly unique, reformist (but anti-communist) political expression, within a strongly anti-imperialist and inclusive nationalist discourse. Without doubt, populist regimes broadened the political field to include the middle classes and to mobilize the working class and, most importantly, women, who gained suffrage throughout the continent between 1932 and 1955. Social reformism was achieved through the construction of broad, relatively inclusive and, some would argue, incompatible alliances between often ideologically opposed groups. As a result, whilst the populist rhetoric may have been radical and inflammatory, policy was as much about compromise and reform as about radical change. Moreover, whilst nationalist populist regimes sought to create unity between contrasting (often irreconcilable) social forces, they were also characterized by authoritarian traits, including censorship and the violent repression of opposition.

The case of Juan Perón in Argentina is illustrative. As head of the Ministry of Labour and Welfare (1943–1945) and President (1946–1955), Perón became an outspoken defender of the previously disenfranchised and excluded urban working class, seeking to strengthen his own position through the introduction of progressive social policies, including the development of social and labour welfare, such as social security, collective bargaining, wage increases, cheap housing and annual holidays. He also encouraged the formation of unions under the General Confederation of Labour (CGT), broadened suffrage to women, encouraged political participation and in particular (alongside his wife Evita) increased the participation of women in society and politics. As Michael Goebel (2006) has argued, Perón's nationalist discourse succeeded in uniting opposing political camps (right and left) and hence became a temporary obstacle to latent political violence, which would erupt after the collapse of the Perónist project.

Yet despite a strongly nationalistic discourse based on national harmony, unity and solidarity, as well as the maintenance of democratic forms, Perón's presidency was also marked by authoritarian practices (Vacs 2002). The CGT was co-opted into the Perónist fold, the press was subject to censorship, power was consolidated through a wide network of patronage and informants, and the armed forces and paramilitary groups, such as Perón's own National Liberating Alliance, subjected the opposition to threats, imprisonment, torture and exile. Nationalism may have espoused unity, solidarity and participation, but it also justified the repression and violence that became increasingly associated with the regime, until its overthrow by the military in 1955 (Rock 1995).

Populism did not necessarily lead to political violence, but it did increase the possibility of future violence in a number of ways. First, the inclusion of the military in the political project reinforced its role as political arbiter and guardian of the national interest, giving it an overtly political remit far beyond its institutional and constitutional role. Second, the broad alliances concealed a lack of long-term stability between competing and irreconcilable interests (reform versus continuity, elitism versus mass participation). Populist policies raised the expectations of previously disenfranchised groups, whilst raising the threat perception of elites, polarizing politics and making the struggle for control of the state a struggle for absolute power. Third, within the discourse of nationalism, the regime saw itself as synonymous with the state and hence the nation. Those who supported the regime were thus patriots, whilst those who legitimately opposed it were portrayed as anti-national, as traitors, whose political activism was in opposition to what were presented as the true interests of the nation. These developments would contribute to the explosion of political violence in the following decades.

Nationalism and the Rise of Military Rule

The irreconcilable differences amongst diverse and often competing forces within populist alliances, combined with mass political mobilization, led to political instability, the perception amongst elites of the breakdown of social order and to an almost inevitable series of military backlashes against populism. The context of the Cold War heightened the perception of threat felt by elites and the military throughout the continent, especially following the success of the Cuban Revolution in 1959, the rise of guerrilla movements, the emergence of organized and radical working-class and peasant movements, and the success of the political left throughout the continent in the 1960s. The victory of Salvador Allende, the democratic Marxist, in the Chilean presidential elections of 1970 confirmed to many, especially in the military, that democracy and the national interest did not necessarily complement each other.

The Cold War environment allowed greater space for military intervention in a number of forms. A more interventionist stance by the USA led to attempts to overthrow a variety of nationalist and socialist regimes, including Guatemala (1954), Cuba (1961), the Dominican Republic (1965) and Chile (1973), as well as support for a range of authoritarian regimes, from personalist dictatorships to what Guillermo O'Donnell (1973) termed bureaucratic authoritarian regimes (institutionalized military dictatorships). Although this was predominantly in the form of military and economic aid, political support and intelligence coordination (such as through the infamous Operation Condor),[11] it also included ideological

---

11 Operation Condor was a coordinated campaign of repression and intelligence sharing, established in 1975 between authoritarian regimes in South America. It included Argentina, Paraguay, Bolivia, Uruguay, Chile, Brazil and, later, Peru and Ecuador, with the USA playing a supervisory role.

military training in the form of the National Security Doctrine, which became a key factor in the facilitation of and ideological justification for political repression.

This doctrine, widely adopted by the armed forces of Latin America, held that the enemy was not necessarily external, but rather internal, in the form of insurgents or civilians who sought to undermine the state through subversion. This distorted, exclusive form of nationalism reinforced the self-perception of the armed forces as the sole guardians of national interest, the last defence of the nation. As such, the military could justify political intervention and, once in power, operate with impunity, claiming to represent the true interests of the nation. In the most extreme examples, military rulers, such as Trujillo, Somoza and Stroessner, sought to develop a cult of personality around themselves that projected them as living personifications of the nation. To paraphrase Eduardo Galeano, if the system – however corrupt and repressive it may be – presents itself as the nation, then those who oppose the system are by definition traitors to the fatherland, a subversive threat to the national interest (Galeano 1973: 307).

The logical consequence was the rise of military authoritarianism across the continent, affecting even those countries, such as Chile and Uruguay, which had long-established democratic traditions. There were of course exceptions; Colombia, Venezuela, Mexico and Costa Rica managed to retain civilian rule with varying degrees of democracy and repression, but by 1976, over two-thirds of the continent was under military rule. The systematic use of repression, abuse of human rights, political assassination, torture, imprisonment and exile were all justified under a nationalist discourse in which repression was presented as defence of the national interest. In the worst cases, regimes launched 'dirty wars' against their own people, with arbitrary repression used to defeat real or imagined opposition in the name of nationalism, anti-communism and the protection of democracy. Democracy collapsed as 'from Guatemala to Argentina the dictatorships declared war on their populations in the name of freedom and the preservation of western Christian values' (Koonings and Kruijt 1999: 10).

In Argentina, the military junta (1976–1982) unleashed a brutal campaign of state violence, terrorism and repression through a variety of interconnected, legitimized, but often extra-legal, groups, including the police, the armed forces, the intelligence services, paramilitaries and death squads (Garretón 1992). The result was the annihilation not only of armed guerrilla groups and their sympathizers, but also of any kind of dissent, resulting in between 10,000 and 30,000 'disappeared' (Vacs 2002: 409). What differentiated this wave of violence from previous forms was not only its supranational nature (as reflected in Operation Condor), but also the sophistication of the technology, its effectiveness and the horror of its consequences – what has been termed the 'trivialization of horror' (Torres-Rivas 1999: 291) and the creation of 'societies of fear', in which the state creates a climate of insecurity and fear to crush all dissent (Koonings and Kruijt 1999).

All sides in the Argentinian conflict sought legitimacy through reference to the nationalist cause. The military junta justified the disappearance of thousands in the name of protecting a traditional, ordered, Catholic and hierarchical vision of the nation from the threat of subversion and social disintegration. The right-wing paramilitary Argentinian Anticommunist Alliance (Triple A) justified its death squad activities under an authoritarian, anti-communist interpretation of Perónism, whilst the left-wing Montonero guerrilla movement was strongly influenced by an anti-imperialist, revolutionary nationalism also inspired by Perónism. The political violence was not caused by nationalism – the roots were far deeper. However, once political violence had gripped Argentine society, its practices dovetailed with the symbolically violent discourse of the many forms of nationalist expression, which divided the political field into irreconcilable dichotomies (Goebel 2006: 219).

As the case of Argentina illustrates, the nationalist discourse used by the military to justify its actions was not left uncontested. The emergence of Dependency Theory[12] in the 1960s, associated with Andre Gunder Frank (1969) among others, strengthened the anti-imperialist orientation of nationalism, already established amongst various left-wing groups. This coincided with the impact of the Cuban Revolution (and the spread of Cuban-inspired guerrilla groups) and a growing anti-imperialist, anti-capitalist and revolutionary nationalism. Whilst mainstream left-wing parties may have turned towards nationalism in the form of the rediscovery of popular national identity (for example, through music, literature and poetry) and a rejection of cultural imperialism, repression of legitimate protest led some on the Left to become involved in guerrilla organizations. Anti-imperialism, nationalism, national sovereignty and Marxism seemed to go hand in hand within left-wing guerrilla movements, as in Alain Touraine's words, 'class and nation ... appeared as nothing but the two faces of the same protagonist of the struggles for national liberation' (Touraine 1989: 141). Such counter-hegemonic interpretations of nationalism saw political violence as justified against what was portrayed as an unholy alliance between the military, national elites and US imperialism, aligned against the interests of the poor majority and hence the nation.

Most of the guerrilla movements that emerged in the 1960s were defeated by highly trained and well-equipped counter-insurgency forces. However, in Nicaragua, the FSLN (Sandinista Front for National Liberation) overthrew the corrupt and repressive dictatorship of Anastasio Somoza in 1979 and then held power until its electoral defeat in 1990. Key to its success was the coordination of a broad, cross-class alliance, with a strongly nationalist rhetoric which was dissident (in that it challenged the official nationalism promoted by Somoza), anti-imperialist (highlighting the strong US support for the dictatorship since the 1930s) and inclusive (especially of the poor majority) (Smith 1993). Also drawing on influences from liberation theology and socialism, it developed a revolutionary nationalism, based on a conscious celebration of national identity through art, music, literature and popular history, that sought to offer meaning to the political

---

12 Dependency Theory rejected the concepts behind modernization that the integration of developing countries into the international capitalist system would promote development. Instead, due to the nature of structural dependency, for example, in the form of transnational corporations and foreign investment, it would bring continued underdevelopment.

violence of the revolution and later (1981–1990) to the ongoing war against the US-backed *contras*.[13]

Violence in Post-authoritarian Latin America

The collapse of authoritarianism and the subsequent 'wave' of democratization that spread across the continent from the late 1970s led to the belief that there would be a parallel reduction in political violence and that conflict would henceforth tend to be channelled through new democratic institutions and procedures, especially following the end of the Cold War (Huntington 1991). Indeed, political conflict, in the form of state terrorism and civil wars between the state and ideologically inspired guerrilla movements, did largely disappear during the 1990s, with the notable exception of Colombia.

However, transitions to democracy in Latin America were not smooth, but rather were difficult and uneven processes, especially given the contextual problems of the debt crisis, the 'lost decade of development' in the 1980s and the imposition of structural adjustment programmes (Stallings and Kaufman 1989). In a region already characterized by endemic poverty and extreme inequalities, the prolonged crisis led to an increase in social inequality and poverty, social disintegration and the growth of the informal sector – all of which contributed to the exclusion of large sectors of the population from the benefits of democratization (Green 1996; Pinheiro 1996). Such 'fault-lines of democracy' (Aguero and Stark 1998) undermined citizenship, the legitimacy of the political order and the democratic process itself.

In part as a result of this, and despite progress in terms of the consolidation of democratic institutions and procedures, 'since the mid-1980s democratic rule has been accompanied by increasing levels of social and organized violence in which armed actors of all kinds have frustrated the efforts to achieve a peaceful social and political order. Instead violent disorder has permeated many Latin American societies' (Silva 2004: 186). What has emerged is a new form of violence that is fundamentally different from established patterns (Pereira and Davis 2000). This new violence – ranging from the drugs trade to small- and large-scale organized crime, to the *maras* of Central America, to social cleansing in the *favelas* of Brazil[14] – is linked to the emergence of an 'uncivil society', which exists alongside civil society, but uses force or coercion to maintain or pursue its interests against the legitimate work of other societal groups (Keane 1997). It is different from previous

---

13 Despite internal failings of the incumbent government, the failure of the Nicaraguan Revolution is widely seen as principally due to the interventionist stance of the USA in the form of the organization and funding of the infamous *contra* war, the establishment of an economic embargo on Nicaragua (1985–1990) and diplomatic isolation, including the freezing of credit and loans (see Smith 1993).

14 *Maras* are armed gangs in Central America, Mexico and the USA; *favelas* are very poor areas, often shanty towns.

forms of violence, not only in the diversity of its forms of expression but also in that in terms of intent, it does not seek to challenge, conquer or defend the power of the state or the regime and is therefore not easily classified as overtly political violence. True, in some cases, such as in El Salvador, gang violence including extortion, kidnapping, drug trafficking and revenge killings may be linked in some cases to ex-combatants involved in the overtly political violence of the 1980s, but this is not a common explanatory factor throughout the continent. However, the consequences of this new violence are clearly political in that it undermines the rule of law, active citizenship and democratic procedures and institutions.

In addition, the collapse of military rule might have led to reduced military budgets and an end to direct military influence in domestic politics in most countries, but it did not alter the deeply rooted self-perception of the armed forces as guardians of the national interest with a mission to safeguard the nation (Loveman 1994). The blurring of roles under authoritarianism between the legitimate security sector (armed forces) and connected extralegal or illegal services (military intelligence, private security, civilian informants and, in some cases, death squads) has still not been resolved. Indeed, links between official security forces on the one hand and unofficial or private forces – security, vigilante or paramilitary – on the other continue as a key feature of this new violence (Koonings and Kruijt 2004: 9).

If violence has undergone a process of transformation and fragmentation, so too has nationalism. The hegemonic forms of nationalism promoted under military rule have to a great extent been discredited and rejected during the process of transition and globalization, especially in those countries most damaged by state repression. Indeed, the scars of authoritarian rule have led to the emergence of a crisis of national identity in some countries such as Chile (Mullins 2006) and the emergence of multiple, less exclusive and non-hegemonic primary forms of identity, not necessarily based on the nation. As violence has fragmented and taken on new and diverse forms, motives and expressions, so too has national identity.

However, despite predictions that globalization would gradually undermine and erode nationalism (Hobsbawm 1990, Tomlinson 1991), there has there has been a resurgence in formally dissident forms of nationalism since the late twentieth century. The rise of centre-left and left-leaning governments throughout the region between 1998 and 2008 has led to the re-emergence of nationalist discourse strongly associated with previously counter-hegemonic ideas of dependency, anti-imperialism, pan-Americanism and national sovereignty. Moreover, the emerging narratives are generally inclusive, based on ideas of social justice and citizenship, and, rhetorically at least, seek to offer a protagonistic role to previously excluded majority groups. While violence has yet to erupt on a large scale in any of the nations within the so-called 'pink tide', the subsequent polarization of politics has raised the spectre of potential violence between new governments and elites who now find themselves excluded both from power and from the emerging nationalist project – especially in Bolivia and Venezuela. This would suggest that despite the fragmentation of identities implicit in the globalization of culture, politics and economics, it would be mistaken to underestimate the power of regional and national identities.

There are of course exceptions to this trend. In the 1980s and 1990s, Colombia became almost synonymous with political violence, as long-running conflicts between guerrilla movements and the state broadened to include a vast array of armed actors with interrelating interests, including paramilitary groups and narcotics mafias. As a result, the lines between official and unofficial armed groups, and state-sanctioned and non-sanctioned violence were almost entirely blurred. This fragmentation of violence, referred to earlier, was further exacerbated in the 1990s by the rise of vigilante groups involved in social cleansing, *sicarios*[15] and slum gangs. The result was that the conflict gathered a momentum of its own and became almost routinized (Richani 2002). Between 1995 and 2005, Colombia suffered the highest rates of kidnapping, political assassinations, abuses of human rights (by official and non-official forces) and internal displacement in Latin America.

Whilst the causes of such protracted internal violence are complex and have multiple historical social and political roots, Marisol Dennis (2006) has argued convincingly that the historical unwillingness of Colombian elites to accommodate competing identities has prevented the creation of an inclusive, unifying, legitimate and accepted version of national identity with which to unite diverse groups in society. The elite nature of the hegemonic form of nationalism has constrained social change, excluded the poor majority and undermined social cohesion, resulting in a self-perpetuating system of violence that in turn precluded any resolution of the problems underlying the conflict. With almost all sides in the conflict appealing to differing versions of nationalism, the case of Colombia clearly highlights the dangers of the promotion of non-inclusive forms of national identity in the post-authoritarian era.

National Identity and Political Violence

Nationalism should not be solely associated with xenophobia, discrimination, subordination of diversity and dissidence or military confrontation. It has also been a necessary and at times dynamic force in terms of state creation, economic modernization, the entry of the masses into politics and struggles for national liberation against authoritarianism and in favour of greater equality, rights, democracy and freedom. To use the phrase of Tom Nairn, it is Janus-faced (Nairn 1997), essentially contested, with both regressive and progressive features, and lending itself to both violent conflict and peaceful coexistence. However, from the case of Latin America it is possible to highlight four areas of interrelation between nationalism and violence, based on Anthony Smith's concepts of autonomy, identity and unity (Smith 1999: 18).

First, central to the concept of national identity is the relationship between the rise of the nation-state, national identity and conflict, what Smith has termed 'political autonomy'. As Dandeker has argued, 'the creation of the modern nation-

---

15 Hired assassins, generally from poorer areas.

state system has been intimately connected with violence' (1998: 24) through struggles for political and economic power and survival, as well as for the undisputed coercive monopoly over the national territory (Giddens 1985). In Latin America, the creation of new independent nation-states in the nineteenth century was characterized by multiple forms of political violence, including inter-elite conflict, rebellion from below, internal pacification and, in a few cases, international conflict. The proliferation of domestic conflicts over a prolonged period had an adverse effect on the development of a consensual, inclusive national identity under a recognized state. Moreover, it led to the emergence of armed forces with an exaggerated sense of their role as the guardians of undefined and contested national values, as political arbiters and the source of political power. In this sense, independence brought political autonomy, but not the associated creation of an inclusive national identity or accepted state monopoly on force.

Second, nationalism is related to issues of legitimacy. As Barry Buzan has argued, the state is composed of constructed 'organizing ideologies' which provide social and political cohesion and legitimacy (Buzan 1983: 50). In the absence of other, stronger 'organizing ideologies', weaker states tend to resort to political violence (repression, coercion and fear) which is then justified through the development of a hegemonic nationalism to tie the incumbent regime with higher national interests, aims and purposes. This was repeatedly the case with authoritarian regimes in Latin America throughout the twentieth century, which, in the absence of popular legitimacy or any organizing ideology, looked to nationalism (conservative, traditional and intolerant) for legitimacy of existence and action, and in order to reduce the political debate to one of ally or enemy, patriot or subversive. Nationalism gave legitimacy to normally unacceptable levels of state violence, excessive use of force and repression for regimes that lacked alternative forms of ideological legitimacy.

Third, national identity has been used as a political tool to reinforce concepts of unity and community, binding together diverse and often conflicting interests, and (as in the case of Perón in Argentina) acting as an obstacle to political violence between irreconcilable social forces. However, ideas of community and unification within nationalism are of course also premised on concepts of exclusion, difference and otherness. Nationalism is based on the identification of differences of values, customs, ideas and modes of life which underlie identity, and is thus as much about difference and alterity as about unity and community. The accentuation of difference can be rapidly transformed into a process of increasing opposition, from distrust and exclusion to aggression and violence, in order to seek a 'temporary unity of purpose by putting an imagined us against an inevitably hostile other' (Stern 1995: 117). This may be the foreigner or just the outsider, the subversive or the internal enemy, as regimes use difference to justify 'a struggle to mobilize the people, to purify their ranks, to expel the "others" who threaten their identity and power' (Hall 1992: 295). The exaggeration of difference in exclusionary forms of nationalism has been a constant underlying factor in the continuation of political violence, nowhere more obviously than in the case of Colombia.

And this leads to the final point, which is the ability of nationalism to mobilize diverse interests and identities behind a certain political project (Breuilly 1993;

Gellner 1983). Indeed, nationalism demands and achieves a level of commitment unparalleled by other forms of identity. As Benedict Anderson has argued, it draws parallels not only with concepts of family loyalties or a 'metaphoric kin group' (Erikson 2004: 59), but also with religion, in terms of myths, traditions, sense of community, destiny and sacrifice to a higher cause (Anderson 1983: 18–19). In this sense, nationalism is more akin to a political religion than an ideology (Smith 2001: 35). The sacrality of national identity, the concept of fighting for a greater good, permits the unleashing (and exploitation) of intense and violent emotions, which in part explain why so many are willing to tolerate or even participate in political violence, kill or be killed for the greater good of the nation.

The causes of political violence are multiple, historical and contextual. Factors such as the role of the military, the absence of democratic experience and the prevalence of authoritarian traditions, vast disparities of wealth, land and opportunity, ethnic and class discrimination, the lack of socio-economic reform due to entrenched and conservative elites, high levels of poverty and illiteracy and, of course, foreign intervention cannot be underestimated in the case of Latin America. The absence of a consensual national identity in Colombia or the adoption of a virulently anti-communist and traditional form of nationalism in Argentina may contribute to and exacerbate political violence, but they are not the cause.

Yet nationalism clearly maintains a close relationship with political violence in Latin America. As an essentially contested concept (reflecting conflicting issues of class, ethnicity, gender and politics) open to constant challenge and re-interpretation, it has been repeatedly transformed and manipulated by very different and often opposing political projects to provide legitimacy and justification not only for the ends (national unity and development), but also for the means (political violence). Time and again nationalism has been invoked to unite and then mobilize people to condone, suffer and exert violence. It is in this use – as an instrument in the struggle for political power – that nationalism and political violence become fused, with nationalism producing the passions, emotions and loyalties which in turn have repeatedly legitimized and justified normally unacceptable acts of political violence.

References

Aguero, F. and Stark, J. (1998) *Fault Lines of Democracy in Post-Transition Latin America* (Miami: North-South Center Press).
Anderson, B. (1983) *Imagined Communities* (London: Verso).
Barthes, R. (2000) *Mythologies* (London: Vintage).
Breuilly, J. (1993) *Nationalism and the State* (Manchester: Manchester University Press).
Buzan, B. (1983) *People, States and Fear* (Brighton: Wheatsheaf Books).
Centeno, M.A. (2002) 'The Centre Did Not Hold', in Dunkerley, J. (ed.), *Studies in the Formation of the Nation State in Latin America* (London: ILAS), 54–76.
Dandeker, C. (ed.) (1998) *Nationalism and Violence* (New Jersey: Transaction Press).

Dennis, M. (2006) 'National Identity and Violence: The Case of Colombia', in Fowler, W. and Lambert, P (eds), *Political Violence and National Identity in Latin America* (New York: Palgrave Macmillan), 91–110.
Dix, R.H. (1985) 'Populism: Authoritarianism and Democratic', *Latin American Research Review* 20(2), 29–52.
Ericksen, T.H. (2004) 'Place, Kinship and the Case for Non-ethnic Nations', *Nations and Nationalism* 10(1), 49–62.
Fowler, W. (2002) *Latin America 1800–2000* (London: Arnold).
Fowler, W. (2006) 'The Children of the Chingada', in Fowler, W. and Lambert, P. (eds), *Political Violence and National Identity in Latin America* (New York: Palgrave Macmillan), 1–18.
Fowler, W. and Lambert, P. (eds) (2006) *Political Violence and National Identity in Latin America* (New York: Palgrave Macmillan).
Frank, A.G. (1969) *Capitalism and Underdevelopment in Latin America* (New York: Monthly Review Press).
Galeano, E. (1973) *The Open Veins of Latin America: Five Centuries of the Pillage of a Continent* (New York: Monthly Review Press).
Garretón, M.A. (1992) 'Fear in Military Regimes: An Overview', in Corradi, J.F., Fagan, P.W. and Garretón, M.A. (eds), *Fear at the Edge: State Terror and Resistance in Latin America* (Berkeley: University of California Press), 13–25.
Gellner, E. (1983) *Nations and Nationalism* (Oxford: Blackwell).
Giddens, A. (1985) *The Nation State and Violence* (Cambridge: Polity Press).
Goebel, M. (2006) 'Some Historical Observations on the Relationship between Nationalism and Political Violence in Argentina', in Fowler, W. and Lambert, P. (eds), *Political Violence and National Identity in Latin America* (New York: Palgrave Macmillan), 207–26.
Green, D. (1996) *Silent Revolution: The Rise of Market Economics in Latin America* (London: Latin America Bureau).
Hall, S. (1990) 'Cultural Identity and Diaspora', in Rutherford, J. (ed), *Identity, Community, Culture, Difference* (London: Lawrence & Wishart).
Hall, S. (1992) 'The Question of Cultural Identity', in Hall, S., Held, D. and McGrew, T. (eds), *Modernity and its Futures* (Cambridge: Polity Press), 273–326.
Hamnett, B. (1999) *A Concise History of Mexico* (Cambridge: Cambridge University Press).
Hobsbawm, E.J. (1983) 'Invented Tradition', in Hobsbawm, E.J. and Ranger, T. (eds), *The Invention of Tradition* (Cambridge: Cambridge University Press), 1–24.
Hobsbawm, E.J. (1990) *Nations and Nationalism since 1870: Programme, Myth, Reality* (Cambridge: Cambridge University Press).
Huntington, S.P. (1991) *The Third Wave: Democratization in the Late Twentieth Century* (Norman: University of Oklahoma Press).
Keane, J. (1997) *Reflections on Violence* (London: Verso).
Kedourie, E. (1960) *Nationalism* (London: Hutchinson).
Keen, B. and Haynes, K. (2000) *A History of Latin America* (New York: Houghton Mifflin).
Knight, A. (1986) *The Mexican Revolution* (Cambridge: Cambridge University Press).

Koonings, K. and Kruijt, D. (eds) (1999) *Societies of Fear: The Legacy of Civil War, Violence and Terror in Latin America* (London: Zed Books).
Koonings, K. and Kruijt, D. (eds) (2004) *Armed Actors: Organised Violence and State Failure in Latin America* (London: Zed Press).
Larrain, J. (2000) *Identity and Modernity in Latin America* (Cambridge: Polity Press).
Loveman, B. (1994) 'Protected Democracies and Military Guardianship: Political Transitions in Latin America 1978–1993', *Journal of Interamerican Studies and World Affairs* 36(2), 105–89.
Mullins, M. (2006) 'The Effects of State Violence on National Identity: The Fate of the Chilean Historical Narratives Post-1973', in Fowler, W. and Lambert, P. (eds), *Political Violence and National Identity in Latin America* (New York: Palgrave Macmillan), 167–86.
Nairn, T. (1997) *Faces of Nationalism: Janus Revisited* (London: Verso).
O'Donnell, G.A. (1973) *Modernization and Bureaucratic-Authoritarianism: Studies in South American Politics* (Berkeley: University of California Press).
Paz, O. (1985) *The Labyrinth of Solitude* (New York: Grove Press).
Pereira, A. and Davis, D. (2000) 'New Patterns of Militarized Violence and Coercion in the Americas', *Latin American Perspectives* 27(2), 3–17.
Pinheiro, P.S. (1996) 'Democracies without Citizenship', *NACLA Report on the Americas* 30(2), 17–23.
Richani, N. (2002) *Systems of Violence: The Political Economy of War and Peace in Colombia* (New York: State University of New York Press).
Rock, D. (1995) *Authoritarian Argentina: The Nationalist Movement, its History and its Impact* (Berkeley: University of California Press).
Rodó, J.E. (1988) *Ariel* (Austin, Texas: University of Texas Press) (first published in 1900).
Rosenberg, T. (1992) *Children of Cain: Violence and the Violent in Latin America* (New York: Penguin).
Sarmiento, D.F. (1998) *Facundo: or, Civilization and Barbarism* (New York: Penguin) (first published in 1845).
Silva, P. (2004) 'Violence and the Quest for Order in Contemporary Latin America', in Koonings, K. and Kruijt, D. (eds), *Armed Actors: Organised Violence and State Failure in Latin America* (London: Zed Press).
Smith, A.D. (1998) *Nationalism and Modernism* (London: Routledge).
Smith, A.D. (ed.) (1999) *Myths and Memories of the Nation* (Oxford: Oxford University Press).
Smith, A.D. (2001) *Nationalism* (Cambridge: Polity Press).
Smith, H. (1993) *Nicaragua: Self Determination and Survival* (London: Pluto).
Stallings, B. and Kaufman, R. (1989) *Debt and Democracy in Latin America* (Boulder: Westview Press).
Stern, P.C. (1995) 'Why do People Sacrifice for their Nations?', in Comaroff, J.L. and Stern, P.C. (eds), *Perspectives on Nationalism and War* (Amsterdam: Gordon and Breach Science Publishers), 99–122.
Tella, T. (1972) 'Populism and Reform in Latin America', in Véliz, C. (ed.), *Obstacles to Change in Latin America* (Oxford: Oxford University Press).

Tomlinson, J. (1991) *Cultural Imperialism* (London: Pinter Publishers).

Torres-Rivas, E. (1999) 'Epilogue: Notes on Terror, Violence, Fear and Democracy', in Koonings, K. and Kruijt, D. (eds), *Societies of Fear: The Legacy of Civil War, Violence and Terror in Latin America* (London: Zed Books), 285–300.

Touraine, A. (1989) *América Latina: Política y Sociedad* (Madrid: Espasa-Calpe).

Vacs, A.C. (2002) 'Argentina', in Vanden, H.E. and Prevost, G. (eds), *Politics of Latin America: The Power Game* (Oxford: Oxford University Press), 399–435.

Vanden, H.E. and Prevost, G. (eds) (2002) *Politics of Latin America: The Power Game* (Oxford: Oxford University Press).

Wiarda, H. (ed.) (1992) *Politics and Social Change in Latin America: Still a Distinct Tradition?* (Boulder: Westview Press).

Zea, L. (1993) *Fuentes de la Cultura Latinoamericana* (Mexico City: Fondo de Cultura Económica).

Staying Alive while Conducting Primary Research: Fieldwork on Political Violence

Jeffrey A. Sluka

British sociologist Robert Moore recounts how, during his fieldwork, the police told him to leave the site of a racially charged affray. 'What does the eager researcher do when moved on?', he asks. 'I ran around the block, took my coat off and strolled innocently into the middle of the battle again.'
Lee 1995, 1

Socio-political violence can be approached in many ways. At some level, however, to be able to discuss violence, one must go to where violence occurs, research it as it takes place.
Robben and Nordstrom 1995, 4

A moment's reflection should indicate that to witness physical violence is in itself extremely dangerous and necessarily entails complex ethical judgements as to how (and whether) such events should be described and published.
Whitehead 2002, 17

The dangerous field imposes an even greater limitation on our vision as it reminds us that as we observe, we participate – and when we do so in the midst of violence, we become part and parcel of it.
Kovats-Bernat 2002, 10

Pursuing the truth is a highly political endeavour! It is not the way of safety, of security, of sweet dreams. It is jihad.
Mahmood 2008, 5

Today, political violence and armed conflict have grown to epidemic proportions and have become globally endemic. There are approximately 25 'major' wars and 80–100 lesser armed conflicts, and if we include other forms of political violence in many people's lives such as riots, civil disorder, coups, terrorism and particularly state terrorism such as extrajudicial killings, torture and intimidation, then the number of people directly affected runs into the hundreds of millions or even billions. As a result, more researchers are studying violence, and more who are not studying violence per se are finding themselves working in violent contexts. As a result, managing danger in fieldwork has become a pressing issue for those conducting primary research on political violence or in locations characterised by such violence. While much has now been written about the conduct of fieldwork (see Robben and Sluka 2007), relatively little has formally been written about handling or managing danger as a methodological issue. In line with Kovats-Bernat's (2002) call for developing pragmatic strategies for negotiating danger in fieldwork on and amidst violence, this chapter identifies the best strategies that have emerged in the literature so far. I briefly review the key literature on this topic and draw on it to make recommendations for developing strategies primarily for managing physical dangers from human sources (research participants, authorities and others), and believe that what I say here is generally applicable to all qualitative social science researchers who conduct fieldwork on or amidst violence.

Two significant corollaries or consequences of the increasing research on violence are that safety in the field has begun to emerge as an important topic in social sciences methodology and even introductory textbooks, and has become a central issue for university ethics committees and Institutional Review Boards (IRBs). Since the 1990s, universities have recognised a legal duty to provide supervision which ensures the health and safety of postgraduate students. This duty primarily devolves onto supervisors, who are required to provide appropriate information, instruction and training in occupational safety and health issues. In the UK in 1998, the Committee of Vice-Chancellors and Principals (CVCP) recommended a system of risk assessment in which supervisors and their students agree on the level of risk inherent in any proposed research, the level of supervision necessary and the precautions that need to be taken (Lee 1995, 66).

Universities require ethical clearance for all research with human beings, and these processes now include maintaining the safety of the researcher. This has been partly dictated by legal concerns surrounding workplace health and safety and employer liability for these, and partly by ethical concerns regarding protecting researchers, research participants and the institution from potential harm. For example, at my university the first question on the ethics review application is: 'Does the proposed research entail situations in which the researcher may be at risk of harm?'

Other relevant recent developments include the publication of a popular press 'gonzo survival guide', *How to Avoid Being Killed in a War Zone* (2011) by journalist Rosie Garthwaite, which presents practical advice on living in dangerous places, and the emergence of private sector companies, such as UK-based Humanitrain Ltd., which provide practical training in security, safety, health and well-being mainly to journalists and overseas humanitarian aid field workers.

Thus, in line with the growing awareness of health and safety issues in a number of disciplines and professions, and within universities and research institutions, 'there has been increasing discussion and an increasing level of informed awareness about the hazards of fieldwork' (Stanko and Lee 2003, 4). At the same time, all of those who have written specifically about managing danger in fieldwork have agreed on the need for greater awareness of safety in social research as a matter of normative practice. They have called for greater reporting of such issues by fieldworkers to build up a wider range of available information and a more explicit commitment to improving awareness of safety issues among graduate students, and they have also stressed the role of supervisors, who 'have an obligation to advise and, if necessary, prevent graduate students from entering violent social settings unprepared' (Lee 1995, 65).

Literature Review on Managing Danger in Fieldwork

In 1986, Nancy Howell was the first to call attention to the need to formally discuss the issue of danger in fieldwork in a conference paper on 'Occupational Safety and Health in Anthropology', and in 1989 I was the first to publish on this topic in a prologue titled 'I'm Alive and Well, My Kneecaps are Still Intact, and My Research is Coming Along Fine' in my ethnography on popular support for the IRA and Irish National Liberation Army in Northern Ireland. This is what I wrote home from the field to my supervisor and family to reassure them that I was safe, since a previous graduate student from my university (Berkeley) had been shot by the IRA while conducting fieldwork in Belfast in 1974. In 1990, Howell's research on health and safety in fieldwork was published as a special report for the American Anthropological Association (AAA) entitled *Surviving Fieldwork*, and I published 'Participant Observation in Violent Social Contexts' based on my fieldwork on the conflict in Northern Ireland.

Howell began her report by noting the paucity of information available on the risks faced by researchers or on how those risks might be managed, and she presented the first serious effort to appraise the multitudinous hazards and threats encountered in the field in a systematic, objective fashion. She evaluated 80 separate risks and, with regard to human ones, found that 42 per cent of anthropologists reported experiencing 'criminal interpersonal hazards' including robbery, assault, rape and murder; 9 per cent reported 'arrests in the field'; 22 per cent reported 'living through political turmoil' such as revolution, war, rioting and military attack; 15 per cent reported that they were 'under suspicion for spying'; 12 per cent reported experiencing 'factional conflict' or acute hostilities within the group they studied; and 2 per cent reported 'hostage-taking incidents'. Howell makes a number of suggestions about improving safety in fieldwork, including stressing the importance of being able to summon help or to leave the setting in the event of an emergency, particularly when working in remote or isolated locations.

In my 1990 article on managing danger in fieldwork, I observed that fieldwork was more dangerous than it had been in the past and that few anthropologists would be able to avoid conflict situations and instances of socio-political violence in the course of their professional lives. I argued that while special sensitivities are required when working on and in sites of political conflict and violence, the dangers can be mediated through foresight and planning. I presented a reflexive account of my fieldwork with Irish nationalist militants and presented practical recommendations on how to enhance personal safety. I suggested that, rather than embracing dangerous situations, field researchers had mostly selected themselves out of potentially hazardous research and that dangerous research had been avoided. That avoidance was rationalised by exaggerating the difficulties involved in researching dangerous situations and was buttressed by a neglect to develop strategies for coping with danger while in the field. I argued that while dangers are never totally manageable, researchers should make a concerted effort to maximise skilful handling of the situation.

In particular, in this and subsequent publications (Sluka 1989, 1990, 1995), I argued that it was important to evaluate explicitly the possibility of danger, its potential sources and how it might be managed or exacerbated by the actions of the researcher. Researchers approaching such settings should seek detailed knowledge, particularly from people with first-hand experience of the situation. The risks involved should be discussed with colleagues or supervisors and, if at all possible, an exploratory visit should be made to the field location before formal research begins. I warned that there were areas where security and danger overrode asking questions. For example, in my research, although I asked respondents about their support for the republican militants, I was careful to avoid subjects such as arms and explosives or the identity of members. Similarly, Feldman (1991, 12), who also carried out fieldwork in Belfast, observed that: 'In order to know I had to become expert in demonstrating that there were things, places and people I did not want to know.'

In 1995, Lee published an excellent study, *Dangerous Fieldwork*, loaded with good advice on managing danger. In 1993, Lee had published a related book, *Doing Research on Sensitive Topics*, and in this study he drew on his fieldwork experience in Northern Ireland and the emerging accounts and reports of researchers from diverse disciplines in other high-conflict or high-risk environments in order to document and compare the personal dangers they experienced. He offered grounded advice regarding what researchers and their advisors could do to reduce such risks. In particular, he discussed issues surrounding access, gatekeepers, conflict, insiders and outsiders, personal safety, espionage, mishaps, counter-insurgency, drug-related violence (including sponsors, safety zones and relations with police), studying 'deviant groups' such as gangs and outlaws, occupational hazards, sexual harassment and assault, and he included a section offering advice on reducing risk, including safety awareness, funding and training.

Lee distinguished between two kinds of dangers that may arise during fieldwork on conflict and violence – *ambient* and *situational*. Ambient danger arises when the researcher is exposed to otherwise avoidable dangers simply from having to be in a dangerous setting for the research to be carried out, while situational danger arises when the researcher's presence or action evokes aggression, hostility or violence from those within the setting (1995, 3–4). He argued that 'the strategies researchers adopt to manage potential hazards, both to themselves and to those they study, are strongly implicated in the ethics and politics of field situations' (1995, 4) and concluded by suggesting that 'field researchers need to approach potentially dangerous research with a stance of resolute awareness. By so doing they maintain the appropriate balance between the prudence necessary to avoid hazard, and the potential complacency inherent in a failure to take justifiable risks' (1995, 5).

Lee particularly warned against covert research: 'Covert researchers are vulnerable to mistakes and misunderstandings about who they are and what they are doing. Because some clandestine organizations combine an endemic concern about concealed identities with the use of violence as a routine protective device, misattributions can have deadly consequences' (1995, 75). With regard to female researchers, he commented that 'there remains a clear need for the issues raised by the sexual harassment and sexual assault of female researchers to be discussed more widely' (1995, 75–6) and he suggested, after Williams et al. (1992), that:

> Research in dangerous situations depends on the maintenance of safety zones that allow researcher and researched to operate in a secure manner .... the researcher should feel able to remain within the setting, provided a set of environmental and social conditions are met. The safety zone encompasses a physical area that extends for a short distance around the fieldworker. Within this area the researcher should feel physically secure and psychologically at ease, free from environmental hazard or interpersonal danger. The safety zone also permits others in the setting to feel that the researcher is not intruding upon them or presenting a threat to their security. Establishment of a safety zone depends in part on the social acceptance of the researcher by those within the setting. It also depends, however, on the researcher's carefully, even subliminally, sizing up the setting and entering and remaining in it only if it seems that the safety zone can be maintained. (1995, 44)

Finally, since current ethical standards 'encourage researchers to minimize the potential usefulness of their research for intelligence purposes', Lee suggested a strategy of 'research disutilization' (1995, 38) including self-censorship, such as choosing to not publish research findings, public sharing or dissemination of information so that it is available to everyone and refusing to produce secret reports. He noted that: 'Perhaps the most common strategy is to omit or garble specific details, to make identification of research participants or research sites more difficult' (1995, 38).

In 1995, Carolyn Nordstrom and Antonius Robben edited *Fieldwork Under Fire: Contemporary Studies of Violence and Survival*, which contains much material on methods of examining and coping with violence as a fieldworker. In their introduction, they observed that 'there are few social prescriptions on how to cope and survive in violent situations' (1995, 3) and they identified three principal concerns addressed in the book: 'the everyday experiences of people who are the victims and perpetrators of violence; the relationship between field-workers and the people studied, including the distinct research problems and experiences of ethnographers who study situations of violence; and the theoretical issues that emerge from studying topics that involve personal danger' (1995, 3–4).

In their introduction, Robben and Nordstrom note that implicit in all the chapters in the book is the notion that:

> The ontics of violence – the lived experience of violence – and the epistemology of violence – the ways of knowing and reflecting about violence – are not separate. Experience and interpretation are inseparable for perpetrators, victims, and ethnographers alike. Anthropology on this level involves a number of responsibilities above and beyond those associated with more traditional ethnography: responsibilities to the field-worker's safety, to the safety of his or her informants, and to the theories that help to forge attitudes toward the reality of violence, both expressed and experienced. (1995, 4)

They discuss the 'existential shock' most researchers have reported when they study violence directly, caused by tension and 'disorientation about the boundaries between life and death, which appear erratic rather than discrete' (1995, 13). This risk is exemplified in Green's chapter on her research on the culture of fear in Guatemala, where she found that:

> One cannot live in a constant state of alertness, and so the chaos one feels becomes infused throughout the body. It surfaces frequently in dreams and chronic illness. Sometimes in the mornings my neighbours and friends would speak of their fears during the night, of being unable to sleep or being awakened by footsteps or voices, of nightmares of recurring death and violence. After six months of living in Xe'caj, I, too, started to experience night-time hysteria, dreams of death, disappearances, and torture. (1995, 109)

However, Robben and Nordstrom also stress the countervailing and equally powerful experience of encountering 'the creative and the hopeful in conditions of violence' (1995, 14).

The chapters in Nordstrom and Robben's book look at some of 'the realities of studying dangerous topics in dangerous locales' (1995, 14). Taken as a whole, it 'illustrates many of the core features of what one is likely to confront in experiencing and studying socio-political violence' and is offered in the hope that it might 'help ethnographers of violence and socio-political conflict to recognise these existential problems, to solve them, and to turn them to their advantages … We also hope that this book will take away some of the anxieties of doing fieldwork on violence and will encourage anthropologists to carry out more research projects on this topic' (1995, 14).

The chapters in the book address a variety of issues, such as dealing with rumours, and provide more practical suggestions and advice on how to manage danger and enhance personal safety in fieldwork. In a particularly poignant chapter, Green discusses silence and secrecy as both a strategy of survival and instrument of repression and, as Robben and Nordstrom put it: 'Silence and secrecy are the concomitants ethnographers face when they want to carry out fieldwork in a country that is still under authoritarian control, where counterinsurgency units have a free hand and death squads intimidate and assassinate citizens and foreigners alike' (1995, 15).

Five years later, Lee-Treweek and Linkogle published another edited volume entitled *Danger in the Field: Risk and Ethics in Social Research* (2000). Like those in *Fieldwork Under Fire*, the contributors analyse the experience of different forms of danger in various qualitative research settings through reflexive case studies of their own encounters with dangers while conducting their fieldwork. This book not only addresses physical danger, but also emotional, ethical and professional dangers as well. Lee-Treweek and Linkogle make the important point that threats to the researcher and to participants are connected: 'Our experience of risk as researchers frequently parallel[s] those of the people we are studying' (2000a, 1–2). They observe that 'although risk in the field is a frightening experience for the researcher, it does on many occasions enrich our understandings of the research site and enables us to think and write about social life as insiders' and they emphasise the importance of 'building safeguards and precautions into the research strategy, and of planning, team work and colleague support in countering physical risk' (2000a, 2–3). In another chapter in the book (2000b), they present a framework for conceptualising dangers that qualitative researchers must negotiate in their fieldwork, which identifies four key areas of danger – physical, emotional, ethical and professional.

They identify 'emotional danger' as a 'serious threat or danger to researchers brought on by negative feeling states induced by research with participants undergoing stressful or traumatic life events' (Lee-Treweek and Linkogle 2000a, 4). This threat becomes serious when it 'spill[s] over into other areas of the researcher's life, such as their family and personal relationships or connections with colleagues at work' (Lee-Treweek and Linkogle 2000b, 13). Emotional stress results from living with and experiencing danger and violence first-hand, and gathering potentially distressing information such as graphic accounts by victims of the violence they suffered.

While a central ethical concern is 'the need to manage the emotions of research participants and not leave them with painful baggage from the research experience', this goes for protecting the researchers as well (Lee-Treweek and Linkogle 2000b, 15). This is identified as another significant feature of dangerous settings which is shared by both researchers and participants. They stress 'the importance of seeking support and guidance on the emotional impact of research when fieldwork experiences are very distressing' and suggest 'the use of colleague support, personal counselling and specialised study [or debriefing] groups' as means of coping (Lee-Treweek and Linkogle 2000a, 5).

'Ethical dangers' are identified by Lee-Treweek and Linkogle as the temptation to employ unethical or risky methods to acquire information. Today, the main ethical dangers are directly addressed in codes of research ethics, but they note that this is another element of dangerous situations which 'ties together the experience of the researcher and the researched by recognising the wider effects of carrying out unethical research, including the impact upon both participants and the researcher' (2000a, 5).

Lee-Treweek and Linkogle identify 'professional danger' as 'serious risk associated with the consequences of challenging or deviating from existing occupational dynamics and collegial preoccupations' (2000b, 20). Researching powerful groups and controversial, unfashionable or 'taboo' topics can be 'professionally dangerous' to career development: 'The professional danger arising from one piece of research can "menace" a researcher for years after completion. It may be impossible to think through completely the range of professional dangers a paper might provoke. Once published, research findings assume a life of their own with the researcher often having little control over their use or interpretation' (Lee-Treweek and Linkogle 2000b, 23; see also Brettell 1993). For example, Swedenburg has written about researchers being tainted by the dangerous images associated with their research participants and found that working with Palestinians, as he did, 'was not always considered the best career move for aspiring academics' because 'guilt by association' with them affected academic hiring and promotion, and 'the taboo on this subject severely circumscribed academic discussion of the issues' (1995, 26).

The contributors in Lee-Treweek and Linkogle's book also draw out a number of fieldwork lessons and strategies for managing risk, including the use of practical equipment like mobile phones, the careful selection of settings for interviews, letting someone know your whereabouts and being 'artful' and skilled in impression management in the field, for example, by creating cover stories when necessary. In her chapter, Jamieson concludes that 'the necessary preparations for undertaking potentially dangerous fieldwork include: planning research thoroughly, working in a safety-conscious way, remaining constantly alert to potential risks, and being prepared to take action to respond to threat, even if this means leaving the field' (2000, 69). With regard to the maintenance of a fieldwork safety zone, she suggests that 'the provision of safe spaces in which to undertake interviews is also a prime importance, as travelling to and from, and interviewing inside respondents' homes can be a source of danger' (2000, 70).

In their chapter, Jipson and Litton add another warning against covert research and argue that 'the most effective and ethical approach is an overt, known researcher. In this way organizations under study can verify the identity of the researcher as a genuine academic who is interested in the topic. It has been our experience that the known researcher builds a rapport with extremists over time'. Covert research raises the serious risk of exposure and 'because the covert researcher cannot be open about their research project, significant problems arise'. On learning of the deceit, research participants may 'act on their sense of violation by threatening or even physically attacking the researcher' (2000, 153). Jipson and Litton connect safety to informed consent because 'while engaging in informed consent the researcher has an opportunity to explain the research project to those most affected by the outcome and presentation of the research' (2000, 153).

Jipson and Litton also recommend impression management because in dangerous contexts, local people are quick to judge researchers as a possible threat, and researchers have to establish themselves as non-threatening in order to gain access and their consent. Researchers have to gain and subsequently maintain trust, and this is problematic considering that they have no legal protection from being compelled to testify against research participants engaged in violence or illegal activity: 'Social scientists cannot claim protection akin to a doctor/patient or attorney/client privilege. A researcher might be compelled to turn over notes and code books created during the project to the authorities. This is a very real problem for researchers studying social movements or research participants who may be involved with illegal activities' (2000, 155). Because of the potential for notes and research material to be forcibly taken from the researcher, they stress that coding and screening them for confidentiality and anonymity is crucial both for maintaining safety and engendering trust.

Jipson and Litton suggest honesty, openness and good ethics as danger management strategies, and recommend checking research material with research participants (2000, 158). With regard to honesty, it is important that research participants understand that 'there is no real legal protection for your research or your presence in these groups' and with regard to ethics that 'if the dangers to your own person, to the group or to the community become unacceptably large you must remove yourself from the situation' (2000, 164).

Finally, in another important chapter, Peterson observes that the ethnographic literature shows that risk and danger have a shifting or variable nature, and suggests that 'this fluidity is an important part of the nature of work in the field. Because the definition of danger shifts constantly, the researcher needs to be acutely aware of the transitions of his/her perceptions of danger' (2000, 181). While the risks can be managed, the emergent quality of danger means that we cannot always foresee all of the risks or how risky a situation may become, and the real challenge is to not only identify important safety issues prior to embarking on fieldwork, but also to resolve unanticipated issues as they arise.

In 2001, Smyth and Robinson published *Researching Violently Divided Societies: Ethical and Methodological Issues*, in 2003, Lee and Stanko published *Researching Violence* and in 2005 Porter et al. published *Researching Conflict in Africa: Insights and Experiences*, all edited volumes presenting reflexive accounts from researchers who have worked on a variety of projects related to violence in many locations around the world, which provide considerable practical guidance on how to conduct such research safely.

In a chapter in *Researching Violence*, Knox and Monaghan, who conducted fieldwork in Northern Ireland and South Africa, advise that:

> Sensible security planning can involve working out entry and exit routes, opting, where possible, for safe(ish) locations to conduct interviews (for example, administrative headquarters of political parties linked to paramilitaries and the offices of non-governmental organisations), taking taxis to venues as opposed to using personal transport with car registration details, doing fieldwork in pairs, and informing other members of the research

team of your schedule. The venue for conducting interviews is particularly important. Participants and researchers must feel safe. (2003, 170)

However, they found that finding 'neutral' locations was not always easy, and I would add that they are not always necessary or even appropriate, as in some cases participants may interpret this as meaning that you feel at risk from them and therefore do not trust them.

Knox and Monaghan found that a key aspect of convincing research participants of their bona fides as researchers 'was the source of funding for the research', and they state that had their funding come from the government, 'political/paramilitary 'endorsement' for the fieldwork would have been impossible' (2003, 169). If research funding is tied to the government, participants are likely to believe that the researcher is intelligence gathering (spying) under the guise of academic research. They suggest that being funded by independent sources attributes independence to your motives and is a positive contribution in negotiating access with potential participants.

Knox and Monaghan sought the support of respected community members before commencing their research. Experience has shown that these individuals provide invaluable assistance, frequently acting 'not only as guides and "gatekeepers" but also as "sponsors" and thereby ensuring safe passage in the community' (2003, 169). Once access was secured, 'the key problems encountered were suspicion of the researcher's motives, how the information would be utilised and, importantly, who would have access and how it would be stored' (2003, 172). Knox and Monaghan took a number of exemplary precautionary measures, including feeding back research material with research participants and informing political representatives of paramilitary groups about the research, which is tantamount to securing their 'approval'.

Other researchers who have undertaken fieldwork in Northern Ireland have had very similar experiences and employed similar strategies for managing the dangers they experienced. Because more has been written about managing danger in fieldwork in Northern Ireland than any other location in the world, it holds a special place in the literature (e.g. Burton 1978; Jenkins 1984; Sluka 1989, 1990, 1995; Feldman 1991; Brewer 1991, 1993; Bruce 1992; Lee 1995; Weitzer 1995; Hockey 1996; Dowler 2001; Feenan 2002; and Knox and Monaghan 2003).

Feenan, who researched paramilitary 'punishment' activity, describes how he managed to conduct his research safely by 'maintenance of political sensitivity, good faith and cautious security protocols ... While risks of physical injury were minimal, successful research in the field was achieved through transparency about the impartiality and funding independence of the researchers, and a strategic sensitivity towards community and political backgrounds' (2002, 147). Feenan also found that 'it is essential to secure "approval" from key stakeholders. Undertaking the research required tacit acceptance by paramilitaries or, at the very least, making them aware that fieldwork of this nature was being undertaken and its purpose' and satisfying them that he was not involved with the security forces (2002, 153). Similarly, Dowler has recounted how:

> Upon my arrival in Belfast, I was advised by certain community members to meet with IRA representatives from the area. I simply walked to a neighbour's house, where I met with several local men and women who asked general questions about my work. I was asked to present my passport and university identification, which were examined in another room. I was then told if I needed anything to just let them know. Later, when I started to frequent IRA prisoners' clubs, I was checked out more thoroughly. (2001, 421)

Feenan also remarks on the obvious need to take extra caution when violence flares up and explains that:

> where challenges to the impartiality of the project did arise ... my reassurance focused on the independence of the researcher, its public policy orientation and the commitment to understanding and reflecting individuals' and communities' experiences and perspectives. This, together with an offer to meet to discuss any concerns, led, without exception, to further contact with those who initially expressed wariness or resistance. (2002, 155)

In 2002, Christopher Kovats-Bernat, who has 'at various times been present at street shootings, threatened, searched, suspected of subversion and in the midst of crossfire; none of which is an experience unknown to anthropologists who have worked in dangerous fields', wrote about managing danger in his research with street children in Haiti and describes how he was eventually forced to evacuate the field when violence became too threatening to continue his research safely. He argues for the adoption of new research methods and tactics for survival which challenge conventional research ethics, 'reconfigure the relationship between anthropologist and informant, and compel innovation in negotiating the exchange of data under hazardous circumstances' (2002, 1).

One of the hazards of data collection in dangerous fields that Kovats-Bernat discusses is the temptation 'to employ a computation of risk versus desired data' (2002, 3): 'This formula suggests that the amount of data that can be safely collected derives from the balance of what information is important to the study weighed carefully against how much that information is "worth" in terms of the anthropologist's and informants' personal attitudes concerning the relative possibility of dying or being arrested to exchange it' (2002, 4). While he sympathises that it is a 'common and understandable tactic in dangerous fields', he warns that 'in the midst of violence, it becomes surprisingly easy to weigh one's life against the raw material of one's livelihood' (2002, 4).

Kovats-Bernat begins by observing, as Robben and Nordstrom (1995) did, that:

> It is only through the lived witnessing that comes from submersion in the violence – whether it remains threatened or emerges in punctuated bursts – that we are able to experience the dangerous field in a meaningful way and write anthropology from and of it. But on a very practical level, this observational perspective can only be accomplished and maintained if the

> fieldworker is able to survive the violence. Work in dangerous fields implies an ability to negotiate daily a spectrum of social encounters with a diverse host of individuals, some of whom may be helpful, some of whom may be dangerous, and some of whom may be simply indifferent. (2002, 6)

He argues that dangers need to be negotiated over time with innovation and improvisation, not just recognised and avoided, and that 'sharing the responsibilities of security with informants, selective deception, and a variety of techniques for low-profile data collection can effectively empower the ethnographer coping with danger in the field' (2002, 3).

As I and others have strongly recommend, Kovats-Bernat also advocates the importance of asking for, respecting and applying advice given by participants and locals on how to keep safe: 'I quickly got the impression that my informants were better equipped than I to foresee the deadly consequences of participation in my study; and as such I relied on street children, my Haitian research assistant, and a host of other local associates in negotiating my own safety and the ethical issues of my study' (2002, 7). He took stock of:

> the good advice and recommendations of the local population in deciding what conversations (and silences) were important, what information was too costly to life and limb to get to, the amount of exposure to violence considered acceptable, the questions that were dangerous to ask, and the patterns of behaviour that were important to follow for the safety and security of myself and those around me. I preferenced the will and wishes of my informants (who were certainly better at anticipating danger than I was) over any arrogant presumptions as to what was supposed to be best for them. (2002, 7)

Kovats-Bernat argues that the 'normative practice' in dangerous fieldwork should be the development of adaptive strategies that emerge during the process of fieldwork itself, particularly early on in the 'acculturation' phase. These strategies generally entail modifying the methodological approach. For example, 'rather than presupposing a safe location for an orderly, guided interview, the techniques used were informed by a minute-to-minute reassessment of what was going on around the neighbourhood, and I adjusted my methods accordingly. At one moment, I could speak freely with informants and might even be able to take notes. But the next moment, in the midst of abrupt danger, we would have to *pa dan nou* – "shut our mouths", hide the notes' and employ silence as a survival strategy (2002, 6).

More than any other author, Kovats-Bernat describes how the traditional methods and ethics of ethnographic fieldwork may have to be modified to adapt to dangerous fields, and how a 'localised' or negotiated ethics adapted to the specific context should be applied. For example, while respecting the desire for openness and honesty, he recognises that 'selective deception' may be necessary, such as the fact that it is not always prudent or necessary to completely accurately represent the research to everyone encountered in the field or to let everyone in the community know about sensitive aspects and topics of research.

Normally, ethics and danger management are maximised when there is transparency in field relations, avoiding deception and suspicion through complete or honest disclosure of the terms of the research. Researchers in dangerous fields should seek to abide by the *spirit* of this to the best of their abilities, but experience has shown that there are instances where it may be necessary to misrepresent themselves and their research, not in order to conduct the research clandestinely, but because it is necessary to protect participants who might be endangered if there was full public disclosure of all research aims. Kovats-Bernat admits that 'I lied about who I am to a number of individuals over the course of my fieldwork in Haiti, usually when a complicated or confusing description of what anthropologists do could have resulted in me getting arrested, shot, or worse' and he engaged in a degree of measured misrepresentation as a 'posture for protecting myself in the field' (2002, 8).

With regard to the ethical injunction to 'do no harm', Kovats-Bernat states the reality that 'the ability to protect from harm or to offer aegis is not the exclusive domain of the anthropologist but, rather, must be regarded as a power shared among the actors in the field toward the well-being of everyone concerned' (2002, 7). With respect to informed consent, he concludes that the normal instruments of informed consent are poorly adapted to and problematic in dangerous fields (2002, 8). For example, oral consent is usually preferable because signed forms may put the anonymity and confidentiality of research participants at risk; gaining 'group' or 'community' consent is problematic; and, as described above, there is frequently the need for a degree of covertness to disguise dangerous aspects of the research to protect particular participants.

With regard to the ethics of data collection and data protection, Kovats-Bernat discusses the fact that traditional data-recording techniques such as taking detailed field notes, recording interviews and taking photographic and video images may jeopardise the lives and interests of both research participants and researchers, and so these generally have to be adapted or modified. 'Most anthropologists who work in dangerous fields are well aware of the sensitivity, vulnerability, and potentially malign uses of their field notes' and 'we must remind ourselves daily that some of the things that we jot down can mean harassment, imprisonment, exile, torture, or death for our informants or for ourselves and take our notes accordingly' (2002, 9). Because all forms of encryption are fallible, Peritore (1990) has suggested that you should always presume the worst and assume that field notes will be confiscated and the anonymity of informants compromised or lost. Jenkins (1984) suggests that you should be selective in recording sensitive material, not record some things at all and rely on memory instead, carry around only the current day's notes, not keep more than a few weeks' worth of notes in the field and keep them under lock and key in a secure location until they can be sent home.

It is generally accepted that voice and image recording is difficult if not impossible to obscure in the field, and Kovats-Bernat 'took pains to ensure that the notes and recording that I did take were hidden in a secure place while they were in my field residence and that they were meticulously codified, protected, and irregularly and unpredictably sent out of Haiti. The prudence of this tactic was evidenced when it became clear that I was under the surveillance of state authorities' (2002, 9).

In 2007, Dennis Rodgers, in a striking article on how he managed the risks of fieldwork on gangs in Nicaragua, recounts how he joined the gang he was researching and even fought with them – participating or engaging in the violence he was studying – as a means of managing the risks of his fieldwork. In other words, it was safer for him to actually join the gang and even fight with them than it was to remain isolated as an outside observer. He observes that it has always been generally recognised that ethnographic or other fieldwork with humans can never be subject to firm control, and consequently having to adapt to unexpected circumstances is more or less 'standard procedure' (2007, 446) and he points out that 'researchers must always adapt and sensitise themselves to the realities of their field locations, and more importantly, the inherently dialogical nature of ethnographic research' (2007, 444). He comments on the existential shock, identified by Robben and Nordstrom (1995, 13), which normally results from active confrontation with violence in a way – particularly an intensity or level – not experienced before. Rodgers identifies this 'shock' as a central aspect of the 'uneasy process' of acclimatisation to fieldwork in dangerous situations (2007, 447).

Rodgers also stresses the proven strategy of relying on the advice of locals on how to keep safe, recounting how he learned a lot from his gang member participants in 'very practical terms [including hand-to-hand combat techniques] that helped me to extricate myself from several nasty situations during my fieldwork, and also assisted in my developing certain instincts that regularly allowed me to avoid danger spots. Without these, it is unlikely that I would have left Nicaragua physically unscathed as I did' (2007, 456).

Experience has shown that women researchers face the threat of sexual harassment and assault during fieldwork (Warren 1988; Mahmood 2008), and Lee-Treweek and Linkogle have argued that 'we need to consider the gender dynamics of physical theat. Although it is possible for both male and female researchers to experience physical risk, gender shapes the forms such dangers take as well as the ways in which researchers are able to counter these threats' (2000b, 12). In recent years, discussion of the dangers facing female researchers has become more open, and in 2009 Huggins and Glebbeek published *Women Fielding Danger*, which presented reflexive accounts of women researchers from diverse disciplines negotiating multiple dangers in fieldwork locations around the world.

The evidence we have suggests that sexual harassment encountered during fieldwork is a significant and probably under-reported danger, and Warren (1988) has speculated that female researchers may seek to conceal fieldwork difficulties, particularly those related to gender, for fear of harming their career prospects. While this has now been identified as a real risk to female researchers in the field, not much has been written about how to manage this risk, though those who have done so have suggested that female researchers may choose to acquire 'local protectors of various kinds or be taken under the wing of a local family' or 'work with a husband or as part of a team of researchers' (Lee 1995, 56).

However, as Golde (1986) elucidates, this and other forms of protection and concerns about fieldworker safety may also represent a latent form of social control which may constrain the researcher's actions and limit her freedom to conduct research. As Lee observes: 'Nor is social control operating under the guise of protectiveness solely a prerogative of those within the research setting. It may also operate in academic and administrative circles, shaping the research topics and settings typically open to female researchers' (1995, 57). For example, male colleagues and supervisors may discourage female researchers from conducting dangerous fieldwork, and university ethics committees have sometimes exhibited sexism against women compared to men proposing such research. On the other hand, Golde (1986, 8) has noted that female researchers have sometimes been accepted into a research setting with less suspicion than might have greeted a male colleague because women can be perceived as less of a threat than men in some situations of violent conflict.

In 2008, Mahmood published a deeply personal and disturbing, but also moving and ultimately inspiring, account of how she was beaten and raped by a gang of hired thugs or rogue police while conducting fieldwork in India in 1992 in an attempt to prevent her from doing research on Sikh and Kashmiri militants. As Winkler has observed, 'few people have placed in writing the hideous description of a rape attack. To write these words is to relive the pain – in full' (1995, 157). Mahmood warns her readers:

> You do not want to read the rest of this story. Not if you want to avoid confronting the utter disgrace of a world in which some people think they can threaten, pummel, and punish scholars into studying 'the right' topics. Not if you want to believe that knowledge is found in ivory towers and quiet libraries, that it comes without pain, that it is always welcome. (2008, 1)

She also warns that 'those who actually try to study "the wrong" topics – the silenced, the tabooed, the dangerous topics that challenge the power holders of the world – may find out just what it takes to be a truly independent scholar' (2008, 5). She writes that after the attack, she was confronted by:

> many basic ambiguities that were never resolved, ambiguities I later recognised as characteristic of the arenas of terror in which many of the people I now study (Sikhs, Muslims) live themselves, never quite clear who is an ally and who is an enemy, perhaps doubting their own complicity in the suffering they endure. Did they bring it on themselves? (As many say.) It took me years after that to sort through what I should have, could have, or might have done as a victim-survivor who is also a scholar. What was not a grey area for me was whether to continue to work in this region, on those topics. I had to. Every scar, as it faded, begged me to. (2008, 8)

As Robben and Nordstrom have commented, 'very few turn their personal tragedies into research' (1995, 18), but this is precisely what Mahmood did. She utterly subverted her attackers' intentions by doing exactly what they hoped to prevent – publish brilliant ethnographic research presenting the 'tabooed' perspectives and experiences of Punjabi Sikhs and Kashmiri Muslims in India (Mahmood 1996).

Mahmood asks 'is it not time to think more critically about our institutional discourse of "safety" and "risk assessment" and how it guides us securely away from the martyring truths that might really unseat the powerful and change the status quo? How it is part of the machine that keeps academia complicit in the silencing of abuses, the turning away from suffering?' (2008, 9). When she originally went to India, she intended to study tribal development and 'had no stake in any religious or political controversies. But when others chose to use their very bodies as weapons, insulting my own at its very core, this ethnography became a very intimate matter indeed. The question is, what does one do with that deeply, literally visceral violent memory' (2008, 9–10). She used that 'shattering intersection to begin a new journey' into her cutting-edge work on political violence in India. 'It's past time, I think, that we talk to our students not only about safety but also about courage. We should ask them what they think it takes to be an anthropologist in this perilous world of ours – not GRE [test] scores but character. *How will you stand up to it*? How will you pursue, teach, and write the truth in a world intent on masking it?' (2008, 10).

Pragmatic Recommendations for Managing Danger in Fieldwork

Prior to beginning fieldwork, evaluate as realistically as possible the degree of danger and try to identify potential sources of danger you may encounter. The best way to do this is to review the reflexive literature on research that has already been conducted in the locale and seek the advice of academics and others with direct experience with the setting. Over the past 30 years, a mass of reflexive accounts of fieldwork around the world has been published (see Sluka and Robben 2007), and today a good literature review of research already conducted in almost any potential field site is likely to be informative with regard to the dangers and risks encountered there.

If at all possible, conduct 'pre-fieldwork fieldwork' via a preliminary or exploratory visit to the proposed research site to see for yourself, and talk to local academics and other people 'on the ground' there about potential risks and dangers.

Decide if you are prepared to accept the risks involved and, if you are, consider both what sorts of action you might take to ameliorate or manage them and what sorts of action might exacerbate them.

Determine what you consider an 'acceptable level' of danger and what sorts of event would be unacceptable, such as unmanageable direct or immediate threats to your safety.

Recognise that one 'danger' of fieldwork on or amidst violence is that situations may develop in which you have to discontinue your research on your own initiative, or that the authorities or other 'powers that be' may compel you to do so.

Always have a plan of escape, a predetermined means of extricating yourself from the situation as quickly as possible, should the need arise. This may be as simple as always having a mobile phone (to call for help or a taxi) and a credit card (to pay for immediate transport from the scene).

Consider your sponsors and sources of funding and their track record. During the 1970s, some researchers discovered only after the fact that their funding came from US Army-sponsored research groups. Today, governments, militaries, and police and state intelligence agencies fund much research, both directly and indirectly through front organisations. Many researchers have discovered that in conflict situations, government funding of any sort is frequently suspect, and direct or indirect funding by state security agencies is obviously so, because it brings into question the motives, purposes and applications of the research. Being funded by independent sources attributes independence to research motives and is a positive contribution in negotiating access and safety with potential participants.

Consider how your research participants, given their experiences, are likely to define you and what you are doing, and how you will present yourself. Throughout the research process, engage in 'impression management' (Goffman 1959; Berreman 1962) to actively counter dangerous rumours and suspicions, and to foster an honest, accurate public perception of who you are and what you are doing. This is best done by avoiding acting in ways that reinforce suspicions and being as honest and straightforward as possible about who you are and what you are doing. In a nutshell, if you do not want to be defined as a spy, try to not act like one.

Seek the consent and support of respected members of the community you wish to study.

Before formally commencing the research, an explicit ethically based 'research agreement' should be negotiated with participants to gain their (usually verbal) consent, including the nature of the research, methods, ethics, care and disposal of data, and dissemination of results. Then maintain, monitor and manage this agreement, and respond effectively to any difficulties and dangers that subsequently may arise.

Particularly early in the research, avoid asking questions about sensitive political topics that spies would be interested in. In 1967, Polsky suggested that a good rule of fieldwork in sensitive contexts is to 'initially, keep your eyes and ears open but keep your mouth shut. At first try to ask no questions whatsoever. Before you can ask questions … you should get the "feel" of their world by extensive and attentive listening' (1967, 126–7).

While in the field, seek and rely on the good advice offered by research participants and other locals on how to keep safe.

Be as open and honest as possible when describing your research to participants, community members and others. In general, dishonesty and evasion undermine trust and may raise dangerous suspicions.

At the same time, recognise that a degree of misrepresentation or 'selective deception' is sometimes necessary as camouflage to protect participants. For example, when I was doing research directly with paramilitary groups, I did not tell this to others in the community.

Along with being honest, be flexible. Be prepared to modify your research interests, methods and goals to adapt to dangerous contingencies that may arise.

Polsky summarised flexibility in fieldwork in the comment that 'a final rule is to have few unbreakable rules' and suggested that you should revise your plans 'according to the requirements of any particular situation' and recognise that you will undoubtedly encounter 'unanticipated and ambiguous situations for which one has no clear behavioural plan at all' (1967, 133).

Recognise that it may be necessary to not tape interviews or use other sound, photo or video-recording devices, or even take notes. But if these are employed, extra precautions must be taken to secure them and ensure they do not fall into the wrong hands. When sensitive information is recorded, it is imperative to protect the anonymity of research participants. Be selective in information gathering and recognise that some information should be kept only in one's head or not used at all. Notes and research materials should be kept in a secure location, preferably under lock and key or computer password, and periodically removed from the field for safekeeping. Be aware that no computer connected to the worldwide web is safe from being broken into or 'hacked'.

One might think that neutrality is a good danger management strategy, but this has generally proven not to be the case in contexts of political violence, and it is difficult to gain access, trust and consent from participants by claiming this status. As Nash famously discovered in her fieldwork in Bolivia, 'no neutrals are allowed' (1976, 150). Researchers usually need to 'take sides' to some degree, and this is inherently dangerous since, in the Manichean logic of war, as former US President George W. Bush famously put it in launching his 'global war on terror', 'you're either with us or against us'. It is better to present yourself to participants as a researcher who is sympathetic to their situation, who is devoted to helping them and who would not do anything knowingly to harm them.

On the other hand, in interactions with state authorities it is generally a good idea to present yourself and your research as neutral. For example, I had no qualms about telling British soldiers on the streets of Belfast who inquired as to my politics that I was 'a neutral social scientist'. Researchers should decide whose 'side' they are on and should seriously consider whether the ultimate purpose of the research is basically one of control or liberation. Rather than being 'neutral', present yourself honesty as an academic dedicated to the pursuit of truth or knowledge and committed to public good rather than private or political interest.

Experience has shown that in situations of conflict and violence, people generally do want their stories and experiences acknowledged and reported. In his fieldwork in El Salvador and Chile, Huizer 'relied mostly on the common human sympathy' he felt for the villagers he worked with. Basically, his approach to handling danger was to gain people's confidence by convincing them that he was 'on their side' (1973, 21, 28). This is done by sincerely identifying with their interests, understanding and sympathising with their problems and grievances, and showing them that you are willing to act accordingly. I believe that this is the most common approach taken by anthropologists in the field and has proven to be effective in ameliorating danger.

Ideally, findings should be fed back to participants before publication in order to eliminate errors, resolve disagreements, ensure anonymity and alter or delete anything that could be harmful, particularly with regard to fieldwork directly with militants.

When working in communities where militants are active, you must learn to walk softly and be careful about asking questions about dangerous topics. Be sensitive to what sorts of questions may be asked and what sorts are taboo, because they are risky and may lead to harm. There are many things you shouldn't even ask about. Anything that is not relevant to the research should not be pursued, and the kinds of information that state police and intelligence agencies are interested in should be avoided.

It may be best to control and limit contact with particular individuals, who it may be dangerous simply to be around. Restricting interactions with research participants is not ideal in primary research, but it may be necessary for security reasons. The actual amount of time spent directly with 'perpetrators' of political violence should be limited to what is necessary and with safety in mind.

In situations of political conflict and insurgency, fieldworkers typically have to deal with both the insurgents and state authorities combating them at the same time, and this can be a very difficult if not dangerous 'juggling act'. For example, researchers usually need the permission of the authorities to reside in such areas. Often, if you become publicly associated with one side, this alienates you from the other. Experience has also shown that in most field situations, the authorities rather than the research participants represent the most significant source of danger. In his famous study of underground life, *Hustlers, Beats, and Others,* Polsky found that most of the risk in his fieldwork came from the authorities rather than from his research participants and he observed that 'most of the danger for the field worker comes not from the cannibals and head-hunters but from the colonial officials' (1967, 145). This 'top down' threat or 'danger from above' includes the risks of intimidation, physical assault, arrest, interrogation, torture, prosecution, imprisonment, confiscation of research materials and even execution or assassination, and is exemplified in the experience of Philippe Bourgois (1991), who was forced to run for his life from the army while conducting fieldwork in El Salvador and was assaulted and jailed by the police while conducting fieldwork with crack addicts in Philadelphia.

As the Mahmood case illustrates, if you independently conduct research on political violence, authorities and other 'powers that be' may become a threat if they perceive you as a danger to their interests, for example, by producing alternative or competing interpretations, explanations and 'definitions of reality'. If you do 'partisan' research on behalf of insurgents, state authorities will treat you as an enemy combatant or 'terrorist' and, conversely, if you do research for the authorities, then research participants may perceive you as a threat to their interests – that is, a 'spy' or 'social engineer' complicit with elite interests out to control, exploit, oppress or otherwise harm them.

While in the field, never grow complacent about the dangers. View managing them as both an integral part of the research process and an ongoing relationship with research participants.

Do not ignore potential threats when they arise. For example, dangerous rumours may emerge at almost any time while in the field and these should be immediately dealt with. If they are false, they should be publicly denied. If there is some truth to them, work to reassure people that you are not a threat, and if you become a direct threat, get out.

Throughout the fieldwork process, make a concerted effort to define and re-define the risks and dangers in light of actual experiences, and work to reduce such dangers by improving old methods and developing new ones as your network of contacts and degree of experience expand over time. With time, you may be able to allay suspicions and reduce some of the dangers, but new ones will probably arise.

Recognise that some dangers may not end once you return from the field and consider the risks which might eventuate *after* the research is completed, for example, the possibility that ethical and other considerations may mean that you will not be able to publish your findings. There may also be people at home who object to your research and may threaten you as well, and, as discussed above, certain 'professional dangers' may also emerge at this stage. It is also advisable to consider how the media is likely to portray your research findings. It is a common experience, particularly when dealing with controversial political topics, that results are misreported in the media, and when research participants 'read what we write' – or, more likely, what the media has reported about it – they may be upset, offended or feel betrayed (Brettell 1993).

Consider that not all tactics for managing danger are necessarily positive and that some may inadvertently increase risk rather than ameliorate it. Some 'negative recommendations' of things to generally avoid are covert research, hiring security guards and carrying weapons for protection. More often than not, these are likely to generate more suspicion than security. However, as with covert research, this is not a hard-and-fast rule, and there may be a few situations where such protection is justified. With respect to carrying a gun, the general perception is that spies or other state security agents carry guns, not academics conducting research, but in a few cases researchers have felt justified in arming themselves because the groups they worked with were subject to attack by enemies and they needed to defend themselves in that context (see Rodgers 2007). However, in general, if you need a gun for protection in the field, in most cases you probably should not be doing the research.

Finally, remember that while most dangers can be mediated to a substantial degree by skilful manoeuvre, some dangers may be beyond management. For example, despite your best efforts at danger management, simple bad luck can sometimes result in the termination of research or, worse yet, of the researcher. In short, danger is not a purely 'technical' problem and is never totally manageable.

These recommendations are grounded in and have arisen from the direct experience of many researchers who have conducted fieldwork in dangerous contexts. They are by no means exhaustive, but are intended to be thought provoking, consciousness-raising and indicative of some of the problems involved in managing danger and risk, and are designed to be a starting point from which those considering research in dangerous contexts can map out their own strategies for conducting their fieldwork safely.

Conclusion

Much successful research has proven that fieldwork is possible in even the most dangerous contexts. As we have seen, while special ethnographic, methodological, theoretical and ethical sensitivities are required, those who have written on this topic have agreed that the dangers faced in most fieldwork – including primary research on political violence – can be successfully and safely negotiated, mediated and managed through foresight, prior planning, sensible precautions, skilful manoeuvres and an acute awareness of political sensitivities. They have also all concluded that research in dangerous contexts requires 'adaptability and strategic sensitivity, an awareness of the predictable dangers, and flexibility in approach to problems which arise in the field' (Feenan 2002, 161); that 'the safety and well-being of the researcher should always be placed as equal to protecting participants when planning research' (Lee-Treweek and Lingkogle 2000b, 12–13); and that 'if risk is an accepted element of fieldwork then it should be included as part of early instruction on research and students should be taught to evaluate risk consciously' (Peterson 2000, 192). They have also emphasised the critical importance of fundamental research ethics and the necessity of reflecting on the potential for abuse of research by sponsors and funding agencies, particularly when working for coercive state institutions such as the military and police in contexts marked by political violence, but also when working for many private corporations, institutions and organisations. They have also concluded that managing danger in fieldwork frequently requires unconventional ethics and the development of a localised or negotiated ethics which emerges from interaction with research participants in the field, and Fleuhr-Lobban (2009) has produced a set of 'guiding ethical principles' specifically adapted to research in dangerous contexts derived in part from *Guiding Principles for Human Rights Field Officers Working in Conflict and Post-Conflict Environments* (O'Neil 2009).

It is not possible to completely eliminate danger in fieldwork on or amidst political violence and conflict, but just as the risks of everyday life can be managed effectively, so can dangerous research. After all, for the research participants, these dangers are part and parcel of their 'normal' or everyday life which they have had no choice but to learn to adapt to. However, the shifting quality of danger means that we cannot always foresee all of the potential risks or how risky a situation might become. Managing danger in fieldwork should be viewed as a dialogic *ongoing process* based on an *ethical relationship* with research participants, which requires recognising the shifting nature of danger and risk. The challenge is to both identify important safety issues prior to embarking on fieldwork and to resolve unanticipated issues as they arise, and arrangements regarding personal safety may have to be almost continuously re-negotiated.

Whitehead has observed that to witness violence is not only dangerous but also necessarily involves ethical judgements not only about how but *whether* it should studied and reported, and refers to 'the right to raise the possibility that such things might be better left alone' (2002, 37). Similarly, Kovats-Bernat observes that: 'Given the possibility of grave consequences for involvement by participants and our true inability to guarantee their safety or anticipate threats to them, there is at present some question as to whether research in dangerous fields should be engaged in at all' (2002, 8). The ability to protect from harm should be considered a power shared among the actors in the field, and if the dangers become unacceptably large for participants or the researcher, they should remove themselves from the situation.

The world is not becoming a safer place for the pursuit of fieldwork. We can meet this challenge, but we should do so rationally by considering danger as an essential methodological issue in its own right. The intention of this chapter has been to further our consideration of danger as a methodological and ethical issue, and contribute to developing ways of minimising risks and protecting researchers while they are in the field. It is no exaggeration to say that this is, in fact, a matter of life and death.

References

Bell, C. and Roberts, H. (eds) (1984), *Social Researching: Politics, Problems, Practice* (London: Routledge & Kegan Paul).
Berreman, Gerald (1962), 'Behind Many Masks: Ethnography and Impression Management', prologue in *Hindus of the Himalayas* (Berkeley: University of California Press), xvii–lvii.
Bourgois, Philippe (1991), 'Confronting the Ethics of Ethnography: Lessons from Fieldwork in Central America', in F. Harrison (ed.), *Decolonizing Anthropology: Moving Further Toward an Anthropology for Liberation*. (Washington DC: American Anthropological Association).
Brettell, Caroline (ed.) (1993), *When They Read What We Write: The Politics of Ethnography*. (Westport, CT: Bergin and Garvey).
Brewer, John (1991), *Inside the RUC: Routine Policing in a Divided Society* (Oxford: Oxford University Press).
Brewer, John (1993), 'Sensitivity as Problem in Field Research: A Study of Routine Policing in Northern Ireland', in C. Renzetti and R. Lee (eds), *Researching Sensitive Topics* (London: Sage).
Bruce, Steve (1992), *The Red Hand: Protestant Paramilitaries in Northern Ireland* (Oxford: Oxford University Press).
Burton, Frank (1978), *The Politics of Legitimacy: Struggles in a Belfast Community* (London: Routledge & Kegan Paul).
Carter, K. and Delamont, S. (eds) (1996), *Qualitative Research: The Emotional Dimension*. (Aldershot: Avebury).
CVCP (1993), *Health and Safety Responsibilities of Supervisors Towards Postgraduate and Undergraduate Students* (London: Committee of Vice-Chancellors and Principals of the Universities of the United Kingdom).
Dowler, Lorraine (2001), 'The Four Square Laundry: Participant Observation in a War Zone', *Geographical Review* 91:1–2, 414–22.

Feenan, Dermot (2002), 'Researching Paramilitary Violence in Northern Ireland', *International Journal of Social Research Methodology* 5:2, 147–63.
Feldman, Allen (1991), *Formations of Violence: The Narrative of the Body and Political Terror in Northern Ireland* (Chicago: University of Chicago Press).
Fluehr-Lobban, Carolyn (2009), 'Guiding Principles over Enforceable Standards', *Anthropology News*, September, 8–9.
Garthwaite, Rosie (2011), *How to Avoid Being Killed in a War Zone: The Essential Guide for Dangerous Places* (London: Bloomsbury).
Goffman, Erving (1959), *The Presentation of Self in Everyday Life* (New York: Anchor).
Golde, Peggy (1986), *Women in the Field*, 2nd edn (Berkeley, CA: University of California Press).
González, Roberto (2008), '"Human Terrain": Past, Present and Future Applications', *Anthropology Today* 234:1, 21–6.
Green, Linda (1995), 'Living in a State of Fear', in C. Nordstrom and A. Robben (eds), *Fieldwork Under Fire: Contemporary Studies of Violence and Survival* (Berkeley, CA: University of California Press).
Harrison, Faye (ed.) (1991), *Decolonizing Anthropology: Moving Further Toward an Anthropology for Liberation* (Washington DC: American Anthropological Association).
Hockey, J. (1996), 'Putting Down Smoke: Emotion and Engagement in Participant Observation', in K. Carter and S. Delamont (eds), *Qualitative Research: The Emotional Dimension.* (Aldershot: Avebury).
Howell, Nancy (1986), 'Occupational Safety and Health in Anthropology'. Paper presented at the annual meetings of the American Association of Practicing Anthropologists, 10 April, Albuquerque, New Mexico.
Howell, Nancy (1990), *Surviving Fieldwork: A Report of the Advisory Panel on Health and Safety in Fieldwork* (Washington DC: American Anthropological Association).
Huggins, Martha and Glebbeek, Marie-Louise (eds) (2009), *Women Fielding Danger: Negotiating Ethnographic Identities in Field Research* (Lanham, MD: Rowman & Littlefield).
Huizer, Gerrit (1973), *Peasant Rebellion in Latin America* (Harmondsworth: Penguin).
Jamieson, Janet (2000), 'Negotiating Danger in Fieldwork on Crime', in G. Lee-Treweek and S. Linkogle (eds), *Danger in the Field: Risk and Ethics in Social Research* (London: Routledge).
Jenkins, Richard (1984), 'Bringing it all Back Home: An Anthropologist in Belfast', in C. Bell and H. Roberts (eds), *Social Researching: Politics, Problems, Practice* (London: Routledge & Kegan Paul).
Jipson, Arthur and Litton, Chad (2000), 'Career and Community: The Implications of Researching Dangerous Groups', in G. Lee-Treweek and S. Linkogle (eds), *Danger in the Field: Risk and Ethics in Social Research* (London: Routledge).
Knox, Colin and Monaghan, Rachel (2003), 'Researching Inter-communal Violence in Northern Ireland and South Africa', in R. Lee and E. Stanko (eds), *Researching Violence: Essays on Methodology and Measurement* (London: Routledge).

Kovats-Bernat, J. Christopher (2002), 'Negotiating Dangerous Fields: Pragmatic Strategies for Fieldwork amid Violence and Terror', *American Anthropologist* 104:1, 1–15.
Lee, Raymond (ed.) (1993), *Doing Research on Sensitive Topics* (London: Sage).
Lee, Raymond (ed.) (1995), *Dangerous Fieldwork* (Thousand Oaks: Sage).
Lee, Raymond and Stanko, Elizabeth (eds) (2003), *Researching Violence: Essays on Methodology and Measurement* (London: Routledge).
Lee-Treweek, Geraldine and Linkogle, Stephanie (eds) (2000), *Danger in the Field: Risk and Ethics in Social Research* (London: Routledge).
Lee-Treweek, Geraldine and Linkogle, Stephanie (2000a), 'Overview' in G. Lee-Treweek and S. Linkogle (eds), *Danger in the Field: Risk and Ethics in Social Research* (London: Routledge).
Lee-Treweek, Geraldine and Linkogle, Stephanie (2000b), 'Putting Danger in the Frame', in G. Lee-Treweek and S. Linkogle (eds), *Danger in the Field: Risk and Ethics in Social Research* (London: Routledge).
Mahmood, Cynthia Keppley (1996), *Fighting for Faith and Nation: Dialogues with Sikh Militants* (Philadelphia: University of Pennsylvania Press).
Mahmood, Cynthia Keppley (2008), 'Anthropology from the Bones: A Memoir of Fieldwork, Survival, and Commitment', *Anthropology and Humanism* 33:1/2, 1–11.
Nash, June (1976), 'Ethnology in a Revolutionary Setting', in M. Rynkiewich and J. Spradley (eds), *Ethics and Anthropology* (New York: Wiley and Sons).
Nordstrom, Carolyn and Robben, Antonius (eds) (1995), *Fieldwork Under Fire: Contemporary Studies of Violence and Survival* (Berkeley, CA: University of California Press).
O'Neil, William (2009), *Guiding Principles for Human Rights Field Officers Working in Conflict and Post-Conflict Environments* (Nottingham: Human Rights Law Centre, University of Nottingham).
Peritore, Patrick (1990), 'Reflections on Dangerous Fieldwork', *American Sociologist* 21:4, 359–73.
Peterson, Jeff (2000), 'Sheer Foolishness: Shifting Definitions of Danger in Conducting and Teaching Ethnographic Field Research', in G. Lee-Treweek and S. Linkogle (eds), *Danger in the Field: Risk and Ethics in Social Research* (London: Routledge).
Polsky, Ned (1967), *Hustlers, Beats, and Others* (Harmondsworth: Penguin).
Porter, Elizabeth, Robinson, Gillian, Smyth, Marie, Schnabel, Albrecht and Osaghae, Eghosa (eds) (2005) *Researching Conflict in Africa: Insights and Experiences* (New York: United Nations University Press).
Renzetti, C. and Lee, R. (eds) (1993) *Researching Sensitive Topics* (London: Sage).
Robben, Antonius C.G.M. and Nordstrom, Carolyn (1995), 'The Anthropology and Ethnography of Violence and Socio-political Conflict', in C. Nordstrom and A. Robben (eds), *Fieldwork Under Fire: Contemporary Studies of Violence and Survival* (Berkeley, CA: University of California Press).
Robben, Antonius C.G.M. and Sluka, Jeffrey (eds) (2007), *Ethnographic Fieldwork: An Anthropological Reader* (Malden, MA: Blackwell).

Rodgers, Dennis (2007), 'Joining the Gang and Becoming a *Broder*: The Violence of Ethnography in Contemporary Nicaragua', *Bulletin of Latin American Research* 26:4, 444–61.
Rynkiewich, M. and Spradley, J. (eds) (1976), *Ethics and Anthropology* (New York: Wiley and Sons).
Sluka, Jeffrey (1989), 'I'm Alive and Well, My Kneecaps are Still Intact, and My Research is Coming Along Fine', prologue in *Hearts and Minds, Water and Fish: Popular Support for the IRA and INLA in a Northern Irish Ghetto* (Greenwich: JAI Press).
Sluka, Jeffrey (1990), 'Participant-Observation in Violent Social Contexts', *Human Organization* 49:2, 114–205.
Sluka, Jeffrey (1995), 'Reflections on Managing Danger in Fieldwork: Dangerous Anthropology in Belfast', in C. Nordstrom and A. Robben (eds), *Fieldwork Under Fire: Contemporary Studies of Violence and Survival* (Berkeley, CA: University of California Press).
Sluka, Jeffrey and Robben, Antonius (2007), 'Fieldwork in Cultural Anthropology: An Introduction', in A. Robben and J. Sluka (eds), *Ethnographic Fieldwork: An Anthropological Reader* (Malden, MA: Blackwell).
Smyth, Marie and Robinson, Gillian (eds) (2001), *Researching Violently Divided Societies: Ethical and Methodological Issues* (New York: United Nations University Press).
Stanko, Elizabeth and Lee, Raymond (2003), 'Introduction: Methodological Considerations', in R. Lee and E. Stanko (eds), *Researching Violence: Essays on Methodology and Measurement* (London: Routledge).
Swedenburg, Ted (1995), 'With Genet in the Palestinian Field', in C. Nordstrom and A. Robben (eds), *Fieldwork Under Fire: Contemporary Studies of Violence and Survival* (Berkeley, CA: University of California Press).
Warren, Carol (1988), *Gender Issues in Field Research* (Newbury Park, CA: Sage).
Weitzer, Ronald (1995), *Policing Under Fire: Ethnic Conflict and Police–Community Relations in Northern Ireland* (Albany, NY: State University of New York Press).
Whitehead, Neil (2002), *Dark Shamans: Kanaima and the Poetics of Violent Death* (Durham, NC: Duke University Press).
Williams, T., Dunlap, E. Johnson, B. and Hamid, A. (1992), 'Personal Safety in Dangerous Places', *Journal of Contemporary Ethnography* 21, 343–74.
Winkler, Cathy (with Hanke, Penelope) (1995), 'Ethnography of the Ethnographer', in C. Nordstrom and A. Robben (eds), *Fieldwork Under Fire: Contemporary Studies of Violence and Survival* (Berkeley, CA: University of California Press).

PART IV
Manifestations of Political Violence

17

ASHGATE
RESEARCH
COMPANION

Genocide as Political Violence

Adam Jones

Introduction

Examining genocide as political violence transports us directly to some core debates in *genocide studies* – the field invented by the Polish jurist Raphael Lemkin in the 1940s and transformed by successive waves of comparative genocide scholars from the late 1970s onwards. First and most fundamentally, what *is* genocide? Given that virtually all scholars and legal theorists agree that genocide above all means the destruction of human *groups* through a targeting of their actual or alleged members, which collectivities merit inclusion in scholarly analyses, and protection under international law? And how do *multiple* identities overlap, including – perhaps – political ones? In other words, how do such identities blend and interweave, both in the minds of those who claim them as their own and those who impute negative identities to their targets, paving the way for the marginalization and massacre of people who are often utterly mystified by such mythical constructs as 'witch', 'enemy of the people', 'Judeo-Bolshevik' and so on.

The place of political groups, identities and sympathies in the discussion is a pivotal one. For the purposes of this discussion, I define *political groups and identities* as those that revolve around visions of how human collectivities ought to be organized and governed. I define *political violence* as resulting from clashing visions of the same, while recognizing that political affiliations and identities are always bound up with other, analytically distinct identities.

But if political groups are also central in this discussion, their centrality is often hotly disputed. The most common arguments raised *against* including political groups in genocide, from the earliest days of the drafting of the United Nations Genocide Convention (1948) to the present, are broadly threefold.

First, political identities are seen as *consciously adopted rather than ascribed at birth*, as national, ethnic and often religious identities supposedly are. Second, they lack the 'permanence' or durability of these other designations. Third, they are allegedly less common targets of mass violence and repression than the other groups. Such arguments are nicely encapsulated in the justification offered by Raphael Lemkin for his decision to exclude political groups in his foundational understanding of genocide. This understanding, as published in the seminal Chapter X of *Axis Rule in Occupied Europe*, emphasized that genocide was a multi-faceted assault against all aspects of a designated group's existence: 'The objectives of such plan would be disintegration of the *political* and social institutions of culture, language, national feelings, religion, and the economic existence of national groups' (Lemkin 1944, emphasis added; see also the discussion in Shaw 2007, 69–71). However, this is one of only two passing appearances of 'political' in Lemkin's chapter. While he recognized the political nature of some genocidal targeting, he also limited the application of his new concept to 'the destruction of a nation or an ethnic group'. Writing to Sir Hartley Shawcross in July 1947, Lemkin argued 'that political groups have not the permanency and the specific characteristics of the other groups referred to [ethnic, racial, national, religious] and … the Convention on Genocide being of general interest, it should not run the risk of failure by introducing ideas on which the world is deeply divided' (quoted in Cooper 2008, 91).[1]

The final words in the passage also hint at the political pressures Lemkin was under as he sought to sway a critical mass of countries to his nascent, and still rather novel, Convention. He was an adept manoeuverer and manipulator, as was probably required for such solitary and heroic efforts at legal institution-building. Even at the time, though, criticisms were raised relating to the exclusion of political groups from the Convention's protections. One of the most distinguished early scholars on genocide and crimes against humanity, Henri Donnedieu de Vabres, argued that 'genocide was an odious crime, regardless of the group which fell victim to it and … the exclusion of political groups might be regarded as justifying genocide in the case of such groups' (quoted in Cooper 2008, 91). We will see later in this chapter that others, before and since, have echoed de Vabres' concerns.

In fact, the core suppositions of Lemkin's thinking about political groups – and of the wider critiques of protecting political groups – can be challenged, especially in the light of several decades of thinking and theorizing on such previously unproblematic concepts as 'race', 'ethnicity' and 'identity'. We will turn shortly to the international-legal aspect of genocide and how the debate over political groups has evolved from the 1940s to the present. But let us first consider the essential criticisms that Lemkin and others have made to justify excluding political groups: namely, their supposed impermanence, instability and voluntarism, along with the empirical question of whether political groups are actually less vulnerable than 'national', 'ethnic', 'racial' and 'religious' groups to campaigns of mass violence and extermination.

It is true that political identities are *usually* adopted consciously and voluntarily rather than ascribed at birth, and are consciously and voluntarily changed in adult life. But so too are national, ethnic and religious identities. We are by now amply familiar with changes of citizenship, hybrid and hyphenated identities, and plural nationalisms. As for religion, clearly I may move from being a Christian to a Buddhist, or vice versa, from one moment to the next, if my conversion

---

1 Cooper also cites a November 1948 cable from Lemkin: 'Because inclusion political groups Latin Americans losing interest convention while England Belgium intriguing among them' (167).

experience is powerful.[2] More gradually, one may evolve from an ethnic identity (e.g. indigenous Maya in Guatemala) towards another (e.g. 'ladino', identified in Guatemala with Spanish language and dress).

In addition, political identifiers overlap and interpenetrate in intricate ways with ethnoreligious labels (i.e. with the 'national', 'racial' and 'ethnical' groups protected under the Genocide Convention). One would be hard-pressed to draw a line between religion and political affiliation among Hindu or Serbian nationalists, for example, or among activists on either side of Northern Ireland's political-religious-ethnic conflict, now mercifully muted.

As for 'race', its deployment in an unproblematized way in the Genocide Convention seems much less persuasive to contemporary observers than it did to Lemkin and the Convention's framers. Many are dubious that such a thing exists in any form other than that claimed by individuals or ascribed to them by others. To the extent that we *can* usefully employ a terminology of 'race' – for example, to understand the mindset of fanatics on the subject, like Hitler and his crew – we must again acknowledge the blurring and overlapping of racial identities. In his seminal study of Nazi propaganda, *The Jewish Enemy*, Jeffrey Herf argues provocatively that the Nazi preoccupation with the Jew was *primarily* a political one: 'the radical anti-Semitic ideology that justified and accompanied the mass murder of European Jewry was first and foremost *a paranoid political, rather than biological, conviction and narrative*' (Herf 2006, 150–51, emphasis in original). Bolshevism, for Hitler, was:

> the Jews' 'declaration of war' against culture. It would bring about 'the absolute destruction' of the accomplishments of the West in the interest of a 'rootless and nomadic international clique of conspirators.' A small Jewish cabal had come to dominate the Soviet Union. The mission of National Socialism was to prevent the 'Bolshevization of the world.' In fact, 'the Bolshevik International' was 'a Jewish international'. (Herf 2006, 41–2)

Even if we question the centrality that Herf accords to (imputed) political identifications – it is possible that he underplays the 'racial' dimension in the regime's policies and propaganda – we can agree that *the political aspect* of Hitler's genocidal campaign against European Jewry is important in filling out the portrait of the Nazi regime's varied, overlapping motivations and world views. As I have argued elsewhere: 'If the génocidaires do not feel constrained by mutually exclusive categories, I see no reason why the analyst of their actions should be' (Jones 2004, 260).

---

2   The UK delegate to the Genocide Convention deliberations (see further below) pointed this out, calling for the Convention to 'provide protection to groups the members of which were as free to leave them as they were to join them. *National or religious groups were obvious instances of that kind*'. Quoted in Van Schaack 1997, 2265, emphasis added.

The Question of Severity

As contemporary observers, we have a strikingly different perspective on mass atrocity from that of the Genocide Convention's architects and Raphael Lemkin himself. In the mid-1940s, with the Nazi atrocities still fresh in the minds of the framers, racial-ethnic murder was very much uppermost in their thoughts. To the (vast) extent that politically-motivated murder had also occurred, vested interests prevented its serious consideration, since the principal political murderer was a permanent member of the United Nations Security Council (see further below). The delegates of many states unsympathetic to the Soviet Union likewise feared the constraints that protection for political groups might place on their own acts of domestic discipline and punishment.[3]

The Soviet purges and terror under Joseph Stalin from the 1930s to the 1950s truly kick-started the modern era of politically targeted mass killing. In the immediate post-Second World War period, such campaigns of extermination still carried an aura of novelty. Today, our understanding of mass political crimes, and the huge toll of death and suffering they inflict, is starkly greater. The communist atrocities of Stalin and Mao are by now well documented. The terror-states of Latin America, the Middle East and Africa, especially during the military dictatorships of the 1960s to the 1980s, overwhelmingly targeted political opponents, often under the cover of 'ethnic' or ethnoreligious warfare against groups deemed oppositionist *tout court* (e.g. Tibet after the 1959 rebellion, Biafra, Syria[4] and Guatemala). Again, though, political and ethnic identities – both actual and alleged – were only one element of a complex mix. It also included religious and national dimensions, in that 'communist' dissidents and activists were often depicted as irreligious and ungodly, as well as politically traitorous and ethnically suspect.

A broad democratizing trend since the 1980s, and the waning of the conflicts resulting from the collapse of the state-socialist bloc, has reduced the number of overtly political mass murders. Nevertheless, the vicious repressions of dissidents and activists in Burma/Myanmar, Sri Lanka and Colombia, to cite three egregious cases, not only constitute some of the most destructive and inhumane acts perpetrated anywhere, but also evince a powerfully political aspect to the killings. In many of the world's 'extremely violent societies', then – to use the term coined by Christian Gerlach (2006) – conflict-generating schisms are either predominantly or significantly *politicized*.

---

3   To cite just one example, Colombia's genocide law, which Congress approved in 2000, defines genocide 'as including the "partial or total destruction of a group for political reasons and causing death to its members for belonging to such groups"'. According to the International Justice Tribune, the law was the result of lobbying by the leftist Union Patriotica (UP) party, which suffered more than 1,100 extrajudicial killings of its members and political candidates from 1985 to 1993. At the time of writing, the Inter-American Court of Human Rights was studying the matter with a view to bringing proceedings based on a submission from the UP (see International Justice Tribune 2007).

4   The Hama massacre of 1982, with up to 25,000 killed. See Wiedl 2006.

The International Law Dimension

How did the architects of modern international law, and the Genocide Convention specifically, handle the question of political victims as a potential protected category under an anti-genocide covenant? The most detailed exploration of the trajectory is that of the eminent legal scholar and genocide specialist William A. Schabas. In his exhaustive overview of *Genocide in International Law*, Schabas notes that political groups made a surprising and sudden appearance as a protected category in the *travaux préparatoires* for the Genocide Convention, some two years before the Convention was finalized and passed. The initial draft of General Assembly Resolution 96(I), adopted on 11 December 1946, 'did not include political groups', according to Schabas. But then 'a sub-committee of the Sixth Committee' added them – and, even more surprisingly, chose to exclude ethnic and national groups from the equation! The result was a definition of genocide as 'the denial of the right of existence of entire human groups, as homicide is the denial of the right to live of individual human beings ... Many instances of such crimes of genocide have occurred when racial, religious, *political* and other groups have been destroyed, entirely or in part' (cited in Schabas 2000, 45, emphasis added). Including political groups, wrote the drafters, would produce 'a broader concept of genocide ... one that reflects customary law' (cited in Schabas 2000, 45, emphasis added). The trend was mirrored in the language of the US delegation in September 1947, which cited 'criminal acts directed against a racial, national, religious, or *political* group of human beings'. The French, a few months later, offered protection for those targeted 'by reason of their ... opinions', stating that 'whereas in the past crimes of genocide had been committed on racial or religious grounds, it was clear that in the future they would be committed mainly on political grounds' (Schabas 2000, 27, emphasis added; French statement in Kuper 1981, 27).

However, this formulation ran into strong opposition, especially from the Soviet Union and its Polish satellite. The Soviets were intent on demonstrating that genocide was 'organically bound up with Fascism-Nazism and other similar race "theories"' (to quote the Soviets' 'Basic Principles' as presented to the UN subcommittee). But the Soviets and their allies, among others, were also concerned that offering protection to political targets could rebound to their detriment by denying them the right to suppress politically threatening minorities. In the end, the Sixth Committee voted strongly (29:13, nine abstaining) in favour of including political groups. But the staunch protests of the opposing minority proved decisive. Delegates from Egypt, Iran and Uruguay re-opened the question in November 1948 and it became clear to some that to pass the Convention, political groups would have to go. The US delegation, originally a strong supporter of moves to protect political victims, then backed away, declaring that it was doing so 'in a conciliatory spirit and in order to avoid the possibility that the application of the convention to political groups might prevent certain countries from acceding to it' (cited in Schabas 2000, 139).

This settled the matter and, for evidently political reasons, political groups were thereafter frozen out of the Genocide Convention and have remained so ever since. Nonetheless, the clear preference expressed by many countries for including political groups led several, including 'Ethiopia ... Bangladesh, Panama, Costa Rica, Peru, Slovenia and Lithuania', to include political forms of genocide when ratifying the Convention in domestic statutes (Schabas 2000, 141). The first significant legal scholar to explore genocide after the passing of the Convention – the Dutchman Pieter Drost, writing in *The Crime of State* in 1959 – lamented the exclusion of political groups. 'By leaving political and other groups beyond the purported protection', Drost declared, 'the authors of the Convention also left a wide and dangerous loophole for any Government to escape the human duties under the Convention by putting genocide into practice under the cover of executive measures against political or other groups for security, public order or any other reason of state' (Schabas 2000, 144). These groups, and Drost's precise formulation, also factored into the sole substantial attempt to revisit the language of the Genocide Convention – the Whitaker Report of 1985.

The Whitaker Report

The 'Revised and Updated Report on the Question of the Prevention and Punishment of the Crime of Genocide', known as the Whitaker Report after the British parliamentarian who conducted it, was submitted to the UN in July 1985. As the excerpts in the box below indicate, Whitaker acknowledged the contentious issue of the targeting of groups beyond those protected under the Convention. He devoted attention to the issue of 'sexual groups' ('such as women, men, or homosexuals') – a groundbreaking move which I have often cited in my own work on gender and genocide (see Jones 2009). For our purposes, however, what is significant is Whitaker's eloquent caution that excluding 'political and other groups' from 'the purported protection of the Convention offers *a wide and dangerous loophole* which permits any designated group to be exterminated, ostensibly under the excuse that this is for political reasons' (emphasis added; note that the italicized phrase, as well as the entire thought, is a direct lift from Pieter Drost's 1959 language, quoted above). Interestingly, although Whitaker bluntly 'recommended that the definition [of genocide] should be extended to include a sexual group such as women, men, or homosexuals' (his words), he was slightly more recondite on the question of political groups. What he did supply, however, was a remarkably nuanced evaluation of the arguments for and against the inclusion of political groups in the Convention, and one senses his overriding disposition to extend protection to them where possible, for example, through the addition of an optional protocol to the Convention.

Revised and Updated Report on the Question of the Prevention and Punishment of the Crime of Genocide (The Whitaker Report)
Prepared by Mr. B. Whitaker
E/CN.4/Sub.2/1985/6 – 2 July 1985

...

34. A considerable number of commentators on the Convention have also criticized its omission to protect political, economic, sexual or social groups, despite the inclusion in the examples of genocide cited in resolution 96/1 of the destruction of 'racial, religious, political and other groups.'

35. After considerable debate, the Sixth Committee decided not to include political groups among those protected by the Convention. Opposition to the proposal was forcefully led by the Soviet Union's representative. The arguments advanced against the inclusion of political groups were, in essence, that:
(a) a political group had no stable, permanent and clear-cut characteristics in that it did not constitute an inevitable and homogeneous grouping, being based on the will of its members and not on factors independent of that will;
(b) the inclusion of political groups would preclude the acceptance of the Convention by the greatest possible number of States and the acceptance of an international criminal jurisdiction, because it would involve the United Nations in the internal political struggles of each country;
(c) such inclusion would create difficulties for legally established Governments in their preventive actions against subversive elements;
(d) the protection of political groups would raise the question of protection under the Convention for economic and professional groups; and
(e) the protection of political and other groups should be ensured outside the Convention, under national legislation and the Universal Declaration of Human Rights.

36. In support of the inclusion of political groups it was and is argued that it is logical and right for them to be treated like religious groups, a distinguishing mark of both types of group being the common beliefs which unite their members. Specific examples culled from the recent-history of Nazism prove that political groups are perfectly identifiable and, given the persecution to which they were subjected in an age of ideological conflict, protection is essential. During the debate the French representative presciently argued that 'whereas in the past crimes of genocide had been committed on racial or religious grounds, it was clear that in the future they would be committed mainly on political grounds,' and this view received strong support from other representatives. In an era of ideology, people are killed for ideological reasons. Many observers find difficulty in understanding why the principles underlying the Convention would not be equally applicable in the case of mass killings intended to exterminate, for instance, communists or kulaks. In addition, in some cases of horrendous massacre it is not easy to determine which of overlapping political, economic, national, racial, ethnical or religious actors was the determinant one. Is, to take but two examples, the crime of Apartheid primarily racial, political or economic? Or was the selective genocide in Burundi intrinsically political or ethnic in its intent? Most genocide has at least some political tinge, and a considerable number of the Nazis' mass-killings were political. It has been argued that leaving political and other groups beyond the purported protection of the Convention offers a wide and dangerous loophole which permits

> any designated group to be exterminated, ostensibly under the excuse that this is for political reasons.
> 37. One possible solution to the problem of killings of political and other groups which would be considered in the absence of consensus, would be to include this provision in an additional optional protocol.
> http://www.preventgenocide.org/prevent/UNdocs/whitaker/section6.htm.

Recent Legal Innovations and Remaining Quandaries

A couple of recent trends in the international law of genocide and other mass crimes should be noted for the insights they provide into the way the legal winds have been blowing since the great wave of institutional innovation in the 1990s (the criminal tribunals for the former Yugoslavia and Rwanda, the 'mixed tribunals', the International Criminal Court (ICC), and sundry domestic indictments and trials under the principle of universal jurisdiction).

In the first place, we should note that the language and law of genocide has increasingly been complemented – some would say displaced – by an emerging emphasis on *crimes against humanity*. This potent concept, relatively little-studied and little-appreciated until now, offers a number of advantages to a prosecutor seeking to put a perpetrator of mass atrocities behind bars. Most significantly, the 'crimes against humanity' framework, as first codified at Nuremberg and as updated and re-worked in the Rome Statute of the International Criminal Court (1998), prohibits persecution on 'political, racial or religious grounds' (Nuremberg Charter, cited in Van Schaack 1997, 2283) and extends protection to all civilian populations. Its 'extermination' provision, which mirrors the language of the Genocide Convention, *does not require a demonstrated intent to destroy a particular group*. These two elements – limited applicability to targeted groups and the proviso of evident genocidal intent – have proved the most vexing aspects of prosecutions for genocide. With crimes against humanity, it is only required that atrocities be widespread *or* systematic and target civilians in order to be applicable.

Accordingly, though genocide still retains a sense of the 'crime of crimes' (in part because of the memetic power of the word that Raphael Lemkin coined), the framing of crimes against humanity is increasingly preferred. This was evident, for example, in the ICC's original 2008 decision to indict the Sudanese President, Omar al-Bashir – but for crimes against humanity rather than genocide (for which clear evidence of intent was again said to be lacking). I have suggested elsewhere that crimes against humanity prosecutions and intellectual/legal framings may well be the wave of the future (see Jones 2008). Their significance for the protection of political groups merits further investigation.

A related development is that the overriding feature of many high-profile prosecutions or would-be prosecutions, extraditions or would-be extraditions relates to precisely the kind of politically tinged genocidal actions we have considered in this chapter. Chile, Argentina, Guatemala, East Timor, Spain (during and after the Spanish Civil War, the bodies only now being exhumed),[5] Chechnya/Ingushetia, Burma, Iraq ... the list could be extended, but it is hard to deny that the atrocious record of the past couple of decades has featured political persecutions on a scale and of a character comparable to the slaughters generally coded 'ethnic' and 'racial' during the same period.

As I have already mentioned, the temptation to adopt a crimes against humanity framing in lieu of a genocide framing is considerable. But to the extent that genocide is preferred, wriggle-room in the Genocide Convention may exist in the phrase 'to destroy *in whole or in part* a national, ethnical, racial or religious group, as such ...'. Recent prosecutions for genocide in both Spain and Latin America have emphasized that the *part* of a national group targeted for genocide may be politically defined. The trend appears to have begun with the 1997 decision by the crusading Spanish judge Baltasar Garzón to charge the Argentine naval officer Adolfo Scilingo with genocide, based on accusations that Scilingo had thrown political prisoners out of planes into the ocean. Scilingo was convicted and sentenced to 640 years in jail in 2005, but in that decision the Spanish Supreme Court threw out the charge of genocide. Garzón subsequently deployed the genocide framework in his famous but failed attempt to extradite the former Chilean dictator Augusto Pinochet from his house arrest in England.

Since then, the legal cutting edge has shifted to South America. Argentina, which lacks domestic genocide legislation, has used the Genocide Convention's framing in prosecuting military officers. A 2006 decision against Miguel Angel Etchecolatz, the police chief of Buenos Aires under the dictatorship, found him guilty of crimes against humanity for his role in the systematic campaign of repression against Argentina's leftist guerrilla movement in the 1970s. But the tribunal alleged that the crimes against humanity 'had been committed in the context of the "genocide" that took place during those years, in which at least 10,000 guerrilla members and dissidents disappeared. On October 10, 2007, former police chaplain Christian von Wernich received a similar sentence from the same tribunal'. According to Juan E. Mendez, who served a term as Special Adviser on genocide to the UN Secretary General:

> the Etchecolatz and von Wernich sentences represent a good evolution because [the two] were found guilty of crimes against humanity within the context of a genocide, which, in the context of international law, means nothing. But what these sentences add is the recognition of the character of the repression in Argentina, by giving it the name of genocide ... It adds to a tendency and perhaps in the future it can find its way into the body of international law. (International Justice Tribune 2007)

---

5   In October 2008, the Spanish judge Baltasar Garzón launched investigations into the deaths of 100,000 victims of nationalist firing squads and death squads in Franco's Spain, though he later retreated from the inquiry in the face of intense political pressure (see BBC 2009).

Another possible point of entry also exists: the Genocide Convention's protection of *religious* groups. Because perpetrators like Argentina's military right-wingers defined political communism as 'godless', did this mean they were targeting them in significant part as an (ir)religious group? Baltasar Garzón argued along these lines in bringing his genocide case against alleged military perpetrators of the 'Dirty War' against leftist opponents. As Marguerite Feitlowitz notes: 'The generals repeatedly stressed that, "the repression is directed against a minority we do not consider Argentine." The "subversive", likened to the Antichrist, was the destroyer of "Western, Christian civilization" and of the *ser nacional* (the collective national essence, soul, or consciousness)' (Feitlowitz 2000).

Despite such provocative arguments, however, it is hard to avoid a sense that this levering of the Genocide Convention to accommodate political groups is a somewhat inelegant exercise. The more capacious framing of crimes against humanity would seem to render such considerations moot, though this still leaves genocide scholars free, as they always have been, to deploy their own understandings of genocide. I explore some of these scholarly contributions further in the next section.

Whether we prefer a genocide or crimes against humanity framing, we should acknowledge certain moral and practical quandaries in the protection of political groups. One of them was first raised by the Romanian jurist and diplomat Vespasian Pella at the time of the debates over the Genocide Convention: how could protection reasonably be granted to openly Nazi or other fascist (today, perhaps, neo-Nazi or terrorist-affiliated) organizations? But if such groups were to be consigned beyond the pale, why wouldn't a self-interested authority like the Soviet government simply proclaim such forces to be 'fascist', and repress them violently? This wider issue of the limits of liberal freedoms for extremist speech and mobilization has challenged Western and other societies ever since the founding human rights instruments came into being in the mid-twentieth century.

A final question can be raised concerning the well-established international right to self-defence and liberation from a colonial oppressor (see Toros, Chapter 7, this volume). Many colonial resistance movements have used violence against (ethnoreligiously and politically defined) groups of colonizers. At times, this has spilled over into terrorism and vigilantism; at others – such as in Saint-Domingue (Haiti) during the great slave uprising of the late eighteenth century or in Central Europe with the killings and expulsions of ethnic Germans at the end of the Second World War – these may have amounted to cases of *subaltern genocide*, 'genocides by the oppressed' against their oppressors (Robins and Jones 2009). How are we to guarantee the right to resistance, including violent resistance, against occupation and suppression of sovereignty, while stopping short of sanctioning 'righteous' expressions of political-ethnic vengeance? Recent events in Palestine, Iraq, Sri Lanka, Xinjiang and Tibet – again to name only a few cases – attest that this is no abstract issue.

Political Violence in Comparative Genocide Studies

As Raphael Lemkin and, after him, the framers of the Genocide Convention wrestled with the matter of defining genocide, so have scholars of comparative genocide studies sought to re-interpret existing definitions (usually the Convention's) or substitute their own preferred one. Like these forebears, they have engaged with the vexed issue of including or excluding political groups from the agenda. Space considerations do not permit a detailed survey of thinking in the field, but I want to point to a couple of general features that have encouraged or discouraged genocide scholars from extending their framing to political groups.

First, the willingness (or not) to include political groups of course indicates that the scholar is probably moving beyond the language of the Genocide Convention – and therefore substituting language without legal force. In two prominent cases, scholars who accept the Convention as canonical have offered alternative terminology to encompass the targeting of victims on political grounds. This is addressed at the end of the section. The inclusion of political targeting as genocidal per se, however, is limited to those scholars who may feel the Convention has its place as a legal instrument, but consider other framings more useful for analytical and theoretical purposes.

I am one of them. My personally preferred definition of genocide adapts (slightly but significantly) the one advanced by Steven Katz in his epic study, *The Holocaust in Historical Context, Volume 1*. Katz's essential purpose was show that the Jewish Holocaust was 'phenomenologically unique' in human history, and for this reason he stressed that genocide must involve intent to 'murder a group *in its totality*'. But he wished to allow, theoretically, for something approaching the (allegedly) totalistic extermination campaign of the Holocaust to recur in the future – and against just about any definable human group, which was important in drawing me to his language. Katz thus defined genocide as:

> The actualization of the intent, however successfully carried out, to murder in its totality any national, ethnic, racial, religious, *political*, social, gender or economic group, as these groups are defined by the perpetrator, by whatever means. (Katz 1994, 131, emphasis added)

In my own work, I substitute 'in whole or in substantial part' for 'in its totality'. What I otherwise admire about the framing is not only its inclusiveness, but its emphasis on the *perpetrator's* definition of the group, as noted earlier. Other scholars from the dawn of comparative genocide studies have stressed the importance of including political groups, or at least not arbitrarily excluding them. So Pieter Drost, who in his 1959 work had eloquently stressed the vulnerabilities of political victims, defined genocide as 'the deliberate destruction of physical life of individual human beings by reason of their membership of *any human collectivity as such*'. Irving Louis Horowitz, in his 1976 work *Taking Lives: Genocide and State Power*, at least understood politics as essential to the genocidal enterprise: genocide 'functions as a fundamental political policy to assure [sic] conformity and participation of the citizenry'. In a re-formulation offered in 1996, Horowitz extended protection to any 'innocent people' subjected to 'structural and systematic destruction'.[6]

Leo Kuper's field-defining 1981 work, *Genocide: Its Political Use in the Twentieth Century*, gave the game away in the title. In some of the most insightful and influential comments on the subject, Kuper strongly regretted 'the exclusion of political groups from the list of groups protected' in the Genocide Convention. This was a 'major omission' in light of the fact that 'in the contemporary world, political differences are at the very least as significant a basis for massacre and annihilation as racial, national, ethnic or religious differences. Then too, the genocides against racial, national, ethnic or religious groups are generally a consequence of, or intimately related to, political conflict'. For pragmatic reasons, he felt it was not 'helpful to create new definitions of genocide' when the Genocide Convention 'might become the basis for some effective action, however limited'. However, in his seminal book, he devoted full attention to political mass killings as he perceived them: 'it would vitiate the analysis to exclude political groups', and thus he chose to 'refer freely ... to liquidating or exterminatory actions against them' (Kuper 1981, 39).

Perhaps no genocide scholar since Kuper has so focused on the targeting of political groups.[7] But many, apart from Steven Katz and myself, have incorporated them into their definitions of genocide. For Jack Nusan Porter, publishing in 1982, genocide was 'the deliberate destruction, in whole or in part ... of a racial, sexual, religious, tribal or *political* minority'. In 1987, John L. Thompson and Gail A. Quetz stressed the need to protect 'a social collectivity' against destruction 'by whatever agents, with whatever intentions, by purposive actions which fall outside the recognized conventions of legitimate warfare'.

The Cambodia 'Autogenocide' Debate

A critical moment in the evolution of genocide scholarship on political violence was the debate over the mass atrocities inflicted by the Khmer Rouge regime of Cambodia between 1975 and 1978.[8] The crux of the matter, intellectually speaking,

---

6   These definitions, and those that follow, are compiled on pp. 15–18 of Jones 2006.
7   Mention should be made, however, of Van Schaack's important 1996–1997 article, cited above. Van Schaack argues 'that the Genocide Convention is not the sole authority on the crime of genocide. Rather, a higher law exists: The prohibition of genocide represents the paradigmatic *jus cogens* norm, a customary and peremptory norm of international law from which no derogation is permitted'. She accordingly suggests that 'when faced with mass killings evidencing the intent to eradicate political groups in whole or in part, domestic and international adjudicatory bodies should apply the *jus cogens* prohibition of genocide and invoke the Genocide Convention vis-à-vis signatories only insofar as it provides practical procedures for enforcement and ratification' (Van Schaack 1996–1997, 2261–2).
8   For a fine analysis of the Cambodian events and their aftermath in an international-

was that although the Khmer Rouge conducted classically genocidal campaigns against ethnic minorities (notably Vietnamese and Muslim Chams), the majority of its violence was directed against 'fellow Khmers', i.e. members of the same ethnonational grouping. Was it then genocidal? Was it *autogenocidal* – the frankly infelicitous term (suggestive of collective suicide) that was proposed to resolve the conundrum? Or were only certain aspects of it genocidal – the intentional targeting of ethnonational and religious minorities – while the remaining acts of slaughter were perhaps 'exterminatory', under the crimes against humanity provisions reviewed earlier?

This final option seems both to be most in keeping with the Genocide Convention (whose 'drafters did not appear to have contemplated the mass killing of one segment of a group by another segment of that same group': Ratner and Abrams 2001, 287). It is also the one preferred by the field's leading Cambodia scholar, Ben Kiernan of Yale University, who hews to the Genocide Convention definition but includes 'extermination' in the subtitle of his magnum opus, *Blood and Soil* (2007). Most scholars, though, have refrained from making such fine distinctions. For the most part, and aided by the phenomenon of the film *The Killing Fields* in the 1980s,[9] Cambodia has been incorporated as a canonical case of genocide alongside the Jewish Holocaust, the Armenian genocide and the Rwandan apocalypse of 1994. Relatively few distinctions seem to be made among its victims, most of whom are assumed to be victims of the political paranoia and fanaticism of the Khmer Rouge, with occasional nods in the direction of their ethnic animosities. The term 'autogenocide', meanwhile, has largely fallen by the wayside – and deservedly so.[10]

Alternative Framings: 'Politicide' and 'Democide'

I mentioned earlier that scholars who accept the Genocide Convention as a broad reference point have occasionally sought to *supplement* a genocide framework with terminology that incorporates political killings. The two most prominent of these are *politicide*, coined by Barbara Harff, and R.J. Rummel's concept of *democide*. Harff and Gurr, both political scientists, acknowledged that political killings were ubiquitous around the world. They proposed the term 'politicide' – killings of individuals because of 'their hierarchical position or political opposition to the regime and dominant groups' – to supplement 'genocide'. Harff, in a 2003

---

legal context, see Ratner and Abrams 2001, 267–345.

9 According to Elizabeth Becker: 'In a matter of months, *The Killing Fields* [released in 1984] catapulted Cambodia from Cold War politics to mass culture. Black-pajamaed Khmer Rouge joined the brown-shirted Nazis as recognizable villains of the twentieth century. The term killing fields became part of the American vocabulary' (Becker 1998, 459).

10 In charging former Argentine military officials in 1996, Baltasar Garzón also referred to the events of the 'Dirty War' in Argentina as an 'auto-genocide.' See Feitlowitz 2000.

re-formulation, deployed both genocide and politicide to cover acts amounting to 'the promotion, execution, and/or implied consent of sustained policies by governing elites or their agents – or, in the case of civil war, either of the contending authorities – that are intended to destroy, in whole or part, a communal, *political, or politicized ethnic group*'.

Rummel, also a political scientist, established himself as the premier (though politically highly partisan) quantifier of *democide*, the term he devised to refer to 'the murder of any person or people by a government, including genocide, politicide, and mass murder' (Rummel 1997). Reflecting his right-wing political sympathies, he was especially attentive to the immense atrocities inflicted by communist regimes like those of Stalin, Mao and Pol Pot, with tens of millions killed in political purges and campaigns against 'enemies of the people'. He was far less persuasive in addressing (or, rather, failing to address) the politically tinged slaughters inflicted and abetted by capitalist and ostensibly democratic polities, notably his own country, the USA. The equation of democracy with peace is essential to Rummel's thesis and it leads him systematically to downplay 'democratic' depredations, suggesting that they occur only when delinquent individuals occasionally take power. But, as I contended and documented in 2006, it is the USA, the world's leading democracy, that in the post-Second World War period has been far and away the most belligerent and destructive of the world's nations, internationally speaking. Among its greatest crimes were the saturation bombings and ecocidal assaults on the countries of Indochina in the 1960s and the 1970s. But for Vietnam, where probably two million and as many as three million people were killed, Rummel calculates that 'the US democide in Vietnam seems to have killed at least 4,000 Vietnamese civilians, POWs, or enemy seeking to surrender, maybe as many as 10,000 Vietnamese' (Rummel 1994, 277)! Despite Rummel's useful contributions, then, his treatment of favoured states' actions was disappointingly patchy and cursory; he displayed, as Mark Levene has argued, 'an almost wilful myopia about mass murders committed directly or indirectly by liberal democratic regimes' (Levene 2005b, 54).

Genocide, War and Political Violence

One of the most fertile lines of inquiry in recent genocide studies, conducted by a range of political scientists, historians and sociologists, concerns the intimate connection between war and genocide. If war is the continuation of politics by other means, to oversimplify Clausewitz, then genocide often has been viewed as a continuation of war by other means. In particular, according to the sociologist Martin Shaw, 'degenerate war' – war without rules, targeting civilians not coincidentally but essentially – frequently spills over into genocide (Shaw 2003, 26–9). The 'degenerate war' concept, and its connection with politically inspired mass killing, seems especially relevant to understanding the African conflicts and genocides of the past couple of decades. Complex conglomerations of actors combine in multi-faceted conflicts, like those of eastern Congo, Sudan and Somalia, to produce civilian death tolls that (in Congo's case at least) surpass anything seen since the Second World War. The emphasis here is on the breakdown of formal military-political hierarchies and their replacement by undisciplined, gratuitously cruel bands of paramilitaries, freebooters, child soldiers and so on.

Such is the new face of war, reminiscent in its banditry and savage atrocity of pre-modern war-making. But there is also war as waged by colonial actors against 'primitive' and 'heathen' peoples, often with genocidal consequences,[11] and war as a crucial aspect of nation-state formation. Michael Mann's sprawling study *The Dark Side of Democracy* stresses the link between the emergence of the modern nation-state and the explosive increase in genocides since that time (Mann 1999). Mark Levene has conducted the most penetrating study of the links among nationalism, war and genocide in his two-volume (so far) *Genocide in the Age of the Nation State* (Levene 2005a, 2005b). Indeed, as the subtitle of volume 2 suggests – *The Rise of the West and the Coming of Genocide* – genocide, at least in its modern form, *arrives* with the national consolidation and imperial expansion of the West. Levene considers a pivotal moment to have been the slaughter by French revolutionaries of the people of the Vendée region (1793–1799), with the victims designated as both political (counter-revolutionary) and ethnoreligious enemies. In a full-length monograph, Reynald Secher has explored the Vendée case in similar terms (Secher 2003).

The Vendée also serves as a classic early-modern case of *counter-insurgency as genocide*. This theme has increasingly preoccupied genocide scholars, notably political scientists like Benjamin Valentino (2004) and Manus Midlarsky (2005), along with specialists on key cases like Guatemala, Rwanda and Darfur – all genocides that seem inexplicable without reference to the fear and hatred engendered by confrontation with politically 'subversive' foes, and the atrocities associated with military campaigns (including the waging of degenerate war) against it. Nonetheless, in each of these cases, perpetrators also constructed victims as an ethnonational 'Other', and it is this *blend* of identifications which underpinned the genocides.

The ethnic dimension remains something of an enabling condition for most genocide scholars. While they may be able to incorporate campaigns of political killing if they are on an epic scale (Stalin, Hitler, Mao), there seems to be a preference for cases where the more familiar ethnic variable is also evident. It is notable, for example, that Guatemala has received extended attention in the field, but tends to be depicted as a contemporary manifestation of (ethnic-racial) genocide against indigenous peoples rather than mass killings of diverse sectors based on political and ethnic identifiers that overlapped, but also operated independently (e.g. with the death-squad killings of tens of thousands of urban *ladino* opponents of the regime). The killings occurring at the same time as the Guatemalan genocide (1978–1983) in neighbouring El Salvador were of a similar scale and barbaric nature – these two states, in fact, constitute the worst instances of mass atrocity anywhere in the Americas during the twentieth century. But El Salvador has not,

---

11   The most important collection is Moses 2008.

to my knowledge, been incorporated in a systematic way in the literature. This may partly be because the killings were so intimately assisted and directed by the Reagan regime in the USA,[12] but also because the ethnic variable seems muted or marginal. It is an oversight that merits correction, along with numerous other cases that are still underexplored in the literature. They include Argentina under the generals, Indonesia during the military coup and anti-communist slaughter of 1965–1966, Uganda under Idi Amin, Ethiopia under the Dergue, and the state terror that waxes and wanes in present-day Iraq. Sadly, the list could easily be extended.

Conclusion

The analysis presented in this chapter suggests that the issue of genocide as political violence, and political violence as genocide, has been one of the knottiest conundrums that framers of both genocide law and genocide theory have confronted. How they have chosen to address political groups – by excluding them, incorporating them or assigning them to a separate category of atrocity – says much about the framer's vision of genocide and the atrocities it encompasses. We have seen that the subject has become more pressing with time, as political killings have increasingly come to dominate the mass atrocities of the age. But we have also seen that any concept of 'political killings' or, for that matter, 'ethnic' and 'racial' killings, needs to be unpacked and problematized. Areas of blending and spillover among variables are not only critical to understanding, but are perhaps *definitional* to genocide. In other words, humanity seems never to have been confronted with a case of mass atrocity derived purely from a group's identification by another as exclusively an 'ethnic', 'national', 'racial', 'religious' or 'political' enemy – where these labels can even survive searching inquiry into their substance and viability.

An eclectic approach thus seems warranted – one that evaluates certain motivations and strategies of genocidal perpetrators as primarily 'political', but remains alive to the diverse ways that political identities (especially imputed ones) are mapped onto ethnonational and religious identities.[13] The best justification for doing so is the opportunity to develop more nuanced models of genocide, which may lead to more effective and multi-faceted strategies of intervention and prevention. Any anti-genocide scholar or activist would be foolish to ignore the insights to be gleaned from a careful consideration of the political element in these campaigns of wanton human destruction.

---

12   Vital sources include Bonner 1984; McClintock 1984; and Americas Watch 1991.
13   I have argued that 'a given campaign of mass killing can easily be labelled as genocidal, democidal, politicidal, eliticidal, and gendercidal all at once – with each of these designations representing an analytical cut that exposes one aspect of the campaign and serves to buttress comparative studies of a particular "cide"' (Jones 2004, 260).

References

Americas Watch 1991. *El Salvador's Decade of Terror: Human Rights since the Assassination of Archbishop Romero*. New Haven, CT: Yale University Press.
BBC 2009. 'Profile: Judge Baltasar Garzon', 9 September. http://news.bbc.co.uk/2/hi/europe/3085482.stm [accessed 25 June 2012].
Becker, E. 1998. *When the War Was Over: Cambodia and the Khmer Rouge Revolution*. Jackson, TN: Public Affairs.
Bonner, R. 1984. *Weakness and Deceit: U.S. Policy and El Salvador*. New York: Times Books.
Cooper, J. 2008. *Raphael Lemkin and the Struggle for the Genocide Convention*. London: Polity.
Feitlowitz, M. 2000. 'The Pinochet Prosecution: The Genocide Controversy. Crimes of War', May. Website no longer available. PDF available from author: mfeitlowitz@bennington.edu.
Gerlach, C. 2006. 'Extremely Violent Societies: An Alternative to the Concept of Genocide', *Journal of Genocide Research*, 8(4), 455–71.
Harff, B. and Gurr, T.R. 1988. 'Toward Empirical Theory of Genocides and Politicides: Identification and Measurement of Cases Since 1945', *International Studies Quarterly*, 32(3), 359–71.
Herf, J. 2006. *The Jewish Enemy: Nazi Propaganda during World War II and the Holocaust*. Cambridge, MA: Belknap Press.
International Justice Tribune 2007. 'Latin America Extends the Definition of Genocide, Radio Netherlands Worldwide', 5 November. http://www.rnw.nl/print/22179 [accessed 25 June 2012].
Jones, A. 2004. 'Problems of Gendercide: A Response to Stein and Carpenter', in A. Jones (ed.), *Gendercide and Genocide*. Nashville, TN: Vanderbilt University Press.
Jones, A. 2006. *Genocide: A Comprehensive Introduction*. London: Routledge.
Jones, A. 2008. *Crimes Against Humanity: A Beginner's Guide*. London: OneWorld.
Jones, A. 2009. *Gender Inclusive: Essays on Violence, Men, and Feminist International Relations*. London: Routledge.
Katz, S.T. 1994. *The Holocaust in Historical Context, Volume 1: The Holocaust and Mass Death before the Modern Age*. Oxford: Oxford University Press.
Kiernan, B. 2007. *Blood and Soil: A World History of Genocide and Extermination from Sparta to Darfur*. New Haven, CT: Yale University Press.
Kuper, L. 1981. *Genocide: Its Political Use in the Twentieth Century*. Harmondsworth: Penguin.
Lemkin, R., 1944. 'Genocide', in *Axis Rule in Occupied Europe, Carnegie Endowment for International Peace*. Available online at http://www.preventgenocide.org/lemkin/AxisRule1944-1.htm [accessed 25 June 2012].
Levene, M. 2005a. *Genocide in the Age of the Nation State, Volume 1: The Meaning of Genocide*. London: I.B. Tauris.
Levene, M. 2005b. *Genocide in the Age of the Nation State, Volume 2: The Rise of the West and the Coming of Genocide*. London: I.B. Tauris.

McClintock, M. 1984. The *American Connection, Volume 1: State Terror and Popular Resistance in El Salvador*. London: Zed Books.
Mann, M. 1999. *The Dark Side of Democracy: Explaining Ethnic Cleansing*. Cambridge: Cambridge University Press.
Midlarsky, M.I. 2005. *The Killing Trap: Genocide in the Twentieth Century*. Cambridge: Cambridge University Press.
Moses, A.D. 2008. *Empire, Colony, Genocide: Conquest, Occupation, and Subaltern Resistance in World History*. Oxford: Berghahn Books.
Ratner, S.R. and Abrams, J.S. 2001. *Accountability for Human Rights Atrocities in International Law: Beyond the Nuremberg Legacy*, 2nd edn. Oxford: Oxford University Press.
Robins, N.A. and Jones, A. (eds) 2009. *Genocides by the Oppressed: Subaltern Genocide in Theory and Practice*. Bloomington, IN: Indiana University Press.
Rummel, R.J. 1994. *Death by Government*. Piscataway, NJ: Transaction Publishers.
Rummel, R.J. 1997. 'Statistics of Democide'. http://www.hawaii.edu/powerkills/SOD.CHAP6.HTM [accessed 25 June 2012].
Schabas, W.A. 2000. *Genocide in International Law: The Crime of Crimes*. Cambridge: Cambridge University Press.
Secher, R. 2003. *A French Genocide: The Vendée*, trans. George Holoch. Notre Dame, IN: University of Notre Dame Press.
Shaw, M. 2003. *War & Genocide*. London: Polity.
Shaw, M. 2007. *What is Genocide?* London: Polity.
Valentino, B.A. 2004. *Final Solutions: Genocide and Mass Killing in the Twentieth Century*. Ithaca, NY: Cornell University Press.
Van Schaack, B. 1997. 'The Crime of Political Genocide: Repairing the Convention's Blind Spot', *Yale Law Journal*, 106, 2259–91.Wiedl, K.N. 2006. *The Hama Massacre: Reasons, Supporters of the Rebellion, Consequences*. GRIN Verlag.

War as Political Violence

R. Gerald Hughes[1]

War is a social activity as old as civilisation itself. To refer to so unpleasant an activity as being 'social' is something of a misnomer, but nearly all societies have known war (Keegan 1994; Keeley 1996). Raymond Aron (1905–1983) discussed the biological and psychological roots of war and concluded 'that man is by *nature* dangerous to man' (Aron 1981: 344). Most famously, war was defined by the Prussian philosopher of war, Carl von Clausewitz (1780–1831), as 'a continuation of political intercourse, carried on with other means' (Clausewitz 1976: 87). This chapter will concern itself with certain aspects of the evolution of the conduct and study of war. It will deal with inter-state and sub-state conflict (the latter encompassing civil wars). It will also highlight a number of major debates about the history of warfare and outline a preliminary approach for those wishing to study it.

The waging of war has led to an ever-increasing requirement to claim just cause to an ever wider audience (von Elbe 1939; Fotion 2007). War is normally justified in the name of attaining (and then maintaining) peace. Such aspirations have been reflected across the centuries. In the first century AD, the Roman historian Tacitus criticised the Roman Empire on this score by the device of placing a comment in the mouth of Calgacus, a defiant British chief: 'To robbery, butchery and rapine, they give the lying name of "government"; they create a desolation and call it peace' (*Agricola*, 30; Tacitus 1970: 81). The Romans waged warfare in ruthless fashion and Julius Caesar (100 BC–44 BC), a great general in his own right, understood and exploited the inherently political nature of war to great effect (Caesar 2008).

In the twentieth century, the First World War, often invoked as *the* war to have finally demonstrated the futility of large-scale intra-state warfare, was described by US President Woodrow Wilson as the war 'to end all wars' (Zinn 2003: 364). Following the Second World War, US Strategic Air Command (which, along with Soviet strategic forces, was capable of ending all life on earth) adopted the motto 'Peace is our profession' (Sagan and Turco 1990: 207). Many see the adoption of such slogans as, at best, hypocritical and, at worst, designed to serve the ends of those who would perpetuate the notion that war is a natural state of affairs for

---

1 The author wishes to thank Ken Booth, Peter Lambert, Simon Rushton and Björn Weiler for their helpful comments on this chapter.

humankind. In their writings, philosophers of war such as Sun Tzu, Machiavelli and Clausewitz have operated on the implicit assumption that if societies wish to eradicate war, then it is their own responsibility to do so. This abrogation of responsibility for initiating war is often encapsulated in the phrase 'War is hell' (usually accredited to US General William T. Sherman (1820–1891)). In other words, the morality of actually going to war lies outside of the responsibility of those tasked with waging war. In the nuclear age this has mattered as never before in human history. As Albert Einstein noted: 'Bullets kill men, but atomic bombs kill cities. A tank is a defence against a bullet, but there is no defence against a weapon that can destroy civilization' (Granoff 2000: 1413). Although technological advances have always stood at the very centre of war's evolution (McNeil 1982), ethical attitudes are also omnipresent. US General Omar Bradley stated in the late 1940s:

> We live in an age of nuclear giants and ethical infants, in a world that has achieved brilliance without wisdom, power without conscience. We have solved the mystery of the atom and forgotten the lessons of the Sermon on the Mount. We know more about war than we know about peace, more about dying than we know about living. (Granoff 2000: 1441)

The existence of nuclear weapons has not eliminated war, although it has changed the lens through which war as a tool of policy is viewed. Throughout history, the powerful have presented war as both a necessary last resort and as a social activity conducted with at least some reference to societal norms. Its persistence has spurred pacifists to argue that only an absolutist position will ever end wars (Roberts 2005: 330–335). Those actually waging wars have *always* been seen to have a responsibility to behave according to the norms of their society (or at least that is the high-minded expectation at the outset of wars). Thus, American excesses in Vietnam were seen by many contemporaries in the USA as 'war crimes' (Nelson 2003). German conduct in the war against the Soviet Union between 1941 and 1945, on the other hand, was fully reflective of the violent racist ideology that characterised the National Socialist state (Bartov 2001).

The conduct of war often transforms societies and individuals alike. The First World War, for example, saw four years of slaughter and massive social and political upheaval. This destroyed four empires and propelled the ideologies of fascism and communism to global prominence in a challenge to the international order (Stevenson 1991). As Trotsky noted, 'war is the locomotive of history' (Bousquet 2009: 78). Indeed, since war is omnipresent in history, it has long been institutionalised as humankind has sought to regulate it as least as much as it has tried to understand it.

The moral compass which the Western tradition in warfare has adopted is the doctrine of military ethics known as 'just war' theory. This provides the justification for war (*casus belli*). The roots of this theory are complex, but it is derived from the thinking of classical scholars, such as Plato and Cicero, and that of later Christian theologians such as Augustine and Thomas Aquinas. The theory of 'just war', well established by the Middle Ages, eventually formed a major constituent of the rationale for war-making in any political community (Russell 1977). In essence, the doctrine of the 'just war' rests on *jus ad bellum* (justification for war) and *jus in bello* (just conduct within wars) (Childress 1978). These continue to inform many of the public debates about war-making (Brough, Lango and van der Linden 2007) – although they are rarely invoked directly today.

In the modern world, war has come to be 'regulated' by so-called 'laws of war'. The Geneva (1864, 1906, 1929 and 1949) and the Hague Conventions (1899 and 1907) represent the most prominent examples in international law (Roberts and Guelff 2000: 59–370). In contemporary societies, debates about what constitutes *casus belli* have often led to grotesque simplifications (especially in the highly de-militarised societies of Western Europe). For liberal internationalists, just cause can simply mean that approval from the United Nations will grant any given war legitimacy as it will be seen to have accorded with the notion of the *jus ad bellum* (Lango 2005). Against this, for the more traditionally minded, a simple demonstration to the people (*demos*), or their law-makers, of a real national security need will be sufficient to justify going to war (Brook and Epstein 2006).[2]

In the study of war, the criteria for chronological or thematic demarcation of wars and warfare vary. Categorisation can be done by technology, political organisation or the duration of the wars themselves (e.g. Childs 1982; Harari 2007; Urban 2006). There are certain constants in the study of war but, as Clausewitz notes, 'every age had its own kind of war, its own limiting conditions, and its own peculiar preconceptions' (Clausewitz 1976: 593). The era of ancient warfare (seen to have ended with the fall of the Western Roman Empire in AD 476) saw the institutionalisation of the state as the organising entity for the conduct of warfare (Bradford 2001). The success of political structures was the key to success in the military sphere and Ancient Egypt, for instance, owed its longevity to this (Spalinger 2005). The ancient world also saw the specialisation of certain types of fighting men (most basically, infantry, cavalry and naval warriors) and the beginnings of an informed literature on warfare (both in terms of its history and its conduct). Thus, the Greek scholar Herodotus (c.484 BC–c.425 BC), dubbed the 'father of history' by Cicero (Herodotus 2004: notes, 505), wrote extensively about the Greek wars against Persia (Herodotus 2004).

The ancient era also gave rise to a number of other studies of war that have stood the test of time and remain in print to this day. Most notable here is the history of the Peloponnesian War written by the first historian of war, Thucydides (c.460 BC–c.395 BC) (Thucydides 1974). This war, fought in Greece between 431 BC and 404 BC, pitted Athenian naval power against Spartan military dexterity and has fascinated scholars ever since (Hanson 2005). Much of the reason for this continued engagement lies in the abilities of Thucydides as storyteller, historian and military

---

2   In Vietnam, for example, US policy-makers justified escalating their military presence by virtue of the (supposedly defensive) Congressional Gulf of Tonkin Resolution of August 1964 (Moise 1996).

analyst (Dover 1983). No mere chronicler, Thucydides can be regarded as a thinker in a philosophical tradition that stretches to the present day (Murray 1997a).

Whilst this chapter largely focuses on Europe, it is important to remember the very great developments made in ancient warfare elsewhere on the globe – especially in China. Chinese military thought was recorded and developed by Sun Tzu in his classic *The Art of War* (written c.500 BC). Sun Tzu's book is laden with succinct maxims. The most notable of these is that 'all warfare is based on deception' (Sun Tzu 2006: 64), which is a principle underpinning a great deal of subsequent military thought (Bellamy 1990: 28–9). Sun Tzu also stressed the importance of intelligence, manoeuvre, morale, political-military demarcation and national unity. He was an acute observer of society and he advocated the limitation of the duration of wars and, if at all possible, of bending an enemy to one's will without recourse to force (Sun Tzu 2006: 63).

Certain concepts of war, as developed by Thucydides and Sun Tzu, have continuing contemporary relevance. The late Michael Handel, an outstanding scholar of military thought, argued 'that the logic of strategy and waging war is universal rather than parochial, cultural, or regional' (Handel 2001: xxiv).[3] In addition to certain philosophical approaches, specific battles and campaigns are held up as 'must study' classics in the history of war. The battle tactic of double-envelopment, enacted by Hannibal's Carthaginian army in their crushing victory over the Romans at Cannae in 216 BC, is a notable example here (Goldsworthy 2000). This battle, a masterpiece of generalship, continues to influence military thinking to this day (Rothenberg 1986; Hanson 2008: 48–9). General Alfred von Schlieffen (Chief of the Imperial German General Staff, 1891–1905) asserted that: 'A battle of annihilation can be carried out today according to the same plan devised by Hannibal in long forgotten times' (Curtis 2003: 59). This formed the basis of his Schlieffen Plan, designed to deal with enemies on two fronts (Foley 2003: 208–18) by knocking out France in six weeks and allowing Germany to turn east to face Russia (Ritter 1958; Foley 2006).[4] General Dwight D. Eisenhower believed that: 'Every ground commander seeks the battle of annihilation; so far as conditions permit, he tries to duplicate in modern war the classic example of Cannae' (Jarymowycz 2008: 17). The coalition commander in the Gulf War of 1991, Norman Schwarzkopf, regarded Cannae as the greatest military manoeuvre in history and the liberation of Kuwait employed a strategy that drew heavily on the long-established lessons of Cannae (Boot 2006: 338). As General Leroy Suddath, a contemporary of Schwarzkopf, later recalled: 'Norm's favourite battle was Cannae ... It was the first real war of annihilation, the kind Norman wanted to fight' (Engler Anderson, Fischer and van Voorst 1991).

The fall of the Western Roman Empire and the advent of what was traditionally termed the 'Dark Ages' in Europe did not diminish the prevalence of warfare. For many centuries the orthodoxy held that, since the West had renounced certain

---

3   Handel notes that Mao Zedong shared this view (Mao Zedong 1972).
4   Hence Bismarck's assertion that: 'The secret of politics' was to 'Make a good treaty with Russia' (Taylor 1955: 210).

tenets of 'civilised' behavioral norms, warfare logically became more 'barbaric'. For those adhering to the notion of a 'barbarisation' of warfare, the Vikings, highly effective in war, were held up as a case in point. This negative view of the Vikings began to be challenged in the West only in the nineteenth century (Palmer 2005: 21). This was later accompanied by increasing criticism of the term 'Dark Ages' for the manner in which it encouraged the falsehood that civilisation had somehow ceased with the fall of Rome (Wells 2008). In truth, the Vikings were no more barbaric than the Romans and their main crime, as in the case of the Moors in the Mediterranean, was to have come from outside a dominant West European Christian community and to have achieved military success against it (Griffith 1995). Confident of their moral and martial superiority, the West Europeans saw Moors, Vikings and others as only ever being able to prevail by violating the laws of war – which were, of course, defined by the Christian West and the Church of Rome's theological worldview (Elias 1978).[5]

From 989 AD onwards, the Roman Catholic Church attempted to limit violence in society by sanctions applied in accordance with the auspices of the so-called Peace and Truce of God. The Church adhered to versions of this arrangement until the thirteenth century. Of course, the medieval behavioural norms of warfare and the standards of conduct demanded of Christian warriors were rarely applied to the treatment of non-believers. The Second Lateran Council of 1139 supposedly outlawed the use of crossbows by Christians against Christians proclaiming that: 'We prohibit under anathema [excommunication] that murderous art of crossbowmen and archers, which is hated by God, to be employed against Christians and Catholics from now on' (Alberigo and Tanner 1990: 187). The conduct of warfare with a clearly defined ethical base eventually ossified into the code known as chivalry (Keen 2005).[6] In modern terms we might also see such a code as glorifying the conduct of war (and raising the social status of the warrior class to the kind of heights it had enjoyed in ancient Greece and Rome). Originating from about the year 1000 AD, chivalry was intimately related with the prevailing political-social organisation in Western Europe, Feudalism (Bouchard 1998). Although most often associated with warfare, chivalry actually provided a moral and religious compass for life (Kaeuper 2009), superficially similar to that of the contemporary warrior caste of the Samurai in Japan (Farris 1995). By the later Middle Ages, adherents to the code of chivalry were expected to conduct themselves with the utmost virtue in their everyday lives. In the heat of battle, such standards were often cast aside (although one might usefully speculate as to the prospect of limiting violence in war in any era), for, as Cicero wrote in 52 BC: 'In times of war, the laws fall silent' (Cicero 1931: 16–17).

The Middle Ages saw great changes in the conduct of warfare, not least because of enormous technological advances. The evolution of weaponry had an effect on

---

5 Although, of course, it should be remembered that the destruction of church property and violence against Christians were central features of war-making by the Moors and the Vikings.
6 From the French word *chevalier* (i.e. one who rides a horse).

tactics which were, in turn, increasingly sophisticated. Technology, when wedded to a studied awareness of the battlefield space, led to some spectacular military victories. During the Hundred Years' War (1337–1453), the English inflicted three particularly crushing defeats on the French by the skilful deployment of the longbow at Crécy, Poitiers and Agincourt (in 1346, 1356 and 1415 respectively). Advances in military technology (DeVries 1992), along with the relative strength of European state structures, also ensured that, by the early modern period, the Christian West would eventually enjoy a real advantage over non-European opponents (Parker 1996). The impact of technology upon warfare is reflected in a burgeoning literature on so-called Revolutions in Military Affairs (RMAs) (Gray 2002). There are any number of these 'revolutions' and there are a number of debates as to whether or not the term is a useful one, given its highly subjective nature. In 1997 Williamson Murray listed what he termed 'Possible RMAs' (Murray 1997b: 70).

Table 18.1   Revolutions in military affairs (RMA), AD 1301–2000

Dates	RMA	Nature of RMA
1301–1400	The longbow	*Cultural*
1401–1500	Gunpowder	*Technological and financial*
1501–1600	Fortifications	*Architectural and financial*
1601–1700	Dutch and Swedish military reforms	*Tactical, organisational and cultural*
	French military reforms	*Tactical, organisational and administrative*
1601–1800	Naval warfare	*Administrative, social, financial and technological*
1701–1800	British Industrial Revolution	*Financial, organisational and conceptual*
1789–1815	French Revolution	*Ideological and social*
1701–1900	Industrial Revolution	*Financial, technological, organisational and cultural*
1861–1865	American Civil War	*Ideological, technological, administrative and operational*
1861–1900	Naval warfare	*Technological, administrative and cultural*
1801–2000	Advances in medicine	*Technological and organisational*
1914–1918	First World War: combined arms	*Tactical, conceptual, technological and scientific*
1939–1943	German *Blitzkrieg*	*Tactical, operational, conceptual and organisational*
1939–1945	British, Japanese and American naval warfare by means of aircraft carrier	*Conceptual, technological and operational*
1942–1945	Strategic air war	*Technological, conceptual, tactical and scientific*

1901–2000	Submarine warfare	*Technological, scientific and tactical*
	Amphibious warfare	*Conceptual, tactical and operational*
	Intelligence in war	*Conceptual, political and ideological*
	Nuclear weaponry	*Technological*
	People's war	*Ideological, political and conceptual*

At certain times, the impact of technology (and the subsequent focus on this by commentators and scholars) has obscured the unchanging requirements for the prosecution of war to a victorious end. The Middle Ages saw the English crown attempt to maximise its potential as a military power by rigorous organisation (Prestwich 1980, 1999, 2004, 2007).[7] Unsurprisingly, domestic stability and good government were key factors in the maintenance of a formidable English war machine. This was exemplified during the reign of Edward I between 1272 and 1307 (Prestwich 1972; Carpenter 2003: 466–94). A superior army could not, however, guarantee victory. Poor leadership and inferior strategy could still lead to disaster as the English, under the unimpressive Edward II, learned against the Scots at Bannockburn in 1314 (Brown 2008: 115–36). This battle, which led to the recognition of Scottish independence by the English (Brown 2008: 171–91), can be seen as a 'decisive battle' in that it attained far-reaching *political* ends by *military* means.[8] Such events live long in the national memory and Bannockburn occupies a place in the Scottish national psyche akin to that occupied by the Battles of the Marathon and Salamis (where Persian invasions were defeated in 490 and 480 BC respectively) in the collective memory of the Greek people (Green 1996).

The evolution of the nation-state in the early modern period (i.e. from c.1500 AD onwards) only accelerated the trend towards making security (and warfighting) the central rationale for the ever-more powerful state (Elias 2000: 387–97). Niccolò Machiavelli recognised this and, in 1521, published a companion volume to *The Prince* entitled *The Art of War* (Machiavelli 2001). In the eighteenth century Voltaire (1694–1778) asserted that 'Machiavelli taught Europe the art of war; it had long been practised, without being known' (Machiavelli 2001: introduction, xxxii). Machiavelli's work certainly represents an important reference point in the evolution of thinking about war, and his legacy is obvious in the later writings of Clausewitz and others (Gilbert 1986: 31). By the sixteenth century, all of the major powers of Europe had acquired formidable military capabilities, often specialising in areas of particular strength (Black 2002). Spain was the superpower of the day – the military capabilities of its infantry were legendary (Parker 1998). But the failure of the Spanish state to provide the necessary infrastructure for maintaining its hegemony meant that it would find itself surpassed by France in the seventeenth

---

7   Although it was France that eventually won the Hundred Years' War (Sumption 1999, 2001).
8   By contrast, the defeat of the rebellion of Owain Glyndŵr in the fifteenth century meant that Wales failed to achieve a similar political end by military means (Davies 1995).

century. In these two centuries, wars were often waged with extreme brutality (not least because of religious zeal).[9] The violence associated with war reached its apex in the Thirty Years' War[10] (Parker 1984; Wilson 2009, 2010) in which perhaps one-third of the population of Germany perished. Changes in European society, not least the ascendancy of the secular (reflected by the Peace of Westphalia in 1648), helped ensure that religion was no longer the central factor in European international politics. In addition, certain philosophies, such as the writings of the Dutch lawyer Hugo Grotius (1583–1645), initiated a number of debates on the necessity of an 'international' law (Bull, Kingsbury and Roberts 1990; Tuck 1999). In his 1625 work *The Law of War and Peace*, Grotius asserted that there was:

> [A] common law among nations, which is valid alike for war and in war, I have had many and weighty reasons for undertaking to write upon the subject. Throughout the Christian world I observed a lack of restraint in relation to war, such as even barbarous races should be ashamed of; I observed that men rush to arms for slight causes, or no cause at all, and that when arms have once been taken up there is no longer any respect for law, divine or human; it is as if, in accordance with a general decree, frenzy had openly been let loose for the committing of all crimes. (Grotius 1957: 21)

The eighteenth century saw the conduct of warfare becoming, in some ways, rather more restrained (Veale 1953: 57–8; Rothenberg 1994: 86–97). This, so the argument runs, was brought to an abrupt end when the French Revolution brought nationalism to the fore as *the* prime factor in a renewed barbarisation of war. In truth, the eighteenth century had seen plenty of wars that could hardly be described as civilised. In the Seven Years' War (1756–1763), for instance, Prussia was faced with a multitude of enemies and endured extensive devastation and near-destruction (Clark 2006: 198–210). That Prussia and its warrior-king, Frederick II, survived against overwhelming odds was, in the minds of its people, down to the fact that Prussia had invested heavily in its army and had exalted military virtues above all others. This ascendancy of arms in Frederick's domains led the French statesman the Comte de Mirabeau (1749–1791) to comment that: 'Most states have an army; the Prussian Army is the only one that has a state' (Nef 1963: 305).

The faith invested by the Prussian (and the German) people in military solutions was heightened by the eventual defeat of Napoleon in 1815 and Otto von Bismarck's skilful use of three short wars to unify Germany by 1871 (Craig 1955: 180–217; Showalter 2004). This demonstration of the utility of military power was to elevate the prestige of the army to new heights in Germany. Eventually this was to have dire consequences, but when Frederick II died in 1786, war was more than

---

9   As a factor in leading states to wage war in the early modern period, the role of religion should not be overstated. There were major exceptions to this 'rule'. Thus, for example, Spain and France were at war between 1635 and 1659 despite the fact that they were the leading Catholic powers in Europe.

10   The Thirty Years' War was fought in Europe between 1618 and 1648.

ever a rational and normal tool of state policy. And, after the French Revolution of 1789, war really did become an 'affair of the people' (Schama 1990):

> Suddenly war again became the business of the people ... instead of governments and armies as heretofore, the full weight of the nation was thrown into the balance. The resources and efforts now available for use surpassed all conventional limits; nothing now impeded the vigor with which war could be waged, and consequently the opponents of France faced the utmost peril. (Clausewitz 1976: 592)

The advent of the era of mass war was given added impetus by virtue of the fact that, in Napoleon Bonaparte (1769–1821), the European state system was soon to witness the harnessing of the French national will to a man with a 'genius' for war (Bell 2007). Napoleon utilised the massive changes in French and European society to wage unlimited wars for unlimited goals. He was central to the further expansion of the social activity of war in European society (Paret 1986: 141–2). Napoleon was perhaps the greatest military leader since Alexander the Great and his brilliance prompted his near-contemporary Clausewitz to conceive the notion of 'military genius' in war (Clausewitz 1976: 100–112; Rogers 2002: 1167–76). Yet, even in respect of this concept, Clausewitz stressed the inherent link between war and politics. He thus remarked that Charles XII, King of Sweden (r.1697–1718), 'is not thought of as a great genius, for he could never subordinate his military gifts to superior insights and wisdom, and could never achieve a great goal with them' (Clausewitz 1976: 111). This is because although Charles XII took Sweden to the peak of its power through brilliant victories against a range of enemies, his limitless ambition during the Great Northern War (1700–1721) led to Sweden's total defeat and the loss of its empire (Lisk 1967).

In the early evolution of modern military thinking, there is one other figure that stands with Clausewitz and Napoleon – Antoine-Henri Jomini (1779–1869). Jomini, a Napoleonic general who later served with the Russian army, declared that strategy was derived from 'invariable scientific principles' which 'prescribe offensive action to mass forces against weaker enemy forces at some decisive point if strategy is to lead to victory' (Shy 1986: 146). This acceptance of the supposedly scientific nature of the study of the waging of war reflected a wider faith in 'progress', by universal laws, inherent in nineteenth-century European society. And, given the success of Prussian arms in that century (most notably in defeating Austria in 1866 and France in 1870–1871), the great powers were provided with a post-Napoleonic model of military efficiency. The Prussian Military Academy (*Preußische Kriegsakademie*), founded by Gerhard von Scharnhorst in 1810 in response to the crushing defeat by Napoleon at Jena and Auerstädt in 1806, was thus emulated throughout Europe (Craig 1955: 38–53). In terms of managing the business of waging war, the Prussian (and then German) General Staff (*Großer Generalstab*) became the model (Goerlitz 1985).[11] The *Kriegsakademie* produced highly professional officers who ensured that

---

11 The *Großer Generalstab* was unofficially founded in 1806 (and established in law in 1814).

the *Großer Generalstab* could process the massive amount of information flowing into its headquarters in Berlin. This material was then systematically analysed and employed so as to enhance German military prowess. War was regarded as both *art* and *science* and the process was constantly refined whilst creative thought, within certain parameters, was encouraged and nurtured. Of Germany, the Swiss journalist Victor Tissot noted:

> In this vast factory war is prepared just like some chemical product; within these walls all the various directing strings that regulate the German army are made to meet in order to be under the control of one master-hand, so that the troops in fact scarcely march a step, explode a cartridge, or fire a cannon shot without orders from here, while not so much as a military gaiter button can be sewn on anywhere in Europe without a note being taken of it. (Vizetelly 1879: 409)

Unfortunately, the German army's successful assertion of the demand for a clear division of politics and strategy, designed to free the military from civilian 'interference', produced a fatal flaw in the understanding of the nature of war in generations of German staff officers (Craig 1955: 216). Thus, while Germany may have possessed superb armed forces between 1871 and 1945, its decision-makers neglected many of the basic dictums laid down by the greatest thinkers on war (Geyer 1986).

By the latter part of the nineteenth century, what Handel terms a 'classical strategic paradigm for the understanding and direction of war' had emerged out of the works of Sun Tzu, Machiavelli, Clausewitz and Jomini. These Handel summarised in six points. First, since war serves the political interest, it must always be controlled at the highest level by the political elite and not the military. Second, war should not be the first or the last resort of any political community. Third, wars should be fought with clear goals and employ a cost/benefit analysis. Ideally, they should thus be won as quickly as possible for the lowest possible material outlay. Fourth, there are limitations on the rationality that can be brought to bear in terms of the analysis of the conduct of wars. Indeed, given factors like emotion and ideology, wars can even be fought rationally for non-rational ends. Fifth, wars cannot be won simply in military terms: political and diplomatic factors must continue to play a role even after the onset of hostilities.[12] And, finally, Handel's paradigm is based upon the observation of human nature and a reading of human history. It is fatalistic, accepting that war can never be abolished (although some wars can be prevented) and that violence is an integral part of the relationships between nations (Handel 2001: xviii–xix). As a logical corollary of this, Clausewitz noted that even military victory is rarely final as the 'defeated state often considers

---

12 Here, one can again highlight the deficiencies of Charles XII, who once declared: 'Gentlemen, I have resolved never to start an unjust war but never to end a legitimate one except by defeating my enemies' (Voltaire 1976: 51).

the outcome merely as a transitory evil, for which a remedy may still be found in political conditions at some later date' (Clausewitz 1976: 80).

The history of warfare from the second half of the nineteenth century onwards is often referred to as the era of 'Total War' (a term usually traced back to General Erich Ludendorff's memoir of the First World War (Ludendorff 1935)). 'Total War' involves the mobilisation of the entire effort of a nation or state to destroy the capacity of another to resist. It is generally agreed that this form of warfare rejects the traditional distinction between combatant and non-combatant. There are other distinctive features of 'total war' (such as mass conscription), but, as Ian Beckett notes, the notion of 'total war' has its limits and is subject to contestation as a concept (Beckett 1988: 21). Thus, the debate as to whether the American Civil War (1861–1865), for example, was a 'total war' continues to this day (Neely 2004).

The Second World War is seen as the culmination of the escalating violence and savagery that characterised the conduct of warfare in the modern era (Weinberg 2005). Although the brutal nature of the defeated regimes means that many hesitate to question the justification of fighting for the Allies in the Second World War (Overy 1997: 282–313), the hideous cost demonstrated that humankind needed to re-think the whole institution of war. This was given added impetus by the existence of nuclear weapons after 1945. In mainstream strategic thinking, mindsets came to be dominated by notions of 'deterrence' – i.e. dissuading not coercing opponents through psychological pressure (Snyder 1961: 3–51; Jervis, Lebow and Stein 1985). Bernard Brodie, the first and perhaps the greatest of all nuclear strategists, recognised that technological change had fundamentally altered the nature of war (Booth 1991). Brodie predicted that a new rationale for war would emerge: 'Thus far the chief purpose of our military establishment has been to win wars. From now on its chief purpose must be to avert them. It can have almost no other useful purpose' (Brodie 1946: 76). Despite the widespread alarm that nuclear weapons were eventually to generate amongst populations, many politicians and strategists tried to make sense of them in Clausewitzian terms (Kaplan 1983; Freedman 1986, 2003).

The American nuclear strategist Herman Kahn (1922–1983) suggested that we 'think the unthinkable' (Kahn 1962) by means of systematic thought. Kahn's belief that he was operating in the Clausewitzian tradition was clear from the title of his 1960 book, *On Thermonuclear War* (Kahn 1960). The prospect of a nuclear war had also led Kahn to ask 'Will the survivors envy the dead?' (Kahn argued that they would not: he believed that nuclear war was survivable (Kahn 1960: 40–95)). Kahn's fellow countryman, the economist and strategist Thomas C. Schelling, pioneered the study of bargaining and strategic behaviour (Schelling 1960). Schelling recognised the fact that, while Clausewitz had seen war as a rational part of the business of the state, nuclear weapons had wrought a revolution in warfare. In *Arms and Influence*, he developed his theory of 'compellence', asserting that the purpose of nuclear weapons lay in using the threat of their employment to coerce an adversary into a particular course of action (Schelling 1966). With the basic philosophical tenets of nuclear war-making now in place, policy-makers sought to maintain freedom of action by prescribing conditions whereby any given political community might resort to military means. Nevertheless, the reversion to more aggressive American nuclear war-fighting doctrines during the Second Cold War naturally caused great alarm in the Soviet Union (Lockwood and O'Brien Lockwood 1999: 24–6).

By the latter part of the twentieth century, fundamental changes in society across the world (such as the rise of the mass media), allied to a massive increase in the destructive potential of weapons, had called into question the very notion of war as having any real utility at all (Mueller 1989). Many hoped that the end of the Cold War in 1989 would usher in an era where populations did not live in constant dread of war. This was not to be the case, as John J. Mearsheimer perceptively forecast less than one year after the fall of the Berlin Wall (Mearsheimer 1990). Once again, international society witnessed the ability of war to endure social and political change. In Europe, much of the post-Cold War optimism was blown away by the Yugoslav Wars of Succession (1991–1995) in which over 100,000 died and the term 'ethnic cleansing' entered the lexicon of war. The West looked on as what had been termed an 'ethnic civil war' (Glenny 1996) raged. In the light of this prolonged civil war, nobody would have suggested that any of the protagonists had come to the 'end of history'.

Since 1945, war has little direct meaning for only a small minority of populations in the modern West (McInnes 2002). Today it is clear that major war, in the sense of the two world wars, has little utility for states (Smith 2005). But the Clausewitzan insistence upon the utility of force, and of the necessity of keeping political and military goals in alignment, remains. Military victory is still attainable (witness NATO's victory in Kosovo in 1999 and the Sri Lankan state's defeat of the Tamil Tiger rebellion in 2009). Very few strategists would therefore advocate the abrogation of the right to resort to violence as a policy option. Thus, while it is very unlikely that Russia, China and the USA would ever get involved in war with each other in whatever combination, it is even less likely that such powers will ever foreswear war. Russia gave Georgia a sharp lesson in *Realpolitik* in a brief war in South Ossetia in 2008; China makes ominous references to its military options should Taiwan ever formally secede from the mainland (Tsang 2006); and the USA is embroiled in a 'Global War on Terror' (GWOT) (Clarke 2004). As part of this 'War on Terror', US forces (and their allies) have engaged in low-intensity warfare against sub-state insurgents in Iraq and Afghanistan (Barnett 2003). The massive firepower of the USA, sufficient to sweep away the Taliban and Saddam Hussein in 2001 and 2003 respectively, was rendered impotent by virtue of the political failings of the global strategy pursued by the USA since 2001 (Cassidy 2008). What Russell F. Weigley termed the 'American way of war' (Weigley 1973) has been the subject to scrutiny for many years now (Booth 1978). These debates have been given added impetus by the GWOT (Boot 2003; Record 2006). In this war, American *military* difficulties have encouraged a certain amount of successful innovation (such as the extensive use of Special Forces). American *political* difficulties, on the other hand, may well be insurmountable.

States have been involved in fighting insurgency in innumerable wars, and since 1945 these have often been related to decolonisation (Beckett 2001, 2007; Marston and Malkasian 2008). This is not a recent development, as guerilla warfare has matured over 200 years (Laqueur 1975). Examples of its use against great powers include Spanish insurgency against Napoleon between 1808 and 1814[13] (Glover 2001: 10) and the Boer struggle against the British Empire between 1899 and 1902 (Pakenham 1992: 472–3, 534–5). Today, great powers continue to have enormous difficulty in subduing smaller rivals or sub-state insurgents – witness the experience of the Soviet Union in Afghanistan (Braithwaite 2011) and of Russia in Chechnya (German 2003; Russell 2007). Part of the reason for this lies in the way in which modern globalised society has delivered a number of new weapons, and other assets, into the hands of those who seek to defy the state's traditional claim to a monopoly on violence. There are an infinite variety of means here – both lethal and non-lethal. They include the Internet, the global media, anti-war movements, West European timidity, terrorism and a proliferation of advanced weaponry and Improvised Explosive Devices (IEDs). The greater availability of such lethal resources has caused states to suffer a diminution in their ability to impose their will upon well-equipped non-state opponents – the 2006 Israeli campaign against Hezbollah being a case in point (Harel and Issacharoff 2008).

Given the trends outlined above, it is small wonder that 'asymmetrical warfare' is now such a rich field of scholarly enquiry (Arreguin-Toft 2005). Less fettered by the (admittedly oft-violated) restraints imposed upon the regular armed forces of states, insurgent groups can employ a number of methods to counter the firepower of the state (Sullivan 2007). Tactics such as terrorism are designed to strike at the very heart of the political will of governments and populations to endure war. Terrorism, in one form or another, is as old as war itself. It can achieve spectacular results (Chaliand 2007; Steinhoff 2007). One recent example is the Budyonnovsk hostage crisis of June 1995, in which Chechen terrorists killed over 150 civilians and provoked a major political crisis in Russia (Stone 2006: 245). Such acts demonstrate nothing so much as the continuing attraction of violence to those seeking to attain political ends.

In 1967, it was noted that 'if force ... lost its utility, its condemnation on moral grounds [would be] superfluous' (Osgood and Tucker 1967: 224). Since then, huge waves of moral condemnation have had little effect on the utility of force. The limited Western military intervention in Libya in 2011, which assisted the (ultimately successful) rebellion against Colonel Gaddafi, demonstrated the limitations of military power as an instrument for modifying the behaviour of any given state, especially when that state's vital interests, or survival, is at stake (Schnaubelt 2011). Yet the use of force, and the threat of the use of force, remains at the heart of the conduct of international politics. As long as that continues to be the case, it will be impossible to disagree with Plato's maxim that 'Only the dead have seen the end of war'.

---

13   The term *guerrilla* ('little war') is derived from this conflict.

References

Alberigo, G. and Tanner, N. (eds) (1990), *Decrees of the Ecumenical Councils*, volume II (Washington DC: Georgetown University Press).
Aron, R. (1981), *Peace and War: A Theory of International Relations* (Malabari, FL: Krieger).
Arreguin-Toft, I. (2005), *How the Weak Win Wars: A Theory of Asymmetric Conflict* (Cambridge: Cambridge University Press).
Barnett, R.W. (2003), *Asymmetrical Warfare: Today's Challenge to U.S. Military Power* (Washington DC: Brassey's).
Bartov, O. (2001), *The Eastern Front 1941–1945: German Troops and the Barbarisation of Warfare*, 2nd revised edn (Basingstoke: Palgrave Macmillan).
Beckett, I.F.W. (1988), 'Total War', in McInnes, C. and Sheffield, G.D. (eds), *Warfare in the Twentieth Century: Theory and Practice* (London: Unwin Hyman), 1–23.
Beckett, I.F.W. (2001), *Modern Insurgencies and Counter-Insurgencies: Guerrillas and their Opponents since 1750* (London: Routledge).
Beckett, I.F.W. (ed.) (2007), *Modern Counter-Insurgency* (Aldershot: Ashgate).
Bell, D.A. (2007), *The First Total War: Napoleon's Europe and the Birth of Modern Warfare* (London: Bloomsbury).
Bellamy, C. (1990), *The Evolution of Modern Land Warfare: Theory and Practice* (London: Routledge).
Black, J. (ed.) (2002), *European Warfare, 1494–1660* (London: Routledge).
Boot, M. (2003), 'The New American Way of War', *Foreign Affairs* 82:4, 41–58.
Boot, M. (2006), *War Made New: Technology, Warfare and the Course of History, 1500 to Today* (New York: Gotham Books).
Booth, K. (1978), 'American Strategy: The Myths Revisited', in Booth, K. and Wright. M. (eds), *American Thinking about Peace and War* (New York: Barnes and Noble), 1–35.
Booth, K. (1991), 'Bernard Brodie', in Baylis, J. and Garnett, J. (eds), *Makers of Nuclear Strategy* (London: Pinter), 19–56.
Bouchard, C.B. (1998), *Strong of Body, Brave and Noble: Chivalry and Society in Medieval France* (Ithaca, NY: Cornell University Press).
Bousquet, A.J. (2009), *The Scientific Way of Warfare: Order and Chaos on the Battlefields of Modernity* (Irvington, NY: Irvington).
Bradford, A.S. (2001), *With Arrow, Sword, and Spear: A History of Warfare in the Ancient World* (Santa Barbara, CA: Praeger).
Braithwaite, R. (2011), *Afgantsy: The Russians in Afghanistan 1979–89* (London: Profile).
Brodie, B. (1946), *The Absolute Weapon: Atomic Power and World Order* (New York: Harcourt).
Brook, Y. and Epstein, A. (2006), '"Just War Theory" vs. American Self-Defence', *The Objective Standard: A Journal of Culture and Politics*, 1:1. http://www.theobjectivestandard.com/issues/2006-spring/just-war-theory.asp [accessed 25 June 2012].

Brough, M.W., Lango, J.W. and van der Linden, H. (eds) (2007), *Rethinking the Just War Tradition* (Albany, NY: SUNY Press).
Brown, M. (2008), *Bannockburn: The Scottish War and the British Isles, 1307–1323* (Edinburgh: Edinburgh University Press).
Bull, H., Kingsbury, B. and Roberts, A. (eds) (1990), *Hugo Grotius and International Relations* (Oxford: Oxford University Press).
Caesar (2000), *The Gallic War*, seven commentaries on *The Gallic War* with an eighth commentary by Aulus Hirtius, trans. C. Hammond (Oxford: Oxford University Press).
Caesar (2008), The Gallic War: Seven Commentaries on The Gallic War with an Eighth Commentary by Aulus Hirtius, trans. and intro. C. Hammond (Oxford: Oxford University Press).
Carpenter, D. (2003), *The Struggle for Mastery: Britain 1066–1284* (Oxford: Oxford University Press).
Cassidy, R.M. (2008), *Counterinsurgency and the Global War on Terror: Military Culture and Irregular War* (Stanford, CA: Stanford University Press).
Chaliand, G. (2007), *The History of Terrorism: From Antiquity to al Qaeda* (Berkeley, CA: University of California Press).
Childress, J.F. (1978), 'Just War Theories: The Bases, Interrelations, Priorities, and Functions of their Criteria', *Theological Studies* 39, 427–45.
Childs, J. (1982), *Armies and Warfare in Europe, 1648–1789* (Manchester: Manchester University Press).
Cicero (1931), *The Speeches of Cicero*, trans. and ed. N.H. Watts (London: William Heinemann).
Clark, C. (2006), *Iron Kingdom: The Rise and Downfall of Prussia 1600–1947* (London: Penguin).
Clarke, R.A. (2004), *Against All Enemies: Inside America's War on Terror* (New York: Free Press).
Clausewitz, C. von (1976 [1832]), *On War*, Howard, M. and Paret. P. (trans. and eds) (Princeton, NJ: Princeton University Press)
Collins, R. (1995), *The Arab Conquest of Spain: 710–797* (London: Wiley-Blackwell).
Craig, G.A. (1955), *The Politics of the Prussian Army 1640–1945* (Oxford: Oxford University Press).
Curtis, V.J. (2003), 'Understanding Schlieffen', *Army Doctrine and Training Bulletin* 6:3, 56–65.
Davies, R.R. (1995), *The Revolt of Owain Glyn Dŵr* (Oxford: Oxford University Press).
DeVries, K. (1992), *Medieval Military Technology* (Toronto: University of Toronto Press).
Dover, K.J. (1983), 'Thucydides "as History" and "as Literature"', *History and Theory* 22:1, 54–63.
Elbe, J. von (1939), 'The Evolution of the Concept of the Just War in International Law', *American Journal of International Law* 33:4, 665–88.
Elias, N. (1978 [1939]), *The Civilizing Process*, volume I, *The History of Manners* (Oxford: Blackwell).

Elias, N. (2000 [1939]), Dunning, E., Goudsblom J. and Mennell, S. (eds), *The Civilizing Process: Sociogenetic and Psychogenetic Investigations* (Oxford: Blackwell).
Engler Anderson, A., Fischer, D. and Voorst, B. van (1991), 'The Commander: Stormin' Norman Schwarzkopf on Top', *Time* (4 February), http://www.time.com/time/magazine/article/0,9171,972270,00.html [accessed 25 June 2012].
Farris, W.W. (1995), *Heavenly Warriors: The Evolution of Japan's Military, 500–1300* (Cambridge MA: Harvard University Press).
Foley, R.T. (ed. and trans.) (2003), *Alfred von Schlieffen's Military Writings* (London: Frank Cass).
Foley, R.T. (2006), 'The Real Schlieffen Plan', *War in History* 13:1, 91–115.
Fontana, B. (1993), 'Tacitus on Empire and Republic', *History of Political Thought* 14:1, 29–40.
Fotion, N. (2007), *War and Ethics* (London: Continuum).
Freedman, L. (1986), 'The First Two Generations of Nuclear Strategists' in Paret, P. (ed.), *Makers of Modern Strategy: From Machiavelli to the Nuclear Age* (Oxford: Clarendon Press), 735–78.
Freedman, L. (2003), *The Evolution of Nuclear Strategy*, 3rd revised edn (Basingstoke: Palgrave Macmillan).
German, T.C. (2003), *Russia's Chechen War* (London: RoutledgeCurzon).
Geyer, M. (1986), 'German Strategy in the Age of Machine Warfare, 1914–1945', in Paret, P. (ed.), *Makers of Modern Strategy: From Machiavelli to the Nuclear Age* (Oxford: Clarendon Press), 527–97.
Gilbert, F. (1986), 'Machiavelli: The Renaissance of the Art of War', in Paret, P. (ed.), *Makers of Modern Strategy: From Machiavelli to the Nuclear Age* (Oxford: Clarendon Press), 11–31.
Glenny, M. (1996), *The Fall of Yugoslavia: The Third Balkan War*, 3rd revised edn (New York: Penguin).
Glover, M. (2001), *The Peninsular War 1807–1814: A Concise Military History* (London: Penguin).
Goerlitz, W. (1985), *History of the German General Staff, 1657–1945* (Boulder, CO: Westview Press).
Goldsworthy, A. (2000), *The Punic Wars* (London: Weidenfeld & Nicolson).
Granoff, J. (2000), 'Nuclear Weapons, Ethics, Morals, and Law', NGO Presentation for the Nuclear Non-Proliferation Treaty Prepcom of 1999, http://www.gsinstitute.org/gsi/docs/gran_12-9-00.pdf [accessed 25 June 2012].
Gray, C.S. (2002), *Strategy for Chaos: Revolutions in Military Affairs and the Evidence of History* (London: Frank Cass).
Green, P. (1996), *The Greco-Persian Wars* (Berkeley, CA: University of California Press).
Griffith, P. (1995), *The Viking Art of War* (Mechanicsburg, PA: Stackpole).
Grotius, H. (1957), *Prolegomena to the Law of War and Peace*, trans. F.W. Kelsey (New York: Liberal Arts Press).
Handel, M.I. (2001), *Masters of War: Classical Strategic Thought*, 3rd revised edn (New York: Frank Cass).

Hanson, V.D. (2005), *A War Like No Other: How the Athenians and Spartans Fought the Peloponnesian War* (New York: Random House).
Hanson, V.D. (2008), 'From Phalanx to Legion 350–250 BC', in Parker, G. (ed.), *The Cambridge Illustrated History of Warfare: The Triumph of the West* (New York: Cambridge University Press), 32–49.
Harari, Y.N. (2007), *Special Operations in the Age of Chivalry, 1100–1550* (Rochester, NY: Boydell Press).
Harel, A. and Issacharoff, A. (2008), *34 Days: Israel, Hezbollah, and the War in Lebanon* (New York: Palgrave Macmillan).
Herodotus (2004), *The Histories*, trans. C.G. Macauley, ed. and notes by D. Lateiner (New York: Barnes and Noble).
Holland, T. (2005), *Persian Fire: The First World Empire and the Battle for the West* (London: Abacus).
Jarymowycz, R.J. (2008), *Cavalry from Hoof to Track* (Westport, CT: Praeger Security International).
Jervis, R., Lebow, R.N. and Stein, J.G. (eds) (1985), *The Psychology of Deterrence* (Baltimore, MD: Johns Hopkins University Press).
Kaeuper, R.W. (2009), *Holy Warriors: The Religious Ideology of Chivalry* (Philadelphia, PA: University of Pennsylvania Press)
Kahn, H. (1960), *On Thermonuclear War* (Princeton, NJ: Princeton University Press).
Kahn, H. (1962), *Thinking about the Unthinkable* (London: Weidenfeld & Nicolson).
Kaplan, F.M. (1983), *The Wizards of Armageddon* (Stanford, CA: Stanford University Press).
Keegan, J. (1994), *A History of Warfare* (London: Pimlico).
Keeley, L.H. (1996), *War Before Civilization: The Myth of the Peaceful Savage* (Oxford: Oxford University Press).
Keen, M. (2005), *Chivalry* (New Haven, CT: Yale University Press).
Lango, J.W. (2005), 'Preventive Wars, Just War Principles, and the United Nations', *Journal of Ethics* 9:1, 247–68.
Laqueur, W. (1975), 'The Origins of Guerrilla Doctrine', *Journal of Contemporary History* 10:3, 341–82.
Lisk, J. (1967), *The Struggle for Supremacy in the Baltic: 1600–1725* (New York: Funk & Wagnalls).
Lockwood, J.S. and O'Brien Lockwood, K. (1999), *The Russian View of US Strategy* (New York: Transaction Publishers).
Ludendorff, E. (1935), *Der totale Krieg* (Munich: Ludendorff Verlag).
Machiavelli, N. (2001 [1521]), *The Art of War*, intro. Neal Wood [1965] (New York: Da Capo).
McInnes, C. (2002), *Spectator Sport War: The West and Contemporary Conflict* (Boulder, CO: Lynne Rienner).
McNeil, W.H. (1982), *The Pursuit of Power: Technology, Armed Force, and Society since A.D. 1000* (Chicago: University of Chicago Press).
Mao Zedong (1972), *Six Essays on Military Affairs* (Peking: Foreign Languages Press).
Markusen, E., and Kopf, D. (1995), *The Holocaust and Strategic Bombing: Genocide and Total War in the Twentieth Century* (Boulder, CO: Westview Press).

Marston, D. and Malkasian, C. (eds) (2008), *Counterinsurgency in Modern Warfare* (London: Osprey).
Mearsheimer, J.J. (1990), 'Back to the Future: Instability in Europe after the Cold War', *International Security* 15:1, 5–56.
Moise, E.E. (1996), *Tonkin Gulf and the Escalation of the Vietnam War* (Chapel Hill, NC: University of North Carolina Press).
Mueller, J. (1989), *Retreat from Doomsday: The Obsolescence of Major War* (New York: Basic Books, 1989)
Murray, W. (1997a), 'War, Theory, Clausewitz, and Thucydides: The Game May Change but the Rules Remain', *Marine Corps Gazette* 81, 62–9.
Murray, W. (1997b), 'Thinking about Revolutions in Military Affairs', *Joint Force Quarterly* 16, 69–76.
Neely Jr., M.E. (2004), 'Was the Civil War a Total War?', *Civil War History* 50:4, 434–58.
Nef, J.U. (1963), *Western Civilization since the Renaissance: Peace, War, Industry and the Arts* (New York: Harper & Row).
Nelson, D. (2003), *The War Behind Me: Vietnam Veterans Confront the Truth about U.S. War Crimes* (New York: Basic Books).
Osgood, R. and Tucker, R. (1967), *Force, Order, and Justice* (Baltimore, MD: Johns Hopkins University Press).
Overy, R. (1997), *Why the Allies Won: Explaining Victory in World War II* (New York: W.W. Norton).
Pakenham, T. (1992), *The Boer War* (London: Abacus).
Palmer, A. (2005), *Northern Shores: A History of the Baltic Sea and its Peoples* (London: John Murray).
Paret, P. (1986), 'Napoleon and the Revolution in War', in Paret, P. (ed.), *Makers of Modern Strategy: From Machiavelli to the Nuclear Age* (Oxford: Clarendon Press), 123–42.
Parker, G. (ed.) (1984), *The Thirty Years' War* (London: Routledge & Kegan Paul).
Parker, G. (1996), *The Military Revolution: Military Innovation and the Rise of the West* (Cambridge: Cambridge University Press).
Parker, G. (1998), *The Grand Strategy of Philip II* (New Haven, CT: Yale University Press).
Prestwich, J.O. (2004), *The Place of War in English History, 1066–1214*, ed. M. Prestwich (Rochester, NY: Boydell Press).
Prestwich, M. (1972), *War, Politics and Finance under Edward I* (London: Faber & Faber).
Prestwich, M. (1980), *The Three Edwards: War and State in England, 1272–1377* (London: Weidenfeld & Nicolson).
Prestwich, M. (1999), *Armies and Warfare in the Middle Ages: The English Experience* (New Haven, CT: Yale University Press).
Prestwich, M. (2007), 'The Enterprise of War', in Horrox, R. and Ormrod, W.M. (eds), *The Social History of England, 1200–1500* (Cambridge: Cambridge University Press), 74–90.

Record, J. (2006), 'The American Way of War: Cultural Barriers to Successful Counterinsurgency', *Policy Analysis* 577 (Washington, DC: Cato Institute), http://www.cato.org/pubs/pas/pa577.pdf [accessed 25 June 2012].
Ritter, G. (1958), *The Schlieffen Plan: Critique of a Myth* (London: Oswald Wolff).
Roberts, A. (2005), 'Against War', in Townshend, C. (ed.), *The Oxford History of Modern War* (Oxford: Oxford University Press).
Roberts, A. and Guelff, R. (eds) (2000), *Documents on the Laws of War*, 3rd revised edn (Oxford: Oxford University Press).
Rogers, C.J. (2002), 'Clausewitz, Genius, and the Rules', *Journal of Military History* 66:4, 1167–76.
Rothenberg, G.E. (1986), 'Moltke, Schlieffen, and the Doctrine of Strategic Envelopment', in Paret, P. (ed.), *Makers of Modern Strategy: From Machiavelli to the Nuclear Age* (Oxford: Clarendon Press), 296–325.
Rothenberg, G.E. (1994), 'The Age of Napoleon', in Howard, M., Andreopoulos, G.J. and Shulman, M.R. (eds), *The Laws of War: Constraints on Warfare in the Western World* (New Haven, CT: Yale University Press), 86–97.
Russell, F.H. (1977), *The Just War in the Middle Ages* (Cambridge: Cambridge University Press).
Russell, J. (2007), *Chechnya – Russia's 'War on Terror'* (Abingdon: Routledge).
Sagan, C. and Turco, R.P. (1990), *A Path Where No Man Thought: Nuclear Winter and the End of the Arms Race* (New York: Random House).
Schama, S. (1990), *Citizens: A Chronicle of the French Revolution* (New York: Knopf).
Schelling, T.C. (1960), *The Strategy of Conflict* (Cambridge, MA: Harvard University Press).
Schelling, T.C. (1966), *Arms and Influence* (New Haven, CT: Yale University Press).
Schnaubelt, C.M. (2011), 'The Limits of Military Force', *New York Times* (18 May), http://www.nytimes.com/2011/05/19/opinion/19iht-edschnaubelt19.html [accessed 25 June 2012].
Showalter, D.E. (2004), *The Wars of German Unification* (London: Arnold).
Shy, J. (1986), 'Jomini', in Paret, P. (ed.), *Makers of Modern Strategy: From Machiavelli to the Nuclear Age* (Oxford: Clarendon Press), 143–85.
Smith, R. (2005), *The Utility of Force: The Art of War in the Modern World* (London: Allen Lane).
Snyder, G.H. (1961), *Deterrence and Defence: Toward a Theory of National Security* (Princeton, NJ: Princeton University Press).
Spalinger, A.J. (2005), *War in Ancient Egypt* (Malden, MA: Blackwell Publishing).
Steinhoff, U. (2007), *On the Ethics of War and Terrorism* (Oxford: Oxford University Press).
Stevenson, D. (1991), *The First World War and International Politics* (Oxford: Clarendon Press).
Stone, D.R. (2006), *A Military History of Russia from Ivan the Terrible to the War in Chechnya* (Westport, CT: Praeger Security International).
Sullivan, P. (2007), 'War Aims and War Outcomes: Why Powerful States Lose Limited Wars', *Journal of Conflict Resolution* 51:3, 496–524.

Sumption, J. (1999), *The Hundred Years War*, volume I: *Trial by Battle* (Philadelphia, PA: University of Pennsylvania Press).
Sumption, J. (2001), *The Hundred Years War*, volume II: *Trial by Fire* (Philadelphia, PA: University of Pennsylvania Press).
Sun Tzu (2006), *The Art of War*, trans. S.B. Griffith (Uxbridge, Ontario: Blue Heron Books).
Tacitus (1970), *The Agricola and the Germania*, trans. H. Mattingly and S.A. Handford (London: Penguin).
Taylor, A.J.P. (1955), *Bismarck: The Man and the Statesman* (London: Hamish Hamilton).
Thucydides (1974), *History of the Peloponnesian War*, trans. Rex Warner, ed. and introduced by M.I. Finlay (London: Penguin).
Tsang, S. (ed.) (2006), *If China Attacks Taiwan: Military Strategy, Politics and Economics* (Abingdon: Routledge).
Tuck, R. (1999), *The Rights of War and Peace: Political Thought and the International Order from Grotius to Kant* (Oxford: Oxford University Press).
Urban, W. (2006), *Medieval Mercenaries: the Business of War* (St Paul, MN: MBI Publishing).
Veale, F.J.P. (1953), *Advance to Barbarism* (Appleton, WI: C.C. Nelson).
Vizetelly, H. (1879), *Berlin under the New Empire: Its Institutions, Inhabitants, Industry, Monuments, Museums, Social Life, Manners, and Amusements*, volume I (London: Tinsley Brothers).
Voltaire (François-Marie Arouet), (1976 [1731]), *The History of Charles XII, King of Sweden*, trans. A. White (London: Folio Society).
Weigley, R.F. (1973), *The American Way of War: A History of United States Military Strategy and Policy* (Bloomington, IN: Indiana University Press).
Weinberg, G.L. (2005), *A World at Arms: A Global History of World War II*, 2nd revised edn (Cambridge: Cambridge University Press).
Wells, P.S. (2008), *Barbarians to Angels: The Dark Ages Reconsidered* (New York: W.W. Norton).
Wilson, P.H. (2009), *Europe's Tragedy: A History of the Thirty Years War* (London: Allen Lane).
Wilson, P.H. (ed.) (2010), *The Thirty Years War: A Sourcebook* (Basingstoke: Palgrave Macmillan).
Zinn, H. (2003), *A People's History of the United States: 1492–Present* (New York: Harper).

PART V
Countering Political Violence

Intelligence and Political Violence: The Case of Counter-Terrorism

Frank Gregory

Introduction

This chapter has its empirical grounding in the widespread attention given to the nature of intelligence and intelligence agency organisation in relation to 9/11 and its continuing legacy in counter-terrorism intelligence work in the USA and the UK. Thus, this chapter concentrates on intelligence as a counter-terrorism tool of Western states directed against terrorism perpetrated by non-state Islamist-type actors such as identified groups (on proscribed lists by established by the UN, the EU, the UK and the USA), loose networks and those the UK counter-terrorism (CT) policy CONTEST called 'radicalized individuals' (HM Government, 2009). It is a task which contains two challenges for intelligence agencies; first, because intelligence gathering is partly a human resource-intensive activity, the counter-terrorism focus entails opportunity costs in terms of other parts of an intelligence agency's remit; and, second, post-9/11 intelligence agency 'failures' will receive extensive media coverage and scrutiny through parliamentary, judicial and other forms of formally constituted accountability mechanisms (on these mechanisms, see, for example, Council of Europe, 2007; Müller-Wille, 2006).

Criticism has been levelled at some terrorism studies for inadequacies in, *inter alia*, quantitative analysis or qualitative analysis through a lack of attention to the issue of the 'outcomes' of counter-terrorism strategies (Lum, Kennedy and Sherley, 2006). Thus, to begin, I will examine how reliable and valid research on intelligence can be conducted. In the subfield of the UK government response to terrorism, these criticisms have, superficially, some validity. It has been noted (Gregory, 2009a, 2009b; Pantazis and Pemberton, 2009) that the published UK official statistics relating to counter-terrorism operations are not easy to interpret and, in some cases, are not published in comparable formats in successive years. On the qualitative analysis approach in the UK, recently Christopher Andrew (2009) was in a unique situation with regard to his access to the MI5 in-house archives and no researcher has had similar access in respect of the UK MI6 archives (Jeffery, 2010, only goes up to 1949) or to the Government Communications Headquarters (GCHQ) and the Defence Intelligence & Analysis Service (DI&AS) archives. However, the current Director General (DG) of MI5 has provided unprecedented recent detail about the intelligence services information and action flows on two of the 7/7 London bombers (Intelligence and Security Committee, 2009). Because of the separation of powers in the USA, more qualitative analysis material is available through sources like the General Accountability Office (GAO) and the Congressional Research Service (CRS) reports.

Since 9/11, research in this subfield in the UK and the USA has been able to draw upon a growing volume of sources (George, 2007). In terms of UK government publications, the basic CONTEST (counter-terrorism policy) document (HM Government, 2006 , 2009, 2011) has grown in size from approximately 30 pages in 2006 to over 170 pages in 2009. Parliamentary scrutiny of counter-terrorism policy and legislation has been carried out by the Joint Committee on Human Rights, the Defence Committee and the Home Affairs Committee (which now has a subcommittee on terrorism), and some of these inquiries have included aspects of the role of intelligence in counter-terrorism. Issues relating to intelligence also feature in the annual UK terrorism law reviews carried out by Lord Carlile. There are also, of course, the annual and special reports of the Intelligence and Security Committee (ISC), though as a non-parliamentary committee appointed under prime ministerial patronage, it has been subject to a number of critical reviews. More specific US and UK intelligence-related information can be derived from the evidence presented in court cases and incident reviews. A similar and indeed wider range of intelligence-related analyses, in addition to the well-known 9/11 Commission, is available in US official and Congressional publications.

Furthermore, under the Chatham House Rule, it is also possible to discuss aspects of the intelligence contribution to counter-terrorism with official participants at small group conferences in the UK organised by, for example, the Foreign & Commonwealth Office agency Wilton Park (see http://www.wiltonpark.org.uk), with the Association of Chief Police Officers (ACPO) and through projects funded by the Economic and Social Research Council (ESRC) and the Airey Neave Trust. These events can be used to develop a programme of fieldwork interviews through the network of contacts from the events. In turn, these interviews can, by snowballing, produce further fieldwork interviews. Similar research openings exist in the USA. Thus, by applying the methodology of triangulation to this growing range of sources, it is possible to produce well-grounded research.

Based on such methods, this chapter commences with a general analysis of intelligence and counter-terrorism which leads on to a discussion of the impact of 9/11 on the field of counter-terrorism intelligence. This discussion also considers the question of whether a 'revolution in intelligence affairs' (RIA) can be discerned. It concludes with brief case studies of the recent histories of counter-terrorism intelligence in the UK and the USA which are related to the concept of a RIA.

Intelligence and Counter-terrorism: General Issues

The significance of intelligence in counter-terrorism stems from three main drivers: its role in, ideally, pre-emption and disruption of terrorist activity, its role in post-incident investigations and the priority given to the maximisation of the efficient use of counter-terrorism resources through intelligence-led counter-terrorism (see Gregory, 2006b). Intelligence-led counter-terrorism is not a new aspiration, but it is given current emphasis within the performance-related Western public service culture and the priority assigned to preventing and pre-empting a 9/11 type of attack. Consequently, the role of intelligence in counter-terrorism needs to be fully understood and appreciated, both in its possibilities and its limitations (see further McCulloch and Pickering, 2009).

Pillar (2004) has provided an important contemporary critique of how the intelligence function can contribute to a comprehension of generic issues. As Pillar aptly points out, the 'bull's eye of this intelligence target – an individual terrorist plot – lacks the size and signatures of most other targets, from nuclear weapons programs to political instability'. Moreover, as he further notes, 'intelligence specific to terrorist plots is often unattainable' (2004, 115). Therefore, a CT response system that relies too much on ratcheting up security only on receipt of actual tactical warnings can be badly caught out.

In developing these introductory points, one should be mindful of the caution expressed in the Butler Report: 'Intelligence is not only – like many other sources – incomplete, it can be incomplete in undetectable ways' (Report of a Committee of Privy Counsellors, 2004, para 50). It is helpful to refer to Hughes-Wilson (2004), who has provided a very sound basic introduction to intelligence work. Hughes-Wilson's breakdown of the 'Intelligence Cycle' is well worth quoting in full, as it helps to identify generic issues. The cycle should start with:

1. Statement of end-user[s] **requirements**. These should lead to:
2. Planned **collection**.
3. **Collation** of all collected information.
4. **Interpretation** by trained *analysts* for *relevance, reliability, credibility* and *accuracy*.
5. Timely **dissemination** to end-user[s]. (Hughes-Wilson, 2004, 10)

The information-gathering part of the intelligence cycle is now much more complex, with an increasing range of both public and private intelligence-sector information 'collectors'. For example, there are international, regional (EU) and national regimes for investigating suspicious financial transactions that might be linked to money laundering or the financing of terrorism that assign suspicious transaction-reporting requirements on, for example, banks and other financial institutions, lawyers, accountants and estate agents.

There are currently five principle means of information gathering for intelligence purposes: SIGINT/ELINT (various forms of communications intercept), MASINT (measurements and signatures intelligence), IMINT (imagery intelligence, for example, from 'spy' satellites), OSINT (open source) and HUMINT (human sources). Over the last two decades, there has been a growing problem of information overload for the human intelligence analyst from the increasing capacity of the technical means of information gathering. Treverton and Renwick comment that in:

> the Cold War, the issue for agencies was a shortage of data; now there is a glut (every few hours the NSA collects enough electronic data to fill the Library of Congress), making it difficult to separate the wheat from the chaff, the meaningful signals from the background noise. (2008, 8)

Moreover, the more emphasis intelligence agencies place on the value of SIGINT/ELINT, the more likely it is that those who seek to avoid detection will utilise PETs (Privacy Enhancing Technologies, such as encryption) and/or PES (Privacy Enhancing Strategies, such as avoidance of the Internet) (see further Levi and Wall, 2004). In turn, this has led, together with other factors, to states placing a renewed emphasis upon HUMINT. Pre-9/11 clampdowns on CIA HUMINT operations and post-9/11 revelations about the US Intelligence Community's HUMINT deficiencies led in 2005 to the setting up of the National Clandestine Service within the CIA to manage all CIA HUMINT operations and with responsibility for coordinating all the US Intelligence Community's HUMINT work (Best, 2009, 10).

The actual use of intelligence as a tool in countering violence in the political realm has to be placed within both a situational and political context. We can distinguish between usage of intelligence in a 'law enforcement' response to terrorism and its usage in a 'war on terror' response mode. In the first mode of response, intelligence ideally leads to the arrest and conviction of terrorists *before* an act of political violence. In this case the intelligence product has an evidentiary role within the criminal justice system in this mode and therefore must pass 'the beyond all reasonable doubt' test in a court trial process. In the second mode of response, intelligence may be used for providing targeting information for a weapons system such as an air strike in Afghanistan by a, unmanned aerial vehicle (UAV) which may be controlled from the USA (on the CIA's use of UAVs, see Ripley, 2011).

However, there are some legitimate concerns about the domestic pre-emptive approach to counter-terrorism. Recent criminological studies (McCulloch and Pickering, 2009; Pantazis and Pemberton, 2009) have raised issues relating to the notion of 'pre-crime' (acts preparatory to terrorism in UK law) and the creation of new 'suspect communities' (on the earlier impact of the UK's Prevention of Terrorism (Temporary Provisions) Act 1974 on the Irish community, see Hillyard, 1993). Moreover, because of source sensitivity and ongoing counter-terrorism operations, a 'key tension exists between covert police and security agency operations aimed at monitoring or disrupting activities and securing convictions on the basis of evidence presented in open court' (McCulloch and Pickering, 2009, 631). A further complication arises because the Western focus on international terrorism has been accompanied by increasing links between their internal (domestic) security issues and external international security issues. As the former US Director of National

Intelligence, John Negroponte, contended: 'What happens abroad can kill us at home' (Randol, 2009a, 3).

Democracies use intelligence for protective purposes and increasingly, both the intelligence process and its usage are governed by formal human rights compliant legal regimes and accountability systems (Council of Europe, 2007). In contrast, authoritarian regimes are seen to have intelligence systems whose task it is to sustain the leader/regime by providing intelligence (including fabricated intelligence) to, first, prevent actions designed to counter state political violence and, second, to identify targets for state-directed political violence. However, the intelligence-related usage of 'extraordinary rendition' by the USA, the Guantanamo Bay detention camp, the woefully inadequately regulated US detention facilities in Iraq and Afghanistan, and the forms of torture sanctioned by the US administration under President George W. Bush are all examples of an unprecedented disregard for the usual due process and rule of law systems found in modern democracies.

9/11 Consequences? Is There a 'Revolution in Intelligence Affairs'? Did National Intelligence Systems Require Major Overhauls?

As Herman has pointed out, CT intelligence is not a new intelligence activity, but:

> its importance now warrants regarding it as an intelligence discipline in its own right, with equal standing to the accepted 'political', 'military' and 'economic' categories of collection and products. (2003, 42)

He also underlines the fact that although CT intelligence's:

> most important and direct value is in providing pre-emptive tactical warning of a terrorist action ... this may not result in immediately observable action such as arresting terrorists or capturing their *materiel*, (2003, 43)

Furthermore, Lahneman notes that:

> [C]alls for intelligence reform have been an almost continuous feature of the security policy landscape since the end of the Cold War, and the volume and frequency of such calls have risen dramatically since the 9/11 attacks. (2007, 1)

The studies relating to these calls for reform have commonly focused on one or more of the following issues: intelligence agency organisation; analytical capacity; the relationship between the analysed intelligence product and policy-makers, and the use of open sources; covert operations and information technologies. From the range of US-related studies, Lahneman (2007, 2) identifies three main clusters of views on intelligence reform: first, the 'no significant reform needed' cluster argues that the occurrence of a 'surprise attack' is not of itself a *prima facie* imperative for organisational reform; second, an albeit small cluster believes that there needs to be a RIA; third, another cluster represents a kind of middle-ground position by advocating significant but evolutionary change. A somewhat similar analysis is also offered by Honig, who identifies an 'orthodox-revisionist dichotomy' but cautions that:

> in the absence of a normative theory for how intelligence should be optimally done, scholars lack the criteria to distinguish between unprofessional mistakes and inherent difficulties that lead to intelligence failure. (2007, 703)

Lahneman (2007, 4) identifies three categories of discourse on the concept of a RIA. First, there are arguments based around the proposition that there has already been a revolution in military affairs (RMA) and that therefore there is a logical requirement for both a RIA and a revolution in diplomatic affairs (RDA). This category of discourse suggests that, without accompanying RIAs and RDAs, decision-makers may over-privilege military methods because they are presented as possessing 'the least uncertainty' (Lahneman, 2007, 4).

The second category of discourse proceeds from the premise that there have been three recent significant 'failures of intelligence': the absence of any 9/11 warning; the posited existence of weapons of mass destruction (WMDs) in Iraq; and the woefully inadequate appreciation of the probable post-conflict conditions in Iraq – to which could be added the failure to appreciate the realities of 'stabilisation assistance' in Afghanistan. This cluster then concludes that a RIA is *required* in order for the intelligence agencies to remain effective, but Lahneman argues that this RIA requirement is posited on the basis of relatively few, albeit significant, 'failures'.

The third category of discourse is based upon predicted intelligence requirements arising out of current security trends and projected security threats, for example, threats to cybersecurity, possible pandemics and Islamist fundamentalism.

Lahneman suggests (2007, 6–7) that a re-working of Cohen's (1996) questions, designed to establish the existence of a RMA, can be used to probe for such a RIA. The re-worked questions are as follows:

6. Will developments in the intelligence enterprise change how intelligence is developed and used (the process)? For Lahenman, the answer is 'yes' because of the need to use more open-source methods, to look inside the state as well outside the state and to explicitly widen the range of agencies which regularly participate in the intelligence enterprise. This requires the skilful balancing of knowledge-sharing imperatives with traditional intelligence agency knowledge about security concerns.
7. Will developments in the intelligence enterprise change the structure of the intelligence community (the organisation)? Again, following from point 1 above, the answer is 'yes', but the degree of change may be variable. An

observable organisation change feature in the USA, the UK, France and Italy is a degree of counter-terrorism intelligence 'centralisation'.
8. Will developments in the intelligence enterprise lead to the rise of new elites in the intelligence community? Or, rather radically, here, Lahneman suggests (2007, 11) that what may be required is the acquisition of a single national intelligence identity as opposed to the more traditional distinct and multiple intelligence agency identities. This is reminiscent of the efforts of defence departments to promote a unitary defence identity as opposed to separate and multiple armed service identities. Another important new skill set may develop around the need for working with experts from outside the public service.
9. Will developments in the intelligence enterprise significantly affect the national security of countries that fail to embrace these developments? The answer here appears to be a guarded 'possibly'. This is because, first, there are no simple military solutions to political violence and, second, there is the need to try to pre-empt possible 'mass-effect' threats from, for example, improvised bio-devices and from within cyberspace.

I will now apply these questions as part of the analytical framework in case studies of the USA and the UK. In the UK case study, I will examine the context of domestic intelligence operations and whether the 7/7 London bombings could have been prevented by intelligence. I will then consider the US context and the outcomes of US CT intelligence operations.

The UK after 9/11

Much of CT intelligence has to focus on the relatively small intelligence footprint of suspect individuals, but to reach this focus, the analytical work has to manage a geographically dispersed, large volume of information. This is a resource-intensive process, using HUMINT, SIGINT, IMINT and intercept sources. It is also an extremely complex task in relation to the al-Qaeda-inspired groups and their supporters, which are made up of a mixture of nationals, non-nationals, unknown illegal immigrants, people using false identities (anything up to 200 false identities for one person) and, apparently, law-abiding individuals with no criminal records. In the case of some of the suspects in the incidents in London on 21 July 2005, false identities are now known to have been used. In terms of possible intelligence 'gaps' in the London bombings of 7 July 2005, one of the dead bomb suspects, Mohammad Sidique Khan, may have already been tagged as suspects. It has been reported that Khan (and Shaheed Tanveer) did come to the attention of MI5 before 2005 in relation to ammonium nitrate seizures and other matters, but at the time they were not thought to be a priority target for surveillance.

These cases would suggest the need to draw the priority parameters more widely in terms of when CT resources are assigned to a person appearing on the intelligence 'radar'. Indeed, these target priority parameters have been re-formulated following reviews by the intelligence services after the London bombings (Intelligence and Security Committee, 2006). However, there are real practical issues in maximising the effectiveness of intelligence resource allocation to the range of potential targets, which are discussed later in this section.

Currently, a key function of UK CT intelligence is the assessment of the intentions and capabilities of terrorists in relation to the spectrum of 'deadly and determined' threats which were identified after 9/11. For example, assessments are made of the extent to which terrorists seek to add on to the common Improvised Explosive Device (IED) a Chemical, Biological, Radiological or Nuclear (CBRN) component to, first, cause more casualties and longer-lasting effects and, second, to complicate the CT response. In this assessment, CT intelligence specialists most emphatically do not see themselves as looking for the equivalent of WMDs; rather, they have to operate in the comparatively low-visibility intelligence arena, investigating, for example, who is receiving, a Western university training in chemistry.

The UK's Domestic Intelligence System

Until the passing of the Intelligence Services Act 1994, the British intelligence and security services existed in a kind of 'limbo'. The government refused to allow open discussion of their functions, despite a history dating back to the early twentieth century. The UK's intelligence 'community' can be described as a layered, pyramidal structure. At the top there are three civilian security and intelligence agencies (HM Government, 2002): the Security Service (MI5) for domestic security and intelligence; the Secret Intelligence Service (MI6) for external intelligence; and the GCHQ for SIGINT information assurance. In addition, under the Ministry of Defence, there are the three service intelligence organisations, namely the army, navy and air force intelligence organisations and the Defence Intelligence Analysis Staff (DIAS). The UK police forces also have their own specialist criminal intelligence bodies in the specialist national units. Specialist intelligence gathering is also carried out by other public bodies such as the UK Border Agency, HM Revenue & Customs and the Serious Organised Crime Agency (parts of which are scheduled to metamorphose into the National Crime Agency by 2013).

The UK police service's primary relationship is with MI5. Historically, a major function of the police Special Branches (see Clutterbuck, 2006; Denning, 1963; HMIC, 2003), which focus on politically related criminality, was to serve as the inter-agency link for this relationship. This link was codified in Home Office guidelines to chief constables, which stressed the Special Branches' 'interface' role between the Service and the police. The 1994 version of the guidelines highlighted the CT work by the Special Branches for MI5, but also referred to three other important areas of the working relationship: espionage, proliferation and subversion. Former MI5 Director General Stella Rimington noted that 'this relationship has expanded significantly and now includes other parts of the Police Service' (Rimington, 1994).

On a rough calculation, MI5 only has a personnel size equivalent to about 2.3 per cent of the total UK police strength, which is in itself a limiting factor for optimising relationships.

In essence, this relationship exemplifies the separation of organisational roles in monitoring suspect activities in the three main areas of political criminality: espionage, subversion and terrorism. This relationship is governed by two important general principles. First, it is considered to be good practice – as well as legally advisable – to have a functional separation and sterile corridor between investigation (governed by the provisions of the Police and Criminal Evidence Act 1984) and the gathering of intelligence. Second, the UK has always sought to maintain a clear distinction between the intelligence community and the law-enforcement community (Rimington, 1994).

The most significant development in intelligence analysis in the UK's CT operations was the establishment in June 2003 of the Joint Terrorism Analysis Centre (JTAC) on the initiative of Sir David Omand, the then Security and Intelligence Coordinator. In part, this was a response to criticisms of its more narrowly drawn predecessor, the Counterterrorism Analysis Centre (CTAC), which was largely staffed by MI5. The JTAC operates under the authority of the Director General of MI5 with staff drawn from a range of relevant agencies. It has autonomy in its workings and its Director reports to an inter-agency management board. Its remit is to provide long-term studies of international terrorism, for example, on the suicide bomber problem and immediate assessments of current threats. Externally, MI5 and MI6 also participate in a range of networks with similar agencies within, for example, the G8, the USA, the Commonwealth and Europe, especially the Counterterrorism Action Group formed by the G8 nations (see further Intelligence and Security Committee, 2006; Rosand, 2009; Rudner, 2004; Segell, 2004). Not surprisingly, more attention has been paid to the potential significance of such networks after 9/11.

After 9/11, CT has made MI5 more publicly visible through its participation in inter-agency working and, in the wide range of Whitehall inter-agency strategy committees emanating from the UK's CONTEST strategy (on CONTEST, see HM Government, 2006, 2009, 2011). This participation increased with the development of MI5's protective security outreach in the form of the Centre for the Protection of National Infrastructure (CPNI). In the development of anti-terrorist operations, MI5 also worked very closely, at a senior level, with: the ACPO rank officer designated as the National Coordinator of Terrorist Investigations (NCTI) who chairs a group that agrees operational priorities (the Executive Liaison Group); the ACPO rank officer who chairs the National Counterterrorism Tasking and Coordinating Group; and with chief constables. A former NCTI, Peter Clarke, commented that the metaphor of him acting as a 'bridge' between the intelligence services and the police was now obsolete and that what happens is that it is more like 'a very wide two way street, and my job is to make sure that the traffic flows freely' (Clarke, 2007).

The CONTEST emphasis on engaging with communities in tackling terrorism has recently led to more overt forms of engagement between the police Special

Branches and communities in the process of information gathering. This has been done under MI5 tasking (assisted by the development of MI5 regional offices) and may produce more usable intelligence. This joint effort is known as the 'Rich Picture' approach (Metropolitan Police Authority, 2008).

Could the 7/7 London Bombings Have Been Prevented?

Within the UK, there has been considerable controversy over whether the police and MI5 had sufficient information before 7/7 on two of the bombers, Mohammed Siddique Khan and Shaheed Tanveer, and could have used this information to prevent the 7/7 attacks. The intelligence services' oversight committee, the ISC, has twice investigated this issue. Its most recent and detailed inquiry produced a long report in May 2009 (Intelligence and Security Committee, 2009), the wealth of detail in which provides a unique 'window' into the realities of CT intelligence in the UK after 9/11. The unprecedented detail in this report allows us to focus on the process of assigning CT resources to a 'name' (of a suspect) identified from CT information, the scale of major CT investigations and their impact on available CT resources, and the 'lessons learned'.

An individual's name may come up in the course of CT information gathering in a myriad of ways, for example: from surveillance on an existing suspect; from a Driver and Vehicle Licensing Agency (DVLA) check on a vehicle seen at a suspect address; or from accessing phone records. The individual's name itself may be problematic because it might be transcribed inaccurately, it might be one of many aliases or the name may be recorded in different versions. In 2004–2005 (the period when Operation CREVICE, the operation directed at the ammonium-nitrate bomb plot) MI5 was using three categories of threat-related ranking of names in CT intelligence gathering. The three categories were/are: 'essential' (possible life-threatening activities and surveillance resources *may* be assigned); 'desirable' (possible undesirable activities but *no* life-threatening information); and 'other' (simple collateral information). As the DG of MI5 said to the ISC: '[I]n order to get on the "essentials" list you needed to be doing something which suggested you were involved in some form of life-threatening activity ... We had not got to that point with Mohammed Siddique Khan' (Intelligence and Security Committee, 2009, 39, para 135).

As a measure of the strain on resources to provide surveillance on 'potential targets', in 2004 MI5 could only provide reasonable surveillance coverage to six per cent of the known threat and even that required using 'every surveillance officer we [MI5] have' (Intelligence and Security Committee, 2009, 42, para 149).

After the July 2005 London attacks, MI5 revised its rankings into Priority 1–4 categories with Priorities 1 and 2 linked to possible plots and networks (covering both the 'essential' and 'desirable' previous categories). Priority 3 became the former 'other' category. However, on the Priority 2 – formerly 'desirables' – category, the ISC commented that:

for MI5 to have carried out consistent surveillance on the very large numbers who fell into the same category as [for example, Mohammad Sidique Khan and Shaheed Tanveer] ... it would have needed to be a very different organisation, both in terms of its size and how it operates, which would have huge ramifications for our society and the way we live, (Intelligence and Security Committee, 2009, 40, para 143)

The ISC's intensive investigations together with MI5's own self-reflexive process produced a number of 'lessons learnt' from Operation CREVICE and the July 2005 London bombings. These included the need for increased resources for MI5 in order to increase the number of Priority 1 targets subjected to a minimum of 'reasonable' surveillance coverage. Three further lessons related to improved working practices with the police and Special Branches. First, after 2004, MI5 changed the basis of its working relationship with the SBs from one based upon a 'need to know' to one based upon a 'need to share' (Intelligence and Security Committee, 2009, 71). Second, this was further facilitated by the establishment of MI5 regional offices linked to police regional CT and CT intelligence units. Third, there was greater recognition of the contribution that police forces can make to MI5 intelligence gathering from their Borough Command Units (BCU) work in both the CONTEST and PREVENT counter-violent extremism work and from ordinary criminal intelligence, since 60 per cent of terrorists have been found to be involved in some kind of other criminal activity (Intelligence and Security Committee, 2009, 49, para 178). Overall, the ISC found that these three lessons had 'brought considerable improvements to joint investigations and intelligence and information sharing' (Intelligence and Security Committee, 2009. 53, para 201). MI5 also developed its lateral work, whilst being what the DG MI5 described in June 2007 as 'on the operational sort of front edge' (Intelligence and Security Committee, 2009, 36, para 43). This lateral work involves the creation of 'legacy teams' (Intelligence and Security Committee, 2009, 46, para 167) which do follow-up work on past major operations. However, the ISC was critical of MI5's record-keeping and data management, and the DG MI5 admitted that ' our records are not to the level that we would choose them to be' (Intelligence and Security Committee, 2009, 172). The ISC linked this to the need for the UK's various CT IT systems to be better connected (Intelligence and Security Committee, 2009, 53). These critiques emerged from a 2007 evaluation of a 2005 incident and echo some of the post-9/11 concerns in the USA.

Returning to Lahneman's four questions (see above), the UK is clearly now more familiar with open-source research and a wide range of agencies with an intelligence function feed into the JTAC. In contrast to the USA, centralisation has been well established through the Joint Intelligence Committee (JIC) and the JTAC, and a better control of 'feeder' agency intelligence is proposed by the planned introduction of the National Crime Agency (NCA) (on which, see Home Office, 2011a). There are no signs of either new elites or a specific national intelligence identity. Other countries which have not set up structures like the JTAC or centralised intelligence services, like France and Italy, do not seem have encountered proportionately more incidents of terrorism or terrorism-related suspect behaviour.

The USA

In the USA the '9/11 Commission' (National Commission on Terrorist Attacks upon the United States, 2004) identified two intelligence-related factors as possible contributory factors in the failure to prevent the 9/11 attacks. These were 'breakdowns in information sharing and the failure to fuse pertinent intelligence' (Randol, 2009b, 1). Indeed, the current Director of National Intelligence (DNI), John M. McConnell, said in December 2008 that '[we] designed our own system to make the attacks of 9/11 successful' (YaleGlobal Forum, 2009). Thus, much of the US post-9/11 intelligence system reform efforts have been directed at addressing these matters. However, as recently as July 2008, Congress was told that the 'breadth and complexity of the information sharing challenge should not be underestimated. Information silos, cultural issues and other barriers that inhibit sharing still exist today' (Randol, 2009a, 14).

The USA PATRIOT Act was designed to facilitate an 'all sources' intelligence effort and three major developments were designed to implement these reforms. The post of DNI was created to oversee the USA's 16 main intelligence agencies. However, 80 per cent of the intelligence budget is under the control of the Department of Defense. In structural terms, the US Intelligence Community (defined at 50 U.S.C. 401a(4)) comprises 16 agencies. Best (2009, 5) describes the CIA as 'the keystone of the Intelligence Community' because it has all source analytical capabilities, it collects intelligence using HUMINT and it has an overseas covert action capability. The Department of Defense houses three of the major national-level intelligence agencies: the National Security Agency (NSA); the National Reconnaissance Office (NRO); and the National Geospatial-Intelligence Agency (NGA. The DNI produces the National Intelligence Strategy of the US (NIS) and stresses the need for federal, state, local and tribal entities to be 'connected to our homeland security and intelligence effort'. However, as Randol noted (2009a, 7), the definition of 'connected' is of crucial importance. The function of the National Counterterrorism Center (NCTC) established by the Intelligence Reform and Terrorism Prevention Act 2004, is to make maximum use of NSA products from ELINT. The third development was the establishment of the Fusion Centers initiative to further promote intelligence sharing.

Domestically, there are two particularly important intelligence 'players' in the USA: the CIA and the FBI. The long-established FBI has two key intelligence functions: counter-terrorism and counter-intelligence. After 9/11, it was:

> strongly criticized for failing to focus on the terrorist threat, for failing to collect and strategically analyze intelligence, and for failing to share intelligence with other agencies (as well as among various FBI components). (Best, 2004, 18)

As a consequence the FBI has been undertaking some major revisions to its role, organisation and structural approach (Cumming and Masse, 2004). First, in June 2003 the FBI Director, Robert S. Mueller, made counter-terrorism the FBI's top priority. Before that date, counter-terrorism had been listed as merely one of many concerns in the old 'Priority 1' basket of 'National and Economic Security'. Mueller established the new post of Executive Assistant Director for Intelligence (EAD-I) with increased emphasis on the intelligence function. Reporting to the EAD-I is the new Office of Intelligence (OI) with responsibility for implementing an agency-wide FBI intelligence strategy. The OI also oversees the FBI participation in federal level CT bodies and develops career paths for intelligence analysts.

In each of the FBI's 56 field offices, a Field Intelligence Group has been established which co-locates analysts, special agents responsible for intelligence collection and the new post of 'reports officers' who are responsible for sifting and disseminating intelligence. In 2002 the FBI also created a National Joint Terrorism Task Force (NJTTF) to coordinate the works of the 106 FBI-led JTTFs, 71 of which were established after 9/11. It should be noted that prior to 9/11, the FBI only had 154 CT analysts. The agency has also removed an important internal barrier by permitting criminal and intelligence investigators to work together in the same squad. An example of the success of a JTTF is the recent guilty plea of Zakariya Boyd before a federal court in New Bern, North Carolina to conspiracy to provide material support to promote violent jihad. The North Carolina JTTF run by the FBI Raleigh-Durham office included the Department of Defense's Defense Criminal Investigation Service (DCIS), the North Carolina Alcohol Law Enforcement Bureau, the Raleigh Police Department, the Durham Police Department and the North Carolina Information Sharing and Analysis Center (FBI, 2011).

The FBI has two serious problems to overcome if Mueller's goals are to be realised. First, the FBI is quite enmeshed in a law enforcement culture which sees criminal conviction as an end point as opposed to the use of arrest and charging with minor offences to disrupt, which are common in the CT world. In 2003, over 90 per cent of Supervisory Agents in Charge in the FBI had no national security experience. Second, since 9/11, the FBI has been trying to upgrade its IT systems to support a 'Virtual Case File' system. The initial programme, Trilogy, was cancelled in 2005, resulting in millions of dollars having been wasted. It has since been replaced by the 'Sentinel' programme, which, despite further criticisms from the Department of Justice's Inspector-General, has been reported as ongoing (FBI, 2009).

It is also a particular responsibility of the Department of Homeland Security (DHS) under the Homeland Security Act (P.L. 107-296) to ensure the 'fusing law enforcement and intelligence information relating to terrorist threats to the homeland' (FBI, 2009, 4). Thus, homeland security intelligence is a mixture of both domestic and foreign intelligence. Speaking in 2005, the DHS Chief Intelligence Officer, Charles Allen, told Congress that his role and goal was to ensure 'that Homeland Security Intelligence, a blend of traditional and non-traditional intelligence that produces unique actionable insights, takes place alongside the other kinds of intelligence as an indispensable tool for securing the nation' (Randol, 2009a, 1). This goal has been articulated in the DHS Intelligence Enterprise Strategy Plan formulated in 2006.

Fusion centres did exist before 9/11, but they have been broadened in scope beyond criminal intelligence to include a wide range of homeland security issues including the response to natural disasters (Rollins, 2008). Currently there are over 40 fusion centres of varying membership across the USA. Thus, the fusion centres potentially have access to a wider range of information than is available to the JTTFs. The majority of fusion centres have an all-crimes and/or all-hazards focus; less than 15 per cent of fusion centres have solely a CT function. However, Rollins suggests that 'in the absence of a common understanding of what constitutes intelligence fusion center development and progress may be impeded' (2008, 10).

The USA: Outcomes of CT Intelligence

A post-9/11 'outcomes' assessment on the USA has three main types of 'outcome' to consider. The primary outcome category relates to CT intelligence and terrorist threat reduction within the USA. The other two categories fall within the fields of overseas intelligence and intelligence-led covert operations, namely the practice of 'extraordinary rendition' and 'suspect elimination' via covert or 'black' operations (see Best and Feickert, 2006). These fall largely outside the scope of this chapter, but a brief examination of covert operations can show some degree of linkage between CT intelligence and operations aimed at terrorist threat reduction.

Under presidential authority, after 9/11, the CIA managed to obtain all-agency agreement to use UAVs against terrorists (i.e. suspect civilians) rather than just military targets (Tucker-Jones, 2009, 15–16). In the period 2007–2009, CIA-guided Predator strikes are claimed to have killed '20 al-Qaeda commanders' (Tucker-Jones, 2009, 16). However, public sources do not contain hard information linking the deaths of these people with actual terrorist plots against the USA. Most recently, on 1 May 2011, US Navy SEALs from the US Department of Defense Joint Special Operations Command made an intelligence-led helicopter-borne assault on a compound in Abbottabad in the northwest Khyber Pakhtunkwa province of Pakistan and subsequently killed Osama bin Laden, the leader of al-Qaeda. The Bush and Obama administrations have always held that Osama bin Laden was a legitimate target in armed conflict, being part of al-Qaeda's command and control structure (Rollins, 2011). The long-running controversy surrounding 'extraordinary rendition' has generated a wide range of analyses and critiques; indeed, in November 2009, an Italian court convicted 23 Americans *in absentia* for kidnapping Osama Moustafa Hassan Nasr (alias Abu Omar) from Italy and taking him to Egypt (*Intersec*, 2009, 40).

The main category of 'outcomes' of counter-terrorism intelligence that fall within the scope of this chapter relate to domestic CT operations, as discussed in the earlier UK case study. Nearly a decade after 9/11, there is less force to the criticisms of Lum, Kennedy and Sherley (2006) that CT analyses pay insufficient attention to the outcomes of CT strategies and operations. For example, Randol (2009b) has looked at the US experience with regard to the outcomes of the Nationwide Suspicious Activity Reports (SARs) initiative and terrorism information sharing which stemmed from the Intelligence Reform and Terrorism Prevention Act 2004.

At the base level, the SAR is a reporting format used by the 800,000+ US police officers on a daily basis. As an example of the scope of SARs, former Washington State-based US Attorney John McKay said: 'evidence of a potential terrorist threats or organised criminal enterprise is far more likely to be found in the incidental contact with the 10,000 police officers in the state of Washington than by the less than 150 FBI agents assigned to the Seattle Field Division' (Randol, 2009b, 5). However, of course, the effectiveness of the system will depend upon the sophistication of the filters applied to the SARs. For instance, between July 2004 and November 2007, the FBI 'documented approximately 108,000 potential terrorism related threats, reports of suspicious incidents, and terrorist watch-list encounters' (Randol, 2009b, 6). Some further indication of the outcomes of a CT-related SAR management process is given by the data from Los Angeles for the period 3 March 2008– 25 October 2009 provided by the Los Angeles Police Department (LAPD). In that period in the area within the jurisdiction of the LAPD, there were 2,063 SARs generated, of which 26 related to terrorist cases.

On the basis of this, it has been claimed that the USA has pre-empted 19 terrorist attempts on its home ground between 2002 and 2007, and the New York University Center on Law and Security data suggests that 'more than 500 individuals have been convicted (in the US) for terrorism-related charges since 9/11' (Vidino, 2009, 2). Most were US nationals or long-term residents who were radicalised in the USA. However, until the 2005 London bombings, the USA was reluctant to acknowledge the possibility of home-grown radicalisation. In 2009, for example, there were a series of seven counter-terrorism arrests between September and December (Vidino, 2009, 2–3). These included, in September, the cases of two Afghan immigrants, one of whom was Najibullah Zazi, trained in an al-Qaeda camp in Pakistan, who had purchased large quantities of chemicals to construct IEDs for use in the New York area. Their plot was described by the US authorities as the most serious threat against the US homeland uncovered since 9/11.

However, in the same period there have been two incidents which call into question the effectiveness of post-9/11 US intelligence sector reforms and changes. First, there is the case of the shootings at Fort Hood on 5 November 2009 apparently perpetrated by a US Army Major, Nidal Malik Hasan, where it would appear that the FBI had investigated his links with the American-born but Yemeni-based radical cleric Anwar al Awlaqi, but had failed to pass them on to the Army. Second, there was the 25 December 2009 case of Umar Farouk Abdulmutallab, a Nigerian Muslim who allegedly tried to ignite an IED on Northwest Airlines Flight 253 to Detroit. Abdulmutallab was known to UK intelligence for low-level radical leanings and was actually banned from entering the UK for trying to obtain a visa for a course at an unapproved college. Moreover, information passed to the US authorities by Abdulmutallab's father of his concerns about his son's radicalisation had led to Abdulmutallab being placed on the US NCTC Terrorist Identities Datamart Environment (TIDE). However, he was *not* nominated by the NCTC to the FBI for inclusion in the Terrorist Screening Database, which would have led to his name going on a 'no-fly' or screening watch list (Krouse and Elias, 2009, 1). Both of these cases raise two important general intelligence-related counter-terrorism issues: first, the issue of sharing information related to terrorism between national intelligence agencies and between countries; and, second, the criteria for allocating additional intelligence resources or attention to an individual suspect case.

With regard to Lahneman's four questions (see above), in the USA there are already too many intelligence agencies, with 16 main agencies and about 13,000 contributing state and local police forces. Open-source intelligence already yields more data than can be handled effectively. There have been recent important measures of centralisation such as establishing the oversight role of the DNI and the creation of the NCTC. However, 80 per cent of the intelligence budget remains under the control of the federal Department of Defense. Moreover, there are no signs of the development of a single national intelligence identity. As with the UK, states that have not implemented such reforms do not seem to be suffering from more terrorism-related incidents.

Conclusions

Intelligence work is necessarily limited in scope by the capacity of national surveillance systems. Paradoxically, however, it is virtually unlimited in some states in terms of information gathering. Ultimately, it is only when you have an 'eyeball' or the electronic equivalent on a suspect that you have a reasonable chance of a preventive intervention. Technology provides access to a vast array of surveillance information; however, using that information to construct meaningful analyses relies on the training and skills of the analysts and the abilities of individual agencies to disseminate intelligence appropriately. Even if agency A has the requisite skills and analytical methods, it cannot be assumed yet, despite all the reforms, that agencies B and C have necessarily passed agency A all their relevant information. The additional complications of intelligence sharing between countries compound these difficulties. Moreover, if aspiring terrorists or their sympathisers use Privacy Enhancing Technologies or Privacy Enhancing Strategies, uncovering their activities will probably still depend on chance activities such as a surveillance sweep, a police investigation of an apparently unrelated suspect activity, a random customs search or an immigration check at an airport. Overall, the answer to Lahneman's four questions about the existence of a RIA has to be that whilst some trends suggest such a revolution, some do not, and we require further evidence on others.

References

Andrew, C. (2009), *The Defence of the Realm – The Authorized History of MI5*. London: Allen Lane.

Best, R.A. (2004), 'Proposals for Intelligence Reorganization 1994–2004', CRS Report for Congress, RL325000, 24 September.
Best, R.A. (2009), 'Intelligence Issues for Congress', CRS Report for Congress, RL33539, 18 September.
Best, R.A. and Feickert, A. (2006), 'Special Operations Forces (SOF) and CIA Paramilitary Operations: Issues for Congress', CRS Report for Congress RS22017, 6 December.
Cabinet Office (2007), 'Security in a Global Hub – Establishing the UK's New Border Arrangements'. Cohen, E. (1996), 'A Revolution in Warfare', *Foreign Affairs* 75(2), 37–54.
Clarke, P. (2007), 'Learning from Experience', The Inaugural Colin Cramphorn Memorial Lecture, Policy Exchange.
Clutterbuck, L. (2006), 'Countering Irish Republican Terrorism in Britain: Its Origins as a Police Function', *Terrorism and Political Violence* 18, 95–118.
Council of Europe, European Commission for Democracy through Law (Venice Commission) (2007), *Report on the Democratic Oversight of the Security Services*, Study No. 388/2006, CDL-AD(2007)016, Strasbourg, 11 June.
Cumming, A. and Masse, T. (2004), 'FBI Intelligence Reform Since September 11, 2001: Issues and Options for Congress,' CRS report for Congress RL323336, 4 August.
Denning, L.J. (1963), *Lord Denning's Report (Profumo Affair)*. Cm. 2152, London, HMSO.
FBI (2009), 'Response to OIG Audit of the FBI's Sentinel Program', 10 November, http://www.fbi.gov/news/pressrel/press-releases/response-to-oig-audit-of-the-fbi2019s [accessed 23 June 2011].
FBI (2011), 'North Carolina Man Pleads Guilty to Terrorism Charge', 7 June, http:www.fbi.gov/charlotte/press-releases/2011/north-carolina-man-pleads-guily-to [accessed 23 June 2011].
George, R.Z. (2007), 'CSI Meeting the 21st Century Transnational Challenges: Building a Global Intelligence Paradigm', https://www.csi.gov/library/center-for-the-study-of-intelligence/csi-publications/csi-st [accessed 23 June 2011].
Gregory, F., (2006), 'Intelligence-led Counter-terrorism Operations in the UK Summer 2006: Issues and Consequences', ARI Paper 106/2006, Real Instituto Elcano de Estudios Internacionales y Estratégicos, Madrid, October, http://r-i-elcano,org/analisis/1056.asp [accessed 23 June 2011].
Gregory, F. (2008), 'The Police and the Intelligence Services: With Special Reference to the Relationship with MI5', in C. Harfield, A. MacVean, J. Grieve and D. Phillips (eds), *The Handbook of Intelligent Policing: Consilience, Crime Control and Community Safety*. Oxford: Oxford University Press.
Gregory, F. (2009a), *UK Border Security: Issues, Systems and Recent Reforms*. London: IPPR.
Gregory, F. (2009b), 'CONTEST: An Evaluation of Revisions to the UK Counter-Terrorism Strategy with a Special Focus on the CBRNRE Threat', ARI Paper 130/2009, Real Instituto Elcano de Estudios Internacionales y Estratégicos, Madrid.

Herman, M. (2003), 'Counter-Terrorism, Information Technology and Intelligence Change', *Intelligence and National Security* 18(4), 40–58.

Hillyard, P. (1993), *Suspect Communities: People's Experience of the Prevention of Terrorism Acts in Britain*. London: Pluto Press.

HM Government (2002), National Intelligence Machinery, London. http://webarchive.nationalarchives.gov.uk/+/http://www.cabinetoffice.gov.uk/media/136045/national_intelligence_booklet.pdf [accessed 30 August 2012].

HM Government (2006), *Countering International Terrorism: The United Kingdom Government Strategy*. Cm. 6888, London: The Stationery Office.

HM Government (2009), *CONTEST: The United Kingdom's Strategy for Countering International Terrorism*. Cm. 7547, London: The Stationery Office.

HM Government (2011), *CONTEST: The United Kingdom's Strategy for Countering Terrorism*. Cm. 8123, London: The Stationery Office.

HMIC (2003), 'A Need to Know: HMIC Thematic Inspection of Special Branches and Ports Policing', Communications Division, Home Office, January.

Home Office, Scottish Executive, Northern Ireland Office (2004), Guidelines on SPECIAL BRANCH WORK in the United Kingdom. http://www.scotland.gov.uk/Resource/Doc/47171/0025036.pdf [accessed 30 August 2012].

Home Office (2011), *Prevent Strategy*. Cm. 8092, London: The Stationery Office

Home Office (2011), *The National Crime Agency: A Plan for Creating a National Crime-Fighting Agency*. Cm. 8097, London: The Stationery Office.

Honig, Or Arthur (2007), 'A New Direction for Theory-Building in Intelligence Studies', *International Journal of Intelligence and Counterintelligence* 20(4), 699–716.

Hughes-Wilson, J. (2004), 'Pre-war Intelligence and Iraq's WMD Threat', *RUSI Journal* 149(1), 10–15.

Intelligence and Security Committee (2006) *Report into the London Terrorist Attacks on 7 July 2005*. Cm. 6785, London: The Stationery Office.

Intelligence and Security Committee (2009), *Could 7/7 Have Been Prevented? Review of the Intelligence on the London Terrorist Attacks on 7 July 2005*. Cm. 7617, London: The Stationery Office.

Intersec (2009), 'News – Europe' 19(10), November/December, 40.

Jeffery, K. (2010), *MI6: The History of the Secret Intelligence Service 1909–1949*. London: Bloomsbury.

Krouse, W.J. and Elias, B. (2009), 'Terrorist Watchlists Checks and Air Passenger Prescreening', CRS Report for Congress RL37645, 30 December.

Lahneman, W.J. (2007), 'Is a Revolution in Intelligence Affairs Occurring?', *International Journal of Intelligence and Counter-Intelligence* 20, 1–17.

Levi, M. and Wall, D.S. (2004), 'Technologies, Security, and Privacy in the Post – 9/11 European Information Society', *Journal of Law and Society* 31(2), 194–220.

Lum, C., Kennedy, L.W. and Sherley, A.J. (2006), 'Are Counter-terrorism Strategies Effective? The Results of the Campbell Systematic Review on Counter-terrorism Research', *Journal of Experimental Criminology* 2, 489–516.

McCulloch, J. and Pickering, S. (2009), 'Pre-crime and Counter-terrorism', *British Journal of Criminology* 49, 628–45.

Manningham-Buller, E. (2003), James Smart Memorial Lecture, http://www.mi5.gov.uk/output/Page380.html [accessed 23 June 2011].

Masse, T. (2003), 'Domestic Intelligence in the United Kingdom: Applicability of the MI5 Model to the United States', CRS report for Congress, RL33539, September.

Metropolitan Police (2006), 'Special Branch Introduction and Responsibilities', Freedom of Information Act Publication Scheme Document.

Metropolitan Police Authority (2007), 'Community Engagement to CounterTerrorism', Report 8b by the Commissioner, 27 July 2007. http://www.mpa.gov.uk/committees/mpa2006/060727/08b.htm, accessed 19 October 2007.

Metropolitan Police Authority (2008), 'MPS Prevent Delivery Strategy', Report: 8, Date: 24 July 2008 By: Assistant Commissioner Specialist Operations on behalf of the Commissioner.

Müller-Wille, B. (2006) 'Improving Democratic Accountability of EU Intelligence', *Intelligence and National Security*, 21, 100–128.

National Commission on Terrorist Attacks upon the United States (2004), *The 9/11 Commission Report*. New York: W.W. Norton.

News Europe (2009), 'Italy Convicts CIA Agents', *Journal of International Security* 19(10), 40.

Pantazis, C. and Pemberton, S. (2009), 'From the "Old" to the "New" Suspect Community', *British Journal of Criminology* 49, 646–66.

Pillar, P.R. (2004), 'Intelligence', in A.K. Cronin and J.M. Lendes (eds), *Attacking Terrorism – Elements of a Grand Strategy*. Washington DC: Georgetown University Press, 115–39.

Randol, M.A. (2009a), 'Homeland Security Intelligence: Perceptions, Statutory Definitions and Approaches', CRS Report for Congress, RL33616, 14 January.

Randol, M.A. (2009b), 'Terrorism Information Sharing and the Nationwide Suspicious Activity Report Initiative: Background and Issues for Congress', CRS Report for Congress R40901, 5 November.

Report of a Committee of Privy Counsellors (2004), *Review of Intelligence on Weapons of Mass Destruction, Chairman Lord Butler*. HC 898, London: The Stationery Office.

Rimington, S. (1994), 'Intelligence, Security and the Law', James Smart Lecture, 3 November.

Rimington, S. (2002), *Open Secret*. London: Arrow.

Ripley, T. (2011), *Air War Afghanistan*. Barnsley: Pen & Sword.

Rollins, J. (2008), 'Fusion Centers: Issues and Options for Congress', CRS Report for Congress RL34070, 18 January.

Rollins, J. (2011), 'Osama bin Laden's Death: Implications and Considerations', CRS Report for Congress R41809, 5 May.

Rosand, E. (2009), 'The G8's Counterterrorism Action Group', Policy Brief, May, Center on Global Counterterrorism Cooperation, www.globalct.org [accessed 25 June 2012].

Rudner, M. (2004), 'Hunters and Gatherers: The Intelligence Coalition against Islamic Terrorism', *International Journal of Intelligence and CounterIntelligence* 17, 193–230.

Segell, G.M. (2004), 'Intelligence Agency Relations between the European Union and the U.S.', *International Journal of Intelligence and CounterIntelligence* 17, 81–96.

Treverton, G.F. and Gabbard, C. Bryan (2008), 'Assessing the Tradecraft of Intelligence Analysis', RAND, TR-293.

Treverton, G.F. and Renwick, J. (2008), 'The Challenge of Trying Terrorists as Criminals', Proceedings of a RAND Colloquium, RAND Center for Global Risk and Security.

Tucker-Jones, A. (2009), 'The Great Escape', *Intersec* 19(2), 16.

Vidino, L. (2009), 'The Homegrown Terrorist Threat to the US Homeland', Real Instituto Elcano, ARI 171/2009, 18 December.

YaleGlobal Forum (2009), 'EU and USA Intelligence Community', https://forums.globalyale.yale.edu/threat.jspe?threatID-1850 [accessed 2 November 2009].

20

Counter-Terrorism and its Effectiveness in the UK since 1969: Does It Pay to Be Tough on Terrorism?

Robert Lambert

Introduction

My aim in this chapter is to demonstrate that UK governments since 1969 have consistently fallen into a trap set for them by a variety of non-state actors who have chosen to adopt the tactics of terrorism and political violence to further their political aims. This is to conceive terrorism as a tactic intended to provoke overreaction by governments that will harm communities where the terrorists seek recruits and supporters. It would conceivably pay to be tough on terrorism, but by failing to keep counter-terrorism policies tightly focused on lawfully targeting legitimate terrorist suspects, and instead invoking extrajudicial and 'emergency' measures that have too often harmed, alienated and criminalised minority communities, governments have routinely invoked counter-terrorism practices that have become counter-productive. Counter-productivity does not follow simply because counter-terrorism policies have been too tough, but rather because they have been poorly focused and have sought military and extrajudicial means instead of normal investigative responses led by the police.

Such counter-productivity, I argue, has often been unwitting but rarely unforeseeable. In the case of the New Labour government's enthusiastic embrace of a neo-conservative war on terror after 9/11, such a wilful refusal to ignore the cumulative lessons of the UK counter-terrorism experience since 1969 reached an extraordinary level of irresponsibility. As a result on the tenth anniversary of the war on terror, the Coalition government, inspired by neo-conservativism in the same way as New Labour, was unable to point to a significant reduction of the terrorist threat that a US/UK alliance had set out to destroy. To understand the basis for such apparent indifference to UK counter-terrorism lessons learned prior to 9/11, it is necessary to appreciate the power of a prevailing notion that the war on terror was responding to 'new terrorism' and that all prior experience was therefore redundant (Lambert 2011a). This was a necessary basis on which to launch the war on terror and one that does not stand up to close scrutiny.

In contrast, I argue that to be effective, all UK counter-terrorism policies should aim to achieve a degree of legitimacy in minority, often alienated, communities where terrorist movements who plan to carry out bomb attacks in UK towns and cities seek recruits and support (Tupman and O'Reilly, 2004; Lambert 2011a). Since 1969, this hypothetical objective has entailed achieving legitimacy in Irish republican and nationalist communities in Belfast, London, Liverpool, Manchester, Glasgow and other UK towns and cities. Since 2001, the same objective has existed in respect of Muslim communities in the same towns and cities. Successive governments have failed to appreciate that both objectives arise from an analysis that acknowledges the crucial importance the Provisional IRA (PIRA), al-Qaeda and most other terrorist movements place upon their strategies for propaganda, recruitment, retention and support (Schmid, 2004; Lia, 2007). It is not always clear whether governments wilfully ignore this kind of analysis and adopt ineffective counter-terrorism policies that appear tough under pressure from sections of the media or whether they genuinely believe in their ability to declare war on 'terror'. Central to the analysis consistently ignored by governments in respect of PIRA and Al-Qaeda movements is the understanding that all UK citizens and residents have a potential stake in reducing violence in their towns and cities, whether it is inspired by politics or not.

To the extent that this approach to counter-terrorism policy may be described as soft, it has not won favour with UK political leaders, who have generally preferred to be seen to be tough on terrorism instead – especially in the aftermath of terrorist bomb attacks. 'Tough' in this context invariably means seeking retribution and punishment in the aftermath of bomb attacks where innocent civilians have been killed and injured while going about their daily business. *Realpolitik* demands tough political responses at such times, but it is regrettable that UK political leaders have not devised coherent strategies to present soft and effective counter-terrorism strategies to the public and media in ways that would make them legitimate to majority communities as well as minority communities. Although UK governments have invested millions of pounds in contingency planning to prepare responses to terrorist attacks, virtually none of the expenditure has been allocated to explore ways of explaining to the public what terrorist strategies are and what the most effective ways of responding to them might be. UK security and police chiefs would face the same difficulties if they tried to adopt soft instead of hard counter-terrorism strategies. Generally speaking, they have preferred instead to follow the tone set by Conservative and Labour prime ministers and home secretaries and have often supported or lobbied for extraordinary powers and special legislation in respect of PIRA, al-Qaeda and other terrorist movements over the last 40 years. It is, however, important to note that outstanding success has been achieved by UK security and police officers in innumerable counter-terrorism cases during the same period, regardless of the political rhetoric in Westminster (Jackson 2008; Lambert 2011a).

In most instances, success in these cases arises from the application of specialist intelligence and investigative skills that focus narrowly on legitimate terrorist suspects without recourse to exceptional police powers granted by Parliament. In terms of operational counter-terrorism, this is no different from success in other areas of detective work tackling serious violent crime where perpetrators of murders and assaults are investigated, tried and convicted at trials where the evidence is tested by a judge and jury. Where miscarriages of justice have arisen – the Birmingham Six and the Guildford Four being the most notable examples – they have been due in part to the political notion that being tough on terrorism licenses derogations from normal police practice. In contrast, the significant body of successful UK terrorist prosecutions since 1969 where junior security and police officers have behaved professionally and proportionately owes everything to specialist detective and security skills and not extended or exceptional police powers (Lambert 2011a).

In response to dramatic investigative failings identified by Lord Macpherson in the Stephen Lawrence Inquiry in 1999, John Grieve, a senior and highly regarded detective in the Metropolitan Police, led a government-backed attempt to eliminate institutional racism in policing and restore confidence in policing amongst minority ethnic communities (Sharp, 2002; Souhami, 2007). He was especially focused on ensuring that mistakes in the Stephen Lawrence murder investigation were never repeated (Grieve and French, 2000). Two years later, Tony Blair, the UK Prime Minister, Jack Straw and David Blunkett, Home Secretaries who backed Grieve, showed no appreciation or appetite for ensuring that the same sensitivity was extended by police to Muslim communities in a post-9/11 counter-terrorism context. On the contrary, 9/11 licensed a global war on terror that ensured several UK Muslims would receive treatment – most especially outside UK jurisdiction – that fell way below the standards demanded by Lord Macpherson and John Grieve. Thus, building confidence in policing became problematised in respect of Muslim communities (Spalek, 2005; Spalek and Lambert 2007; Spalek, El-Awa and McDonald, 2008). While such a failing might be dismissed by influential political commentators as being a mere failure of 'political correctness' (Gove, 2006; Phillips, 2006), it was, from Grieve's perspective, an issue that went to the heart of legitimate and effective counter-terrorism policing.

It is also noteworthy that former UK Prime Minister Margaret Thatcher denied the political status of PIRA prisoners while simultaneously licensing extrajudicial counter-terrorism responses against them that would not be sanctioned in responses to criminals unmotivated by politics. By refusing to acknowledge the reality of the political grievances that distinguished PIRA prisoners from prisoners convicted of ordinary crimes, Thatcher sought to appear tough and was indeed unyielding in her response to a hunger strike that ultimately proved more beneficial to PIRA recruitment than to UK counter-terrorism. To a significant extent, by licensing extrajudicial counter-terrorism responses against PIRA, Thatcher undermined her simultaneous claim that their prisoners should be treated as ordinary criminals. For a political leader who otherwise could pride herself on a remarkable consistency of policy and conduct, such ill-conceived responses pay tribute to the power of terrorist strategists to induce disproportionate and counter-productive responses from UK governments.

Thatcher's close involvement with UK counter-terrorism policy, together with her role as terrorist victim in PIRA's bombing of the Conservative Party Conference in Brighton in 1984, highlights a symbiotic relationship between terrorists who target the UK and the UK political leaders who wish to appear tough in confronting them. Strictly speaking, when PIRA planned to plant and explode a bomb in the heart of the UK government, it was conceiving an act of political violence that sits beyond the normal definition of terrorism in which innocent civilians are the proxy victims intended to prompt a government reaction. The fact that Thatcher narrowly escaped death herself did little to dampen the success of the operation from a PIRA perspective. It was more than sufficient to draw Thatcher into a direct confrontational engagement which boosted PIRA's profile despite her simultaneous attempt to deny it 'the oxygen of publicity'. Thatcher in relation to the Provisional IRA and Blair in relation to al-Qaeda have adopted policies and postures that appear tough but which negligently boost support for the terrorist tactics being adopted by their non-state opponents against the UK (Lambert 2011a). This chapter focuses on political responses to terrorist campaigns conducted by PIRA and allied Irish republican groups from 1969 onwards, and by al-Qaeda and allied groups and individuals from 2001 onwards by political leaders who have been more concerned with impressing their own supporters rather than potential supporters in communities where the terrorists seek support. It also analyses the tactics of PIRA and al-Qaeda bombing campaigns in the UK and the failure of political leaders to interpret them correctly and to respond effectively.

UK Political Leaders Act Tough on Terrorism

Both terrorist movements have targeted London and other UK cities in which their own supporters are resident, yet have benefited from similar retributive approaches by UK governments determined to be seen to be tough on terrorism in the aftermath of terrorist outrages. In particular, Margaret Thatcher and Tony Blair led government responses to terrorist attacks that were insufficiently focused on the terrorist conspiracies themselves and liable thereby to stigmatise surrounding communities that hitherto only shared the terrorists' political grievances, not their terrorist tactics. In both instances, disproportionate government responses were seized upon by terrorist propagandists who sought to bolster their claims that communities adversely affected by draconian counter-terrorism measures should join or support their movement. The fact that Tony Blair was able to adopt a tough posture after 9/11 and repeat mistakes made by Margaret Thatcher speaks volumes for the power of terrorist outrages to impede rational responses by politicians who are generally persuaded to appease tabloid anger and outrage instead. Blair's blinkered adherence to Thatcher's failed model might also be explained in part by what Dr David Owen has professionally diagnosed as 'hubris syndrome', a condition in which politicians lose their moral compass when they become overly attached to the trappings of power (Owen, 2007).

Over the last four decades, UK political leaders who have responded to terrorist bomb attacks by PIRA or al-Qaeda in the UK have perforce reflected the moral outrage of the public and the media. Although there is an understandable need for political leaders to be seen to be 'tough on terrorism', such reactions have generally resulted in knee-jerk legislative responses that have not achieved a reduction in the terrorist threat but have often unintentionally benefited the strategists planning the terrorist attacks more than the police and security services seeking to detect and disrupt them. Rarely have political leaders felt inclined to advise the public or the media that softer, often counter-intuitive responses to terrorist attacks are inherently more likely to achieve success than the draconian measures invariably adopted instead. Whether this failure results from ignorance or political expediency or a combination of the two is a moot point that does not need to be resolved for the purposes of this chapter.

Instead, it will serve to illustrate the point by highlighting the febrile atmosphere in the House of Commons in the aftermath of a PIRA bomb attack on 21 November 1974 in which 21 civilians were killed and 182 were injured. Two improvised explosive devices exploded in two central Birmingham pubs – the *Mulberry Bush* and the *Tavern in the Town* – and a third device, left outside a bank in Hagley Road, failed to detonate. Noting parallels with the atmosphere in the House of Commons after 7/7, the al-Qaeda tube bombings in July 2005, the *New Statesman* usefully marked the first anniversary of 7/7 by reprinting an article written by Mary Holland after she witnessed the House of Commons debate on the introduction of the Prevention of Terrorism (Temporary Provisions) Act 1974. The following extract from Holland's 30-year-old article certainly resonated in 2006:

> The most depressing aspect of the House of Commons debate on Mr. Jenkins' new laws against terrorism was not the desire of most MPs to be seen as more vociferous in their demands for retribution than all but the most vengeful of their constituents, Holland noted. Nor was it the fact that so few seemed to have given thought to how Mr. Jenkins's measures might work in practice. The character of the debate which should have induced near despair was the passionate desire of a British Parliament to batten down the hatches, to shut out the ugly, dangerous infection which threatens us from the outside ... If the new laws are seen as labelling all Irish people here as potentially suspect, that is what those people could become. (Holland, 2006)

Most tellingly, Holland captures the wilful failure of the Labour government to acknowledge the legitimacy of the political grievances that PIRA sought to exploit for terrorist recruitment. Before examining the parallels between this Old Labour knee-jerk response in 1974 and its New Labour counterpart in 2005, it will be useful to examine parallels with an equally tough though more considered Conservative response to another kind of tactic, the hunger strike, adopted by Irish republican prisoners convicted or suspected of terrorism offences. During the course of

1981, PIRA hunger striker Bobby Sands emerged as a high-profile opponent of Conservative Prime Minister Margaret Thatcher, and their battle of wills became the media focal point for a hunger strike that was itself the culmination of a five-year protest by Irish republican prisoners (Taylor, 1997).

The protest began as the blanket protest in 1976, when the British government withdrew special category status for convicted paramilitary prisoners. In 1978 the dispute escalated into the dirty protest, where prisoners refused to wash and covered the walls of their cells with excrement. Bobby Sands was elected as a Member of Parliament during the strike, but instead of using that as a basis for negotiation, Margaret Thatcher stood firm and refused to give concessions to Sands and his fellow hunger strikers. Thatcher argued that she was not prepared to 'consider special category status for certain groups of people serving sentences for crime' because, as she put it, 'crime is crime, it is not political' (BBC, 2006a). She maintained this hardline position in the face of last-ditch efforts by intermediaries, Pope John Paul II's personal envoy John Magee and European Commission of Human Rights official, to negotiate a compromise (Taylor, 1997: 242–3). With Sands close to death, the Secretary of State for Northern Ireland Humphrey Atkins noted that if Sands 'persisted in his wish to commit suicide that was his choice'. 'The Government', he declared, 'would not force medical treatment upon him' (Taylor, 1997: 242–3).

Over 100,000 people lined the route for Sands' funeral, which was conducted with full IRA military honours. The unintended consequence of Thatcher's role in terms of increased recruitment and support for PIRA resulted from the pressure to maintain prestige with government supporters and allies, not with the communities where PIRA sought recruits. This tendency towards hardline counter-terrorism responses was first evidenced in Northern Ireland when a Conservative government introduced the Special Powers Act in 1971 so as to facilitate the internment of suspected PIRA members and supporters. According to George Churchill-Coleman, a former head of the Metropolitan Police Anti-Terrorism Branch, this draconian measure had the unintended consequence of boosting PIRA recruitment. He also argued that the detention of suspected al-Qaeda terrorists under similar emergency powers ran the same risk (Travis, Dyer and White, 2005).

Counter-productive Counter-terrorism

In both instances, Churchill-Coleman based his assessment on his practitioner experience of terrorist recruitment strategies that sought to capitalise on draconian or disproportionate counter-terrorism policies that alienated communities where they sought support. PIRA and al-Qaeda strategists take a long-term view. They aspire to overcome inevitable, substantial operational setbacks on the basis that they have nurtured sustainable grassroots support. In this context, tacit community support is highly valued as a vehicle for sustaining terrorist activity. More than anything else, though, the aim of terrorist propaganda is to maintain a pool of potential recruits; if the pool dries up, there is no one left to plant their bombs (Lambert 2010).

It is axiomatic to all forms of non-state terrorism that the perpetrators are seeking to elicit a response from government that will further publicise their cause. A terrorist act or terrorist campaign that achieves no publicity has largely failed. For all that is new in the terrorism of al-Qaeda, much remains familiar, especially in relation to terrorist propaganda. While the wider Irish public might have been appalled by or indifferent to terrorist activity, PIRA strategists always calculated that as long as recruitment from a small section of the community was invigorated by it, the long-term effort was safeguarded. Al-Qaeda strategists make the same calculation (Lia, 2007). Alex Schmid argues that terrorism is helpfully viewed from a terrorist's perspective as 'communication':

> Terrorism cannot be understood only in terms of violence. It has to be understood primarily in terms of propaganda. Violence and propaganda, however, have much in common. Violence aims at behaviour modification by coercion. Propaganda aims at the same by persuasion. Terrorism can be seen as a combination of the two. Terrorism, by using violence against one victim, seeks to coerce and persuade others. The immediate victim is merely instrumental, the skin on a drum beaten to achieve a calculated impact on a wider audience. (Schmid, 2004: 205–6)

As Louise Richardson argues, terrorist movements 'pursue two sets of long and short-term motivations simultaneously' (Richardson, 2006: 105–6). The long-term motivations belong to 'the leadership of the movements', while 'the followers tend to be attracted by the more near-term appeal of revenge, renown and reaction' (Richardson, 2006: 105–6). 'Terrorist groups', she concludes, 'have been singularly unsuccessful in delivering the political change they seek, but they have enjoyed considerable success in achieving their near-term aims. It is this success which appeals to disaffected youth with time on their hands who seek a means of rapid redress' (Richardson, 2006: 105–6). The reaction that terrorist propagandists seek to exploit is that of emulation among its target audience. Thus, according to Carlos Marighela in 1971, repressive counter-terrorist measures turn communities towards the terrorists:

> From the moment a large proportion of the population begin to take [an urban guerrilla's] activities seriously, his success is assured. The Government can only intensify its repression, thus making the life of its citizens harder than ever: homes will be broken into, police searches organised, innocent people arrested, and communications broken; police terror will become the order of the day, and there will be more and more political murders – in short a massive political persecution ... the political situation of the country will become a military situation. (Marighela, 1971: 95)

Conservative and Labour prime ministers have consistently failed to anticipate the adverse unintended consequences of deploying military responses to Provisional IRA and al-Qaeda terrorist threats. Twenty-seven civil rights protesters were shot by British soldiers belonging to the Parachute Regiment during a Northern Ireland Civil Rights Association march in Derry in 1972. Thirteen people, seven of whom were teenagers, died immediately, while the death of another person four months later has been attributed to the injuries he received on the day (McClean, 1997). Academics have long realised that the recourse to military action at a civil rights protest boosted rather than reduced the influence of PIRA (Silke, 2003; Horgan, 2005; Richardson, 2006). Andrew Silke has observed a similar failing in Tony Blair's enthusiastic support for the Bush administration's poorly focused, retaliatory military response to 9/11:

> The US aggressively chasing down al-Qaida and its affiliates throughout the world may find that a last resolution to the chase eludes it, regardless of how much energy and military force it invests in the campaign ... If past experience is anything to go by, defeating or diminishing the overall threat of terrorism is not something that either small – or large-scale retaliations have yet been able to achieve. (Silke, 2003: 230)

Given Blair's support for the Saville Inquiry and a negotiated settlement with PIRA, it might appear surprising that he did not apply the lessons from Northern Ireland when considering responses to al-Qaeda. Certainly, the initial failure of military overreaction to the terrorist tactics of PIRA and the belated success of law enforcement and negotiation against that sustained terrorist threat might have been at the forefront of his mind as he travelled to Washington to offer his support and counsel to George Bush in the immediate aftermath of 9/11:

> Indeed, the UK prime minister's key role in the negotiation process with PIRA placed added weight on his experience and ensuing informed counsel to his transatlantic counterpart. Which is not to suggest that all the lessons learned in combating PIRA are easily or immediately transferable to al-Qaida, merely that the experience provided a potentially sound basis for avoiding overreaction of the kind that terrorists universally seek to provoke. (Lambert, 2008a)

Suffice to say that Blair endorsed the view that al-Qaeda represented a wholly different kind of terrorist threat from PIRA and that this 'new' kind of terrorist threat was well beyond the scope of negotiation or 'soft' investigation. However, the failure of the military-led war on terror can be linked directly to a wilful determination by the neo-conservative cabal guiding it to misrepresent the real nature of the terrorist threat (Lustick, 2006). While the invasion of Iraq is the most notable example of this misrepresentation, it is the extent to which al-Qaeda has been purposefully misconstrued as an entity that is so opposed to Western interests as to be beyond the scope of law enforcement and negotiation that characterises

Blair's conceptualisation of the threat (Lambert, 2008a). In *The Lesser Evil*, Michael Ignatieff expresses the political wisdom that prevailed in Washington and Whitehall and facilitated the neo-conservative agenda in which wholesale human rights abuses against al-Qaeda suspects are permitted on the premise of their exceptional threat (Ignatieff 2004). Ignatieff also licenses the scope and methodology of the war on terror by endorsing the prevailing view that al-Qaeda is beyond politics and thereby beyond negotiation:

> The nihilism of their [al-Qaeda's] means – the indifference to human costs – takes their actions out of the realm of politics, but even out of the realm of war itself. The apocalyptical nature of their goals makes it absurd to believe they are making demands at all. They are seeking the violent transformation of an irremediably sinful and unjust world. (Ignatieff, 2001)

According to Isabelle Duyvesteyn, the argument that 'religious terrorists have no motivation because the achievement of their goals is impossible' is logically untenable (Duyvesteyn, 2004). More importantly, the argument that al-Qaeda constituted an existential threat to Western civilisation failed to take account of the extent to which al-Qaeda terrorist strategists followed well-established terrorist tactics, especially in relation to propaganda. Al-Qaeda propagandist Saif al-Adl illustrates the point when claiming that 9/11 was intended to provoke the USA to 'lash out militarily against the ummah in the manner if not the scale of the war on terror' (Gerges, 2005: 270). 'The Americans took the bait', he continues, 'and fell into our trap', doubtless using hindsight to describe al-Qaeda's ability to predict the massive scale and range of the response to 9/11 (Gerges, 2005: 270). Apart from falling for a familiar terrorist ploy – and thereby boosting al-Qaeda propaganda and recruitment strategy – responses such as that of Blair fail to distinguish between inveterate al-Qaeda ideologists like Saif al-Adl who may well be beyond the scope of immediate negotiation and local activists who may be susceptible to skilful intervention strategies (Lambert, 2008a). More importantly, the war on terror failed to take account of the extent to which young recruits to al-Qaeda might easily be rehabilitated to non-violent politics if credible figures in their communities were encouraged or facilitated to undertake negotiations to that end (Lambert, 2008a, 2008b, 2010).

In contrast to Blair, when the experienced al-Qaeda strategist Abu Mus'ab al-Suri reflected on the successes and failures of PIRA's bombing campaign in the UK, he was not unlike a British military strategist reviewing earlier campaigns so as to learn from the experience of history (Lia, 2007). The sophisticated attention high-calibre strategists like al-Suri pay to the conduct of terrorism should come as no surprise, given the level of commitment they have invested in such high-risk activity. To take such an empathetic view of terrorist strategists is to adopt a counter-terrorism position that was not in evidence during Blair's stewardship of the war on terror. Indeed, when Blair stood up in the House of Commons to respond to al-Qaeda's terrorist attack in London in July 2005, he appeared to be unaware that his overreaction might aid al-Qaeda recruitment and support (BBC

News, 2005). Echoing Roy Jenkins in 1974, he was careful to deny any legitimacy to the political grievances the terrorist enemy sought to exploit. More specifically, he described the al-Qaeda threat as existing independently of British foreign policy and as having ideological motivation that pre-dated 9/11 (Ahmed, 2006; Oborne 2006; Rai, 2006). Instead, Blair was at pains to describe 7/7 as an 'attack on our way of life' when delivering high-profile media messages that explicitly excluded political grievance from an analysis of the root causes of al-Qaeda terrorism:

> But, coming to Britain is not a right. And even when people have come here, staying here carries with it a duty. That duty is to share and support the values that sustain the British way of life. Those that break that duty and try to incite hatred or engage in violence against our country and its people, have no place here. Over the coming months, in the courts, in parliament, in debate and engagement with all parts of our communities, we will work to turn those sentiments into reality. That is my duty as Prime Minister. (BBC News, 2005)

Similarly, in a speech to the World Affairs Council in Los Angeles on 1 August 2005, Blair located the 7/7 attacks within a global struggle between 'reactionary Islam and moderate, mainstream Islam' (Blair, 2006). On reflection, Peter Bergen's analysis of root causes having far more to do with a violent political response to US (and after 9/11 UK-backed) policies in the Middle East appears more plausible (Bergen, 2002). In contrast, Blair has been able to rely on neo-conservative analysts for support, most crucially when implausibly linking the al-Qaeda threat with the threat posed by other 'Islamist' groups such as Hamas and Hizbollah (Pipes, 2003). Significantly Bergen's analysis has been endorsed by experienced counter-terrorism practitioners (Scheuer, 2003; German, 2007). Certainly, for the conspirators who killed 52 London commuters on 7 July 2005, suicide bombing was a tactical choice informed by the guiding strategy of an influential terrorist movement – al-Qaeda. In the suicide bombers' post-dated videos there is clear evidence that they drew inspiration from Osama bin Laden's propaganda statements claiming legitimacy for the tactic. The attacks of 7/7 would be justified by the men who carried them out in exactly the same way as bin Laden rationalised 9/11 and 3/11 (an al-Qaeda terrorist attack in Madrid):

> What happened in September 11 [New York/Washington] and March 11 [Madrid] is your own merchandise coming back to you. We hereby advise you ... that your definition of us and of our actions as terrorism is nothing but a definition of yourselves by yourselves, since our reaction is of the same kind as your act. Our actions are a reaction to yours, which are destruction and killing of our people as is happening in Afghanistan, Iraq, and Palestine. (Lawrence, 2005)

Legitimacy here is premised on reciprocity (Richardson, 2006). Political grievance and the shame of defeat are assuaged in an act of reciprocal violence:

> By what measure of kindness are your killed considered innocents while ours are considered worthless? By what school [of thought] is your blood considered blood while our blood is water? ... Therefore, it is [only] just to respond in kind, and the one who started it is more to blame. (Lawrence, 2005)

The point of interest is that grievance and shame appear to be key motivational factors for both PIRA and al-Qaeda terrorists who have attacked UK targets with bombs at different times and in respect of campaigns that are otherwise conceptualised as belonging to separate typologies – most typically 'radical nationalism' (in the case of PIRA) and 'religious and quasi-religious extremism' (in the case of al-Qaeda) (Stepanova, 2008). However, the possibility that grievance and shame were key factors in the mindsets of two distinct terrorist movements who chose to attack commuters in the same city at different times was denied by Blair, and his refusal to hold any authoritative inquiry into 7/7 has led to uncertainty and confusion about the motivation to the attacks (Lambert, 2010). In addition, an unintended outcome of the government's position has been an alarming growth of conspiracy theories gaining root in British Muslim communities. Instead of the clarity and transparency that Lord Scarman and Lord Macpherson brought to bear on events of equal concern to minority communities, in respect of 7/7, Muslim communities have been forced to rely instead on government narratives that carry no credibility (Scarman, 1982; Macpherson, 1999). Early investigative accounts of 7/7 were similarly dismissive of government credibility but were perhaps overly focused on the Iraq War as a single explanatory cause (Ahmed, 2006; Rai, 2006).

Denying the Political Grievances that Al-Qaeda and PIRA Exploit

For the purposes of this chapter, it is helpful to consider how Blair's response to 7/7 might have been assessed had it become the subject of an independent judicial inquiry. On that basis it is reasonable to suppose that a High Court judge inquiring into the causes of 7/7 would have examined the veracity and meaning of the video messages left by the perpetrators. Muslim community witnesses might have been called to comment on them. Indeed, on the evidence of community interviews conducted by the author, it is fair to suggest that the judge would have been encouraged to understand that the frustrations about a lack of any effective response to state violence against Muslims – as enunciated by the bombers – was commonplace:

> Oh Muslims of Britain – you day in day out on your TV sets watching and hearing about the oppression of the Muslims. From the east to the west yet you turn a blind eye as if you never heard anything or as if it does not concern

you. You have preferred the duniya (world) to Allah and his messenger (PBUH) and to the hereafter. (BBC, 2006b)

Moreover, a High Court judge, it is reasonable to speculate, might have come to appreciate that the legitimacy of 7/7 in the eyes of the conspirators would have turned on their willingness to accept that the tactic was *halal* (lawful) in the context of their religious understanding. The bomber Mohammad Sidique Khan argued that it is *halal*, ridiculing Muslim scholars who say it is *haram* (unlawful) as cowards (BBC, 2006). In the same way, it is reasonable to suggest that an experienced High Court judge might have been willing to hear evidence from counter-terrorism practitioners who dissented from prevailing 'new terrorism' wisdom and 'war on terror' paradigms that dismissed experience of PIRA terrorism as irrelevant (Jackson 2008; Spalek, El-Awa and McDonald, 2008). Instead, the judge might have been reminded that a tough government response to the demands of terrorist prisoners for political status was turned into a successful recruitment strategy by PIRA and that one of al-Qaeda's aims was that Mohammad Sidique Khan, the eldest 7/7 bomber, should achieve the same heroic status as Bobby Sands and for the same purpose. Certainly, this propaganda purpose becomes patently clear when analysing an al-Qaeda video in which its spokesmen addresses a UK audience to explain the purpose of 7/7 (Lambert, 2010). This, at least some counter-terrorist practitioners would have argued, was the prime purpose of the video in which Khan explained the reasons for his pending terrorist enterprise (Lambert, 2010).

Intriguingly, Khan's explanation both for taking part in terrorism and for taking his own life bears striking similarities to Bobby Sands' case. To demonstrate this, it is helpful to compare extracts from Khan's video performance with extracts from Bobby Sands' prison diary – a record written in secret that had a subsequent major impact in elevating him to heroic status for a generation of PIRA volunteers (Sands, 1998). Both terrorists (Khan and Sands) insist they are part of oppressed communities that have to resort to violence to oppose the overwhelming might and treachery of an inherently hostile neo-colonialist power. In Khan's words: 'until you stop the bombing, gassing, imprisonment and torture of my people we will not stop this fight' (BBC, 2006). In Sands' words: 'I am a casualty of a perennial war that is being fought between the oppressed Irish people and an alien, oppressive, unwanted regime that refuses to withdraw from our land' (Sands, 1998).

Both are self-consciously approaching death as a form of martyrdom so as to elevate themselves to an imagined moral high ground. In Khan's words: 'I and thousands like me have forsaken everything for what we believe' (BBC, 2006). In Sands' words: 'I am a political prisoner because I believe and stand by the God-given right of the Irish nation to sovereign independence, and the right of any Irishman or woman to assert this right in armed revolution. That is why I am incarcerated, naked and tortured' (Sands, 1998). Interestingly, in the prison diaries of al-Qaeda suspects, there are self-conscious references to Bobby Sands and other non-Muslim 'freedom fighters' (Lambert, 2010). Both Khan and Sands highlight the significance of their respective religious allegiances. Both aspire to lead by example. In Khan's words: 'Our words are dead until we give them life with our blood ... By preparing ourselves for this kind of work, we are guaranteeing ourselves for paradise and gaining the pleasure of Allah' (BBC, 2006). In Sands' words: 'I have considered all the arguments and tried every means to avoid what has become the unavoidable: it has been forced upon me and my comrades by four-and-a-half years of stark inhumanity' (Sands, 1998).

Moreover, both men, follows, are self-evidently addressing themselves to supporters and would-be recruits rather than a wider public. This brief comparison between statements made by Khan and Sands is merely to suggest that the two men shared one key commitment that marks them out from the majority of their compatriots who shared their unremarkable attachment to anti-colonial politics – a willingness to become martyrs for their cause. Moreover, it may be prudent not to place too much emphasis, as Blair did, on the fact that only one of the two terrorists was a suicide bomber.

The Political Impact on Counter-terrorism Policing

Despite a tendency to toe the government line, officers from the Association of Chief Police Officers (ACPO) have regularly proclaimed their political neutrality on issues of counter-terrorism policy. Thus, Peter Clarke protested that his support for a 90-day period of pre-trial terrorist detention in 2005 no less than his support for a 42-day period of pre-trial terrorist detention in 2008 should be seen as wholly apolitical (Porter, 2008). As Kleinig notes, valuable government support of this kind is often presented under the guise of political neutrality, never more so than when the notoriously compliant Metropolitan Police Commissioner Sir David McNee articulated his case for electoral abstention:

> The political neutrality of the police service and the political independence and impartiality of chief police officers is central to the British policing system. I personally regard it as so important that I no longer exercise my right to vote, nor have I since I was appointed a chief officer of police. Police officers must be men and women of the middle, bound only by the rule of law.
> (Kleinig, 1996: 214)

Like Clarke, McNee was fully supportive of extrajudicial measures in counter-terrorism – in his day against Irish republican terrorism – and was similarly unaware or dismissive of any notion that they might be counter-productive. While reducing the risk of alienating *Daily Telegraph* and *Daily Mail* readers, such approaches jar with counter-terrorism policing initiatives that are more focused on countering the unintended impact on terrorist recruitment of such measures (Lambert, 2010). For police officers willing to challenge the prevailing wisdom, John Alderson, the founding figure of British community policing, remained a positive role model (Alderson 1979, 1998). In 1982 he confounded his conservative colleagues by giving a frank interview to the far-left journal *Marxism Today* in which he addressed tensions between community policing and intelligence gathering in both counter-terrorism and public order policing contexts (*Marxism Today*, 1982). Most notably, he responded to a quote in which Tony Bunyan argued that a community police officer's role entailed gathering intelligence 'on the people on their patch' for the benefit of all police departments including Special Branch:

> Community policing, despite its high-sounding purpose, is a double-edged tool to penetrate the community through other professional agencies and by spying on the community under the guise of offering a protective, friendly approach. Consent is thus to be engineered and, in case this fails, intelligence is gathered to pre-empt dissent. (*Marxism Today*, 1982)

Significantly, similar allegations were made at the Muslim Safety Forum in 2006 by a Muslim community leader (Lambert, 2010) and again in a research report published by the Institute of Race Relations (Kundnani, 2009), whereas in a thoroughgoing Home Office review of community policing literature in 2006, the issue of spying was not raised once (Myhill, 2006). In the circumstances, Alderson's reply is worth quoting in full:

> If one accepts, as I do, that what Tony Bunyan describes is a corruption of community policing, then you've got to build in safeguards to prevent that. There has to be a form of social contract, there have to be codes, there have to be bills of rights, there have to be scrutineers – I would accept all that. (*Marxism Today*, 1982)

Significantly, notwithstanding a grudging respect for Alderson, many senior police officers have not moved far from the naturally conservative position outlined by Assistant Commissioner David Powis in 1977 in which 'political radicals', 'intellectuals who spout extremist babble' and 'people in possession of "your rights" cards such as those issued by the National Council for Civil Liberties (NCCL)' are deemed to be innately suspicious and subversive (Reiner, 1985: 92). In the circumstances, Reiner's observations about the inherent conservatism of policing remain relevant notwithstanding and perhaps even because of the close association of Sir Ian Blair (Metropolitan Police Service Commissioner 2005–2008 and Metropolitan Police Service Deputy Commissioner 2000–2005) with his New Labour namesake, the UK architect of the war on terror. Certainly, the two Blairs stood shoulder to shoulder in endorsing Gilles Kepel's suggestion that UK counter-terrorism should adopt the tougher policies of European partners, most especially France, in the wake of 7/7 (Kepel, 2005). Just as Ignatieff licensed derogation from the rule of law as a proportionate response to an exceptional terrorist threat, so too did both Blairs insist on the unprecedented scale of threat to London, the police chief arguing that al-Qaeda represented a 'far graver threat in terms of civilians than either the Cold War or the Second World War' (Morris, 2006).

As Darren Thiel illustrates, the notion that a grave terrorist threat licensed extraordinary legislation and exceptional strategies and tactics in respect of intelligence, disruption and target hardening became an accepted premise in UK counter-terrorism policing (Thiel, 2009). That it might reduce or weaken the legitimacy and effectiveness of counter-terrorism policing in Muslim communities was sometimes acknowledged, but was invariably viewed as a necessary consequence within policing (Thiel, 2009). In a Metropolitan Police Authority report, the same concern was raised in connection with both 'low policing' activities such as 'stop and search' and also with regard to 'high policing' activities often carried by Special Branch and the Security Service (MI5) (Metropolitan Police Authority, 2007). 'Thus for students to hear that Special Branch officers have been talking to university vice-chancellors behind closed doors about extremist activity on campus was troubling', the report notes, 'rather than reassuring' (Metropolitan Police Authority, 2007).

To add substance to the police maxim 'communities defeat terrorism', it would be necessary for counter-terrorism policing to ensure that Irish and Muslim communities in the UK were not unwittingly alienated by a perception of bias against them, all the more so given a history of alienation from police amongst minority communities most likely to be criminalised. As the former Labour cabinet minister Peter Hain noted as a researcher before entering Parliament, 'members of minority or marginalised communities were especially prone to poor service from a minority of officers who failed to uphold the highest standards of the police service on this fundamental issue of professional service' (Hain, 1979). Phil Cohen offers the testimony of Detective Sergeant Holland of West Yorkshire Police giving evidence against Asian political activists in the 'Bradford 12' appeal case in 1981 in support of this viewpoint:

> Police officers must be prejudiced and discriminatory to do their job ... to search long-haired youths in bedraggled clothing ... and West Indian youths wearing tea cosy hats and loitering in city centres ... The police are expected to act against those people who, by their conduct, mode of life, dress, associates and transport are most likely to be criminals. (Cohen, 1982)

Any suggestion that there was not still a minority of police officers capable of stigmatising marginalised communities during the post-Macpherson period would have to take cognisance of the evidence of a small number of cases pointing to the contrary (London Metropolitan University Research Unit, 2005). As Bernard Harcourt has noted, there is also evidence of a form of ethnic profiling to the detriment of Muslim communities in a post-9/11 policing environment (Harcourt, 2006).

All of this explains why Paddy Hillyard's claim that the war on terror created 'suspect Muslim communities' in the same way that Irish communities had been treated by counter-terrorism policing during 'the troubles' (Hillyard, 1993, 2005) has resonated so strongly in Muslim communities (Commission for Racial Equality Safe Communities Initiative, 2006). According to Hillyard, for three decades, Irish Catholic communities in London, as well as in Northern Ireland, were regularly stigmatised and conflated with the terrorism of PIRA (Hillyard, 1993). In particular,

Hillyard highlighted the adverse impact of much coercive policing and security activity licensed by the Prevention of Terrorism (Temporary Provisions) Act (first introduced in 1974 and then renewed on an annual basis) on minority Irish communities. It is not necessary to accept all the accounts presented by Hillyard at face value to grasp that it was problematic for the vast majority of over 7,000 Irish 'suspects' who were arrested and detained under the emergency legislation and subsequently released without charge. By detailing individual, often harrowing, personal accounts of suspects' arrest, detention and questioning, Hillyard was expressing a minority and poorly funded academic interest in the notion that such extraordinary and draconian police powers (first enacted by Parliament in the aftermath of the Birmingham pub bombings, as recorded by Mary Holland above) might unfairly alienate and stigmatise minority sections of Irish communities. More specifically, Hillyard argues that government policy was counter-productive in that it sent out a signal that 'demands for a more fair and just society in Northern Ireland could no longer be carried forward through dialogue and persuasion' and also 'led to hundreds of young men ... joining the IRA and creating one of the most efficient insurgency forces in the world' (Hillyard, 1993). Nothing that was being said about the 'exceptional' nature of the al-Qaeda threat following 9/11 persuaded Hillyard that this lesson might not apply equally in relation to it (Hillyard, 2005).

Conclusion

In his review of post-9/11 counter-terrorism policing in the UK, Thiel describes three main areas of activity: intelligence collection, analysis and distribution (what he calls 'high policing' following Brodeur, 1983); target-hardening activity including 'stops, searches and screening practices administered by uniformed police'; and the 'generation of community intelligence and community co-operation through uniformed "low-policing" consultation with British Muslim community members', including 'a related policy to intensify and develop neighbourhood policing-style practices in areas deemed at risk of producing violent Islamists' (Thiel, 2009: 31–4). In theory there may be no inherent conflict between each field of activity, but, as Thiel demonstrates, in practice tensions have arisen between the notions of high and low policing; between the notions of community intelligence and community support; and between the notions of 'neighbourhood policing as risk reduction' and as spying on 'suspect' communities (Thiel, 2009: 31–4). Moreover, a post-7/7 shift in focus towards 'home-grown' terrorism and 'radicalisation' raised a number of issues concerning the legitimacy and effectiveness of counter-terrorism policing practice, in particular in relation to a tension that was perceived to exist between 'hard' investigative counter-terrorism and 'soft' community policing in support of counter-terrorism (Innes, 2006; Innes et al., 2007).

In fairness, these were issues that a small number of academics had raised in the aftermath of 9/11 (de Guzman, 2002; Murray, 2005; Pelfrey, 2005). Thus, for instance, in arguing that 'strategies against terrorism negate assumptions of community cooperation and trust that are implicit in community policing', Melchor de Guzman highlighted a dilemma that UK counter-terrorism policing struggled to overcome (de Guzman 2002: 13). In addition, by arguing that 'the war on terror necessitates broader collaborative policing' than 'parochial' community policing, de Guzman drew attention to a key issue of police legitimacy and effectiveness (de Guzman, 2002). Similarly, William Lyons was concerned that the need to build trust with marginalised communities where terrorists sought support was insufficiently understood by the architects and administrators of the war on terror:

> Until we learn to police in ways that build trusting relationships with those communities least likely to willingly assist the police – those often marginalized communities where criminals and terrorists can more easily live lives insulated from observation – no amount of additional funding or legal authority, consistent with living in a free society, will increase the capacity of our police forces to gather the crime and terror-related information we desperately need. (Lyons, 2002: 530)

Implicit in Lyons' observation is the notion that counter-terrorism policing (whether hard or soft) needs to achieve legitimacy in marginalised, distrustful communities in order to become effective. However, Lyons' concerns did not appear to feature in UK government counter-terrorism strategy, which was instead designed to support US military action at every turn (Scratton, 2002; Gregory and Wilkinson, 2005). Given, however, the extent to which the UK emerged as a major contributor to al-Qaeda's global campaign in terms of terrorist recruits, it is not fanciful to suggest that the oversight proved costly – most especially for the UK itself. Although after Blair's tenure as Prime Minister, New Labour government policy was far more attuned to winning Muslim community support, there was a strong sense that considerable alienation may already have been caused by the government's close association with the worst excesses of the war on terror.

Regrettably, the Coalition government has not only adopted Blair's neo-conservative approach to UK counter-terrorism, it has enhanced it. As a result, several Muslim organisations with impeccable records of tackling al-Qaeda's influence in the UK have been branded 'extremist' and consequently unfit for partnership or funding (Lambert, 2011b). A modest withdrawal from New Labour's craven support for corrupt regimes that conducted torture in the name of the war on terror is to be welcomed, but should be seen in the context of the weakening of those regimes internally during the Arab Spring. Similarly, the Coalition government's greater regard for civil liberties in a counter-terrorism context is generally to be welcomed. However, there is no evidence at all to suggest that David Cameron, Prime Minister at the time of writing, will avoid the same mistakes made by his predecessors if he is suddenly faced with a terrorist attack that is designed to prompt disproportionate counter-terrorism measures in order to alienate potential terrorist recruits and supporters.

References

Ahmed, Nafeez Mosaddeq (2006). *The London Bombings: An Independent Inquiry*. London: Duckworth.
Alderson, John (1979). *Policing Freedom*. Plymouth: Macdonald & Evans.
Alderson, John (1998). *Principled Policing: Protecting the Public with Integrity*. Winchester: Waterside Press.
Alonso, R. (2007). *The IRA and Armed Struggle*. Abingdon: Routledge.
Ansari, Farhad (2005). *British Anti-Terrorism: A Modern Day Witch-Hunt*. London: Islamic Human Rights Commission.
Bamford, Bradley W.C. (2004). The United Kingdom's 'War Against Terrorism', *Terrorism and Political Violence* 16(4), 737–56.
BBC News online (2005). Full text: Blair speech on terror, 5 August, http://news.bbc.co.uk/1/hi/uk/4689363.stm [accessed 25 June 2012].
BBC News online (2006a). What Happened in the Hunger Strike?, 5 May, http://news.bbc.co.uk/1/hi/northern_ireland/4941866.stm [accessed 25 June 2012].
BBC News online (2006b). Bomber Video Released, 6 July, http://news.bbc.co.uk/1/hi/5154714.stm [accessed 25 June 2012].
Bergen, Peter (2006). *The Osama bin Laden I Know*. London: Free Press.
Blair, Tony (2006). Transcript of speech on Middle East to Los Angeles World Affairs Council, 1 August, http://news.bbc.co.uk/1/hi/uk/5236896.stm [accessed 18 July 2012].
Blears, Hazel (2008). Speech at Policy Exchange, 17 July. London: Policy Exchange.
Briggs, Rachel, Fieschi, Catherine and Lownsbrough, Hannah (2006). *Bringing it Home: Community-based Approaches to Counter-terrorism*. London: Demos.
Bright, Martin (2006). *When Progressives Treat with Reactionaries*. London: Policy Exchange.
Brodeur, Jean-Paul (1983). High Policing and Low Policing: Remarks about the Policing of Political Activities, *Social Problems* 30(5), 507–20.
Brodeur, Jean-Paul (2007). High Policing and Low Policing in Post-9/11 Times, *Policing: A Journal of Policy and Practice* 1(1), 25–37.
Brodeur, Jean-Paul and Dupont, Benoit (2006). Knowledge Workers or 'Knowledge' Workers?, *Policing & Society* 16(1), 7–26.
Cohen, Phil (1982). Bradford 12, *Marxism Today*, August, 2–3.
Commission for Racial Equality Safe Communities Initiative (2006). Anti-Terrorism Laws: The Experiences of the Irish and Muslim Communities in the UK. Report from a seminar held at the University of Birmingham, 21 April, http://83.137.212.42/sitearchive/cre/downloads/birmingham_seminar_report.pdf accessed 18.5.09.
De Guzman, Melchor C. (2002). The Changing Roles and Strategies of the Police in Time of Terror, *ACJS Today* 22(3), 8–13.
De Lint, Willem (2006). Intelligence in Policing and Security: Reflections on Scholarship (editorial), *Policing & Society* 16(1), 1–6.
Deibert, Ronald and Stein, Janice Gross (2002). Hacking Networks of Terror, *Dialog-IO*, Spring, 1–14.

Duyvesteyn, Isabelle (2004). How New is the New Terrorism?, *Studies in Conflict & Terrorism* 27, 439–54.
Gerges, Fawaz A. (2005). *The Far Enemy: Why Jihad Went Global.* Cambridge: Cambridge University Press.
German, Mike (2007). *Thinking Like a Terrorist: Insights of a Former FBI Undercover Agent.* Washington DC: Potomac Books.
Gill, Peter (2006). Not Just Joining the Dots But Crossing the Borders and Bridging the Voids: Constructing Security Networks after 11 September 2001, *Policing & Security* 16(1), 27–49.
Githens-Mazer, Jonathan (2010). Mobilisation, Recruitment and Violence: Radical violent takfiri Islamism in early 21st century Britain. In Roger Eatwell and Matthew Goodwin (eds), *The New Extremism in 21st Century Britain.* Oxford: Routledge.
Gove, Michael (2006). *Celsius 7/7.* London: Weidenfield & Nicholson.
Gregory, Frank and Wilkinson, Paul (2005). Riding Pillion for Tackling Terrorism is a High-Risk Policy. In Christopher Browning (ed.), *Security, Terrorism and the UK.* London: Chatham House, 2–3.
Grieve, John G.D. and French, Julie (2000). Does Institutional Racism Exist in the Metropolitan Police Service? In David G. Green (ed.), *Institutional Racism and the Police: Fact or Fiction?* London: Institute for the Study of Civil Society (Civitas).
Haggerty, Kevin D. and Kauger, Erin (2006). Review Essay: Intelligence Exchange in Policing and Security, *Policing & Society* 16(1), 86–91.
Hain, Peter (ed.) (1979). *Policing the Police,* vols. 1 and 2. London: John Calder.
Harcourt, Bernard (2006). Muslim Profiles Post-9/11: Is Racial Profiling an Effective Counterterrorist Measure and Does it Violate the Right to be Free from Discrimination? Paper presented at the Oxford Colloquium on Security and Human Rights, University of Oxford, 17 March, http://papers.ssrn.com/sol3/papers.cfm?abstract_id=893905 [accessed 8 July 2012].
Hillyard, Paddy (1993). *Suspect Community: People's Experience of the Prevention of Terrorism Acts in Britain.* London: Pluto Press.
Hillyard, Paddy (2005). The 'War on Terror': Lessons from Northern Ireland. *Essays for Civil Liberties and Democracy in Europe.* London: ECLN, available at http://www.ecln.org/essays/essay-1.pdf [accessed 25 June 2012].
Holland, Mary (2006). Commons Terrorism Debate 1974. *New Statesman,* July.
Horgan, John (2005). *The Psychology of Terrorism.* London: Routledge.
Ignatieff, Michael (2001). It's War. *The Guardian,* 1 October. http://www.guardian.co.uk/Archive/Article/0,4273,4267406,00.html [accessed 25 June 2012].
Ignatieff, Michael (2004). *The Lesser Evil: Political Ethics in an Age of Terror.* Princeton, NJ: Princeton University Press.
Innes, Martin (2006). 'Policing Uncertainty: Countering Terror through Community Intelligence and Democratic Policing', *Annals of the American Academy* 605, 1–20.
Innes, Martin, Abbot L., Lowe, T. and Roberts, C. (2007). *Hearts and Minds and Eyes and Ears: Reducing Radicalisation Risks Through Reassurance-Oriented Policing.* London: ACPO.

Jackson, Richard (2008). Counter-terrorism and Communities: An Interview with Robert Lambert, *Critical Studies on Terrorism*, August, 293–308.
Kauffman, Phillipa (2009). Counsel for Claimant: Opening Submission to High Court. *Babar Ahmad v. Commissioner of Metropolitan Police*, 18 March, http://www.freebabarahmad.com [accessed 25 June 2012].
Kepel, Gilles (2004). *The War for Muslim Minds: Islam and the West.* Cambridge, MA: Harvard University Press.
Kepel, Gilles (2005). Radical Secularism. *The Independent* opinion page, 22 August, 12.
Kleinig, John (1996). *The Ethics of Policing.* Cambridge: Cambridge University Press.
Kohlmann, Evan F. (2004). *Al-Qaida's Jihad in Europe: The Afghan-Bosnian Network.* Oxford: Berg.
Kundnani, A. (2009). *Spooked! How Not to Prevent Violent Extremism.* London: Institute of Race Relations.
Lambert, Robert (2008a). Empowering Salafis and Islamists Against Al-Qaida: A London Counter-terrorism Case Study, *PS: Political Science and Politics* 41(1), 31–5.
Lambert, Robert (2008b). Salafi and Islamist Londoners: Stigmatised Minority Faith Communities Countering al-Qaida, *Crime, Law & Social Change* 50, 73–89.
Lambert, Robert (2010). *The London Partnerships: An Insider's Analysis of Legitimacy and Effectiveness.* Unpublished PhD, University of Exeter.
Lambert, Robert (2011a). *Countering Al-Qaeda in London: Police and Muslims in Partnership.* London: Hurst.
Lambert, Robert (2011b). Competing Counter-Radicalisation Models in the UK. In Coolsaet, Rik (ed.), *Jihadi Terrorism and the Radicalisation Challenge. European and American Experiences.* Aldershot: Ashgate, 215–26.
Lawrence, B. (ed.) (2005). *Messages to the World: The Statements of Osama bin Laden.* London: Verso.
Lia, Brynjar (2007). *Architect of Global Jihad: The Life of al-Qaida Strategist Abu Mus'ab al-Suri.* London: Hurst.
London Metropolitan University Research Unit (2005). Suspect Communities: The Real War on Terror, http://www.eldh.eu/fileadmin/user_upload/ejdm/events/archive/Suspect%20Communitites%20Conference%20Report.pdf [accessed 18 July 2012].
Lustick, Ian S. (2006). *Trapped in the War on Terror.* Philadelphia: University of Pennsylvania Press.
Lyons, William (2002). Partnerships, Information and Public Safety: Community Policing in a Time of Terror, *Policing: An International Journal of Police Strategies & Management* 25(3), 530–42.
McClean, Raymond (1997). *The Road To Bloody Sunday*, revised edn. Guildhall: Printing Press.
Macpherson, Lord (1999). *The Stephen Lawrence Inquiry: Report.* Cm. 4262-1. London: The Stationery Office.
Marighela, Carlos (1971). *Minimanual of the Urban Guerilla.* London: Penguin.

Marxism Today (1982). Policing in the Eighties. Interview with Chief Constable John Alderson. April, 8–14.
Metropolitan Police Authority (2007). *Counter-Terrorism: The London Debate*. London: MPA.
Morris, Nigel (2006). Met Chief Warns of Christmas Terror Threat. *The Independent*, 23 December, http://www.independent.co.uk/news/uk/crime/met-chief-warns-of-christmas-terror-threat429633.html [accessed 25 June 2012].
Murray, John (2005). Policing Terrorism: A Threat to Community Policing or Just a Shift in Priorities?, *Police, Practice and Research* 6(4), 347–61.
Myhill, Andy (2006). *Community Engagement in Policing: Lessons from the Literature*. London: The Stationery Office.
Neumann, Peter R. (2008). Joining al-Qaeda: Jihadist Recruitment in Europe. *Adelphi Paper 399*. International Institute for Strategic Studies, 31–4.
O'Brien, Brendan (1995). *The Long War: The IRA and Sinn Féin*. Syracruse, NY: Syracuse University Press.
Oborne, Peter (2006). *The Use and Abuse of Terror: The Construction of a False Narrative on the Domestic Terror Threat*. London: Centre for Policy Studies.
Owen, David (2007). *The Hubris Syndrome: Bush, Blair and the Intoxication of Power*. London: Politicos.
Pelfrey, William V. (2005). Parallels between Community Oriented Policing and the War on Terrorism: Lessons Learned, *Criminal Justice Studies* 18(4), 335–46.
Phillips, Melanie (2006). *Londonistan: How Britain is Creating a Terror State Within*. London: Gibson Square.
Pipes, Daniel (2003). *Militant Islam Reaches America*. London: W.W. Norton & Company.
Porter, Andrew (2008). 'Terror Law Should Allow 42 Days' Detention, Says Former Police Chief Peter Clarke', *Daily Telegraph*. 2 June, http://www.telegraph.co.uk/news/uknews/2066861/Terror-law-should-allow-42-days-detention-says-former-police-chief-Peter-Clarke.html [accessed 18 July 2012].
Rai, M. (2006). *7/7: The London Bombings Islam and the Iraq War*. London: Pluto Press.
Reiner, Robert (1985). *The Politics of the Police*. Brighton: Wheatsheaf.
Richardson, Louise (2006). *What Terrorists Want: Understanding the Terrorist Threat*. London: John Murray.
Sands, Bobby (1998). *Writings from Prison*. Dublin: Mercier.
Scarman, Lord (1982). *The Scarman Report: The Brixton Disorders 10–12 April, 1981*. London: Pelican.
Scheuer, Michael ('Anonymous') (2003). *Through Our Enemies' Eyes: Osama bin Laden, Radical Islam, and the Future of America*. Washington DC: Brassey's.
Schmid, Alex P. (2004). Frameworks for Conceptualising Terrorism, *Terrorism and Political Violence* 16(2), 197–221.
Scraton, Phil (2002). In the Name of a Just War. In Phil Scraton (ed.), *Beyond September 11: An Anthology of Dissent*. London: Pluto Press, 216–33.
Sharp, Douglas (2002). Policing after Macpherson: Some Experiences of Muslim Police Officers. In Basia Spalek (ed.), *Islam, Crime and Criminal Justice*. Cullompton: Willan, 76–93.

Silke, Andrew (2003). Retaliating Against Terrorism. In Andrew Silke (ed.), *Terrorists, Victims and Society: Psychological Perspectives on Terrorism and its Consequences*. Chichester: Wiley, 231–56.

Souhami, A. (2007). Understanding Institutional Racism: The Stephen Lawrence Inquiry and the Police Service Reaction. In Rowe, M. (ed.), *Policing beyond Macpherson: Issues in Policing, Race and Society*. Cullompton: Willan, 66–8.

Spalek, Basia (2005). Muslims and the Criminal Justice System. In T. Choudhury (ed.), *Muslims in the UK: Policies for Engaged Citizens*. Budapest: Open Society Institute, 253–340.

Spalek, Basia, El-Awa, Salwa and McDonald, Laura (2008). Partnerships for the Purposes of Counter-Terrorism: An Examination – Summary Report, University of Birmingham, 18 November.

Spalek, Basia and Lambert, Robert (2007). Terrorism, Counter-Terrorism and Muslim Community Engagement Post 9/11. *Social Justice and Criminal Justice Conference Papers*, Centre for Crime & Justice Studies, Kings College, London, July, 202–15.

Stepanova, E. (2008). *Terrorism in Asymmetrical Conflict: Ideological and Structural Aspects*, Stockholm International Peace Research Institute (SIPRI) Research Report No. 23. Oxford, Oxford University Press.

Stevenson, Jonathan (2004). Law Enforcement and Intelligence Capabilities, *The Adelphi Papers* 44(367), 47–71.

Taylor, P. (1997). *Provos, the IRA and Sinn Fein*. London: Bloomsbury.

Thiel, Darren (2009). *Policing Terrorism: A Review of the Evidence*. London: The Police Foundation.

Travis, Alan, Dyer, Clare and White, Michael (2005). Britain 'Sliding into Police State'. *The Guardian*, 28 January, http://www.guardian.co.uk/uk/2005/jan/28/terrorism.humanrights1 [accessed 25 June 2012].

Tupman, W.A. and O'Reilly, C. (2004). Terrorism, Hegemony and Legitimacy: Evaluating Success and Failure in the War on Terror. *Political Studies Association Conference*, Lincoln, August 2004, http://www.psa.ac.uk/cps/2004/tupman.pdf [accessed 25 June 2012].

21

ASHGATE
RESEARCH
COMPANION

Counter-Terrorism and Human Rights since 9/11

Michael McClintock

Introduction

Good intelligence, a sophisticated criminal justice system and targeted military strikes overseas were the principal mechanisms of the US for dealing with the threat of terrorism in the last quarter of the twentieth century. Outrages at home by international actors (the 1993 World Trade Center bombing) and domestic (the 1995 Oklahoma City bombing) were both met with effective criminal investigations, prosecutions and severe punishments.

The domestic and the international approaches were framed in terms of accepted norms of international law, even as some military actions were harshly criticized. The US also criticized even close allies for abuses in the name of counter-terrorism, documenting and condemning foreign practices of torture and ill-treatment, unfair trials and systems of detention without trial.

This approach changed after the attacks of 11 September 2001. Due process guarantees and other fundamental rights inside the US were eroded or set aside. Human rights and humanitarian norms applying to international operations were disparaged and blatantly violated. Measures taken in the name of the new counter-terrorism undermined human rights observance both inside the US and internationally.

The 9/11 Attacks on the US

On 11 September 2001, 19 hijackers took control of four civilian airliners in coordinated attacks on the US. The hijackers, later identified as members of the al-Qaeda network, crashed two planes into New York's World Trade Center, bringing the Twin Towers to the ground. A third targeted the Pentagon, causing deaths and serious damage, while a fourth crashed into a field in Pennsylvania. The attacks killed 2,973 people, the vast majority of them civilians. There were no survivors among the airliner passengers, and the attack on the World Trade Center alone killed at least 2,751 people (Alfano 2006; CBS News 2008). The attacks led to a redirection of American domestic and foreign policies aimed at countering terrorism but that ultimately undermined human rights protection both at home and abroad.

The administration of George W. Bush responded to the 9/11 attacks on multiple fronts, initially with little dissent. Congress gave the President a sweeping mandate for global action and enacted an omnibus emergency law curtailing civil liberties. Americans and immigrants alike faced a new order in which rights to due process of law, freedom of association, non-discrimination and privacy – among other fundamental rights – were undermined or set aside. A series of executive orders and secret legal memoranda opened the way to torture, secret detention, clandestine international transfers, special courts and indefinite detention without charge or trial.

Almost eight years later, President Barack Obama took office on a platform of change and moved rapidly to reverse some of the policies conducive to gross and persistent human rights violations. Obama took rapid action to repudiate the post-9/11 policies regarding torture and ill-treatment and programmes of secret detention, but issues of domestic surveillance, preventive detention, fair trial and government secrecy remain at the top of the human rights agenda (Finn 2009; Greenwald 2009a; Risen and Lichtblau 2008).

A Changing Consensus on Fundamental Rights

The public response to 9/11 combined fear and anger with a determination to support whatever government action was necessary to meet the new threats to national security. Senior officials asserted that the scale of the 9/11 atrocities and the level of the continuing threat meant that there was no alternative but to recur to extraordinary means in response. On 16 September 2001, Vice President Dick Cheney set the tone in a television interview, saying that to be successful, the US would need to turn to 'the dark side' – 'to use any means at our disposal' (Russert 2009).

Those involved directly in security matters spoke in similar terms, suggesting that in the fight against terrorism the USA would be obliged to fight fire with fire. One officer charged with capturing and transferring suspected terrorists told a reporter that: 'If you don't violate someone's human rights some of the time, you probably aren't doing your job' (Federation of American Scientists 2002; Priest and Gellman 2002). Others acknowledged, and took pride in asserting, that the rules of the game had changed after 9/11. Cofer Black, the Director of the CIA's Counterterrorism Centre, told congressional hearings that that 'there was "before" 9/11 and "after" 9/11. After 9/11 the gloves came off'.

The enemy was defined largely in terms of its extremist religious background, often described as 'Islamist', and its use of tactics commonly defined as terrorism – deliberately attacking civilians in order to achieve political goals. By recurring to terrorism, the enemy was held to have forfeited any claim to rights. As the enemy had jettisoned the rules, US leaders considered themselves largely unfettered by law in their response.

To many Americans, the fear engendered by the 9/11 attacks brought with it a readiness to give up certain rights in exchange for increased security. This included an acceptance of such inconveniences as enhanced security screening in public buildings, airports and virtually all aspects of public life, as well as greater demands for individuals to surrender personal information about themselves. Measures that most directly affected foreigners, whether inside the US or abroad, found particular support as being necessary for self-defence in a time of terror and deadly peril.

In the days and weeks after the attacks, national policy-makers framed both an omnibus security law to provide new counter-terrorism powers at home and a new approach to taking the fight to the enemy abroad. The USA PATRIOT Act (hereinafter 'the Patriot Act') provided a basis for increased surveillance, enhanced detention powers, greater government secrecy and tools such as increased powers of search and seizure to address subversion domestically.

International action was set in motion through the Authorization for Use of Military Force (AUMF), a law passed on 18 September 2001 that provided a broad framework of war powers with which to counter international terrorism. This authorized the president to use force against 'those nations, organizations, or persons he determines planned, authorized, committed, or aided' in the 9/11 attacks (US Congress 2001).

Behind the scenes, the administration issued secret orders so that suspects could be detained, aggressively interrogated and swiftly brought to justice without the impediments of either domestic due process of law or the constraints of international human rights and law of war treaties. These included memoranda mounting a legal defence for torture by US personnel and a framework for the torture and systematic ill-treatment of detainees as a policy of the US, as discussed below.

In the new order, powers of arrest and indefinite detention were determined to be virtually unlimited, justified by the congressional authorization of the use of force. Norms for the treatment of detainees were adjusted to permit whatever was deemed necessary to break a detainee's will in what was a process that often took months or years. This included protracted detention in cruel, inhuman and degrading conditions that in itself could constitute torture, as well as interrogation under torture that could stretch out over a month or more. The administration of justice, finally, was to be assumed by special military courts, the military commissions, as discussed below.

The Rise of Racism and Xenophobia

The attacks created an immediate climate of fear and uncertainty that for some found expression through racism and xenophobia. A rash of random attacks, including arsons, serious assaults and murders, was reported on Arabs, South Asians and others thought to be Muslims. Official hate crime statistics compiled by the FBI showed a 1,700 per cent rise in hate crimes against Muslims within a year, from 28 in 2000 to 481 in 2001, though the real levels were believed to be much higher (Human Rights First 2005a: 135; Human Rights Watch 2002). The levels of violence fell dramatically by the end of the year, although relatively high levels of violence would continue in the ensuring years, with periodical surges in response to developments in the wars in Afghanistan and Iraq (Human Rights First 2005a: 137).

Hate crime violence came in the context of government operations to round up Muslim immigrants for registration, detention and often deportation; to establish new controls at airports and on the borders, where Muslims were singled out for special attention; and to conduct new and aggressive forms of surveillance (Lawyers Committee for Human Rights 2002: 13–14). The beginning of the war with Afghanistan on 7 October 2001, with the launch of the US military's Operation Enduring Freedom and the British Operation Herrick, and the launch of Operation Iraqi Freedom on 19 March 2003 brought new threats of insecurity to the Muslim minorities in the US.

In the immediate aftermath of the attacks, nearly 1,200 people were detained, mostly Muslim men of Arab and South Asian origin who were not US citizens; many were subjected to prolonged detention without charge and without notification of their families. Few were ever charged with an offence related to terrorism and, ultimately, many were deported without access to a judicial hearing (Lawyers Committee for Human Rights 2002: 13–14). A federal programme required all male non-citizens over 16 years of age from 25 Muslim countries to go to special registration centres for questioning, where many were detained and some were ill-treated (American Immigrant Lawyers Association 2003; Amnesty International 2003; Lawyers Committee for Human Rights 2003c).

Civil rights groups warned that the government's actions represented a revival of racial profiling and that a hard-won consensus on halting racial profiling had been reversed (Leadership Conference on Civil Rights Education Fund 2002; Amnesty International 2004). In a Gallup poll just weeks after the attacks, 'a majority of Americans surveyed supported greater scrutiny of Arabs' and, specifically, that 'most white, black, and other non-white Americans expressed support of profiling of Arabs at airports and of requiring Arabs to carry special identification cards' (New York Advisory Committee to the U.S. Commission on Civil Rights 2004: vi).

A Climate Conducive to Torture

In the wake of the attacks, those calling for extreme measures to combat those responsible had ready access to the mainstream media. Commentators declared that the very survival of the US could rest upon its readiness to be as ruthless as its foreign adversaries. As part of this new reality, torture was portrayed as disagreeable but necessary (Alter 2001: 45). Even intellectuals who portrayed themselves as civil libertarians presented arguments that there was sometimes no alternative to torture and that, however abhorrent, it could be for the greater good (Dershowitz 2002a, 2002b; Ignatieff 2004: 136–55).

Opinion polls would subsequently report a disturbing readiness of the American public to contemplate torture – a consequence both of the real horror and dislocation caused by the 9/11 attacks and the drumbeat of calls to 'take the gloves off' in the fight against terror (Associated Press 2005; Rejali and Gronke 2009). An 'anything goes' message was also received within the armed forces, particularly by ordinary soldiers who took the tough talk of senior officials to heart. A former brigadier general later recalled that '[f]or young soldiers', statements like Vice President Cheney's reference to the 'dark side' were like 'the dissolute uncle up there winking, telling him he's got license' (Dwyer 2009).

Promoted by distinguished political pundits and high-adrenaline television series, the theme of torture as the answer to the terrorist conspirator and the ticking bomb became a leitmotif of popular culture (Human Rights First 2009a). Human Rights First's Prime Time Torture programme monitored and responded to popular television, notably series such as *24* and *Alias*, that made the ticking bomb syndrome a central plot device, presenting torture as a sovereign remedy to uncertainty (Human Rights First 2009a). The number of scenes of torture on television rose dramatically after September 2001, while monitors observed that '[o]n TV, torture almost always works'. While 'only villains on television tortured' before 9/11, in the new programming '"good guy" and heroic American characters torture – and this torture is depicted as necessary, effective and even patriotic' (Human Rights First 2009a).

The media's ubiquitous legitimating of torture was also of concern to military professionals. The former director of the law of war programme at West Point described classroom discussions of torture in which cadets cited the television show *24* in arguing that torture was effective (Human Rights First 2009b). Similarly, a former US Army intelligence officer with decades of experience as an interrogator said that young soldiers he trained frequently asked about techniques they had seen on television (Human Rights First 2009b).

Over time, public awareness of the extent and consequences of torture in US policy, in Iraq and in relation to the detainees at Guantanamo Bay, may have been decisive in turning the public against torture. In the 2008 presidential elections, both Barack Obama and John McCain, a former prisoner of war, came out strongly against torture under any circumstances. In the first year of the Obama administration, polls showed an important shift in attitudes. A *Washington Post-ABC News* poll conducted in January 2009 in the weeks before Obama took office found that by a wide margin, 'Americans say that torture should never be used, no matter the circumstances' (Greenwald 2009b).

A National Security Doctrine at Home

The Patriot Act was the omnibus security law enacted in the wake of the attacks. Signed into law on 26 October 2001, it granted the executive sweeping new powers of surveillance and search and seizure. The new powers allowed government agents to open the doors of private homes, offices, churches and businesses without warrant and without notification, while new secrecy norms barred access to information on the use of the new powers. The most sweeping measures expanded pre-existing powers of electronic surveillance and search and seizure (including access to digital information), and provided for the assembly of vast government databases on individuals on which no suspicion had previously been cast. Other programmes encouraged neighbours to spy upon neighbours (Lawyers Committee for Human Rights 2002: 1–12; 2003b: 1–15).

New government structures were also introduced in order to better implement expanded national security powers. The Department of Homeland Security was created in March 2003, consolidating 22 agencies, including the immigration service, into a single organization dealing with domestic security. Its rationale was to bring under central direction principal border and transportation security agencies, among others, and to create a central point for analysis and dissemination of intelligence and other information pertaining to terrorist threats. The FBI and CIA, however, remained outside the new super-agency (White House 2004a).

Warrantless Search and Seizure

The Patriot Act significantly loosened existing procedures for the authorization of domestic intelligence gathering, opening the way to the search and seizure of records and property, and the monitoring of the communications of US citizens without probable cause (Podesta 2002), as well as establishing new norms for surreptitious searches (Electronic Frontier Foundation 2006) and lowering the legal standard for initiating telephone and Internet surveillance measures (FBI 2002). An initial surge of protests also centred upon provisions under the Act to access the card-holder records of local public libraries – although the records that could be secretly accessed ranged from video rentals to the attendance records of churches or mosques to Internet access data (Lithwick and Turner 2003; Department of Justice, Office of the Inspector General 2008a: 1, 14).

The Act gave new authority to the Federal Bureau of Investigation (FBI) to secretly issue administrative subpoenas, called National Security Letters (NSLs), to demand access to personal customer records, including Internet information. Nearly 200,000 secret NSLs were issued between 2003 and 2006 alone to financial institutions, credit agencies, Internet Service Providers and other private bodies, including public libraries (in contrast to the 8,500 issued in 2000) (American Civil Liberties Union 2008; Sánchez 2009). In the vast majority of cases, recipients of the NSLs are barred from disclosing that they have received the letters. In 2008, the Department of Justice's Inspector General issued two reports finding that FBI agents misused the provision on a broad scale (Department of Justice, Office of the Inspector General 2008a, 2008b; Eggen 2008).

Data Mining and Domestic Spying

In July 2002, Attorney General John Ashcroft announced a new programme called Operation TIPS (the Terrorism Information and Prevention System) that the Justice Department had designed to 'encourage citizens to report on the "suspicious activities" of people in their communities' (Lawyers Committee for Human Rights 2003a: 15–16). TIPS was intended to recruit for domestic spying 'people whose everyday activities put them in daily contact with people in their homes and businesses, for example telephone repairmen, cable television installers, postal workers, delivery truck drivers, and workers for courier services' (Lawyers Committee for Human Rights 2002: 12). A pilot phase was scheduled to recruit one million workers in 10 cities, but media exposure drew immediate protests from all parts of the political spectrum and brought the programme to a halt (Black 2002). Congress subsequently banned funding for TIPS, even as dramatically increased domestic surveillance was achieved through other means (Lawyers Committee for Human Rights 2003a: 16).

The Pentagon initiated the Total Information Awareness (TIA) project in January 2002 in what was widely described as a new system of 'data mining'. TIA pulled together previous defence projects intended to combine data from private and government data sources in a central database. Healthcare, employment, school and library records, the credit card records of consumer purchases, and the records of domestic and international email traffic were all to be tapped with a view to compiling 'a comprehensive data profile of citizens and noncitizens'. Data to be incorporated included 'biometric, financial, education, travel, medical, veterinary, country entry, transportation, housing, government, critical resources, and communications data' (Electronic Privacy Information Center 2002). Public outcry over the project's threat to privacy rights led in September 2003 to congressional action to deny it funding (Electronic Frontier Foundation 2003). However, much of this programme reportedly continued more discreetly under less politically explosive names (Electronic Frontier Foundation 2003; Department of Defense 2004).

Similarly, an anti-terrorism data mining tool called ADVISE (Analysis, Dissemination, Visualization, Insight and Semantic Enhancement) was developed by the Department of Homeland Security, but was suspended in September 2007 for having inadequate privacy safeguards (Singel 2007a, 2007b). In March 2007, the Government Accountability Office concluded that 'the ADVISE tool could misidentify or erroneously associate an individual with undesirable activity such as fraud, crime or terrorism' (Sniffen 2007).

Other data-mining programmes undertaken by the FBI threatened new levels of intrusion into personal privacy that would have application far beyond their counter-terrorism rationale. A new order from the Attorney General after 9/11 declared that 'the FBI shall retain' all records it collects; that it 'may disseminate' them freely among federal agencies; and that it should develop 'data mining technology' to identify links between individuals on whom data was held. A FBI status report said a computerized 'Investigative Data Warehouse' was operational in January 2004 (Gellman 2005). The new projects gave the state a vast new capacity to monitor – and control – citizens' lives. The promotion of seemingly omnipresent government surveillance as necessary for public security in turn created a chilling effect on public life, particularly for those from minority groups.

Government Secrecy

Post-9/11 policies were characterized by a commitment to increasing government secrecy, while stripping away the privacy rights of the ordinary citizens. A presumption of secrecy surrounded all aspects of the new security order. The Freedom of Information Act (FOIA), a keystone of open government in the USA, for a time threatened to become a dead letter – with new norms by which executive agencies would presumptively deny FOIA requests. Court challenges gradually wore away at government non-compliance with the FOIA, winning the release of crucial documentation concerning secret policies and concealed abuses. The overall record of declassification, however, was extremely limited by the new norms of denial (Lawyers Committee for Human Rights 2003a: 2; Bain 2009).

Secrecy concerning detainees, both domestic and abroad, became a norm almost immediately, with information concerning detainees in the first panicky weeks after the attacks being withheld for months. Detention operations overseas, in turn, were cloaked in secrecy even from the International Committee of the Red Cross (ICRC), with the acknowledgement of detentions the exception rather than the rule.

Detainees in CIA custody effectively 'disappeared', their detentions denied, as they were transferred between detention centres that themselves had no formal recognition and the secret facilities of allies. The facilities employed included CIA 'black sites' on the island of Diego Garcia, and in Djibouti, Jordan, Morocco, Poland, Romania and Thailand, as well as at US bases in Afghanistan and Iraq (Human Rights First 2008; Priest and Gellman 2002). The CIA also used the interrogation cells of allies in Egypt, Jordan, Libya, Morocco and Syria, through which suspects were rotated using the system of covert international transfers called 'extraordinary rendition' (Human Rights Watch 2008; Horton 2009). Transfers to countries in which torture was known to occur violated the 1984 Torture Convention as well as US law – and most of the states in question had previously been criticized in the Department of State's annual human rights reports for torture and ill-treatment (United Nations 1984; Department of State 1975–2009).

Eroding the Framework of International Law

The Bush administration's rejection of the norms of international law in the conduct of the 'war against terrorism' provoked criticism both at home and abroad. Close allies protested that, through its actions in the name of national security, the US had 'severely undercut progress everywhere toward a rights-respecting global order'. European and Latin American governments were among the most vocal (Lawyers

Committee for Human Rights 2002: 41–2). The President's determination that the US would not comply with the Geneva Conventions was a point of departure from which most subsequent decisions on co
mpliance with domestic and international law would derive.

The Geneva Conventions of 1949, which codify the laws of war, are the principal instrument of international humanitarian law that protects those caught up in war – both soldiers and civilians. They apply to all international armed conflicts without exception, while establishing minimum standards for non-international armed conflict (in Article 3 common to the four conventions, known as Common Article 3) that cannot be set aside (Human Rights First 2005b). Accordingly, the Bush administration's unilateral disavowal of the Geneva Conventions in the 'war against terrorism' struck a blow at one of the most universally accepted pillars of international law.

President Bush determined that the Geneva Conventions would not apply to either the conflict with al-Qaeda or the ongoing war in Afghanistan on 18 January 2002, in a measure that provoked immediate dissent from other senior officials left out of the decision-making process. In a subsequent meeting, Secretary of State Colin Powell pressed for a reversal of the decision, backed by Defense Secretary Donald Rumsfeld and the chairman of the Joint Chiefs of Staff (Golden 2004; Fogarty 2005).

The determination was re-affirmed, however, in part on the basis of a 25 January 2002 memorandum in which White House general counsel Alberto Gonzales declared the posture setting aside the Geneva Conventions 'definitive' (White House 2002). On 7 February 2002, the President issued a further Confidential Presidential Determination that declared that 'none of the provisions of Geneva apply to our conflict with al-Qaeda in Afghanistan or elsewhere throughout the world'. Similarly, Bush determined that 'the Taliban detainees are unlawful combatants and, therefore, do not qualify as prisoners of war' (Department of Defense 2003: 4; Human Rights First 2005b).

In making this determination, the President reversed long-standing US policy and practice (Golden 2004; Fogarty 2005). Powell and senior military officials had protested that to undermine the Geneva Conventions was to strip US soldiers themselves of its protection, while undermining a fundamental basis for international cooperation (Human Rights First 2005b). There was also a concern that the US was sending a signal that it in fact *saw a need* 'to commit – and countenance – war crimes in its counterterrorism efforts', with its circumvention of the Geneva Conventions done expressly to shield US personnel from accountability for such crimes (Human Rights First 2005b).

The assertion that the Geneva Conventions did not apply led directly to subsequent legal memoranda and political determinations that re-interpreted the limits of international human rights law and US law itself. After putting the Geneva Conventions on the shelf, the administration argued that other legal norms too could be disregarded – including by reason of military necessity or as ultimately subordinate to the president's conduct of the war. For example, a March 2003 Department of Defense report echoed earlier White House and Department of Justice memoranda, concluding that it was ultimately up to the president whether to abide by the law (Department of Defense 2003: 3). It maintained that the president's war powers cannot be checked either by the laws passed by Congress, international treaties or even *jus cogens* (a peremptory norm under international law) (Department of Defense 2003: 21). (The prohibition of torture is widely accepted as *jus_cogens*.) The most notorious legal memoranda of this kind, produced in August 2002, concerned the legitimation of torture itself (see below)

The White House position on the Geneva Conventions was challenged before the federal courts, and in June 2006, the Supreme Court rejected the position that Common Article 3 was inapplicable to the armed conflict with al-Qaeda (Supreme Court 2006; Garcia 2009: 1–2). The President responded by pressing for congressional action that would assert a narrow interpretation of the Common Article 3 of the Conventions (White House 2006). The Military Commissions Act, signed into law on 17 October 2006, did just that, while barring those before the commissions from invoking the Geneva Conventions as a source of rights – or the right to habeas corpus (a position that would stand until overturned by the Supreme Court on June 2008 in *Boumediene v. Bush*) (Babington and Weisman 2006; US Congress 2006).

Undermining Global Rights Protection

The posture of the US towards the Geneva Conventions and international human rights law had the inevitable effect of a bad example, seeming to extend to others a similar licence to expedience over law. International progress towards making torture as unthinkable as slavery suffered a serious setback. A green light for US forces to carry out torture can only have reassured those governments whose use of torture and ill-treatment had previously been exposed by US human rights reports. At the same time, the Patriot Act and other domestic security measures were taken as an endorsement of ever more draconian anti-terrorism laws and decrees around the world (Lawyers Committee for Human Rights 2002: 41–9; 2003b: 73–80).

The US also took on an adversarial relationship with the principal international bodies responsible for the implementation of international human rights norms, exacerbating the estrangement already apparent in early 2001 (Crossette 2001). At the same time, the USA's role in ongoing negotiations to develop new international instruments changed from that of an advocate for higher standards to that of a criminal defence lawyer concerned that stronger international law would put its clients at risk.

In July 2002, for example, US representatives in Geneva sought to undermine efforts to finalize an optional protocol to the Torture Convention that would provide for independent inspections of detention facilities (Cassel 2002). (The protocol was adopted by the General Assembly on 18 December 2002.) Similarly, while the US had long supported an International Convention for the Protection of All Persons from Enforced Disappearance, declassified documents show that between 2003 and 2006, it actively sought to exclude from its scope then-current US practices such as extraordinary rendition and holding detainees without acknowledgement or the release of their names (Department of Defense 2004, 2005a).

In drafting sessions, US negotiators fought for language that would have exempted from prosecution those who thought they were following lawful orders in carrying out 'disappearances', supporting what was called in internal memoranda 'the good soldier' or the 'superior orders' defence. A September 2005 guidance sheet for negotiators continued to highlight concern at the 'Lack of [a] Defence of Superior Orders' clause (Department of State 2005b). A further 'serious concern', with its implication of potential international trials, was the proposed inclusion of the term 'crimes against humanity' in the preamble to the declaration (Department of State 2005c). The US delegation also fought against the creation of 'an unqualified 'right of families and others with a legitimate interest to know' the whereabouts and other circumstances of a disappeared person', while acknowledging that it stood 'virtually alone on this issue' (Department of State 2005c). (The Convention on Enforced Disappearances was adopted, largely intact, by the UN General Assembly on 20 December 2006.)

The Detainees

Policy-makers decided to hold long-term detainees from the 'war against terrorism' at the Guantanamo Bay Naval Station (GTMO) on the southeast coast of Cuba. The administration said that indefinite detention without charge was authorized by the presidential 'use of force' authority extended by Congress. The legal fiction would be maintained that, as the base was on Cuban territory, detainees were out of reach of the American courts – a position the Supreme Court would not conclusively overturn until 2008.

There is considerable evidence that Guantanamo was chosen expressly to allow US forces to deal with terrorism detainees with no legal constraints whatsoever. An inter-agency working group was tasked with identifying a place detainees could be denied rights at will – what one participant (Department of Security legal advisor David Bowker) described as 'the legal equivalent of outer space' (Isikoff and Taylor 2006; NYU School of Law 2008). The White House representation on the group reportedly said that it would accept nothing less (Isikoff and Taylor 2006). The Department of Defense also considered the legal advantages and Guantanamo was the choice (Department of Defense 2003). In fact, Guantanamo was not the 'legal equivalent of outer space', and both domestic US law and international law would eventually be found to hold there by the US's own courts. But Guantanamo was in practice a place in which the US for many years denied the law held sway – what was called in a British court judgment a 'legal black hole' (Court of Appeal 2002; Borelli 2005: 41).

The Bush administration denied those detained in the 'war against terrorism' any status under the laws of war. The terms of international human rights law, in turn, were rendered inapplicable by non-compliance, open disdain and virtual (but not formal) repudiation. The detainees were also denied any status under US law. Constitutional due process safeguards were circumvented both through executive orders and the courts and by keeping most security detainees physically outside the country's borders. The names of detainees were systematically withheld, although the ICRC would eventually be permitted to conduct visits to most – under its normal conditions of strict confidentiality.

Most of the prisoners were detained in the course of the initial phase of the conflict in Afghanistan, including individuals handed over by allied warlords there and by the authorities in Pakistan – often for cash payments. Others were detained as far afield as Bosnia, often on highly questionable grounds. Those detained ranged from children as young as 13 to men in their eighties and nineties (Auster and Whitelaw 2003). US officials said all were hardened terrorists: what Secretary Rumsfeld called the 'worst of the worst' (Warrick 2008).

The first prisoners arrived at the Guantanamo facility on 11 January 2002. Soon afterwards, a photograph broadcast around the world showed prisoners kneeling on the ground in leg shackles and handcuffs with their eyes, ears and mouths covered and wearing mittens (Ifill 2002). Human rights monitors found conditions at Guantanamo to constitute cruel, inhuman or degrading treatment that was harmful to detainees' health, aggravated by the psychological stress of indefinite detention without charge. Monitors tied pattern of abuse to numerous prisoner suicide attempts and recurrent hunger strikes (Physicians for Human Rights 2005; Amnesty International 2009).

By 2008, some 800 men and boys had been transferred to Guantanamo, of 37 nationalities. The US military acknowledged a peak prisoner population of slightly over 750 at any one time. As of May 2009, approximately 540 detainees had been returned to their home countries, where some were detained and have since been released. Some 240 detainees remained (CNN 2007; Global Security 2009). Only a very small minority of the Guantanamo detainees were found to be tied to terrorist groups, charged with a crime or otherwise shown to represent a danger to the US (Lawyers Committee for Human Rights 2003b: 59).

As evidence emerged that many had been detained on the say so of unreliable allies, there was a reluctance to admit that mistakes had been made. The presence of hundreds of detainees at Guantanamo was the administration's primary exhibit with which to convince a still-nervous electorate that something was being done to combat a largely invisible enemy. To backtrack was politically untenable. Even as the majority of the detainees were released after years of detention, a handful at a time, the fact that many of them never should have been detained was never acknowledged and no public explanation of what went wrong was forthcoming.

The Right to a Fair Trial

The Bush administration argued that the due process safeguards of the federal court system, and indeed those of the ordinary military courts, would pose insuperable obstacles to the prosecution of detainees suspected of terrorism. This largely disregarded the numerous successful prosecutions before the US federal courts of criminal cases arising from terrorism inside the US both before and after 9/11 (Human Rights First 2009c: 1, 6). Despite the availability of the federal courts, the vast majority of security detainees seized overseas were held indefinitely without charge. However, the administration retained the option to bring detainees before special military courts, the military commissions.

The Military Commissions

In November 2001, President Bush authorized the trial of suspected terrorists by a new system of military courts to be established to try 'violations of the laws of war and other applicable laws'. The order extended to the Department of Defense the power to detain and prosecute non-US citizens anywhere, so long as the president or his representative determined they had 'engaged in, aided or abetted, or conspired to commit acts of international terrorism' (White House 2001). New procedures permitted 'secret evidence, hearsay, hearings closed to the public, limitations on defendants' choice of counsel, and denial of review of commission determinations by the U.S. federal courts' (Lawyers Committee for Human Rights 2002: 33).

In 2006, the Supreme Court ruled that the military commissions as they were then constituted were illegal under both the Uniform Code of Military Justice and the Geneva Conventions, and could not continue (Supreme Court 2006). In creating the basis for new commissions, through the Military Commissions Act of 2006, Congress re-established a special court system that restricted the right to defence, lowered standards of evidence and was institutionally neither independent nor impartial. The Act made evidence obtained through torture admissible as long as certain conditions are met. In cases in which 'the degree of coercion is disputed', it is up to the judge to consider whether 'the totality of the circumstances renders the statement reliable' and whether 'the interests of justice' would be served by its admission into evidence. A second provision declared that detainees before the commissions would have no rights to habeas corpus before any court – a provision finally overturned by the Supreme Court in 2008 (US Congress 2006).

Torture

The US was unique in the world during the Bush administration not for the fact that its military and intelligence forces employed torture, but for its formal adoption and regulation of torture as a policy, as subsequently confirmed by declassified White House, CIA and military documents, and for its public apologia for the use of methods almost universally condemned as torture. No aspect of the US human rights record was more emblematic of the post-9/11 years than the issue of torture. The evidence of torture by US forces, including deaths under torture, emerged through inadvertent exposés, notably the photographs taken by American soldiers at the Abu

Ghraib detention facility in Iraq: the leaks of top-level legal memoranda seeking to justify torture; declassified documents detailing interrogation policies and practices; and through investigations by the ICRC, human rights monitors and the media.

Already in December 2002, investigative journalists were filing detailed reports of torture or ill-treatment at Guantánamo, at the US air base at Bagram, Afghanistan, and at secret CIA sites (Priest and Gellman 2002). Some of the most extraordinary evidence of torture came from documents that were declassified under the FOIA – or leaked – detailing the interrogations under torture of individuals identified as 'high value detainees' and held in prolonged CIA custody. This included interrogation logs, indepth reviews of interrogation techniques, and secret reports on the CIA's own detainee programme.

Declassified government documents ultimately revealed both the details of torture in particular cases and the elaborate efforts of civilian and military authorities to devise, regulate and rationalize specific forms of torture. The documents are important in terms of exposing the reality of the practice of torture as well as the elaborate institutional framework established for its implementation. Some of the technical memoranda, for example, reflect a banalization and bureaucratization of torture, with specifications that might be compared to those for a government motor pool.

A report from the CIA's Office of Medical Services (OMS) gave specific technical specifications for breaking a prisoner's resistance: this included the optimum wattage of lights, the decibel level for constant noise, the calorific intake and the temperatures to be used in deliberately exposing prisoners to 'an uncomfortably cool environment'. The combination of instructions made up a package, with each component specified. Even a routine in which prisoners were periodically doused with cold water was to be carefully calibrated (with the water temperature at 41 degrees Fahrenheit, dousing was to continue for no more than 20 minutes) (CIA 2004a; Shane and Mazzetti 2009a). Similarly, the specifications gave the number of hours a prisoner could be kept in 'awkward boxes, specifically constructed for this purpose' (two hours for the small one and eight consecutive hours in the large one for up to 18 hours a day) (CIA 2004a).

Guidance is also given on the risk of hypothermia to prisoners held in enforced nudity – including references to scientific studies on the exposure to cold. Medical officers were also to file detailed questionnaires on the conduct of waterboarding – suggesting a research and experimentation role (the Geneva Conventions define medical experiments as 'grave breaches') (CIA 2004b). The role of the CIA's medical personnel is described as central to the programme, with physicians and psychologists involved in both calibrating the pain and suffering to be inflicted (and charged with certifying that it falls short of torture) and standing by to bring detainees back from the brink when necessary to continue interrogations (CIA 2004a: 17). The organization Physicians for Human Rights has raised concerns that the involvement of CIA medical staff in 'data collection and analysis' on interrogations 'may amount to human experimentation', thus constituting a grave breach of the Geneva Conventions (Physicians for Human Rights 2009).

The waterboard technique is described like an industrial process: 'A stream of water is directed at the upper lip. Resistant subjects ... have the cloth lowered to cover the nose and mouth, as the water continues to be applied, fully saturating the cloth, and precluding the passage of air. Relatively little water enters the mouth.' Each session is, optimally, to last no more than a few minutes and to involve 'up to 15 canteen cups of water' (CIA 2004a: 17). Medical personnel are required to be on hand and are warned that 'extensive sustained use' introduces serious risks, including 'excessive filling of the airways and loss of consciousness'. If a subject is unresponsive, 'the interrogator should deliver a sub-xyphoid thrust to expel the water'; if this is insufficient, 'aggressive medical intervention' is required. The same document notes that as of December 2004, high-level approvals for waterboarding remain in force for just 30 days, with sessions on no more than five days within this period.

The declassified reports also show administrative requirements that torture be exhaustively documented, with reports on the CIA's 'enhanced interrogations' sent to the top of the CIA hierarchy. Considerable detail comes from the CIA Inspector General's May 2004 report on interrogations, which examines the record of the interrogation of 'high value' detainee Zayn Abidin Muhammed Hussein abu Zubaida, including an hour-by-hour video record and 'logs and cables' documenting the interrogations (CIA 2004c: 42–3). The CIA subsequently said the tapes had been destroyed to conceal the identities of interrogators 'at a time [when] the Justice Department was debating whether or not the tactics used during the interrogations were legal' (Barrett 2009).

Some of the most detailed descriptions of the actual practice of torture were also revealed in the CIA Inspector General's report, which focuses upon 'enhanced interrogation techniques' (EITs) and the guidelines and training provided for their employment (CIA 2004c; Shane and Mazzetti 2009b). It includes details of interrogations, including the use of near-drowning (waterboarding), stress positions, suspension by the arms, exposure to cold, threats to sexually abuse family members and to kill children, mock executions, and threats of maiming and death. Other techniques used, but not considered 'enhanced', included dousing with water, sleep deprivation, hooding and enforced nudity (CIA 2004c: 75).

The record shows that interrogators did not follow clinical prescriptions for the use of particular techniques. In particular, waterboarding was not the antiseptic and carefully controlled process described by agency spokesmen and policy-makers. Two individuals were subjected to 83 and 119 'waterboard applications' respectively in the space of a month: Khalid Shaykh Muhammad was waterboarded 183 times (and denied sleep for 180 consecutive hours) (CIA 2004c: 51, 110). Techniques described as 'unauthorized or undocumented' included the threat of summary execution with a handgun while the suspect 'sat shackled in his cell', and threatening a detainee with a power drill ('the debriefer ... revved the drill while the detainee stood naked and hooded. The debriefer did not touch [the detainee] with the power drill') (CIA 2004c: 48).

New details continued to emerge. In April 2009, reporter Mark Danner published extensive sections of a 2007 report that had been submitted by the ICRC to the Bush administration (Danner 2009; Warrick, Finn, and Tate 2009). The report, which was based on ICRC access to 14 'high value' detainees after their transfer to Guantanamo in 2006, concluded unambiguously that their treatment 'constituted torture'. Detainee interviews described beatings, being slammed head-first into walls, being forced to stand with their arms shackled above them, near-drowning, sleep deprivation for days and being exposed to extreme temperatures. They said they were deprived of solid food, stripped of clothing, held for days in adult diapers and bombarded with loud music (the ICRC did not dispute the authenticity of the report, but expressed dismay that it had been leaked) (Warrick, Finn, and Tate 2009). The ICRC accounts were consistent with the government's own declassified records, although the latter were more chilling insofar as they described a programme of torture as if it was an ordinary function of government.

The Military and Torture

In October 2002, the US armed forces had already begun to adopt the new interrogation norms endorsed for the CIA, with Guantanamo's military commanders seeking formal permission from Secretary of Defense Donald Rumsfeld to employ specific harsh new interrogation techniques. Sixteen techniques were approved, including 'hooding, stress positions, isolation, stripping, deprivation of light, removal of religious items, forced grooming, and use of dogs' (Human Rights Watch 2005). These procedures, incorporated into Standard Operating Procedures (SOPs) in Guantanamo, subsequently 'migrated', with top-level Pentagon approval, to regular army units in Iraq and Afghanistan (Department of Defense 2006: 28).

Torture and ill-treatment in military custody combined special techniques for indepth interrogation with a comprehensive programme for the ongoing treatment of detainees intended to *prepare* detainees for interrogation, weakening their bodies and breaking their spirits. Major General Antonio Taguba, in his secret, pre-scandal report on Abu Ghraib, traced the abuses there in part to recommendations by Guantanamo commander Major General Geoffrey Miller that detention be used as 'an enabler for interrogation' and that 'the guard force be actively engaged in setting the condition for the successful exploitation of internees' (Hersh 2004; Human Rights Watch 2005). Miller visited Iraq in August–September 2003 expressly to share the lessons of Guantanamo with commanders in Iraq (Department of Defense 2006; Koppelman 2009), and told senior commanders 'we had to get tougher with the detainees' (Senate. Date redacted). Miller's mission was to apply Guantanamo's 'operational procedures and interrogation authorities to Iraq' (Department of Defense 2006: 33).

The treatment described in the military investigations showed that torture was not just a matter of particular techniques in isolation, but often involved a combination of elements over time that in isolation might have been considered forms of ill-treatment falling short of torture. It was its nature, purpose and severity that made this systematic treatment torture – one reason that cruel, inhuman or degrading treatment is also prohibited under any circumstances by the Geneva Conventions and human rights law (United Nations 1966; Rodley 2002). The ongoing treatment of detainees at Abu Ghraib was deliberately designed to inflict severe physical and psychological pain and suffering in order to 'break' prisoners. This was in part what distinguished this as torture – which must be deliberate – from other cruel or inhuman treatment, which does not (Rodley 2002).

The first photographs from Iraq's Abu Ghraib prison were broadcast around the world on 28 April 2004, showing American soldiers torturing and mocking Iraqi detainees in their custody. The pictures showed smiling, uniformed soldiers posing with cringing naked prisoners. President Bush condemned what he called the 'disgraceful conduct' at Abu Ghraib, but attributed this to 'a few American troops who dishonoured our country and disregarded our values' (White House 2004b).

It was soon after the scandal broke over Abu Ghraib that the news media received a leaked copy of the 1 August 2002 'torture memo' that grappled with a legal rationale for torture – while setting out arguments that could be used in the legal defence of American torturers. This and other official documents, once published, made clear that reports of torture by US forces revealed more than a problem of 'a few bad apples' and required urgent remedial action (Hersh 2004). Although a rash of military and congressional inquiries followed, a pattern of torture and systemic ill-treatment of security detainees continued to be reported throughout the Bush administration (Human Rights Watch 2006).

The exposure of torture at Abu Ghraib generated a series of high-level military inquiries and the prosecution of a handful of low-ranking troops who took the photographs and posed in them. More than 300 criminal, military and administrative investigations were set into motion after Abu Ghraib hit the headlines, but no senior officials – or civilian policy-makers – were held accountable for the crimes committed there (Human Rights First 2004). As of March 2005, just 14 people had been convicted by court-martial in relation to the Abu Ghraib investigations, while others received non-judicial punishments such as 'reprimands, rank reductions, or discharge from the military' (Human Rights Watch 2005: 16).

Major investigations by senior military officers into abuses at Abu Ghraib each looked at just a part of the problem (Human Rights First 2004). Each confirmed large-scale patterns of abuse. The report by Major General Antonio Taguba, for example, found 'numerous incidents of sadistic, blatant, and wanton criminal abuses' constituting 'systematic and illegal abuse of detainees' at Abu Ghraib (Human Rights Watch 2005: 16). But none of the inquiries was empowered to address the totality of the abuse, the underlying policies and operating procedures or, most significantly, the role of senior commanders and civilian policy-makers. Terms of reference that prevented the three officers from addressing 'civilian command responsibility' for flawed and unlawful policies endorsing torture were a crucial failing of the internal military reports (Human Rights First 2004: 17).

The Torture Memoranda

Some of the most damning evidence of a policy of torture comes from legal memoranda to assess and deem permissible specific interrogation techniques intended to cause pain and suffering (Bilder and Vagts 2004: 691; Physicians for Human Rights 2004). Prepared for and endorsed by the White House, these were then passed on to military and civilian counter-terrorism authorities as guiding principles (Danner 2004). The legal memoranda on what torture consists of and how it was justified are widely available on the Internet, notably on the websites of the Federation of American Scientists and the National Security Archive.

The post-9/11 legal memoranda exhaustively consider possible legal defences to be put forward should the abusive treatment of detainees become known. The 'legal exposure' of US personnel under domestic and international law prohibiting torture was a primary concern, with the memoranda crafted with the express purpose of minimizing this exposure (Department of Defense 2003: Recommendations).

One of the most authoritative of the documents now known as the 'torture memos' was prepared by Assistant Attorney General Jay S. Bybee for the Department of Justice Office of the Legal Counsel and dated 1 August 2002 (Department of Justice 2002a). Bybee found that laws barring torture 'may be unconstitutional if applied to interrogations [in wartime]'; that doctrines of 'necessity and self-defence could provide justifications that would eliminate any criminal liability' for US personnel who carried out torture; and that only the highest levels of pain and suffering should be considered to constitute torture ('physical pain amounting to torture must be equivalent in intensity to the pain accompanying serious physical injury, such as organ failure, impairment of bodily function, or even death') (Department of Justice 2002a).

The Bybee memorandum set the tone for subsequent legal memoranda that sought both to re-define torture in terms that would exclude abusive US methods, while asserting that authorized interrogation methods, however brutal, could never lead to prosecutions. It found that even if a technique was to violate US law, 'the statute would be unconstitutional if it impermissibly encroached on the President's constitutional power to conduct a military campaign' (Department of Justice 2002a).

Other key legal memoranda were drafted by Deputy Assistant Attorney General John Yoo, including a 14 March 2003 'torture memo' on *military* interrogations, which echoed the reasoning of the Bybee memo (Department of Justice 2003). Already in October 2001, Yoo had advised the President that US law barring the engagement of the armed forces domestically could be disregarded in the context of the 'war on terror', and that the Fourth Amendment, which prohibits unreasonable searches and seizures, would not apply to domestic military operations (Department of Justice 2001; Kamiya 2009). In a March 2002 memorandum, preparing the way for 'extraordinary rendition', Yoo advised that 'captured terrorists' could be transferred to the control and custody of foreign nations without restraint, in that the Geneva Conventions and the Torture Convention 'do not apply to the factual situation posed by the transfer of al Qaeda or Taliban prisoners to third countries' (Department of Justice 2002b).

The torture memos also repeatedly addressed concerns that US personnel employing sanctioned interrogation techniques might one day face an international tribunal. The naming of the members of the first International Criminal Court (ICC) in March 2003 occurred just as torture was becoming institutionalized at Guantanamo, Iraq and Afghanistan (International Criminal Court undated). The crime of torture is one of universal jurisdiction, and for the first time a permanent international court (the ICC) existed to investigate and prosecute such crimes when governments were unwilling or unable to do so.

The 2003 Department of Defense report on the treatment of detainees makes special reference to the ICC, warning that states party to the arrangements may find the interrogation techniques employed by US personnel to constitute torture or inhuman treatment and accordingly seek to prosecute such individuals for these crimes should they be found in their territory (Department of Defense 2003: 68–9). Its conclusion stresses that it may in fact be 'major partner nations' that seek such prosecutions, in their own courts or in international tribunals, to the extent that this might 'impact future operations and overseas travel of such personnel' (Department of Defense 2003: 68–9).

Efforts by military lawyers to reverse the course set by the torture memos, notably by Navy General Counsel Alberto Mora, were largely disregarded (Mora 2004; Mayer 2006). In 2004 Mora condemned what he called the 'catastrophically poor legal reasoning' of the memos and said the new legal theories granting the President the right to authorize abuse were 'unlawful', 'dangerous' and 'erroneous' (Mayer 2006). Although the Yoo and Bybee memoranda were formally repudiated after they were leaked to the press, their basic arguments would be repeated throughout the Bush years, with internal dissidents sidelined (Rosen 2007).

Restoring Fundamental Rights

A series of court decisions were instrumental in bringing about a gradual restoration of the fundamental rights curtailed after 9/11. The Supreme Court first ruled that the rights of security detainees, including those held at Guantanamo, did in fact fall under the jurisdiction of the courts in two cases on 28 June 2004. In its ruling on *Hamdi v. Rumsfeld*, the Court ruled that notwithstanding Congress' authorization of the use of force, 'due process demands that a citizen held in the United States as an enemy combatant be given a meaningful opportunity to contest the factual basis for that detention before a neutral decision maker' (Supreme Court 2004a). In *Rasul v. Bush*, the Court further found that the 'United States courts have jurisdiction to consider challenges to the legality of the detention of foreign nationals captured abroad in connection with hostilities and incarcerated at Guantanamo Bay' (Supreme Court 2004b).

The court rulings re-affirming the rights of Guantanamo detainees to seek judicial review by US courts led directly to congressional action to block such appeals through the Detainee Treatment Act 2005 (DTA) and the Military Commissions Act 2006

(MCA). The DTA provided that 'no court, justice, or judge shall have jurisdiction' to consider habeas corpus filed by a Guantanamo detainee (US Congress 2005), while a clause in the MCA barred judicial review in similar terms (US Congress 2006).

The new legal constructions were in turn rejected by a Supreme Court ruling on 12 June 2008 in the case of *Boumediene v. Bush* as an unconstitutional bar on the right to habeas corpus. The Court rejected the Bush administration's position that the constitution afforded detainees at Guantanamo Bay 'no rights because the United States does not claim sovereignty over the naval station' (Supreme Court 2008).

President Obama's First Year

In January 2009, incoming President Barack Obama acted almost immediately to draw a line across the past with respect to government secrecy, adherence to international law and the treatment of detainees. On 21 January, Obama issued a memorandum to heads of executive agencies on open government, declaring that the FOIA should be administered 'with a clear presumption: In the face of doubt, openness prevails'. Henceforth, all agencies are instructed to 'adopt a presumption in favour of disclosure, in order to renew their commitment to the principles embodied in FOIA, and to usher in a new era of open Government' (National Security Archive 2009; White House 2009a).

Three executive orders were issued in public sessions on 22 January 2009 to address the most egregious human rights issues of the post-9/11 period. They addressed interrogation, the disposition of the Guantanamo detainees and a review of the basis on which security detainees would be held.

In 'Ensuring Lawful Interrogation', Obama repudiated the previous administration's policies regarding torture and ill-treatment, barring US officials, employees and agents 'from relying on any interpretation of the law governing interrogation (including Common Article 3) that was issued by the Bush Administration following September 11, 2001' (White House 2009b). The order also instructed the CIA to 'expeditiously' close 'any detention facilities that it currently operates' and bars its future operation of such facilities. The President also instructed all federal departments and agencies to provide the ICRC 'with notification of, and timely access to, any individual detained in any armed conflict' by the US (White House 2009b).

The executive order makes Common Article 3 a minimum baseline for detainee treatment, while also requiring compliance with domestic law, the Convention Against Torture and other international norms (White House 2009b). The order is also prescriptive regarding specific allowable techniques, making the standard in any armed conflict the norms established in the Army's field manual on interrogation. Accordingly, any treatment related to interrogation 'that is not authorized by and listed in Army Field Manual 2-22.3' is prohibited (White House 2009b). The Army field manual expressly forbids many of the techniques authorized by the Bush administration, including waterboarding, hooding, sleep deprivation or forced standing for prolonged periods (Department of the Army 2006; Garcia 2009).

In a further order, Obama ordered a review of the status of the Guantanamo detainees and the closure of the detention facilities there within one year (White House 2009c). A third executive order required a review of policy options available for detention in armed conflict and counter-terrorism situations and established an inter-agency task force to develop these options (White House 2009d).

In its first year, the Obama administration continued to support prosecutions for some detainees suspected of terrorism, before both the federal criminal courts and military commissions, while holding others without trial. The administration had initially considered the introduction of new legislation providing for indefinite administrative detention without charge or trial, drawing upon past proposals under the previous administration (Glaberson 2009; Waxman 2008). In September 2009, spokesmen for the administration said that it would not be seeking further authorization from Congress to this end (Baker 2009). Critics had held that proposals to legislate administrative detention (sometimes called preventive detention) had a ring of totalitarianism to them and were almost certainly unconstitutional (Greenwald 2009c).

The Department of Justice subsequently announced that detainees would continue to be held without charge under the resolution authorizing the president to use force against al-Qaeda and the Taliban. In contrast to the position of the Bush administration, it did not maintain that the president had an inherent constitutional power to detain suspects of terrorism indefinitely without congressional authorization. Some 50 detainees were held at Guantanamo without charge or apparent intention of trial in September 2009, and the Department of Justice said their cases would continue to be subject to habeas corpus and review by the courts (Baker 2009).

In September 2009, progress towards the announced closure of Guantanamo within one year of President Obama's taking office was looking uncertain. In May 2009, the Senate voted 90:6 to block funding for the closure of the Guantanamo facility, with many members responding to constituent concerns about the possible relocation of detainees in their districts (Kornblut and Linzer 2009).

As of June 2008, 15 months after the Supreme Court had ruled the bar on habeas corpus unconstitutional, the federal courts had considered 36 of some 200 outstanding habeas corpus cases, ordering the release of 29 detainees and supporting the continued detention of seven. In general, the courts were finding that the administration's assertion that the detainees held there were only 'the worst of the worst' was unfounded (Rosenberg 2009). The administration had determined by September that some 50–60 prisoners there who could not be tried because of legal impediments could not be released, on the grounds that they posed continuing threats. Alternative detention facilities within the US had not yet been identified and obstacles remained to any prisoner transfer, including congressional opposition (Kornblut and Linzer 2009). In mid-2012, Guantanamo remained open.

In October 2009, when it was announced that President Obama was the recipient of the Nobel Peace Prize, Obama himself acknowledged this as recognition of both what he had achieved and what he might yet achieve, declaring that he would 'accept this award as a call to action' (Erlanger and Stolberg 2009). As presidential elections approached in 2012, it remained an open question whether Obama's presidency would meet the expectations of the Nobel Committee.

Conclusion

Outrage and fear after the 9/11 attacks led the American people to accept the curtailing of their own rights and to acquiesce in the secret detention and torture of others. The administration took advantage of a door opened by al-Qaeda to expand executive power at home and to go outside the law abroad in the name of counter-terrorism.

A cowed Congress accepted an argument that respect for human rights was an obstacle to security and gave carte blanche to a presidency prepared to take extraordinary measures at home and abroad. The Patriot Act and administrative acts curtailed the rights to privacy and due process of law. The courts, not Congress, curbed some of the administration's excesses with regard to the rights of detainees, but new government powers introduced by the Patriot Act remained intact.

The Obama administration moved quickly to disassociate itself from the most brutal and damaging of US policies concerning overseas operations, abjuring the practice of torture and re-affirming adherence to the Geneva Conventions. It stopped short of establishing accountability for past abuses, opposing broad criminal investigations or any form of truth commission, and it failed to end detention without trial or to close Guantanamo within the promised timeframe. Nor in its first year did the new administration indicate that it would revisit the new norms of secrecy, surveillance and enhanced executive powers introduced in the name of security at home.

The cost to human rights protection and promotion of post-9/11 counter-terrorism was severe and can be expected to be lasting. Regaining the ground lost in the global fight against torture and detention without trial will in itself be a long-term challenge. Inside the US, push-back from the public emerged gradually, turning back some serious challenges to liberties at home, such as neighbour-on-neighbour spying programmes. But much of the structural transformation concerned the expansion of government powers behind the scenes: powers of surveillance, search and seizure, and 'data mining' through which government can oversee, overhear and interfere with the private lives of citizens. These post-9/11 innovations and the erosion of civil liberties that they represent appear to be here to stay.

References

Alfano, S. 2006. 'War Casualties Pass 9/11 Death Toll'. CBS News, 22 September.
Alter, J. 2001. 'Time to Think About Torture'. *Newsweek*, 5 November.

American Civil Liberties Union (ACLU). 2008. 'FBI Withdraws Unconstitutional National Security Letter ater ACLU and EFF Challenge'. Press Release, 7 May: http://www.aclu.org/safefree/nationalsecurityletters/35202prs20080507.html [accessed 1 July 2012].

American Immigration Lawyers Association (AILA). 2003. 'AILF Q and A About "Call-In" Special Registration', 3 March: http://www.aila.org/content/default.aspx?bc=1016%7C6715%7C20852%7C20854%7C8023 [accessed 20 August 2009].

Amnesty International (AI). 2003. Letter to Attorney General John Ashcroft, 10 January.

Amnesty International. 2004. 'Threat and Humiliation: Racial Profiling, Domestic Security and Human Rights in the United States', September: http://www.amnestyusa.org/racial_profiling/report/rp_report.pdf [accessed 1 July 2012].

Amnesty International. 2009. 'USA', in *Amnesty International Report 2008*: http://archive.amnesty.org/air2008/eng/regions/americas/usa.html [accessed 1 July 2012].

Associated Press (AP). 2005. 'Poll Finds Broad Approval of Terrorist Torture'. MSNBC, 9 December: http://www.msnbc.msn.com/id/10345320/ [accessed 1 July 2012].

Auster, B.B. and Whitelaw, K. 2003. 'Terror's Cellblock: Complaints over the Handling of Suspects at Guantanamo are Raising Hackles in Washington'. *U.S. News and World Report*, 4 May: http://www.usnews.com/usnews/news/articles/030512/12gitmo.htm [accessed 1 July 2012].

Babington, C. and Weisman, J. 2006. 'Senate Approves Detainee Bill Backed by Bush: Constitutional Challenges Predicted'. *Washington Post*, 29 September.

Bain, B. 2009. 'Obama Reverses Course on FOIA'. *FederalComputerWeek*, 17 April: http://www.fcw.com/Articles/2009/04/20/policy-FOIA-open-government.aspx [accessed 1 July 2012].

Baker, P. 2009. 'Obama to Use Current Law to Support Detentions'. *New York Times*, 24 September.

Barrett, D. 2009. 'CIA Destroyed 12 Harsh Interrogation Tapes'. *Washington Post*, 7 March.

Bilder, R.B. and Vagts, D.F. 2004. 'Speaking Law to Power: Lawyers and Torture'. *American Journal of International Law*, 98, 689.

Black, J. 2002. 'Some TIPS for John Ashcroft', *BusinessWeek*, 25 July: http://www.businessweek.com/stories/2002-07-24/some-tips-for-john-ashcroft [accessed 1 July 2012].

Borelli, S. 2005. 'Casting Light on the Legal Black Hole: International Law and Detentions Abroad in the "War on Terror"'. *International Review of the Red Cross*, 87(857): http://www.icrc.org/eng/assets/files/other/irrc_857_borelli.pdf [accessed 1 July 2012].

Cassel, D. 2002. 'Do Unto Others ... America Fights International Covenants Against Torture'. *Chicago Tribune*, 1 September.

CBS News. 2008. 'Official 9/11 Death Toll Climbs by One', 10 July.

Central Intelligence Agency (CIA). 2004a. *OMS Guidelines on Medical and Psychological Support to Detainee Rendition, Interrogation, and Detention*, December: http://documents.nytimes.com/c-i-a-reports-guidelines-for-interrogators#p=13.

Central Intelligence Agency. 2004b. 'Appendix A. Medical Rationales for Limitations on Physical Pressures', in *OMS Guidelines on Medical and Psychological Support to Detainee Rendition, Interrogation, and Detention*, December.

Central Intelligence Agency. 2004c. 'CIA Inspector General, Special Review, Counterterrorism Detention and Interrogation Activities (September 2001–October 2003), (2003-7123-IG)', 7 May:. http://documents.nytimes.com/c-i-a-reports-on-interrogation-methods#p=1 [accessed 1 July 2012].

CNN. 2007. 'Inside Guantanamo Bay': http://i.cdn.turner.com/cnn/interactive/world/0807/explainer.guantanamo/explainer.swf [accessed 1 July 2012].

Court of Appeal, Supreme Court of Judicature Judgment. 2002. *Abbasi and another v. Secretary of State for Foreign and Commonwealth Affairs & Secretary of State for the Home Department*. Case No. C/2002/0617A; 0617B, 6 November: www.law.utoronto.ca/documents/Mackin/AbbasiUKCA.doc [accessed 1 July 2012].

Crossette, B. 2001. 'For First Time, U.S. is Excluded from U.N. Human Rights Panel', 4 May: http://www.nytimes.com/2001/05/04/world/for-first-time-us-is-excluded-from-un-human-rights-panel.html?pagewanted=all&src=pm [accessed 1 July 2012].

Danner, M. 2004. *Torture and Truth: America, Abu Ghraib, and the War on Terror*. New York: New York Review of Books.

Danner, M. 2009. 'US Torture: Voices from the Black Sites'. *New York Review of Books*, 56(6), 9 April.

Department of the Army 2006. Headquarters. 2006. FM 2-22.3 (FM 34-52), *Human Intelligence Collector Operations*, September: http://www.army.mil/institution/armypublicaffairs/pdf/fm2-22-3.pdf [accessed 15 September 2009].

Department of Defense (DOD). 2003. 'Working Group Report on Detainee Interrogations in the Global War on Terrorism', National Security Archive, 6 March: http://www.gwu.edu/~nsarchiv/NSAEBB/NSAEBB127/03.04.04.pdf [accessed 1 July 2012].

Department of Defense. 2004. *Safeguarding Privacy in the Fight Against Terrorism: Report of the Technology and Privacy Advisory Committee*, March: http://www.cdt.org/security/usapatriot/20040300tapac.pdf [accessed 1 July 2012].

Department of Defense. 2006. Office of the Inspector General. Report No. 06-INTEL-10, *Review of DoD-Directed Investigations of Detainee Abuse*, 25 August.

Department of Justice, Office of the Inspector General (DOJ/OIG). 2001. Deputy Assistant Attorney General John Yoo and Robert J. Delahunty, Special Counsel, U.S. Department of Justice, Office of Legal Counsel, Memorandum for Alberto R. Gonzales, Counsel to the President and William J. Haynes, II, General Counsel, Department of Defence, Authority for Use of Military Force to Combat Terrorist Activities Within the United States, 23 October: http://www.usdoj.gov/opa/documents/memomilitaryforcecombatus10232001.pdf [accessed 1 July 2012].

Department of Justice, Office of the Inspector General. 2002a. Memorandum from Jay S. Bybee, Assistant Attorney General, Office of Legal Counsel, U.S.

Department of Justice, to Alberto R. Gonzales, Counsel to the President, regarding Standards of Conduct for Interrogation under 18 U.S.C. §§ 2340–2340A, 1 August: http://www.washingtonpost.com/wp-srv/nation/documents/dojinterrogationmemo20020801.pdf [accessed 1 July 2012].

Department of Justice, Office of the Inspector General. 2002b. Deputy Assistant Attorney General John Yoo, U.S. Department of Justice, Office of Legal Counsel, Memorandum for William J. Haynes, II, General Counsel, Department of Defence, Re: The President's power as Commander in Chief to transfer captured terrorists to the control and custody of foreign nations, 13 March: http://www.salon.com/news/primary_sources/2009/03/03/bushmemos/index2.html [accessed 1 July 2012].

Department of Justice, Office of the Inspector General. 2003. Deputy Assistant Attorney General John Yoo, U.S. Department of Justice, Office of Legal Counsel, Memorandum for William J. Haynes, II, Re. Military Interrogation of Alien Unlawful Combatants Held Outside the United States, 14 March: http://www.aclu.org/pdfs/safefree/yoo_army_torture_memo.pdf [accessed 1 July 2012].

Department of Justice, Office of the Inspector General. 2008a. *A Review of the FBI's Use of Section 215 Orders for Business Records in 2006*, March: http://www.justice.gov/oig/special/s0803a/final.pdf [accessed 1 July 2012].

Department of Justice, Office of the Inspector General. 2008b. *A Review of the FBI's Use of National Security Letters: Assessment of Corrective Actions and Examination of NSL Usage in 2006*, March: http://www.usdoj.gov/oig/special/s0803b/final.pdf [accessed 1 July 2012].

Department of State (DOS). 1975–2009. *Country Reports on Human Rights Practices*. Washington DC: USGPO.

Department of State. 2003. 'Working Group Report on Detainee Interrogations in the Global War on Terrorism', 6 March: http://www.gwu.edu/~nsarchiv/NSAEBB/NSAEBB127/03.04.04.pdf [accessed 1 July 2012].

Department of State. 2004.'Cable, Subject: Reporting Cable on Forced Disappearances Treaty Negotiations, Fm US Mission Geneva to SecState, February: http://www.washingtonpost.com/wp-srv/nation/documents/declassified_assessment_of_negotiations.pdf [accessed 1 July 2012].

Department of State. 2005a. Non-Paper, to French Chair, undated (c.2005). Declassified 30 July 2009: http://www.state.gov/documents/organization/134071.pdf [accessed 25 August 2009].

Department of State. 2005b. Forced Disappearances Treaty Negotiations. Guidance for Closing Statement of the United States, September. Declassified 22 June 2009: http://www.washingtonpost.com/wp-srv/nation/documents/forced_disappearances_treaty_negotiations_090309.pdf [accessed 1 July 2012].

Department of State. 2005c. Cable. Subject: Reporting Cable on Forced Disappearances Treaty Negotiations, undated: http://www.state.gov/documents/organization/134857.pdf [accessed 1 July 2012].

Dershowitz, A.M. 2002a. *Shouting Fire: Civil Liberties in a Turbulent Age*. Boston, MA: Little Brown & Co.

Dershowitz, A.M. 2002b. *Why Terrorism Works*. New Haven, VT: Yale University Press.
Dwyer, J. 2009. 'An Honour Guard Comes Out for Obama's Ban on Torture'. *New York Times*, 23 January.
Eggen, D. 2008. 'FBI Found to Misuse Security Letters', *Washington Post*, 14 March.
Electronic Frontier Foundation (EFF). 2003. 'Total/Terrorism Information Awareness (TIA): Is It Truly Dead? EFF: It's Too Early to Tell', 3 October, http://w2.eff.org/Privacy/TIA/20031003_comments.php [accessed 1 July 2012].
Electronic Frontier Foundation. 2006. 'Sneak and Peak' Search Warrants: https://ssd.eff.org/your-computer/govt/sneak-and-peek [accessed 1 July 2012].
Electronic Privacy Information Center (EPIC). 2002. Briefing on Total Information Awareness, EPIC: http://www.epic.org/events/tia_briefing/ [accessed 1 July 2012].
Erlanger, S. and Stolberg, S.G. 2009. 'Surprise Nobel for Obama Stirs Praise and Doubts'. *New York Times*, 9 October.
Federal Bureau of Investigation (FBI). 2002. Memorandum, to Counterterrorism, Counterintelligence, From Office of the General Council, 29 March 2002, declassified 6 November 2002: http://epic.org/privacy/terrorism/usapatriot/foia/fbi_fisa_pen_proc.pdf [accessed 1 July 2012].
Federation of American Scientists (FAS). 2002. 'Testimony of Cofer Black, 26 September 2002, Before Joint Hearing of the House and Senate Intelligence Committees': http://www.fas.org/irp/congress/2002_hr/092602black.pdf [accessed 1 July 2012].
Finn, P. 2009. 'Obama Endorses Indefinite Detention Without Trial for Some'. *Washington Post*, 22 May: http://www.washingtonpost.com/wp-dyn/content/article/2009/05/21/AR2009052104045.html [accessed 1 July 2012].
Fogarty, G.P. 2005. 'Is Guantanamo Bay Undermining the Global War on Terror?' *Parameters*, Autumn, 54–71.
Garcia, M.J. 2009. 'The War Crimes Act: Current Issues', 22 January, Congressional Research Service: http://www.fas.org/sgp/crs/intel/RL33662.pdf [accessed 1 July 2012].
Gellman, B. 2005. 'The FBI's Secret Scrutiny'. *Washington Post*, 6 November: http://www.washingtonpost.com/wp-dyn/content/article/2005/11/05/AR2005110501366.html [accessed 1 July 2012].
Glaberson, W. 2009. 'President's Detention Plan Tests American Legal Tradition'. *New York Times*, 22 May.
Global Security. 2009. 'Guantánamo Bay Detainees': http://www.globalsecurity.org/military/facility/guantanamo-bay_detainees.htm [accessed 1 July 2012].
Golden, T. 2004. 'After Terror: A Secret Rewriting of Military Law'. *New York Times*, 24 October.
Greenwald, G. 2009a. 'Keith Olbermann's Scathing Criticism of Obama's Secrecy/Immunity Claims'. *Salon*, 8 April: http://www.salon.com/opinion/greenwald/2009/04/08/criticism/ [accessed 1 July 2012].
Greenwald, G. 2009b. 'New Poll on Torture and Investigations Negates Beltway Conventional Wisdom'. *Salon*, 22 January: http://www.salon.com/opinion/greenwald/2009/01/22/torture/ [accessed 1 July 2012].

Greenwald, G. 2009c. 'Backlash Grows Against Obama's Preventive Detention Proposal'. *Salon*, 25 May: http://www.salon.com/opinion/greenwald/2009/05/25/obama [accessed 1 July 2012].

Hersh, S.M. 2004. 'Gray Zone: How a Secret Pentagon Program came to Abu Ghraib'. *New Yorker*, 24 May: http://www.newyorker.com/reporting/2007/06/25/070625fa_fact_hersh?currentPage=all [accessed 1 July 2012].

Horton, S. 2009. 'New CIA Docs Detail Brutal "Extraordinary Rendition" Process'. *Huffington Post*, 28 August: http://www.huffingtonpost.com/2009/08/28/new-cia-docs-detail-bruta_n_271299.html [accessed 1 July 2012].

Human Rights First. 2004. *Getting to Ground Truth: Investigating U.S. Abuses in the 'War on Terror'*. New York: Human Rights First.

Human Rights First. 2005a. *Everyday Fears: A Survey of Violent Hate Crimes in Europe and North America*. New York: Human Rights First.

Human Rights First. 2005b. 'Gonzales and the Geneva Conventions', 24 January: https://secure.humanrightsfirst.org/us_law/etn/gonzales/briefs/brief_20041209_Gonz_%20GC.pdf [accessed 1 July 2012].

Human Rights First. 2008. 'The CIA's Secret Detention Program', 1 May: http://www.humanrightsfirst.org/2008/05/01/the-cias-secret-detention-program [accessed 1 July 2012].

Human Rights First (HRF). 2009a. 'Prime Time Torture', undated: http://www.humanrightsfirst.org/our-work/law-and-security/torture-on-tv/what-can-be-done/ [accessed 1 July 2012].

Human Rights First. 2009b. 'Soldiers Have Imitated What They See on TV': http://www.humanrightsfirst.org/2007/11/10/soldiers-have-imitated-what-they-see-on-tv/ [accessed 1 July 2012].

Human Rights First. 2009c. *In Pursuit of Justice: Prosecuting Terrorism Cases in the Federal Courts – 2009 Update and Recent Developments*. New York: Human Rights First.

Human Rights Watch (HRW). 2002. 'We Are Not the Enemy: Hate Crimes Against Arabs, Muslims, and Those Perceived to be Arab or Muslim after September 11', November: http://www.hrw.org/reports/2002/usahate/ [accessed 1 July 2012].

Human Rights Watch. 2005. 'Getting Away with Torture?', 23 April: http://www.hrw.org/en/node/11765/section/2 [accessed 1 July 2012].

Human Rights Watch. 2006. '"No Blood, No Foul": Soldiers' Accounts of Detainee Abuse in Iraq', 22 July: http://www.hrw.org/en/node/11282/section/1 [accessed 1 July 2012].

Human Rights Watch. 2008. 'Fighting Terrorism Fairly and Effectively', 16 November: http://www.hrw.org/en/node/75959/section/9 [accessed 1 July 2012].

Ifill, G. 2002. 'Prisoners of War?'. PBS News Hour, 22 January: http://www.pbs.org/newshour/bb/terrorism/jan-june02/pow_1-22a.html [accessed 1 July 2012].

Ignatieff, M. 2004. *The Lesser Evil: Political Ethics in an Age of Terror*. Princeton, NJ: Princeton University Press.

International Criminal Court (ICC). Undated. 'Chronology of the International Criminal Court': http://www.icc-cpi.int/Menus/ICC/About+the+Court/ICC+at+a+glance/Chronology+of+the+ICC.htm [accessed 1 July 2012].
Isikoff, M. and Taylor Jr., S. 2006. 'The Gitmo Fallout'. *Newsweek*, 27 July: http://www.newsweek.com/id/46764 [accessed 1 July 2012].
Kamiya, G. 2009. 'John Yoo is Sorry for Nothing'. *Salon*, 8 October: http://www.salon.com/opinion/kamiya/2009/03/10/john_yoo/ [accessed 1 July 2012].
Koppelman, A. 2009. 'Gitmo General Told Iraq WMD Search Team to Torture'. *Salon*, 15 May: http://www.salon.com/politics/war_room/2009/05/15/miller/ [accessed 1 July 2012].
Kornblut, A.E. and Linzer, D. 2009. 'White House Regroups on Guantanamo', *Washington Post*, 25 September, http://www.washingtonpost.com/wp-dyn/content/article/2009/09/24/AR2009092404893.html [accessed 1 July 2012].
Lawyers Committee for Human Rights (LCHR). 2002. *A Year of Loss*. New York: Lawyers Committee for Human Rights.
Lawyers Committee for Human Rights. 2003a. *Imbalance of Power*. New York: Lawyers Committee for Human Rights
Lawyers Committee for Human Rights. 2003b. *Assessing the New Normal; Liberty and Security for the Post-September 11 United States*. New York: Human Rights First.
Lawyers Committee for Human Rights. 2003c. 'Special Registration (National Security Entry-Exit Registration System)': http://www.humanrightsfirst.org/wp-content/uploads/pdf/Special%20Registration%20-%20Background.pdf [accessed 1 July 2012].
Leadership Conference on Civil Rights Education Fund (LCCREF). 2003. 'Wrong Then, Wrong Now', February: http://www.civilrights.org/publications/wrong-then/ [accessed 1 July 2012].
Lithwick, D. and Turner, J. 2003. 'A Guide to the Patriot Act'. *Slate*, 8 September: http://www.slate.com/id/2087984/ [accessed 1 July 2012].
Mayer, J. 2006. 'The Memo: How an Internal Effort to Ban the Abuse and Torture of Detainees was Thwarted'. *New Yorker*, 27 February: http://www.newyorker.com/archive/2006/02/27/060227fa_fact [accessed 1 July 2012].
Mora, A. 2004. Navy General Counsel Alberto Mora, Memorandum for Inspector General, Department of the Navy, Subj: Statement for the Record: Office of General Counsel Involvement in Interrogation Issues, 7 July: http://www.newyorker.com/images/pdf/2006/02/27/moramemo.pdf [accessed 1 July 2012].
National Security Archive. 2009. 'President Obama Embraces Openness on Day One, as Urged by the National Security Archive and a Coalition of More Than 60 Organizations', Press Release, 21 January: http://www.gwu.edu/~nsarchiv/news/20090121/index.htm [accessed 1 July 2012].
New York Advisory Committee to the US Commission on Civil Rights. 2004. 'Civil Rights Implications of Post-September 11 Law Enforcement Practices in New York', March: http://www.usccr.gov/pubs/sac/ny0304/ny0304.pdf [accessed 1 July 2012].

NYU School of Law. 2008. 'Former State Department Attorney-Adviser Bowker Visits Law and Security Colloquium', 17 November: http://www.law.nyu.edu/news/BOWKER_COLLOQUIUM [accessed 1 July 2012].

Physicians for Human Rights (PHR). 2004. 'Lawyer's Statement on Bush Administration's Torture Memos', 4 August: http://physiciansforhumanrights.org/library/documents/non-phr/lawyers-statement-on-bush.pdf [accessed 1 July 2012].

Physicians for Human Rights. 2005. *Break Them Down: Systematic Use of Psychological Torture by US Forces*. Cambridge, MA: Physicians for Human Rights.

Physicians for Human Rights. 2009. 'Aiding Torture: Health Professionals' Ethics and Human Rights Violations Demonstrated in the May 2004 CIA Inspector General's Report', 31 August: http://physiciansforhumanrights.org/library/news-2009-08-31-pr.html [accessed 1 July 2012].

Podesta, J. 2002. 'USA Patriot Act: The Good, the Bad, and the Sunset', American Bar Association, *Human Rights* magazine, Winter: http://www.abanet.org/irr/hr/winter02/podesta.html [accessed 1 July 2012].

Priest, P. and Gellman, B. 2002. 'U.S. Decries Abuse but Defends Interrogations: "Stress and Duress" Tactics Used on Terrorism Suspects Held in Secret Overseas Facilities'. *Washington Post*, 26 December.

Rejali, D. and Gronke, P. 2009. 'U.S. Public Opinion on Torture, 2001–2009'. Reed College, 2 May: http://academic.reed.edu/poli_sci/faculty/rejali/articles/US_Public_Opinion_Torture_Gronke_Rejali.pdf [accessed 1 July 2012].

Risen, J. and Lichtblau, E. 2008. 'Early Test for Obama on Domestic Spying Views'. *New York Times*, 17 November.

Rodley, N.S. 2002. *The Treatment of Prisoners under International Law*. Oxford: Oxford University Press.

Rosen, J. 2007. 'Conscience of a Conservative'. *New York Times Magazine*, 9 September: http://www.nytimes.com/2007/09/09/magazine/09rosen.html?_r=1 [accessed 1 July 2012].

Rosenberg, C. 2009. 'Judges Siding with Detainees in Guantanamo Habeas Sases'. *Miami Herald*, 7 September.

Russert, T. 2001. 'Interview with Vice President Richard Cheney'. *Meet the Press*, 16 September: http://georgewbush-whitehouse.archives.gov/vicepresident/news-speeches/speeches/vp20010916.html [accessed 1 July 2012].

Sánchez, J. 2009. 'New Bill Would Tighten Rules for National Security Letters'. *Ars Tecnica*, 31 March: http://arstechnica.com/tech-policy/news/2009/03/nsl-reform-legislation-reintroduced.ars [accessed 1 July 2012].

Senate. Date redacted. Senate Armed Services Committee, Inquiry into the Treatment of Detainees in U.S. Custody [dateline redacted]: http://media.washingtonpost.com/wp-srv/nation/pdf/12112008_detaineeabuse.pdf [accessed 1 July 2012].

Shane S. and Mazzetti, M. 2009a. 'Report Shows Tight C.I.A. Control on Interrogations'. *New York Times*, 25 August.

Shane S. and Mazzetti, M. 2009b. 'C.I.A. Abuse Cases Detailed in Report on Detainees'. *New York Times*, 25 August.

Singel, R. 2007a. 'Homeland Data Tool Needs Privacy Help, Report Says'. *Wired*, 20 March: http://www.wired.com/threatlevel/2007/03/homeland_data_t/ [accessed 1 July 2012].
Singel, R. 2007b. 'DHS Data Mining Program Suspended After Evading Privacy Review, Audit Finds'. *Wired*, 20 August: http://www.wired.com/threatlevel/2007/08/dhs-data-mining/ [accessed 1 July 2012].
Sniffen, M.J. 2007. 'DHS Ends Criticized Data-Mining Program'. *Washington Post*, 5 September.
Sternstein, A. 2009. 'Obama's Secrecy Record is Mixed'. *Tech Insider*, 9 August: http://techinsider.nextgov.com/2009/09/obamas_secrecy_record_is_mixed.php [accessed 1 July 2012].
Supreme Court. 2004a. *Hamdi v. Rumsfeld* (03-6696) 542 U.S. 507 (2004).
Supreme Court. 2004b. *Rasul v. Bush* (03-334) 542 U.S. 466 (2004): http://www.law.cornell.edu/supct/html/03-334.ZS.html [accessed 1 July 2012].
Supreme Court. 2006. *Hamdan v. Rumsfeld* 05-184, decided 29 June: http://caselaw.lp.findlaw.com/scripts/getcase.pl?court=us&vol=000&invol=05-184 [accessed 1 July 2012].
Supreme Court. 2008. *Boumediene v. Bush* 06-1195, decided 12 June: http://www.law.cornell.edu/supct/html/06-1195.ZS.html [accessed 1 July 2012].
United Nations (UN). 1966. International Covenant on Civil and Political Rights, General Comment, Article 7(2).
United Nations. 1984. Convention against Torture and Other Cruel, Inhuman or Degrading Treatment or Punishment, Article 3.
US Congress. 2001. 'Authorization for Use of Military Force, 18 September, Public Law 107-40 [S. J. RES. 23]', Findlaw: http://www.gpo.gov/fdsys/pkg/PLAW-107publ40/pdf/PLAW-107publ40.pdf [accessed 1 July 2012].
US Congress. 2005. 'Detainee Treatment Act of 2005 (DTA)', 30 December, *Jurist Legal News and Research*: http://jurist.law.pitt.edu/gazette/2005/12/detainee-treatment-act-of-2005-white.php [accessed 1 July 2012].
US Congress. 2006. 'Military Commissions Act of 2006', 3 January: http://www.govtrack.us/congress/billtext.xpd?bill=s109-3930 [accessed 1 July 2012].
Warrick, J. 2008. 'A Blind Eye to Guantanamo?' *Washington Post*, 12 July.
Warrick, J., Finn P. and Tate, J. 2009. 'Red Cross Described "Torture" at CIA Jails: Secret Report Implies that U.S. Violated International Law'. *Washington Post*, 16 March.
Waxman, M.C. 2008. 'Administrative Detention: The Integration of Strategy and Legal Process. Legal Architecture for the War on Terror, Justice and Law, Terrorism, Courts, U.S. Judiciary'. Brookings Institution, Counterterrorism and American Statutory Law, 24 July: http://www.brookings.edu/papers/2008/0724_detention_waxman.aspx [accessed 1 July 2012].
White House. 2001. Military Order of November 13, 2001, Detention, Treatment, and Trial of Certain Non-Citizens in the War Against Terrorism: http://www.fas.org/irp/offdocs/eo/mo-111301.htm [accessed 1 July 2012].
White House. 2002. Memorandum of Alberto Gonzales, White House General Counsel to President George W. Bush, Re: Decision Re Application of the Geneva

Convention on Prisoners of War to the Conflict with Al Qaeda and the Taliban, 25 January: http://www.gwu.edu/~nsarchiv/NSAEBB/NSAEBB127/02.01.25.pdf [accessed 1 July 2012].

White House. 2004a. 'Department of Homeland Security': http://www.whitehouse.gov/omb/rewrite/budget/fy2004/homeland.html [accessed 22 September 2009].

White House. 2004b. 'Remarks on Iraq and the War on Terror at the U.S. Army War College, Carlisle, Pennsylvania', 24 May. Weekly Compilation of Presidential Documents, 944, 947 (2004): http://www.gpo.gov/fdsys/pkg/WCPD-2004-05-31/html/WCPD-2004-05-31-Pg944.htm [accessed 1 July 2012].

White House. 2006. 'President Discusses Creation of Military Commissions to Try Suspected Terrorists', 6 September: http://georgewbush-whitehouse.archives.gov/news/releases/2006/09/20060906-3.html [accessed 1 July 2012].

White House. 2009a. Memorandum for the Heads of Executive Departments and Agencies, SUBJECT: Freedom of Information Act, 21 January 2009: http://www.whitehouse.gov/the_press_office/FreedomofInformationAct/ [accessed 1 July 2012].

White House. 2009b. Executive Order – Ensuring Lawful Interrogations, 22 January, Section 3(c): http://www.whitehouse.gov/the_press_office/EnsuringLawfulInterrogations/ [accessed 1 July 2012].

White House. 2009c. Executive Order – Review and Disposition of Individuals Detained at the Guantánamo Bay Naval Base and Closure of Detention Facilities, 22 January: http://www.whitehouse.gov/the_press_office/ClosureOfGuantanamoDetentionFacilities [accessed 1 July 2012].

White House. 2009d. Executive Order – Review of Detention Policy Options, 22 January: http://www.whitehouse.gov/the-press-office/review-detention-policy-options [accessed 1 July 2012].

Counter-Terrorism and Human Rights in the UK

Clive Walker

Introduction

Within the dominion of counter-terrorism, policy choices can be stark. One must determine in institutional terms whether the response is to be predominantly military or policing and, cutting across that boundary, who is to generate and own intelligence and where financial support should be directed. There are also choices to be made in corresponding legal regimes around counter-terrorism, ranging from the rules of war and legal states of emergency through to nuanced versions of criminal justice. These counter-terrorism policy choices can determine not only the nature of a society whilst it deals with terrorism, but also, as illustrated by the variant experiences of countries such as South Africa or Sri Lanka, compared to Germany and Italy, the nature of that society and its residual scars if and when it emerges from terrorism. It is the thesis of this chapter that human rights discourse has grown in importance as a determinant of counter-terrorist strategic choices and modes of tactical delivery. The meaning and impact of this will be assessed alongside other normative considerations such as democratic accountability.

This promise of human rights impact appears somewhat ambitious, for counter-terrorism has historically been barren ground for the flourishing of human rights. A more evident product of counter-terrorism is its baleful litany of atrocities and abuses, which include numerous British misdeeds in Ireland, such as Bloody Sunday in 1972 (Bloody Sunday Inquiry, 2010), and the contemporary abuses of prisoners in Iraq (Baha Mousa Inquiry, 2010). Yet, the thesis adopted in this chapter is that rights protection within counter-terrorism has strengthened since the entry into force (in October 2000) of the Human Rights Act 1998. This Act of Parliament has engendered within the UK a culture of rights more pervasive than its technical legal requirements (Walker and Weaver, 2000: 560).

There are three institutional support mechanisms boosted by the Human Rights Act: internal governmental 'Strasbourg proofing'; parliamentary scrutiny; and judicial review, which observes a decreasing level of deference. These mechanisms add to the explicit reviews set up under the counter-terrorism legislation itself. By these means, the Act has ensured that relevant parts of an established international treaty, the European Convention on Human Rights and Fundamental Freedoms (1950), must be treated as legally relevant in all legal and administrative transactions to which it applies. Observance is most tightly scrutinised within the domestic sphere, but, as will be illustrated, human rights duties are applied by the legislation to any sphere where effective British control exists – even if overseas. Beyond the Human Rights Act, the European Convention still exerts influence in international law, and decisions from the European Court of Human Rights provide an important final check against wayward nationalistic pleading of national security, whether in regard to detention without trial, rendition or otherwise, as shall again be illustrated later in this chapter. Beyond even the European Convention and other formal instruments, human rights philosophy has proven potent, as evidenced, for instance, by the annual human rights review of foreign policy, the twelfth of which was delivered in 2011 (Foreign & Commonwealth Office, 2011). While taking due cognisance of these wider emanations of human rights discourse, the primary focus in this chapter will be on the impact of the Human Rights Act as the most important legal development in counter-terrorism over the past decade.

The principal impacts of all these systemic mechanisms will be considered from several perspectives. The first is a framing perspective by which human rights considerations rule in and rule out potential approaches to counter-terrorism. At the same time, the suppression of terrorism can itself be founded on rights-based arguments, and special laws are certainly not debarred per se. The second perspective is rights-specific – how individual rights fare in circumstances of terrorist threat. The interpretation adopted in this chapter is that activities which are seen as within the purview and expertise of courts (such as procedure) are subjected to stricter standards than activities which rarely trouble the courts (such as surveillance). The third perspective is temporal – that human rights scrutiny gains traction as counter-terrorism campaigns mature. The fourth perspective is that the treatment of rights in counter-terrorism can have socially transformative impacts by affecting negatively or positively the mobilising factors for or against terrorism.

Prior to these inquiries, a brief overview of UK counter-terrorism legislation will be provided so as to appreciate the overall nature of the core materials which are being discussed with reference to human rights.

Overview of UK Counter-Terrorism Legislation

Special laws against terrorism have provided a constant feature of political and legal life within the UK for many years. As described more fully elsewhere (Walker, 2009), the catalogue is now marked by its complexity, depth and range. The current legislative collection also builds upon long experience. The notion that it represents an 'emergency' or 'temporary' code is belied by its close links to predecessors such as the Civil Authorities (Special Powers) Acts 1922–1943 (Northern Ireland), the Prevention of Violence (Temporary Provisions) Act 1939, the Northern Ireland (Emergency Provisions) Acts 1973–1998 and the Prevention of Terrorism (Temporary Provisions) Acts 1974–1989.

The Terrorism Act 2000

The Terrorism Bill reflected a new dispensation – a considered, comprehensive and principled code rather than hastily considered and fragmented emergency laws. The period of gestation involved the Lloyd Report (1996) as well as the government's response (Home Office, 1998). The passage of the Human Rights Act 1998 also made it advisable to conduct some revision. The government claimed that the Bill was compatible with European Convention rights, especially as it provided for judicial scrutiny of arrest powers instead of the ministerial system, which had breached the protection for liberty under Article 5(3) of the European Convention in *Brogan v. UK* (1988). The derogation notice issued in 1988 was therefore withdrawn, though the Act has since been found wanting in other respects (most notably by denying effective access to lawyers: *Brennan v. UK* (2001)). The substantive themes covered by the Act comprise proscribed organisations, terrorist property, special investigatory and policing powers, special offences and extra measures under Part VII, mainly in the form of wide policing powers and special 'Diplock' non-jury criminal trials confined to Northern Ireland. The latter were replaced with the Justice and Security (Northern Ireland) Act 2007, but still provide for non-jury trials.

The Anti-terrorism, Crime and Security Act 2001

There was no immediate rush to legislation following the 9/11 attacks and the 2001 Act was in fair part constructed around the Terrorism Act, rather than striking out in the new and alarming direction set by the US 'war on terror' (US Presidential Order, 2001). Nonetheless, a major innovation was the revival of detention without trial. This 2001 variant was couched in terms of immigration legislation and was aimed exclusively at foreign suspects who, following the determination of the European Court of Human Rights in *Chahal v. UK* (1996), could not be deported without breach of international law where a real risk of torture in their country of origin was established. Given the manifest incursion into the right of liberty under Article 5 which was entailed by detention without trial, the enforcement of Part IV could only be justified by a declaration of an emergency threatening the life of the nation, which was pronounced with due legal formality by means of a 'notice of derogation' under Article 15 of the European Convention.

The Prevention of Terrorism Act 2005

The policy of detention without trial under Part IV encountered fierce criticism from a Privy Counsellor Review Committee (2003); it viewed the system as objectionable because of the lack of safeguards, because it did not extend to British terrorists and because viable alternatives existed. In response, the Home Office Consultation Paper (2004, Pt I, paras 8, 34; Pt II, para 31) regarded Part IV as indispensable and depicted any alternatives as unworkable. There the matter might have rested were it not for the declaration of incompatibility under section 4 of the Human Rights Act 1998 issued by the House of Lords in *A v. Secretary of State for the Home Department* (2004). A majority of their Lordships did not condemn the reliance upon the derogation notice. However, two features of Part IV – that foreigners were the exclusive target while ignoring threats from British citizens and that it comprised only a 'prison with three walls' (since those foreign detainees were allowed to leave the prison if willing to move abroad) – meant it was disproportionate, discriminatory and irrational. In response, lesser executive restrictions, 'control orders', were introduced via the Prevention of Terrorism Act 2005. Following the Macdonald Report (2011), control orders have been replaced by marginally less restrictive measures under the Terrorism Prevention and Investigation Measures Act 2011.

The Terrorism Act 2006

The London bombings of 7 July 2005 galvanised apprehension about the radicalisation of British-born 'neighbour terrorists' (Walker, 2008). Great controversy ensued around two proposals – an offence of the glorification of terrorism and a maximum police detention period of 90 days (up from the 14-day limit set by the Criminal Justice Act 2003. This Act, through section 306, had already doubled the seven days allowed by the Terrorism Act 2000 and went far beyond the four days in the 'normal' regime of the Police and Criminal Evidence Act 1984). Parliamentary opposition forced the refinement of the first measure to the notion of 'indirect incitement', while the second measure was defeated, albeit with a compromise of 28 days being substituted. The extension beyond 14 days has since been reversed, again endorsed by the Macdonald Report (2011) and implemented by the Protection of Freedoms Act 2011.

The Counter-Terrorism Act 2008

No overarching theme or trigger emerged for the most recent Act – it deepens and widens existing strands of laws rather than inserts new initiatives (Home Office, 2007). As a result, anti-terrorism laws are ever-widening, but the process remains unprincipled, incomplete and fragmented. Notable political battles in 2008 saw the defeat of the 42-day detention proposal but the acceptance of post-charge questioning.

Institutional Support Mechanisms

Since the Terrorism Act 2000 is largely a permanent code, there is no requirement for periodic renewal. According to the former government minister Charles Clarke (2000):

> We have had so-called temporary provisions on the statute book for 25 years. The time has come to face the fact of terrorism and be ready to deal with it for the foreseeable future. We need to make the powers permanently available, although the fact that those powers are available does not mean that they have to be used.

It follows that the review mechanisms appear relatively weak. Section 126 simply requires that the Secretary of State shall lay before Parliament an annual report on the working of the legislation. Yet, extraordinary powers should be subjected to extraordinary scrutiny, so it is welcome that the government has adopted the practice of appointing an independent reviewer (Lord Carlile of Berriew from 2001 to 2011, succeeded by David Anderson, for UK legislation and Robert Whalley for Northern Ireland legislation) to assist with the annual reports. At the same time, the independent review schemes are muddled and beset by 'pragmatic incrementalism' (Carlile, 2008). The Terrorism Act 2000 is fully reviewed and there was a specific review for the special Northern Ireland measures under Part VII, now replaced by ongoing review of sections 21–32 of the Justice and Security (Northern Ireland) Act 2007. The reviewer can also be commissioned to undertake thematic reviews and has reported on proposals in 2005 and 2007 for extended detention of 90 and then 42 days and on the definition of terrorism (Carlile, 2005, 2007a, 2007b). There is now no review specific to the Anti-terrorism, Crime and Security Act 2001, since the Privy Counsellor Review Committee (2003), set up under section 122, completed its work in 2003. As for the Prevention of Terrorism Act 2005, annual independent review is required under section 14, while section 13 provides for annual renewal subject to parliamentary approval. The Justice and Security (Northern Ireland) Act 2007 is partially reviewed according to section 40. But there is no independent review of sections 1–9 (non-jury trials), which were time limited by section 9 to two years but were extended in 2009. There is no specialist review of the Counter-Terrorism Act 2008.

Aside from the Northern Ireland review, which was allocated to Robert Whalley (2008), most scrutiny work has been undertaken by Lord Alex Carlile (Carlile, 2002–2010, 2006–2011). His appointment in relation to the Terrorism Act 2000 has now been formalised by section 36of the Terrorism Act 2006. The criteria for review make no explicit reference to human rights, but was considered by Lord Carlile (2009, para 26) to be the same as those of the very first independent reviewer in 1984 (Elton, 1984):

> First, he would not be an appellate authority ... It would be his task to look at the use made of the powers under the Act. To consider, for example, whether

he saw emerging any change in the pattern of their use which required to be drawn to the attention of Parliament.

However, Lord Carlile has always treated compliance with human rights as an important topic, and his reviews are accurate, diligent and based on considerable fieldwork. Though influential in government and parliamentary circles, the review process suffers from several faults, including limited coverage and the lack of commitment of resources. Lord Carlile views himself as a watchdog and commentator whose main constituency is Parliament and the government. One implication of these target audiences is that reports must be short and relatively shorn of arguments. If there were to be a commitment of resources to set up a panel of reviewers, they could address different audiences, such as the communities most affected by the legislation, the lawyers who work with it and even the general public. A panel could also adopt specialities, with a deeper analysis of human rights impact being one such aspect. However, the government has been resistant to reform (Joint Committee on Human Rights, 2008b: 20).

Aside from the work of specialist reviewers, the Human Rights Act 1998 has triggered a number of institutional support mechanisms, not all strictly required by the Act but in keeping with its desire to foster a human rights culture. The first feature involves explicit departmental scrutiny of draft legislative from the perspective of its compliance with the European Convention. Though 'Strasbourg proofing' occurred before the Human Rights Act (Walker and Weaver, 2000: 559), it has formalised this process and made it more transparent. The formality is that section 19 of the Act requires that the minister in charge of presenting a new bill must before the Second Reading make 'a statement of compatibility' as to whether the provisions of the bill are compatible with Convention rights. Any doubts should lead to questioning and debate which will hopefully deter the minister from sponsoring inimical measures in the first place. To nobody's surprise, most ministers at most times have claimed compatibility for terrorism legislation – the sole exception was Part IV of the Anti-terrorism, Crime and Security Act 2001. However, their claims of compatibility have become the subject of explicit parliamentary inquisition, and this process has been latterly assisted by the willingness of ministers to state reasons for their declaration in the explanatory notes which accompany the bill (Cabinet Office, 2009, para 12.27; Joint Committee on Human Rights, 2008a, para 226).

Aside from debates on the declaration of compatibility, Parliament has also improved its scrutiny of human rights issues by increased attention from select committees. Most notable has been the work of the Joint Committee on Human Rights. Though not a creature of the Human Rights Act, the Joint Committee represents a government commitment given during the passage of that legislation (Irvine, 1997) and seeks to ensure that the human rights implications, *inter alia* of counter-terrorism, can be subjected to detailed comment and the testimony of independent expert witnesses. For example, even the legislative passage of the Prevention of Terrorism Act 2005, completed in the highly partisan and often confused period of three weeks set by the tight deadline of the expiration of Part IV (Walker, 2007a: 1395), was assisted by two reports from the Joint Committee on Human Rights (2005a, 2005b). The

House of Commons Home Affairs Committee has also often considered the impact of counter-terrorism legislation on human rights, such as the community perceptions of stop and search powers (House of Commons Home Affairs Committee, 2004).

The next aspect of institutional support which has been boosted by the Human Rights Act concerns judicial review. A positivist viewpoint suggests that the executive knows best in an emergency on grounds of secrecy, speed and flexibility (Posner and Vermeule, 2007). By contrast, judges are said to be 'amateurs playing at security policy' (Posner and Vermeule, 2007: 31). In reply, the primacy of the executive and legislature in policy initiative and invocation is accepted. However, the application of policy to individuals in cases which affect absolute or unqualified rights, such as liberty or due process, should appropriately fall for the ultimate determination of the courts as 'a cardinal feature of the modern democratic state, a cornerstone of the rule of law itself' (*A v. Secretary of State for the Home Department* (2004), para 42, *per* Lord Bingham). On the grounds of training, skills and impartiality, the reported cases on security implementation reveal a generally creditable performance and one which is far superior to the amateurish and unprincipled efforts of executive ministers (Feldman, 2006). The UK judges have moved away from the treatment of security matters as non-justiciable or as subject to thick layers of deference to the executive, as occurred even during the 1990s (Walker, 1997). A jurisprudence of the control of security powers has begun to develop, encouraged by the statutory requirement of judicial confirmation of ongoing security measures, such as control orders (Walker, 2010) and police detention powers (*In re Duffy* (2009)), as well as by the subsequent facility of judicial review of these and other security-related decisions, such as the proscription of organisations (*Secretary of State for the Home Department v. Lord Alton of Liverpool* (2008)) and financial listing (*A v. HM Treasury* (2008)). The emergent jurisprudence is highly tempered by the values of individual rights and constitutionalism and by practical experience, which demonstrates the value of judicial review and the executive exaggeration of security concerns (Dyzenhaus, 2006: Chapter 1). Those like Agamben (2005) who articulate an emergency, executive-dominated constitution 'neglect how the judicial habitus, in its rearticulation of the rule of law via individual cases, affirms due process values and continues to provide some protection from arbitrary state power' (Vaughan and Kilcommins, 2008: 13). As will be further illustrated in this chapter, the judges have forcefully resisted 'legal back holes' (Steyn, 2004). Whilst shades of grey remain, the executive can no longer count on judicial indulgence.

The Impacts of Human Rights

The Framing of Narratives and Legislation

The first claim made regarding the impact of human rights is that human rights operate as important framing devices. They perform this role in several respects, but just three examples will be provided here.

The first links to the issue just covered above – that of systemic review. Though Lord Carlile's brief does not explicitly require regard for rights, more episodic reviews have clearly been set in the context of human rights. Thus, Lord Lloyd asserted as a guiding principle that: 'Additional statutory offences and powers … must strike the right balance between the needs of security and the rights and liberties of the individual' (1996, para 3.1). Likewise, the last major review of the counter-terrorism legislation by the Privy Counsellor Review Committee, while directed neither by section 122 of the Anti-terrorism, Crime and Security Act 2001 nor by any further ministerial direction (2003, Pt I, para 68) to have regard to rights, endorsed the views of Lord Lloyd (2003, Pt I, para 94).

The second aspect of framing is that the government itself views human rights as shaping the environment for its own proposals and actions, as indeed is required under section 6 of the Human Rights Act. In regard to proposals, the Home Office response to the Privy Counsellor Review Committee's report, while rejecting much of what was proposed in detail, did at least propound that 'the Government is willing to consider any realistic alternative proposals and approaches which take account of the Government's human rights obligations' (Home Office, 2004, para 44).

As regards the importance of human rights in the delivery of official counter-terrorism action, the strongest signal is delivered in the strategy against international terrorism, 'CONTEST' – Countering International Terrorism (Home Office, 2006, 2009a, 2010, 2011), whereby:

> The protection of human rights is a key principle underpinning our counterterrorism work at home and overseas. A challenge facing any government is to balance measures intended to protect security and the right to life, with the impact on other rights which we cherish. The Government has sought to find that balance at all times. (Home Office, 2009a, para 0.30)

The ultimate aim of CONTEST – 'to reduce the risk to the UK and to its interests overseas from international terrorism, so that people can go about their lives freely and with confidence' (Home Office, 2009a, para 0.73) – thus reflects the enjoyment of human security in a broad sense. Of course, these official claims to give meaning to human rights must be treated with caution, and the commitment to training and practical implementation should be gauged. One instance of excellent practice concerns the Human Rights Programme of Action of the Police Service of Northern Ireland, which involves contributions by independent advisers, an Oversight Commissioner and an internal Human Rights Champion (Police Service of Northern Ireland, 2008: 1). However, no other security organisation has emulated this level of commitment and effort.

The third aspect of framing is at the level of tactical legal response to terrorism. As has been mentioned previously, the perspective of human rights does not rule out an ongoing need for distinct anti-terrorist laws. They can be justified at three levels. The first level concerns the powers and duties of states. In principle, it is justifiable for liberal democracies to be empowered to defend their existence, and it might be truly claimed that: 'The first priority of any Government is to ensure the security and safety of the nation and all members of the public.' (Home Office, 2009a: 4) This approach is reflected in Article 17 of the European Convention on Human Rights (prohibiting the engagement in any activity aimed at the destruction of rights and freedoms) and the power of derogation in time of emergency threatening the life of the nation under Article 15. There is next a state responsibility to act against violence in order to safeguard the protective right to life of citizens (under Article 2 of the Convention). Under United Nations (UN) instruments, such as UN Security Council Resolution 1373 of 28 September 2001, states must not harbour or condone terrorism. The second level of justification for special laws is more morally grounded and points to the illegitimacy of terrorism as a form of political expression. Many of its emanations are almost certainly common crimes, crimes of war or crimes against humanity, even if the political cause of the terrorist is deemed legitimate. The third level of justification is that terrorism may be depicted as a specialised form of criminality which presents peculiar complications for policing and criminal justice processes because of its structure, capacity to intimidate and sophistication. A specialist response is thereby legitimised to surmount these complications.

Having justified the persistence of counter-terrorism codes, some repressive states have treated them as an excuse for the repression of dissent rather than terrorism. The UN's Special Rapporteur on the promotion and protection of human rights, while countering terrorism (an office devised by the Human Rights Commission in 2005), does not wholly absolve the UK of blame on this score because of the use of offences of incitement in the Terrorism Act 2006 (Special Rapporteur on the promotion and protection of human rights while countering terrorism, 2006, para 7). But the handful of relatively obscure prosecutions under this measure (Walker, 2011: Chapter 8) hardly compares with the state's past harrying of political leaders, such as the exclusion from Britain of Gerry Adams until 1994 (Walker, 1997) or the prosecution in the name of terrorism in other countries of the likes of Leyla Zana in Turkey (*Sadak and others v. Turkey (No. 2)* (2002); EU Turkey Civic Commission, 2008) or Roy Bennett in Zimbabwe (*Zimbabwe Times*, 2009). Of course, the avoidance of some of these extremes of policy does not mean that the delivery of counter-terrorism activity in the UK has always been faultless. The tragic error of the lethal shooting of Jean Charles de Menezes in 2005 is a stark example of an excessive state response. However, even in this case, and perhaps mindful of the standards of respect for the right to life and due process set by Articles 2 and 6, there has been no official move to modify the rules on lawful force in favour of security forces or to curtail the subsequent independent investigation into the events, or to intervene in the prosecution of the Commissioner of the Metropolitan Police for health and safety breaches (*R (da Silva) v. Director of Public Prosecutions* (2006); Independent Police Complaints Commission, 2007a, 2007b).

More fundamentally, human rights considerations have weighed against any further resort to departure from normal rights standards by the issuance of a notice of derogation. This is evidenced by the determination to issue only non-derogating control orders, even though derogating orders remain an equal possibility under the Prevention of Terrorism Act 2005. The trend contrasts with those in the past. In the context of terrorism in Northern Ireland, the derogation facility was repeatedly invoked – up to 1984 and from 1988 until 2001. It was upheld in relation to a scheme of seven days police detention in *Brannigan and McBride v. UK* (2001). The Terrorism Act 2000 allowed that notice of derogation to be withdrawn. A further derogation was entered in respect of the detention under Part IV of the Anti-terrorism, Crime and Security Act 2001, but was in turn withdrawn on 14 March 2005.

The current abeyance from derogation consequently stands in stark contrast to the experiences of previous decades and persists despite two contraindications favouring a new notice. One indication is the bombings in London on 7 July 2005, more patent evidence of public danger even than at the time of the derogation notice in 2001. In addition, the 2001 notice of derogation was upheld as lawful in *A v. Secretary of State for the Home Department* (2004). A majority found that the lower court (the Special Immigration Appeals Commission) had not misdirected itself. Next, the jurisprudence of the European Court of Human Rights did not seem to require the actual experience of widespread loss of life as opposed to a clear and present danger. Lord Bingham was content to apply the Strasbourg approaches, including the recognition of a 'margin of appreciation' for executive discretion on the recognition of an emergency (para 29). The approach of the House of Lords was largely endorsed by the Strasbourg court in *A v. UK* (2009), taking due notice of the later attacks in 2005, of a standard which did not require the life of the nation to be threatened in its entirety, and of being 'acutely conscious of the difficulties faced by states in protecting their populations from terrorist violence' (para 126). Though the terrorism threat level was downgraded in July 2009 (Home Office, 2009b), the prevailing conditions could arguably justify a derogation, taking account of the involvement in *jihadi* terrorism by British citizens and the continuing involvement of British security forces in operations in Afghanistan and elsewhere which terrorists have interpreted as an enduring justification for their violence (Khan, 2005).

Aside from deterring resort to derogation, another aspect of tactical restraint due to human rights concerns is counter-terrorism abroad. As already mentioned, a 'war on terror' approach cannot be applied within the domestic jurisdiction. Even in extreme times, there must be observance of the terms of derogation under Article 15, which requires scrutiny and ongoing justification, and rules out coercive interrogation techniques such as waterboarding (*A v. Secretary of State for the Home Department (No. 2)* (2005)) or extraordinary rendition (*R v. Horseferry Road Magistrates' Court, ex parte Bennett* (1994); *R (Mohamed) v. Secretary of State for Foreign and Commonwealth Affairs* (2009); *Al Rawi v. Security Service* (2009)). A further indication of the onward emboldening of human rights jurisprudence is that human rights standards must even be applied during overseas counter-insurgency activity. This phase of recognition was sustained in *R (Al-Jedda) v. Secretary of State for Defence* (2007), which related to a long-term internee in Iraq. His detention was found to be justiciable but lawful under the UN Security Council Resolution 1546 of 8 June 2004. This verdict sanctions an abdication from Article 5 standards, but on the explicit condition of clear UN authority. The consequence is that British authorities cannot unilaterally establish any detention regime equivalent to Guantanamo Bay, but must act within one international law regime or another.

The extension of domestic rights norms has been taken a stage further wherever it can be established that there is effective control of territory or facilities by British state forces. The point is illustrated by *R (Al-Skeini) v. Secretary of State for Defence* (2007), which concerned Baha Mousa, who died from physical injuries consistent with severe assaults while held in British military custody in Basrah in 2003. The House of Lords held that his death required a full investigation compliant with Article 2 of the European Convention. The same level of enhanced human rights standards can equally apply to the potential mistreatment of soldiers, as in *R (Smith) v. Assistant Deputy Coroner for Oxfordshire* (2009).

By contrast, the Canadian courts have been reluctant to apply domestic standards abroad (*Amnesty Canada International v. Chief of the Defence Staff for the Canadian Forces* (2008)). The US courts have only just begun to grapple with the position of foreigners held abroad in detention facilities such as in Bagram (*Maqaleh v. Gates* (2009)), though they have taken some momentous decisions to enforce habeas corpus review in respect of foreigners detained in US territory (*Rasul v. Bush* (2004); *Boumediene v. Bush* (2008)) and US citizens detained abroad (*Munaf v. Geren* (2008)).

This is not to give the impression that human rights are wholly thriving at the hands of the UK government in its pursuit of terrorism. One important deficit concerns the machinations to bring about the deportation of foreign suspects at risk of torture abroad. The UK government has sought unsuccessfully to challenge the case of *Chahal v. UK* (1998), but was rebuffed by the European Court of Human Rights in *Saadi v. Italy* (2008). The latter judgment was applied against the UK government in *NA v. UK* (2008), where intended deportation of an asylum seeker linked to the Tamil Tigers was declared to be a potential breach of Article 3. The UK government's alternative tactic has been to seek diplomatic assurances about the regime to be applied on return (Walker, 2007b). In *AS v. Secretary of State for the Home Department* (2008), the Court of Appeal refused to sanction a return to Libya. By contrast, misgivings about assurances relating to the deportation to Jordan of Abu Qatada were dismissed by the House of Lords in *RB and OO v. Secretary of State for the Home Department* (2009), but await the verdict of the European Court of Human Rights in *Othman v. UK* (2009). As far as the European Court of Human Rights is concerned, the weight to be placed on assurances depends on the circumstances obtaining at the material time in the receiving state; in *Saadi*, the Tunisian authorities did not provide assurances other than in unsatisfactory general terms ((2008), paras 147, 148).

Variable Rights-Specific Impacts

The second perspective to be considered is rights-specific – how affected individual rights fare in circumstances of terrorist threat. The thesis is that activities which are perceived as within the expertise of courts – such as their own procedures for preparing and holding trials – are subjected to stricter standards than activities which rarely trouble the courts and occur without their sanction or supervision (such as surveillance). An example from each category –judicial activism and judicial in activism – will now be given.

An example of a low-level terrorism policing power which has proven to be of low judicial visibility (in activism) is the power of stop and search under section 44 of the Terrorism Act 2000. Any police constable in uniform can stop a vehicle and search it, the driver or any passenger, and also stop and search a pedestrian if located within an area or at a place specified in an authorisation. An authorisation may be granted only if the senior police officer giving it considers it 'expedient for the prevention of acts of terrorism.' (section 44(3)) An authorisation, which may be valid for up to 28 days and can be renewed, may be given by an assistant chief constable or a commander of a London force. Section 46 requires the police to inform the Secretary of State as soon as is reasonably practicable. The authorisation lapses if not confirmed within 48 hours.

It is made clear in section 45(1)(b) that there can be a random or blanket search – the power 'may be exercised whether or not the constable has grounds for suspecting the presence of articles of that kind'. There are some limits to the exercise of the powers. By section 45, powers must be exercised only for the purpose of 'searching for articles of a kind which could be used in connection with terrorism' (section 45(1)(a)). They may not involve a person being required 'to remove any clothing in public except for headgear, footwear, an outer coat, a jacket or gloves' (section 45(3)) Next, when exercising stop and search powers, police officers must have regard to Code A of the Police and Criminal Evidence Act 1984. According to para 1.1 of Code A, powers to stop and search must be used 'fairly, responsibly, with respect for people being searched and without unlawful discrimination'; para 1.2 provides that the 'intrusion on the liberty of the person stopped or searched' has to be brief and that any detention 'must take place at or near the location of the stop'. On the other hand, since the power is not applied on the basis of reasonable suspicion, there may be some doubts as to the applicability of the warning in para 2.2 not to exercise the powers based on 'generalisations or stereotypical images [or] a person's religion'.

These extraordinary powers were considered by the House of Lords in *R (Gillan) v. Metropolitan Police Commissioner* (2006). An Assistant Commissioner of the Metropolitan Police gave an authorisation under section 44(4) covering the whole of the Metropolitan Police District. This authorisation was confirmed and was then renewed on a continuous basis from February 2001. Both applicants were stopped near an arms fair being held at the ExCel Centre, Docklands. Nothing incriminating was found; the length of the transaction was up to 30 minutes. The House of Lords accepted that an authorisation might be expedient under section 44(3) if, and only if, the person giving it considered it likely that the stop and search powers would be 'of significant practical value and utility in seeking to achieve ... the prevention of acts of terrorism.' (para 15) Lord Bingham was satisfied that the authorisation and confirmation processes had not become a 'routine bureaucratic exercise' (para 18), even though a London-wide authorisation had repeatedly been enforced.

At the stage of implementation, some of their Lordships were troubled by the dangers of discrimination. Lord Bingham emphasised that the implementing constable is not free to act arbitrarily and must not stop and search people who are 'obviously not terrorist suspects' ((2006), para 35) while, in Lord Hope's view (para 45), 'the mere fact that the person appears to be of Asian origin is not a legitimate reason for its exercise'. But these formulae do not rule out racial or ethnic profiling as one lawful element in decision-making (Moeckli, 2008: 198, 200).

An even more stark aspect of the indulgence in this judgment is that the House of Lords even denied that the stop and search process had involved any intrusion into rights to liberty under Article 5. However, the court's depiction of the stop and search process as no more threatening or oppressive than waiting until the light turns green at a pedestrian crossing ((2006), para 25) is wholly unconvincing for two reasons. First, section 45 involves the exercise of an official coercive power, not a directive power – the person waiting for the green light can give up and try another route. Second, the time of 'non-detention detention' pending search (which was alleged to endure for up to 30 minutes) is not as fleeting as suggested.

In conclusion, the treatment of section 44 exemplifies the attitude of the courts to low-level policing, including the growth of profiling. As a result, like the imaginary American crimes shaped by racial profiling or racial prejudice, such as 'driving while Black' or 'flying while Arab', section 44 created the nasty British equivalent of 'perambulating while Muslim' (Walker, 2008: 298). The liberty of the individual is of prime concern to the judges, as signalled in the 'remarkable' (Arden, 2005: 606) case of *A v. Secretary of State for the Home Department* (2004). As already recounted in connection with the Anti-terrorism, Crime and Security Act 2001, the House of Lords declared the policy of detention of foreign terror suspects to be incompatible with human rights standards, an outcome which deserves to be counted as 'the finest assertion of civil liberties' (Gearty, 2005: 37). But the *Gillan* case equally illustrates that what counts as 'liberty' may be affected by judicial disinterest in surveillance. As a result, it has been the government and Parliament which have been at the forefront of the reform of section 44, which has now been repealed and replaced by a slightly more restricted power in section 47A, as substituted by the Protection of Freedoms Act 2011.

The contrasting approach of judicial activism, whereby the judges are assertive of the rights of individuals, despite counter-claims relating to national security imperatives, concerns the enforcement of due process rights within the context of control orders. The key case is *Secretary of State for the Home Department v. MB and AF* (2007). The material which justified MB's control order included open (disclosed) and closed (secret) statements. The open allegations were admitted to be 'relatively thin' (paras 39, 66). The essence of the Secretary of State's case against AF was in the closed material (para 42). The House of Lords concluded that neither suspect had enjoyed a substantial measure of procedural justice and so there was a breach of Article 6. Lord Bingham accepted that 'the application of the civil limb of art 6(1) does in my opinion entitle such person to such measure of procedural protection as is commensurate with the gravity of the potential consequences' (para 24).

The outcome was not wholly in favour either of the controlled persons or the Home Office but has significantly aided the former. The High Court will have to assess whether 'a substantial measure or degree of procedural justice' ((2007), para 32) has been accorded. Since Article 6 protects fundamental rights, any obstacles to its enjoyment must be counterbalanced by the procedures adopted by the judicial authorities such as extra disclosure or the appointment of special advocates.

Thus, the Home Office now faces a stark decision as to whether to compromise compelling security arguments in favour of disclosure or whether to avoid reliance on the sensitive information and hope that less sensitive submissions will carry the day, or to abandon the control order option altogether. The House of Lords has since confirmed in *Secretary of State for the Home Department v. AF (No. 3)* ((2009), para 59) that there must always be some level of disclosure, so that:

> the controlee must be given sufficient information about the allegations against him to enable him to give effective instructions in relation to those allegations ... Where, however, the open material consists purely of general assertions and the case against the controlee is based solely or to a decisive degree on closed materials the requirements of a fair trial will not be satisfied.

Several control orders have been abandoned by the Home Office as a result of these strictures, though speculation that the device is becoming unworkable has proven exaggerated (Walker, 2010).

Temporal Transitions

The next assertion about the impact of rights on counter-terrorism laws is that it is temporal – that rights gain traction as counter-terrorism campaigns mature. One might speculate that the factors behind this effect arise from a growing public understanding of the conflict and a better estimation of its threat and severity, whereas information is at a premium at the time of attack either because the details are unknown or because of the imposition of state security. The judiciary and legislature might also become emboldened by the revelation of executive mistakes made in the earliest phases of conflict.

The performance of the courts on security matters in previous decades has been characterised as involving short judgments, which relied upon bald assertion, which sought refuge in narrow technical issues and which adopted the perspective of dangers to security rather than to rights (Gearty, 1994; Livingstone, 1994). Evidence of a transition in these judicial attitudes can be plotted in several cases. For instance, Lord Hoffman commented in *Secretary of State for the Home Department v. Rehman* ((2001), para 62):

> Postscript. I wrote this speech some three months before the recent events in New York and Washington. They are a reminder that in matters of national security, the cost of failure can be high. This seems to me to underline the need for the judicial arm of government to respect the decisions of ministers of the Crown on the question of whether support for terrorist activities in a foreign country constitutes a threat to national security.

But events since 2001 gave substantial pause for thought about the viability of a policy of holding in detention suspected international terrorists without trial and without any overall time limit (Walker, 2005), not least on the part of Lord Hoffman, who in *A v. Secretary of State for the Home Department* ((2004), paras 96, 97) stated:

> Terrorist violence, serious as it is, does not threaten our institutions of government or our existence as a civil community ... The real threat to the life of the nation, in the sense of a people living in accordance with its traditional laws and political values, comes not from terrorism but from laws such as these. That is the true measure of what terrorism may achieve. It is for Parliament to decide whether to give the terrorists such a victory.

The performance of Parliament in 2001 might be contrasted with its efforts in later years. Select committees have become more vigorous. For example, in the febrile atmosphere of the 2001–2002 session, the Joint Committee on Human Rights produced two terrorism-related reports. In session 2007–2008, which also witnessed new legislation, albeit shorter and less draconian in nature, there were nine such reports. The debates have also become more assertive, with major changes inflicted on the legislation in 2005, 2006 and 2008 (notably, the rejection of the 42- and 90-day periods of police detention). Earlier victories were more minor or peripheral (House of Commons Home Affairs Committee, 2001, paras 56–61).

Social Transitions

The final assertion concerns the socially transformative impacts of the treatment of rights in counter-terrorism – that their treatment can negatively or positively affect the level of conflict either as a source of recruitment for terrorism or as part of conflict resolution.

During the time of 'The Troubles', the impacts of what were perceived to be human rights breaches in Ireland proved to be important waypoints in the conflict. Four such illustrations may be cited. One concerns the imposition of internment and the selective use of inhuman treatment through 'deep interrogation' in 1971, as later condemned in *Ireland v. UK* (1978). This security crackdown galvanised IRA opposition to the security forces and removed nationalist community acquiescence in their presence, processes which were boosted by the killings on Bloody Sunday in 1972 (Bishop and Mallie, 1987: Chapter 10). The next example arose through the prisoner hunger strikes in 1981, which 'marked a dramatic improvement in the fortunes of the republican movement ... with the IRA restoring their credentials among sections of the Catholic community as freedom fighters' (Bishop and Mallie, 1987: 299). The final example concerns the impact of routine exercises of security powers, such as house searches and vehicle check points, which produced resentment (both individual and communal) and thereby mobilised violent challenges (Campbell and Connolly, 2006: 948).

This mobilising effect is perhaps less apparent with *jihadis*. Though concern has been expressed about stop and search powers, the sanctioned intrusions into personal liberty and privacy are on a much lower scale and duration than the operations suffered in Northern Ireland. Furthermore, *jihadis* do not emanate from any ethnically united, socially cohesive or geographically concentrated community, the entirety of which can then be treated as a suspect community (Greer, 2008: 169). While perceptions of inequitable treatment may not be a prime generator of *jihadi* sentiment, deleterious effects are experienced in terms of police–community relations and the willingness of the latter to volunteer information to the former (Mythen et al., 2009). Furthermore, perceived breaches of human rights abroad rather than at home – in Afghanistan, Iraq and Palestine – formed the core of the complaint in the suicide video of Mohammad Sidique Khan, one of the four 7/7 bombers: 'Until you stop the bombing, gassing, imprisonment and torture of my people we will not stop this fight ... We are at war and I am a soldier. Now you too will taste the reality of this situation' (Khan, 2005).

Conversely, human rights observance and restoration can be major elements of conflict resolution and transitional justice (Bell, 2000). Examples already cited include the emphasis within the Northern Ireland police on human rights audit. The tempering effects of judicial and legislative review also encourage an impetus towards conflict resolution by, first, ruling out militaristic solutions which involve grievous breaches of international law and, second, by maintaining the recognition of common humanity between protagonists (Dickson, 2006). Mention has also been made of the inquiries into past controversial events, such as the Bloody Sunday Inquiry, which were established in the expectation that fair and open inquiry into historical wrongs and then asserting justice and human rights over them can assist a peace process. Of course, the actual delivery of such idealistic goals is often hugely problematic. The Bloody Sunday Inquiry was established in 1998, but took until 2010 to deliver its report (Bloody Sunday Inquiry, 2010). While unequivocally damning of the actions of the British Army, the belated Report could hardly impact on the protagonists (with no soldiers being charged or disciplined and no compensation yet being paid) or strongly influence the course of events in the peace process. Even the impact of the paradigmatic Truth and Reconciliation Commission in South Africa remains contested (Wilson, 2001).

Conclusions

Counter-terrorism laws have become no more transitory than other 'special' laws dealing with other forms of serious criminality such as organised crime, sexual violence or serious frauds (Gross and Ní Aoláin, 2006: Chapter 1). In this context, human rights can be counted as 'one of the greatest civilizing achievements of the modern era' (Gearty, 2006: 1) and their impact upon crises of national security has been growing. Despite the broadly progressive picture depicted in this chapter, there remain substantial paradoxes and weaknesses in the protection of human rights (Gearty, 2007; Starmer, 2007). However, that proviso is a far cry from claims about the 'futility' of human rights (Ewing, 2004; Ewing and Tham, 2008), which misreads the emergent jurisprudence of national security controls now being devised by courageous High Court judges such as Collins, Mitting and Wilkie. The lessons of recent history and the prospects for the future of national security jurisprudence also point towards the rejection of the gullible belief (Campbell, 2009) that a return to positivism in which the executive dominates the security agenda on the basis of subjective and secretive assessments will afford better protection for individuals and for collectives against the excesses of counter-terrorism or indeed a better chance of success against terrorism.

References

A v. HM Treasury [2008] EWCA Civ 1187 (London).
A v. Secretary of State for the Home Department [2004] UKHL 56 (London).
A v. Secretary of State for the Home Department (No. 2) [2005] UKHL 71 (London).
A v. UK (2009) Application number 3455/05, 19 February (Strasbourg).
Agamben, G. (2005), *The State of Exception* (Chicago: University of Chicago Press).
Al Rawi v. Security Service [2009] EWHC 2959 (QB) (London).
Amnesty Canada International v. Chief of the Defence Staff for the Canadian Forces (2008) FCA 401 (Ottawa).
Arden, M. (2005), 'Human Rights in the Age of Terrorism', *Law Quarterly Review* 604.
AS v. Secretary of State for the Home Department [2008] EWCA Civ 289 (London).
Baha Mousa Inquiry (2010), *The Report of the Baha Mousa Inquiry* (2010–12 HC 1452).
Bell, C. (2000), *Peace Agreements and Human Rights* (Oxford: Oxford University Press).
Bishop, P. and Mallie, E. (1987), *The Provisional I.R.A.* (London: Heinemann).
Bloody Sunday Inquiry (2010), *Report of the Bloody Sunday Inquiry* (2010–12 HC 29).
Boumediene v. Bush (2008) 128 S. Ct. 2229 (Washington).
Brannigan and McBride v. UK (2001) Application nos. 14553/89, 14554/89, Ser. A. 258-B (Strasbourg).
Brennan v. UK (2001) Application no. 39846/98, 2001-X (Strasbourg).
Brogan v. UK (1988) Application no. 11209, 11234, 11266/84, 11386/85, Ser. A 145-B (Strasbourg).
Cabinet Office (2009), *Guide to Making Legislation*, http://www.cabinetoffice.gov.uk/resource-library/guide-making-legislation [accessed 1 July 2012].
Campbell, C. and Connolly, I. (2006), 'Making War on Terror?', 69 *Modern Law Review* 935–57.
Campbell, D. (2009), 'The Threat of Terrorism and the Plausibility of Positivism', *Public Law* 501.
Carlile, Lord Alex (2002–2010), *Reports on the Operation of the Terrorism Act 2000* (London: Home Office).
Carlile, Lord Alex (2005), *Proposals by Her Majesty's Government for Changes to the Laws against Terrorism* (London: Home Office).
Carlile, Lord Alex (2006–2011), *Reports of the Independent Reviewer pursuant to Section 14(3) of the Prevention of Terrorism Act 2005* (London: Home Office).

Carlile, Lord Alex (2007), *Report on Proposed Measures for Inclusion in a Counter-Terrorism Bill*, Cm. 7262 (London: Home Office).
Carlile, Lord Alex (2007a), *The Definition of Terrorism*, Cm. 7052 (London: Home Office and Government Reply, Cm. 7058, London: Home Office).
Carlile, Lord Alex (2008), *Conference on the Regulation of Criminal Justice* (Manchester: University of Manchester, 9 April).
Carlile, Lord Alex (2009), *Report on the Operation of the Terrorism Act 2000* (London: Home Office).
Chahal v. UK (1996) Application no. 22414/93, Reports 1996-V (Strasbourg).
Clarke, C. (2000), *Hansard* (House of Commons), volume 346, column 363, 15 March.
Dickson, B. (2006), 'The House of Lords and the Northern Ireland Conflict – A Sequel', 69 *Modern Law Review* 383.
Dyzenhaus, D. (2006), *The Constitution of Law* (Cambridge: Cambridge University Press).
Elton, Lord R. (1984), *Hansard* (House of Lords), volume 449, column 405, 8 March.
EU Turkey Civic Commission (2008), 'Kurdish Spokesperson and EUTCC Patron Leyla Zana Convicted to Ten Years in Prison by a Turkish Court', http://www.eutcc.org/articles/7/document368.ehtml [accessed 1 July 2012].
Ewing, K.D. (2004), 'The Futility of Human Rights', *Public Law* 829.
Ewing, K.D. and Tham, J-C. (2008), 'The Continuing Futility of the Human Rights Act', *Public Law* 668.
Feldman, D. (2006), 'Human Rights, Terrorism and Risk', *Public Law* 364.
Foreign & Commonwealth Office (2011), *Human Rights and Democracy: The 2010 Foreign & Commonwealth Office Report*, Cm. 8017 (London: Home Office).
Gearty, C. (1994), 'The Cost of Human Rights' *Current Legal Problems*, 47, 19.
Gearty, C. (2005), 'Human Rights in an Age of Counter-terrorism', *Current Legal Problems*, 58, 25.
Gearty, C. (2006), *Can Human Rights Survive?* (Cambridge: Cambridge University Press).
Gearty, C. (2007), 'Rethinking Civil Liberties in a Counter-terrorism World', *European Human Rights Law Review* 111.
Greer, S. (2008), 'Human Rights and the Struggle Against Terrorism in the United Kingdom', *European Human Rights Law Review* 163.
Gross, O. and Ní Aoláin, F. (2006), *Law in Times of Crisis* (Cambridge: Cambridge University Press).
Home Office (1998), *Legislation Against Terrorism*, Cm. 4178 (London: Home Office).
Home Office (2004), *Counter Terrorism Powers*, Cm. 6147 (London: Home Office).
Home Office (2006), *Countering International Terrorism*, Cm. 6888 (London: Home Office).
Home Office (2007), *Possible Measures for Inclusion into a Future Counter-Terrorism Bill* (London: Home Office).
Home Office (2009a), *Pursue, Prevent, Protect, Prepare: The United Kingdom's Strategy for Countering International Terrorism*, Cm. 7547 (London: Home Office).
Home Office (2009b), http://www.homeoffice.gov.uk/about-us/news/terror-threat-level-substantial [accessed 1 July 2012].

Home Office (2010), *Pursue Prevent Protect Prepare: The United Kingdom's Strategy for Countering International Terrorism*, Cm. 7833 (London: Home Office).
Home Office (2011), *CONTEST: The United Kingdom's Strategy for Countering Terrorism*, Cm. 8123 (London: Home Office).
House of Commons Home Affairs Committee (2001), *The Anti-terrorism, Crime and Security Bill* (2001–02 HC 35).
House of Commons Home Affairs Committee (2004), *Terrorism and Community Relations* (2003–04 HC 165).
Independent Police Complaints Commission (2007a), *Stockwell One – Investigation into the Shooting of Jean Charles de Menezes at Stockwell Underground Station on 22 July 2005* (London).
Independent Police Complaints Commission (2007b), *Stockwell Two – An Investigation into Complaints about the Metropolitan Police Service's Handling of Public Statements Following the Shooting of Jean Charles de Menezes on 22 July 2005* (London).
In re Duffy [2009] NIQB 31 (Belfast).
Ireland v. UK (1978) Application number 5310/71 (Strasbourg).
Irvine, Lord Derry (1997), *Hansard* (House of Lords), volume 583, column 1150 (27 November).
Joint Committee on Human Rights (2005a), *Prevention of Terrorism Bill: Preliminary Report* (2004–05 HL61/HC 389).
Joint Committee on Human Rights (2005b), *Prevention of Terrorism Bill* (2004-5 HL68/HC334).
Joint Committee on Human Rights (2008), *Twenty-Ninth Report, A Bill of Rights for the UK?* (2007–08 HL 165-I/HC 150-I).
Joint Committee on Human Rights (2008a), *Government Responses to the Committee's Twentieth and Twenty First Reports and Other Correspondence* (2007–08 HL 127, HC 756).
Khan, M.S. (2005), http://news.bbc.co.uk/1/hi/uk/4206800.stm [accessed 1 July 2012].
Livingstone, S. (1994), 'The House of Lords and the Northern Ireland Conflict', 57 *Modern Law Review* 333.
Lloyd Report (1996), *Inquiry into Legislation against Terrorism*, Cm. 3420 (London: HMSO).
Macdonald Report (2011), *Review of Counter-Terrorism and Security Powers*, Cm.8003 (London: HMSO).
Maqaleh v. Gates (2009) 620 F. Supp. 2d 51 (DC Cir) (Washington).
Moeckli, D. (2008), *Human Rights and Non-Discrimination in the 'War on Terror'* (Oxford: Oxford University Press).
Munaf v. Geren (2008) 129 S. Ct. 19 (Washington).
Mythen, G. et al. (2009), '"I'm a Muslim, but I'm Not a Terrorist": Victimization, Risky Identities and the Performance of Safety' 49 *British Journal of Criminology* 736–54.
NA v. UK (2008) Application number 25904/07 (Strasbourg).
Othman v. UK (2009) Application number 8139/09 (Strasbourg).
Police Service of Northern Ireland (2008), *Human Rights Programme of Action 2007–2008* (Belfast).

Posner, E.A. and Vermeule, A. (2007), *Terror in the Balance* (New York: Oxford University Press).
Privy Counsellor Review Committee (2003), *Anti-Terrorism, Crime and Security Act 2001 Review, Report* (2003–04 HC 100).
R (Al-Jedda) v. Secretary of State for Defence [2007] UKHL 58 (London).
R (Al-Skeini) v. Secretary of State for Defence [2007] UKHL 27 (London).
R (da Silva) v. Director of Public Prosecutions [2006] EWHC 3204 (Admin) (London).
R (Gillan) v. Metropolitan Police Commissioner [2006] UKHL 12 (London).
R v. Horseferry Road Magistrates' Court, ex parte Bennett [1994] 1 AC 42 (London).
R (Mohamed) v. Secretary of State for Foreign and Commonwealth Affairs [2009] EWHC 152 (Admin) (London).
R (Smith) v. Assistant Deputy Coroner for Oxfordshire [2009] EWCA 441 (London).
Rasul v. Bush (2004) 542 U.S. 466 (Washington).
RB and OO v. Secretary of State for the Home Department [2009] UKHL 10 (London).
Saadi v. Italy (2008) Application number 37201/06, 28 February (Strasbourg).
Sadak and others v. Turkey (No. 2) (2002) Application nos. 25144/94, 26149/95 to 26154/95, 27100/95 and 27101/95, 11 June (Strasbourg).
Secretary of State for the Home Department v. AF (No. 3) [2009] UKHL 28 (London).
Secretary of State for the Home Department v. Lord Alton of Liverpool [2008] EWCA Civ 443 (London).
Secretary of State for the Home Department v. MB and AF [2007] UKHL 46 (London).
Secretary of State for the Home Department v. Rehman [2001] UKHL 47 (London).
Special Rapporteur on the promotion and protection of human rights while countering terrorism (2006), *Report* (New York: A/61/267, United Nations).
Steyn, J. (2004), 'Guantanamo Bay: The Legal Black Hole', 53 *International & Comparative Law Quarterly* 1–15.
Starmer, K. (2007), 'Setting the Record Straight', *European Human Rights Law Review* 123–32.
US Presidential Order (2001), Detention, Treatment, and Trial of Certain Non-Citizens in the War Against Terrorism (Washington DC: 66 Federal Register 57831).
Vaughan, B. and Kilcommins, S. (2008) *Terrorism, Rights and the Rule of Law* (Cullompton: Willan).
Walker, C. (1997), 'Constitutional Governance and Special Powers Against Terrorism', 35 *Columbia Journal of Transnational Law* 1–62.
Walker, C. (2005), 'Prisoners of "War All the Time"', *European Human Rights Law Review* 50–74.
Walker, C. (2007), 'Keeping Control of Terrorists Without Losing Control of Constitutionalism', 59 *Stanford Law Review* 1395–463.
Walker, C. (2007a), 'The Treatment of Foreign Terror Suspects', 70 *Modern Law Review* 427–57.
Walker, C. (2008), '"Know Thine Enemy as Thyself": Discerning Friend from Foe under Anti-terrorism Laws', 32 *Melbourne Law Review* 275–301.
Walker, C. (2009), *The Anti-Terrorism Legislation*, 2nd edn (Oxford: Oxford University Press).

Walker, C. (2010), 'The Threat of Terrorism and the Fate of Control Orders', *Public Law* 3–15.
Walker, C. (2011), *Terrorism and the Law* (Oxford: Oxford University Press).
Walker, C. and Weaver, R. (2000), 'The United Kingdom Bill of Rights', 33 *University of Michigan Journal of Law Reform* 497–560.
Whalley, R. (2008), *Report of the Independent Reviewer: Justice and Security (Northern Ireland) Act 2007* (Belfast: Northern Ireland Office).
Wilson, R.A. (2001), *The Politics of Truth and Reconciliation in South Africa* (Cambridge: Cambridge University Press).
Zimbabwe Times (2009), 'Bennett in High Court on Terrorism Trial', 9 November, http://www.thezimbabwetimes.com/?p=24734 [accessed 1 July 2012].

PART VI
Ending Political Violence

The State's Role in the Management and Resolution of Violent Conflict: Learning from Northern Ireland?

Bill Rolston

Introduction

It has become customary in recent years to represent the successes of the Northern Ireland peace process internationally as a model to be seriously considered by other conflict-ridden or transitional societies. A healthy academic scepticism about such claims (Guelke 2008; English 2009) has not prevented politicians and media commentators in particular from presenting the transformation in Northern Ireland as miraculous. If such an intransigent conflict as the long-lasting Irish one could be thus solved, why not other such conflicts?

This chapter seeks to examine this wisdom in depth, looking particularly at the British state's role during the distinct periods of violent political conflict dating from the late 1960s and the subsequent peace process from the 1990s to the present day. Specifically, it will interrogate the state's own claims about its contribution both to conflict management in the earlier period and conflict resolution in the more recent period. On the basis of that interrogation, the question of the exportability of the lessons of Northern Ireland can perhaps be assessed in a more sober fashion.

Selling Conflict Management

It was clear from the beginning that Britain had to deal with the Northern Ireland conflict within the context of international opinion. At times it had to justify its actions to a sceptical or even critical world, as in the case of the hunger strikes of 1981, where the international media were practically unanimous in criticism of its intransigence

(Mulcahy 1995; von Tangen Page 1996), or the case of the costly campaign of counter-propaganda in the face of the successes of the MacBride lobby on fair employment throughout the USA in the 1980s (Cochrane 2007; McNamara 2009). The international law left loopholes for justifications to be made, as in the case of Britain's derogation from European human rights protocols in relation to internment in Northern Ireland in the early 1970s (Marks 1995). But legal fora could work the other way, as when the Irish government successfully brought the British government to the European Court of Human Rights over the torture of internees (Mowbray 2007).[1]

Thus, the eventual abandonment of internment without trial was partly instigated by the need of the British state, with one eye on international opinion, to represent the management of the violent political conflict in Ireland as being under the rubric of normal democratic law. The corollary of this representation was that the violence in Ireland was not a war, but rather a criminal conspiracy and/or a terrorist onslaught. The latter explanation was more likely to emerge from indigenous forces such as the Royal Ulster Constabulary (RUC), while the former was the preferred British government explanation. The cost of preserving the fiction of normality was massive: the criminalisation of prisoners who previously had had political status and the subsequent hunger strike (Campbell, McKeown and O'Hagan 1994), the 'Ulsterisation' of security, wherein the role of the British army was represented as being 'in support of the civil power' (Newsinger 1995) and the British state's inability to acknowledge that the British army could not beat the IRA until over a decade after the admission by Brigadier James Glover in 1978 that 'in no way can or will the Provisional IRA ever be defeated militarily' (quoted in Miller 1993: 76).[2]

Once the situation had settled into what the IRA termed 'the long war' (Kelley 1982; Guelke, Cox and Stephen 2000), the British state had two stories to tell to the international community: first, that it was succeeding in maintaining the rule of law despite the political violence and that any supposedly temporary derogations from this rule of law were emergency measures. This meant that the state had to scale back its more militaristic, and especially its illegal, methods in favour of the rule of law. Toolis concluded:

> The rules of engagement in a white island off the shores of Europe that enjoyed good media links precluded the British armed forces' usual brutal response, used in previous anti-colonial struggles. Military force had to be cloaked in civilian law, thus ruling out widespread assassination campaigns against

---

[1] Initially, the European Commission on Human Rights (*Ireland v. United Kingdom* (1976) Y.B. Eur. Conv. on Hum. Rts. 512, 748, 788–94) found for Ireland that techniques used against some internees in 1971 amounted to torture. On appeal, the European Court of Human Rights (*Ireland v. United Kingdom* (1978) ECHR 1, 18 January, Case No. 5310/71) overturned the finding of torture and concluded that the victims had been subjected to 'inhuman and degrading treatment' in breach of Article 3 of the European Convention on Human Rights.

[2] For its part, the IRA (Irish Republican Army) also admitted that it could not defeat the British militarily. See the speech of senior republican Jimmy Drumm in June 1977 (Moloney 2002: 151).

IRA leaders or draconian mass screening operations against the nationalist community. Torturing suspects was illegal. (2003: 31)

Not quite so. The role of law in counter-insurgency had been succinctly summed up early in the conflict by Brigadier Frank Kitson; his ideas proved to be very influential as Britain faced urban warfare in its neighbouring 'white island':

> There are two possible alternatives, the first one being that the law should be used as just another weapon in the government's arsenal, and in this case it becomes little more than a propaganda cover for the disposal of unwanted members of the public ... The other alternative is that the courts should remain impartial and administer the laws of the country without any direction from the government. (Kitson 1971: 69)

Kitson, and at times the British state, favoured the latter option. Thus, 'assassination campaigns' (Stalker 1988) and mass screening operations (Boyle, Hadden and Hillyard 1983: 37–54) occurred, as well as tacit support for loyalist death squads (Sluka 1999: 127–57; Rolston 2005).

The second story that the state had to tell was that British military forces were now among the most sophisticated and successful at counter-insurgency, especially in the urban terrain. The key question related to explaining the nature of that insurgency. From time to time, Britain represented its task as standing up to international communism – but this view was mostly confined to the fringes of the Conservative Party (Harwood, Guinness and Biggs-Davison 1970), only appearing in more official rhetoric for a Reaganite US audience. For example, Secretary of State Tom King claimed in a speech to the Association of American Correspondents in London that the IRA was 'a dedicated group of extreme Marxist republican terrorists' determined to 'establish a Marxist revolutionary government in a 32-county republic' (Northern Ireland Information Service 1988). More common was the argument that Britain was facing up to international terrorism of which the IRA campaign was the regional example. The IRA's links – real, exaggerated and imaginary (Sterling 1981) – with other insurgents in Libya, Lebanon, Palestine, Germany, the Basque country and South Africa were grist to the mill of this representation.

No other advanced democratic state, with the possible exception of Spain in relation to the Basque region, had had to deal with a major insurgency such as that in Northern Ireland. Thus, in the European and North American context, the British ploughed a relatively lonely furrow in terms of counter-insurgency. However, as a leading member of that community of democratic states, it was able to ensure itself a sympathetic hearing in terms of its successful management of conflict in Ireland. For the most part it had succeeded in containing the problem militarily – to the island of Ireland, to the northern part of the island and to certain districts of that region (Rolston 1991) – while at the same time holding on to enough of the characteristics of the democratic state as not to be confused with, say, a contemporaneous Latin American dictatorship.[3]

As Britain's 'Northern Ireland problem' moved toward a solution, suddenly other states found themselves in a similar position, especially in the aftermath of 9/11. In this situation, Britain could now represent itself as the quintessential expert on counter-insurgency and conflict management as a result of its Northern Ireland experience. Former British soldiers who had served in Northern Ireland segued into running or working for private security firms in Iraq and elsewhere. An example is former Lieutenant Colonel Tim Spicer whose Aegis Defence Services was awarded a $293 million security contract by the US military in October 2004. He had been in charge of a unit which had killed an unarmed teenager in Belfast in 1992 (Pat Finucane Centre 2004). Former members of the RUC were similarly involved; 250 such people were employed by two security firms alone, ArmorGroup and Control Risks Group, comprising 10 per cent of their workforce (Ellison and O'Reilly 2008: 417). The only branch of the Northern Ireland Retired Police Officers' Association outside Northern Ireland is in Baghdad! And such was the concern in the Police Service of Northern Ireland (PSNI) in 2003 over officers taking sabbaticals to pursue lucrative security duties in Iraq and Afghanistan that a moratorium on sabbaticals was introduced (Ellison and O'Reilly 2008: 417). At least one officer managed to work in Afghanistan for five weeks at £275 per day while officially on sick leave (*Belfast Telegraph*, 26 January 2006).

The newly reformed PSNI quickly became a global brand in terms of conflict management and counter-terrorism. Numerous fact-finding delegations arrived in Northern Ireland to hear the story of the how the beleaguered 'force' had turned itself into an acceptable 'service'. And the organisation carried this same message abroad, spending £1.5 million in 2006–2007 alone on air travel (Ellison and O'Reilly 2008: 409). Part of this marketing involved the PSNI's value as a model of a thoroughly modern police service, attuned to all the correct requirements of human rights awareness, etc. Thus, a PSNI representative was sent to Latvia in August 2006 to promote the organisation's successes in countering hate crime (Ellison and O'Reilly 2008: 411).[4] Yet, to take one example, the PSNI's response to attacks which led to 100 members of the Roma community being forced out of Belfast was 'not up to scratch' (Northern Ireland Assembly Debates 2009) according to local politicians. As such, the international esteem attributed to the PSNI as expert in managing political violence was perhaps more due to the promotional activities

---

3   At the same time, see the comments of Assistant Chief Constable John Stalker, sent from Manchester to investigate shoot-to-kill operations by the RUC: 'if a police force of the United Kingdom could, in cold blood, kill a seventeen-year-old youth with no terrorist or criminal convictions, and then plot to hide the evidence from a senior policeman deputed to investigate it, then the shame belonged to us all. This is the act of a Central American assassination squad' (Stalker 1988: 67).

4   A Criminal Justice Inspection report on hate crime in Northern Ireland noted of the PSNI that 'delay is a problem in relation to hate crime, as it is for the criminal justice system at large' (Criminal Justice Inspection Northern Ireland 2007: vii). It also found that some police officers were unaware of PSNI policy in relation to hate crime (2007: 23).

of the government in selling the 'success' of Northern Ireland and less due to the inherent merits or effectiveness of its policies and practices.

The PSNI was also involved in direct action in both policing and training abroad. The RUC in its final days was involved in policing missions in Bosnia, Kosovo, Mongolia, Ethiopia and Dominica (Ellison and O'Reilly 2008: 409). But it was Iraq which became the main base abroad for many PSNI officers (Quinn 2004). Stephen White, a PSNI assistant chief constable, was in charge of the establishment of the academy for the new Iraqi police force near Basra (*Sunday Times*, 28 December 2003). During the same period, police officers from Northern Ireland also held the key posts of chief of police mentors and of regional training coordinator in Iraq (Ellison and O'Reilly 2008: 418). In 2005 former RUC Chief Constable Ronnie Flanagan was posted to Iraq to oversee police reform (BBC Online 2005), while PSNI Assistant Chief Constable Duncan McCausland served in 2007 as a commissioner for the US government in Iraq (PSNI 2008).

For the PSNI, policing in Iraq was relatively straightforward; the organisation did not have to face the constraining effects of accusations, as it did on the home front, of human rights abuses laid at the door of its predecessor, the RUC. In Iraq it could get on with the job of counter-insurgency without the encumbrances of an Ombudsman or an Oversight Commissioner. At home it also faced cold case reviews by the Historical Enquiries Team, inquiries and tribunals, most of which derived from the reform of the policing and justice system in Northern Ireland and which were deemed necessary to restore public confidence in the system and to ensure that the police did not repeat the human rights offences of the past. Despite the fact that, due to the Patten Report (1999), which led *inter alia* to the reform of the police in Northern Ireland, safeguards for human rights had been built into the new system in Northern Ireland, this was not the immediate expertise which was sought from these officers. As PSNI Chief Inspector Kevin Smith, tasked with training new police recruits in Basra, put it: 'The tactics which I am teaching are straight off the streets of Belfast' (Ellison and O'Reilly 2008: 418). These were the tactics and skills which were also foregrounded by former head of the RUC Special Branch Bill Lowry when he provided training at 20 homeland security seminars in the US or his former boss, RUC Chief Constable Ronnie Flanagan and Chris Albiston, former Assistant Chief Constable of the PSNI with responsibility for counter-terrorism, when they shared their skills in high-powered seminars on the war on terror at Harvard and elsewhere (Ellison and O'Reilly 2008: 414).

The British army was also able to represent itself as being better situated to counter-insurgency in Iraq and Afghanistan because of its long experience in Northern Ireland. Thus, at the start of the war in Iraq, General Sir Mike Jackson, commander of British troops, stated: 'We are not interested in gratuitous violence', the implication being that not all coalition partners were so disposed. To elaborate on the implication, senior British military officers on the ground were at pains to point out to journalists that they were dismayed by the failure of US troops to understand the need to 'win the hearts and minds' of local Iraqis. This public relations offensive in Basra was contrasted with the more brutal tactics used by American forces around Nassiriya. 'Unlike the Americans, we took our helmets and sunglasses off and looked at the Iraqis eye to eye', said a British officer. And where did this skill come from? 'The British military put the difference in approach down to decades of training as well as experience – first in colonial insurgencies in Malaysia, then in Northern Ireland and peacekeeping operations in the Balkans' (Norton-Taylor and McCarthy 2003).

This message was often delivered directly to American forces. Thus, US Colonel Mansoor, Commander of the First Brigade Combat Team, First Armoured Division, in Baghdad (2003–2004), notes that they started the tour with a briefing from the British Army's Operational Training and Advisory Group, all with experience in Northern Ireland (Mansoor 2008: 144). And in 2006, British Army Brigadier Nigel Aylwin-Foster, who served alongside US forces in Iraq from December 2003 to November 2004, published a hard-hitting article in a key US military journal accusing the American military in Iraq of damaging cultural insensitivity in Iraq, unrealistic optimism and a predisposition towards using maximum force. Undoubtedly influenced by the Macpherson Report (1999) on the killing of black teenager Stephen Lawrence in London, he accused US forces in Iraq of 'institutional racism' (Aylwin-Foster 2005).

Despite this self-congratulatory message to the international community, it soon became clear that there was an underbelly of British army mistreatment of civilians. As *The Observer* came to admit, 'quietly, out of the sight of the media, abuses were taking place' (Beaumont 2006). In time, the failure of the British army approach was admitted by the army itself. In 2007 a leaked internal British army report acknowledged that the British were unable to win the 'hearts and minds' of the Iraqis because, it was argued, they had failed to understand Arab culture (Rayment 2007).[5]

Notwithstanding the admission of failure, the blueprint continued to be widely disseminated as the key one to emulate, especially in the USA, where the war on terror was at the forefront of state policy. Thus, in 2006 'Gen. C. Redmond Watt, Britain's top land forces commander who headed government troops in Northern Ireland when the Irish Republican Army announced disarmament last year' addressed an audience in the Pentagon on 'how Britain won in Northern Ireland after 37 years of fighting insurgents and how those lessons might be applied to Iraq'. He told them that the '37-year campaign offered a textbook of lessons on how to defeat armed groups who used unconventional warfare to kill people, military and civilian alike' (Scarborough 2006).

A year later, the Royal United Services Institute held a seminar in London which repeated the claims from Basra (RUSI 2007):

> Since Malaya the British Army has had a long experience of dealing with insurgency and urban warfare in Northern Ireland. This has informed the British Army's attempts to 'win the battle for hearts and minds' in Iraq which

---

5   By 2010 the claim of British army superiority became untenable with an official inquiry appointed to investigate the role of British soldiers in the torture and murder of Baha Moussa in Iraq in 2003: http://news.bbc.co.uk/1/hi/uk/10285258.stm [accessed 2 July 2012].

included the use of 'minimum force' and operating among the people rather than in armoured vehicles.

And more generally, at a ceremony in St Paul's Cathedral, London to honour the 300,000 soldiers who were involved at some point during the Northern Ireland conflict, the Bishop of London stated:

> I've been able to see personally in other theatres how the lessons of Northern Ireland have entered the DNA of the British armed forces, who in my view combined a remarkable degree of military efficiency with a capacity to engage in a humane way with the civilian population. (BBC Online 2008a)

Selling Conflict Resolution

For years, global coverage of Northern Ireland comprised stories related to major atrocities, from Bloody Sunday in 1972 to the Omagh bomb in 1998. But as the peace process took root, increasingly these stories were of the remarkable advances in the process: the IRA and loyalist ceasefires of 1994, the Good Friday Agreement of 1998 and the first power-sharing executive of the devolved administration in 1999. There were numerous reverses, usually relating to demands for the decommissioning of IRA weapons, which led to the executive being suspended on four occasions, most seriously in 2002. But in the next five years significant developments occurred: the IRA eventually decommissioned and later disbanded, and the two hardline parties, the Democratic Unionist Party and Sinn Féin, became the two largest parties in the North. Subsequently, and to the surprise of many commentators, in March 2007 these parties formed a new executive, with the DUP's Ian Paisley as the First Minister and Sinn Féin's Martin McGuinness as his deputy.

There was widespread international media interest in this event; Northern Ireland seemed to be succeeding where many other societies had failed in coming out of a protracted period of intense political violence into a new era of peace. The fact that Paisley and McGuinness were not merely sharing power but seemed genuinely to respect each other's position was eminently newsworthy. Some of the reporting was relatively sober. 'Two life-long enemies, mellowed by age, by the sorrow of loss and by political realities, have at long last found common ground', announced the *Boston Herald* (8 May 2007). 'Peace is for real', assured the *Cleveland Plain Dealer* (9 May 2007), probably because it is 'built on solid foundations' (*Albany Times Union*, 10 May 2007). For its part, the *Toronto Star* (9 May 2007) opted for hyperbole – 'It was the most unlikely tea party since Alice in Wonderland sat down with the Mad Hatter' – and was quickly surpassed by others. The phenomenon was no less than 'a miracle', according to both the *Washington Times* (10 May 2007) and the *Ottawa Citizen* (12 May 2007), while for the *Springfield Republican* (9 May 2007), 'the unimaginable became reality yesterday'. 'Hate has suffered an amazing defeat', concluded the *Charleston Post and Courier* (9 May 2007), while for the *New*

York Daily News (10 May 2007), 'now we know what happens when hell freezes over'.

Credit for the progress was copiously distributed by these and other papers – to Paisley and McGuinness, Sinn Féin President Gerry Adams, Bertie Ahern, Taoiseach (the Prime Minister) of the Republic of Ireland, John Hume of the SDLP and even Canadian retired General John de Chastelain, head of the international body tasked with overseeing decommissioning, the last not surprisingly by a Canadian paper (*Toronto Star*, 9 May 2007). But the person singled out for the most widespread praise was British Prime Minister Tony Blair (*Canberra Times*, 10 May 2007; *Nelson Mail*, 11 May 2007).

Many of the papers announced that what had happened in Northern Ireland was a 'beacon' of 'hope' for the rest of the world (*Star Tribune*, 9 May 2007; *Washington Post*, 9 May 2007; *New Haven Register*, 14 May 2007), but beyond that, there is precious little in all of this coverage to indicate what exactly the practical lessons of the Northern Ireland peace process for the rest of the world might be. There are a few notable exceptions. For the *Ottowa Citizen* (12 May 2007) and the *Canberra Times* (10 May 2007), the lesson is that peace, whether in Northern Ireland or Iraq, is built not on the middle ground, but on the extremes. According to the Australian paper, in Northern Ireland 'there is no middle ground; instead there is an agreement to work together within tightly specified guidelines for the greater good of a community that has suffered too much'. For the *American Chronicle* (8 May 2007), the lesson for America is that it is necessary to talk – to Hamas and Hezbollah, in Cuba and Iran. For its part, *Time* magazine (9 May 2007) stressed that there were three main components of success: the use of both carrots and sticks; flexibility (especially in relation to the timing of decommissioning); and patience and determination.

Newspapers in other conflict zones seemed more eager to draw practical lessons. Thus, the *Times of India* (15 May 2007), with one eye towards the Punjab, saw the Irish developments as a 'glimmer of hope' for the rest of the world. But, moving beyond rhetoric, it concluded that adopting the Irish model would require the Israelis to talk to Hamas and would also set an example for places like Sri Lanka and Iraq.

The *Cyprus Mail* (13 May 2007) contained a lengthy interview with former Taoiseach Garret Fitzgerald: 'The IRA has changed completely. They realised they couldn't win. The British also knew they couldn't win. And it is when both sides knew they couldn't win that they had to move closer to a settlement.' In the same edition of the newspaper, the British High Commissioner in Cyprus, Peter Millett, tried to square the circle of representing Northern Ireland as a model without seeing it as a general blueprint: 'through dialogue, building trust, making compromises and taking risks, essential steps were made to reach a solution. We are deliberately not drawing parallels with Cyprus but the above message applies to all conflicts around the world'.

In Sri Lanka, the *Colombo Daily Mirror* (11 May 2007) argued that the peace process succeeded because 'the negotiations were conducted within the framework of a broad political framework or solution which gave hopes to all stakeholders. The political solution dangled over the peace table made everyone to feel that nobody would be a loser'. The lack of such a political solution is the main obstacle to peace in Sri Lanka, it concluded. A second lesson was this: 'The British and Irish governments pursued their search for peace and maintained their communication links with Sinn Féin even as the IRA was carrying out its violent campaign.'

In relation to the Israeli–Palestinian conflict, politicians there were already keeping a close eye on Irish developments even before March 2007. Thus, in November 2006 Ahmed Yousef, an adviser to the Hamas Palestinian Prime Minister, Ismail Haniyeh, wrote in the *New York Times* suggesting a temporary truce to allow for political negotiations. His reference point was Northern Ireland:

> the Irish Republican Army agreed to halt its military struggle to free Northern Ireland from British rule without recognizing British sovereignty. Irish Republicans continue to aspire to a united Ireland free of British rule, but rely upon peaceful methods. Had the IRA been forced to renounce its vision of reuniting Ireland before negotiations could occur, peace would never have prevailed. Why should more be demanded of the Palestinians, particularly when the spirit of our people will never permit it?. (Quoted in *Jerusalem Post*, 10 November 2006)

In response to the establishment of the power-sharing executive in Northern Ireland, Israel's liberal newspaper *Haaretz* (16 May 2007) opined that both the Israelis and the Palestinians needed leadership of the calibre of Blair if there was to be any hope for progress in the Middle East peace process. It did not allude to Blair's role in relation to the Iraq war, a role which did not endear him to Palestinians. In the event, *Haaretz*'s wish came true. One month later, on 27 June, Blair was appointed as a special envoy to the region on behalf of the USA, Russia, the UN and the EU.

Also in response to the Irish developments, an influential article appeared in the *International Herald Tribune*, written by two former US envoys to Northern Ireland, George Mitchell and Richard Haass (2007). Mitchell had chaired the peace negotiations from 1996 and was widely credited as the architect of the Good Friday Agreement of 1998. The article was extremely upbeat. Laying out some ground rules for peace building on the basis of their Northern Ireland experience, the authors stressed the necessity of inclusiveness. The goal was to convince protagonists that violence will not succeed while at same time building up the confidence of all: 'Parties should be allowed to hold on to their dreams.' Including formerly violent groups in dialogue is essential, they argued: 'Sometimes it's hard to stop a war if you don't talk with those who are involved in it.'

Although the article did not refer to the Middle East, the *Jerusalem Post* (16 May 2007) seized the opportunity to report on it at length. In doing so, it played down the optimism of the original while focusing on perhaps the only negative point in Mitchell and Haass' analysis: 'Sanctions should be introduced when there is backsliding. In the case of Northern Ireland it meant public criticism, stopping diplomatic contacts, the suspension of local institutions. There must be a clear price for unacceptable actions.' The *Jerusalem Post* article went on to conclude that Mitchell and Haass' advice regarding compromise and inclusiveness cannot work in the Middle East for, while Israeli leaders have compromised repeatedly, for example, in relation to Jerusalem, no Palestinian political leader has ever reciprocated, for example, in relation to the right of return.

The debate was fired up again when in January 2009 Mitchell was appointed by President Barack Obama as a special envoy to the Middle East. *Haaretz* (29 January 2009) welcomed his appointment and emphasised the importance of the Mitchell Principles in relation to the Irish peace process. These specified a cessation of violence in return for peace talks. On this basis, *Haaretz* urged dialogue with Hamas.

The *Jerusalem Post* (4 February 2009) was less supportive and instead carried a major piece by Ed Moloney, a prolific journalistic commentator on the Irish conflict, which stressed that Mitchell had not been the main architect of Irish peace. That honour, said Moloney, should go to Tony Blair and Bertie Ahern, the leaders of the British and Irish governments respectively. These governments could not sell the Good Friday Agreement to the divided clientele in Northern Ireland; the unionists would not have accepted Ahern's credentials, nor would the nationalists have accepted Blair's. So Mitchell became 'the chosen channel through which the British and Irish achieved their goal. The draft agreement introduced at the talks had been composed and written by British and Irish officials, but it was presented as if it had come from Mitchell's own hand'.

The following day, the offensive continued with an article by Sean Gannon, Chairman of the Irish Friends of Israel. He argued that the Irish peace process was based on a fiction devised by the British and Irish governments that there was a distinction between Sinn Féin and the IRA, so that they would not have to be seen negotiating with those advocating and conducting terrorism. Gannon warned that Mitchell and Blair would impose the same fiction on Israel, so that Hamas' political wing could be brought in from the cold while its militarists continue to terrorise.

If Northern Ireland has a lesson for the Middle East conflict, it is this. Terrorists will not lay down their weapons until they feel they are left with no choice. Sinn Féin/IRA's decision to renounce violence was largely the result of exhaustion, an exhaustion born both of repeated military reversals and increasing pressure to end its campaign from elements of its own wider community – in other words, its effective defeat (Gannon 2009).

In recent years, the messages about the Northern Ireland peace process to Israel have been contradictory. On the one hand, there are those who urge at least caution and scepticism. Thus, former Northern Ireland First Minister David Trimble advised the Israelis to 'Stand firm on Hamas'. He told the *Jerusalem Post* (29 October 2007) that whereas the majority in Israel wanted 'accommodation', Hamas might still be on the lookout for 'victories'. And Jonathan Tobin, neoconservative executive editor of the US Jewish monthly *Commentary Magazine*, warned readers of the *Jerusalem Post* (5 April 2007) that the Irish peace process was a 'misleading analogy': 'the Irish never begrudged the right of the British to rule Britain; they just wanted them out of Ireland. The Arabs still oppose the existence of Israel within any borders, including the cease-fire lines of 1949'.

On the other hand, there were those who presented Northern Ireland as a blueprint. Writing in *The Guardian,* Jonathan Freedland urged the Israeli government to issue a declaration similar to that of the British government which had been crucial in opening up the Irish peace process. In 1990, Secretary of State Peter Brooke had stated that the British government had no 'selfish strategic or economic interest' in relation to Northern Ireland. According to Freedland, both sides in Israel-Palestine, as in Northern Ireland, needed to realise that a solely military solution is impossible. And Israel needed to negotiate with Hamas on the same basis as the British negotiated with Sinn Féin, namely, the renunciation of violence. Freedland concluded: 'Northern Ireland offers paradoxical advice: each side must strengthen its adversary' (Freedland 2009). Israel's ambassador to the Republic of Ireland, while less open to some aspects of this 'blueprint' approach, itemised seven lessons from the Northern Ireland experience which were potentially applicable to Israel, including third-party mediation and adoption of the 'Mitchell Principles' (Evrony 2010).

In practice, the international community has tended towards the 'Northern Ireland as blueprint' view. It has pointedly sent two key players in the Northern Ireland peace process as envoys, thus underlying the message of the potential value of the Irish experience to that in the Middle East. At the same time, programmes have been funded which underscored the same message.[6] For example, the Irish government's Conflict Resolution Unit of the Department of Foreign Affairs supported a visit of Palestinian and Israeli negotiators to Ireland in August 2008, and in April 2009 funded a visit by 'Combatants for Peace', an organisation of Israeli and Palestinian ex-combatants, to meet republican and loyalist counterparts in Donegal (DFA 2009). The Irish ex-combatants have also visited Israel and Palestine on a number of occasions.

The two-way traffic between Ireland and some of the world's major conflict zones has been heavy over recent years. While some on the Irish side have sought to learn lessons from elsewhere – for example, regarding the possibility of a truth commission for Northern Ireland – for the most part the encounters present the Irish peace process as a model. Usually this is prefaced by the acknowledgement that no two conflicts are identical and therefore neither are any two peace processes; that said, the supposed lessons of Northern Ireland then loom large in any exchange.[7]

David Alderdice, former speaker of the Northern Ireland Assembly, visited Kashmir in 2007 with the message for politicians there that there was no alternative to dialogue for finding the solution to a problem (*The Statesman* (India), 9 September 2007). Former Secretary of State for Northern Ireland Paul Murphy visited Sri Lanka in 2006, where he announced somewhat oddly that:

> there are striking similarities between Northern Ireland and the Sri Lanka conflict. Firstly and primarily is the loss of life – 3,500 people died in Northern

---

6   On 13 May 2011, George Mitchell resigned as Special Envoy to the Middle East, citing 'personal reasons'. At the same time, unlike in Northern Ireland, there was little to show for the two years he had devoted to the task.

7   As O'Kane (2010: 240) points out, this has not just been confined to Irish commentators or those directly involved in the Northern Ireland peace process such as Blair and Mitchell, but also advocates as diverse as Hillary Clinton and the Pope. The author also analyses the extent to which most of the comparisons to the peace process rest on hope rather than the type of robust model required by political science.

Ireland. In Sri Lanka, 65,000 people have died. Discrimination and human right issues were prevalent during the Northern Ireland conflict, and remain so in the conflict in Sri Lanka. The war absolutely cannot be won by either side. (Reddy 2006)

Murphy's visit followed a meeting in August where Tony Blair discussed with President Mahinda Rajapakse ways in which the UK could support the Sri Lanka peace process (TamilNet 2006).

In the same year, Martin McGuinness, chief negotiator for Sinn Féin in the peace process, who was to become Deputy First Minister a year later, was taken by military helicopter to territory controlled by the Tamil Tigers in Sri Lanka to try to persuade the rebels and the government to return to peace talks. 'I was able to share with the Tamil leadership the experiences of the Irish peace process', he said. 'The reality is that, just as in Ireland, there can be no military victory and that the only alternative to endless conflict is dialogue, negotiations and accommodation' (Huggler 2006).[8]

McGuinness was later involved in the Iraqi situation. In 2007 the US National Democratic Institute brought nine members of the Iraqi Council of Representatives to Belfast to meet Paisley and McGuinness (Baron 2009). There followed a meeting in Finland, co-chaired by Martin McGuinness and former South African government minister Roelf Meyer, with Sunni and Shi'ite leaders from Iraq to discuss non-violence and the peace process. Also present were Democratic Unionist Party (DUP) politician Jeffrey Donaldson, David Alderdice, Billy Hutchinson, a loyalist ex-prisoner, and Mac Maharaj from the African National Congress (ANC). The meeting was arranged by the former Finnish President Martti Ahtisaari's organisation Crisis Management Initiative along with University of Massachusetts Professor Padraig O'Malley, who had previously been involved in similar meetings during the Irish peace process (McKittrick 2007). This was followed by a further meeting in July 2008 when McGuinness travelled to Baghdad to seek to convince the leaders to sign up to an equivalent of the Mitchell Principles (BBC Online 2008b).

One further example reveals the orchestration involved in the selling of Northern Ireland. In 2009, Jonathan Powell, a close adviser to Blair during the Irish peace process, and Sinn Féin's Gerry Kelly met in the Philippines with members of the Moro Islamic Liberation Front (MILF) Central Committee (Kelly 2009). This followed a meeting of four MILF members in Belfast with Kelly in June 2009. This is the sort of contact which would have been grist to the mill for 'terrorologists' at an earlier stage in Northern Ireland (Sterling 1981). But the measure of how far the landscape had changed was that the MILF had come to Belfast in June at the invitation of the British government (Alanto 2009).

---

8   It is worth pointing out that, in this instance at least, the 'lessons from Northern Ireland' message fell on some deaf ears in Sri Lanka. The government subsequently pursued a policy of straightforward military victory over its Tamil opponents. See 'Tamil Tigers admit defeat after battle reaches "bitter end"', *The Times*, 18 May 2009; http://www.timesonline.co.uk/tol/news/world/asia/article6305401.ece [accessed 2 July 2012].

Not everyone was in agreement that the British state had a legitimate product to sell. Bew argues that, beginning as early as 1972, the British had frequently tried to engage republicans in peace talks. The difference in the 1990s was, according to Bew, that the IRA 'only came to the negotiating table after a hugely successful campaign of intelligence and policing forced them to recognise that their military campaign was failing'. The lesson in relation to the exportability of the Irish peace process, Bew argues, is therefore clear: 'There is a great difference in talking to terrorists who are on the crest of a wave and believe they have momentum on their side and talking to those who have been made to realise – by hard power as well as soft power – that their aims are unattainable through violence' (Bew 2009; see also Bew, Frampton and Gurruchaga 2009).

Simon and Stevenson conclude that the comparison between Northern Ireland and Iraq is 'ludicrous' and 'disingenuous'. It falls down on a number of points: the size of the insurgency (500 IRA personnel at any one time versus 30,000 plus insurgents in Iraq), the Iraq insurgents' connection to an international conspiracy compared to the IRA's nationalist revolt, the indigenous support for the state from loyalists in Northern Ireland compared to the absence of such support in Iraq, and the absence of anything approximating stable and legitimate government in Iraq. 'When it comes to Iraq, the appeal of invoking Northern Ireland ... lies in its ability to sustain false hope' (Simon and Stevenson 2007).

The View in the Mirror: The State and Radicalisation

There is an element of continuity in these two phases of the British state's representation of itself in relation to its involvement in Northern Ireland. The common factor is that the state gets to promote its view of things – its centrality in countering insurgency in the first phase and pursuing the peace process in the second. Within this representation, needless to say, it casts itself in a flattering light.

It has to be acknowledged that there is some substance to this trumpet blowing when it comes to the Irish peace process. The commitment of not just the British state, but also the Irish and US states, was indispensible; nowhere is this more obvious than in the final deliberations which led to the Good Friday Agreement, involving as they did Blair, Ahern and Mitchell. There is indeed a tale to tell about how their tenaciousness ensured a number of elements which were key to peace in Northern Ireland, in particular, inclusiveness, and the emergence of a solution to the thorny issue of decommissioning. Undoubtedly there are lessons there for other conflicted or transitional societies.

At the same time, such a tale of success hides the fact that some of the exemplary good practice which emerged only did so after protracted clashes in which the states concerned were not always exemplary. In this sense, the two elements emphasised as the main reason for self-congratulation – inclusiveness and decommissioning – were among those over which most disagreement occurred during the peace process. Inclusiveness came to be central to the peace process and was propagated as being at the core of New Labour's approach, but in practice it took some time for the concept to be established (Breen-Smyth 2008). Thus, in 1996 'all-party' talks took place which excluded Sinn Féin. The party's exclusion was on basis of the lack of decommissioning of arms on the part of the IRA.

Labour's priority after its election in 1997 was to bring the republicans back into the process. To do so, it accepted an earlier suggestion of George Mitchell which had been rejected by the previous Conservative government. Mitchell had proposed a twin-track approach: the issues of decommissioning and peace talks would be separated and each would be negotiated at its own speed. In February 1997 decommissioning became the responsibility of the Independent International Commission on Decommissioning (IICD), headed by John de Chastelain, and the peace process was reinvigorated. The total decommissioning of IRA weapons finally occurred in August 2005.

Told as briefly as this, the story of decommissioning shows Labour in a good light. However, such a shorthand account fails to acknowledge the extent to which Blair's landslide victory gave him a relatively free hand in relation to Northern Ireland, unlike the case with his predecessor John Major, whose narrow parliamentary margin left him highly dependent on unionist MPs in Parliament (Breen-Smyth 2008: 1146–7). Nor were all the obstacles on the road to a solution solely due to Conservative government actions. Thus, it was under Labour Party Secretary of State Peter Mandelson that the devolved arrangements in Northern Ireland were suspended in 2000 on the grounds that there had not been 'sufficient progress' in relation to IRA disarmament. This was despite the fact that at the last minute Sinn Féin claimed that the IRA had made a substantial breakthrough, a claim later acknowledged by John de Chastelain (*The Independent*, 11 February 2000).

But a more telling criticism relates to how little the British state itself appears to have learned from its experience in Northern Ireland. As one theatre closed, another opened; the Northern Ireland conflict was moving towards some solution as the 'war on terror' was opening up. As part of that latter war, the British state has had to manage political Islam, not least within its own borders. In this context much attention was focused on Muslim 'radicalisation'. In attempting to understand this phenomenon, the British state had at least two places to which it could turn for guidance: one was the increasing literature on 'pathways' to terror (McCauley and Moskalenko 2008) and the other was its own experience in Northern Ireland.

Writers on radicalisation, who differ on many points, seem agreed on one: the rejection of simplistic notions of poverty or psychopathology in the explanation of why people turn to terror. Terrorists are not necessarily drawn from the poorest levels in any society (Kimhi and Even 2004: 817; Speckhard and Ahkmedova 2006: 454; Abbas 2007: 111; Brighton 2007: 2), although marginalisation and inequality can be an important element in the creation of a collective condition which can spawn radicalisation (Rehman 2007: 847). Also, although some terrorists may have psychological problems (Kimhi and Even 2004: 819–20), most are motivated by factors which, while often personal, are much more linked to the collective and social dimension than the individualist explanation of psychological disorder would indicate. For example, a major study of Palestinian suicide bombers suggested four types of activists: those motivated by religious belief, those who are vulnerable and are exploited by more powerful groups, those seeking retribution and those inspired by social/nationalist ideology (Kimhi and Even 2004: 817). While psychological factors are central to the exploited and retribution categories, social aspects of motivation explain the religious and the ideologically motivated.

More fundamentally, it is in the interconnection between the personal and the social that the motivation of suicide bombing appears most explicable. Thus, a study of Chechen suicide bombers found that most (82 per cent) were secular prior to a direct experience of trauma affecting them, their family or friends. Violent jihadism was thus a reaction to trauma. Put simply, 'Chechen suicide bombers for the most part are simply traumatized men and women turned misguided warriors, following a jihadist ideology that has taught them this strategy to avenge themselves' (Speckhard and Ahkmedova 2006: 486).

The most sophisticated explanations of radicalisation acknowledge that the phenomenon emerges not from the individual activist but from the dyadic relationship between the individual and the state. For example, there is an acceptance that the state's actions in countering terror, if too severe, can in fact fan the flames of radicalisation. The state can thus cause what it claims to be suppressing, namely an escalation of insurgent violence (Foster 2007). Sometimes this can be done through 'hard power', naked military suppression and sometimes by 'soft power'. A prime case in point is current British counter-terrorism policy and practice.

Following the London bombings of July 2005, the Home Office set up seven working groups under the title PET (Preventing Extremism Together). One of the groups focused on 'tackling extremism and radicalization' and reported with recommendations in autumn 2005. Although the group noted a range of factors which could lead to the radicalisation of British Muslim youth, such as inequality and disapproval of British foreign policy, it concluded that these matters were beyond its brief and focused instead on what it saw as the main reason for the bombers' actions, namely that they were 'inadequately integrated' into British society. According to Brighton, this is a standard flaw in British explanations of radicalisation:

> The issue of foreign policy is raised, its central importance is noted, but little if any account is offered of its relationship with domestic radicalization. Instead, there is a return to the need for 'integration' and by extension for a reworking of the domestic framework of multiculturalism. (2007: 3)

There is, he concludes, a 'retreat to multiculturalism'. This underpinned British policy in relation to Islam. The task is to locate and empower the voices of supposed mainstream Islam as a counterweight to the radicals. The measure of being mainstream is the acceptance of the legitimacy of British social norms and by extension of foreign policy (Brighton 2007: 4). They are bound to the pre-existing state of affairs as a measure of their integration.

According to this view, all Muslims thus fall into one of two opposing categories: the radical and the respectable. Those who do not engage with or are not allowed to engage with the state are judged as a threat, while the others are expected not merely to engage enthusiastically with the state but are also mobilised to isolate the radicals in their midst (Spalek and Imtoual 2007: 196). Similarly, in Germany, radicalisation is said to arise because of a lack of integration with German norms. This lack of integration is seen as an individual failure, not a structural failure. The burden on expectation is on Muslims to integrate, not on the state to facilitate diversity. In this context it is difficult for Muslims to rise above the generalised label of being a national security risk (Dornhof 2009).

Thus, while in the British context the Home Office may tackle radicalisation in part through dealing with disadvantage and engaging in the battle of ideas, it does not and cannot see radicalism as a form of insurgency, arising from a deep sense of injustice felt by many (especially young) Muslims, coupled with the sense of collective identity and collective agency which radical Islam can offer (Githens-Mazer 2008: 555). The state's refusal to acknowledge the effects of foreign policy, especially in the Middle East and Afghanistan, on young British Muslims is particularly noteworthy. The present coalition government's re-launch of the Prevent anti-radicalisation strategy has only four references to British foreign policy in a 113-page document (HM Government 2011; see also Kundnani 2009).

And behind all of this 'soft power' there is of course 'hard power': stop and search, profiling, deportation of 'suspects', house arrest, extraordinary rendition, torture, indefinite detention, etc. (Brittain 2009; Hizb ut-Tahrir 2007) – in short, the treatment of wide swathes of the Muslim population of Britain as a 'suspect community' (Hillyard 1993; Ansari 2006; Pantazis and Pemberton 2009; Hickman et al. 2011).

The British state has copious prior experience in dealing with the radicalisation in Ireland. Thus, there is ample evidence of community intervention as a tool of counter-insurgency. While it is possible to exaggerate the direct influence of Brigadier Kitson's strategy of counter-insurgency in Northern Ireland (Faligot 1983), it is undeniable that the logic at the heart of that strategy matched closely what he advised at an early stage in the conflict. For Kitson, in a guerrilla situation, the first target must be the disorientation of the community because it is the community which harbours the guerrilla. Naked force can be counter-productive. As such, the army must involve itself in community work in order to disorient the community (McGuffin 1974: 144–5; Rolston 1975). The army must have control of community work at central and local levels. As a result of coordination, the army can, and in Northern Ireland tried to, recommend only 'good' groups for grant aid, and thus divided the community; for the 'bad' groups not only would not receive help, but would come to resent the 'good' groups for receiving it (Kitson 1971: 32). A similar policy was enacted by the Northern Ireland Office in the late 1980s and early 1990s: 'political vetting', whereby funds for community development were denied to groups with alleged connections to republicans and were channelled instead through 'respectable' organisations, especially the Catholic Church (Rolston 1990).

Direct intervention in the community was also practised. In the 1970s the British army received 100 per cent grants under Social Needs legislation (the equivalent of Urban Needs legislation in England) for 'community work'. This included at one point Operation Wham – Win Hearts and Minds – which was at once a public relations and intelligence-gathering exercise. Similar purposes were at the heart of the RUC's community involvement. In 1980 the RUC claimed to have worked with 1,061 teenagers in 35 separate four- to seven-day camping expeditions; 1,366 teenagers in 76 separate weekend camps; and to have run 1,281 Blue Lamp Discos with 185,000 teenagers in attendance, the 'Top of the Form' Quiz League in secondary and grammar schools, and 546 Blue Lamp Football League matches (Belfast Bulletin 1982: 14). Their involvement in community recreational provision for teenagers continued into the 1990s (Ellison 2000).[9]

The British state cannot claim ignorance of the reasons for the radicalisation of Irish youth, despite the sustained campaign in the 1970s to deny political motivation to offenders and to label them simply as criminals (Campbell, McKeown and O'Hagan 1994). For a start, many commentators have noted the youth of Irish combatants, especially on the republican side. For example, in 1975, 70 per cent of republicans prosecuted were under 21 years old. In 1979, it was 53 per cent (Alonso 2003: 9). Another study found that almost 70 per cent of republican ex-prisoners had been jailed first between the ages of 16 and 20; for loyalists the figure was 30 per cent (Shirlow and McEvoy 2008: 79). Furthermore, it is known that the level of political sophistication of such young prisoners was not high when they first entered prison. So the question which follows is: why did they join insurgent or pro-state paramilitary groups in the first instance?

Campbell and Connolly (2006: 947) interviewed 16 republican ex-prisoners and found two clusters of reasons for involvement. The first related to personal experiences of repression from childhood onwards, such as house raids and stop and search. The second centred on the experience of repression inflicted on the group with which the respondent identified; the most notable events mentioned were Bloody Sunday (1972) and the republican hunger strikes (1981).

Hamber (2005: 24), who interviewed 21 ex-prisoners from Derry who had been on the no-wash protest[10] in the late 1970s, adds two other factors: first, joining was due to family connections and traditions; and, second, it was a normal occurrence in the community where they lived; joining the IRA was a 'natural process of development'.

Not every young man in Derry joined up, but the experience of one illustrates the importance of state actions in the radicalisation of a whole generation. Don Mullan was a 15-year-old boy who witnessed the British army massacre of civil rights protesters in Derry in 1972:

---

9   On the reluctance of young Muslims to participate in similar contemporary Prevent programmes in the UK, see Breen-Smyth (2010).
10   In the early 1970s, politically motivated prisoners in Northern Ireland had what was termed special category status. As a result, for example, they were not required to wear a prison uniform. That policy was changed in the mid-1970s, when eventually hundreds of republican prisoners refused to wear the uniform, then dressed only in towels or blankets. When, in an escalation of the confrontation, prison authorities decreed that they could not leave their cells to wash or go to the toilet without a uniform, they did not wash and were left with no option to wipe their excrement on the walls in a bid to dry it out and thus reduce the possibility of disease. See Campbell, McKeown and O'Hagan 1994.

Bloody Sunday was the beginning of the end of British colonialism in my heart and soul. Henceforth, whenever I looked at the Union Jack flying in Ireland, it became symbolic of one abiding memory of that day: our blue-and-white civil rights banner stained by the blood of Barney McGuigan. Any faint hope of purchasing my loyalty to the British Crown through superficial reforms died on that day. My identity became sharply focused. I am Irish, not Northern Irish. Partition had failed forever. (Mullan 1999: 41)

To some extent there is a similar story on the loyalist side. Crawford (1999) interviewed 50 loyalist ex-prisoners who provided a range of reasons for joining armed groups. They had experienced the killing of a family member (30 per cent) or friend (90 per cent), or were reacting to various incidents where the IRA had killed large numbers of unionists – for example, Bloody Friday (1972), when 22 bombs exploded in Belfast, or the bombing of the La Mon House Hotel in 1978. More generally, they had a political motivation; they believed they were advancing the cause, defending the community, defending the constitution, bringing the war to republicans and terrorising the nationalist community in order to have them give up support for the IRA; in fact, loyalist violence had the opposite effect, reinforcing the nationalist community view of the IRA as protectors.

The British state's subsequent reaction to radicalisation was to compound the problem. The outlets for political expression by republicans were increasingly closed down, culminating most spectacularly in the broadcasting ban between 1988 and 1994, whereby the actual words of spokespersons for Sinn Féin (and a number of other, smaller organisations) were banned from the airwaves (Moloney 1991). The irony was that within four years of the ending of the ban, leading Sinn Féin member Martin McGuinness was Minister for Education in Northern Ireland, and nine years after that became Deputy First Minister. Prior to this, however, British policy was in effect an outright denial of rational political agency on the part of republican opponents of the state. The dominant political response deemed appropriate by the British state was therefore one of 'hard power' in the form of counter-insurgency, mass imprisonment,[11] suspension of major elements of the rule of law and on occasion unlawful killing – the end result of which was the creation of a suspect community out of Irish nationalists. In this respect, there was no distinction drawn between criticism of state policy and actions and outright insurrection; criticism of the state and its actions, even if it was not armed, was regarded as 'playing into the hands of terrorists'. At the very least, such an approach alienated the very communities the state needed to work with if it was to encourage systemic change (Campaign on the Administration of Justice 2008: 102).

It took a long time for the British state to acknowledge officially that the insurgency in Ireland had political roots and that consequently any hope of solution had to be in the political rather than the military sphere. Accepting the primacy of politics leads inexorably to conceding the rational political agency of one's

---

11   A minimum of 10,000 republicans and 5,000 loyalists were imprisoned during the 30-year conflict. See Rolston 2007.

opponents, talking to those opponents and ultimately seeking to engage with those opponents in political institutions. If this sounds remarkably like a description of the peace process of the late 1990s in Northern Ireland, it has to be remembered that in the longer view the conversion of the British state to this viewpoint was at least as miraculous as that of the IRA.

Conclusion

On 15 June 2010, the Saville Report – 12 years in the making and running to 5,000 pages – into the deaths of 14 civil rights marchers in Derry on 30 January 1972 at the hands of British paratroopers was published. Saville concluded:

> The immediate responsibility for the deaths and injuries on Bloody Sunday lies with those members of Support Company whose unjustifiable firing was the cause of those deaths and injuries ... none of the casualties was posing a threat of causing death or serious injury, or indeed was doing anything else that could on any view justify their shooting. (Saville Report 2010: vol. 1, chapter 4, section 1 and vol. 1, chapter 3, section 79)

Speaking to the Report on the same day in the House of Commons, British Prime Minister David Cameron was astonishingly hard-hitting.

> the conclusion of this report are absolutely clear. There is no doubt. There is nothing equivocal. There are no ambiguities. What happened on Bloody Sunday was both unjustified and unjustifiable. It was wrong ... on behalf of the government – and indeed our country – I am deeply sorry ... this report and the inquiry itself demonstrate how a state should hold itself to account and how we are determined at all times – no matter how difficult – to judge ourselves against the highest standards.[12]

This is not the place to wonder how history would have been different if this, instead of the findings of the official Widgery Tribunal, had been the conclusion drawn 38 years previously, but it is to say that states, like large oil tankers, can only turn very slowly.

What the British state did for many years in managing the Northern Ireland problem arguably not only did not end the conflict but in fact prolonged it. This is not necessarily a message that the British state is likely to broadcast internationally in a period when it is seen as central to conflict resolution in Northern Ireland. It would require a level of honesty and self-criticism which few contemporary states possess, but it would be a powerful alternative message to promulgate. It would

---

12 *Hansard*, 15 June 2010; http://www.publications.parliament.uk/pa/cm201011/cmhansrd/cm100615/debtext/100615-0004.htm#10061522000002 [accessed 2 July 2012].

raise questions which the British state did not ask itself at the height of the Irish conflict; more tellingly, the state resisted answering those questions when they were asked by others.

One such question relates to the timing of talking to armed activists. This was resisted for many years in Northern Ireland and denied by the British Prime Minister John Major even as secret talks were in progress.[13] And it is a question which became more difficult after 9/11 and the escalation of the 'war on terror'. Yet it is a question which raises its head and which must be answered in the interests of conflict transformation (see, for example, Perry 2010). Similarly, questions must be asked about the rational basis of the motivation of those who oppose the state. Their beliefs cannot simply be dismissed as irrational. The state's role in perpetuating the terrorism which it claims to oppose is also a difficult issue facing those in power, yet it is a timely question not least in relation to the actions of the Israeli state. These are questions which an understanding of the history of recent conflict in Ireland can help answer. There is no single blueprint, no magic formula in the Irish situation which can be simply read across as a solution for other violent conflicts. At the same time, there are lessons which are there for those who know how to read them.

References

Abbas, T. (2007) 'A theory of Islamic political radicalism in Britain: sociology, theology and international political economy', *Contemporary Islam* 1: 109–22.

Alanto, M. (2009) 'The Belfast Agreement: a lesson in political maturity', 10 July, http://www.luwaran.com/index.php?option=com_content&view=article&id=849:the-belfastagreement-a-lesson-in-political-maturity&catid=60:maulana-bobby-alonto&Itemid=346 [accessed 24 September 2009].

Alonso, R. (2003) *The IRA and Armed Struggle*. New York: Routledge.

Ansari, F. (2006) *British Anti-Terrorism: A Modern Day Witch-hunt*. London: Islamic Human Rights Commission.

Aylwin-Foster, N. (2005) 'Changing the army for counterinsurgency operations', *Military Review*, November–December: 2-15; http://www.scribd.com/doc/8593846/Changing-the-Army-for-Counterinsurgency-Operations-By-Brigadier-Nigel-Foster-British-Army [accessed 2 July 2012].

Baron, K. (2009) '"Divided Cities" leaders to gather, advise Iraqis', *Stars and Stripes*, 21 March.

BBC Online (2005), 'Ex-RUC head to review Iraq police', 4 December, http://news.bbc.co.uk/1/hi/northern_ireland/4497128.stm [accessed 2 July 2012].

BBC Online (2008a) 'Service for Troubles soldiers', 10 September, http://news.bbc.co.uk/1/hi/northern_ireland/7607360.stm [accessed 2 July 2012].

---

13 In November 1993 in the House of Commons, John Major stated that talking to Sinn Féin would turn his stomach. It quickly emerged that his government had been doing precisely that for some time. See Miller and McLaughlin 1996.

BBC Online (2008b) 'Iraq talks possibly in Ireland', 7 July, http://news.bbc.co.uk/1/hi/northern_ireland/7489785.stm [accessed 2 July 2012].
Beaumont, P. (2006) 'How the British Army's capture of hearts and minds turned sour', *The Observer*, 12 February.
Belfast Bulletin (1982) *The Law in Northern Ireland*. Belfast: Workers' Research Unit.
Bew, J. (2009) 'Talking to the Taliban: lessons from Northern Ireland', *History and Policy*, 29 July, http://www.historyandpolicy.org/opinion/opinion_12.html [accessed 2 July 2012].
Bew, J., Frampton, M. and Gurruchaga, I. (2009) *Talking to Terrorists: Making Peace in Northern Ireland and the Basque Country*. London: Hurst.
Boyle, K., Hadden, T. and Hillyard, P. (1983) *Law and State: The Case of Northern Ireland*. London: Martin Robertson.
Breen-Smyth, M. (2008) 'Frameworks for peace in Northern Ireland; an analysis of the 1998 Belfast Agreement', *Strategic Analysis* 32(6): 1–23.
Breen-Smyth, M. (2010) 'Between intelligence-gathering and social engineering: can government legitimately mingle its social interventions with intelligence-gathering, as the UK's Prevent counter-terrorism strategy stands accused of doing?', Royal United Services Institute Analysis Online, http://www.rusi.org/analysis/commentary/ref:C4AE8359535743/ [accessed 2 July 2012].
Brighton, S. (2007) 'British Muslims, multiculturalism and UK foreign policy: "integration" and "cohesion" in and beyond the state', *International Affairs* 83(1): 1–17.
Brittain, V. (2009) 'Besieged in Britain', *Race and Class* 50(3): 1–29.
Campaign on the Administration of Justice (2008) *War on Terror: Lessons from Northern Ireland*. Belfast: CAJ.
Campbell, B., McKeown, L. and O'Hagan, F. (1994) *Nor Meekly Serve My Time*. Belfast: Beyond the Pale Publications.
Campbell, C. and Connolly, I. (2006) 'Making war on terror? Global lessons from Northern Ireland', *Modern Law Review* 69(6): 935–57.
Cochrane, F. (2007) 'Irish-America, the end of the IRA's armed struggle and the utility of "soft power"', *Journal of Peace Research* 44(2): 215–31.
Crawford, C. (1999) *Defenders or Criminals? Loyalist Prisoners and Criminalisation*. Belfast: Blackstaff Press.
Criminal Justice Inspection Northern Ireland (2007) *Hate Crime in Northern Ireland: A Thematic Inspection of the Management of Hate Crime by the Criminal Justice System in Northern Ireland*. Belfast: Criminal Justice Inspection Northern Ireland.
DFA (Department of Foreign Affairs) (2009) 'Lesson-sharing', http://www.dfa.ie/home/index.aspx?id=82474 [accessed 2 July 2012].
Dornhof, S. (2009) 'Germany: constructing a sociology of Islamist radicalisation', *Race and Class* 50(4): 75–82.
Ellison, G. (2000) 'Reflecting all shades of opinion', *British Journal of Criminology* 40(1): 88–111.
Ellison, G. and O'Reilly, C. (2008) 'From empire to Iraq and the "war on terror": the transplantation and commodification of the (Northern) Irish policing experience', *Police Quarterly* 11(4): 395–426.

English, R. (2009) *Terrorism: How to Respond*. Oxford: Oxford University Press.
Evrony, Z. (2010) 'From Ireland to Israel', *New York Times*, 5 March.
Faligot, R. (1983) *Britain's Military Strategy in Ireland: The Kitson Experiment*. London: Zed Books.
Foster, D. (2007) 'The "Balancing Act": counterterrorism and domestic overreaction in democratic states', Paper presented at International Studies Annual Convention, Chicago, 2 March, http://citation.allacademic.com/meta/p_mla_apa_research_citation/1/8/1/5/4/pages181548/p181548-1.php [accessed 1 July 2012].
Freedland, J. (2009) 'Amid the horror and doom of Gaza, the IRA precedent offers hope', *The Guardian*, 14 January.
Gannon, S. (2009) 'Resist the Irish model', *Jerusalem Post*, 2 May.
Githens-Mazer, J. (2008) 'Islamic radicalisation among North Africans in Britain', *British Journal of Politics and International Relations* 10: 350–370.
Guelke, A. (2008) 'The lure of the miracle? The South African connection and the Northern Ireland peace process', in C. Farrington (ed.), *Global Change, Civil Society and the Northern Ireland Peace Process: Implementing the Political Settlement*. London: Palgrave Macmillan, 73–90.
Guelke, A., Cox, M. and Stephen, F. (2000) *A Farewell to Arms: From 'Long War' to Long Peace in Northern Ireland*. London: Macmillan.
Hamber, B. (2005) *Blocks to the Future: An Independent Report into the Psychological Impact of the 'No Wash Blanket' Prison Protest*. Derry, Cunamh.
Harwood, J., Guinness, J. and Biggs-Davison, J. (1970) *Ireland: Our Cuba?* London: Monday Club.
Hickman, M., Thomas, L., Silvestri, S. and Nickels, H. (2011) *'Suspect Communities'? Counterterrorism Policy, the Press, and the impact on Irish and Muslim Communities in Britain*. London: Institute for the Study of European Transformations, London Metropolitan University.
Hillyard, P. (1993) *Suspect Community*. London: Pluto Press.
Hizb ut-Tahrir (2007) *Radicalisation, Extremism and 'Islamism': Realities and Myths in the 'War on Terror*. London: Hizb ut-Tahrir.
HM Government (2011) *Prevent Strategy*. Cm 8092. London: The Stationery Office.
Huggler, J. (2006) 'McGuinness on peace mission to Sri Lanka', *The Independent*, 5 July.
Kelley, K. (1982) *The Longest War: Northern Ireland and the IRA*. Dingle: Brandon.
Kelly, G. (2009) 'Building peace in the Philippines', *An Phoblacht*, 29 January.
Kimhi, S. and Even, S. (2004) 'Who are the Palestinian suicide bombers?', *Terrorism and Political Violence* 16(4): 815–40.
Kitson, F. (1971) *Low Intensity Operations: Subversion, Insurgency and Counter Insurgency*. London: Faber.
Kundnani, A. (2009) *Spooked! How Not to Prevent Violent Extremism*. London: Institute of Race Relations.
McCauley, C. and Moskalenko, S. (2008) 'Mechanisms of political radicalization: pathways toward terrorism', *Terrorism and Political Violence* 20: 415–33.
McGuffin, J. (1974) *The Guinea Pigs*. Harmondsworth: Penguin.

McKittrick, D. (2007) 'Conquering sectarianism: can Ulster be a model for Iraq?', *The Independent*, 5 September.
McNamara, K. (2009) *The MacBride Principles: Irish America Strikes Back*. Liverpool: Liverpool University Press.
Macpherson Report (1999) *The Stephen Lawrence Inquiry: Report of an Inquiry by Sir William Macpherson of Cluny*, Cm 4262-I. London: The.Stationery Office.
Mansoor, P. (2008) *Baghdad at Sunrise, a Brigade Commander's War in Iraq*. New Haven, CT: Yale University Press; cited in (2009) *Canadian Army Journal* 12(1): 144.
Marks, S. (1995) 'Civil liberties at the margin: the UK derogation and the European Court of Human Rights', *Oxford Journal of Legal Studies* 15(1): 69–95.
Miller, D. (1993) *Getting the Message*. London: Routledge.
Miller, D. and McLaughlin, M. (1996) 'The media politics of the peace in Ireland', *Harvard International Journal of Press/Politics* 1(4): 116–34.
Mitchell, G. and Haass, R. (2007) 'Irish lessons for peace', *International Herald Tribune*, 15 May.
Moloney, E. (1991) 'Closing down the airwaves: the story of the broadcasting ban', in B. Rolston (ed.), *The Media and Northern Ireland: Covering the Troubles*. London: Macmillan, 8–50.
Moloney, E. (2002) *A Secret History of the IRA*. New York: Norton.
Mowbray, A. (2007) *Cases and Material on the European Convention on Human Rights*. Oxford University Press, 77–93.
Mulcahy, A. (1995) 'Claims-making and the construction of legitimacy: press coverage of the 1981 Northern Irish hunger strike', *Social Problems* 42(4): 449–67.
Mullan, D. (1999) 'Blood, white and blue', in Trisha Ziff (ed.), *Hidden Truths: Bloody Sunday 1972*. Santa Monica, CA: Smart Art Press.
Newsinger, J. (1995) 'British security policy in Northern Ireland', *Race and Class* 37(1): 83–94.
Northern Ireland Assembly Debates (2009) http://archive.niassembly.gov.uk/record/reports2008/090629.pdf, 29 June, p. 279 [accessed 1 July 2012].
Northern Ireland Information Service press release (1988), 13 May.
Norton-Taylor, R. and McCarthy, R. (2003) 'British military critical of US troops' heavy-handed style with civilians', *The Guardian*, 1 April.
O'Kane, E. (2010) 'Learning from Northern Ireland? The uses and abuses of the Irish "model"', *British Journal of Politics and International Relations* 12: 239–56.
Pantazis, C. and Pemberton, S. (2009) 'From the "old" to the "new" suspect community: examining the impacts of recent UK counter-terrorist legislation', *British Journal of Criminology* 49: 646–66.
Pat Finucane Centre (2004) 'Aegis Defence Services, Lt Col Tim Spicer and the murder of Peter McBride track record of British mercenary uutfit in Iraq', http://www.globalresearch.ca/index.php?context=va&aid=1399 [accessed 2 July 2012].
Patten Report (1999) *A New Beginning. Independent Commission on Policing for Northern Ireland*. London: Independent Commission on Policing for Northern Ireland.
Perry, M. (2010) *Talking to Terrorists: Why America Must Engage with its Enemies*. New York: Basic Books.

PSNI/Police Service of Northern Ireland (2008) 'Assistant Chief Constable Duncan McCausland OBE', http://www.psni.police.uk/index/aboutus/senior_officer_profiles/about_assistant_chief_constable_duncan_mccausland_obe_criminal_justice_department_.htm [accessed 1 July 2012].

Quinn, K. (2004) 'Policing the new Iraq – how the PSNI are leading the way', *Newsletter*, 4 August.

Rayment, S. (2007) 'Iraq war was badly planned, says army', *Daily Telegraph*, 5 November.

Reddy, B. (2006) 'Sri Lanka peace process needs to be inclusive', *The Hindu*, 17 November.

Rehman, J. (2007) 'Islam, "war on terror" and the future of Muslim minorities in the United Kingdom', *Human Rights Quarterly* 29(4): 831–78.

Rolston, B. (1975) 'Iron fists, kid gloves', *Case Con* 20: 25–6.

Rolston, B. (1990) 'Political vetting: an overview', in *Political Vetting of Community Work Group, The Political Vetting of Community Work in Northern Ireland*. Belfast: Northern Ireland Council for Voluntary Action, 3–12.

Rolston, B. (1991) 'Containment and its failure: the British state and the control of conflict in Northern Ireland', in Alexander George (ed.), *Western State Terrorism*. Oxford, Polity Press, 155–79.

Rolston, B. (2005) '"An effective mask for terror": democracy, death squads and Northern Ireland', *Crime, Law and Social Change* 44(2): 181–203.

Rolston, B. (2007) 'Demobilisation and reintegration of ex-combatants: the Irish case in international perspective', *Social and Legal Studies* 16(2): 259–80.

RUSI (Royal United Services Institute) (2007) *'Hearts and Minds': British Counter-Insurgency from Malaya to Iraq*, http://rusi.org/go.php?structureID=S4332E5804C30C&ref=E466804A9E83DD [accessed 2 July 2012].

Saville Report (2010) *Report of the Bloody Sunday Inquiry*. London: The Stationery Office, HC 29-I – HC 29-X, Volumes 1–10. http://www.bloody-sunday-inquiry.org [accessed 2 July 2012].

Scarborough, R. (2006) 'Northern Ireland holds Iraq lessons', *Washington Times*, 23 October.

Shirlow, P. and McEvoy, K. (2008) *Beyond the Wire: Former Prisoners and Conflict Transformation in Northern Ireland*. London: Pluto Press.

Simon, S. and Stevenson, J. (2007) 'Northern Ireland's arch irrelevance', *The American Prospect*, 25 July.

Sluka, J. (ed.) (1999) *Death Squad: The Anthropology of State Terror*. Philadelphia: University of Pennsylvania Press.

Spalek, B. and Imtoual, A. (2007) 'Muslim communities and counter-terror responses: "hard" approaches to community engagement in the UK and Australia', *Journal of Muslim Minority Affairs* 27(2): 185–202.

Speckhard, A. and Ahkmedova, K. (2006) 'The making of a martyr: Chechen suicide terrorism', *Studies in Conflict and Terrorism* 29: 429–92.

Stalker, J. (1988) *The Stalker Affair*. London: Penguin.

Sterling, C. (1981) *The Terror Network*. London: Weidenfeld & Nicolson.

TamilNet (2006) 'Northern Ireland peacemaker to visit Sri Lanka this week', 13 November; http://www.tamilnet.com/art.html?catid=13&artid=20258 [accessed 2 July 2012].

Toolis, K. (2003) 'Iraq will be Blair's Northern Ireland', *New Statesman*, 20 October, 31–2.

Von Tangen Page, M. (1996) 'The inter-relationship of the press and politicians during the 1981 hunger strike at the Maze Prison', in P. Catterall and S. McDougall (eds), *The Northern Ireland Question in British Politics*. London: Macmillan, 162–73.

Political Violence and Peace Processes

Roger Mac Ginty

Introduction

The relationship between political violence and peacemaking processes in civil war contexts is close and complex. The peace process may be a reaction to the level of violence and may expressly aim to lower the cost of that violence. The process may spark a violent reaction, often termed 'spoiler violence', which may attempt to derail efforts to reach an accommodation. Violence during a peace process may even act as a spur to those at the negotiating table and intensify their efforts to strike an accord. A peace process may also create a space in which other forms of violence, for example, crime or the illicit trading of weapons or people, may take place or gain new prominence. For the purposes of this chapter, a peace process is regarded as a sustained attempt by the main actors in a violent conflict to reach some sort of negotiated outcome (Darby and Mac Ginty, 2008: 2–4). The peace process may become conflict by other means and the parties to it may be seeking very different political outcomes (Richmond 1998: 707–22). In some circumstances, they may reach a mutual understanding that the peace process can be a vehicle through which they can reduce the costs of the conflict and attain some of their political or economic goals. A peace accord and programme of implementation, perhaps overseen by third parties, may follow. This chapter seeks to outline the different forms that political violence takes during peacemaking processes. Following a brief conceptual discussion on the nature of violence in peace processes, it concentrates on three issues: the relationship between violence, ceasefires and peace processes; spoiler violence; and crime during and after peace processes.

It is worth noting that the international context shaped by the war on terror has helped embolden a number of states to seek military outcomes to conflicts. As a result, some states have not seriously investigated the options for negotiated settlements. In the 1990s, some peace processes were characterised by inclusiveness and seemingly endless patience with armed non-state actors. In more recent years, a number of states have favoured a more coercive model of peacemaking. Sri Lanka, India, Russia, Colombia, Spain, Israel, Pakistan, Thailand and the Philippines have used hard security measures in efforts to militarily defeat separatist or identity groups within or adjacent to their territory. In a number of cases, these security-first approaches have been encouraged by large powers which themselves have been engaged in security-first adventurism in Iraq, Afghanistan and elsewhere. The key point is that the international environment has increasingly legitimised state and official violence and has downgraded the importance of negotiated outcomes if these are seen to contradict the security imperative.

Parties may also seek to precede attempts to reach a peace settlement with strategic violence. They may seek to gain an advantageous battlefield or security situation prior to engaging in peace initiatives. Guelke (2008: 63) notes how South Africa sought to use this 'negotiation from strength' or 'thump and talk' strategy in the 1980s. This combination of coercion with negotiation illustrates that it is useful to be cautious when attempting to separate violence from peace processes. The close bonds between the two mean that it is useful to see them on the same continuum rather than existing in separate spheres.

Conceptualising Violence in Peace Processes

Six points are worth making to help conceptualise the types and role of violence in peace processes. The first point is to underline how political violence is context-specific and so we must take care in generalising between cases. A near-limitless range of factors combine to create specific environments in which certain types of violence take place. Crucial here are the social-moral frameworks in operation in particular conflicts and how they may help deem certain types of violent activity and targets as acceptable or non-acceptable. So, for example, civilians or places of worship might be regarded as legitimate targets in one context, but 'off limits' in another. While there may be codification of such rules through the 'laws of war' and intricate debates on proportionality, just war theory and pre-emption, much comes down to expediency or the calculation by combatants that they can pursue a course of action with limited censure or cost (Evans, 2005: 5). Important too are the range of prosaic factors that determine the capability of antagonists to inflict and withstand violence: weather and topography; access to weaponry and the technological sophistication of that weaponry; public support; external support, including that of a diaspora; international tolerance of armed non-state actors; the effectiveness of the state in countering armed non-state actors; and the ability of states and their opponents to hold territory. The main point is that each conflict is attended by a peculiar set of circumstances that facilitate and restrict certain types of violent behaviour.

A second conceptual factor concerns the tendency of political violence to be fluid. Even protracted conflicts rarely conform to the 'stalemate' cliché favoured in some journalistic accounts of civil wars. Instead, the types and intensity of violence will change with circumstances and capability. The potential and real costs of political violence mean that individuals, groups and institutions adopt a mix of reactive and proactive strategies to protect themselves, maximise gains and attempt to diminish opportunities for their opponents. For example, antagonists may have to switch from previously successful roadside bombs when they find their opponent has developed a counter-measure. Thus conflicts develop, as antagonists change tactics and seek new vulnerabilities. The fluidity of political violence may also reflect a conflict with multiple actors. Rather than a simple state versus insurgent dyadic conflict, a conflict might involve a state with multiple competing law-enforcement agencies, a number of external parties and several insurgent groups, each with different sub-motives, leaderships, political platforms and capabilities. The result might be an extremely complex situation with much fluidity. Matters might be complicated still further in that violent actors may be infiltrated by their opponents or operating as double agents. It is worth conceptualising violent conflicts in terms of 'variable geometry', with multiple actors operating in multiple spheres. No actor is likely to have anything approaching full knowledge. In the peculiar context of a peace process, in which there is potential for substantial political, economic, security and social upheaval, political violence actors may seek to modulate their activities as a reaction to real or perceived change.

Third, political violence during peace processes is usually instrumentalist. Although it may be reported as 'senseless' or 'random', it attempts to effect some form of change or response. Given the political context of a peace process and the potential for major change, the instrumentalist nature of the violence may become more urgent. In a sense, political violence may become more political during a peace process. Yet the outcomes that combatants seek from violent acts may not always be apparent. Violent actors may have multiple target audiences: the direct victims of the attack, the media who will report it, state forces who will react to it, support constituencies, rival political and militant groups within their own side, etc. Interpreting the precedence of these audiences (i.e. those who are the primary and secondary targets, and what the perpetrators want to achieve in relation to each target audience) is a difficult task. Adding to this difficulty, the antennae of many political actors may be poorly 'tuned' and unable to interpret the intentions of the perpetrators of violence. David Keen (2008: 15) notes how many orthodox analyses of civil wars are guilty of 'a neglect of local agendas, an overemphasis on ideological motivations and on fixed identities among the warring parties, and an adoption of overly rigid distinctions between combatants and non-combatants'. The interpretive tools one uses will determine the conflict that is seen. For example, if one side in a conflict uses the shrill discourse of 'terrorism' to interpret the actions of their opponents and categorises the world into simplistic them/us, good/bad categories, then they are unlikely to be able to recognise the nuances in violence. This lack of awareness may be especially limiting in the context of a peace process in which violent actors may modulate and calibrate their activities quite precisely to react to events within a talks chamber. Clumsy lenses like 'terrorism' or 'security' are likely to lead to predictable and not very illuminating analyses of violence.

Fourth, violence in peace processes is not always effective in terms of political outcomes. A peace process may have too much momentum, be supported by too many external and internal actors, and have too much legitimacy to be seriously impacted by some types and levels of violence. This can make the violence appear all the more pathetic; serious harm can be caused to individuals, groups and inter-group perceptions, but the impact on the meta-level peace process may well be negligible. In South Africa, a right-wing extremist assassinated Chris Hani, the leader of the South African Communist Party and a prominent figure in the movement to overturn authoritarianism, in March 1993. The murder occurred at a delicate time in the South African transition, and although it caused an increase in tension and civil unrest, it did not derail the transition process (Höglund, 2004: 25). Similarly, the political impact of violence by republican 'dissidents' in post-Belfast Agreement Northern Ireland has largely been contained.

A final conceptual point is to underline the role of structural or indirect violence in peace processes. One of the remarkable features of contemporary civil war is the extent to which direct violence is often limited to certain geographical areas, gender, age and socio-economic groups, and particular individuals that Tilly refers to as 'violence specialists' (2002: 20). In parts of Sri Lanka, the UK, Israel, Colombia, Uganda and India, selected classes have been able to live virtually unaffected by vicious conflicts occurring only a few hundred miles away. Shaw and Mbabazi (2009) identified 'two Ugandas': one in the south a model African developmental state that was increasingly connected with the global economy, and the other in the north mired in a civil war between the state and the Lord's Resistance Army. Beyond the mass-level violence of genocide and ethnic cleansing, many people in civil war contexts experience direct violence episodically or by proxy. A more typical experience of civil war might involve extended periods of political tension, harassment from state or non-state forces, a sense of grievance or marginalisation, discrimination in relation to resources and the denial of life opportunities as a result of the potential of direct violence to break out. While indirect violence may not inflict physical harm, it retains enormous capacity to shape political, social, economic and cultural life. Many peace processes concentrate (for understandable reasons) on containing direct violence (through, for example, ceasefires and disarmament programmes). Attention towards indirect violence, which might be regarded as somehow 'ancillary' or secondary, may be less pressing.

The chief point is the need to see the totality of conflict and violence in civil wars. David Keen advises that:

> Rather than listing the causes of war or famine and rather than portraying war as fundamentally irrational or as an aberration or interruption, it would be more helpful to investigate how violence is generated by particular patterns of development, by particular political economies which violence in turns modifies (but does not destroy). Indeed, part of the problem in much existing analysis is that conflict is regarded as, simply, a breakdown in a particular system, rather than as the emergence of another, alternative system of profit, power, and even protection. Yet events, however horrible and catastrophic, are actually produced, they are made to happen by a diverse and complicated set of actors who may well be achieving their objectives in the midst of what looks like failure and breakdown. (2008: 14–15)

The task for this chapter is to explain how political violence shapes, and is shaped by, peacemaking processes in civil war contexts.

Ceasefires and Peace Processes

A ceasefire is a common precondition for the beginning of formal negotiations between adversaries. Secret pre-negotiations may take place while violence continues, but it is very rare for formal negotiations to get under way while violence continues unabated. At a minimum, the ceasefire provides the physical security for delegates to attend talks. More substantively, a ceasefire is a confidence-building measure, signalling the trustworthiness of parties as partners in a peace process: if parties can be trusted to maintain a ceasefire over the short term, then they may be trusted on more complex issues over the longer term (Kriesberg, 2005: 80). It may also contribute to an atmosphere in which delicate negotiations can take place without negotiators feeling that they have to react to the last outrage (Egeland, 1999: 538–9). A sustained ceasefire may assist a period of 'normalisation' through which states, armed groups and communities become used to the absence of direct violence, and so become supportive of the benefits that a sustained peace process may bring. Ceasefires usually involve an element of mutuality, either with parties agreeing to cease hostilities against each other or one party (a state) recognising a ceasefire by a non-state armed actor. Right-wing Spanish governments, however, have declined to recognise unilateral ceasefires from the Basque separatist group ETA (Euskadi Ta Askatasuna/Basque Homeland and Freedom) as they believe that such a move would legitimise a group they regard as 'criminal'.

Ceasefires require discipline, something that may be in short supply in conflicts with multiple actors or in which antagonists are loosely organised and have little central control. There were repeated failures of ceasefires in the Lebanese civil war to the extent that the whole notion of ceasefires became devalued. In some cases, ceasefires and the promise of a peace process have provided a cover for antagonists to re-arm and continue the conflict. Notionally, the Sri Lankan government and the separatist LTTE (Liberation Tigers of Tamil Eelam) were on ceasefire between 2000 and 2008. For a time, the ceasefire was relatively well observed, with a Norwegian-led team monitoring alleged breaches and preliminary high-level negotiations underway between both sides. When peace talks stalled (in late 2003), both sides engaged in violence, with this violence reaching very substantial proportions. Yet the fiction of a ceasefire was maintained. Both sides were happy to reap the benefits that a stalled peace process brought them: an opportunity to attract international legitimacy and assistance, as well as an opportunity to re-arm. When the government revoked the ceasefire in January 2008 and launched what would ultimately become a victorious military offensive against the LTTE, it became clear that it had used the ceasefire interregnum most effectively. The Sri Lankan army had been re-equipped and re-trained, with foreign assistance, and had the qualitative (mainly technological) edge on its opponent.

Inter-group suspicions may be so chronic, especially in protracted conflicts, that immense weight is placed on the observance of ceasefires. This should not be surprising given the enmity between antagonists and the discourses used by political and military leaders which dehumanise and delegitimise their foes. There is a danger that the ceasefire is fetishised within the peace process, in that political actors award it singular attention, ready to interpret every action of their opponents as a ceasefire breach. Such 'ceasefire-watching' can be particularly prominent in intra-group debates in which 'ethnic outbidding' is under way. In such cases, parties in the same group attempt to portray themselves as the vigilant 'true' defenders of group interests and their in-group rivals as weak and negligent. As we will see below, spoiler groups often seek to exploit this dynamic. In a number of peace processes, antagonists have sought to transcend the security dilemma inherent in ceasefire-watching through independent ceasefire monitors. For example, an international monitoring team drawn mainly from Asian states adjudicated on alleged ceasefire breaches between the government of the Philippines and the Moro Islamic Liberation Front.

In a number of cases, 'humanitarian pauses' have been negotiated to allow food or medical supplies to populations in war-affected regions. The Henri Dunant Centre for Humanitarian Dialogue negotiated a ceasefire in 2000 and 2002 between the Indonesian government and the Free Aceh Movement, while the UN brokered 'Operation Lifeline' between the Sudanese government and the Sudan People's Liberation Movement (SPLM/A) from 1989 onwards (Aall, 2007: 478–80; Barbelet 2008). In both cases, the prior humanitarian stoppage had a wider impact on the conflict, especially in terms of the debates within groups on the attractiveness of exploring more serious peace options. Barbelet notes that sustained humanitarian interaction helped the government of Sudan realise that 'the SPLM/A was a not a mere guerrilla movement, that it was a strong military and political force in southern Sudan' (2008: 423–4). Moreover, the communication channels that existed during the conflict enabled both sides to gain 'a more practical and thorough understanding of the type of formula for a peace agreement that could work, as well as the safeguards that were needed in order for it to be sustainable'.

Spoiling

Spoilers have been seminally defined by Stephen Stedman (1997: 5) as 'leaders and factions who view a particular peace as opposed to their interests and who are willing to use violence to undermine it'. In the classic case, spoilers are groups like the Real Irish Republican Army in Northern Ireland or Islamic Jihad in the occupied Palestinian territories that have sought to use violence to undermine a peace process that involves their traditional enemy (respectively, the British and Israeli states) and their more mainstream in-group rivals (respectively the Irish Republican Army and Sinn Féin, and the Fatah faction of the Palestine Liberation Organization). Perhaps the most effective weapon in the armoury of such groups is timing. Their violence has the capacity to puncture the national and international public and political optimism that might attend a peace process, especially in the early phases of a process when political actors and communities are becoming acclimatised to more relaxed security conditions.

Spoiling attacks might be regarded as blunt rejectionism, as an angry statement of contempt for efforts to reach a negotiated accommodation and as an attempt to bring a society back to the 'bad old days'. On closer examination, however, such violence is often highly sophisticated in its political intentions. It often has multiple targets stretching beyond the direct victims of the attacks. It may first attempt to make a statement of disdain for the peace process. This might especially be the case if the militant group and its political confederates have been locked out of the peace talks. Second, a spoiling attack may attempt to embarrass in-group rivals, depicting them as selling their own group short. The attack may be a recruiting advertisement, alerting the in-group community of the readiness of the armed group to stand up for the community and its willingness to attract support. Third, it may seek to goad the opposing group (whether a community, a non-state armed group or the state security apparatus) into a reaction. In many cases, the hope will be for an overreaction so that those involved in spoiling can make recourse to traditional narratives of the perfidy and heavy-handedness of their out-group rivals. All of this depends on the delicate psychology that can develop during a peace process, in which individuals, communities and institutions are poised between hope and suspicion. Those engaged in spoiling will hope to play on the security dilemma and prevent the spread of inter-group trust that might assist those wishing to reach a political accommodation (Booth and Wheeler, 2008: 80).

Heightened suspicions may mean a readiness to over-interpret the actions of the other side and those involved in spoiling may seek to exploit this. Yet, in many cases, those involved in spoiling are marginal in terms of their capacity. While able to attract headlines and inflict human suffering, their military and political effectiveness may be limited. The peace process may be too far advanced, and have too much material and moral support from internal and external sources, to be seriously derailed by the actions of small groups. Moreover, it may have significant popular support, both internally and externally, among constituencies who are war-weary and wish to lower the costs of the conflict. Indeed, in some cases there may be what Tim Sisk (2006) refers to as 'silver linings', or acts of violence so egregious that it shocks the peace process participants into redoubling their efforts to find an accommodation.

The term 'spoiler' is problematic for at least four reasons and should be approached with circumspection. First, like the term 'terrorism', 'spoiler' is immediately pejorative and morally positions both the user and target of the term in relation to the conflict and the peace process. Rather than an objective descriptor, the term strays into the territory of condemnation and so is conceptually and analytically limited. The term also risks assuming that all peace processes are normatively 'good' and that the actions of 'spoilers' are injurious to the common good. Under certain circumstances, however, antagonists may be entirely justified in their suspicions of a peace process: it may promise an unjust peace in which their key grievances are left unaddressed, their vulnerability to insecurity persists and basic power relations remained unaddressed. The term 'spoiler' steers us towards an overly simplistic dyadic world in which there are guardians and wreckers of peace. Peace processes, however, are more complex than such binary combinations.

Edward Said's powerful warnings on the hollowness of the Oslo Peace Process between Israel and Yasser Arafat's Palestine Liberation Organization provide a good example of warnings of 'bad peace'. Said (2002: 19) saw the internationally feted peace process as a fraudulent exercise through which a corrupt clique surrounding Arafat were jockeying to administer Israeli rule over Palestinians:

> Arafat and his advisers have closed themselves off to their own people. They have no conception at all either of accountability or of democratic and free debate. The worst thing of all is that in his disastrous policy of capitulating to the Israelis and then signing all sorts of crippling limits on his people into agreements with his occupiers, Arafat has mortgaged the future of his people to their oppressors. It is as if in his haste to get things for himself and a few symbols for his Authority, Arafat has thrown away his people's future, leaving it for future generations to try to extricate themselves from the mess he has now created.

If we accept that not all peace processes are normatively 'good', then the utility of a judgemental term like 'spoiler' is open to question.

Second, the term does not describe a particular type of violence. Again echoing the failure of the term 'terrorism', it says more about the political orientation of the user of the term. A bomb planted by a so-called spoiler group is no different from one planted by the same group in the pre-peace process days. What has changed is the political context and the position of those who use the term 'spoiler'. It becomes a label for political positions on groups and causes rather than a descriptor of violence. If the term is to be used at all, then this chapter advocates the use of the verb 'spoiling' rather than the noun 'spoiler'. Actors may be labelled as 'spoilers', but they may have little real capacity to 'spoil' the peace: their threats are not matched by deeds, their plots are disrupted or they gain little support (Mac Ginty, 2006a: 153–72). As a result, it seems more sensible to make judgements on the actual impact of groups and individuals in relation to the peace process.

Third, the orthodox use of the term 'spoiler' is biased towards applying the term to non-state actors. States, through sovereignty and international recognition, have advantages over non-state actors in terms of mobilising legitimacy and labelling political processes (such as peace processes) 'official'. States are more able than many other actors to legitimise themselves as official custodians of a peace process. In such a context, non-state actors are more likely to be delegitimised and labelled as 'spoilers'. Höglund and Zartman (2006: 13) identify 'official spoilers' or 'state spoilers', and highlight the vested interests that stand to lose resources and legitimacy in a post-war dispensation. They point to Israel, Congo-Brazzaville, Haiti, Guatemala, South Africa and Northern Ireland as cases in which agents of the state, or their proxies, used violence in official and unofficial capacities to subvert a peace process.

A fourth point relates to the extent to which spoiling behaviour can be non-violent. In the classic definition, 'spoilers' are violent actors. Yet, in many cases, spoiling behaviour does not involve direct violence. Political actors may drag their feet, establish unrealistic preconditions for opponents or fail to create conditions conducive for a comprehensive peace accord. None of this activity may involve direct violence, but it may be effective in stymieing an accommodation. Can this activity be defined as 'peaceful spoiling'? Consider the example of the Northern Ireland peace process after the Irish Republican Army (IRA) ceasefire in 1994. The IRA expected that its political cousins in Sinn Féin would have immediate access to political negotiations. Instead, the British government insisted that the IRA disarm. This pre-condition, and the perception that the British government was unnecessarily prolonging the pre-talks phase, led the IRA to rescind its ceasefire in February 1996 (de Chastelain, 1999: 436–8). To the extent that the British government was a gatekeeper on access to talks by one of the main protagonists, it is possible to argue that the British government was engaged in 'spoiling' behaviour.

The labelling of politico-militant actors aside, the fact remains that some groups do attempt to undermine peace processes using violence or threats of violence. This creates a series of dilemmas for those actors committed to a negotiated settlement. To react robustly to violence from out-group actors might risk driving moderate out-groups away and jeopardising a settlement. To exercise restraint and persevere with the peace process may equally risk accusations of weakness. In some cases, external actors, for example, a UN peacekeeping force, can help calm the security dilemma (Zahar, 2008: 169).

Crime During and After Peace Processes

In a number of cases, crime levels have increased markedly during peace processes and after peace accords have been reached. South Africa and Guatemala provide startling examples in which post-accord or transition crime levels were much greater than the violence during the preceding civil war or national liberation struggle. Despite the new dawn of a post-apartheid South Africa, the crime statistics for 1995 make for grim reading: 220,990 assaults, 26,637 murders, 47,506 cases of rape and 120,952 robberies. To put this into context, the number of murders was more than the number of political fatalities for the decade 1984–1994 (du Toit, 2001: 47). In Guatemala, post-civil war violence has included over 200 people killed by lynching – mob justice – between 1996 and 2002 (Garcia, 2004). The implications of crime associated with peace processes and peace accords are serious. If people's everyday experience of 'peace' is marked by insecurity and a decline in the quality of life because of crime, then they will have few incentives to express political support for a post-peace accord political dispensation.

Yet discussion of crime during peace processes is anything but straightforward. The concept of 'crime' may well be blurred in a society that has experienced a protracted civil war. In most stable societies it is relatively clear what constitutes a crime and what does not, and a political and social consensus will be assisted by an established legal code, a capable, efficient and transparent legal enforcement system, a separation of the judiciary from the executive, scrutiny from civil society, professional associations and safeguards for minorities. In societies experiencing or emerging from civil war, most of these factors will be absent. Indeed, it worth asking the following question: if the state is dysfunctional and incapable, if there is effectively no law and order, can there really be crime? It can be argued that the concept of crime only makes sense if there is a context of order. Moreover, it will take time and money to rectify many of the shortcomings in the judicial system of a post-civil war society, hence the enormous efforts invested in transitional justice schemes in some societies emerging from civil war.

At least three factors complicate the identification of what does and does not constitute crime in societies undergoing a peacemaking process. The first arises from the nature of the principal activities of many combatants during a civil war. Intimidation, arson, theft, assault and sexual violence comprise the core violent activities in many civil wars. As such, the *modus operandi* of many combatants in a civil war could be labelled crime in a post-civil war period. At a minimum, many individuals and groups in the post-civil war society may be equipped with skills that would be described as 'criminal' in a post-civil war context. Former combatants may believe they have no choice but to fall back on these 'skills' if economic opportunities in the post-civil war period are severely constrained. This situation may be exacerbated by access to military-style weapons which can both increase the capacity of criminal gangs to effect injury and intimidation, and can impede efforts to civilianise a police force. Demobilisation, disarmament and reintegration (DDR) programmes offer some hope of managing the transition for former combatants and directing them towards alternatives (Gamba, 2008). However, such schemes have not always met with success, and many attempts at disarmament have underestimated the cultural importance of retaining weapons, especially when militias/armed gangs are one of the few economically viable social structures available for young men in post-war societies. As a member of the White Army militia in southern Sudan observed: 'If you have a gun, you believe you can get something. If you don't have a gun, you don't feel like you have anything at all' (cited in Arnold and Alden, 2007: 366).

A second complicating factor stems from what citizens believe constitutes crime in the post-civil war period. During a civil war, citizens may engage in activities or tolerate activities that they would not engage in or tolerate during peacetime. Certain activities might become routine and socially accepted to the extent that they are not regarded as criminal. At the extreme end of the spectrum, this might involve the abuse or denial of rights to certain groups. In a deeply divided society under threat, one community might regard the other community as responsible for evildoing or as less than human. To do harm to members of the other community might be widely accepted. At the other end of the spectrum, we might find the illegal tapping into the electricity network. For example, about one-third of Lebanese households avoid electricity charges by independently hooking up to the network. Most do not see this as a crime, and they and their neighbours have been doing this for years. It is socially accepted and routinised. The perception of what constitutes a crime, and the extent to which this perception is shared across society, is especially important in transitional societies. While some citizens might be genuinely confused as to what does and does not constitute a crime in a post-civil war dispensation, others might be more willing to exploit the confusion (Mac Ginty, 2006b: 112). A persistent civil war may mean that a 'culture of violence' becomes embedded within social relations to the extent that activities regarded as 'deviant' in other contexts would be regarded as permissible (Steenkamp, 2009: 29–53).

A third complicating factor relates to the transitional nature of the legal code in the post-peace accord period. Peace accord implementation often contains programmes of security sector reform (SSR) and DDR, as well as changes to the constitution and criminal justice system. Such upheavals may present (short-term) difficulties for the construction of a uniform legal code, certainty and transparency. People may be genuinely unsure as to what constitutes legal and illegal activity in the context of reform. In a number of cases, international actors have taken the lead in reforming the criminal justice system, with the United Nations, for example, providing an interim force of police officers while the new indigenous police force was trained (Murray, 2006).

Post-peace accord crime has not brought down a peace accord. Instead, in a number of cases, crime and insecurity have been so pervasive as to help erode popular and international faith in a peace accord and the public institutions charged with upholding it. Haiti, Afghanistan, the Solomon Islands, El Salvador and Chechnya have all undergone political transitions and major 'peace support' interventions (a hugely violent intervention by Russia in the case of Chechnya). In all cases, however, public insecurity is rife. Militant groups that may have once had a political position have transformed into gangs whose main rationale is the perpetuation of the gang and the livelihood of its members. Simultaneously, those institutions charged with upholding law and order have suffered from practical and legitimacy problems. This raises a dilemma for those interested in peace implementation: should freedoms be restricted after a peace accord so that security can be ensured? Roland Paris' (2004) much-criticised 'institutionalisation before liberalisation' formula prescribed just such a strategy. The danger with such an approach, however, is that it relies on benign authoritarianism and the liberty versus order trade-offs inherent in such a system.

Conclusion

By way of conclusion, it seems important to emphasise the totality of violence and to include structural and other forms of violence in the context of societies transitioning towards lower levels of violence. To concentrate only on direct violence can lead to a distorted view of conflict and the strategies required to ameliorate the impact of conflict. Such a view is likely to be overwhelmingly statist, male and confined to clashes between or involving organised armed groups. Instead, a more representative picture of violence in societies emerging from civil war would include violence within the private sphere, economic violence in the form of child labour or sex trafficking, and corruption whereby political leaders siphon off public funds. An exhortation to take account of the totality of violence may seem daunting as this will include violence that may be labelled as direct, indirect, public, private and structural. The logic of this broader view is that strategies to deal with violence and its effects must operate in the social and economic spheres, as well as in the more traditional security and political spheres.

It is also worth underlining the capacity of states to be violent actors. Distinctions between state 'force' and non-state 'violence' are Jesuitical. Both state and non-state actors are capable of extreme forms of direct and indirect violence, and as such are capable of preventing or derailing peacemaking processes. Indeed, in many violent conflicts, states are often the most violent actors, being responsible for more deaths and human misery than other so-called 'terrorist' or 'criminal' actors. Moreover, given the prizes associated with statehood (notionally, sovereignty, legitimacy and access to resources), it seems appropriate that the bar, in terms of respect for the law, is set higher for states than for non-state actors. Derogation from the International Criminal Court by leading states, thereby undermining the idea of universal laws, gives positive assistance to those states who routinely abuse human rights.

A final concluding point relates to the status of civilians in war and peace. There is nothing new in the blurring of the distinction between combatants and non-combatants. The post-Cold War wars and insurgencies are not particularly different from wars of previous centuries in their use of indiscriminate violence. Hugo Slim (2007) shows how 'civilian ambiguity' and 'anti-civilian ideology' are central parts of modern warfare and counter-insurgency. Taliban car bombs in Kabul or US predator strikes on 'high value insurgent targets' in northwest Pakistan (which often involve the flattening of housing compounds and the obliteration of entire families) share a disregard for civilians. One of the urgent tasks for peace processes is to assert the sanctity of civilians. Peace processes give many opportunities for the privileging of civilians: ceasefires, peace zones, new constitutions, DDR, reform of the state 'security' apparatus and the institution of political processes that help re-civilianise politics, governance and the state.

References

Aall, P. (2007), 'The power of nonofficial actors in conflict management', in C. Crocker, F.O. Hampson and P. Aall (eds), *Leashing the Dogs of War: Conflict Management in a Divided World*. Washington DC: United States Institute of Peace Press, 477–94.

Arnold, M. and C. Alden, (2007), '"This gun is our food": disarming the White Army militias of southern Sudan', *Conflict Security and Development* 7(3): 361–85.

Barbelet, V. (2008), *Engaging with Armed Non-state Actors on Humanitarian Issues: A Step Towards Peace?* PhD thesis, University of York.

Booth, K. and N. Wheeler (2008), *The Security Dilemma: Fear, Cooperation and Trust in World Politics*. Basingstoke: Palgrave.

Darby, J. and R. Mac Ginty (2008), 'Introduction: what peace, what process?', in J. Darby and R. Mac Ginty (eds), *Contemporary Peacemaking: Conflict, Peace Processes and Post-war Reconstruction*, 2nd edn. Basingstoke: Palgrave, 1–8.

De Chastelain, J. (1999), 'The Good Friday Agreement in Northern Ireland', in C. Crocker, F.O. Hampson and P. Aall (eds), *Herding Cats: Multiparty Mediation in a Complex World*. Washington DC: United States Institute of Peace Press, 435–68.

Du Toit, P. (2001), *South Africa's Brittle Peace: The Problem of Post-settlement Violence*. Basingstoke: Palgrave.

Egeland, J. (1999), 'The Oslo Accord: multiparty facilitation through the Norwegian channel', in C. Crocker, F.O. Hampson and P. Aall (eds), *Herding Cats: Multiparty Mediation in a Complex World*. Washington DC: United States Institute of Peace Press, 529–46.

Evans, M. (2005), 'Moral theory and the idea of a just war', in M. Evans (ed.), *Just War Theory: A Reappraisal*. Edinburgh: Edinburgh University Press, 1–21.

Gamba, V. (2008), 'Post-agreement demobilization, disarmament, and reconstruction: towards a new approach', in J. Darby and R. Mac Ginty (eds), *Contemporary Peacemaking: Conflict, Peace Processes and Post-war Reconstruction*, 2nd edn. Basingstoke: Palgrave, 178–91.

Garcia, M.C.F. (2004), *Lynching in Guatemala: Legacy of War and Impunity*. Weatherhead Centre for International Affairs, Harvard University.

Guelke, A. (2008), 'Negotiations and peace processes', in J. Darby and R. Mac Ginty (eds), *Contemporary Peacemaking: Conflict, Peace Processes and Post-war Reconstruction*, 2nd edn. Basingstoke: Palgrave, 63–77.

Höglund, K. (2004), 'Negotiations amidst violence: explaining violence-induced crisis in peace processes', Interim Report from the International Institute for Applied Systems Analysis IR-04-002, http://www.iiasa.ac.at/Admin/PUB/Documents/IR-04-002.pdf [accessed 18 July 2012].

Höglund, K. and I.W. Zartman (2006), 'Violence by the state: official spoilers and their allies', in J. Darby (ed.), *Violence and Reconstruction*. Notre Dame, IN: University of Notre Dame Press, 11–31.

Keen, D. (2008), *Complex Emergencies*. Cambridge: Polity Press.

Kriesberg, L. (2005), 'Nature, dynamics and phases of intractability', in C. Crocker, F.O. Hampson and P. Aall (eds), *Grasping the Nettle: Analyzing Cases of Intractable Conflict*. Washington DC: United States Institute of Peace Press, 65–97.

Mac Ginty, R. (2006a), 'Northern Ireland: a peace process thwarted by accidental spoiling', in E. Newman and O. Richmond (eds), *Challenges to Peacebuilding: Managing Spoilers During Conflict Resolution*. Tokyo: United Nations University Press, 153–72.

Mac Ginty, R. (2006b), 'Post-accord crime', in J. Darby (ed.), *Violence and Reconstruction*. Notre Dame, IN: University of Notre Dame Press, 101–19.

Murray, D. (2006), 'Post-accord police reform', in J. Darby (ed.), *Violence and Reconstruction*. Notre Dame, IN: University of Notre Dame Press, 77–100.

Paris, R. (2004), *At War's End: Building Peace after Civil Conflict*. Cambridge: Cambridge University Press.

Richmond, O. (1998), 'Devious objectives and the disputants' view of international mediation: a theoretical framework', *Journal of Peace Research* 35(6): 707–22.

Said, E. (2002), *The End of the Peace Process*. London: Granta.

Shaw, T. and P. Mbabazi (2009) 'Two Ugandas and a "liberal peace"? Lessons from Uganda about conflict and development at the start of a new century', in R. Mac Ginty and O. Richmond (eds), *The Liberal Peace and Post-war Reconstruction: Myth or reality?* London: Routledge, 76–88.

Sisk, T. (2006), 'Political violence and peace accords: searching for the silver linings', in J. Darby (ed.), *Violence and Reconstruction*. Notre Dame, IN: University of Notre Dame Press, 121–42.

Slim, H. (2007), *Killing Civilians: Method, Madness and Morality in War*. London: Hurst.

Stedman, S. (1997), 'Spoiler problems in peace processes', *International Security* 22(2): 5–53.

Steenkamp, C. (2009), *Violence and Post-war Reconstruction: Managing Insecurity in the Aftermath of Peace Accords*. London: I.B. Tauris.

Tilly, C. (2002), 'Violent and non-violent trajectories in contentious politics', in K. Worcester, S.A. Bermanzohn and M. Ungar (eds), *Violence and Politics: Globalization's Paradox*. London: Routledge, 13–31.

Zahar, M.J. (2008), 'Reframing the spoiler debate in peace processes' in J. Darby and R. Mac Ginty (eds), *Contemporary Peacemaking: Conflict, Peace Processes and Post-war Reconstruction*, 2nd edn. Basingstoke: Palgrave, 159–77.

Civil Society Actors and the End of Violence

Avila Kilmurray

The Northern Ireland state has been a contested entity since its establishment in 1921. The longest period of consistent, and increasingly violent, opposition to the state emerged out of the suppression of the non-violent civil rights movement (1968–1971) and developed into a full-blown republican campaign, which was to last over the 25 years, from 1969 to 1994. The British Army was introduced on to the streets of the North in 1969, to both bolster the state and to counter the inter-communal clashes between the largely Protestant unionists and loyalists (who were committed to maintaining the union with Britain) and the predominantly Catholic nationalists and republicans. Loyalists were to join two main paramilitary organizations – the long-established Ulster Volunteer Force (UVF) and the Ulster Defence Association (UDA), giving rise to a three-cornered confrontation between republican and loyalist paramilitaries and the forces of the state (the British Army, the Royal Ulster Constabulary (RUC) and the Ulster Defence Regiment). By 1972, direct rule under the British government had been introduced and, with the hiatus of five months in 1974, was to remain in place until the restoration of a power-sharing Executive in December 1999. The instability of the Executive arrangement was to result in a stop-start direct rule interregnum until May 2007, when devolution was reinstated.

The declaration of ceasefires by both republican and loyalist paramilitaries in autumn 1994 marked a decisive shift from open warfare into a prolonged period of conflict transformation and peace building, with elections to peace talks – chaired by US Senator George Mitchell – being held in 1996. Two years later, the Belfast/Good Friday Agreement[1] was concluded and accepted by a popular referendum. However, the conflict transformation years had seen the breakdown of the IRA (Irish Republican Army) ceasefire over the period 1996–1997, a bitter loyalist paramilitary feud in 2000–2001 and continuing incidences of violence within both republican and loyalist communities over issues of community control and

---

1   There is no agreement on how the Agreement should be named. As a general rule, nationalists and republicans term the agreement the Good Friday Agreement, whilst unionists and loyalists speak about the Belfast Agreement.

criminality, particularly prior to the re-structuring of policing in Northern Ireland. In short, a distinction was to be drawn between the end of violence as a political strategy and its use on a tactical basis. The availability of weaponry, and the motivation and willingness to use it, was to be a longer-term legacy that was to bedevil the implementation of the Belfast/Good Friday Agreement, although the IRA put its weapons 'beyond use' in October 2001 and issued a formal statement announcing the end of its armed campaign in July 2005. Republican demands for British 'demilitarization' accompanied this protracted process.

Whatever the complexities around the point when violence ended, the main emphasis in this chapter is on the contribution made by civil society actors to the ending of that violence. This contribution will be examined within the categories of a civil society role as catalyst, cheerleader, communicator and change agent. It will consider how these roles were applied over the years of early community division, as well as over the years of open violence and into the period of peace building and conflict transformation. These time periods include: (a) 1968–1975; (b) 1976–1994; and (c) 1995–2007. While the beginning of 'the Troubles' (the colloquial name for the conflict) and the 1994 ceasefires are clear, 1976 saw the introduction of a British government meta-narrative of 'Normalization, Ulsterization and Criminalization',[2] which was to influence the framing of societal reaction to the ongoing conflict. It was within this context that civil society actors operated and, given the multiplicity of such actors and their often very different perspectives, acted in both opposition, compliance and, at times, in enthusiastic acceptance of the official narrative. This chapter, however, will focus on organizations within the community and voluntary sectors, and to a lesser extent on social formations such as trade unions and employers' associations, that showed the ability to question – or at the very least nuance – the government narrative. Clearly, the sphere of civil society includes a much wider range of social organizations – the 'multiplicity of micro worlds and micro power relations' that Morison and Livingstone (1995) commented on – but analytical focus requires prioritization.

The chapter will conclude that while the contribution made by civil society actors to the ending of political violence was arguably important, it was by no means decisive in an overall context that was dominated by a large number of political actors. The latter included the British and Irish governments as well as local political parties and the array of paramilitary organizations referred to above. It also encompassed the externalizing interest and influence of states such as the USA and institutions like the European Union (EU). On this often crowded stage, the civil society actors were more often to be found positioning the lighting, adjusting the scenery or providing a supportive accompaniment from the orchestra pit, although

---

2   This narrative, which framed the Northern Ireland situation until the 1996–1998 peace talks, was introduced by Merlyn Rees as Secretary of State for Northern Ireland in 1976 and was reinforced by his successor, Roy Mason (1976–1999), who asserted that 'I wanted criminals caught by the RUC and punished as criminals not "Politicals"' (Mason 1999: 164).

every so often they worked as stage prompts or took action to prevent the curtain falling at inappropriate moments in the production of conflict transformation.

Casting the Roles of Civil Society Actors

It is important to distinguish between the community sector (made up of the very many area-based tenants' associations, community councils, women's groups and community networks) and the voluntary sector (largely interest- or issue-based) given the increasing tendency for both sectors to be described jointly as the third sector or as non-governmental organizations (NGOs) (Acheson et al. 2004). The regional umbrella body for voluntary action in Northern Ireland, the Northern Ireland Council for Voluntary Action (NICVA), adopts this approach when reporting on the 'State of the Sector' on a regular basis. At a community level, however, the distinction between the voluntary sector and community action is often clearly drawn, with the former being depicted as external to local neighbourhoods and often middle class and professionalized. Notwithstanding this stereotype, a range of community actors and voluntary organizations were notable for their respective roles in addressing the political dimension of the Troubles, as well as taking supportive action in seeking alternatives to political violence.

Groups within local neighbourhoods as often as not reflected local political opinions and had variable relations with the prevailing political forces – which might, of course, include paramilitary organizations. Indeed, the flourishing locally based community sector has often been attributed to the communal disturbances of the 1969–1972 period, which resulted in major forced population movements due to intimidation and the establishment of a number of 'no-go' areas in Catholic neighbourhoods in opposition to the state forces (McCready 2001). This, in effect, gave rise to the self-organization of communities in the face of virtual political breakdown, but also set the context for the development of many 'single identity' community organizations to reflect the increasing number of 'single identity' communities.[3] A second factor was the proactive community development role of the Northern Ireland Community Relations Commission (1969–1974) that had been set up at the behest of the British government in an attempt to promote more harmonious relations between disadvantaged local communities that were experiencing the brunt of the violence. Although the Commission was disbanded in 1974 by local politicians,[4] who were concerned at the potential challenging nature of participative democracy to their elected mandates, it was reported by 1975 that some 500 community groups

---

3   By 1995, almost half of Northern Ireland's 1.5 million people lived in areas more than 90 per cent Protestant or 95 per cent Catholic. Of Belfast's 51 wards, 35 were at least 90 per cent one religion or the other – cited in Pollak (1993: 42).

4   The decision to disband the Northern Ireland Community Relations Commission was taken during the five-month rule of the short-lived power-sharing Executive of 1974, which itself fell victim to the loyalist Ulster Workers' Council strike in May 1974.

were active in local areas (Duffy and Percival 1975). The next three decades saw an expansion in the number of active, community-based groups, although with a bias towards their establishment in Catholic/nationalist/republican urban working-class and rural areas. Indeed, by 1990/1991, concerns were expressed by a number of community activists from a Protestant/unionist/loyalist (PUL) background that community development appeared less effective in single-identity PUL areas (Burrows 1991). This was attributed to the nature of the relationship between PUL communities with both the state and their elected political representatives. If there are some 98 definitions of 'community' (Dominelli 1991: 133–43), then the experience and practice of community action within that sector was equally diverse in nature, although what the many groups did bring was an understanding of the hopes, fears and concerns held by their particular communities, not only on social and economic issues but also regarding political perspectives and possibilities.

The voluntary sector also was multi-faceted, ranging from single-issue service delivery that was often deliberately apolitical in nature to advocating for aspects of social justice and change. It is organizations in this latter range that played a part in contributing to the end of political violence. Specific examples referred to in this chapter include the NICVA, the Northern Ireland Association for the Care and Resettlement of Offenders (NIACRO), the Campaign for the Administration of Justice (CAJ) and the Corrymeela Community and the Community Foundation for Northern Ireland (previously known as the Northern Ireland Voluntary Trust), to mention but a few. Finally, while the trade union movement was not without internal political tensions –which were often linked to the dominant communal identity of the members of any specific union – it also played its part in the ending of political violence by moving from a non-sectarian to an anti-sectarian policy position, and through its various campaigns for peaceful alternatives to armed struggle. In some cases the contribution made was to place a marker that violence was neither acceptable nor the only strategy for change, while in others it was to offer a change process and space. However, notwithstanding the differences, the overall contribution of this complex civil society can be described in terms of its role as catalyst, cheerleader, communicator and change agent.

The Role of Civil Society as Catalyst

There is a song that was written by the Rostrevor singer-songwriter Tommy Sands entitled 'Whatever You Say, Say Nothing' that captured the atmosphere prevailing over the period 1976–1994. There were the internal community tensions and fears, but there was also the societal context framed by the British government meta-narrative of 'Normalization, Ulsterization and Criminalization'. This was shorthand for a reductionist presentation of the ongoing conflict as an aggravated crime wave that could be effectively managed by the RUC, with just a little help from British Army friends. The outworkings of this official narrative were to lead to media censorship, the politicization of the criminal justice and prison system, the virtual sidelining of victims of the violence and the attempted isolation of the political 'extremes'. The manifestation of the policy in practice was recalled by one retired civil servant: 'Me and mine were the official hand shakers. We had to get out at all ministerial [events] and get in the way. If there was a hand coming out we had to grab it ... I mean it seems ridiculous now, but it was awfully important at the time.'[5] This was to ensure that a British minister did not unwittingly shake hands with a 'political extremist', notwithstanding the fact that the latter might have been the democratically elected MP for the area.

In these circumstances, a number of civil society initiatives were designed as a means of providing a voice to groups and sections of society that had been officially silenced. The purpose of these projects went beyond that of communication, being motivated by an understanding that unless people could state their views, demands and fears, it was unlikely that political negotiation could develop as a realistic option.[6] Two examples of open, formal processes that challenged the politics of exclusion were the 'Beyond Hate' conference, organized in Derry in September 1992 by the community-based Hollywell Trust and the Opsahl Citizens' Inquiry, also launched that same year. The 'Beyond Hate' gathering was subtitled 'Living with our Deepest Differences' and brought together participants from 25 countries over four continents. Alongside having an impressive list of international contributors (including broadcasted messages from Nelson Mandela, former US President Jimmy Carter and Archbishop Desmond Tutu), the floor and platform were thrown open to anyone who wished to make a contribution (Deane and Ritter 1994). Representatives of Sinn Fein took up the offer.

The Opsahl Citizens' Inquiry was a more ambitious venture which involved some 3,000 people making 554 written and taped submissions to a seven-person distinguished panel under the chairpersonship of Professor Torkel Opsahl. A large number of public meetings and oral hearings were also held over the period May 1992–June 1993. In an impressive published report, the organizers noted: 'We have made a recommendation about bringing Sinn Fein into the political process, partly because we were struck by how many authors of submissions and presenters at hearings mentioned the alienation of whole communities who believe they are excluded because they support Sinn Fein' (Pollak 1993: 5). Both Sinn Fein and the Ulster Democratic Party (closely aligned with the loyalist UDA) as well as a group of loyalist ex-prisoners attended Oral Hearings of the Commission, with their views being recorded in the subsequent report. The sense of perceived alienation that the report referred to was acutely reflected by a community activist from the nationalist/republican West Belfast area when she said: 'If you look back we were very much the community that was totally alienated and marginalized. We were the terrorist community, basically, who normally people didn't want to touch with a bargepole – and the full weight of the British propaganda machine was working

---

5   Interview conducted by the author, 20 February 2007. In the case described, the minister was avoiding shaking hands with Sinn Fein leader and West Belfast MP Gerry Adams.
6   Historical hindsight has shown that political contact was ongoing at a range of 'deniable' levels.

against you in those days ... There was all that criminalization, marginalization, alienation and I suppose anybody who was looking after themselves was afraid of being involved.'[7] This feeling was reiterated by a community worker from rural South Armagh, also known as 'Bandit country': 'We were all tarred with that one brush ... Whenever I was going to go anywhere you could see people think "Oh my God, she's from Crossmaglen" and ... it really would undermine your confidence. And oh the peasant would rise up in you ... but still you just went, "Oh my God, not again" ... I think if there had been some way to talk about that somewhere.'[8]

In fulfilling the role as catalyst, civil society actors were facilitating the meeting and interaction of individuals and groups that were either isolated through policies of political marginalization, divided through the segregated nature of society – carved up by peacelines[9] or that were at odds due to antagonistic political positions and the impact and nature of the ongoing violence. The creation of space and opportunities for exchange were important, but so too were the reputations of the actors who designed and initiated these opportunities. In a sharply divided society, it was all too easy to be labelled as one of 'them' as against being one of 'us'; consequently, the identification of international speakers and commentators to speak from their experience was crucial in a situation where a sub-text agenda would be quickly ascribed to local people. The creation of space had to be considered in physical, psychological and even symbolic terms. Thus, the Opsahl Inquiry deliberately held oral hearings in the nationalist/republican Falls area and the unionist/loyalist Shankill area, as well as in many less aligned locations.

The role of catalyst, however, could also be played out in less formal and more secluded settings. The long-established Corrymeela Community made a point of facilitating cross-community exchange as well as opening the doors of its residential centre to diverse groups of people to encourage the honest discussion that the Crossmaglen community worker cited above craved. Equally, Quaker House, then conveniently situated in a studentville suburb of South Belfast, hosted private and confidential discussions between apparent political antagonists over the years in a quiet and studied manner. The practice of a small number of civil society actors being prepared to 'hold the ring' and offer safe space was one that was available over the course of the conflict and, while this was often carried out by individuals with an institutional standing, this did not necessarily imply institutional approval. This was true in many of the various dialogue and facilitative initiatives engaged in by members of the clergy of various religious denominations, but also applied to individual entrepreneurs for peace within both the private and the community sectors. The most successful of these approaches were always hedged around by confidentiality and a firm grasp of the imperative of political deniability, particularly where political or paramilitary representatives were involved. However, the participation of community activists wearing a number of hats (which could be

---

7   Interview conducted by the author, 7 February 2006.
8   Interview conducted by the author, 27 March 2009.
9   The 'peacelines' often took the form of over 20-foot high reinforced walls, but could also be a road or a river in other locations.

both political and community) offered opportunities for an exchange of views, which in turn could inform policies and political positions.

If civil society actors could fulfil a catalytic role in a range of varying contexts, the locating of this role in a recognizable frame often proved helpful. On a thematic basis, and with less of the macro political edge, a peer consortium of women's centres (the Belfast Women's Support Network) worked together on shared priorities, winning in the process a respect for difference, which was arguably important given their location in very different politically sensitive community settings. In a strategic approach that Cockburn (1998) has termed 'transversal politics' – which roots dialogue and exchange in one's own identity while at the same time seeking to understand the communal perspective and identity of 'the other' – the Network broke the silence around political difference by organizing workshops called 'Let's Talk Politics' and fought to obtain funding, and official recognition, for the work of the various neighbourhood-based centres, irrespective of community location. As one initiative in a very varied and nuanced women's movement, the Belfast Women's Support Network experience highlighted the need to develop strategies to address and cope with political difference where it proved impossible to ignore it. Cross-community differences were only one facet of the issues at hand; there was also the pressing impact of political and policy differences within single-identity communities. Arguably, the shared frame of an interest in women's issues helped to develop the transversal approach that, in turn, allowed a shift from joint working on the basis of functionality to the ability to address sensitive and more controversial issues in a supportive manner.

As events in Northern Ireland moved from open violence into a process of conflict transformation, the role of civil society actors, acting as a catalyst for collective discussion and change, was augmented. Buoyed up with fresh sources of funding to underpin the peace process from the EU,[10] there were a plethora of academic, voluntary sector and community-organized gatherings to acknowledge the ravages of the conflict and to chart various political imperatives and remedial approaches for the future. Civil society actors produced research reports focused on the needs of victims and survivors of the conflict, conferences were held on the impact of the violence as experienced by children and young people, funding programmes were developed to support the reintegration of former political prisoners into society, and the 'peace dividend' became the subject of endless discussion and debate. The NICVA and the Community Foundation for Northern Ireland, amongst others, argued that this dividend should be more than a focus on economic development. The Community Foundation linked up with the Project on Justice in Times of Transition (Harvard University) and organized residential conferences and workshops, on an annual basis, for a large number of community-based activists on issues related to the transition from violence, as well as issues that were deemed politically sensitive. The Project on Justice in Times of Transition provided an international panel of speakers, who were respected and experienced

---

10 Largely delivered through the EU Special Support Programme for Peace and Reconciliation (1995–1999).

through their work in their own societies that were emerging from violence. The Community Foundation used its network of over 3,000 community projects throughout the North to ensure a broad range of participation that reflected a wide variation of political positions. The hope was that this approach would act as a catalyst for participation and identification with issues; there was even talk about participatory democracy and the development of structures that might achieve this in practice.[11] During the course of the 1990s, the catalytic role of civil society actors shifted from one of engagement and inclusion to one of generating ideas; righting the wrongs instituted by the official governmental meta-narrative and testing the socio-economic parameters of the peace process itself.

Civil Society Actors as Cheerleaders

The role of cheerleader in the transition from violence is evident in those civil society initiatives that called for an end to violent conflict – such as the range of church and trade union demonstrations in this regard, as well as the much-publicized Peace People of earlier years – but it can also refer to the various coalitions of interest that came together to safeguard the move towards positive political negotiation in the immediate aftermath of the 1994 ceasefires. At the invitation of the Northern Ireland Voluntary Trust – now the Community Foundation for Northern Ireland – the Rural Community Network and the NICVA supported a community survey carried out by the Trust with hundreds of community and voluntary organizations. The survey sought to identify the main priorities and opportunities facing Northern Ireland as perceived within this constituency in order to give local groups a sense of ownership of a possible peace dividend which was then under discussion. Issues raised ranged from the social to the economic, but also touched on the protection of human rights and the need for inclusive political structures (Northern Ireland Voluntary Trust 1995). More localized consultation exercises were organized in West Belfast, Derry, Newry and West Belfast by community-based networks as well as amongst organizations in the women's sector. The recommendations emerging from these initiatives were relayed to the officials responsible for the design of the EU Special Support Programme for Peace and Reconciliation that was being formulated at that time. It was felt important to generate a sense of movement, of responsiveness to the needs of areas and groups most adversely affected by the violence, and to argue that there should be an identifiable peace dividend in local communities to greet the end of violence.

The fragility of the peace process by the summer of 1996 prompted a significant linkage of seven major bodies representative of business, labour, agriculture,

---

11 The Civic Forum, provided for in the Belfast/Good Friday Agreement, was one such structure put forward by the Northern Ireland Women's Coalition to act as a deliberative second chamber to the Northern Ireland Assembly. With the return of devolution, the Civic Forum remains under long-term review.

economic development and the NICVA to come together as the G7 (later extended to the G8) to engage with all the political parties that were involved in the ongoing peace negotiations. This civil society alliance issued a press statement warning of the dangers posed to the Northern Ireland economy and society by the threat of political breakdown, and they then met with representatives of political parties the following October. One of those who participated in the meeting described it as 'a major occasion ... never before had so disparate a group of business and other interests united to meet such a broad range of political opinion' (Quigley 2002: 15–16). The emphasis was placed on the importance of a successful outcome to the peace process: 'We invited the parties to seek fresh solutions to problems that had hitherto proved intractable and to tackle areas where agreement might be easier, if only to encourage people to have trust that the talks process could deliver results' (Quigley 2002: 16). The group continued to meet over a period of time to monitor the situation and to make supportive public comments when necessary.

While acting as a cheerleader celebrating the end of violence, the principle of social partnership also became written into the operation of the EU Special Support Programme for Peace and Reconciliation, which was self-consciously innovative, inclusive and promoted cross-community initiatives. Local authority-based Partnership Boards were constituted with representatives from trade unions, the private sector, agriculture, the community and voluntary sectors, public bodies and elected political representatives. This offered a forum not only for decision-making around the allocation of resources, but also brought groups within both participative and representative democracy into a direct working relationship on a cross-community basis (Greer 2001). When the subsequent draft EU PEACE 11 Programme (2001–2006) diluted this process, a number of the former G8 organizations came together under the title Concordia to get the proposed guidelines re-written in favour of civil society involvement. Concordia consisted of the NICVA, the Irish Congress of Trade Unions, the Ulster Farmers' Union, the Northern Ireland Agricultural Producers' Association and the Confederation of British Industry. While not directly related to the political dimensions of the end of violence, there was still a strong civil society sense that the uncertainty of the implementation of the Belfast/Good Friday Agreement required the public exercise of continued active citizenship.

The exercise of the cheerleader role took on a new dimension when many of the individuals who had been active through the G8 initiative provided resources, expertise and support to the broadly based Yes Campaign which was initiated to campaign for a yes vote in the 1998 Referendum on the Belfast/Good Friday Agreement. Most associated with Quintin Oliver, the previous Director of the NICVA, the Yes Campaign worked with the cross-section of political parties that were advocating a positive response to the Agreement. While civil society more generally reflected all the contradictions and differences that were evident in the body politics as a whole, both the Yes Campaign Group and the Northern Ireland Women's Coalition – a cross-community political party formed in 1996 by women activists from the community and voluntary sectors that then had representatives elected to both the peace talks and the subsequent Northern Ireland Assembly[12] – were an example of cheerleaders turned political actors when the occasion required it.

Civil Society Actors Maintaining Communication

Given that one of the first casualties in a violently divided society is trust, and the second is invariably any sense of complexity, the importance of developing and maintaining lines of communication within and between communities cannot be over-exaggerated. Both during the Troubles and in the uncertain period of transition from violence, the prevalence of rumour and misinformation was a constant factor. However, communication can also be seen as a more active process than the simple provision of information. In this latter context, it can include creating opportunities for people to meet and exchange views and experiences, and it can also take a proactive role in flagging up shifts in political positions and opinions. Despite the physical divisions of the 'peacewalls' and the fear and distrust that acted as barriers to communication, at least one initiative within the women's sector was to highlight that while such long-term divisions could result in stereotypes and prejudice, they could also give rise to a sense of curiosity about 'the other'. One woman, a resident of a single-identity community in West Belfast, attended a Women's Information Day at a youth centre and described her experience: 'There was a newspaper – just the "Shankill News" – and I would have loved to know what was happening on the Shankill but I was scared to go and buy the paper so when they weren't looking I took one ... only because I was afraid they thought I might be up to something devious, but I really wanted to know what was happening on the Shankill.'[13] Coming together initially in 1980, the Women's Information Day network was a brave step, bringing together locally based women's groups who met around shared issues of interest. It started by meeting in 'neutral' venues and providing transport and childcare for the monthly gatherings. However, with developing relationships and confidence, the network took the decision to alternate its venues between community settings in single-identity Catholic and Protestant neighbourhoods across the Greater Belfast area. In this way the meetings broke down misperceptions and satisfied curiosity, as a participant reported: 'The Information Days gave women the chance to go into another area ... because even just crossing the road, the colour of the flag changes, the murals change – a different type of gunman is up, the curbstones be a different colour, and that alone can put a fear into women – the fear that they're not in their own territory. We can overcome that at Information Days.'[14] This particular civil society initiative was to continue throughout the years of the Troubles and during the years of the transition from violence, bringing many hundreds of women from

---

12 For further information, see Fearon 1999.
13 Interview conducted by the author, 11 February 2004.
14 Interview conducted by the author, 11 February 2004.

disadvantaged areas together on a monthly basis. Unlike the more deliberately catalytic initiatives, the cross-community dimension of the Women's Information Day network succeeded by largely avoiding divisive political issues in its open sessions; however, this was an example of work to build relationships and a degree of understanding and trust on a personal level.

Cross-community communication was arguably floating around in the policy ether since the work of the Northern Ireland Community Relations Commission (1969–1974) with its strategy of community development which prioritized work in the most disadvantaged areas. The Commission argued that if community confidence and leadership could be built, then issues of common concern might be identified that could, in time, offer the basis for cross-community action. This was based on the hope that the constitutional and ideological issues that divided people could be put on hold while communities got on with the ordinary business of living, and that joint working on 'bread and butter' issues could build trust and garner the potential for a less divisive approach to politically contentious challenges. As a philosophy of action, this approach was to have more purchase within the private, trade union and voluntary sectors. On the other hand, whilst a number of religious denominations accepted the need for communication, the churches were arguably rooted in ideological division, and local communities were seeing the price of constitutional divisiveness being played out on their physically divided streets. Within the private, trade union and voluntary sectors, policies and approaches were eventually inspired by a consciously non-sectarian approach – although the private sector often had to be chivied in this regard by the introduction of statutory fair employment legislation. Within the community sector, there were always examples of cross-community communications and working alignments, as well as from time to time the establishment of more structured organizational relationships between local community activists.[15] However, by the late 1980s, those local communities that identified themselves with the republican movement became more openly critical of a community relations strategy that seemed to place an emphasis on improved relations between the two communities in Northern Ireland (an endogenous approach) as compared to setting the ongoing conflict within the frame of the British–Irish–Northern Ireland constitutional relationship (the exogenous interpretation).[16] Thus, by the time the Northern Ireland Community Relations Council was set up in 1990, as a result of a combination of civil society pressure (Fitzduff and Frazer 1986) and a policy response from government, it was plunged into a maelstrom in which cross-community work and communication was to be attempted with 'extremely cross communities'.

In the earlier phase of the conflict, over the period 1969–1975, a number of cross-community initiatives were attempting to identify straws in the wind for

---

15 The Community Organizations of Northern Ireland (CONI) brought many local community activists together on a cross-community basis from 1975 to 1979, whilst the membership of the NICVA, as well as being drawn from the voluntary sector, also reflected a cross-community range of community organizations.
16 See O'Leary and McGarry 1997.

peace. Community education lecturer Tom Lovett worked with CONI, the Greater West Belfast Community Association and various community activists in the northwest to hold discussions and conferences on 'The Way Forward' in Magee College, Derry. A Community Conference Council gathering was also organized in Port Salon (Donegal) in September 1974, which brought together a number of leading businesspeople, religious leaders, legal representatives and 'community workers' who 'had an insight' into the thinking of the official and republican IRA, the UDA and other political interests. The agenda for the three-day residential included items such as internment, detainees' welfare, political freedom, causes of problems, analysis of republican demands and effects of violence, amongst others (Camplisson 1974). Community activists loosely identified with the loyalist UDA were proactively supported to set up the Ulster Community Action Group (UCAG) in 1975 in order to encourage greater loyalist engagement in political discussion, and individuals drawn from a wide spectrum of civil society supported the UDA as they moved to develop their 'Commonsense' and 'Beyond the Religious Divide' documents which had the potential to take the organization beyond the militarism of the Ulster Freedom Fighters, who were aligned with the UDA. A leading member of the UDA who was supportive of these developments remembered: 'We used everyone there that was prepared to listen ... From our point of view we were prepared [to work with] anyone who wanted to help ... We tried to talk to people from the nationalist community.'[17] However, the range of informal rounds of communication, contact and exchange – often conducted under the inclusive guise of community action – was to be stymied during the Secretary of Stateship of Roy Mason (1976–1979) and the official meta-narrative being spun. Notwithstanding this, a small number of conduits continued to operate on an individual basis to facilitate communication and counter political demonization.

The contribution of civil society organizations to communication within and between communities, and between communities and political decision-makers, was to take place at a number of levels during the course of the conflict, although some of the issues addressed were not always of a macro-political nature in themselves. The movement of individual trade unions and voluntary organizations from a non-sectarian position to an anti-sectarian stance was significant, as was the willingness of at least some trade unions to incorporate this policy position into their shop stewards' training.[18] The cross-community communication and campaigns around poverty and human rights issues were to develop in the face of the determinedly conservative Thatcher government in the 1980s. By the period of conflict transformation, in the mid- to late 1990s, the plethora of political agreements, commissions and consultative documents resulted in the cross-community Community Dialogue organization taking it upon itself to facilitate participative democracy by providing comprehensible versions of the official documents so that local communities could meet and discuss the implications for themselves. Communication was also a priority for the Farset Community Think Tank Project, which recognized the importance

---

17 Interview with the author in Belfast, 6 April 2005.
18 See also the work of Counteract (NI), City Bridges, and Trademark (NI).

of recorded memory, taped and published the reflections of community activists and ex-combatants from differing backgrounds, and then circulated them for wider discussion through a series of pamphlets.[19] And then there was the development of the community Mobile Phone Network, which worked to dispel unfounded rumours generated on the opposite sides of the peacewalls about the intentions of 'the other' community. Finally, throughout the decades of conflict, there were always those individuals drawn from civil society who made contact with 'the outsider', who suggested alternative conceptual frameworks or who went into the prisons during times of stress. The trustable intermediary was to continue to hold a position of importance in terms of promoting communication links.

The Role of Civil Society Actors as Change Agents

If politics is a struggle for people's imagination, then the role of change agents is to fire that imagination with new possibilities. There are a number of indicative examples that had an impact on the ending of violence. Two examples discussed here were at community level: the first was when a local community organization created space for loyalist ex-prisoners to liaise over a community issue in order to build pre-ceasefire space and confidence; and the second was a case of a community organization providing political cover to an important change opportunity.

In the first case, the Springfield Inter-Community Development Project (SICDP), which worked on both sides of the peacewall on the Springfield Road in West Belfast, employed a recently released Ulster Volunteer Force prisoner, Billy Hutchinson, on a community planning project. His management committee was drawn from both sides of the sectarian divide and his contacts on the republican side of the wall included leading republican ex-hunger striker Pat McGeown. Billy described what happened: 'We tried to get people together, you know, from the same social and economic background; forget about the religious stuff, if people wanted to walk and talk about that, then we had other strands in the project that could actually do that.'[20] Links were made between community development and community relations, but then went one step further, into conflict resolution and transformation. In 1990 not everyone was on board with these developments, but Billy fulfilled another important role: he gave the Ulster Volunteer Force representatives comfort that their tentative involvement in political talks with go-betweens had a value. Again, the deniability factor was important: 'I think they were quite happy to have somebody like me, you know, talking, because they could actually wash their hands of it and say "Nothing to do with us".'[21]

---

19 Hall (various dates), who worked with the community-based Farset Enterprises located on the Springfield interface in west Belfast.
20 Interview with the author, 15 December 2005.
21 Interview with the author, 15 December 2005.

The other example was when the Falls Community Council was used as a vehicle to enable the then Irish President Mary Robinson's visit to West Belfast in 1992. This, in turn, facilitated a public handshake between the President and the Sinn Fein leader, Gerry Adams – then still demonized. Again, a community activist who was involved in the arrangements held: 'That would have been regarded as one of the milestones, breaking the log jam … They [the government] knew that once she'd shook his hand somebody had to deal with him … Once you open the door a crack you push the door open as far as you can get to bring everyone into the room with you.'[22] The fate of the Windsor Women's Centre in a loyalist area of South Belfast, which was set on fire when it had the temerity to welcome the Irish President, highlighted the continuing complexity of civil society reaction.

Two very different models of civil society actors as change agents were reflected in the initiatives taken by two voluntary organizations: NIACRO and the CAJ. Financially supported by the pioneering Joseph Rowntree Charitable Trust, NIACRO enabled two of its staff to undertake a study of the early release of political prisoners in a range of societies in conflict (Gormally and McEvoy 1995), and then extended this work into an innovative restorative justice initiative undertaken with individuals with affiliations to the republican movement. After extensive discussion, a non-violent community mediation project was established on human rights principles in an attempt to replace the more traditional kneecapping that had been meted out by both republican and loyalist paramilitaries. The model – Community Restorative Justice – was to spread to loyalist areas and was one important step in the movement away from of violence and engagement in a broader debate over criminal justice, policing and community ownership.

The CAJ, on the other hand, took the lead in drawing together a thematic platform of four leading human rights organizations across Ireland and Britain in the immediate aftermath of the 1994 ceasefires to launch 'The Declaration on Human Rights, the Northern Ireland Conflict and the Peace Process', which called for human rights to become a core principle of any political settlement (Mageean and O'Brien 1999). The declaration was followed up with a skilled advocacy strategy to ensure the centrality of the issues raised. The coalition of NGOs built on earlier campaigns on equality, fair employment and rights issues (Campbell 2008: 48–103) that had often been politically controversial, but that were now set to become part of the scenery of the ongoing peace talks.

Acting as an effective change agent entailed adopting the often uncomfortable position of challenging the prevailing common sense of broader society, which invariably invited the sharp edge of political tongues and media coverage. In a society in conflict, all civil society actors had to be prepared to take the risk of putting their reputational capital into the balance. The Community Foundation for Northern Ireland was heavily criticized when it adopted an inclusive process of working with former political prisoners – with both loyalist and republican allegiances – bringing them into its decision-making processes over the period 1995–2005 by establishing a Grant Advisory Panel made up of representatives of

---

22 Interview with the author, 7 February 2006.

both loyalist and republican former prisoner groups.[23] Although answering an avalanche of parliamentary questions and media queries was not the norm for a charitable foundation, the Community Foundation believed that the importance of creating the space for these politically critical constituencies to meet and exchange views warranted the risks taken. Both the former political prisoners (a number of who are now elected members of the Northern Ireland Assembly) and the victims and survivors of the Troubles that the Community Foundation was also working with were participants in the broader peace-building initiative that the Foundation had put in place to encourage cross-community discussion and engagement.

Finding Space on a Crowded Stage

The respective roles adopted by civil society actors shifted and changed over the course of both the violent conflict and the more recent period of conflict transformation. Table 25.1 below summarizes the menu of roles adopted by such actors over the course of the Northern Ireland Troubles.

While the progression of violent conflict is rarely linear in nature, there are always phases on the continuum between the more balanced and unbalanced political power relations when intervention at a civil society level can be at the very least supportive and at best a form of innovative risk-taking in promoting exits out of violent confrontation. When civil society actors operate most effectively, they can make a judgement – informed by their broad range of contacts – about the kind of intervention that will maximize the possibilities at any particular moment in time, and they take action on the basis of confidentiality and/or solidarity, given the potential of the time. The experience of Northern Ireland would suggest that multi-layered interventions involving a range of different civil society actors, operating in various contexts, are important, although, as noted in the introduction to this chapter, they should not be over-exaggerated given the range of local, national and international actors and the heterogeneous nature of civil society itself.[24]

If all the world's a stage, as Shakespeare once wrote, then notwithstanding the role played by civil society actors, at various stages in the conflict, experience drawn from a number of divided societies would suggest that the final curtain call will be taken by the cast of political and governmental players. This is as it should be, given the imperative of representative democracy and the very real risks taken by a political leadership prepared to play leading roles. Where the contribution of civil society actors should not be forgotten is where audiences are small and the political theatricals restricted. It is in these conditions that there is a need to challenge meta-narratives of oversimplification and pessimism. Civil society actors, whatever their guise, are often in a prime position to mount these challenges and to keep the stage lights fixed firmly on possibilities for change.

---

23   Leat 2007: 116–31. See also Kilmurray (2004) and Shirlow et al. (2005).
24   As noted in Seligman 1995.

Table 25.1 Summary of the menu of roles adopted by such actors over the course of the Northern Ireland troubles

Date	Actor	Cheerleader	Communication	Catalyst	Change agent
1968	Community		Engaging in cross-community dialogue on shared concerns.	Ensuring local views are heard by policy makers and political actors.	Questioning of the status quo and providing trusted intermediaries with paramilitaries and political decision-makers.
to	Voluntary		Developing communication resources to facilitate community interchange.	Creating space for cross-community contacts.	Redefining the parameters of voluntary/community-level engagement.
1975	Other		Being prepared to listen and hear the views of marginalized groups and communities.	Working to maintain a level of neutral space. Offering resources to explore alternatives to violence.	Identifying contentious issues to be addressed by political decision-makers.
1976	Community		Continuing to engage with 'the other' and countering stereotyping.	Developing opportunities for inclusion of marginalized voices.	Creating space to counter demonization due to governmental narrative and/or sectarian stereotyping.
to	Voluntary	Supporting those who question community certainties and stereotypes.	Offering opportunities for cross-community communications around various issues.	Continuing to facilitate cross-community contacts and bringing forward new approaches/ideas.	Raising issues of human rights and justice notwithstanding the divisive politicization of such issues.
1994	Other	Rallies and campaigns to question violence and suggest alternate strategies.	Individuals fulfilling a role as 'back channel' communicators.	Create specific projects to address issues such as intimidation and anti-sectarian training.	

Date	Actor	Cheerleader	Communication	Catalyst	Change agent
1995 to 2005	Community	Modelling cross-community engagement and initiatives.	Ensuring that communities have information on political development. Communication to limit interface violence (mobile phone networks, etc.).	Demystifying political developments.	Offering structures and forums to facilitate political understanding and inclusion.
	Voluntary	Working to ensure that the needs of communities/groups most affected by violence are met.	Mobilizing inter-sectoral communication to build alliances.	Bringing in experiences from other societies in transition from violence.	Providing reputational cover for initiatives that question the official narrative.
	Other	Highlighting the costs of any return to violence.	Supporting cross-border communications.		Supporting initiatives to address inclusion of marginalized groups and communities.

References

Acheson, N. et al (2004) *Two Paths, One Purpose: Voluntary Action in Ireland, North and South*. Dublin, Institute of Public Administration.
Burrows, R. (ed.) (1991) *Community Development in Protestant Areas*. Belfast, Northern Ireland Community Relations Council.
Campbell, B. (2008) *Agreement – The State, Conflict and Change in Northern Ireland*. London, Lawrence & Wishart.
Camplisson, J. (ed.) (1974) 'Community Conference Council '74: Report on Port Salon Conference'. Belfast, unpublished paper.
Cockburn, C. (1998) *The Space Between Us – Negotiating Gender and National Identities in Conflict*. London: Zed Books.
Deane, E. and Ritter, C. (eds) (1994) *Beyond Hate: Living with our Differences*. Derry: YES Publications.
Dominelli, L. (1995) 'Women in the Community: Feminist Principles and Organizing in Community Work', *Community Development Journal* 30(2): 133–43.
Duffy, F. and Percival, R. (1975) *Community Action and Community Perceptions of the Social Services in Northern Ireland*. Coleraine: Department of Social Administration, New University of Ulster.
Fearon, K. (1999) *Women's Work – The Story of the Northern Ireland Women's Coalition*. Belfast: Blackstaff Press.
Fitzduff, M. and Frazer, H. (1986) *Improving Community Relations*. Belfast: Standing Advisory Commission on Human Rights.
Gormally, B. and McEvoy, K. (1995) *Release and Reintegration of Politically Motivated Prisoners in Northern Ireland – A Comparative Study of South Africa, Israel/Palestine, Italy, Spain, the Republic of Ireland and Northern Ireland*. Belfast: Northern Ireland Association of the Care and Resettlement of Offenders.
Greer, J. (2001) *Partnership Governance in Northern Ireland – Improving Performance*. Aldershot: Ashgate.
Hall, M. (various dates) *Island Pamphlets*. Newtownabbey: Island Publications.
Kilmurray, A. (ed.) (2004) *Taking Calculated Risks for Peace*. Belfast: Community Foundation for Northern Ireland.
Leat, D. (2007) *Just Change – Strategies for Increasing Philanthropic Impact*. London: Association of Charitable Foundations.
McCready, S. (2001) *Empowering People – Community Development and Conflict, 1969–1999*. Belfast: HMSO.
Mageean, P. and O'Brien, M. (1999) 'From the Margins to the Mainstream – Human Rights and the Good Friday Agreement', *Fordham International Law Journal* 22: 1499–538.
Mason, R. (1999) *Paying the Price*. London: Robert Hale.
Morison, J. and Livingstone, S. (1995) *Reshaping Public Power: Northern Ireland and the British Constitutional Crisis*. London: Sweet & Maxwell.
Northern Ireland Council for Voluntary Action (2002) *State of the Sector 111*. Belfast: Northern Ireland Council for Voluntary Action.

Northern Ireland Voluntary Trust (1995) *Response to Community Priority Survey*. Belfast: NIVT.

O'Leary, B. and McGarry, J. (1997) *The Politics of Antagonism – Understanding Northern Ireland*. London: Athlone Press.

Pollak, A. (ed.) (1993) *A Citizens' Inquiry – The Opsahl Report of Northern Ireland*. Dublin: Lilliput Press.

Quigley, G. (2002) 'Achieving Transformational Change', in M. Elliott (ed.), *The Long Road to Peace in Northern Ireland*. Liverpool: Liverpool University Press.

Seligman, A. (1995) *The Idea of Civil Society*. Princeton, NJ: Princeton University Press.

Shirlow, P. et al. (2005) *Politically Motivated Former Prisoner Groups: Community Action and Conflict Transformation*. Belfast: Northern Ireland Community Relations Council.

PART VII
Dealing with the Aftermath

26

Defining and Building the Rule of Law in the Aftermath of Political Violence: The Processes of Transitional Justice

Richard J. Goldstone and Adam M. Smith

Introduction

'Rule of law' and 'transitional justice' are simultaneously analytically distinct notions with vastly divergent histories *and* concepts that have been increasingly brought to bear together, responsive to the same sorts of problems. Rule of law, broadly speaking the idea that the most just manner of state management is for all to be subject to legal edict rather than human caprice, is a concept as old as political theory itself. It first appeared in the writings of Aristotle and Plato, and has played a role in the work of theorists ever since. Transitional justice, meanwhile, which speaks to the 'processes ... associated with a society's attempts to come to terms with a legacy of a prior regime's ... abuses', is of much more recent vintage (United Nations 2004, 4). Though there were sputtering attempts after the First World War, our modern understanding of transitional justice can only be traced to the post-Second World War era when the Allies wrestled with the most effective means to address the violence that had been perpetrated by the German Reich and the Japanese Empire.

Despite their different ages and provenances, rule of law and transitional justice share several features. First, until recently both concepts were largely confined to the philosophical domain rather than being thought applicable to practical policy-making. Rule of law has been the subject of debate and discussion for millennia with limited departure from the Ivory Tower throughout. Transitional justice was briefly a policy choice with the creation of the post-Second World War Nuremberg and Tokyo Trials. Yet, these proceedings were *sui generis* and gave way to decades of academic debate on transitional justice but on-the-ground inaction. A primary connection between rule of law and transitional justice is that they both only emerged as fully fledged *policy tools* after the Cold War. So long as the Soviet Union and the USA remained at loggerheads, there could be little international policy agreement on what 'rule of law' or 'transitional justice' entailed. Major international bodies, such as the United Nations (UN) and the Organization for Security and Co-operation in Europe (OSCE), which have played such central roles in promoting the policies of rule of law and transitional justice in the post-Cold War era, were hamstrung by this geopolitical intransigence. It was only with the emergence of a brief *Pax Americana* in the early 1990s that multi-stakeholder institutions were able to move forward on the ground, implementing policy from long-brewing theory.

A second similarity is that when they emerged, they did so as linked policies, one following from the other: states emerging from political violence and eager to establish rule of law were counselled to undertake a process of transitional justice.

Third, since the beginning of the 1990s, both rule of law and transitional justice have attempted to make up for lost time, becoming ubiquitous policy prescriptions and enjoying near-universal support. It would be hard to find other concepts that have achieved so global an endorsement.

A final, often unstated feature shared by rule of law and transitional justice is that there is limited agreement, either worldwide or even within a given society, as to what either concept actually entails. In a sense it is at least partly due to their inherent flexibility that rule of law and transitional justice have had such wide appeal. In many respects, they are what their proponents wish them to be. The combination of widespread deployment, near unanimity of support and definitional uncertainty has led to an industry of policy-makers and scholars explicitly pursuing the same goals in motley states overcoming the legacy of political violence, but with often radically different means and ends.

This chapter will focus on the different strategies employed by practitioners of transitional justice and will provide some context and assessment regarding how successful they have been in achieving rule of law. To do so, we will begin by briefly examining the wide range of definitions policy-makers have ascribed to rule of law and the equally broad range of techniques transitional justice practitioners have relied upon in seeking rule of law. As we shall see, examining rule of law through the lens of transitional justice can help focus and narrow both concepts, more firmly grounding each in policy practice rather than philosophical discourse.

Understanding Rule of Law through Transitional Justice

Since it came of age as a policy tool, rule of law has been applied as a stated policy objective in countries emerging from diverse forms of political violence. Initially, policy-makers warmed to rule of law as the goal for the post-communist transitions in Europe. Once the Berlin Wall fell, Central and Eastern European states were essentially viewed as the 'lawless' cousins of Western Europe, with establishing rule of law the key both to their overcoming the overhang of communist violence and their integration into the West.

As the early 1990s progressed and more concentrated political violence in the form of genocides and other mass crimes erupted in the Balkans and then in the African Great Lakes, rule of law was again called upon. The argument echoed the post-communist application and the Balkans and Rwanda were criticized for lacking rule of law. The establishment of rule of law was thought to be critical to addressing and reconciling these states.

The application of rule of law would expand further towards the end of the 1990s – appearing in Northern Ireland as a mode to move past its 'Troubles', in Mozambique and Guatemala as a bookend to their civil wars, and in numerous other situations. By the end of the 1990s, rule of law had become such a policy reflex that a leading scholar quipped that one could not engage in a foreign policy debate on almost any topic without someone suggesting 'rule of law as a solution to the world's troubles' (Carothers 1998, 95). Rule of law has only continued its expansion since 2000 and has been suggested to 'solve' problems in both the world's seemingly lawless areas such as Somalia and the tribal belts of Afghanistan and Pakistan, as well as in those states where law exists and state hegemony is not seriously questioned, such as in Russia, China and Venezuela. In both sorts of environments, observers have argued that rule of law is lacking, political violence has been furthered and rule of law must thus be sought.

As is evident from its expansive usage, rule of law is multi-faceted and not amenable to easy definition. This fact may account for the uneven success of rule of law programmes since the beginning of the 1990s; there has been little accord regarding exactly what promoters of rule of law were seeking. The difficulty in finding a useful definition has meant that for many it is easiest to 'find' rule of law in hindsight, after rule of law has broken down and violence has erupted. Such a definition sees rule of law as much as a prescription for moving forward as it is a diagnosis of what went wrong. This is intuitively satisfying, given that political violence and especially mass crimes often seem to go along with an absence of rule of law. The apparent anarchy of Rwanda's genocide in 1994, the marauding 'irregular' forces in the 1991–2001 Yugoslav wars that perpetrated so many of that conflict's horrific crimes, and the existence of the Nazi *Schutzstaffel* (SS) operating outside the comparatively legally-bound German *Wehrmacht* during the Second World War, are all leading examples of an absence of rule of law catalysing (or at least allowing) unchecked violence.

The challenge for this definition is that it does not speak to the meaning of 'rule of law', but rather to 'absence of violence'. Evidently peace that emerges after violence subsides does not of its own accord produce rule of law. Consequently, this 'hindsight' definition does not adequately explain what was missing from rule of law in the first place that allowed these violations. As a policy tool it is lacking, providing limited direction and no clear metric for recognizing rule of law when it appears. A similar ambiguity pervades perhaps the most common definition of rule of law relied upon by policy-makers: an 'institutional' understanding. Carothers, for instance, speaks of rule of law 'as a system in which the laws are public knowledge, are clear in meaning, and apply equally to everyone' (Carothers 1998, 95). Such a system is buttressed by state institutions that enforce, adjudicate and punish. There is much to recommend an 'institutional' definition and the formalization and predictability of this understanding of rule of law counters the ad hoc, arbitrary application of regulations that pervades many states without rule of law. Indeed, it calls to mind the original Aristotelian understanding of 'rule of law' as a rejection of the 'Rule of Man' (Aristotle 350 BC).

Yet the limitations of this definition are many. Most prosaically, the existence of law 'on the books' may not translate into 'law in action' (Stephenson 2009). A seemingly robust, dense legal system and set of supporting state institutions may officially exist, but they may not actually function, returning rule of law to philosophical construct rather than societal reality. For example, as of this writing, the Federal Charter of the Somali Republic provides citizens, *inter alia*, with the right to personal liberty and security (Republic of Somalia 1961, Arts. 24, 26). However, the current Somali government is so weak that any legal protections remain solely *de jure*, with little to no law actually existing on the ground. A different dimension of this problem comes in states where the governments' deeds do not match its laws. The 1977 Constitution of the Soviet Union legally granted Soviet citizens rights which were abrogated more than enforced: citizens had the putative rights to freedom of speech, assembly, and religion, yet would pay dearly if they attempted to practice any of these 'rights' (Soviet Union 1977, Arts. 50, 52). The current constitution of the Democratic People's Republic of Korea (North Korea) provides similarly hollow rights to civil and political expression, with often deadly consequences endured by any who dare assert them (Democratic People's Republic of Korea 1998, Chapter 5).

A further limitation of the institutional understanding of rule of law concerns situations in which states do bring their laws on the books into action, but the laws themselves are suspect. The legal edifice that upheld South Africa's Apartheid or promulgated the degradation of Jews under the Nuremberg Laws, or Blacks under the USA's 'Jim Crow' regulations, would fit many institutional definitions of rule of law. However, these legal systems were not only perversions of rule of law, but in themselves countenanced the commissioning of political violence of the most egregious kinds.

The difficulties of the institutional definition are a microcosm of the challenges inherent in defining rule of law, challenges which coalesce around three central questions for policy-makers. First, is 'rule of law' an end to itself or a means to greater ends? For their part, UN officials have argued the latter. In 2003, Jean-Marie Guéhenno, then Under-Secretary General for Peacekeeping Operations, stated that 'the restoration of … rule of law is *sine qua non* for the sustainable resolution of conflict and the rebuilding of secure, orderly and humane societies' (United Nations 2003). Others argue that rule of law can only emerge as an end goal, once conflict has been sustainably resolved and society is secure and orderly.

The second question, as made clear by the practitioners of Apartheid and the Nuremberg and Jim Crow laws, relates to the practice of political violence *through* rule of law. This presents a thorny difficulty for rule of law adherents in that it necessitates making a judgment that some laws do not make for 'rule of law'. But what are the parameters of 'real' rule of law?

Third, and finally, speaking to the disjuncture between the statement of rule of law and its application, in what direction does rule of law flow? Is it only from the government onto the people or does true rule of law imply some aspect of societal involvement in the creation and enforcement of rule of law? Though some formalists disagree, most scholars have concluded that rule of law must imply a societal ethic and not solely a governmental form. A rule of law that does not enjoy acceptance, application and legitimacy by the populace strains to be called rule of law.

In the abstract, even responding to these three questions does little to limit the breadth of the concept. One could logically answer these queries and pursue a rule of law so extensive and so culturally bound and politically complex as to be nearly impossible to establish and susceptible to collapsing under its own weight. Alternatively, one could pursue a rule of law that is thin and brittle, comparatively easy to achieve but difficult to sustain.

Fortunately for practitioners, transitional justice provides some limitation to the potential range of rule of law. In as much as the goal of transitional justice is to aid in building rule of law, transitional justice as a policy concept has come to refer to the techniques employed to allow a state to transition in a sustaining, 'liberalizing direction' (Teitel 2000, 5). In other words, only transitions seeking to move away from illiberal environments, those replete with bigotry, crime and/or other political violence, and towards states that are in line with more universal notions of 'the good' as articulated in various international conventions and human rights understandings, are included in an appropriate understanding of transitional justice.

In line with the fundamental limitations imposed by transitional justice, a powerful and useful definition for rule of law emerges. One can find that a state enjoys rule of law when it 'successfully monopolizes the means of violence, and in which most people, most of the time, choose to resolve disputes in a manner ... that respects fundamental human rights norms' (Stromseth, Wippman and Brooks 2006, 78). In such a 'thick' definition, rule of law is an end in itself, it must comport with 'fundamental [notions of] human rights' and it must not only be applied *on* the populace but also actually be used by citizens to 'resolve disputes'. In short, there must be local ownership. The difference between true 'rule of law' and Apartheid, the Nuremberg and Jim Crow laws is manifest – none of these suspect 'rules of law' comport with human rights and it would strain the notion of 'ownership' to claim that the subject of these regulations 'owned' them.

Despite the seeming simplicity of the 'thick' definition, the transitional justice employed to develop rule of law can be politically fraught, and the profile of the specific system chosen depends in large measure upon the circumstances from which it emerges. Whether transitional justice occurs in the process of regime change or regime 're-alignment' (compare Argentina after the 'dirty war' with post-Second World War Japan), whether it receives near-universal domestic support or not (compare post-communist Eastern Europe with Northern Ireland after the Troubles), and the role, if any, of the international community in the process (compare the former Yugoslavia after the Balkan wars with post-Apartheid South Africa) can be determinative factors.

Though it is clear that each situation will be unique, the thick understanding of rule of law as seen through transitional justice serves as a powerful lens through which to examine the various means of transitional justice that have been used to pursue rule of law. How successful have they been?

The Transitional Justice Spectrum

While the Nuremberg prosecutions after the Second World War set the initial standard for modern transitional justice processes, the world of transitional justice is almost as varied and broad as are definitions of rule of law. As an analytical exercise, one can speak of five broad categories of transitional justice, describing the various classes of transitional justice that have been practised:

1. amnesties;
2. lustrations/exclusions;
3. truth commissions;
4. prosecutions;
5. retributive political violence.

A brief review of the successes and failures of the various models of transitional justice demonstrates that no single solution holds the secret to the successful establishment of rule of law. Each transitional system has seen achievements and failures. However, in the following analysis, broad trends can be seen, and the chapter will conclude with the key lessons learned from these experiences.

Amnesties

No other variety of transitional justice has been practised so often and with such controversy as 'amnesty'. The term derives from the Greek word 'amnestia', which means 'oblivion'. Exactly what an amnesty can cast into 'oblivion' – essentially the obliteration of 'all legal remembrance' of a crime – is what has made the issuance of amnesties controversial. For many, the very notion of 'amnesty' does violence to rule of law by allowing past transgressions to disappear and past abusers to remain unpunished. Some argue that widespread amnesties allow others to calculate that they too can 'get away with it'; thus, the practice dulls the deterrent effect of any punishments that are meted out on those who do not receive amnesties.

Amnesties have played a part in the treatment of old regimes by new leadership for millennia. More recently:

> Governments from every region of the world have decided to grant amnesties to persons who committed serious crimes ... In the past twenty years, Argentina, Chile, Uruguay, El Salvador, Guatemala, Peru, Zimbabwe, South Africa, Haiti, Sierra Leone, Colombia, Afghanistan, and Algeria have granted amnesty to persons who had [committed such] crimes. (Trumbull 2007, 296–7)

While the exact legal process of amnesty – whether achieved by legislative or executive decree or in the course of a negotiated peace accord – may differ, the end result is similar. The only substantive variation concerns the scope of which crimes qualify for amnesty and consequently which perpetrators receive it. It is in this regard that significant debate and discord has emerged. Notably, such dissonance has been seen both within and between organizations. In 2000 the UN Secretary-General stated that the UN had 'consistently maintained the position that amnesty cannot be granted in respect of international crimes' (United Nations 2000, 5; Schabas 2006, 347). Though this limitation is widely accepted as the correct outer bound for amnesties, in reality the UN's support for amnesties for even international crimes has been more varied. In the early 1990s – alongside the UN's development of international criminal tribunals to address Rwanda and the Balkans (institutions designed, at least in part, to deny amnesty to violators) – the UN and other international organizations actively or tacitly supported amnesties for often equally horrific crimes perpetrated in Haiti, El Salvador, Guatemala and Sierra Leone. In the Balkans themselves and despite the jurisdiction of the UN's tribunal and the presence of horrific crimes, various international organizations have thought amnesties would be a promising option. For instance, during the height of the Yugoslav wars, Philippe Morillon, the commanding general of the North Atlantic Treaty Organization (NATO) forces, stated that a 'general amnesty' was critical to calming the region (Smith 2009, 217).

There are two sorts of arguments supporters use in promoting amnesties, one applicable to a post-violent state and the other to a state that remains in the throes of violence. For a state that has begun to emerge from political violence, the argument is that amnesties allow a new regime (and its people) to 'draw a line through the past' and start again. The concern these supporters have is that compelling a legal reckoning would freeze the state, forcing the new regime into a long-winded and perhaps debilitating retrospective assessment of its history. Robert Mugabe made this determination upon assuming power as the first leader of independent Zimbabwe in 1980. He decided not to prosecute the abuses committed by Ian Smith's regime, arguing that 'it was a war' and that both sides were guilty of 'trying to kill each other' (Roht-Arriaza 1995, 254). The same view prevailed in the days after the Franco dictatorship in Spain when Spanish writer Jorge Semprun argued that: 'If you want to live a normal life, you must forget. Otherwise those wild snakes freed from their box will poison public life for years to come' (Michnik and Havel 1993, 24).

Others argue, however, that if one does not address the past in some manner, a state cannot move forward regardless. A robust rule of law cannot be built on the uncertain foundations of pent-up feelings of neglect by victims and unacknowledged harms. While the success and stability of post-Franco Spain may represent the counter case, Zimbabwe is a self-evident illustration of this potential weakness of amnesties. Opponents of amnesties could look to those granted by the Mugabe government as laying the groundwork for a regime that in its latter days of rule has itself committed awful acts of violence.

The other argument for amnesties arises in the process of trying to end violence, and speaks to the debate over 'Peace vs. Justice'. Amnesties have often been offered to warring parties as sweeteners in peace deals. At times they have worked and parties came to peace; at other times, belligerents have used the negotiations towards amnesties solely as a stalling tactic, with a cessation in violence and even amnesties themselves providing them the opportunity to regroup rather than return to the fold. Amnesties have allowed them to play spoiler rather than peacemaker.

This is a live issue in today's Uganda where Kampala has been battling the Lord's Resistance Army (LRA) for two decades. Members of the LRA leadership have been indicted by the International Criminal Court (ICC), but Uganda's President Yoweri Musevini has continued negotiations with the LRA seeking a cessation to its violence. As a part of the negotiations, he has offered amnesties and even suggested asking the ICC to withdraw its indictments. While there has been significant debate about the propriety (legal or otherwise) of the ICC withdrawing an issued indictment in such circumstances, there have been equally heated arguments suggesting that the LRA is merely using the offer of amnesties to gain some breathing space to continue its fighting rather than come to peace.

There are two further variables in amnesties that have become increasingly evident concerning the scope of amnesties' effects. First, there is the question of the duration of an amnesty. While casting something into legal 'oblivion' seems to imply the permanence of amnesties, in recent years, amnesties appear to have a far more limited life. For example, in Chile and Argentina, amnesties granted in the wake of their *junta*s' rule (in 1983 and 1990, respectively) have been recently abrogated by those nations' highest courts and prosecutions begun against those who were officially granted amnesty. Regional human rights courts have also acted to declare amnesties void – in 2001, in its *Barrios Altos* ruling, the Inter-American Court of Human Rights held that amnesties granted by Peru to human rights violators were incompatible with Peru's obligations under the American Convention on Human Rights and consequently they must be stricken (Pasqualucci and Buergenthal 2003, 248; *Chumbipuma Aguirre et al. v. Republic of Peru* (2001), 43–4).

The second aspect of the scope of amnesties is the effect of an amnesty on another jurisdiction's desire or ability to prosecute individuals. Again, Chile plays a central role. Two years before the Chilean courts stripped former *junta* leader Augusto Pinochet of his amnesty, the Spanish government sought to prosecute him for crimes his regime committed (and for which the subsequent Chilean government had granted him 'permanent' amnesty). In this case, the Chilean amnesty had no force before Spanish courts, which issued a warrant for his arrest. Similarly, the Special Court for Sierra Leone refused to recognize the amnesties provided by the Lomé Agreement, stating, *inter alia*, that they may 'be of doubtful validity under international law' (Special Court for Sierra Leone 2004, 34). The steady globalization of law and justice – in which, *inter alia*, international and domestic tribunals share jurisdiction and countries practise 'universal jurisdiction' – means that some amnesties may have increasingly limited geographic and temporal effect (Trumbull 2007, 304–6).

With all of these variables and variations, it is hard to find a prototypical case of an amnesty, let alone to definitively conclude whether amnesties aid the establishment of rule of law. Despite this, it is evident that this technique *alone* cannot build rule of law. Amnesties, after all, are in some senses counter-law, allowing known violators to escape punishment. Such an escape may be necessary in order to secure societal peace and justice, and eventual rule of law, but more is clearly needed. Perhaps the best way to view amnesties is not as a tool towards rule of law, but, at best, as an instrument that can help create enough political space in order for rule of law to be allowed to grow. In the case of South Africa, it has been said that amnesty (as a part of the truth commission process – see below) was a critical incentive and allowed the 'county [to] begin the long and necessary process of healing the wounds of the past' (*Azanian People's Organization* 1996, 17). The policy-relevant inquiry thus becomes whether, in any particular case, amnesties uniformly serve as fertile ground for the 'healing' needed for robust growth of rule of law or whether in some cases they salt the soil to such a degree that rule of law struggles to be established. The outcome of the process is contingent upon the conditions under which amnesties have been granted – the range of potentials is significant, ranging from the most basic of 'blanket amnesties' (which cover a select class of individuals automatically) to more selectively prescribed varieties that refuse amnesties for specific, especially serious infractions and/or require applicants for amnesties to express remorse and/or fully confess to their crimes. Each type of amnesty has its own benefits and drawbacks depending upon the social and political environment in which it is implemented.

There have been some clear cases in which the process of amnesty allowed space and sustainable rule of law to emerge; in fact, 'a survey of 200 constitutional reforms since 1975 ... found that amnesty was strongly associated with the durability of civil peace' (Snyder and Vinjamuri 2006, 9). Uruguay is a heartening example of this success. At the end of its military regime in the mid-1980s, the new democratic government provided the *junta*'s leadership a far-reaching amnesty. The amnesty provision was controversial, but President Julio Sanguinetti was convinced that this was the only way to consolidate democracy. Though causation is difficult to demonstrate, it is hard to quibble with Uruguay's success since the amnesty – democratic vibrancy and enviable economic growth and stability. Rule of law, and its attendant benefits, has thrived.

Lustrations/Exclusions

This transitional process seeks to identify and punish wrongdoers from the prior regime by exposing them and excluding them from a range of public offices in the new regime (Boed 1999, 357). Lustration is a unique transitional technique for two reasons. First, unlike the other models, it has few champions outside the regions in which it has been practised. It has become widely disfavoured by the international human rights community, with many critical of the process as potentially violative of individual rights (because it has often based an individual's exclusion on sources of dubious accuracy and has often denied lustrated individuals the right of appeal). Consequently, many are sceptical of its ability to build rule of law (Boed 1999, 359, 398–9).

Second, lustration is the only transitional technique that has become identified almost exclusively with a particular region at a particular time: post-communist Central and Eastern Europe. It is true that the lustration processes can be seen elsewhere (as in post-Saddam Hussein Iraq, discussed below), but nowhere has it been practised so extensively as in the former Warsaw Bloc.

These two features – limited international support and high geographical concentration – derive from the characteristics of both the political violence endured by Central and Eastern European states during their five decades of totalitarian control and of the challenges these states faced in the years immediately following the fall of the Berlin Wall. The political violence endured in this region was of a different type from that seen in many other transitioning states. While Latin American and African dictatorships have regularly practised outright violence, with killings and torture a mainstay of their operations, especially after Stalin (post-1953), the violence in Central and Eastern Europe was in general less physical and more 'psychological', revolving around social control (Huyse 1995, 72–3). The key to this control was in states developing an Orwellian network of oversight, using a bloated secret police to 'creat[e] widespread mistrust in which individuals were encouraged to feel suspicious of their fellow citizen, neighbour, or even family member' (Horne and Levi 2002, 7).

The European transitions that began in 1989 were largely peaceful, another unique factor in the decision to pursue lustration. In fact, in many cases the change in regime from communist to post-communist appeared to be only evolutionary (rather than revolutionary), with *ante bellum* leaders remaining in power, acknowledging the new reality simply by renaming and re-branding their 'communist' parties. However, a backlash against the former regimes soon arose. Newly free citizens became angry at both the continuing power of those former communists who aided or participated in the past regimes' violence and the fact that it was unknown who else outside government had acted in concert with the state (as informers) to similarly assist in the perpetration of the regimes' crimes. As Ellis notes, it was in 'this context, [that] debate surfaced that focused on questions of culpability for crimes committed by former Communist regimes' (Ellis 1996, 181). Though other transitional options were mooted and even partially pursued, lustration laws quickly became the preferred tool. While the form of lustration:

> varie[d] among different countries in Central and Eastern Europe, [lustration] … universally [refers to the process by which new governments] assess[ed the involvement of individuals in] past regime[s' wrongdoing] based on accounts

from the information in the secret police files of the former regime. (Horne and Levi 2002, 15)

Lustration uniquely matched the needs of the post-Cold War situation. The process focused on the primary instrument of oppression employed by these totalitarian regimes: the bureaucracy, and in particular willing bureaucrats and their allies. Lustration, as it was often implemented, denied those implicated in cooperating with the past regime from again wielding this instrument of power. Lustration also served a truth-telling and shaming function. The opening of the secret police files in all of the post-communist countries helped to answer long-held questions and in so doing publicly branded those who betrayed friends and family.

Even if clear in hindsight, at the time it was not evident that lustration was the 'right' transitional process. Lustration was not immediately embraced by states. The first post-communist Polish government explicitly rejected the policy, with Prime Minister Tadeusz Mazowiecki pledging to draw a 'thick line' under the communist past. Other states only came to lustration slowly and ambivalently. Czechoslovakia passed lustration laws in 1991, Hungary in 1994 and Poland, despite Mazowiecki's pledge, came around to lustration in 1997. The scope of lustration changed over time, with the early adopters usually implementing narrow screening processes, while the latter expanded it markedly. Hungary, for instance, initially saw just 12,000 officials subjected to screening for potential lustration, while in Romania, which has one of the most recently enacted lustration processes (in 2005), 1.35 million files were placed under review for potential lustration.

Though the role of lustration in the post-1989 development of rule of law in Central and Eastern European states is debatable, there is no doubt that the states where lustration has been practised have by and large successfully built rule of law. Several of these states are now members of the European Union and/or NATO, and all have vibrant political, civic and legal cultures.

Yet, there are counter-examples in which the lustration process itself had collateral effects that have hindered the pursuit of rule of law. The Iraqi process is emblematic of this risk. Iraq under Saddam Hussein was more violent than most European communist states, though the process of control exercised by Baghdad and the crimes committed by the regime would be recognizable to any citizen who lived behind the Iron Curtain. A combination of a cult of personality and hegemonic control exercised through the vehicles of the secret police and apparatchiks of the ruling Baath Party kept dissent at bay while providing a ready source of patronage to supporters. As one of his initial acts, Paul Bremer, the administrator of the Coalition Provisional Authority (the American-led occupational government that administered Iraq from shortly after the March 2003 invasion until June 2004) ordered a mass lustration, outlawing the Baath Party and dismissing as many as 30,000 Baathists from ministerial positions. While the act enjoyed some early support, over time, and especially as Iraq became more violent and fractured, it was clear that lustration had been short-sighted. The process removed the only trained members of the bureaucracy, including those critical to state management, missed an opportunity to co-opt into the new democratic state many who had only joined the Baath Party because they were forced to do so and, perhaps most importantly, effectively denied local, Iraqi ownership of the transition. In fact, a large part of Iraqi lustration was actually reversed over time, as former Baathists were welcomed back into the bureaucracy. Rule of law that may yet develop in Iraq was arguably retarded by the seemingly reflexive move towards lustration (Otterman 2005).

Truth Commissions

The third potential transitional justice technique is a process that tasks a usually non-judicial body with uncovering the truth of what transpired during the prior regime (Hayner 2002, 1–49). Given that political violence throughout the world has often incurred unsolved crimes and 'disappeared' individuals, finding the 'truth' has frequently been a critical goal for successful transition.

The South African Truth and Reconciliation Commission, which operated from 1995 to 1998, is viewed by some as the paragon for this model and it has been credited with helping post-Apartheid South Africa come to terms with its brutal past. Truth commissions, however, have been established throughout the world, as a part of transitions seen in states as diverse as Ghana, the Solomon Islands, South Korea, Morocco, Guatemala and East Timor.

Because commissions are explicitly not courts oor *stricto senso* 'legal', many have asked exactly how they fit into the transitional justice canon. What is it that they hope to achieve? Popkin and Roht-Arriaza identify four main goals for the process:

1. creating an authoritative record of what happened;
2. providing a platform for the victims to tell their stories and obtain some form of redress;
3. recommending legislative, structural or other changes to avoid a repetition of past abuses; and
4. establishing who was responsible and providing a measure of accountability for the perpetrators (Popkin and Roht-Arriaza 1995, 262).

In addition, practitioners often use truth commissions as a tool of reconciliation. In fact, many truth commissions are explicitly 'Truth and Reconciliation Commissions'. The reconciliation component comes from their allowing:

> [t]he families of those unlawfully tortured, maimed or traumatised [to] become more empowered [once they] discover the truth, the perpetrators [to] become exposed to opportunities to obtain relief from the burden of ... guilt or ... anxiety they might be living with for many long years, [and] the country [to] begin the long and necessary process of healing the wounds of the past, transforming anger and grief into a mature understanding and creating the emotional and structural climate essential for ... 'reconciliation and reconstruction'. (*Azanian People's Organization* 1996, 17)

Though each commission has been unique, in general the process undertaken by the various bodies can be divided into several discrete steps. First, much like lustration, this transitional technique has emerged only after political violence has ceased, and usually after a new regime has been put in place. A commission is established by legislative or executive decree and is given a mandate to 'bear witness' to violations that occurred during the tenure of the prior regime. Commission membership varies between different commissions, and they have often included eminent citizens from home and/or abroad. In order to achieve the fullest picture of the 'truth', most commissions are charged with hearing the stories of crimes committed by all sides, and not just those of the old regime's leadership. As such, the South African Commission heard from both officials of the Apartheid government and leaders of the African National Congress, and learned about crimes committed by each group. In order to secure the participation of witnesses, commissions are often provided with either subpoena power (in that they can force witnesses to testify) and/or the power to provide witnesses amnesties in exchange for testimony. In South Africa, the Commission had broad discretion to grant amnesties to those who appeared before it, but only if they offered a 'full confession' and the crimes about which they spoke were 'politically motivated' and not a 'gross violation of human rights' (South Africa 1994, No. 34). Though controversial, it was evident that '[w]ithout that incentive there [was] nothing to encourage such persons to make the disclosures and to reveal the truth' which was 'so desperately desire[d]' (*Azanian People's Organization* 1996, 17).

The final step in all commissions is the presentation of a report. These reports have often been very moving and many have been published and disseminated not just locally but also throughout the world (see, for example, Argentine National Commission on the Disappeared 1986).

In several cases, truth commissions have indisputably played an important role in building and solidifying rule of law. The South African experience is noteworthy, but so too are those of Ghana and Argentina. Some suggest that one of the reasons why truth commissions can serve as an important foundation for rule of law is that they provide acknowledgement for victims and, even if they do not further the right of victims to see their assailant prosecuted (see below), they vindicate another right: the independent right to 'know what happened' (Naqvi 2006, 245–73). Despite their many benefits, some scholars are quick to note that truth commissions are 'clearly not [always] necessary' for building rule of law and:

> one can point to a number of cases of relatively peaceful transitions to democracy in which the past has not been systematically examined. In places like Mozambique ... there appears to be a consensus that the past should be left alone [and there] is a sense ... that rehashing the past will bring a return of violence. (Brahm 2004)

Moreover, there are some observers who criticize truth commissions for their reliance on specific political environments. Whatever their promise, plainly truth commissions cannot be implemented in many situations.

Prosecutions

The fourth mode of transitional justice involves the prosecutions of those who perpetrated political violence. Directly recalling the Nuremberg model, states have either independently or with the assistance of the international community brought wrongdoers before judicial bodies, held trials and sentenced the convicted. Since the establishment of the International Criminal Tribunals for the former Yugoslavia (ICTY) and Rwanda (ICTR) in 1993 and 1994, respectively, for many, this mode of transition has become the *primus inter pares* of all processes. Some have called prosecution of prior political violence 'the appropriate and necessary goal' of *any* successful transition. Supporters posit that in as much as transitional justice aims to build rule of law, and the violent conduct of the prior regime was a radical departure from the law, a *legal* reckoning of the past is a uniquely potent tool towards that end. Pressure for states to undertake prosecutions (as opposed to any other transitional process) was seen by keen observers even before the ICTY and ICTR were established. Reiter argued that 'countries transitioning in the post-Nuremberg environment [since the Second World War] have [all] been confronted with ... international and domestic pressure to hold past perpetrators [legally] accountable' (Reiter, Olsen and Payne 2007, 2).

Some proponents of investigations and trials argue that states should always heed such pressure and that denying victim's legal, punitive redress would itself violate victims' rights. Several regional human rights bodies seem to concur. The European Court of Human Rights held in *X and Y v. The Netherlands* that a 'state's failure to provide for prosecution of [a victim's] assailant violated [her rights, and that] only the criminal law [was] an adequate means of protecting the crucial values at stake' (Orentlicher 1991, 2580). Likewise in *Velásquez Rodríguez*, the Inter-American Court of Human Rights found an affirmative obligation of prosecution in the American Convention of Human Rights. The Court held that the Convention charged states party to it with a 'legal duty to take reasonable steps to prevent human rights violations and to use the means at its disposal to carry out a serious investigation of violations committed within its jurisdiction, to identify those responsible [and] to impose ... punishment' (Orentlicher 1991, 2576; *Velásquez Rodríguez v. Republic of Honduras* (1988), 174).

Similar to the other models of transitional justice, even within the prosecutorial mode one finds significant variation in institutional structure and the scope of crimes that can be addressed. There are 'pure' international modes of justice, relying on institutions such as the ICTY and the ICTR, and more recently the ICC. These courts exist above states, are usually geographically detached from the region in which violations occurred and operate under international law. This means, *inter alia*, that the type of political violence under their jurisdiction is limited to international crimes such as genocide, war crimes and crimes against humanity. 'Lesser' crimes, even if equal in scale and horror, need to be addressed elsewhere.

In addition to the 'pure' international model, there are also 'hybrid' prosecutions in which international institutions are paired with domestic bodies, prosecuting violators under a mix of international and domestic law and usually (but not always) convened in the country where political violence occurred. Among other locations, hybrid models have been undertaken in East Timor, Sierra Leone, Cambodia, and Bosnia and Herzegovina (Goldstone and Smith 2009, 106–10).

And, finally, prosecutorial transitional justice has increasingly taken place in the purely domestic arena before local judges. From a legal perspective, this has encountered some difficulties regarding jurisdiction, especially if the political violence being addressed consisted of international crimes, which may correlate exactly to domestic law (especially the domestic law in force at the time the crimes were committed). The solution to this jurisdictional quandary has seen some states opt to simply define alleged violations under domestic law with no reference to international code (for example, 'mass murder' rather than 'genocide'), others explicitly incorporate international code into domestic law, such as France in its prosecution of Klaus Barbie, while others, such as Israel in its prosecution of Adolf Eichmann, assert that such incorporation is unnecessary when dealing with crimes against 'the whole of mankind' (Goldstone and Smith 2009, 77).

Prosecutions as a transitional process have achieved an undeniable measure of global support (seen no more clearly than by the fact that more than 110 states are now members of the ICC). In at least some cases, their success in aiding the achievement of rule of law seems similarly undeniable. Post-Second World War Germany and Japan are perhaps the leading examples of such states. However, we acknowledge that prosecutions are not *sine qua non* for rule of law (as seen in Mozambique, for example) and that even in manifest cases of success such as Germany and Japan, the nature of rule of law and the details of specific transition processes make it difficult to establish clear causation between transitional process and ensuing rule of law. For instance, in Germany and Japan, the fact that the Nuremberg and Tokyo Trials brought justice to some members of the regimes' senior leadership was undoubtedly important to rule of law. Trials served to re-establish rule of law in the wake of horrifying crime, but in their focus on senior leaders avoided indicting the entire German or Japanese people. Both factors were critical to the post-Second World War development of rule of law in each country. However, the impact of the prosecutions in each state must also be viewed in light of the fact that each state was occupied after the war by Western forces. The occupying powers worked hard building rule of law with tools other than prosecutions, such as writing robust constitutions and establishing rule of law-promoting public and private institutions. Another complexity in linking prosecutions *qua* prosecutions to developing rule of law is that in no case of a prosecution-based transition have all violators (even all senior violators) been brought to justice. Pragmatics and politics have dictated otherwise. In post-War Japan, for example, the Tokyo Trials prosecuted only 28 officials and no members of the Imperial Household. In Rwanda, which 18 years after the genocide is still undergoing a primarily prosecution-based transition, there are thought to be many tens of thousands of perpetrators of the 1994 genocide. Not all violators will face the courts. Official or *de facto* amnesties have always played a role in prosecution-based transitions. The impact of prosecutions on the development of rule of law is thus muddied by the impact of other transitional processes that have necessarily accompanied it.

Retributive Political Violence

There is a final model of transitional 'justice' that is disfavoured but is both more common than most may be willing to admit and shares with amnesties the title of having the longest history of state practice. While vigilantism and random violence have been seen in many transitions, retributive political violence as a tool of transitional justice entails a new regime engaging in violence, in what it publicly states is a first step towards rule of law. Practitioners of this transitional process are often animated by the notion that rule of law can be built on the twin foundations of catharsis and deterrence. There have been two primary means by which states have engaged in this transition process. The first is to explicitly and immediately punish certain members of the prior regime. After Mussolini's fascist government collapsed in spring 1945, *Il Duce* was detained by the new government and summarily executed. The second (and more common means) is to stage at least a quick proceedings (calling it a 'trial' would often be overstating the summary nature of the process) before public punishment. This occurred in Romania in 1989 when the communist leader Nicolae Ceauşescu was subjected to the briefest of proceedings before a military tribunal and was then taken before a firing squad. Images of his 'trial' and body were broadcast throughout the country, providing proof that the Ceauşescu era was over.

While victims and survivors may exact some satisfaction from the knowledge that a tyrant is no more, as a basis for establishing rule of law, this fifth model is perilous. Romania and Italy may be exceptions that prove the rule, as those states managed to develop rule of law after their initial flush of new regime violence. History demonstrates, however, that no matter how unjust a prior regime, violent retribution rarely provides a solid foundation for developing rule of law. That the 1789 French Revolution began with a string of executions no doubt helped set the stage for the Reign of Terror four years later and the resulting Thermidorian Reaction, which together saw as many as 40,000 French people killed. Though the Bolshevik Revolution in 1917, the Polish May Coup and Lithuanian Coup in 1926, and the coups and counter-coups of the 1960s and 1970s in Nigeria and in Pakistan all replaced violent, unjust prior regimes, the fact that the coups and their aftermaths included violent retribution made it difficult to establish rule of law. And, indeed, in each of these cases (and in numerous others), despite the stated intentions of the new government, true rule of law did not emerge under their watch.

Conclusion: Embracing the Diversity of Transitional Justice and Moving Towards a 'Thick' Rule of Law

The nuances of various transitional justice techniques and their successes and limitations in providing for rule of law present a complicated picture of the most effective strategies for policy-makers to undertake. At first blush, it may even seem that the depth of their institutional, operational and legal complexities revert 'transitional justice' and 'rule of law' to theory rather than policy practice. Yet, for policy-makers, the diversity can, and should, be embraced. As challenging as the bevy of options makes building rule of law, such complexity makes the task possible. The history of transitional justice and rule of law provides a rich menu of choices that can be selected to suit the individual context and, just as importantly, three overarching lessons to guide the policy-maker.

First, in as much as rule of law is a social and cultural construct – and not solely an institutional one – designers of transitional justice techniques must heed the unique cultural, political and historical realities in transitioning countries before devising the most appropriate transitional techniques. The importance of the environment cannot be overstated. The success of Eastern European lustration was due to it being directly responsive and calibrated to the specific blend of the political violence endured, the peaceful nature of the post-communist transitions and the expressed desires of the populace. Comparing European and Iraqi lustration reveals that the political and cultural environment can be determinative, allowing the same transitional technique to aid rule of law in one iteration and impede it in another.

Second, though transitional techniques have been discussed in distinct categories, in practice the categories are neither discrete nor mutually exclusive. Some of the models can be practised simultaneously. For instance, lustration can be practised with little to no resort to criminal trials, as occurred in post-Cold War Czechoslovakia. Alternatively, lustration could be paired with a robust prosecution process, as was the case in post-Cold War Poland and in post-Saddam Hussein Iraq. As noted previously, prosecutions are always practised alongside (at least *de facto*) amnesties, and participation in truth commissions by perpetrators often brings with it official amnesty. Meanwhile, other transitions have practised various transitional models sequentially, even if unwittingly. Over the past 25 years, Argentina has experienced a dizzying set of transitional processes which began when democracy was restored after the fall of the military *junta* in 1983. That year saw President Raúl Alfonsín undertake both a truth commission and trials of leading members of the *junta*. Convictions against several leaders were handed down in 1985. In 1989, when Alfonsín was replaced as president by Carlos Menem, the *junta* convictions were overturned and amnesties were granted. Since then, several *junta* leaders have died and those who remain have been subjected to a litany of continued processes with new charges of wrongdoing (presumably not covered by the amnesties) surfacing in the late 1990s and early 2000s, repeated requests for extradition to Spain (which did not respect the amnesties) to stand trial for human rights violations and, since 2006, the legal undoing of their Menem amnesties as the Argentine President and courts have declared them invalid. Though a confusing and arguably unstable transitional process, since the return of democracy, Argentina has by and large maintained a commitment to real rule of law, and the admonishment of its truth commission, which entitled its final report *'Nunca Más'* (Never Again), has been followed.

Third, and finally, even a combination of regime-appropriate transitional strategies, effectively and widely deployed, will not, on their own, provide rule of law. While the requirement for additional efforts towards rule of law is perhaps clearest with amnesties, it is true regardless of which transitional processes are undertaken. True rule of law will not emerge without efforts to inculcate, educate and acculturate a population to rule of law. In the absence of such strong buttressing efforts, even 'successful' transitions can fade and political violence can re-emerge. As such, while the success of countries like Poland and South Africa in their transitions can be partly traced to their initial, divergent transitional justice choices (reflecting as they did the specific environments in which their transitions occurred), in both cases these processes were bolstered by substantial subsequent investments in solidifying rule of law and ensuring local ownership of the process. In Poland, private-sector organizations such as the Foundation for Education for Democracy worked alongside public programmes such as the Education for Democratic Citizenship project. Their efforts were key to teaching and formalizing rule of law, moving the Poles from being passive *Homo Sovieticus* to active, engaged citizens of a democratic society. In South Africa, the private sector has also played a part, though arguably the most noteworthy aspect of rule of law promotion has been the public sector's constitutionally prescribed role in the process. Chapter 9 of the post-Apartheid constitution established several 'state institutions' explicitly designed to nurture democracy and rule of law, including a Public Protector, a Commission for Gender Equality, an Electoral Commission, an Auditor General, a Commission for the Promotion and Protection of the Rights of Cultural, Religious and Linguistic Communities, and a Human Rights Commission (South Africa 1996, Chapter 9).

Establishing rule of law in the wake of political violence is a challenging task. Transitional justice is a critical tool in the process, but what that tool will look like in any particular case, how it is employed and what else is provided ancillary to and supportive of a transition will differ, often significantly across cases. Rule of law may be the common destination and political violence the common starting point, but the path a state takes on its transitional justice journey will be as unique as the state itself.

References

Argentine National Commission on the Disappeared (1986), *Nunca Mas: The Report of the Argentine National Commission on the Disappeared* (New York: Farrar Straus Giroux).

Aristotle (350 BC), *The Politics* (trans. Jowett B. (2000)) (Mineola, NY: Dover Publications).

Azanian People's Organization (AZAPO) v. Republic of South Africa, Constitutional Court of South Africa, Case 17/96, 25 July 1996.

Boed, R. (1999), 'An Evaluation of the Legality and Efficacy of Lustration as a Tool of Transitional Justice', *Columbia Journal of Transnational Law* 37, 357–402.
Brahm, E. 'Truth Commissions', *Beyond Intractability*, http://www.beyond intractability.org/essay/truth_commissions/ [accessed 3 July 2012].
Carothers, T. (1998), 'The Rule of Law Revival', *Foreign Affairs* 77(2), 95–107.
Chumbipuma Aguirre et al. v. Republic of Peru (2001) (Barrios Altos Case), Inter-American Court of Human Rights, (Ser. C) No. 75.
Democratic People's Republic of Korea (1998), Constitution.
Ellis, M. (1996), 'Purging the Past: The State of Lustration Laws in the Former Communist Bloc', *Law and Contemporary Problems* 59, 181–96.
Goldstone, R.J. and A.M. Smith (2009), *International Judicial Institutions: The Architecture of International Justice at Home and Abroad* (London: Routledge).
Hayner, P.B. (2002), *Unspeakable Truths: Facing the Challenge of Truth Commissions* (London: Routledge).
Horne, C. and M. Levi (2002), 'Does Lustration Promote Trustworthy Governance?' Budapest Collegium, 'Truth and Honesty Project'.
Huntington, Samuel (1991), *The Third Wave: Democratization in the Late Twentieth Century* (Norman: University of Oklahoma Press).
Huyse, L. (1995), 'Justice after Transition: On the Choices Successor Elites Make in Dealing with the Past', *Law and Social Inquiry* 20, 51–78.
Michnik, A. and V. Havel (1993), 'Confronting the Past: Justice or Revenge?', *Journal of Democracy* 4, 20–27.
Naqvi, Yasmin (2006), 'The Right to the Truth in International Law: Fact or Fiction?', *International Review of the Red Cross* 88(862), 245–73.
Orentlicher, D. (1991), 'Settling Accounts: The Duty to Prosecute Human Rights Violations of a Prior Regime', *Yale Law Journal* 100, 2537–615.
Otterman, S. 'Iraq: Debaathification', *Council on Foreign Relations*, http://www.cfr.org/publication/7853/iraq.html [accessed 3 July 2012].
Pasqualucci, J.M. and T. Buergenthal (2003), *The Practice and Procedure of the Inter-American Court of Human Rights* (Cambridge: Cambridge University Press).
Popkin, M. and N. Roht-Arriaza (1995), 'Truth as Justice: Investigatory Commissions in Latin America', in N.J. Kritz and N. Mandela (eds), *Transitional Justice* (Washington DC: US Institute of Peace).
Reiter, A.G., T. Olsen and L. Payne (2007), 'In Defence of Amnesty? An Analysis of Transitional Justice and State Practice from 1974–2003', Paper presented at the Midwest Political Science Association Conference, April.
Republic of Somalia (1961), Constitution.
Roht-Arriaza, N. (1995), *Impunity and Human Rights in International Law and Practice* (Oxford: Oxford University Press).
Schabas, W. (2006), *The UN International Criminal Tribunals: The Former Yugoslavia, Rwanda, and Sierra Leone* (Cambridge: Cambridge University Press).
Smith, Adam M. (2009) *After Genocide: Bringing the Devil to Justice* (Amherst, NY: Prometheus Books).
Snyder, J. and L. Vinjamuri (2006), 'A Midwife for Peace: Amnesty', *International Herald Tribune*, 27 September, 9.

South Africa (1994), Office of the President, Bill No. 34 of 1995: Promotion of National Unity and Reconciliation Act.
South Africa (1996), Constitution.
Soviet Union (1977), Constitution.
Special Court for Sierra Leone (2004), *Prosecutor v. Morris Kallon and Brima Buzzy Kamara, Decision on Challenge to Jurisdiction*, SCSL-2004-15AR72(E), 13 March.
Stephenson, M. 'Rule of Law as a Goal of Development Policy', *World Bank – Law and Justice Institutions*, http://go.worldbank.org/DZETJ85MD0 [accessed 3 July 2012].
Stromseth, J., Wippman, D. and Brooks, R. (2006), *Can Might Make Rights? Building the Rule of Law After Military Interventions* (Cambridge: Cambridge University Press).
Teitel, R.G. (2000), *Transitional Justice* (New York: Oxford University Press).
Trumbull, C.P. (2007), 'Giving Amnesties a Second Chance', *Berkeley Journal of International Law* 25, 283–345.
United Nations (2000), 'Report of the Secretary General on the Establishment of a Special Court for Sierra Leone', UN Doc. S/2000/915.
United Nations (2003), 'Restoring Rule of Law Essential for Resolving Conflict', Press Release UN Doc. SC/7884, 30 September.
United Nations (2004), 'Report of the Secretary-General. The Rule of Law and Transitional Justice in Conflict and Post-Conflict Societies'. UN Security Council, UN Doc. S/2004/616, 23 August.
Velásquez Rodríguez v. Republic of Honduras (1988), Inter-American Court of Human Rights, (Ser. C) No. 4.

Political, Economic and Social Reconstruction after Political Violence: The Case of Afghanistan

William Maley

Afghanistan's transition process following the overthrow of the Taliban regime in October–November 2001 offers an instructive case study of the difficulties of re-assembling functioning institutions in an environment marked by massive social dislocation and low levels of trust between different actors. It reminds us that transitions often occur in an environment marked by continuing violence rather than a cessation of armed conflict, something which has prompted several experienced scholars to highlight the challenges of 'conflictual peacebuilding' (Suhrke and Strand 2005). It also provides a salutary warning that the commitment of international actors to assist such a transition can easily drift as new issues take shape and demand attention. But perhaps most depressingly, it also suggests that after a seismic political shift of the kind that occurred in late 2001, there may only be one opportunity to set things right. There is thus a need for very careful reflection at the beginning of a transition as to how it might proceed (Maley 2002a).

My aim in this chapter is to elaborate some of these complexities. It is divided into seven sections. The first shows how the historical development of the Afghan state and its subsequent collapse, combined with the impact of war in the 1980s and 1990s, framed the challenges confronted by those seeking to lay the foundations for transition after 2001. The next three sections examine the particular approaches to political, economic and social development that were taken from 2001 onwards, and identify their particular strengths and weaknesses. The fifth section addresses the impact of the wider international environment that Afghanistan faced, noting that transitions such as Afghanistan's never occur in a vacuum, but instead are also shaped by events far beyond the control of local actors. The sixth section offers an overview of where Afghanistan finds itself after close to a decade of reconstruction efforts. The final section draws some lessons from this case that are worth bearing in mind if other such endeavours are to be undertaken.

Some Context: State and War

Afghanistan's post-2001 transition was preceded by more than two decades of high-level violence triggered by a communist coup in April 1978 (Maley 2010). It should not be forgotten that for almost five decades before the coup, from 1929 to 1978, Afghanistan was one of the most peaceful countries in Asia, avoiding entanglement in the carnage of both the Second World War and of the partition of the Indian subcontinent. However, the April 1978 coup, and the December 1979 invasion of Afghanistan by the Soviet Union, led to mayhem on an extraordinary scale. A study of war-related mortality in Afghanistan between 1978 and 1987 pointed to 876,825 unnatural deaths, or an average of more than 240 deaths every day for 10 years straight (Khalidi 1991: 107). With violence on this scale striking many parts of the country, it is not surprising that millions of Afghans fled their homes, becoming refugees in the neighbouring states of Pakistan and Iran (see Schmeidl and Maley 2008). Added to these problems were massive damage to infrastructure and to the agricultural sector (Maley 1999: 234–6), and severe challenges arising from internal displacement. There were also the burdens of coping with injured and disabled war victims and of coming to terms with the psychological traumas inflicted on a generation of young Afghans who grew up knowing only war.

A less palpable consequence of these dramatic events was the virtual collapse of the Afghan state. As a territorial unit, Afghanistan took shape well before the end of the nineteenth century, but it was only in the last two decades of that century that more modern forms of state administration began to appear (see Gregorian 1969; Ghani 1978; Kakar 1978a), although more rudimentary power structures had emerged earlier (Noelle 1998). Nonetheless, while the state was ubiquitous, it was a relatively weak instrument for the pursuit of forceful policies, something which Afghanistan's communist radicals learned to their cost after the 1978 coup. Their natural inclination when their policies encountered opposition was to use violence as a way of enforcing their control, but all they succeeded in doing was to produce an escalating insurgency (Maley 1991), reflecting the strength of Afghanistan's 'micro-societies' and the norms of reciprocity that held them together. This struggle was to dominate Afghanistan's political life throughout the 1980s. There was more, however, to the collapse of the Afghan state than just this.

On the one hand, the Afghan state had been facing a creeping loss of capacity for quite some time. Its revenue sources from the 1950s onwards had become increasingly unstable, largely because of the drive by Prime Minister Mohammad Daoud between 1953 and 1963 to pursue rapid, state-driven modernisation. As Rubin has demonstrated, Afghanistan had many of the features of a rentier state, dependent upon foreign aid and the sale of natural resources to sustain its activities. In 1953, some seven per cent of state expenditure was funded by foreign aid, but 93 per cent was met from domestic revenue. By 1963, foreign aid covered 49 per cent of state expenditure; domestic revenue covered a mere 38 per cent, the balance coming from domestic borrowing (Rubin 2002: 296). Afghanistan proceeded to encounter two of the problems for which rentier states are notorious. On the one hand, its revenue sources proved unstable, as donor priorities shifted and the global price of exported resources (especially natural gas) moved in an adverse direction. This deprived it of the ability to meet the expectations of the public that had risen in easier times. On the other hand, its dependence on such income sources diverted it from developing organic relations with the population: nurturing donors was more important than securing the goodwill of the public.

Allied to this was a serious crisis of legitimacy. The importance of legitimacy, which in the sense in which I use the term implies *generalised, normative support*, has long been recognised by political commentators. In *The Social Contract*, written in 1762, Jean-Jacques Rousseau wrote that the 'strongest is never strong enough to be always master, unless he transforms strength into right, and obedience into duty' (Rousseau 1973: 168). This was echoed by Edmund Burke in his 1775 *Speech on Moving Resolutions for Conciliation with the Colonies*: 'the use of force alone is but *temporary*. It may subdue for a moment; but it does not remove the necessity of subduing again: and a nation is not governed, which is perpetually to be conquered' (Burke 1999: 236, emphasis in original). The overthrow of the Afghan monarchy in a palace coup mounted by former Prime Minister Daoud in July 1973 undermined the 'traditional' legitimacy of the state and the April 1978 coup compromised the position of the state still further (Maley 1987), not least because the avowed atheism of those who seized power set them immediately at odds with mainstream opinion in a conservative Muslim society. Following the Soviet invasion of Afghanistan, the regime which the invasion put in place survived by means of *non*-legitimate domination, first through coercion of the population and second through the use of Soviet-supplied resources to purchase prudential loyalty. However, at the end of 1991, these resources dried up, and within four months, the communist regime collapsed (Kalinovsky 2011: 206–8). This inaugurated a period of fierce struggle between different *Mujahideen* (resistance) groups for control of the *symbols* of the state, followed by the takeover of large tracts of Afghanistan by the Pakistan-backed Taliban movement (see Maley 2009b: 162–209). It was the overthrow of the Taliban in late 2001 that set the scene for a major effort at reconstruction of Afghanistan, with significant support from key actors in the international community (Maley 2009a).

Political Reconstruction

The most immediate challenge that arose in the aftermath of the Taliban's overthrow was the need to establish a framework for political activity. This was pursued initially through the brokering by the United Nations (UN) of an elite settlement at a meeting in Bonn, and subsequently through a process that saw an interim administration established in December 2001 headed by Hamid Karzai, a transitional administration from mid-2002, a new Constitution put in place in January 2004, and elections held for a president in October 2004 and the Lower House (*Wolesi Jirga*) of a bicameral parliament in September 2005 (Maley 2006: 31–3). Yet there is much more to political reconstruction than simply meeting benchmarks of this sort, as the Afghan experience was to show.

Predominant among these additional concerns was that of providing security for ordinary Afghans. The collapse of the Taliban regime created a security vacuum of sorts, with an immediate threat arising from criminal elements and from other predatory forces. The Bonn Agreement had anticipated the establishment of an International Security Assistance Force (ISAF) for Kabul, and virtually all informed experts, together with the UN, argued that it should be disseminated swiftly throughout the country. This, however, was initially blocked by the Bush administration (which wished to conserve airlift assets for use in Iraq), and it was not until October 2003 that the wider deployment of ISAF was finally authorised by the UN Security Council in Resolution 1510. By this time, crucial momentum had been lost and President Karzai had been forced to strike deals with unappetising local power-holders in order to prevent them from moving immediately into 'spoiler' mode, in which disgruntled actors seek to disrupt or destroy a peace process as a way of advancing their own political objectives (Stedman 1997). The burden of providing security was thus imposed on a largely embryonic security sector, consisting of the Afghan National Army (ANA) and the Afghan National Police (ANP), with inadequate recognition of just how difficult it was likely to be not simply to train personnel to adequate standards, but also to establish appropriate middle-management structures and inculcate the kind of organisational cultures that civilian policing and a military subordinated to civilian authority would require.

The Bonn Agreement was silent on this deeper issue of how the bureaucratic structures of a revived Afghan state would be put in place. Indeed, at Bonn, there was no reflection at all on what kind of state Afghanistan might require, judged in terms of such key variables as scope and strength (Fukuyama 2004: 6–14). Instead, the Agreement provided for up to 29 'Departments', many with potentially overlapping functions, which were allocated as prizes to the factions that attended the Bonn meeting. Since these factions were more patronage networks than political parties in the Western sense of the term, this set the scene not for the development of 'Weberian' bureaucracies that privileged impartial expertise, but for positions in the state to be distributed as rewards on the basis of political loyalty. While the scale of this problem varied between agencies, the net effect was to marginalise a generation of brighter, younger Afghans who had acquired significant skills while working for non-governmental organisations (NGOs) or international organisations that had been involved for many years in delivering humanitarian assistance for Afghans. Many of these took their skills back to the NGO or international sector, giving rise to what some called a 'second civil service' (World Bank 2005a: 47). A more sinister effect of the allocation of departments to different factions was the fuelling of vicious rivalries between departments, rivalries which inevitably landed on the President's desk for 'solution'.

This, of course, was at one level largely a problem in Kabul, where the central agencies of the state came to be headquartered. However, there were parallel problems in the outlying parts of Afghanistan, where diverse power-holders managed to establish their positions in the chaotic days and weeks that followed the overthrow of the Taliban regime. Some of these actors were formally incorporated by Karzai into the structures of the state, but continued to exercise local power not by virtue of holding state office, but rather on the strength of their capacity to extract and mobilise resources. This created a gulf between what one study called the *de jure* and *de facto* states (Evans et al. 2004: 12–21). Other actors remained outside the state, but nonetheless retained the capacity to exercise significant power. Some prominent larger actors of this sort came to be labelled 'warlords' (see Giustozzi 2009), but arguably the terminology better fitted lesser-known actors, especially in the south of the country, whose predatory behaviour in aggregate created major opportunities for a recrudescence of the Taliban, with Pakistani support.

But perhaps the greatest problem was the dysfunctionality of the constitutional framework developed through the Bonn process, and the matching failure of a democratic culture to take root within the dominant elite. The 2004 Constitution created a strong presidential system with a weak parliament. This had several severely adverse consequences. In an ethnically diverse society, it fostered an environment in which one group came to be seen as the 'winner', with many as 'losers'. It also overburdened the central office in the system, with the president being called on to serve as symbolic head of state, executive head of government and as broker between rival factions and agencies (Saikal and Maley 2008). But most seriously of all, it gave rise to an unelected 'caste' of presidential associates and clients whose own power depended entirely on the capacity of the incumbent president to retain office. This created structural incentives for the truly massive electoral fraud that blighted the 2009 presidential election, handing President Karzai a very suspect 'victory' but leaving his historical reputation in tatters (see Maley 2009c; Ruttig 2009).

Economic Reconstruction

If political reconstruction proved to be a troubled process, so too did economic reconstruction. Here, of course, there was not a *tabula rasa*. For decades preceding the overthrow of the Taliban, the bulk of the Afghan population had survived not on the strength of state activity or of international handouts, but simply through the circular flow of income in a small and fragmented market economy in which custom and culture ensured that for the most part contracts were honoured by those who made them. Nonetheless, in a range of areas, challenges arose that required urgent attention.

One challenge related to the fiscal capacities of the state. In a real sense, the Taliban left the larder totally bare. The Finance Ministry was a shambles. As the economist Michael Carnahan put it:

> At the start of 2002 there were no computers in the ministry – the deputy minister in charge of the budget department provided hand-held calculators to line ministry staff to use when preparing their handwritten budget submissions. The treasury system operated a manual ledger system, so no meaningful reconciliation was ever undertaken ... Anecdotal evidence suggests that the vast majority of the budget was actually not programmed in any conventional sense; rather, it was kept in discretionary funds that were allocated by the finance ministry or the president's office. This provided considerable scope for corruption and, in July 2002, operations of the finance ministry were reportedly under the control of three significant criminal gangs. Senior positions with access to major revenue sources were said to be bought and sold. (Carnahan 2004: 123)

It was a tribute to Dr Ashraf Ghani, who became Finance Minister in June 2002 and served until December 2004, that a modern system of financial management was put in place, encompassing currency reform, tax reform, treasury management and a banking law (see Ghani et al. 2007).

An equally challenging set of issues related to property rights. A functioning market system requires clarity as to property rights so that they can be exchanged to the mutual benefit of participants in a transaction. The economist Hernando de Soto has famously argued that clarification of property rights may liberate entrepreneurial capacities that are otherwise constrained by an individual's lack of clear legal title to an asset that may be mortgaged to raise funds to invest (De Soto 2001: 241) – although the key word here is 'may' (see Otto 2009). In Afghanistan, land title issues have proved unbelievably complicated. Studies in 2003 and 2004 pointed to great diversity in patterns of land ownership in different parts of the country (Wily 2003: 3–4), as well in customary, religious, civil, statutory and constitutional law relevant to tenure (Wily 2004: 29–32). Land itself could be government, public, private, communal or religious. Disputes over land tenure are now extremely common, but notably complex: some involve inheritance, others involve access, others the location of boundaries, and some the fundamental question of ownership. A number in the last category appear to involve 'bad faith', where a powerfully actor seeks to use the legal system to expropriate another's property by fraudulent means (see Deschamps and Roe 2009). Here, the notorious corruption of the Afghan judicial system and the weakness of the rule of law (Watson 2006; Maley 2011a) left many legitimate titleholders in a vulnerable position, limiting their scope to use their land as an economic asset.

Two other complications aggravated the problem of corruption. One has been the impact of foreign aid and defective forms of foreign aid management. Given the flaws of the Afghan state bureaucracy, it is perhaps not surprising that donors, looking for quick results, often bypassed line ministries in order to directly fund projects to be implemented by international organisations, NGOs or private commercial contractors. The result, however, was often a miserable hodge-podge, with multiple sub-contracting eroding the value of what was actually delivered at ground level and the quality of outputs often being highly suspect (see Stephens and

Ottaway 2005; Nawa 2006). This had two further unfortunate effects. Shoddy project delivery helped drive a narrative within Afghanistan to the effect that little positive had resulted from the post-2001 changes and that the Afghan state was ineffectual. But more seriously, the rush to spend large sums in a country with weak audit and anti-corruption controls undoubtedly fuelled corruption at many levels of the state and on a scale which far exceeded the levels of corruption in the state bureaucracy with which Afghans had been familiar before 1978 (see Kakar 1978b: 200).

But even more than through misdirected aid, corruption has been fostered by the emergence of a substantial illicit economy based on the cultivation of the opium poppy. The Taliban, using coercive methods, reduced Afghanistan's opium output in 2001 to 185 tonnes, although cynics suspected that this was more to preserve the value of substantial accumulated stockpiles. By 2008, output had reached 7,700 tonnes, although it was expected to fall to 6,900 tonnes in 2009. There is no doubt that significant sums from this industry made their way into the coffers of the Taliban insurgency (Peters 2009). Nonetheless, the problem of opium is an exceedingly difficult one to address and, indeed, one could argue that there is *no* single 'opium problem', but rather a multiplicity of distinct factors including the difficulty of transporting 'legal' crops without spoilage occurring, and the difficulty of securing loans from legal sources to fund investment in farm equipment, that can drive poppy cultivation and that requires distinctive and specifically crafted responses (see Hafvenstein 2007; Higgins 2007; Mansfield 2007; Rubin and Sherman 2008). The irony here is that targeted eradication of crops, now little more than a recipe for improved Taliban recruiting, might well in the past have sent a valuable signal when opium first began to re-emerge as a problem. Unfortunately, the USA was not prepared to move down this path, reportedly fearing that it would compromise its 'War on Terror' (Felbab-Brown 2005), given that a number of allies in the struggle against al-Qaeda were themselves implicated in the opium trade.

Social Reconstruction

In the aftermath of decades of violent armed conflict, a range of serious issues related to social reconstruction also required attention after 2001. Prolonged and extensive war inevitably disrupts social roles and social relations, albeit in complex ways. Afghanistan arguably contained not one society, but rather a plethora of *microsocieties* with their own histories, authority patterns and cultural practices (Saikal and Maley 1991), and virtually none has gone unaffected by the tumult of the years following the 1978 coup. Four particular areas cried out for attention after 2001.

The first related to refugee repatriation. The fall of the Taliban regime saw nearly 5 million refugees return to Afghanistan from neighbouring countries, with 3.8 million of them receiving assistance from the Office of the United Nations High Commissioner for Refugees (UNHCR) (Schmeidl and Maley 2008: 164). While this undoubtedly reflected the high hopes that surrounded the Bonn process, it threatened to overwhelm the absorptive capacity of the communities to which returnees headed (Turton and Marsden 2002). Particularly vulnerable in this respect was the Afghan capital, Kabul. The infrastructure of the capital was historically designed to cope with a population of roughly 800,000. By 2009, the population had risen to over 4 million, severely straining the transport, energy and waste disposal systems of the capital. Complicating this process still further were the high expectations of returnees. Early Western talk of a 'Marshall Plan' for Afghanistan proved to be little more than talk, but it led to hopes for the future that could not be sustained by either the Afghan government or its international supporters, in turn creating political problems for both.

A further area of serious long-term concern related to education and human capital formation. Afghanistan's education system was one of the principal victims of years of war, and a generation of Afghans grew up deprived of the benefits of anything approaching a modern education. In some cases, Afghan students ended up in the Deobandi *madrassas* (religious colleges) in Pakistan from which the Taliban shock-troops emerged, and in others cases, the English-language classes run by the International Rescue Committee offered windows to a wider world, but in many instances, education proved to be an unattainable dream. One of the principal claims made since 2001 is that millions of Afghans, including girls, have secured access to schooling, which is undoubtedly the case. However, there is arguably less to this claim than meets the eye. In many schools, students attend classes in multiple shifts and thus enjoy only a fraction of the class-contact time that students in Western schools would enjoy. Furthermore, a World Bank study has concluded that 'the available input indicators (teachers' background, curricula, textbook quality and availability, conditions of physical learning space, time on task, etc.) strongly suggest that quality is generally poor' (World Bank 2005b: vol. iv, 24). There is also a huge unmet demand for access to higher education that needs to be addressed urgently if it is not to generate political tensions of the sort that contributed to Afghanistan's slide to disaster in the late 1970s.

Gender issues also required considerable attention. The Taliban regime had won international notoriety on account of its treatment of women, which set benchmarks of expectation for any successor regime enjoying international support. On the one hand, for those who remember the Taliban regime's impact on Kabul, there can be no comparison with the present situation: Afghan women sit in large numbers in the *Wolesi Jirga*, appear on television and fill some important positions (such as the Chair of the Afghan Independent Human Rights Commission, occupied by Dr Sima Samar). On the other hand, Afghanistan remains firmly patriarchal. The Cabinet nominated by President Karzai in December 2009 contained only one female nominee, the Minister for Women's Affairs, and problems of discrimination, domestic violence and disempowerment remain pervasive. This is actually an area of extreme complexity (see Azarbaijani-Moghaddam 2004, 2007), since Afghan women do not live in a social world exclusively defined by gender. Socio-economic status, or ethnic or sectarian identification, can, as elsewhere, also be important determinants of social orientation, as a fierce dispute between some Shiite women over a Personal Status Law for Shiite Muslims showed in 2009 (Oates 2009: 20–22).

One final issue has received very little attention, and this relates to the position of Afghan youth. While there has been no recent census to provide definitive data, it is widely accepted that Afghanistan has a very young population, with perhaps 50 per cent below the age of 25. This creates a range of social challenges. Some confront young refugees (Saito 2009), returning to a country which they hardly know, which in many cases has changed hugely since their parents fled and which may offer a less socially liberal environment than they experienced in exile. This is a particular problem for younger women returning from Iran. But other challenges, less noticed, arise as the young fall increasingly under the influence of new communication media that expose them to very different images of possible worlds from those that dominated the lives of their parents. The current generation of Afghan youth is the first to have been exposed in large numbers to mobile telephones and (in urban areas) to television. What the exact effects of this exposure will be remains unclear, but older Afghans clearly fear the erosion of their social authority as images proliferate of young people doing well in the wider world by following their own pathways.

Afghanistan and the World

The wider world also supplied Afghanistan with a series of challenges in the post-2001 era. Afghanistan is located in an exceptionally troubled part of the world, and the troubles of the region have easily spilled onto Afghanistan's territory. The strife which beset Afghanistan in the post-1992 period was not just internal but transnational in character, as different actors in the region sought to assist parties in Afghanistan that seemed broadly sympathetic to their actions. Pakistan's vigorous support for the Taliban might better be seen as a 'creeping invasion' of Afghanistan (Maley 2002b).

The most important relationship for Afghanistan in the post-2001 period was of course that with the USA (Maley 2011b). US forces were decisive in the overthrow of the Taliban regime and provided the backbone of international support in the years that followed. However, the relationship was not as smooth as one might have expected (Zakheim 2011). While President George W. Bush retained a high level of rhetorical commitment to Afghanistan, it was not matched after 2003 by commitment on the ground. The reason for this was the mounting US preoccupation with the situation in Iraq, invaded by the USA and some of its allies in March 2003 but thereafter increasingly a quagmire, especially from mid-2004 onwards (see Hashim 2006; Allawi 2007). The relative priorities of the two theatres were summed up in a telling comment in 2007 by Admiral Michael G. Mullen, Chairman of the US Joint Chiefs of Staff: 'In Afghanistan we do what we can. In Iraq we do what we must' (Burns 2007). A further complication in the relationship arose from civilian casualties resulting from US military operations. Every one of these created a political problem for the Karzai government, something that was not always fully appreciated by his US allies (see Human Rights Watch 2008).

The US–Afghanistan relationship was also complicated by the resumption of Pakistani meddling in Afghanistan, of which there was a long history (Hussain 2005; Reidel 2011). The Afghan Taliban leadership was not obliterated by Operation Enduring Freedom; rather, it relocated to sanctuaries in Pakistan. The significance of this was admitted even by Pakistani President Pervez Musharraf, speaking in Kabul in August 2007: 'There is no doubt [that] Afghan militants are supported from Pakistani soil. The problem that you have in your region is because support is provided from our side' (Shah and Gall 2007). Keen to block Indian influence in post-2001 Afghanistan, Pakistan's intelligence service (ISI) supported a range of disruptive actors, including the original Taliban leaders, the *Hezb-e Islami* of Gulbuddin Hekmatyar, and the so-called 'Haqqani network', which Pakistan's Army Chief reportedly described as a 'strategic asset' (Sanger 2009: 248). Thus, Pakistan in effect adopted a dual-track approach to Afghanistan, professing support for US objectives but at the same time continuing to support militant groups (see Grare 2007; Rashid 2008; Weinbaum and Harder 2008; Waldman 2010). The Karzai government looked to Washington to address this problem, but found the results far from satisfactory: while Washington pressed Kabul to mute its criticisms, the meddling persisted.

Of course, there were many other powers and actors involved in Afghanistan apart from the USA. The UN had a notable presence organisationally through the United Nations Assistance Mission in Afghanistan (UNAMA), established by Security Council Resolution 1401 of 28 March 2002. It was avowedly an assistance mission (Caplan 2005: 14), rather than an actor exercising delegated sovereignty in a transitional phase to statehood (see Chesterman 2004), and it was not intended to compete with the Afghan government. Rather, as the UN Secretary-General put it, 'UNAMA should aim to bolster Afghan capacity (both official and non-governmental), relying on as limited an international presence and on as many Afghan staff as possible, and using common support services where possible, thereby leaving a light expatriate "footprint"' (United Nations 2002, para. 98). UNAMA's 'golden age' was in the period from 2002 to 2004, when it was headed by the renowned Algerian diplomat Lakhdar Brahimi, who was respected by both Karzai and the USA. However, it did not fare so well after Brahimi departed, since his shoes proved difficult for his successors to fill, and in the aftermath of the 2009 presidential election, it was deeply scarred by a public dispute between the Special Representative of the Secretary-General, Kai Eide of Norway, and his dismissed Deputy, former US Ambassador Peter Galbraith, over how the problem of electoral fraud should have been handled (Smith 2011).

The other organisation that became prominently involved in Afghanistan was NATO, which assumed command of ISAF operations from 9 August 2003. However, the NATO states which assumed that they would be taking part in a peace operation were in for a rude shock, as deteriorating security produced mounting casualties, especially amongst the British in Helmand province and the Canadians in Kandahar. Coordinating the activities of NATO forces proved difficult, as 'national caveats' imposed by contributing governments limited the uses to which soldiers could be put. NATO was also involved in an interesting experiment in civil-military cooperation, namely the deployment of so-called 'Provincial Reconstruction Teams' (PRTs).

These did not fit a single template, but rather reflected the resource endowments and organisational cultures of the different NATO and non-NATO militaries that became involved. The results of the experiment were varied (Hynek and Marton 2012). Some PRTs, such as the New Zealand PRT in Bamiyan, performed very well. Others, however, ran into difficulties because of rapid personnel turnover (see Yaqub and Maley 2008) or because their objectives were not sufficiently matched to wider national priorities (Piiparinen 2007).

Where Afghanistan Finds Itself

After more than a decade of reconstruction activity, Afghanistan nonetheless remains high on any list of failed states and is a major preoccupation of key capitals such as Washington, London, Paris and Berlin. In the final section of this chapter, I attempt to draw some broader lessons from Afghanistan's experience, but before doing so, it is useful to identify where Afghanistan is now positioned in terms of security, state capacity, state legitimacy and international salience.

There is no doubt that Afghanistan remains extremely insecure and that many Afghans feel insecure as they go about their daily lives (Jones 2008). This is not to say that daily life does not go on or that some parts of Afghanistan are not relatively secure compared to others. But to the extent that Afghans do feel insecure, this is likely to translate into some degree of disappointment with the performance of both the Afghan government and its international supporters. The relative silence on the part of the international community over Pakistan's destabilising role has prompted a train of thought in Afghanistan which says that if the USA knows of Pakistan's activities but says nothing about them, then it must somehow be complicit in those activities: this is an ever-present danger for states that opt for 'quiet diplomacy' in addressing a serious problem. The insecure environment in Afghanistan also affects public opinion in troop-contributing states, unprepared for casualties on the scale that the Afghanistan theatre of operations has generated. In the USA in particular, an analogy with Vietnam can all too easily be drawn, prompting President Barack Obama to confront it directly in his West Point address in late 2009. Without progress on this front (which requires direct attention to Pakistan's meddling), it is unlikely that the situation in Afghanistan can be easily salvaged.

Equally troubling are questions about the capacities of the Afghan state. Joel S. Migdal has identified core capacities of the state as including 'the capacities to *penetrate* society, *regulate* social relationships, *extract* resources, and *appropriate* or use resources in determined ways' (Migdal 1988: 4, emphasis in original). In none of these areas could the Afghan state be described as highly capable, although its revenue-raising capacity has improved. One explanation of the weak capacity of the Afghan state is the over-ambitious character of the post-2001 state-building enterprise, to which a number of studies have drawn attention (see Suhrke 2006, 2007, 2011). Arguably, by attempting to do too much, the Afghan state has ended up doing nothing really well: focused attention to a small number of key tasks would have made much more sense. But, that said, it is important in fairness to also note that states are extraordinarily complex structures. Migdal has usefully distinguished four different types of state institution. First are the 'trenches', consisting of 'the officials who must execute state directives directly in the face of possibly strong societal resistance'. Second are the 'dispersed field offices', the 'regional and local bodies that rework and organize state policies and directives for local consumption, or even formulate and implement wholly local policies'. Third are the 'agency's central offices', the 'nerve centers where national policies are formulated and enacted and where resources for implementation are marshaled'. Fourth are the 'commanding heights', the 'pinnacle of the state' where the 'top executive leadership' is to be found (Migdal 1994: 16). To make these different structures work, and more importantly work together, is arguably a task of decades rather than years.

Weak state capacity is unlikely to contribute much to state legitimacy, since legitimacy in Afghanistan is at least as dependent upon the performance of rulers as it is on the process by which rulers are selected. Problems of insecurity in particular have contaminated the reputation of the state. But that is not to say that process is irrelevant. Indeed, one could argue that it operates in a lethally asymmetric fashion – that while even a credible electoral victory does little to legitimate a regime that fails subsequently to perform effectively, a fraudulent 'victory' can *de*legitimate the 'victor'. Some would point to the rejection by the *Wolesi Jirga* of almost three-quarters of President Karzai's proposed Cabinet in January 2010 as evidence of just such a process at work. While the President may not have himself orchestrated the theft of the 2009 presidential election, he risks being seen as little better than a receiver of stolen goods. The Bonn Agreement was premised on the view that no single strategy of legitimation was sufficient to legitimate power in the eyes of all relevant actors. It held that a number of different strategies would need to be woven together. With the 2009 election, this delicate fabric is at risk of unravelling.

In terms of international salience, Afghanistan finds itself in a curious position. On the one hand, it probably received more attention in major capitals in 2009 – the first year of the Obama administration – than almost any other single state. Yet, at the same time, the fear that Afghanistan might be abandoned again, as it was after the Soviet withdrawal in 1989 and again after the communist regime collapsed (Gutman 2008), remains alive in Kabul. This fear was aggravated by President Obama's West Point reference to 2011 as a date by which the USA would begin to withdraw troops. Given that manifest failure in Afghanistan could give a huge boost to radicals and militants in nuclear-armed Pakistan and beyond (O'Hanlon and Sherjan 2010), an 'abandonment' scenario on a grand scale might seem unlikely. But its mere improbability gives rise to another paradox – namely that while President Karzai is in an ultimate sense almost wholly dependent on international support, this does not give his international supporters much leverage, since a threat to withdraw support would not strike Karzai as credible. It is therefore unsurprising that the Cabinet he nominated in December 2009 showed very few signs of the 'renewal' which his international backers had been seeking.

Some Lessons

Generalising from a single case study is always a dangerous undertaking, and this case is no exception. But, that said, there are some lessons which Afghanistan has to offer which can be fruitfully kept in mind by those who might find themselves entangled in roughly similar situations of post-conflict or conflictual peace building.

First, as noted at the beginning of this chapter, in transitions of this sort, there may be only one chance to get things right. If defective arrangements are put in place, a range of interests will likely crystallise that benefit from the new arrangements and seek to defend them, even though they may seriously blight the prospects for political, economic and social progress. In the Afghan case, the combination of the way in which the bureaucratic agencies of the state were structured and the blocking of ISAF expansion created space for a range of predatory or extractive actors to position themselves to benefit from the new state as it took shape. This was at the expense of the security and well-being of civil society. This then accounted for a decidedly mixed performance over such issues as human rights and transitional justice, which ordinary Afghans saw as desirable but a number of political actors saw as threatening (Niland 2004), and for mounting cynicism about political processes.

Second, the Afghanistan case shows how complex the idea of sovereignty is. There is no doubt that Afghanistan is 'juridically' sovereign, in the sense that it occupies a broadly accepted territory and has been recognised as a distinct unit by other international actors. However, its 'empirical' sovereignty, its capacity actually to affect developments on the ground, is much more doubtful. As in many other transitions (Jenkins and Plowden 2006), there have been ongoing tensions between donor priorities and the wishes of local actors. The Afghan government has arguably found itself trapped in the worst of all possible worlds, formally responsible for a whole range of state activities, but in practice incapable of meeting people's expectations in those spheres because of its dependence on others to supply resources and technical assistance. It is perhaps unsurprising that President Karzai has shown vigorous independence in some areas within his control (for example, in nominating officeholders or in denouncing civilian casualties from Coalition air strikes), given that so many 'state-like activities' in Afghanistan lie beyond his control.

Third, the Afghan case clearly shows how devastating the distractions that divert the attention of international actors from situations that remain fragile or tenuous can be. Within months of the overthrow of the Taliban regime, the prospects of US military action in Iraq had begun to suck oxygen out of the Afghan theatre. Yet the notion that after decades of conflict, and in a region as fraught as Afghanistan, the country could be stabilised in a matter of months and with minimal international presence was a pure confabulation. Nonetheless, this drove the Pentagon to neglect Afghanistan's complexities, much to the dismay of the first US Ambassador in Kabul after 2001, Dr Robert P. Finn (Rohde and Sanger 2007). The difficult problems that President Obama inherited in Afghanistan were very much the product of near-criminal neglect on the part of President Bush and his senior colleagues, who in their zeal to remove Saddam Hussein lost touch with Afghanistan's transition while it was still in its infancy and vulnerable to disruption.

Fourth, Afghanistan also illustrates the paradox that one can sometimes have too many friends. This can give rise to coordination or collective-action problems that prove significant. The Taliban enemy are rather more coherent organisationally than is often recognised (Dorronsoro 2009). This gives them a notable advantage over the fragmented and discordant NATO alliance (see Sinno 2008). While NATO soldiers have shown great courage in combat, their political leaders have all too often engaged in blatant buck-passing and burden-shifting, often in public and in full view of an Afghan audience. The spectacle of a NATO Secretary-General requesting more contributions for Afghanistan, with only a fraction of what was sought then being contributed, has more than once sent a dispiriting signal to Afghans about the seriousness with which the wider world views their situation.

Finally, the Afghan case also shows the difficulty of addressing problems that demand long-term commitments in a world of short political cycles. The Taliban's much-quoted statement that 'you have watches but we have time' points to their understanding of this conundrum. If a country has experienced decades of violence and turmoil, it is more than likely to need decades to recover from the experience. Very few governments, however, are configured in such a way as to allow them to make commitments of support for a comparable period, not least because democracy means that voters have periodic opportunities to change governments and their policies. Finding a way of making long-term commitments seem credible has proved an intractable problem in Afghanistan. It seems likely to be intractable in a number of other contexts as well.

References

Allawi, A.A. (2007), *The Occupation of Iraq: Winning the War, Losing the Peace* (New Haven, CT: Yale University Press).
Azarbaijani-Moghaddam, S. (2004), 'Afghan Women on the Margins of the Twenty-first Century', in Antonio Donini, Norah Niland and Karin Wermester (eds), *Nation-Building Unravelled? Aid, Peace and Justice in Afghanistan* (Bloomfield: Kumarian Press): 95–113.
Azarbaijani-Moghaddam, S. (2007), 'On Living with Negative Peace and a Half-Built State: Gender and Human Rights', *International Peacekeeping*, 14(1): 127–42.
Burke, E. (1999), *Select Works of Edmund Burke* (Indianapolis: Liberty Fund) Vol. I.
Burns, R. (2007), 'Mullen: Afghanistan Isn't Top Priority', *Washington Post*, 11 December.
Caplan, R. (2005), *International Governance of War-Torn Territories: Rule and Reconstruction* (Oxford: Oxford University Press).
Carnahan, M. (2004), 'Next Steps in Reforming the Ministry of Finance', in Michael Carnahan, Nick Manning, Richard Bontjer and Stéphane Guimbert (eds), *Reforming Fiscal and Economic Management in Afghanistan* (Washington DC: World Bank): 123–49.

Chesterman, S. (2004), *You, The People: The United Nations, Transitional Administration, and State-Building* (Oxford: Oxford University Press).
Deschamps, C. and A. Roe (2009), *Land Conflict in Afghanistan: Building Capacity to Address Vulnerability* (Kabul: Afghanistan Research and Evaluation Unit).
De Soto, H. (2001), *The Mystery of Capital: Why Capitalism Triumphs in the West and Fails Everywhere Else* (London: Black Swan).
Dorronsoro, G. (2009), *The Taliban's Winning Strategy in Afghanistan* (Washington DC: Carnegie Endowment for International Peace).
Evans, A., N. Manning, Y. Osmani, A. Tully and A. Wilder (2004), *A Guide to Government in Afghanistan* (Kabul: Afghanistan Research and Evaluation Unit).
Felbab-Brown, V. (2005), 'Afghanistan: When Counternarcotics Undermines Counterterrorism', *Washington Quarterly*, 28(4): 55–72.
Fukuyama, F. (2004), *State-Building: Governance and World Order in the 21st Century* (Ithaca, NY: Cornell University Press).
Ghani, A. (1978), 'Islam and State-Building in a Tribal Society: Afghanistan 1880–1901', *Modern Asian Studies*, 12(2): 269–84.
Ghani, A., C. Lockhart, N. Nehan and B. Massoud (2007), 'The Budget as the Linchpin of the State: Lessons from Afghanistan', in J.K. Boyce and M. O'Donnell (eds), *Peace and the Public Purse: Economic Policies for Postwar Statebuilding* (Boulder, CO: Lynne Rienner): 153–83.
Giustozzi, A. (2009), *Empires of Mud: War and Warlords in Afghanistan* (London: Hurst & Co.).
Grare, F. (2007), *Rethinking Western Strategies toward Pakistan: An Action Agenda for the United States and Europe* (Washington DC: Carnegie Endowment for International Peace).
Gregorian, V. (1969), *The Emergence of Modern Afghanistan: Politics of Reform and Modernization 1880–1946* (Stanford, CA: Stanford University Press).
Gutman, R. (2008), *How We Missed the Story: Osama Bin Laden, the Taliban, and the Hijacking of Afghanistan* (Washington DC: United States Institute of Peace Press).
Hafvenstein, J. (2007), *Opium Season: A Year on the Afghan Frontier* (Guilford, CT: The Lyons Press).
Hashim, A.S. (2006), *Insurgency and Counter-Insurgency in Iraq* (Ithaca, NY: Cornell University Press).
Higgins, H.B. (2007), 'To Helmand and Back', *The American Interest*, 3(2): 60–72.
Human Rights Watch (2008), *"Troops in Contact": Airstrikes and Civilian Deaths in Afghanistan* (New York: Human Rights Watch).
Hussain, R. (2005), *Pakistan and the Emergence of Islamic Militancy in Afghanistan* (Aldershot: Ashgate).
Hynek, N. and P. Marton (eds) (2012), *Statebuilding in Afghanistan: Multinational Contributions to Reconstruction* (New York: Routledge).
Jenkins, K. and W. Plowden (2006), *Governance and Nationbuilding: The Failure of International Intervention* (Cheltenham: Edward Elgar).
Jones, S.G. (2008), 'Afghanistan's Growing Security Challenge', in Ruth Rennie (ed.), *State Building, Security, and Social Change in Afghanistan: Reflections on a Survey of the Afghan People* (Kabul and San Francisco: The Asia Foundation): 27–44.

Kakar, H. (1978a), *Government and Society in Afghanistan: The Reign of Amir 'Abd-al Rahman Khan* (Austin, TX: University of Texas Press).
Kakar, H. (1978b), 'The Fall of the Afghan Monarchy in 1973', *International Journal of Middle East Studies*, 9: 195–214.
Kalinovsky, A.M. (2011), *A Long Goodbye: The Soviet Withdrawal from Afghanistan* (Cambridge, MA: Harvard University Press).
Khalidi, N.A. (1991), 'Afghanistan: Demographic Consequences of War, 1978–1987', *Central Asian Survey*, 10(3): 101–26.
Maley, W. (1987), 'Political Legitimation in Contemporary Afghanistan', *Asian Survey*, 27(6): 705–25.
Maley, W. (1991), 'Social Dynamics and the Disutility of Terror: Afghanistan, 1978–1989', in P. Timothy Bushnell, Vladimir Shlapentokh, Christopher K. Vanderpool and Jeyaratnam Sundram (eds), *State Organized Terror: The Case of Violent Internal Repression* (Boulder, CO: Westview Press): 113–31.
Maley, W. (1999), 'Reconstructing Afghanistan: Opportunities and Challenges', in Geoff Harris (ed.), *Recovery from Armed Conflict in Developing Countries: An Economic and Political Analysis* (New York: Routledge): 225–57.
Maley, W. (2002a), 'The Reconstruction of Afghanistan', in Ken Booth and Tim Dunne (eds), *Worlds in Collision: Terror and the Future of Global Order* (Basingstoke: Palgrave Macmillan): 184–93.
Maley, W. (2002b), 'Confronting Creeping Invasions: Afghanistan, the UN and the World Community', in K. Warikoo (ed.), *The Afghanistan Crisis: Issues and Perspectives* (New Delhi: Bhavana Books): 256–74.
Maley, W. (2006), *Rescuing Afghanistan* (London: Hurst & Co.).
Maley, W. (2009a), 'Democracy and Legitimation: Challenges in the Reconstruction of Political Processes in Afghanistan', in Brett Bowden, Hilary Charlesworth and Jeremy Farrall (eds), *The Role of International Law in Rebuilding Societies after Conflict: Great Expectations* (Cambridge: Cambridge University Press): 111–33.
Maley, W. (2009b), *The Afghanistan Wars* (Basingstoke: Palgrave Macmillan).
Maley, W. (2009c), *States of Conflict: A Case Study on State-Building in Afghanistan* (London: Institute for Public Policy Research).
Maley, W. (2010), 'Afghanistan: An Historical and Geographical Appraisal', *International Review of the Red Cross*, 92(880): 1–18.
Maley, W. (2011a), 'The Rule of Law and the Weight of Politics: Challenges and Trajectories', in Whit Mason (ed.), *The Rule of Law in Afghanistan: Missing in Inaction* (Cambridge: Cambridge University Press): 61–83.
Maley, W. (2011b), 'Afghanistan: Grim Prospects?', in Shahram Akbarzadeh (ed.) *America's Challenges in the Greater Middle East: The Obama Administration's Policies* (New York: Palgrave Macmillan): 195–216.
Mansfield, D. (2007), '"Economical with the Truth": The Limits of Price and Profitability in Both Explaining Opium Poppy Cultivation in Afghanistan and in Designing Effective Responses', in Adam Pain and Jacky Sutton (eds), *Reconstructing Agriculture in Afghanistan* (Rugby: FAO and Practical Action Publishing): 213–34.

Migdal, J.S. (1988), *Strong Societies and Weak States: State-Society Relations and State Capabilities in the Third World* (Princeton, NJ: Princeton University Press).
Migdal, J.S. (1994), 'The State in Society: An Approach to Struggles for Domination', in Joel S. Migdal, Atul Kohli and Vivienne Shue (eds), *State Power and Social Forces: Domination and Transformation in the Third World* (Cambridge: Cambridge University Press): 7–34.
Nawa, F. (2006), *Afghanistan, Inc.: A CorpWatch Investigative Report* (Oakland, CA: CorpWatch).
Niland, N. (2004), 'Justice Postponed: The Marginalization of Human Rights in Afghanistan', in Antonio Donini, Norah Niland and Karin Wermester (eds), *Nation-Building Unraveled? Aid, Peace and Justice in Afghanistan* (Bloomfield, CT: Kumarian Press): 61–82.
Noelle, C. (1998), *State and Tribe in Nineteenth-Century Afghanistan: The Reign of Amir Dost Muhammad Khan (1826–1863)* (Richmond: Curzon Press).
Oates, L. (2009), *A Closer Look: The Policy and Lawmaking Process Behind the Shiite Personal Status Law* (Kabul: Afghanistan Research and Evaluation Unit).
O'Hanlon, M.E. and H. Sherjan (2010), *Toughing it Out in Afghanistan* (Washington DC: Brookings Institution Press).
Otto, J.M. (2009), 'Rule of Law Promotion, Land Tenure and Poverty Alleviation: Questioning the Assumptions of Hernando de Soto', *Hague Journal on the Rule of Law*, 1(1): 173–94.
Peters, G. (2009), *Seeds of Terror: How Heroin is Bankrolling the Taliban and al Qaeda* (New York: Thomas Dunne Books).
Piiparinen, T. (2007), 'A Clash of Mindsets? An Insider's Account of Provincial Reconstruction Teams', *International Peacekeeping*, 14(1): 143–57.
Rashid, A. (2008), *Descent into Chaos: The United States and the Failure of Nation Building in Pakistan, Afghanistan, and Central Asia* (New York: Viking Press).
Reidel, B. (2011), *Deadly Embrace: Pakistan, America, and the Future of Global Jihad* (Washington DC: Brookings Institution Press),
Rohde, D. and D.E. Sanger (2007), 'How a "Good War" in Afghanistan Went Bad', *New York Times*, 12 August.
Rousseau, J-J. (1973), *The Social Contract and Discourses* (London: J.M. Dent).
Rubin, B.R. (2002), *The Fragmentation of Afghanistan: State Formation and Collapse in the International System* (New Haven, CT: Yale University Press).
Rubin, B.R. and J. Sherman (2008), *Counter-Narcotics to Stabilize Afghanistan: The False Promise of Crop Eradication* (New York: Center on International Cooperation, New York University).
Ruttig, T. (2009), *Afghanistans Wahlkrise: Die gefälschte Präsidentschaftswahl und Strategien für »danach«* (Berlin: Stiftung Wissenschaft und Politik).
Saikal, A. and W. Maley (1991), *Regime Change in Afghanistan: Foreign Intervention and the Politics of Legitimacy* (Boulder, CO: Westview Press).
Saikal, A. and W. Maley (2008), 'The President Who Would Be King', *New York Times*, 6 February.

Saito, M. (2009), *Searching for My Homeland: Dilemmas Between Borders. Experiences of Young Afghans Returning "Home" From Pakistan and Iran* (Kabul: Afghanistan Research and Evaluation Unit).
Sanger, D.E. (2009), *The Inheritance: The World Obama Confronts and the Challenges to American Power* (New York: Harmony Books).
Schmeidl, S. and W. Maley (2008), 'The Case of the Afghan Refugee Population: Finding Durable Solutions in Contested Transitions', in H. Adelman (ed.), *Protracted Displacement in Asia: No Place to Call Home* (Aldershot: Ashgate): 131–79.
Shah, T. and C. Gall (2007), 'Afghan Rebels Find Aid in Pakistan, Musharraf Admits', *New York Times*, 13 August.
Sinno, A.H. (2008), *Organizations at War in Afghanistan and Beyond* (Ithaca, NY: Cornell University Press).
Smith, S.S. (2011), *Afghanistan's Troubled Transition: Politics, Peacekeeping, and the 2004 Presidential Election* (Boulder, CO: Lynne Rienner).
Stedman, S.J. (1997), 'Spoiler Problems in Peace Processes', *International Security*, 22(2): 5–53.
Stephens, J. and D.B. Ottaway (2005), 'A Rebuilding Plan Full of Cracks', *Washington Post*, 20 November.
Suhrke, A. (2006), *When More is Less: Aiding Statebuilding in Afghanistan* (Madrid: Fundación para las Relaciones Internacionales y el Diálogo Exterior).
Suhrke, A. (2007), 'Reconstruction as Modernisation: The "Post-conflict" Project in Afghanistan', *Third World Quarterly*, 28(7): 1291–308.
Suhrke, A. (2011), *When More is Less: The International Project in Afghanistan* (London: Hurst & Co.).
Suhrke, A. and A. Strand (2005), 'The Logic of Conflictual Peacebuilding', in Sultan Barakat (ed.), *After the Conflict: Reconstruction and Development in the Aftermath of War* (London: I.B. Tauris): 141–54.
Turton, D. and P. Marsden (2002), *Taking Refugees for a Ride? The Politics of Refugee Return in Afghanistan* (Kabul: Afghanistan Research and Evaluation Unit).
United Nations (2002), *The Situation in Afghanistan and its Implications for International Peace and Security: Report of the Secretary-General* (New York: United Nations, A/56/875, S/2002/278, 18 March).
Waldman, M. (2010), *The Sun in the Sky: The Relationship Between Pakistan's ISI and Afghan Insurgents* (London: Discussion Paper No. 18, Crisis States Research Centre, London School of Economics and Political Science).
Watson, P. (2006), 'In Afghanistan, Money Tips the Scales of Justice', *Los Angeles Times*, 18 December.
Weinbaum, M.G. and J.B. Harder (2008), 'Pakistan's Afghan Policies and their Consequences', *Contemporary South Asia*, 16(1): 25–38.
Wily, L.A. (2003), *Land Rights in Crisis: Restoring Tenure Security in Afghanistan* (Kabul: Afghanistan Research and Evaluation Unit).
Wily, L.A. (2004), *Looking for Peace on the Pastures: Rural Land Relations in Afghanistan* (Kabul: Afghanistan Research and Evaluation Unit).
World Bank (2005a), *Afghanistan: State Building, Sustaining Growth, and Reducing Poverty* (Washington DC: World Bank).

World Bank (2005b), *Afghanistan: Managing Public Finances for Development* (Washington DC: World Bank, Report No. 34582–AF).

Yaqub, D. and W. Maley (2008), 'NATO and Afghanistan: Saving the State-Building Enterprise', in Robin Shepherd (ed.), *The Bucharest Papers* (Washington DC: German Marshall Fund of the United States, and London: Chatham House): 5–17.

Zakheim, D.S. (2011), *A Vulcan's Tale: How the Bush Administration Mismanaged the Reconstruction of Afghanistan* (Washington DC: Brookings Institution Press).

Conclusions

The preceding chapters raise a range of issues about political violence; how it is defined; how, if at all, it is distinct from terrorism; whether states engage in political violence and if so, how and under what circumstances; why individuals and groups resort to political violence; whether they have a right to do so when faced with tyranny; the methods they use and why; whether religion is a motivating factor; the way in which men and women are involved in such violence; the legal status of such violence when it is ongoing; how such violence can be countered or prevented; the role of the security forces and ordinary citizens; and how combatants and other participants are pacified and law and order is established or re-instated.

Following these chapters, it is perhaps clearer how political violence might be defined. In his 2012 book, Robert Muchembled defined violence as 'a power relationship aimed at subjecting or constraining another person' (Muchembled 2012: 7), but his definition excluded political violence, which, according to him, required further definition. The chapters assembled in this volume would support a definition of political violence as follows: violence aimed at achieving or resisting regime change in established power hierarchies and orders; asserting or resisting supremacy of one form of national identity over another or others; seizing and controlling economic, political or other resources in the form of mineral, key routes; or resistance to any of these forms of violence. Any of these can be considered political violence.

Is All Violence Political?

Where does political violence start and other forms – interpersonal violence or criminal violence – stop? Surely, all violence can be considered political insofar as all violence can be construed as an attempt to exert power over another party or to unsettle an existing power status quo. The definition and labelling of violence are political acts in themselves. McIntyre in Chapter 9 argued against the construction of Irish republican violence as criminal violence, as Margaret Thatcher would have had it, rather than a liberation struggle as he and other combatants saw it. To revisit Muchembled's definition of interpersonal violence, it is evident that the fields of interpersonal violence and political violence are not entirely separate and distinct fields. Consider, for example, the interpersonal violence visited upon the individual person of Muammar Gaddafi, which ultimately led to his death. Or consider the demobilised combatant recently returned from an engagement in Iraq, Afghanistan, Northern Ireland, Vietnam, Korea, the First World War or the Second World War. When this demobilised combatant returns to his (and he is usually male) family, if he has one, he carries with him his experience of armed combat and his military training. Processes of demobilisation are often brief. Suppose that this demobilised combatant displays some form of aggression or frustration towards his family, using behaviour that was regarded as appropriate or at least unremarkable yesterday on the battlefield. When he behaves today in ways that were appropriate yesterday on the battlefield, the behaviour may well become labelled domestic violence, intimate partner violence or child abuse.

Sjoberg in Chapter 14 has elucidated how political violence is inextricably implicated in the ubiquity of gender subordination and Avila Kilmurray has illustrated how women in civil society have performed particular roles, perhaps most dramatically illustrated by the role of women's organisations in Liberia during the Accra peace talks of 1996.

A great deal more attention has been paid recently to the situation of the demobilised soldier from standing state armies that have seen recent combat. The level of awareness of the intersections between military and civilian life has increased.

Whatever the wisdom of the wars in Iraq and Afghanistan, and the debates surrounding the *jus ad bellum* or *jus in bello* dimensions of these, the stigmatisation of Vietnam veterans in the USA following the loss of public support for that war and anti-war demonstrations in the UK during the 2003 Iraq War has led to an increased consciousness about the 'separation of functions' between the government that declares a war and the troops on the ground who fight it. Whatever the wisdom of or justification for war declared by civilian politicians, public opinion in both the USA and the UK has swung behind the men and women of the military who must do their bidding. In the UK, the Help for Heroes campaign amongst other initiatives has operationalised an additional moral dimension in the ethics of war, *jus post bellum*, and a plethora of equivalent organisations and campaigns in the US espouse similar sentiments, some also supporting the campaign, others focusing on support for military personnel.

Alongside this, new and emerging voices from amongst the military themselves have begun to express opposition to particular wars or to specific tactics. In the USA, organisations such as Iraq Veterans Against the War recruit members currently serving in the US military as well as those who have been demobbed or gone AWOL. In the UK, the articulation of opposition to the 2003 Iraq War, military families in organisations such as Military Families Against the War and the individual cases of Michael Lyon, Joe Glenton and Ben Griffin are part of a longer tradition of refusal, pacifism and political opposition to specific campaigns, and seemingly individual acts such as that of Pfc Bradley Manning who leaked to WikiLeaks US intelligence footage of a US Apache helicopter attack in Baghdad in 2007 that killed 12 civilians. Elsewhere, notably in Israel, organisations such as Yesh Gvul and Breaking the Silence, alongside feminist organisations such as New Profile, engage directly with the issue of conscription, again part of a longer anti-militarism and anti-violence tradition and incorporated at any one time into specific political campaigns.

In the USA, the conflicts in Laos, Cambodia and Vietnam from 1955 to 1975 and events such as the My Lai massacre in 1968 led to an episode of revulsion for war in the American mind and a period of revulsion to committing American lives in foreign military adventures. This was to last through the first Gulf War, which could be celebrated by Americans perhaps because of its brevity and 'surgical' nature. However, twenty-first-century military expeditions into Afghanistan and then Iraq have resurrected the spectres of My Lai in the form of Abu Ghraib, Guantanamo and the various practices of extraordinary rendition, waterboarding and so on. Once again, it seems that American military engagement has fallen out of favour in popular opinion embarrassed if not shamed by details of recent engagements and ever more preoccupied with the domestic and global financial crisis.

In the UK, one of the key allies of the USA in Iraq and Afghanistan, it is on Tony Blair's decision to go to war and the 'sexing up' of dossiers containing – or not containing – evidence of Saddam Hussein's possession of weapons of mass destruction that public attention and opposition to war has focused. The integrity and wisdom of committing a volunteer army, many of whose lives have been ended in these wars, has been publicly and repeatedly questioned formally in events such as the Chilcot Inquiry and in persistent public debate. These considerations have been influential in shaping decisions about military intervention in the Arab revolutions of 2011 onwards.

Scholarship on international intervention and on international law and human rights has engaged in a plethora of related issues. Perhaps the most prolific field is that dealing with terrorism and counter-terrorism debates about what constitutes terrorism, what causes it and how to manage and end it, which has led to a mushrooming of publishing on the topic.

And violence is also good business for some. The increase in professional armies, the privatisation of security and the development of military technology whereby warfare has become more remote – and expensive – mean that money is to be made in industries associated with it. One suspects that those watching for overhead drones in Pakistan or displaced in any of the conflicts in sub-Saharan Africa are not convinced by arguments about diminishing levels of violence.

One of the important issues not addressed in the book is the civilian experience of political violence and how everyday life proceeds in the context of armed conflict and war. When used as a weapon of political violence, fear is a powerful communicative tool between armed actors and the wider society. Fear can re-shape and re-calibrate the landscape of everyday life. Anthropology has paid some attention to the ways in which fear and terror as products of political violence can permeate the lives of ordinary people in violently divided societies. Chaos, terror and fear are diffused but discernable in language, symbols and material culture. The power of such fear in lives lived under occupation, with the daily threat of political kidnappings, torture or the less dramatic but no less violent daily experiences of life in under militarisation, is often concealed by processes of normalisation. Anthropologists have examined fear and terror as instruments of war by other means and have described the cultural, social and material dimensions of fear and terror in order to understand how ordinary people experience these processes –

their resistance to and collusion with fear, terror and violence; the role of memory and silence in shaping their social relations; and how violence and fear are re-worked and internalised within daily life.

Genocide and International Intervention

Yet whilst the terrible consequences of war are to be feared, human society has not seen the end of the great crimes of genocide that shocked the world during the Second World War. In the closing decade of the twentieth century, the Rwandan genocide – and the inaction of the international community in the face of it – shocked the world, and genocidal violence has continued into the twenty-first century.

The issues of propaganda, the production of knowledge and information about political violence and the processes of ideological warfare have not been addressed in this volume. Instances such as the leaking of photographs of scenes of torture in Abu Ghraib or the leaking by Bradley Manning to WikiLeaks highlight the ongoing battle for the hearts and minds not only of populations in regions under occupation by Western troops, but also for the hearts and minds of voters in the West. Such battles and the increased accessibility of social media form an increasingly important aspect of warfare in particular and politics in general, particularly since the advent of the digital age and widespread access to global media. President Obama's re-election campaign in 2012 announced an even greater investment in social media campaigning, a tactic that was credited as playing a part in his 2008 victory.

The ubiquity and accessibility of such media also renders it more difficult than ever for governments to keep secrets or for intelligence services to sift through the legions of social media material and noise to identify suspicious and dangerous individuals. These issues are evident in the failures of intelligence prior to both the 2001 attacks on the World Trade Center in New York and the 2005 attacks on the London transport system, the breaking of scandals such as that of torture of prisoners in Abu Ghraib and in the proliferation of uprisings in the so-called Arab Spring of 2011.

Butler has pointed to a growing acceptance of censorship in the media since 2001. She notes that the media:

> function as 'public voices' that operate at a distance from their constituency, that both report the 'voice' of the government for us, and whose proximity to that voice rests on an alliance or identification with that voice ... it seems crucial to note that a critical relation to government has been severely, though not fully, suspended and that the 'criticism' or indeed, independence of the media has been compromised in some unprecedented ways. (Butler 2004a: 1)

The role of the scholar in providing analysis and grounded research on political violence is perhaps never more important, yet the challenges to be faced when undertaking this work can be daunting. In Chapter 16, Sluka wrote about the difficulties of conducting field research in the context of political violence in terms of the safety of the researchers. This is not only a matter of safety, however important safety might be. The challenge of maintaining or even achieving a perspective in the midst of violence, of overcoming the limitations of being either an insider or an outsider, and the impact of so-called 'embedding' of journalists and other researchers with troops are all topics worthy of further investigation. The challenges and risks discussed by Sluka are pressing, yet other difficulties such as those of collecting valid and reliable information about the situation on the ground present huge difficulties not only for anthropologists such as Sluka, but also for journalists, emergency relief and aid agencies and those who would report casualty figures. However, such data and analysis form a critical part of understanding political violence.

There is currently no legal obligation on military forces to count civilian casualties, giving rise to a situation where many of the casualty figures cited for particular conflicts reflect only the military casualties or those incurred by a particular party to the conflict. The Oxford Research Group's campaign (see http://www.oxfordresearchgroup.org.uk/rcac) to require the counting of civilian casualties is an intervention aimed at altering practice and consequently mindsets when examining the costs of war. As the Oxford Research Group and this author's own work (Fay et al. 1999) can attest, counting deaths due to a conflict is far from a straightforward or obvious process. Whether indirect casualties such as suicides or those killed by military vehicles should be included, what time parameters should be set and drawing geographical boundaries around a particular conflict are all difficult issues on which no universally accepted protocols exist, nor are there legal imperatives to collect such data in the first place. This has implications for the protection and monitoring of human rights compliance and for resisting the moral drift arguably facilitated by relegating civilian lives to the category of 'collateral damage'.

Counting the Injured

The author's own recent work (Breen-Smyth 2012) on injury due to armed conflict presents a further challenge in terms of counting injuries caused by political violence. Currently protocols on counting injuries are even more disparate and diverse, where they exist at all. There are no commonly agreed standards for definition of physical injury, and although post-traumatic stress disorder (PTSD) is commonly regarded as a benchmark for psychological injury, it is only one of a range of possible injuries that can be sustained as a result of political violence. A survey of the literature reveals that although it is easier to locate information and research on military injuries and whilst some information and research exists about the injuries such as limb loss or the psychological traumatisation of troops, comparatively little exists about civilian injury, and what does exist is largely focused on PTSD.

Hidden Costs: Psychologising the Effects

Elsewhere, this author has argued that only a tiny fragment of the experience and effects of political violence is ever examined (Breen-Smyth 2008b). In conducting research in societies where violent political conflict has taken place, the researcher becomes aware of the ubiquity of experience of political violence. Often, only those killed are the focus of attention, and even when attention is focused on the injured, this omits the experience of witnesses, relatives, displaced people and many others. People such as these do not often appear in statistics about the effects of such violence. They do not seek help for the effect of their experiences, nor do they usually speak about them. Their experiences disappear, re-emerging only for a brief moment when they are presented with an opportunity to speak, a stimulus to thinking about themselves in relation to a violent environment. These myriad experiences, ubiquitous, unrecorded yet held in memory, are not counted because of the way we look at political violence and the way in which we 'measure' its effects.

Two institutions form a central part of the societal mechanisms whereby 'relevant experiences' are selected and the focus is narrowed to exclude other experiences and effects. These two institutions are the media and healthcare, specifically psychology and psychiatry. Not only does the media select its focus according to news values, omitting what is not considered newsworthy, it also increasingly employs psychological concepts to explain political violence, its causes and effects.

What has been referred to as the 'psychological turn' in the Western world, psychology has played a central role in 'managing' the impact of political violence through the use of diagnostic paradigms, which are technical, depersonalised and individualised. In these frameworks, psychological sequelae are privileged over other effects. As a result, some effects of political violence are taken into account by translating them into individual pathology – traumatisation – whilst other effects are ignored or are presumed not to exist. By maintaining the focus of concern on a symptomatic minority at the expense of the wider population, other social and political effects – and even physical effects – are de-emphasised and ignored.

Psychological approaches also serve to accentuate notions of vulnerability. Unprecedented levels of public anxiety in the West about the risk of 'terrorist' attack and the 'new global threat' mean that risk is no longer construed as localised in war zones, but is ubiquitous (see Mueller 2009). The process of demonisation has meant that terrorism is represented as the senseless acts of maniacs rather than as symptomatic of a set of political problems amenable to political solutions. Following the attacks on the World Trade Center and the Pentagon in 2001, and the attacks in London in 2005, Western governments warned their citizens about the 'new global threat' and called for vigilance in order to pre-empt further attacks. Prior to the War on Terror, attacks tended to be seen as localised, and the risk of further attacks was calculated according to location, nationality, occupation or affiliations. A suicide attack in Israel or a car bomb in Northern Ireland told us that Israel and Northern Ireland were dangerous places to be – and that some locations in Israel or Northern Ireland were more dangerous than others.

The global war on terrorism ushered in a new regime of risk interpretation. Since then, an attack on London or New York no longer indicates that these are dangerous places; rather, it indicates that no-one in the West is safe from such attacks. It tells those in Yorkshire or Seattle that they are at risk from violent Islamist attack. An attack thousands of miles away, in another country or state no longer purports to tell us that that location is dangerous. It demonstrates that the West is endangered and that Westerners are at risk. In doing so, it constructs 'Westerners' in opposition to the Muslim or Islamist 'Other'.

The ability to make judgments about the level of risk is now considered to be beyond the competence of the individual. Such risk assessments require 'experts' to pronounce on the level of threat (again, see Mueller 2009) based on 'intelligence' which laypeople are not party to. Large amounts of trust must be placed in the authorities in order to accept the legitimacy of such assessments. Yet, as Gregory points out in Chapter 19, it is often difficult to judge the unreliability of such assessments given difficulties in the accessibility of evidence and intelligence gathering, and assessment is at best an inexact science. An increased tendency on the part of governments towards secrecy has compounded this monopoly on the assessment of risk and dependence on 'experts' within government. The falsity of reports on the existence of weapons of mass destruction in Iraq, which were used to justify the invasion, must give rise to questions about the reliability of such assessments and how they are manipulated and presented.

Countering Terrorism and Preventing Political Violence

A range of authors (Gregory in Chapter 19, Lambert in Chapter 20, McClintock in Chapter 21 and Walker in Chapter 22) discuss the challenges, dilemmas and difficulties in countering political violence through a range of means, and the various advantages and shortcomings of these. In the UK, the 2010 public consultation on the government's Programme for Government showed 'an overwhelming perception that anti-terrorism laws were being used excessively'. This led to a stated intention by the government to 'provide a correction in favour of liberty' and the announcement of a reversal of the tide of the erosion of civil liberties, threats to trial by jury, the misuse of anti-terrorism legislation and the proliferation of 'unnecessary new criminal offences'. The government's drive for greater transparency and openness through an extension of the scope of the Freedom of Information Act, the restoration of the right to non-violent protest and the creation of a commission to examine the creation of a British Bill of Rights showed a promise of a turn in government policy in favour of 'balanc[ing] the rights of the citizen and the laws of the state'.

However, the riots in London and other cities in the UK and the advent of the Occupy movement have created political pressures on the government for hardline responses and shifted fickle public opinion in the other direction. This is in spite of a degree of public sympathy for the Occupy movement in the wake of the banking crisis, growing unemployment and deepening global economic crisis.

This reactivity in public policy to notoriously capricious shifts in public opinion in reaction to events, rather than policy formulated on an evidence-driven approach, particularly in relation to countering terrorism, is a long-standing pattern in public policy in this field. The exceptionalising of threats and the consequent justification of exceptional and tougher counter-terrorism measures are rarely balanced with the lessons of previous experience of countering terrorism. Several counter-terrorism professionals (Breen-Smyth 2008a), including Lambert in Chapter 20, argue that the normal criminal law and the wide range of legal instruments already available in criminal law and investigatory practice are sufficient to address the issue of terrorism, with very few exceptions. The use of the ordinary criminal law not only avoids accusations of erosion of civil liberties but also separates out the illegal, dangerous and threatening behaviour from the possession of politically controversial views, which should not be made illegal.

In the UK, Demos, which advocated a community-based approach to counter-terrorism (Lownsbrough, Briggs and Fieschi 2006) has argued the importance of differentiating between radicals who are likely to use violence and those who will not. Radical views, they argue, must be engaged with in debate and with persuasive counter-argument rather than being demonised, and al-Qaeda must be de-glamorised. Whilst the government can do a certain amount, engagement with radicalism is largely a matter for wider society, individuals, groups and communities, Demos contends. Bartlett and Miller (2010) argue for more openness and transparency on the part of the government, investment in programmes that enable young people to think critically and recognise propaganda, and for civil society to play a proactive role. The banning of more groups, the deporting of radical preachers and the outlawing of demonstrations of 'banned ideologies' (see, for example, Chris Grayling's speech in the USA on 2 December 2009: http://www.conservatives.com/News/Speeches/2009/12/Chris_Grayling_Radicalism_is_a_domestic_and_international_challenge.aspx) drive such ideas underground where they become even more attractive to young people seeking an outlet for rebelliousness and anger at authority. On the other hand, radical ideas that do not break the law should be aired and debated, and strong counter-arguments should be produced. Indeed, such debate should be encouraged and supported by government not only at a national but also at a local level.

The particular relevance of government policy and practice, both in the provision of democratic avenues domestically where dissent and opposition can be expressed and in the area of foreign affairs, is addressed by Toros in Chapter 7. Nonetheless, the actions of governments in creating or undermining the conditions in which political violence becomes likely or even inevitable grow ever more evident. The Arab revolutions have demonstrated the danger posed to public order by despotic and totalitarian regimes, whose various attempts to suppress protest has led to a rash of political violence across the Arab world. Within the West, despair and anger at foreign policy, over which citizens feel they have little control or input, is felt particularly within diaspora communities from the Arab world within the West. The uncovering of evidence of the practice of torture, rendition and other human rights abuses in wars prosecuted by the West in their homelands, coupled with the failure to make any meaningful progress in peace negotiations in the Israel/Palestine conflict, has an alienating effect in the domestic politics as well as on the international stage, an alienation that sustains the conditions in which political violence is possible or even likely.

Although there has been some commitment in both the USA and the UK to some improvement in the care of veterans, there seems to be no account taken of the challenges of re-integrating considerable numbers of demobilised soldiers into communities that also contain Muslims and other minorities. These are issues of veterans' welfare but also of community cohesion. The UK perception that 'threats to our security can come from deep-rooted societal divisions' has led the UK government to declare its intention 'to ensure we have integrated communities' through the deployment of its 'Big Society' approach, yet it remains to be seen how this approach will ensure and secure respect for differences of religion, political belief and culture, where difference is seen as a resource and not a threat.

In countering domestic terrorism, the targeting of violence rather than ideology in future policy is an obvious if untried path. Future policy in the USA, the UK and mainland Europe could avoid singling Muslims out as particularly prone to violent extremism by focusing on *violence* (rather than *political views*) as the problem. This would allow the inclusion of right-wing and other forms of violence in future interventions. It would also provide the space in which to develop a range of educational initiatives focused on violence, the conditions under which it arises, the damage it does and its long-term consequences. Such educational initiatives have been almost entirely absent to date. It is assumed that everyone agrees that violence is a bad thing, yet contemporary popular culture often glamourises it and masks its long-term and wide-ranging effects. An education approach is already used in some school-based programmes in the UK and elsewhere to address other violence-related issues such as bullying. Additional forms of violence, such as knife crime and terrorism, could be incorporated into future programmes so that political violence and terror are framed as criminal rather than political activities and as ones that damage life chances.

Conversely, violence can only remain a reasonable option when young people and local communities cannot see a means of achieving political change peacefully or of having their voices heard. Opening up such opportunities could be a powerful prophylactic against political violence and, indeed, perhaps, other forms of violence.

Is Political Violence on the Decline?

Ideas about political violence have changed since the 'war to end all wars' at the turn of the twentieth century to the attack on the World Trade Center in New York shortly after the turn of the twenty-first century. In Chapter 18, Hughes provides a comprehensive historical survey of ideas about war. In the lived experience of the popular mind, the legacy of the total wars of 1914–1918 and 1939–1945 has instituted various ideas and practices. The notion of national unity and community strength in the face of external threat has created a nostalgic sentimentalism about civilian life during those periods, and the practices of memorialisation of the dead have, to some extent, sustained an ideology of sacrifice and heroism.

Stephen Pinker (2011) argues that violence is in decline and that the human race has moved closer to finding ways of overcoming aggression. This trend, he asserts, is linked to factors such as the end of slavery, the empowerment of women, the legalisation of homosexuality, growing revulsion at the punishment of children, the greater availability of contraception and the growth of global communication networks. He attributes the decline in violence to the influence of the Enlightenment, but others have criticised Pinker's identification of 'the Enlightenment' with a carefully chosen but not necessarily representative group of thinkers (Gray 2011). Pinker ignores the many Enlightenment thinkers who have been doctrinally anti-liberal and those who have favoured the large-scale use of political violence, from Engels, who welcomed a world war which would wipe out the Slavs – 'aborigines in the heart of Europe' (Marx and Engels 1975) – to the Jacobins, who insisted on the necessity of terror during the French Revolution (Mayer 2001).

Pinker's liberal humanist stance is taken in the midst of growing Western doubts about the effectiveness (and cost) of military interventions in Iraq and Afghanistan and the emergence of evidence about the conduct of Western governments and their troops in those wars. Pinker issues a challenge to 'a large swath of our intellectual culture [that] is loath to admit that there could be anything good about civilization, modernity and western society' (Pinker 2011). He argues that this encouraging decline in violence is partly attributable to a European enlightenment that has had an Eliasian civilising effect and signals greater human progress – although he does concede that these trends could be reversible.

North American analysts Erica Chenoweth and Maria Stephan (Chenoweth and Stephan 2011) announced that non-violent political movements succeeded 75 per cent of the time whilst the figure for violent movements was 25 per cent. Non-violent resistance, they argue, facilitates tactical innovation and defections among the opposition, including members of the military establishment to the protesters' cause because of the higher levels of moral and physical involvement and the commitment it entails. They assemble a body of empirical evidence to argue that from 1900 to 2006, campaigns of non-violent resistance were more than twice as effective as their violent equivalents, citing examples in Iran, Burma, the Philippines and the Palestinian territories. They conclude that successful non-violent resistance ushers in more durable and internally peaceful democracies, which are less likely to regress into civil war.

Since violence is rarely regarded as a good, it would be comforting to believe these arguments as mitigation of the pessimism surrounding the possibility of climate wars, global warming and nuclear proliferation. So is political violence in decline? Are more successful and less violent methods of achieving change (if that is what such violence is about) about to supersede violence? And is there any rational as opposed to aspirational reason for believing that the world is making moral progress away from such violence and towards a more pacific future?

On closer inspection, both Pinker and Chenoweth and Stephan are heavily reliant on statistical evidence and particular forms of categorisation. For example, Chenoweth and Stephan describe the anti-Apartheid movement as non-violent (and successful). This is in spite of the existence of the military campaign conducted by Umkhonto we Sizwe (on the non-violence question) and the continuing evidence of Black impoverishment and political marginalisation, and the continued existence of *de facto* spatial segregation in contemporary South Africa (on the success question).

Ross Douthat (2011) argues that this putative decline of violence should perhaps more properly be called the 'nationalisation of violence' since it is linked, he argues, to the rise of the modern state. Europe's unparalleled peace over the last 50 years or so can be seen as the outcome of centuries of civil war and ethnic and religious conflict – and this peace has come at the expense of diversity, with ethnic wars targeting minorities and establishing ever more ethnically homogeneous states.

In a related vein, John Gray (2011) wonders whether Pinker's outbreak of peace in the developed world might be somehow connected to 'endemic conflict in less fortunate lands'. Are such conflicts due to 'backwardness', as Pinker suggests, or can they be seen in the light of other international political forces such as world war and the aftermath of neo-colonial conflict? According to Gray, it may be a case not of peace, but of displacement, with rich countries exporting their wars to the developing world in much the same way as they exported their pollution. In evidence, Gray cites a long list of conflicts during the Cold War in Indo-China and other parts of Asia, the Middle East, Africa and Latin America, Korea, Tibet, Malaya, Kenya, Suez, Angola, Congo and Guatemala, the Six Day War, Hungary, Czechoslovakia, the Iran–Iraq War, the Soviet–Afghan War and so on. Since the end of the Cold War, the list includes the first Gulf War, the Balkan wars, Chechnya, the Iraq War, Afghanistan and Kashmir. Pinker minimises the significance of these wars, Gray argues, in favour of focusing on the outbreak of peace in 'advanced' societies and framing it as an unprecedented transformation in human affairs.

For Gray, then, Pinker's 'attempt to ground the hope of peace in science ... testifies to our enduring need for faith' rather than any great scientific denouement. When science points to the violence of the human animal, Gray opines that liberal humanists such as Pinker deploy science to explain away this evidence. The evidence itself is carefully selected, demonstrating to Gray a determined evasion of inconvenient facts.

Whether or not it is in decline, violence is a way of life for some, and cultures of violence develop as humans adapt to long exposure in places like Palestine and previously Northern Ireland. However morally problematic, violence can also often be a quick and effective method of achieving a particular outcome, *pace* Chenoweth. Where other penalties were not available to them, the use of violent punishment by non-state groups to punish criminality in Northern Ireland, for example, attracted the support of the local community, tired of petty crime and vandalism. On a larger scale, the use of suicide attacks is cheap, effective and largely avoids the risks associated with the capture and interrogation of perpetrators, as Hafez has demonstrated in Chapter 10.

Although wide-ranging, this volume cannot pretend to cover comprehensively the plethora of issues that these trends, concerns and changes raise. There are many other worthy issues well deserving of exploration. There is no extensive discussion of the nuclear issue, for example. Nor is there much extensive discussion on the emergent dilemmas of international intervention and the Responsibility to Protect in the light of the Libyan crisis and the Arab Spring of 2011. Neither do we take up the issues raised in Iraq and Afghanistan about what some of my colleagues would term the 'Responsibility to Rebuild'. Nor, indeed, do we provide any account of political violence and war which addresses war and violence as an economic activity, a profit-making venture, which, for some, it undoubtedly is. Nor indeed is there any coverage of new military technologies and the broader revolution in military affairs. Similarly, the activities of the international arms trade, its relationship with governments and its putative role in the proliferation of militarism and conflict is not addressed.

These omissions are perhaps inevitable in a volume that aspires to address such a vast topic and are no reflection on the merits or importance of the topics that have been omitted. They must form the subject of future explorations elsewhere.

References

Bartlett, J. and C. Miller. 2010. *The Power of Unreason: Conspiracy Theories, Extremism and Counterterrorism* (London: Demos, 27 August).
Bartlett, J.J. Birdwell and M. King. 2010. *The Edge of Violence: A Radical Approach to Extremism* (London: Demos).
Breen-Smyth, M. 2008a. 'Lessons Learned in Counter-terrorism in Northern Ireland: An Interview with Peter Sheridan', *Critical Studies on Terrorism*, 1(1): 111–23.
Breen-Smyth, M. 2008b. *The Other End of the Telescope: Reconsidering the Effects of Political Violence in Context*. Paper resented at the 116th Annual Convention of the American Psychological Association, Boston, MA, August.
Breen-Smyth, M. 2012. 'Injury Due to the Northern Ireland Conflict'. Office of the First and Deputy First Minister, Parliament Buildings, Stormont, Belfast.
Butler, J. 2004a. 'Explanation and Exoneration, or What We Can Hear', in *Precarious Life: The Powers of Mourning and Violence* (London: Verso).
Butler, J. 2004b. 'Violence, Mourning and Politics', in *Precarious Life: The Powers of Mourning and Violence* (London: Verso).
Chenoweth, E. and C. Stephan. 2011. *Why Civil Resistance Works: The Strategic Logic of Non-violent Conflict* (New York: Colombia University Press).
Douthat, R. 2011. 'Stephen Pinker's History of Violence', *New York Times*, 17 October, http://douthat.blogs.nytimes.com/2011/10/17/steven-pinkers-history -of-violence [accessed 4 July 2012].
Fay, M.T., M. Morrissey and M. Smyth. 1999. *Northern Ireland's Troubles: The Human Costs*. London: Pluto Press.
Gray, J. 2011. 'Delusions of Peace', *Propect*, 21 September, http://www. prospectmagazine.co.uk/2011/09/john-gray-steven-pinker-violence-review/ [accessed 4 July 2012].

House of Commons. 2010. *Communities and Local Government Committee – Sixth Report Preventing Violent Extremism*, March, http://www.publications.parliament.uk/pa/cm200910/cmselect/cmcomloc/65/6502.htm [accessed 4 July 2012].

Lownsbrough, H., R. Briggs and C. Fieschi. 2006. *Community Based Approaches to Counterterrorism* (London: Demos). Available at http://www.demos.co.uk/publications/bringingithome [accessed 4 July 2012].

Marx, K. and F. Engels. 1975. *Collected Works of Karl Marx & Frederick Engels* (New York: International Publishers).

Mayer, Arno J. 2000. *The Furies: Violence and Terror in the French and Russian Revolutions* (Princeton: Princeton University Press).

Muchembled, R. 2012. *A History of Violence* (Cambridge: Polity).

Mueller, J. 2009. *Overblown: How Politicians and the Terrorism Industry Inflate National Security Threats, and Why We Believe Them* (London: Simon & Schuster).

Pew Research Center. 2006. *The Great Divide: How Westerners and Muslims View Each Other* (Washington DC: Pew Global Attitudes Project).

Pinker, S. 2011. *The Better Angels of Our Nature: The Decline of Violence in History and its Causes* (New York: Allen Lane).

Shiraz Maher and Martin Frampton. 2009. 'Choosing our Friends Wisely: Criteria for Engagement with Muslim Groups', Policy Exchange. Available at http://www.policyexchange.org.uk/publications/publication.cgi?id=108 [accessed 4 July 2012].

Spalek, B., S. El Awa and L.Z. McDonald. 2009. 'Police-Muslim Engagement and Partnerships for the Purposes of Counter-Terrorism: An Examination', University of Birmingham.

Stephan, C. and E. Chenoweth. 2008. 'Why Civil Resistance Works: The Strategic Logic of Non-violent Conflict', *International Security*, 33(1): 7–44.

Turley, A. 2009. 'Stronger Together: A New Approach to Preventing Violent Extremism', New Local Government Network, August.

Index

3/11 events (Madrid bombing) 398
7/7 events
   al-Qaeda justification 398, 400
   Blair, Tony 391, 397–9
   intelligence 275
   Khan, Mohammad Sidique 458
   legitimacy and *halal* 400
   New Statesman 393
   policing in UK 404
   prevention 378–9
9/11 events
   Afghanistan 255
   al-Qaeda 29, 398, 404
   Americans and security 412
   Blair, Tony 392, 396
   Bush, George W. 396, 412
   FBI 380–81
   global context of armed conflicts 29
   'Global War on Terror' 391
   martyrs without borders 188, 190, 193, 198, 200
   New Labour government 389
   'Northern Ireland problem' 470
   outcomes for USA 382–4
   policing in UK 404
   political violence 577
   prevention 371
   responses 373–5, 375–6
   talking to armed activists 486
   terrorism profile 44, 47
   torture 423
   UK academics 404–5
   US
      invasions of Afghanistan/Iraq 99
      provocation 397
      response 411–12, 414–15
   'War on Terror' 486
   see also counter-terrorism and human rights

A v. HM Treasury case 449
A v. Secretary of State for the Home Department 446, 449, 452, 455
Abdel-Haq, J. 193
Abdulmutallab, Umar Farouk 383
abnormal psychology
   atypical personality traits 142–4
   introduction 140
   narcissism 141–2
   paranoia 141
   psychopathy and sociopathy 142
   psychosis 140–41
Abu Ghraib detention facility 74–5, 86, 249, 423–4, 427, 573
Abu Sayef group 142
Achebback, Jonas 194
Adams, Gerry 124, 178, 474, 530
ADVISE (Analysis, Dissemination, Visualisation Insight and Semantic Enhancement)
   Data-mining tool 417
Aegis Defence Services (Northern Ireland) 470
Afalah, Mohammed 191
Afghan National Army (ANA) 552
Afghanistan
   anti-occupation violence 87–90
   constitution, 2004 553
   feminism and victims of political violence 270
   paramilitaries and local proxies 82
   Soviet Union 359

Taliban 551, 553, 555, 558, 561–2
United States 92, 99, 269, 270, 414, 422, 557–8, 559
Afghanistan (political, economic and social reconstruction)
    current situation 559–660
    economic reconstruction 553–5
    education system 556
    foreign aid 554–5
    gender issues 556
    illicit economy 555
    international relations 557–9
    introduction 549–50
    land titles 554
    lessons 561–2
    opium poppy 555
    political reconstruction 551–2
    property rights 554
    social reconstruction 555–8
    state and war 550–51
    youth 557
African National Congress (ANC) 23, 24, 26, 478, 541
Ahern, Bertie 474, 476, 479
Ahtisaari, Maarti 478
AKP (Turkey) 232
al-Adl, Saif 397
Al-Bara, Abu 191
al-Bashir, Omar 336
Al-Falistini, Abu Qatada 199
al-Hakim, Muhammad Bakir 83
Al Jazeera satellite television 198
al-Kurdi, Abu Umar 195
al-Kuwaiti, Abu Ahmad 191
al-Kuwaiti, Abu Salih 191
al-Kuwaiti, Abu Wadha 191
al-Masri, Muhammad 192
al-Nether, Nafiz 147
al-Qaeda
    7/7 events 398, 400
    9/11 events 29, 398, 404
    al-Adl, Saif 397
    al-Suri, Abu Mus'ab 397
    approach to terrorism 44, 49
    bin Laden, Osama 382
    Blair, Ian 402
    Blair, Tony 392
    detention of suspected terrorists 394
    grievance and shame 399
    Hamdan, Salim 158

influence in UK 405
Iraq 85
London underground bombings 393
martyrs 200–201
opposition to Western interests 396
'religious' militants 231
'religious and quasi-religious extremism' 399
responses 396
strategy 390, 394–5
terrorism 392, 396
terrorist recruitment 405
United States 419–20, 432
USA 177
'War against Terror' 29, 49
al-Qaeda in IRQ (AQI) 188, 191
al-Qaradawi, Yusuf 198
al-Qatinah, Khalaf Allah 194
al-Sadr, Muhammad Saqr 83
al-Sharia wal-Hayat (*Islamic law and life*) TV programme 198
al-Suri, Abu Mus'ab 397
al-Tayyeb, Sheikh Ahmed 198
al-Zarqawi, Abu Musab 88, 188, 192
Albiston, Chris 471
Alderdice, David 477–8
Alderson, John 401
Allende, Salvador 288
American Anthropological Association (AAA) 303
American Civil Liberties Union (ACLU) 86
American Court of Human Rights 542
American Declaration of Independence 1776 121
Amin, Idi 344
amnesties 534–7
Amnesty International 67–8
An Phoblacht (IRA publication) 178
Anderson, Benedict 105, 296
Anderson, David 447
Andrew, Christopher 369
Anghie, Antony 91–2
anti-abortion terrorism in United States 255
anti-occupation violence in Iraq and Afghanistan
    counter-insurgency 89–90
    insurgency as 'Terrorism' 87–8
Anticommunist Alliance (triple A) in Argentina 291
Antisocial Personality Disorder (APD) 142

INDEX

Apartheid 532
Aquinas, Augustine 348
Aquinas, Thomas 348
Arab Spring 405, 580
Arafat, Yasser 25
Arévalo, Juan José 287
Argentina
    amnesties 536
    conflict 290–91
    military junta 290
    Nunca Màs 545
    truth commissions 541
Armed Islamic Group (Algeria) 232–3
Arms and Influence 357
Arniel, Barbara 91
Aron, Raymond 347
Arredidj, Bordj Bou 192
Association of Chief Police Officers
    (ACPO) 370, 377, 401
Atkins, Humphrey 394
Authorization for the Use of Military Force
    (AUMF) 413
Axis Rule in Occupied Europe 329–30
Aylwin-Foster, Nigel 472

Baader-Meinhof Gang 275
Baath Party (Iraq) 539–40
Bain, William 110–11
Baldwin, David 100–101
Bandura, Albert 148
Bannockburn battle 353
Barbie, Klaus 543
Barrios Alto ruling in Peru 536
Barthes, Roland 283
Baskin, Gershon 43
Basque conflict 20, 246–7, 250, 253, 469
Beevor, Antony 182
Begin, Menachim 52
Belfast Women's Support Network 513
Bell, Gertrude 92
ben Masaoud, Moncef 194
Bennett, Roy 451
Bergen, Peter 398
Berlin Wall 358, 530, 538
Bew, J. 479
'Beyond Hate' conference 511
Bhatia, Michael V. 181–2
bin Laden, Osama 158, 382, 398
Birmingham pub bombings 393, 404
Birmingham Six (miscarriage of justice) 391

Black, Cofer 412
Blair, Ian 402
Blair, Tony
    7/7 bombings 391, 397–9
    9/11 events 392, 396
    al-Qaeda 392
    Good Friday Agreement 479
    Iraq 89, 571
    Irish peace process 476
    Muslim Community support 405
    PIRA bombing campaign 397
    Sri Lanka peace process 478
    terrorism 392
    weapons of mass destruction 571
    World Affairs Council 398
Blood and Soil 341
Bloody Sunday 175, 457–8, 473, 485
Blunkett, David 391
book summary (political violence)
    aftermath 12–13
    countering 9–11
    definition 2–4
    ending 11–12
    manifestations 8–9
    motivation and goals 4–6
    theory, understanding and research
        6–8
Borough Command Units (BCUs) 379
Boumediene v. Bush case 420, 430, 453
Bowker, David 421
Bowyer Bell, J. 172–3
Boyd, Zakariya 381
Bradley, Omar 348
Brahimi, Lakhdar 558
Brannigan and McBride v. UK case 452
Braungart, R.G. & Braungart, M.M. 149–50
Breaking the Silence (Israeli organisation)
    570
Bremer, Paul 539
Brennan v. UK case 445
Brettell, Caroline 320
British International Studies Association
    (BISA) 50
British Muslim youth 481
Brock-Utne, Brigit 271
Brogan v. UK case 445
Brooke, Peter 477
Budonnovsk hostage crisis (Chechnya) 359
Burke, Edmund 551
Burma and military coup 31

Bush, George W.
 9/11 events 396, 412
 Afghanistan 557, 561
 Blair Tony 396
 counter-insurgency 89–90
 detainees 421
 Geneva Conventions 419–20
 'Global War on Terror' 318
 Iraq 89–90
 military commissions 423
 torture 430
 'war against terrorism' 29, 418
Butler Report 371
Buzan, Barry 295
Bybee, Jay S. 428–9

Calgacus 347
Cambodia 'autogenocide' 340–41
Cameron, David 405, 485
Campaign for the Administration of Justice (CAJ) in Northern Ireland 510, 520
Campbell, C. and Connolly, I. 483
Canadian Courts and domestic standards abroad 453
Cardenas, Lázaro 287
Carnahan, Michael 553–4
Carothers, T. 531
Carranza, Venustiano 286
Carter, Jimmy 511
Cassese, Antonio 131
Ceauşescu, Nicolae 544
Chabarou, Mourad 191
Chalabi, Ahmed 83
Chalal v. UK case 445, 453
Charlesworth, Hilary 267
Chatham House Rule 370
Chechen suicide bombers 481
Chechnya 31, 255, 359
Chemical, Biological, Radiological or Nuclear (CBRN) components and terrorism 376
Cheney, Dick 412
Chenoweth, Erica 578–9
Chiapas Guerillas, Mexico 151
Chile, amnesties 536
China and Taiwan 358
Chinkin, Christine 267
Churchill-Coleman, George 394
CIA (Criminal Intelligence Agency)
 counter-terrorism 380

 detention facilities 430
 government secrecy 418
 HUMINT 372, 380
 Obama, Barack 430
 torture 424–5
 unmanned aerial vehicles 382
Cicero 349, 351
civil society actors and end of violence
 catalyst role 510–14
 change agents 519–21
 cheerleaders 514–16
 communication 516–19
 finding space on crowded stage 521–3
 introduction 507–9
 roles 509–10
civilians and 'War on Terror'
 air strikes 80–82
 anti-occupation violence in Iraq and Afghanistan 87–91
 conclusions: right to political violence 91–2
 paramilitaries and local proxies 82–4
 risk-transfer war to degenerative war 86–7
 torture and killings 86
 urban assault 84–5
Clarke, Charles 447
Clarke, Peter 377, 401
Cloward, Richard A. 245
Coalition government (UK) 405
Coalition Provisional Authority (Iraq) 539
Coetsee, Jacobus 218
Cohen, Philip 403
Colombia
 nationalism 295–6
 political violence 294
 see also FARC
Commentary Magazine 476
Committee of Vice-Chancellors and Principals (CVCP) 302
Community Foundation for Northern Ireland 510, 513–14, 520–21
Conrad, Joseph 177
CONTEST (counter-terrorism strategy) 369, 369–70, 377–8, 379, 450
Corrymeala Community (Northern Ireland) 510, 512
Counter Terrorism Analysis Centre (CTAC) 377

counter-terrorism and human rights in the UK
  anti-Terrorism Crime and Security Act, 2001 445
  coercive interrogation 452
  conclusions 458–9
  Counter-Terrorism Act, 2008 446
  human rights
    legislation 449–53
    social transitions 457–8
    temporal transitions 456–7
    variable rights-specific impacts 453–6
  institutional support mechanisms 447–9
  introduction 443–4
  legislation 444–5
  Terrorism Act, 2000 445, 447
  Terrorism Act, 2006 446
  'War on Terror' 452
counter-terrorism and human rights since 9/11
  9/11 attacks on US 411–12
  conclusions 432
  data mining and domestic spying 417–18
  detainees 421–2
  fundamental rights 429–30
  global rights protection 420–21
  government secrecy 418
  international law 418–20
  introduction 411
  military commissions 423
  military and torture 426–7
  national security doctrine 415–16
  Obama, Barack 430–32
  racism and xenophobia 413–14
  right to a fair trial 422–3
  torture 414–15, 423–6, 426–7, 428–9
  warrantless search and seizure 416
Counter-terrorism and prevention of political violence 575–7
counter-terrorism in the UK since 1969
  conclusions 404–5
  counter-productive actions 394–9
  introduction 389–92
  politics
    grievances of al-Qaeda and PIRA (denial) 399–401
    impact on policing 401–4
    leaders acting tough 392–4

counting the injured 573–4
Crenshaw, Martha 145
critical accounts of terrorism
  approaches 48–9
  critical turn and CTS 50–56
  introduction 47–8
  research agenda 56–9
Critical Studies on Terrorism Working Group (CSTWG) 50
Critical Terrorism Studies (CTS) 48, 50–56
Critical Theory (Social theory) 47
critical turn and CTS
  Critical Studies on Terrorism Working Group 50
  epistemological commitments 52–3
  ethical-normative commitments 54–6
  methodological commitments 53–4
  ontological commitments 51–2
Cronin, Sean 169
Cuban Revolution (1959) 289

Daily Mail 401
Daily Telegraph 401
Dalacoura, Katerina 234
Danger in the Field: Risk and Ethics in Social Research 307
Dangerous Fieldwork 304
Dannatt, Richard 87
Daoud, Mohammad 82, 550
Darío, Rubén 287
'Dark Ages' term 350–51
de Chastelain, John 480, 501
de Guzman, Melchor C. 405
de Klerk (South African prime minister) 218
de Menezes, Jean Charles 451
de Mirabeau, Comte 354
de Soto, Hernando 554
de Vattel, Emerich 91
Defence Intelligence Analysis Staff (DIAS) 376
definition
  political violence 329
  terrorism 113
Demobilisation, disarmament and reintegration (DDR) 502–3
'*democide*' concept 341–2
Democratic Unionist Party (Northern Ireland) 473, 478
Demos (think tank) 576

Dennis, Marisol 294
Department of Homeland Security (DHS) in US 381
Detainee Treatment Act (DTA), 2005 429
Diaz, Dave 80
Director of National Intelligence (DNI) in US 380
from dissent to revolution: politics and violence
   conclusions 133
   introduction 119–20
   rights
      dissention and disobedience 122–3
      practices 131–3
      resistance 123–8
      revolt 121–2
      self-determination 128–31
Doing Research on Sensitive Topics 304
Donaldson, Jeffrey 478
Dostum, Rashid 82
Douthat, Ross 579
Driver and Vehicle Licensing agency (DVLA) 378
Drost, Pieter 334, 339
Duyvesteyn, Isabelle 397

Easter Rising, 1916 173–4
Education for Democratic Citizenship Project (Poland) 546
Egyptian Muslim Brotherhood 232
Eide, Kay 558
Eisenhower, Dwight D. 350
El Amrani, Abdelmoman Amakchar 194
El Salvador
   ethnicity 343–4
   gang violence 293
Eliot, Thomas 180
Ellis, M. 538
Elshtain, Jean 264, 272–3
enhanced interrogation techniques (EITs) 425
Enloe, Cynthia 274
'Ensuring Lawful Interrogation' 430
ETA (Euskadi Ta Askatasuna) separatist group 49, 497
Etchecolatz, Miguel Angel 337
Europe and social movement studies 244
European Commission of Human Rights 394
European Court of Human Rights 444, 445, 453, 468, 542
European Union (EU)
   Eastern Europe 539
   Northern Ireland 508
   PEACE 11 programme 515
   Special Support Programme for Peace and Rehabilitation 514

Facundo: or Civilization and Barbarism 285
Falls Community Council (Northern Ireland) 520
FARC (Colombia) 142, 230
Farset Community Think Tank Project (Northern Ireland) 518–19
Fascism-Nazism 333
Fatah faction (PLO) 498
FBI (Federal Bureau of Investigation)
   data-mining programmes 417
   Field Intelligence Groups 381
   hate crime statistics 413
   intelligence functions 380
   IT systems 381
   National Security Letters 416
   North Carolina JTTF 381
   Terrorist Screening Database 383
Federal Charter of Somali Republic 532
Feenan, Dermot 310–11, 321
Feitlowitz, Marguerite 338
feminist reflections on political violence
   agents 266–70
   conclusions 276
   feminism 262–6
   gender issues 271–4
   introduction 261–2
   victims 270–71
   women who commit political violence 274–5
'Fenian' term (IRA) 169–70
Field Intelligence Groups (FBI) 381
fieldwork on political violence
   conclusions 321–2
   literature review 303–16
   managing danger 316–20
   quotes 301
Fieldwork Under Fire: Contemporary Studies of Violence and Survival 305–6
Finn, Robert P. 561
First World War 348
Fitzgerald, Garret 474

Flanagan, Ronnie 471
Fluehr-Lobban, Caroline 321
Foundation for Education and Democracy (Poland) 546
Frank, Gunder Andre 291
Frankfurt School 47
Frazier, Clyde 122
Freedom of Information Act 575
Freedom of Information Act (FOIA) in US 418
Freeland, Jonathan 476–7
French Declaration of the Rights of Man and the Citizen 121
French Revolution 119, 177
FSLN (Sandinista Front for National Liberation) in Nicaragua 291
functional component of terrorism 36, 41
fusion centres in US 381–2

Gaddafi, Colonel 359
Gaddafi, Muammar 569
Galasco, Marc 80
Gallagher, Willy 180
Gallup World Poll, 2009 156
Galtung, Johann 125, 271
Gammlerbewegung (hippies) 250
Gandhi, Rajiv 146
Gannon, Sean 476
Garthwaite, Rosie 302
Garzón, Baltasar 337–8
GCHQ (Government Communication Headquarters) 370, 376
General Confederation of Labour (CGT) in Argentina 288
Geneva Conventions 349, 419–20, 428, 432
Genocide Convention (1948) 329–4, 337–41
Genocide in the Age of the Nation State 343
Genocide in International Law 333
genocide, international intervention 572–3
Genocide: Its Political Use in the Twentieth Century 340
genocide, mass killings and collective violence
  bystander actions 210–11
  conclusions 218–19
  cultural characteristics 211–13
  evolution of violence and continuum of destruction 209
  identity, scapegoating and ideologies 208–9
  instigators 207–8
  introduction 205–7
  leaders and elites 210
  restraining forces and positive evolution 216–18
  Rwanda 213–18
genocide as political violence
  Cambodia 'autogenocide' 340–41
  comparative genocide studies 339–40
  genocide, war and political violence 342–4
  international law 333–4
  introduction 329–31
  legal innovations and quandaries 336–8
  '*politicide*' and '*democide*' 341–2
  severity 332
  Whitaker report 334–6
genocide studies term 329
Gerlach, Christian 332
Ghani, Ahraf 554
Gilbert, Paul 124
Giostozzi, Antonio 86
Global Policy Forum (GPF) 85
'Global War on Terror' (GWOT) 28–30, 59, 318, 358, 391, 575
Glover, James 468
Golde, Peggy 314–15
Goldman, Emma 137
Goldstein, Baruch 26, 149
Good Friday Agreement, 1998 (Northern Ireland) 26, 473, 475, 479, 507–8, 515
Gosling, D. 123, 125, 128
Gottschalk, M. and Gottschalk, S. 144, 157
Gray, John 579
Grayling, Chris 576
Great Northern War (1700–22) 355
Greenpeace 72
Grieve, John 391
Grosser Generalstab 356
Grotius, Hugo 354
group dynamics
  collective versus individual identity 152
  martyrdom 153
  small group pressures to conform 152–3
  social network theory 153–4
Guantanamo Bay Naval Station (GTMO) 421–2, 430, 431
Guatemala
  collective violence 206
  conflict 20

ethnicity 343
rule of law 531
Guéhenno, Jean-Marie 532
Guildford Four (miscarriage of justice) 391
Gulf War, 1991 72
Gulf War Air Power Surveys 72
Gunning, Jeroen 243–4
Gurr, Ted 19

Haaretz (Israeli newspaper) 475–6
Haass, Richard 475
Hague Conventions 359
Hain, Peter 403
Hamas (Palestine) 49, 152, 225, 232–3, 235, 251, 398, 474–6
Hamber, B. 483
Hamdan, Salim 158
Handel, Michael 350, 356
Hani, Chris 496
Haniyeh, Ismail 475
Harff, Barbara 341–2
Harris, Sam 90
Hasan, Nidal Malik 383
Hegghammer, Thomas 189–90, 192, 199
Henri Dunant Centre for Humanitarian Dialogue 498
Herb-e Islami 558
Herf, Jeffrey 331
Herodotus 349
Hezbollah (Lebanon) 226, 233, 359, 398, 474
hidden costs: psychologising the effects 574–5
Hillyard, Paddy 403–4
Historical Enquiries Team (Northern Ireland) 473
Hitchens, Christopher 90–91
Hitler, Adolf 64, 71–2, 331, 343
Hobbes, Thomas 122
Hobsbawm, Eric 283, 293
Hoffman, J. 265
Holland, Mary 393, 404
The Holocaust 206–7, 341
Homo Sovieticus (Poland) 546
Horowitz, Irving Louis 339
How to Avoid Being Killed in a War Zone 302
Howell, Nancy 303
'hubris syndrome' (politicians and power) 392–3
Hughes, Brendan 174
Hughes-Wilson J. 371

human rights
  Northern Ireland 450
  notice of derogation 451
Human Rights Act, 1998 443–4, 446
Human Rights Watch 426–7
Humanitrain Ltd 302
HUMINT (human sources) 372, 375, 380
Hundred Years' War 352
Huntington, Samuel 90, 227, 292
Hussein, Saddam 538–9, 561, 571
Hustlers, Beats and Other 319
Huston, Nancy 272–3
Hutchings, K. 264–5
Hutchinson, Billy 478, 519

Ignatieff, Michael 397, 402
IMINT (imagery intelligence) 371–5
Improvised Explosive Devices (IEDs) 276, 359, 383
In Religion: The Missing Dimension of Statecraft 229
Independent International Commission on Decommissioning (IICD) 480
Indian Rebellion, 1857 92
Inkatha Freedom Party (IKP) in South Africa 24, 26
Intelligence Enterprise Agency (DHS in US) 381
intelligence and political violence: counter-terrorism
  7/7 bombings prevention 378–9
  9/11 responses 373–5
  conclusions 384
  general issues 371–3
  introduction 369–70
  UK Domestic intelligence system 376–8
  United States 380–82, 382–4
Intelligence Reform and Prevention Act, 2004 382
Intelligence and Security Committee (ISC) 370, 378
Intelligence Services Act, 1994 376
Inter-American Court of Human Rights 542
International Committee of the Red Cross (ICRC) 418, 422, 425–6, 430
International Criminal Court (ICC)
  Lord's Resistance Army 536
  membership 543
  modes of justice 542

Rwanda 336
Sudan 336
torture 429
former Yugoslavia 336
International Criminal Tribunal for Rwanda (ICTR) 535, 542
International Criminal Tribunal for former Yugoslavia (ICTY) 535, 542
International Herald Tribune 475
international human rights law (IHRL) 69, 73
international humanitarian law (IHL) 69
International Rescue Committee (Afghanistan) 556
International Security Assistance Force (ISAF) 552, 561
IRA
   breakdown 507
   Brighton bombing 179
   British Government 132
   cessation of activities 176–7
   decommissioning of weapons 473, 508
   disarmament 480
   Elliot, Thomas 180
   Gallagher, Willy 180
   hunger strikes 457
   insurgents 469
   loyalist violence 484
   Magee, Patrick 179
   O'Rawe, Richard 180
   political violence 128
   prisoners 22, 49
   publications 178
   'rebel' term 169
   renunciation of violence 476
   security crackdown 457
   Sinn Féin 476, 480
   spoiling 501
   terrorism 49, 178–80
   see also Provisional IRA
Iraq
   anti-occupation violence 87–90
   martyrdom 187–190
   paramilitaries and local proxies 83–4
   'Salvador Option' 83
   Special Police Commandos 83–4
   suicide bombers 187–90
   United States (US) 199
   'War on Terror' 358
Ireland v. UK case 457

Irish Catholic Communities and PIRA terrorism 403
Irish National Liberation Army (INLA) 142, 172
Irish rebels (motivation and 'terrorist' label)
   conclusions 181–2
   historical overview 170–72
   introduction 169–70
   motivation 172–6
   terrorism 176–81
Is all violence political? 569–72
Is political violence on the decline? 577–8
Islam 233, 255
Islamic Jihad (Palestine) 498
Islamic Salvation Front (Algeria) 232
Israel
   Hezbollah 359
   Palestine 39, 40–43
Israeli Defence Force (IDF) 41
Israeli–Palestine conflict 39, 40–43, 207, 475
ITERATE database 154, 155

Jackson, Mike 473
Jackson, Richard 89
Jama'a al-Islammiyya (Egypt) 232
Jefferson, Thomas 119
Jenkins, Richard 313
Jenkins, Roy 398
Jerusalem Post 475–6
'Jewish National Suicide' 43
'Jim Crow' regulations in US 532
Jippson, Arthur and Litton, Chad 308–9
Joint Committee on Human Rights 370
Joint Intelligence Committee (JIC) 379
Joint Terrorism Analysis Centre (JTAC) 377, 379
Jomini, Antoine-Henri 355–6
Jones, K. 103
jus ad bellum concept 349
'just war' theory 91, 121, 348–9
Justice and Development Party (Morocco) 232

Kahn, Herman 357
Kaldor, Mary 29
Kant, Immanuel 122
Kapitan, Tomis 128–30
Karzai, Hamid 551–3, 557–8, 560, 561
Katz, Steven 339, 340

Keen, David 495–6
Kennedy, Helena 275
Kepel, Gilles 402
Khadr, Nadim 187–8
Khan, Mohammad Sidique 375, 378, 400–401, 458
Kiernan, Ben 341
King, Tom 469
Kitson, Frank 469, 482
Knox, Colin and Monaghan, Rachel 309–10
Kovats-Bernat, J. Christopher 301, 311–13, 321–2
Kriegsakademie 355
Krueger, Alan 89
Kuper, Leo 340
Kurdish PKK (Turkey) 230
Kurdistan Workers' Party (PKK, KADEK) 132

Lahneman, W.J. 373–5, 379, 384
Laqueur, Walter 33, 34, 36, 41, 65, 90, 140, 359
Latin America (national identity, conflict and political violence)
  introduction 281–4
  mass politics and populism 286–9
  nationalism 282, 288, 294–6
  nationalism and rise of military rule 289–92
  violence and nation building 284–6
  violence in post-authoritarian states 292–4
Lawrence, Stephen 391
'laws of war' 349
Leaky, Louis 92
Lebanon
  IRA 469
  martyrs 188–9, 192, 198, 200
  suicide bombings 226
  see also Hezbollah
Lee, Raymond 301, 304–5
Lee-Treweek, Geraldine and Linkogle, Stephanie 307–8, 314, 321
Lemkin, Raphael 329–30, 336, 339
Levene, Mark 342
Lewis, Bernard 227
Liberation Tigers of Tamil Eelam (LTTE) 18, 25, 497
Libya
  IRA 469

martyrs 189
Responsibility to Protect 580
war 359
Lifton, Robert, Jay 226
Lomé Agreement (Sierra Leone) 536
Lord Bingham 454
Lord Carlile 370, 447–8
Lord Hope 454
Lord Lloyd 450
Lord Macpherson 391, 399
Lord Scarman 399
Lord's Resistance Army (LRA) in Uganda 536
Los Angeles Police Department (LAPD) 383
Lovett, Tom 518
Lowry, Bill 471
Ludedorff, Erich 357
lustrations/exclusions (Eastern Europe) 537–40
Lyons, William 405

McCain, John 415
McCausland, Duncan 471
McCutcheon, Russell 237
Macdonald report, 2011 446
McDonnell, Joe 179
McDonnell, John M. 380
McGeown, Pat 519
McGuinness, Martin 174, 473–4, 478, 484
Machiavelli, Niccolò 353, 356
McKay, John 383
McKearney, Tommy 175, 179
Mackinnon, Catherine 270
McNee, David 401
Macpherson Report 472
MacStiofáin, Sean 182
McVeigh Timothy 131–2
Magee, John 394
Magee, Patrick 179
Maharaj, Mac 478
Mahmood, Cynthia Keppley 301, 315–16, 319
Major, John 480, 486
Makiya, Kanan 83
Mandela, Nelson 52, 124
Mandela, Winnie 218
Mandelson, Peter 480
Mann, Michael 343
Mansoor, Colonel 472

INDEX

Mao 342, 343
Marighela, Carlos 395
Márquez, Garcia Gabriel 281
Marti, José 287
martyrs without borders (transnational suicide bombers)
  conclusions 200–201
  ideology 198–200
  introduction 185–7
  Iraq 187–90
  organization 196–8
  patterns of recruitment 190–95
  structure 195–6
Marxism 230, 234
Marxism Today (journal) 401–2
MASSINT (measurements and signatures intelligence) 371
Mau Mau in Kenya 92
Mazowiecki, Tadeusz 539
Mearsheimer, John J. 358
Mendez, Juan E. 337
Menem, Carlos 545
Mexican Revolution (1910–17) 286
Meyer, Roelf 478
MI5 (security service) in UK 369, 376–7, 378, 403
MI6 (secret intelligence service) in UK 376
Middle Ages 351–2
Midlarsky, Manus 343
Migdal, Joel S. 559–60
Military Commissions Act (MCA), 2006 420, 429–30
Miller, Geoffrey 426
Millet, Peter 474
Minnesota Multiphasic Personality inventory-2 (MMPI-2) 141, 144
'Minorities at Risk' 19
Mitchell, George 475–6, 479, 507
Mobile Phone Network (Northern Ireland) 519
Moloney, Ed 476
Montoneros (Argentina) 251
Mora, Alberto 429
Morillon, Philippe 535
Moro Islamic Liberation Front (MILF) in Philippines 128, 478, 498
Morreall, John 125, 127
Mousa, Baha 453
Muchembled, Robert 569
Mueller, Robert S. 380–81

Mugabe, Robert 535
Muhammad, Khalid Shaykh 425
Mujihadeen (resistance) groups 551
Mulberry Bush (Birmingham pub) 393
Mullan, Don 483–4
Mullen, Michael G. 557
Murphy, Patrick 169
Murphy, Paul 477–8
Musevini, Yoweri 536
Musharraf, Pervez 558
"Muslim Extremism" 90
Muslims, violent extremism 577
Muslims and political violence 90
Mussolini 544

Nairn, Tom 294
Napoleon Bonaparte 354–5, 359
Nash, June 318
Nasr, Obama Moustafa Hassan 382
Nasser regime in Egypt 255
Nation (magazine) 86
National Coordinator of Terrorist Investigations (NCTI) 377
National Council for Civil Liberties (NCCL) in UK 402
National Counterterrorism Center (NCTC) 380, 383–4
National Crime Agency (NCA) 379
National GeoSpatial-Intelligence Agency (NGA) in US 380
National Intelligence Strategy (NIS) of US 380
National Joint Terrorism Task Force (NJTTF) 381–2
National Liberation Alliance (Argentina) 288
National Reconnaissance Office (NRO) in US 380
National Security Agency (NSA) in US 380
National Security Letters (NSLs) 416
national security and political violence
  description 110–12
  non-state violence 112–14
nationalism
  Colombia 295–6
  Latin America 282, 288, 294–6
NATO 216, 358, 535, 539, 558–9, 562
Nazism 206, 247–8, 331, 338, 531
Negroponte, John 373
Netanyahu, Benjamin 43

New Labour Government, UK 389, 405
New Profile (feminist organisation) 570
New Statesman 393
New York Times 476
Newsnight (BBC) 86
newspapers and Northern Ireland conflict resolution 473–5
non-governmental organizations (NGOs)
   Afghanistan 552, 554
   Bosnia 216
   Global Policy Forum 85
   Iraq 85
   Northern Ireland 509, 520
   political violence 251
   political violence in the community 27
normal psychology
   developmental influences 149–50
   humiliation 149
   moral disengagement 148
   perceived injustice 146
   prejudice 147–8
   rational response to political grievance 145
   social identity theory 151–2
   victimization, trauma and revenge 146–7
Northern Ireland
   conflict 216–17, 246–7, 250, 253
   Good Friday Agreement 26
   political violence 507, 579
   rule of law 531
   see also civil society actors
Northern Ireland Association for the Care and Rehabilitation of Offenders (NIACRO) 510, 520
Northern Ireland Community Relations Commission (1969–74) 509
Northern Ireland Community Relations Council 517
Northern Ireland Council for Voluntary Action (NICVA) 509–10, 513, 514–15
Northern Ireland Retired Police Officers' Association 470
Northern Ireland (state role in management of resolution and violent conduct)
   conclusions 485–6
   conflict management 467–73
   conflict resolution 473–9
   introduction 467

   view in the mirror: state and radicalism 479–85
Northern Ireland Women's Coalition 515
Nunca Màs (never again) policy in Argentina 545
Nuremberg Laws 532
Nuremberg Trials (Second World War) 529, 534, 543

Obama, Barack 29, 119, 412, 415, 430–32, 476, 561
Occupy Movement 575
O'Donnell, Guillermo 289
O'Donovan Rossa, Jeremiah 170
Oliver, Quintin 515
Omagh bombing 473
O'Malley, Padraig 478
Omand, David 377
On Thermonuclear War 357
One Hundred Years of Solitude 281
Operation CREVICE 378–9
Operation Enduring Freedom (Afghanistan) 558
Operation Phantom Fury in Iraq 84–5
opium poppy economy in Afghanistan 555
Opsahl Citizens' Inquiry (Northern Ireland) 511–12
Opsahl, Torkel 511
O'Rawe, Richard 180
Organization for Security and Co-operation in Europe (OSCE) 530
orthodox accounts of terrorism
   conclusions 43–5
   discourse 38–9
   introduction 33–4
   Israel and Palestine 40–43
   orthodox terrorism theory 34–8
OSINT (open source) 372
Oslo process (Israel and Palestine) 25
Othman v. UK case 453
overview of political violence
   approaches 28
   in the community 26–7
   contested terms 17–18
   definition 18, 19
   'Global War on Terror' 28–9
   inter-state or intra-state? 18–20
   militants
      internal paramilitary violence 26
      return to political violence 24–5

spoilers: zealots versus dealers 25–6
  'tactical violence' 25
 patterns 27–8
 political conflict or ordinary decent crime? 21–2
 political conflict or political violence? 20–21
 by the state 23–4
 validity, costs and effectiveness 22–3
 violence or negotiation? - exit routes 30–31
Owen, David 392
Oxford Research Group and civilian casualties 573

Paisley, Ian 473–4
Palestine
 IRA 469
 political violence 579
 suicide bombers 198, 480–81
 see also Hamas
Palestine–Israeli conflict 39, 40–43, 207, 475
Palestine Liberation Organization (PLO) 25
Pape, Robert 226
Paris, Roland 503
Patten Report (Northern Ireland) 471
Paz, Octavio 281
Paz, Reuben 188
PEACE 11 Programme (EU) 515
'Peace vs Justice' debate 536
Pearse, Padric 170
Pentagon attacks in 2001 113
Peritore, Patrick 313
Perón, Juan 288, 295
PET (Preventing Extremism Together) working groups 481
Peterson, Jeff 309
PETs (Privacy Enhancing Technologies) 372, 384
Pew Global Attitudes Survey, 2006 156
Phillips, Melanie 90–91
Piazza, James 231
Pillar, P. R. 371
Pinker, Stephen 578–9
Pinochet, Augusto 336, 536
Pisacane, Carlo 36
Pittsburgh-Post Gazette 72
Piven, Francis Fox 245
Plato 359
Pol Pot 342

Poland, rule of law 546
Police Service of Northern Ireland (PSNI) 470–71
political opportunities (social movement studies) 246, 248
political violence and peace processes
 ceasefires 497–8
 concept 494–7
 conclusions 503–4
 crime 501–3
 introduction 493–4
 spoiling 498–501
'*politicide*' concept 341–2
Polsky, Ned 319
Pope John Paul II 394
Popkin, M. and Roht-Arriaza, N. 540
Popular Front for the Liberation of Palestine (PFLP) 37
Porter, Jack Nusan 340
Post, Jerrold 156
post-traumatic stress disorder (PTSD) 573
Powell, Colin 419
Powis, David 402
'pre-fieldwork' fieldwork 316
PREVENT strategy 379
Prevention of Terrorism Act, 2005 447, 451
Prevention of Terrorism (Temporary Provisions) Act, 1974 371, 393, 404
prima facie rights 126
Project on Justice in Times of Transition (Harvard University) 513–14
Prophet Muhammad 199
prosecutions (transitional justice) 542–3
Protection of Freedom Act, 2011 446
'Provincial Reconstruction Teams' (PRTs) in Afghanistan 558–9
Provisional IRA (PIRA)
 attacks in UK 393, 397
 Brighton bombing 392
 grievance and shame 399
 growth 182
 hunger strikes 393–4
 influence 396
 Irish Catholic communities 403
 motivation of Irish rebel and 'terrorist' label 170–72, 174–5
 negotiated settlement 396
 prisoners 391–2
 'radical nationalism' 399
 Sands, Bobby 394

strategy 390, 394–5
terrorism 392, 396, 400, 403–4
terrorist recruitment 393
Thatcher, Margaret 392
Prussian Military Academy 355
psychology of terrorism
  abnormal psychology 140–44
  classification 138–9
  cognitive style 150–51
  discussion 156–8
  group dynamics 152–4
  introduction 137–8
  martyrdom 153–4
  normal psychology 145–51
  socio-political events 154–6
psychopathy 142

Qatada, Abu 453
Quetz, Gail A. 340

R (Gillan) v. Metropolitan Police Commissioner case 454
R (Smith) v. Deputy Coroner for Oxfordshire case 453
Rabin, Yitzhak 26
Rajapakse, Mahinda 478
Rawls, John 120, 123–4
Reagan, Ronald 344
Real Irish Republican Army (Northern Ireland) 498
Reardon, Betty 261
Red Army Fraction (RAF) in Germany 230
Red Army (Japan) 251
Red Brigades (Italy) 230, 251
Reign of Terror (French Revolution) 177
relative deprivation (RD) 155
religion as motivation for political violence
  introduction 225–6
  organization and wider context 231–4
  prevalence of assumption that religion causes violence 236–8
  religious–divide 234–6
  social sciences 226–8
  violence link 228–9, 229–31
'religious terrorism' 225
Republican News 178
Researching Conflict in Africa: Insights and Experiences 309
Researching Violence 309

Researching Violently Divided Societies: Ethical and Methodological Issues 309
'Responsibility to Rebuild' (Iraq/Afghanistan) 580
retributive political violence (transitional justice) 544
'revolution in intelligence affairs' (RIA) 370, 384
'revolutionary immortality' (suicide bombing) 226
Revolutions in Military Affairs (RMAs) 352–3
Rezaq, Amar 150
'Rich Picture' approach (police operation) 378
Richardson, Louise 395, 398
right-wing authoritarianism (RWA) 150
Rimington, Stella 376
Robben, Antonius C.G.M. and Nordstrom, Carolyn 301, 305–6, 311, 314–15
Robinson, Mary 520
Rodgers, Dennis 314, 320
Rodó, José Enrique 287
Roman Catholic Church 351
Rousseau, Jean Jacques 119–20
Roy, Arundhati 1
Royal Ulster Constabulary (RUC) 468, 470, 483, 507, 510
rule of law in aftermath of political violence (transitional justice)
  conclusions 544–6
  description 530–34
  introduction 529–30
  transitional justice spectrum 534–44
'Rule of Man' (Aristotle) 532
Rumman, Abu 188
Rummel, R.J. 341–2
Rumsfeld, Donald 83, 419, 426
Russia
  Chechnya 359
  Georgia 358
Rwanda (genocide)
  anarchy 531
  apocalypse 343
  bystanders 214
  collective violence 206
  conflict 20
  cultural dispositions 215
  elites 214

evolution 213–14
genocide and afterwards 215–16
instigators 213
prosecutions 543
restraining forces and positive evolution 217

Saadi, Fadhal 191
Saadi v. Italy case 453
Sageman, Marc 153, 255
'Salvador Option' in Iraq 83
Sands, Bobby 175, 177, 394, 400–401
Sands, Tommy 510
Sanguinetti, Julio 537
Sarmiento, Domingo Faustino 285
Sassaman, Nathan 85
Saville Report (Bloody Sunday report) 396, 485
Schabas, William A. 333
Schelling, Thomas C. 357
Schmid, Alex 395
Schutzstaffel (SS) and war crimes 531
Schwarzkopf, Norman 350
Second World War 357
Secretary of State for Home Dept. cases v.
    Lord Alton of Liverpool 357
    MB and AF 455–6
    Rehman 456
security
    individual 101–6
    state 107–8, 108–9
security in political violence
    conclusions 114–15
    introduction 99–100
    national security and political violence 110–14
    threats and duties of state 107–9
    what is security? 100–106
security sector reform 503
'Sentinel' (IT system) for FBI 381
Seven Years' War (1756–63) 354
Sexism and the War System 261
Shaw, Martin 86–7, 330, 342
Shawcross, Hartley 330
Sheikh Muhammed Tantawi 198
Shepherd, Laura 272–3
Sherman, William T. 348
Sherzai, Gul Agha 82
SIGINT/ELINT communications intercept system 371–2, 375, 376

Silke, Andrew 64–5, 396
Simon, S. and Stevenson, J. 479
Sinn Féin
    Adams, Gerry 530
    IRA 476, 480
    McGuinness, Martin 484
    Opsahl Citizens' Inquiry 511
    political growth 473
    spoiling 498, 501
    United Ireland vision 171
Sisk, Tim 499
Slim, Hugo 504
Smart, Carol 275
Smith, Anthony 283, 294, 296
Smith, Ian 535
Smith, Kevin 471
Smyth, Marie and Robinson, Gillian 309
social dominance orientation (SDO) 150
social identity theory (SIT) 151
social movement studies and political violence
    conclusions 256
    freedom-fighter identities 252–6
    introduction 243–5
    polarized violence 245–50
    violent entrepreneurs 250–52
Social Needs legislation (Northern Ireland) 482
sociopathy 142
socio-political events
    governance model 155–6
    poverty/relative deprivation 154–5
    societal attitudes 156
Somoza, Anastasio 291
Somoza dynasty (Nicaragua) 287
South Africa
    ANC 23, 24
    Apartheid 532
    conflict 20
    rule of law 546
    truth commissions 541
South African Truth and Reconciliation Commission 540
Soviet Union
    Afghanistan 359
    constitution 532
    United States 530
Spain and Basque region 469
Special court for Sierra Leone 536

Special Police Commandos (SPCs) in Iraq 83–4
Special Support Programme for Peace and Rehabilitation (EU) 514
Spicer, Tim 470
'spoiler' term 499–500
Springfield Inter-Community Development Project (SICDP) in Northern Ireland 519
Sri Lanka
 collective violence 206
 conflict 20
 spoilers 25
 state terrorism 57
 see also Tamil Tigers
Stalin, Joseph 332, 342, 343, 538
Standing Operation Proceedings (SOP) 426
state terrorism 57, 66–7
state violence as state terrorism
 agency 73–5
 conclusions 76
 definition 64, 64–7
 identification 70
 international law 68–70
 introduction 63–4
 secondary effect 70–73
 target audience 67–8
Stedman, Stephen 498
Stephan, Maria 578
Stephen Lawrence Inquiry 391
'Strasbourg proofing' 443, 448
Straw, Jack 89, 391
Students for a Democratic Society (SDS) in US 250
subaltern genocide 338
Sudan People's Liberation Movement (SPLM/A) 498
Suddath, Leroy 350
Sulieman, Muhammed 193
Sun Tzu 350, 356
Supreme Council for the Islamic Revolution in Iraq (SCIRI) 83
Supreme Iraqis Islamic Council (SIIC) 83
Suspicious Activity Reports (SARs) 382–3
symbolic nature of terrorism 36–7, 41

Tacitus 347
tactical component of terrorism 37–8, 41–2
Taguba, Antonio 426–7
Taiwan and China 358

Taking Lives: Genocide and State Power 339
Taliban
 Afghanistan 551, 553, 555, 561–2
 civilian casualties 504
 Dannatt, Richard 87
 female victims of political violence 270
 forces 88
 hreb-e Islami 558
 Pakistan 558
 United States 82
Tamil Tigers (Sri Lanka)
 'Global War on Terror' 29
 human rights 453
 McGuinness, Martin 478
 religion 226, 230, 235
 victimization, trauma and revenge 146
 war 358
Tavern in the Town (Birmingham pub) 393
Tell, Nawaf 192
'Terrorism in the Grip of Justice' (TV programme) 86
'terrorism' term 1, 499
Terrorist Identities Datamart Environment (TIDE) 383
'terrorist' label
 French resistance 182
 see also Irish rebels
Thabit, Adnan 84
Thatcher, Margaret 391–2, 394
The Ambivalence of the Sacred 229
The Art of War 37, 350, 353
The Clash of Civilizations and the Remaking of World Order 227
The Crime of State 334
The Dark Side of Democracy 343
The Guardian 476
The Holocaust in Historical Context, Volume 1 339
The Jewish Enemy 331
The Killing Fields (film) 341
The Lancet (journal) 81
The Law of War and Peace 354
The Observer 472
The Rise of the West and the Coming of Genocide 343
The Secret Agent 177–8
'the terror of war and the horror of peace' 1
'thick' definition (rule of law) 533
Thiel, Daniel 402–3, 404
Thompson, John L. 340

Thoreau, Henry David 122
Thucydides 349
Tiller, George 21
Tilly, Charles 245–6
TIPS (Terrorist Information and Prevention System) 417
Tissot, Victor 356
Tobin, Jonathan 476
Tokyo Trials (Second World War) 529, 543
Total Information Awareness (TIA) 417
Touraine, Alain 287, 291
transitional justice spectrum (rule of law)
   amnesties 534–7
   introduction 534
   lustrations/exclusions 537–40
   prosecutions 542–3
   retributive political violence 544
   truth commissions 540–1
Trilogy (IT system) for FBI 381
Trimble, David 476
Trujillo, Rafael 287
truth commissions 540–1
Truth and Reconciliation Commission in South Africa 458, 540
Tzu, Sun 37

Ubaydah, Abu 193
Ulster Community Action Group (UCAG) 518
Ulster Defence Association (UDA) 142, 507, 518
Ulster Democratic Party 511
Ulster Freedom Fighters 518
Ulster Volunteer Force (UVF) 507, 519
'Ulsterisation' of security 468
United Kingdom (UK)
   7/7 bombings 197
   9/11 response 375–6
   Demos 576
   domestic intelligence system 376–8
   Iraq/Afghanistan and US 571
   Occupy Movement 575
   United States 389
   war veterans 577
   see also counter-terrorism
United Nations Assistance Mission in Afghanistan (UNAMA) 558
United Nations High Commissioner for Refugees (UNHCR) 555
United Nations (UN)
   Afghanistan 551
   amnesties 535
   civilian deaths in Afghanistan 82
   Genocide Convention (1948) *see* Genocide Convention
   transitional justice 530
United States (US)
   9/11 attacks 397, 411–12, 414–15
   Afghanistan 92, 99, 269, 270, 414, 422, 557–8, 559
   al-Qaeda 17, 419–20, 432
   anti-abortion terrorism 255
   civil rights movement 217
   Department of Defence and terrorism 39
   Freedom of Information Act 418
   Geneva Conventions 419–20, 420–21
   intelligence and political violence: counter-terrorism 380, 382–4
   Iraq 92, 99, 199
   Iraq/Afghanistan and UK 571
   'Jim Crow' regulations 532
   Latin America 289, 291
   Northern Ireland 508
   Operation Phoenix in Vietnam 71
   social movement studies 244
   Soviet Union 530
   Students for a Democratic Society 250
   Taliban 82
   United Kingdom 389
   'war crimes' 348
   'War on Terror' 200
   war veterans 577
   Weather Underground 250
   women's crimes 275
Universal Declaration of Human Rights, 1948 121
unmanned aerial vehicle (UAV) 372, 382
Uppsala Conflict Data Program (UCDP) 30
USA PATRIOT Act 380, 413, 415, 416, 432
USS Cole 113

Valentino, Benjamin 343
Valls, Andrew 124, 130
Vasconcelos, José 286, 287
Vélasquez Rodriguez case 542
Vidal, Georges 119
Vietnam war 342
Vitalis, Robert 79
von Bismarck, Otto 354

von Clausewitz, Carl 347, 349, 353, 355–7
von Schlieffen, Alfred 350
von Wernich, Christian 337

Waldron, J. 102
Walid, Abul 84
Walter, Eugene Walter 65–7
'war against terrorism' 29, 418, 421
war as political violence 347–59
'War on Terror'
    9/11 events 486
    abuses 75
    Iraq 358
    political violence, and civilians 79–80, 80–87
    seminars 471, 486
    United States 200
    see also civilians
War of the Triple Alliance (Latin America) 282
Washington Post 88
Watt, Redmond 472
we Sizme, Umkhonto 579
weapons of mass destruction (WMDs) 376
Weather Underground, United States 250, 275
Weinberg, Leonard 226
Weinberg, L.B. and Eubank, W.L. 155
Wellman, Carl 126–7
West German Ministry of the Interior Study 140, 143

Whalley, Robert 447
Whitaker report on genocide 334–6
Whitehead, Neil 301
Widgery Tribunal (Bloody Sunday) 485
Wikileaks 570
Wiktorowicz, Quentin 249, 251
Wilkinson, Paul 66
Wilson, Woodrow 347
Wolesi Jirga (Afghanistan) 560
Wolf Brigade in Iraq 84
Wolfowitz, Paul 84
Women Fielding Danger 314
Women's Information Day network (Northern Ireland) 517
Wright, Shelley 267

X and Y v. The Netherlands case 542

Yes Campaign Group (Northern Ireland) 515
Yesh Gvul (Israeli organisation) 570
Yoo, John 428
Yousef, Ahmed 475
Yugoslav wars 531
former Yugoslavia 31, 255, 534

Zalewski, Marysia 262
Zana, Leyla 451
Zapata, Emiliano 286
Zazi, Najibullah 383